RACIAL AND ETHNIC RELATIONS
Selected Readings

Edited by

Bernard E. Segal

Dartmouth College

THOMAS Y. CROWELL COMPANY
NEW YORK
ESTABLISHED 1834

Library of Congress Catalog Card Number: 66-19316

DESIGNED BY SUSAN GIBSON

Manufactured in the United States of America
by Vail-Ballou Press, Inc., Binghamton, N. Y.

Preface

The readings and editorial comments in this book can serve as a text, or can supplement assignments from standard textbooks, in the field of American ethnic and racial relations. Rather than attempt to duplicate text materials, however, I have tried to choose selections that will allow students to pursue particular topics in greater depth and detail than is usually the case. I have not hesitated to include studies of a rather technical nature; if students are to become accustomed to evaluating research results for themselves, rather than being led to accept them at face value, it is useful for them to see how investigators present and analyze original data. Although certain of the other selections in the volume are occasionally theoretically or methodologically unsophisticated, they are thought-provoking, and as such should encourage readers to re-examine their own attitudes and values, and to reconsider their own personal solutions—sometimes arrived at without much conscious deliberation—to complex social issues. I shall be satisfied if the range of selections represents a healthy balance between technically precise studies with sufficient substance to maintain readers' interest, and more subjective readings with enough basis in reality to seem reasonable

v

and worthy of further investigation. To help achieve this balance, head-notes briefly summarize and relate each of the selections to more general principles.

The book is organized in seven parts. The first, a sampling of theoretical positions, helps to show various ways of finding order in the complex array of ideas and materials in this field of inquiry. As the Introduction makes clear, my own preference is for institutionally-oriented theory that emphasizes how social arrangements help to shape men's personalities and affect their ideologies and behavior. However, I have not attempted to impose this perspective on readers. Where new facts are still being accumulated from new events, the freedom a student finds in healthy and skeptical eclecticism may be of greater value to his development than theoretical closure. Moreover, no social theory is perfect, and the instructor can use the first section of the book to demonstrate strengths and weaknesses of specific theoretical positions and specific ways of theorizing.

The second part introduces the reader to the diversity of American ethnic subcultures. Two features keep it from being a mere potpourri of idiosyncrasies and curiosities. The first is that many of the selections emphasize the relationship between an individual's subculture, on the one hand, and his prospects for social mobility or for fitting himself into the mainstream of American culture, on the other. The second is that half of the studies investigate comparatively two or more ethnic groups, thus enabling the student to contemplate differences between groups more directly and more precisely than if he had to move from one author's study of one group to another's study of a second or third.

In the third part, it becomes clear that these differences among ethnic and racial groups are a focal point for prejudice and ethnocentrism in American society. The selections do more than describe and analyze how dominant groups employ ethnocentrism and prejudice to maintain their convictions of their own superiority. They reveal the ways minority group members respond to prejudice, and indicate that they are not without prejudices of their own.

Because Negroes are the largest and most visible of American minority groups; because they have been the group most victimized by discrimination; and because they play the central role in the civil rights movement, the next three parts concentrate on them and on their place in American society. Part Four is particularly concerned with the way discrimination leads to segregation and exploitation, and the readings show that these issues must be examined in the North as well as in the South. After completing these selections, northern students will probably have difficulty stigmatizing the entire southern white population as the scapegoat solely responsible for American racial inequities. White southern students will find little solace, however, or the readings also demonstrate the sham of romanticizing white supremacy, and the costs of attempting to perpetuate it.

If it is true that segregation is becoming an outmoded pattern of the past, it follows that integration is the pattern of the future. Part Five examines white and Negro attitudes and responses to desegregation and integration, and shows clearly that it is possible, although frequently difficult, to create situations in which whites and Negroes can get to know one another well and live together compatibly.

For the present, however, and for the immediate future, it seems likely that most Negroes will have to go on living between established patterns of discrimination and hoped-for patterns of acceptance and equality. How they try in these circumstances to find order and meaning in their lives is the theme of Part Six. Of the three readings there, the first describes a set of short-run adjustment mechanisms; the second, a movement that looks toward the future; and the third, an organization trying to re-create a world that never was.

Although it might be expected that the last part of the book, which consists of a single selection, would summarize and synthesize all of the papers that preceded it, this is not the case. The paper does touch upon many themes previously alluded to, but by raising many questions and reaching few conclusions, it fittingly demonstrates the unresolved state of the problems those themes represent. For some time to come, Americans concerned about the nation's racial and ethnic relations will have to go on grappling with the question of which ideals they wish to put into practice, and with the question of how best to go about doing so.

The book could not have appeared without the original investigations and observations carried out by the authors whose works appear in it. I am particularly grateful to two colleagues, Pierre van den Berghe and Robert B. Johnson, who allowed me to include works of theirs that had not previously appeared in their present form, and I am indebted to the publishers of books and journals who permitted the remaining papers to be reprinted here. To my secretary Mrs. Davis Jackson, who put up with my delays and my bad typing in order to make sure that I finished assembling the book, formal thanks is hardly sufficient. Finally, as much as for anyone, the book itself is for Anne, who shares my fondness for café au lait.

B.E.S.

Hanover, New Hampshire
March, 1966

Contents

VI. THE SEARCH FOR NEGRO IDENTITY

VII. AND THE FUTURE?

RACIAL
AND
ETHNIC
RELATIONS
Selected Readings

Introduction

This book is not all-inclusive. It does not cover such matters as the physiology of race and the history of civil rights legislation; nor is every American minority group represented by a specific selection. Rather, the selections center on two themes that seem pivotal to any consideration of racial and ethnic relations in American society. The first is the difficulty members of this society have had in deciding what status they wish to assign to *racial* minorities. In the United States today, minority racial status is practically synonymous with not being white, although at times other fallacious judgments of racial differences have been and still are used to justify discriminatory treatment of white ethnic minorities. The second theme, in marked contrast to the first, is the remarkable process by which American society has attracted a great variety of different ethnic and racial stocks, and has gone on to weave them into a broad social fabric. Neither theme has yet been played out in the United States.

Some observers hold that ethnic minorities have been all but assimilated, and that racial minorities are now about to repeat ethnic history, but many of the readings in this collection suggest that such judgments are

1

too facile. Although it does seem clear that the United States has recently grown more aware of the desirability of affording equal political and legal rights to all its citizens, whether prevalent personal and unofficial judgments will parallel these legal and political developments is less clear. Of course, these questions do not mean that we should not expect important changes to continue to occur, as witness the compliance—albeit under strong pressure from the federal government—with recent civil rights legislation even in some areas of the country that were expected to offer hard-core resistance.

In spite of the official efforts to eliminate inequalities based on race or ethnicity, prejudice, broadly defined as a pattern of negative prejudgments of racial and ethnic minority groups, is still a serious obstacle in the path of intergroup harmony. However, the most important first step in removing such inequalities lies in understanding that it is possible to create circumstances in which it is neither profitable nor socially acceptable to express one's prejudice by discriminating—that is, by acting in ways that are unfair and harmful to members of particular ethnic or racial groups. A decade of research in intergroup relations has shown that changed attitudes frequently derive from changed situations, that prejudice and discriminatory behavior can be reduced more effectively by altering the social context in which they arise and are expressed, rather than by attempting first to alter attitudes.

It has also become apparent that efforts to change the context of majority-minority relations must consider that society is a social system in which important transactions occur among various institutional areas. Thus, political action in such fields as education and social welfare, directed specifically toward minority groups, will have as much bearing on the total majority-minority situation as will legal action concerned chiefly with issues of segregation and discrimination. For example, continued deliberate political intervention and economic planning will probably be necessary, not only to create the conditions that will enable occupational mobility to occur on a large scale in an era of extremely rapid technological innovation, but also to foster the cultural conditions that will enable minority group members to take advantage of opportunities thus created.

In earlier periods of American history, members of low-status minority groups achieved their aspirations over the course of time through processes that were assumed to be either natural and spontaneous, or else the results of individual initiative and determination. In retrospect, we are more likely to be struck by the observation that the ability to fulfill their aspirations was in part the consequence of a growing economy that provided employment for relatively large numbers of low-skilled workers and for small businessmen who served the special interests of their own communities. We may also be aware that the varying rates of success of various ethnic groups partially depended on the extent to which their particular cultural backgrounds fitted them for adaptation to the values of the dominant culture.

In comparison to most white American minority groups, Negro Americans did not take a significant part in even these mobility processes of the past. The history of the Negro and the ways that white communities responded to him combined to exclude him systematically from those opportunities for mobility and comfort sought after by so many others. Negro Americans—as well as Puerto Ricans, Indians, Mexicans, and, to a lesser extent, Orientals—have constituted an "American dilemma" in a dual sense. It is not just that the way they have been treated represents the greatest and most obvious gap between the moral ideals and the practical reality of American society. In addition, their disproportionate concentration on the lowest rungs of the American status ladder, their uncommonly low levels of education and of income, are a paradox in economy of abundance. For different reasons depending heavily on large-scale economic dislocation, many white Americans, of whom a good share are "old stock" Appalachians, are findings themselves in similar straits. Although by now many Americans feel guilty over these disparities, and realize that many of the problems of the chronic poor are quite color-blind, one cannot help but wonder whether we were not shamed first, led to feel concern because of the ways the rest of the world reacted to the ironies of our welfare capitalism.

The other side of the American minority experience, of course, is one in which we have taken great pride. Despite periodic episodes of xenophobic patriotism, and decisions taken a generation ago to limit immigration primarily to those who were already most like us, American history provides an unparalleled example of a nation's capacity to absorb great numbers of people from a wide variety of different cultures into an even larger mass in which almost everyone possesses a strong sense of a common national identity.

An observer seeking only the picturesque survivals of traditional lifeways in ethnic enclaves is not especially likely to observe that many subcultural ethnic differences still persist in less obvious fashion, occurring in more private areas of life, expressed as much in norms as in immediately observable details of behavior. Different patterns of family loyalty, different obligations of one generation to another, preferences for living in neighborhoods composed of "my kinds of people," appeals to ethnic identity which affect the ways people vote—these variations still exist. And standards of performance and achievement are still passed on in ethnocentric—not to say chauvinistic—vessels.

Even so, it would be hard to dispute the contention that unique ethnic patterns of expectations and behavior become less binding and less prominent as higher proportions of a minority group's members move from working- to middle-class status, particularly if generational as well as individual mobility is taken into account. With reference to a case that is close at hand, although today's college students come from diverse social backgrounds, most of them are far more preoccupied with wondering who they are than in trying to establish what they are. Few feel constrained to think of their ethnic characteristics as paramount features of their identities, and even when they do think of themselves in ethnic terms, their reflections involve points of pride as often as doubts about personal worth or status. Their very presence at institutions of higher learning does more than testify to opportunities their parents worked to create for them; it also demonstrates that society is open to them, a point so obvious that it is almost always taken for granted. Less obvious is that it is partly because they are not forced by others to consider themselves in a collectivist ethnic fashion that they are able to afford the luxury of surveying their worlds individualistically.

One important relationship between social opportunity and personal identity in American society can be expressed in the proposition that Americans hardly know how to find a sense of worth or dignity without referring to accomplishments that serve to let others know that they have been successful. These tangible bases of prestige and esteem need not be material, though they often are. What is true is that they preeminently depend on social validation. Our reliance on them highlights our feeling that to be cut off from sources of approval is nearly tantamount to having no way of demonstrating our worth to the world. But many Americans have been and still are cut off from the society's dominant, conventional sources of approval. Many of them have therefore tried, frequently with considerable ambivalence, to maintain themselves in their own worlds, where they could sometimes forget the dominant standards and try to capitalize on their own more traditionalistic ones. Some others, with an ascribed status so low as to offer little hope that either the dominant or their own indigenous standards could offer sustenance and dignity, have become bitter and alienated, hollow and lost.

Is the dominant pattern of contemporary American life so noble, so rare, that others have to be kept from sharing it until they have demonstrated their virtue and their commitment to it as it now stands? Or is it far enough from Utopia to enable us to understand why many of those who have not shared in this society's bounty wish to change its moral perspectives even as they strive to participate in its richness?

I have tried to avoid moral judgments in assembling and editing this book, but no man can pretend to avoiding them altogether. Most readers will probably find that sooner or later they will confront these questions and will have to answer them for themselves.

I. THEORETICAL PERSPECTIVES

1. The Problem of Prejudice

Clear discussion calls for precise terms. By showing how prejudiced people express their attitudes, Allport defines the concept of prejudice quite effectively. A prejudiced individual has a relatively rigid set of negatively toned perceptions of and feelings toward a group (or groups) to which he does not belong. Prejudice is only one of several important terms used to discuss cognitive, affective, or evaluative frames of reference relevant to intergroup relations. For example, prejudice is often expressed in the form of a "stereotype." This more specific term generally refers to a set of prejudiced beliefs, or to a fairly common particular belief, about a given minority group (e.g., Jews are clannish; Negroes are unambitious; Italians

SOURCE: Gordon W. Allport, *The Nature of Prejudice* (Cambridge: Addison-Wesley, 1954), pp. 3–15. Copyright 1954 by Addison-Wesley Publishing Co., Inc. Reprinted by permission of the publisher.

Gordon W. Allport is Professor of Psychology in the Department of Social Relations at Harvard University. He is the author of *Personality and Social Encounter*, and many other works in the field of personality development and theory.

5

are over-emotional). Prejudice and stereotypes both represent categorical styles of thought; that is, they reflect the assumption that judgments or feelings about a group apply to all of the group's members. However, as these terms are usually used, prejudice almost invariably connotes negative or hostile judgments, while stereotypes sometimes have a positive connotation. Different from both terms is "ethnocentrism," used to refer to an individual's positive estimate of and feeling toward his own group and its members.

Unquestionably, prejudice, stereotypes, and ethnocentrism prevent objective and accurate assessments of differences and similarities among racial and ethnic groups. However, they are by no means the only determinants of behavior in intergroup situations. Later readings will show that the kinds of situations in which intergroup relations occur frequently affect men's actual behavior more than their attitudes do, in some cases leading to attitude change.

For now, notice how concisely Allport defines significant concepts, and how he uses examples that make his points concrete. He employs the same technique to show what he is not defining. To attempt to achieve such clarity is more than an academic exercise; it is necessary for orderly communication, especially when discussing a topic like ethnic and racial relations, which rapidly provokes many people to intense commitments to particular points of view.

In Rhodesia a white truck driver passed a group of idle natives and muttered, "They're lazy brutes." A few hours later he saw natives heaving two-hundred pound sacks of grain onto a truck, singing in rhythm to their work. "Savages," he grumbled. "What do you expect?"

In one of the West Indies it was customary at one time for natives to hold their noses conspicuously whenever they passed an American on the street. And in England, during the war, it was said, "The only trouble with the Yanks is that they are over-paid, over-sexed, and over here."

Polish people often called the Ukrainians "reptiles" to express their contempt for a group they regarded as ungrateful, revengeful, wily, and treacherous. At the same time Germans called their neighbors to the east "Polish cattle." The Poles retaliated with "Prussian swine"—a jibe at the presumed uncouthness and lack of honor of the Germans.

In South Africa, the English, it is said, are against the Afrikaner; both are against the Jews; all three are opposed to the Indians; while all four conspire against the native black.

In Boston, a dignitary of the Roman Catholic Church was driving along a lonesome road on the outskirts of the city. Seeing a small Negro boy trudging along, the dignitary told his chauffeur to stop and give the boy a lift. Seated together in the back of the limousine, the cleric, to make conversation, asked "Little Boy, are you a Catholic?" Wide-eyed with alarm, the boy replied, "No sir, it's bad enough being colored without being one of those things."

Pressed to tell what Chinese people really think of Americans, a Chinese student reluctantly replied, "Well, we think they are the best of the foreign devils." This incident occurred before the Communist revolution in China. Today's youth in China are trained to think of Americans as the *worst* of the foreign devils.

In Hungary, the saying is, "An anti-Semite is a person who hates the Jews more than is absolutely necessary."

No corner of the world is free from group scorn. Being fettered to our respective cultures, we . . . are bundles of prejudice.

Two Cases

An anthropologist in his middle thirties had two young children, Susan and Tom. His work required him to live for a year with a tribe of American Indians in the home of a hospitable Indian family. He insisted, however, that his own family live in a community of white people several miles distant from the Indian reservation. Seldom would he allow Tom and Susan to come to the tribal village, though they pleaded for the privilege. And on rare occasions when they made the visit, he sternly refused to allow them to play with the friendly Indian children.

Some people, including a few of the Indians, complained that the anthropologist was untrue to the code of his profession—that he was displaying race prejudice.

The truth is otherwise. This scientist knew that tuberculosis was rife in the tribal village, and that four of the children in the household where he lived had already died of the disease. The probability of infection for his own children, if they came much in contact with the natives, was high. His better judgment told him that he should not take the risk. In this case, his ethnic avoidance was based on rational and realistic grounds. There was no feeling of antagonism involved. The anthropologist had no generally negative attitude toward the Indians. In fact he liked them very much.

Since this case fails to illustrate what we mean by racial or ethnic prejudice, let us turn to another.

In the early summer season two Toronto newspapers carried between them holiday advertisements from approximately 100 different resorts. A Canadian social scientist, S. L. Wax, undertook an interesting experiment. To each of these hotels and resorts he wrote two letters, mailing them at the same time, and asking for room reservations for exactly the same dates. One letter he signed with the name "Mr. Greenberg," the other with the name "Mr. Lockwood." Here are the results:

> To "Mr. Greenberg":
>   52 percent of the resorts replied;
>   36 percent offered him accommodations.
> To "Mr. Lockwood":
>   95 percent of the resorts replied;
>   93 percent offered him accommodations.

Thus, nearly all of the resorts in question welcomed Mr. Lockwood as a correspondent and as a guest; but nearly half of them failed to give Mr. Greenberg the courtesy of a reply, and only slightly more than a third were willing to receive him as a guest.

None of the hotels knew "Mr. Lockwood" or "Mr. Greenberg." For all they knew "Mr. Greenberg" might be a quiet, orderly gentleman, and "Mr. Lockwood" rowdy and drunk. The decision was obviously made not on the merits of the individual, but on "Mr. Greenberg's" supposed membership in a group. He suffered discourtesy and exclusion *solely* because of his name, which aroused a prejudgment of his desirability in the eyes of the hotel managers.

Unlike our first case, this incident contains the two essential ingredients of ethnic prejudice. (1) There is definite hostility and rejection. The majority of the hotels wanted nothing to do with "Mr. Greenberg." (2) The basis of the rejection was categorical. "Mr. Greenberg" was not evaluated as an individual. Rather, he was condemned on the basis of his presumed group membership.

> A close reasoner might at this point ask the question: What basic difference exists between the cases of the anthropologist and the hotels in the matter of "categorical rejection"? Did not the anthropologist reason from the high probability of infection that it would be safer not to risk contact between his children and the Indians? And did not the hotelkeepers reason from a high probability that Mr. Greenberg's ethnic membership would in fact bring them an undesirable guest? The anthropologist knew that tubercular contagion was rampant; did not the innkeepers know that "Jewish vices" were rampant and not to be risked?
>
> This question is legitimate. If the innkeepers were basing their rejection on facts (more accurately, on a high probability that a given Jew will have undesirable traits), their action would be as rational and defensible as the anthropologist's. But we can be sure that such is not the case.
>
> Some managers may never have had any unpleasant experiences with Jewish guests—a situation that seems likely in view of the fact that in many cases Jewish guests had never been admitted to the

hotels. Or, if they have had such experiences, they have not kept a record of their frequency in comparison with objectionable non-Jewish guests. Certainly they have not consulted scientific studies concerning the relative frequency of desirable and undesirable traits in Jews and non-Jews. . . .

It is, of course, possible that the manager himself was free from personal prejudice, but, if so, he was reflecting the anti-Semitism of his gentile guests. In either event our point is made.

DEFINITION

The word *prejudice*, derived from the Latin noun *praejudicium*, has, like most words, undergone a change of meaning since classical times. There are three stages in the transformation.

1. To the ancients, *praejudicium* meant a *precedent*—a judgment based on previous decisions and experiences.
2. Later, the term, in English, acquired the meaning of a judgment formed before due examination and consideration of the facts— a premature or hasty judgment.
3. Finally the term acquired also its present emotional flavor of favorableness or unfavorableness that accompanies such a prior and unsupported judgment.

Perhaps the briefest of all definitions of prejudice is: *thinking ill of others without sufficient warrant.* This crisp phrasing contains the two essential ingredients of all definitions—reference to unfounded judgment and to a feeling-tone. It is, however, too brief for complete clarity.

In the first place, it refers only to *negative* prejudice. People may be prejudiced in favor of others; they may think *well* of them without sufficient warrant. The wording offered by the New English Dictionary recognizes positive as well as negative prejudice:

A *feeling, favorable or unfavorable, toward a person or thing, prior to, or not based on, actual experience.*

While it is important to bear in mind that biases may be *pro* as well as *con,* it is none the less true that *ethnic* prejudice is mostly negative. A group of students was asked to describe their attitudes toward ethnic groups. No suggestion was made that might lead them toward negative reports. Even so, they reported eight times as many antagonistic attitudes as favorable attitudes. . . . [A]ccordingly, we shall be concerned chiefly with prejudice *against,* not with prejudice *in favor of,* ethnic groups.

The phrase "thinking ill of others" is obviously an elliptical expression that must be understood to include feelings of scorn or dislike, of fear and aversion, as well as various forms of antipathetic conduct: such as talking against people, discriminating against them, or attacking them with violence.

Similarly, we need to expand the phrase "without sufficient warrant." A judgment is unwarranted whenever it lacks basis in fact. A wit defined prejudice as "being down on something you're not up on."

It is not easy to say how much fact is required in order to justify a judgment. A prejudiced person will almost certainly claim that he has sufficient warrant for his views. He will tell of bitter experiences he has had with refugees, Catholics, or Orientals. But, in most cases, it is evident that his facts are scanty and strained. He resorts to a selective sorting of his own few memories, mixes them up with hearsay, and overgeneralizes. No one can possibly know *all* refugees, Catholics, or Orientals. Hence any negative judgment of these groups *as a whole* is, strictly speaking, an instance of thinking ill without sufficient warrant.

Sometimes, the ill-thinker has no first-hand experience on which to base his judgment. A few years ago most Americans thought exceedingly ill of Turks—but very few had ever seen a Turk nor did they know any person who had seen one. Their warrant lay exclusively in what they had heard of the Armenian massacres and of the legendary crusades. On such evidence they presumed to condemn all members of a nation.

Ordinarily, prejudice manifests itself in dealing with individual members of rejected groups. But in avoiding a Negro neighbor, or in answering "Mr. Greenberg's" application for a room, we frame our action to accord with our categorical generalization of the group as a whole. We pay little or no attention to individual differences, and overlook the important fact that Negro X, our neighbor, is not Negro Y, whom we dislike for good and sufficient reason; that Mr. Greenberg, who may be a fine gentleman, is not Mr. Bloom, whom we have good reason to dislike.

So common is this process that we might define prejudice as:

> an avertive or hostile attitude toward a person who belongs to a group, simply because he belongs to that group, and is therefore presumed to have the objectionable qualities ascribed to the group.

This definition stresses the fact that while ethnic prejudice in daily life is ordinarily a matter of dealing with individual people it also entails an unwarranted idea concerning a group as a whole.

Returning to the question of "sufficient warrant," we must grant that few if any human judgments are based on absolute certainty. We can be reasonably, but not absolutely, sure that the sun will rise tomorrow, and that death and taxes will finally overtake us. The sufficient warrant for any judgment is always a matter of probabilities. Ordinarily our judgments of natural happenings are based on firmer and higher probabilities than our judgments of people. Only rarely do our categorical judgments of nations or ethnic groups have a foundation in high probability.

Take the hostile view of Nazi leaders held by most Americans during World War II. Was it prejudiced? The answer is No, because there was abundant available evidence regarding the evil policies and practices accepted as the official code of the party. True, there may have been good individuals in the party who at heart rejected the abominable program; but the probability was so high that the Nazi group constituted an actual menace to world peace and to humane values that a realistic and justified conflict resulted. The high probability of danger removes an antagonism from the domain of prejudice into that of realistic social conflict.

In the case of gangsters, our antagonism is not a matter of prejudice, for the evidence of their antisocial conduct is conclusive. But soon the line becomes hard to draw. How about an ex-convict? It is notoriously difficult for an ex-convict to obtain a steady job where he can be self-supporting and self-respecting. Employers naturally are suspicious if they know the man's past record. But often they are more suspicious than the facts warrant. If they looked further they might find evidence that the man who stands before them is genuinely reformed, or even that he was unjustly accused in the first place. To shut the door merely because a man has a criminal record has *some* probability in its favor, for many prisoners are never reformed; but there is also an element of unwarranted prejudgment involved. We have here a true borderline instance.

We can never hope to draw a hard and fast line between "sufficient" and "insufficient" warrant. For this reason we cannot always be sure whether we are dealing with a case of prejudice or nonprejudice. Yet no one will deny that often we form judgments on the basis of scant, even nonexistent, probabilities.

Overcategorization is perhaps the commonest trick of the human mind. Given a thimbleful of facts we rush to make generalizations as large as a tub. One young boy developed the idea that all Norwegians were giants because he was impressed by the gigantic stature of Ymir in the saga, and for years was fearful lest he meet a living Norwegian. A certain man happened to know three Englishmen personally and proceeded to declare that the whole English race had the common attributes that he observed in these three.

There is a natural basis for this tendency. Life is so short, and the demands upon us for practical adjustments so great, that we cannot let our ignorance detain us in our daily transactions. We have to decide whether objects are good or bad by classes. We cannot weigh each object in the world by itself. Rough and ready rubrics, however coarse and broad, have to suffice.

Not every overblown generalization is a prejudice. Some are simply *misconceptions,* wherein we organize wrong information. One child had the idea that all people living in Minneapolis were "monopolists." And from his father he had learned that monopolists were evil folk. When in later years he discovered the confusion, his dislike of dwellers in Minneapolis vanished.

Here we have the test to help us distinguish between ordinary errors of prejudgment and prejudice. If a person is capable of rectifying his erroneous judgments in the light of new evidence he is not prejudiced. *Prejudgments become prejudices only if they are not reversible when exposed to new knowledge.* A prejudice, unlike a simple misconception, is actively resistant to all evidence that would unseat it. We tend to grow emotional when a prejudice is threatened with contradiction. Thus the difference between ordinary prejudgments and prejudice is that one can discuss and rectify a prejudgment without emotional resistance.

Taking these various considerations into account, we may now attempt a final definition of negative ethnic prejudice—one that will serve us throughout this book. Each phrase in the definition represents a considerable condensation of the points we have been discussing:

> Ethnic prejudice is an antipathy based upon a faulty and inflexible generalization. It may be felt or expressed. It may be directed toward a group as a whole, or toward an individual because he is a member of that group.

The net effect of prejudice, thus defined, is to place the object of prejudice at some disadvantage not merited by his own misconduct.

Is Prejudice a Value Concept?

Some authors have introduced an additional ingredient into their definitions of prejudice. They claim that attitudes are prejudiced only if they violate some important norms or values accepted in a culture. They insist that prejudice is only that type of prejudgment that is ethically disapproved in a society.

> One experiment shows that common usage of the term has this flavor. Several adult judges were asked to take statements made by ninth-grade children and sort them into piles according to the degree of "prejudice" represented. It turned out that whatever a boy may have said against girls as a group was not judged to be prejudice, for it is regarded as normal for an early adolescent to heap scorn on the opposite sex. Nor were statements made against teachers considered examples of prejudice. This antagonism, too, seemed natural to this age, and socially unimportant. But when the

children expressed animosity toward labor unions, toward social classes, races or nationalities, more judgments of "prejudice" were given.

In brief, the social importance of an unfair attitude entered into the judges' view of its prejudiced character. A fifteen-year-old boy who is "off" girls is not considered as biased as one who is "off" nationalities other than his own.

If we use the term in this sense we should have to say that the older caste system in India—which is now breaking down—involved no prejudice. It was simply a convenient stratification in the social structure, acceptable to nearly all citizens because it clarified the division of labor and defined social prerogatives. It was for centuries acceptable even to the untouchables because the religious doctrine of reincarnation made the arrangement seem entirely just. An untouchable was ostracized because in previous existences he failed to merit promotions to a higher caste or to a supermortal existence. He now has his just deserts and likewise an opportunity through an obedient and spiritually directed life to win advancement in future reincarnations. Assuming that this account of a happy caste system really marked Hindu society at one time, was there then no question of prejudice?

Or take the Ghetto system. Through long stretches of history Jews have been segregated in certain residential zones, sometimes with a chain around the region. Only inside were they allowed to move freely. The method had the merit of preventing unpleasant conflict, and the Jew, knowing his place, could plan his life with a certain definiteness and comfort. It could be argued that his lot was much more secure and predictable than in the modern world. There were periods in history when neither the Jew nor gentile felt particularly outraged by the system. Was prejudice then absent?

Were the ancient Greeks (or early American plantation owners) prejudiced against their hereditary class of slaves? To be sure they looked down upon them, and undoubtedly held fallacious theories concerning their inherent inferiority and "animal-like" mentality; but so natural did it all seem, so good, so proper, that there was no moral dilemma.

Even today, in certain states, a *modus vivendi* has been worked out between white and colored people. A ritual of relations is established, and most people abide unthinkingly by the realities of social structure. Since they merely follow the folkways they deny that they are prejudiced. The Negro simply knows his place, and white people know theirs. Shall we then say, as some writers have, that prejudice exists only when actions are *more* condescending, *more* negative, than the accepted culture itself prescribes? Is prejudice to be regarded merely as deviance from common practice?

Among Navaho Indians, as in many societies on earth, there is belief in witchcraft. Whoever is accused of being a witch is earnestly avoided or soundly punished on the basis of the prevailing erroneous conceptions concerning the dark powers of witches. Here, as in our preceding illustrations, all the terms of our definition of prejudice are met—but few members of the Navaho society make a moral issue of the matter. Since the rejection of witches is an accepted custom, not socially disapproved, can it be called prejudice?

What shall we say about this line of argument? It has impressed some critics so much that they hold the whole problem of prejudice to be nothing more than a value-judgment invented by "liberal intellectuals." When liberals do not approve of a folkway *they* arbitrarily call it prejudice. What they should do is to follow not their own sense of moral outrage, but consult the ethos of a culture. If the culture itself is in conflict, holding up a higher standard of conduct than many of its members practice, then we may speak of prejudice existing within the culture. Prejudice is the *moral* evaluation placed by a culture on some of its own practices. It is a designation of attitudes that are disapproved.

These critics, it would seem, confuse two separate and distinct problems. Prejudice in the simple psychological sense of negative, overgeneralized judgment exists just as surely in caste societies, slave societies, or countries believing in witchcraft as in ethically more sensitive societies. The second problem—whether prejudice is or is not attended by a sense of moral outrage—is a separate issue altogether.

To be sure, countries with a Christian and democratic tradition view ethnic prejudice with disfavor more often than do countries without this ethical tradition. And it is also probably true that "liberal intellectuals" are more likely than most people to become emotionally aroused by the problem.

Even so, there is not the slightest justification for confusing the objective facts of prejudice with cultural or ethical judgment of these facts. The unpleasant flavor of a word should not mislead us into believing that it stands only for a value-judgment. Take the word *epidemic*. It suggests something disagreeable. No doubt Pasteur, the great conqueror of epidemics, hated them. But his value-judgment did not affect in the slightest degree the objective facts with which he dealt so successfully. *Syphilis* is a term flavored with opprobrium in our culture. But the emotional tinge has no bearing whatever upon the operations of the spirochete within the human frame.

Some cultures, like our own, abjure prejudice; some do not; but the fundamental psychological analysis of prejudice is the same whether we are talking about Hindus, Navahos, the Greeks of antiquity, or Middletown, U.S.A. Whenever a negative attitude toward persons is sustained by a spurious overgeneralization we encounter the syndrome of prejudice. It is not essential that people deplore this syndrome. It has existed in all ages in every country. It constitutes a bona fide psychological problem. The degree of moral indignation engendered is irrelevant.

FUNCTIONAL SIGNIFICANCE

Certain definitions of prejudice include one additional ingredient. The following is an example:

> Prejudice is a pattern of hostility in interpersonal relations which is directed against an entire group, or against its individual members; it fulfills a specific irrational function for its bearer.

The final phrase of this definition implies that negative attitudes are not prejudices unless they serve a private, self-gratifying purpose for the person who has them.

. . . In most cases prejudice seems to have some "functional significance" for the bearer. Yet this is not always the case. Much prejudice is a matter of blind conformity with prevailing folkways. . . . For this reason it seems unwise to insist that the "irrational function" of prejudice be included in our basic definition.

ATTITUDES AND BELIEFS

We have said that an adequate definition of prejudice contains two essential ingredients. There must be an *attitude* of favor or disfavor; and it must be related to an overgeneralized (and therefore erroneous) *belief*. Prejudiced statements sometimes express the attitudinal factor, sometimes the belief factor. In the following series the first item expresses attitude, the second, belief:

> I can't abide Negroes.
> Negroes are smelly.
>
> I wouldn't live in an apartment house with Jews.
> There are a few exceptions, but in general all Jews are pretty much alike.
>
> I don't want Japanese-Americans in my town.
> Japanese-Americans are sly and tricky.

Is it important to distinguish between the attitudinal and belief aspects of prejudice? For some purposes, no. When we find one, we usually find the other. Without some generalized beliefs concerning a group as a whole, a hostile attitude could not long be sustained. In modern researches it turns out that people who express a high degree of antagonistic attitudes on a test for prejudice, also show that they believe to a high degree that the groups they are prejudiced against have a large number of objectionable qualities.

But for some purposes it is useful to distinguish attitude from belief. For example, . . . certain programs designed to reduce prejudice succeed in altering beliefs but not in changing attitudes. Beliefs, to some extent, can be rationally attacked and altered. Usually, however, they have the slippery propensity of accommodating themselves somehow to the negative attitude which is much harder to change. The following dialogue illustrates the point:

> MR. X The trouble with the Jews is that they only take care of their own group.
>
> MR. Y But the record of the Community Chest campaign shows that they give more generously, in proportion to their numbers, to the general charities of the community, than do non-Jews.
>
> MR. X That shows they are always trying to buy favor and intrude into Christian affairs. They think of nothing but money; that is why there are so many Jewish bankers.
>
> MR. Y But a recent study shows that the percentage of Jews in the banking business is negligible, far smaller than the percentage of non-Jews.
>
> MR. X That's just it; they don't go in for respectable business; they are only in the movie business or run night clubs.

Thus the belief system has a way of slithering around to justify the more permanent attitude. The process is one of *rationalization*—of the accommodation of beliefs to attitudes.

· · · · ·

ACTING OUT PREJUDICE

What people actually do in relation to groups they dislike is not always directly related to what they think or feel about them. Two employers, for example, may dislike Jews to an equal degree. One may keep his feelings to himself and may hire Jews on the same basis as any workers—perhaps because he wants to gain goodwill for his factory or store in the Jewish community. The other may translate his dislike into his employment policy, and refuse to hire Jews. Both men are prejudiced, but only one of them practices *discrimination*. As a rule discrimination has more immediate and serious social consequences than has prejudice.

It is true that any negative attitude tends somehow, somewhere, to express itself in action. Few people keep their antipathies entirely to themselves. The more intense the attitude, the more likely it is to result in vigorously hostile action.

We may venture to distinguish certain degrees of negative action from the least energetic to the most.

1. *Antilocution.* Most people who have prejudices talk about them. With like-minded friends, occasionally with strangers, they may express their antagonism freely. But many people never go beyond this mild degree of antipathetic action.

2. *Avoidance.* If the prejudice is more intense, it leads the individual to avoid members of the disliked group, even perhaps at the cost of considerable inconvenience. In this case, the bearer of prejudice does not directly inflict harm upon the group he dislikes.

3. *Discrimination.* Here the prejudiced person makes detrimental distinctions of an active sort. He undertakes to exclude all members of the group in question from certain types of employment, from residential housing, political rights, educational or recreational opportunities, churches, hospitals, or from some other social privileges. Segregation is an institutionalized form of discrimination, enforced legally or by common custom.

4. *Physical attack.* Under conditions of heightened emotion prejudice may lead to acts of violence or semiviolence. An unwanted Negro family may be forcibly ejected from a neighborhood, or so severely threatened that it leaves in fear. Gravestones in Jewish cemeteries may be desecrated. The Northside's Italian gang may lie in wait for the Southside's Irish gang.

5. *Extermination.* Lynchings, pogroms, massacres, and the Hitlerian program of genocide mark the ultimate degree of violent expression of prejudice.

This five-point scale is not mathematically constructed, but it serves to call attention to the enormous range of activities that may issue from prejudiced attitudes and beliefs. While many people would never move from antilocution to avoidance; or from avoidance to active discrimination, or higher on the scale, still it is true that activity on one level makes transition to a more intense level easier. It was Hitler's antilocution that led Germans to avoid their Jewish neighbors and erstwhile friends. This preparation made it easier to enact the Nürnberg laws of discrimination which, in turn, made the subsequent burning of synagogues and street attacks upon Jews seem natural. The final step in the macabre progression was the ovens at Auschwitz.

From the point of view of social consequences much "polite prejudice" is harmless enough—being confined to idle chatter. But unfortunately, the fateful progression is, in this century, growing in frequency. The resulting disruption in the human family is menacing. And as the peoples of the earth grow ever more interdependent, they can tolerate less well the mounting friction.

2. The Ideology of Authoritarianism

THEODOR ADORNO,
ELSE FRENKEL-BRUNSWIK,
DANIEL J. LEVINSON, AND
R. NEVITT SANFORD

The Authoritarian Personality *demonstrated how important an interdisciplinary perspective could be to the study of prejudice and discrimination. The book not only investigated the emotional dynamics and surface appearance of personality types differentially susceptible to prejudice, but also considered what social and cultural circumstances might give rise to personalities of different types. In brief, the formulation of the emergence and dynamics of authoritarian personalities is as follows: The process begins with parents who have insecure personalities resulting from a combination of (a) repressed desires to express their sexuality and their hostility toward people or organizations that hold power over them, and (b) an inability to grasp the complex nature of broad institutional and social forces like economic and governmental arrangements. Such parents tend to be extropunitive in raising their own children, and they stringently emphasize that children should honor conventional standards of respectability without inquiring into the character of social arrangements. As a result, the children become "authoritarian personalities," reluctant to consider their own weaknesses, projecting them on to others instead. They tend to think in rigid dichotomies, and ambiguity makes them uncomfortable. They cling to established authority, frowning on deviation, because they are unconsciously afraid to strike out on new paths of their own. These characteristics incline them to vent their antipathies on whatever minority groups their culture defines as scapegoats, notably in American society Negroes and Jews.*

Later studies have called the methodology of The Authoritarian Personality *into serious question (for example, see selection 20). However, few scholars doubt that the book handled significant issues in a disciplined, sensitive, and thought-provoking fashion.*

SOURCE: T. W. Adorno *et al.*, *The Authoritarian Personality* (New York: Harper & Brothers, 1950), pp. 4–11. Copyright © 1950 by The American Jewish Committee. Reprinted with the permission of Harper and Row, Publishers.

Theodor Adorno is Professor at the Institut für Sozialkunde, University of Frankfurt, West Germany. *Else Frenkel-Brunswik*, now deceased, was research associate in the Institute of Child Welfare at the University of California at Berkeley. *Daniel J. Levinson* is Assistant Professor of Psychology and Director of the Center for Socio-psychological Research at the Harvard Medical School. *R. Nevitt Sanford* is Professor of Psychology at the University of California at Berkeley. He is the editor of *The American College*.

What people say and, to a lesser degree, what they really think depends very largely upon the climate of opinion in which they are living; but when that climate changes, some individuals adapt themselves much more quickly than others. If there should be a marked increase in antidemocratic propaganda, we should expect some people to accept and repeat it at once, others when it seemed that "everybody believed it," and still others not at all. In other words, individuals differ in their *susceptibility* to antidemocratic propaganda, in their readiness to exhibit antidemocratic tendencies. It seems necessary to study ideology at this "readiness level" in order to gauge the potential for fascism in this country. Observers have noted that the amount of outspoken anti-Semitism in pre-Hitler Germany was less than that in this country at the present time; one might hope that the potentiality is less in this country, but this can be known only through intensive investigation, through the detailed survey of what is on the surface and the thorough probing of what lies beneath it.

A question may be raised as to what is the degree of relationship between ideology and action. If an individual is making antidemocratic propaganda or engaging in overt attacks upon minority group members, it is usually assumed that his opinions, attitudes, and values are congruent with his action; but comfort is sometimes found in the thought that though another individual expresses antidemocratic ideas verbally, he does not, and perhaps will not, put them into overt action. Here, once again, there is a question of potentialities. Overt action, like open verbal expression, depends very largely upon the situation of the moment—something that is best described in socioeconomic and political terms—but individuals differ very widely with respect to their readiness to be provoked into action. The study of this potential is a part of the study of the individual's over-all ideology; to know what kinds and what intensities of belief, attitude, and value are likely to lead to action, and to know what forces within the individual serve as inhibitions upon action are matters of the greatest practical importance.

There seems little reason to doubt that ideology-in-readiness (ideological receptivity) and ideology-in-words and in action are essentially the same stuff. The description of an individual's total ideology must portray not only the organization on each level but organization among levels. What the individual consistently says in public, what he says when he feels safe from criticism, what he thinks but will not say at all, what he thinks but will not admit to himself, what he is disposed to think or to do when various kinds of appeal are made to him—all these phenomena may be conceived of as constituting a single structure. The structure may not be integrated, it may contain contradictions as well as consistencies, but it is *organized* in the sense that the constituent parts are related in psychologically meaningful ways.

In order to understand such a structure, a theory of the total personality is necessary. According to the theory that has guided the present research, personality is a more or less enduring organization of forces within the individual. These persisting forces of personality help to determine response in various situations, and it is thus largely to them that consistency of behavior—whether verbal or physical—is attributable. But behavior, however consistent, is not the same thing as personality; personality lies *behind* behavior and *within* the individual. The forces of personality are not responses but *readinesses for response;* whether or not a readiness will issue in overt expression depends not only upon the situation of the moment but upon what other readinesses stand in opposition to it. Personality forces which are inhibited are on a deeper level than those which immediately and consistently express themselves in overt behavior.

What are the forces of personality and what are the processes by which they are organized? For theory as to the structure of personality we have leaned most heavily upon Freud, while for a more or less systematic formulation of the more directly observable and measurable aspects of personality we have been guided primarily by academic psychology. The forces of personality are primarily *needs* (drives, wishes, emotional impulses) which vary from one individual to another in their quality, their intensity, their mode of gratification, and the objects of their attachment, and which interact with other needs in harmonious or conflicting patterns. There are primitive emotional needs, there are needs to avoid punishment and to keep the good will of the social group, there are needs to maintain harmony and integration within the self.

Since it will be granted that opinions, attitudes, and values depend upon human needs, and since personality is essentially an organization of needs, then personality may be regarded as a *determinant* of ideological preferences. Personality is not, however, to be hypostatized as an ultimate determinant. Far from being something which is given in the beginning, which remains fixed and acts upon the surrounding world, personality evolves under the impact of the social environment and can never be isolated from the social totality within which it occurs. According to the present theory, the effects of environmental forces in moulding the personality are, in general, the more profound the earlier in the life history of the individual they are brought to bear. The major influences upon personality development arise in the course of child training as carried forward in a setting of family life. What happens here is profoundly influenced by economic and social factors. It is not only that each family in trying to rear its children proceeds according to the ways of the social, ethnic, and religious groups in which it has membership, but crude economic factors affect directly the parents' behavior toward the child. This means that broad changes in social conditions and institutions will have a direct bearing upon the kinds of personalities that develop within a society.

The present research seeks to discover correlations between ideology and sociological factors operating in the individual's past—whether or not they continue to operate in his present. In attempting to explain these correlations the relationships between personality and ideology are brought into the picture, the general approach being to consider personality as an agency through which sociological influences upon ideology are mediated. If the role of personality can be made clear, it should be possible better to understand which sociological factors are the most crucial ones and in what ways they achieve their effects.

Although personality is a product of the social environment of the past, it is not, once it has developed, a mere object of the contemporary environment. What has developed is a *structure* within the individual, something which is capable of self-initiated action upon the social environment and of selection with respect to varied impinging stimuli, something which though always modifiable is frequently very resistant to fundamental change. This conception is necessary to explain consistency of behavior in widely varying situations, to explain the persistence of ideological trends in the face of contradicting facts and radically altered social conditions, to explain why people in the same sociological situation have different or even conflicting views on social issues, and why it is that people whose behavior has been changed through psychological manipulation lapse into their old ways as soon as the agencies of manipulation are removed.

The conception of personality structure is the best safeguard against the inclination to attribute persistent trends in the individual to something "innate" or "basic" or "racial" within him. The Nazi allegation that natural, biological traits decide the total being of a person would not have been such a successful political device had it not been possible to point to numerous instances of relative fixity in human behavior and to challenge those who thought to explain them on any basis other than a biological one. Without the conception of personality structure, writers whose approach rests upon the assumption of infinite human flexibility and responsiveness to the social situation of the moment have not helped matters by referring persistent trends which they could not approve to "confusion" or "psychosis" or evil under one name or another. There is, of course, some basis for describing as "pathological" patterns of behavior which do not conform with the most common, and seemingly most lawful, responses to momentary stimuli. But this is to use the term pathological in the very narrow sense of deviation from the average found in a particular context and, what is worse, to suggest that everything in the personality structure is to be put under this heading. Actually, personality embraces variables which exist widely in the population and have lawful relations one to another. Personality patterns that have been dismissed as "pathological" because they were not in keeping with the most common manifest trends or the most dominant ideals within a society, have on closer investigation turned out to be but exaggerations of what was almost universal below the surface in that society. What is "pathological" today may with changing social conditions become the dominant trend of tomorrow.

It seems clear then that an adequate approach to the problems before us must take into account both fixity and flexibility; it must regard the two not as mutually exclusive categories but as the extremes of a single continuum along which human characteristics may be placed, and it must provide a basis for understanding the conditions which favor the one extreme or the other. Personality is a concept to account for relative permanence. But it may be emphasized again that personality is mainly a potential; it is a readiness for behavior rather than behavior itself; although it consists in dispositions to behave in certain ways, the behavior that actually occurs will always depend upon the objective situation. Where the concern is with antidemocratic trends, a delineation of the conditions for individual expression requires an understanding of the total organization of society.

It has been stated that the personality structure may be such as to render the individual susceptible to antidemocratic propaganda. It may now be asked what are the conditions under which such propaganda would increase in pitch and volume and come to dominate in press and radio to the exclusion of contrary ideological stimuli, so that what is now potential would become actively manifest. The answer must be sought not in any single personality nor in personality factors found in the mass of people, but in processes at work in society itself. It seems well understood today that whether or not antidemocratic propaganda is to become a dominant force in this country depends primarily upon the situation of the most powerful economic interests, upon whether they, by conscious design or not, make use of this device for maintaining their dominant status. This is a matter about which the great majority of people would have little to say.

The present research, limited as it is to the hitherto largely neglected psychological aspects of fascism, does not concern itself with the production of propaganda. It focuses attention, rather, upon the consumer, the individual for whom the propaganda is designed. In so doing it attempts to take into account not only the psychological structure of the individual but the total objective situation in which he lives. It makes the assumption that people in general tend to accept political and social programs which they believe will serve their economic interests. What these interests are depends in each case upon the individual's position in society as defined in economic and sociological terms. An important part of the present research, therefore, was the attempt to discover what patterns of socio-economic factors are associated with receptivity, and with resistance, to antidemocratic propaganda.

At the same time, however, it was considered that economic motives in the individual may not have the dominant and crucial role that is often ascribed to them. If economic self-interest were the only determinant of opinion, we should expect people of the same socioeconomic status to have very similar opinions, and we should expect opinion to vary in a meaningful way from one socioeconomic grouping to another. Research has not given very sound support for these expectations. There is only the most general similarity of opinion among people of the same socioeconomic status, and the exceptions are glaring; while variations from one socioeconomic group to another are rarely simple or clear-cut. To explain why it is that people of the same socioeconomic status so frequently have different ideologies, while people of a different status often have very similar ideologies, we must take account of other than purely economic needs.

More than this, it is becoming increasingly plain that people very frequently do not behave in such a way as to further their material interests, even when it is clear to them what these interests are. The resistance of white-collar workers to organization is not due to a belief that the union will not help them economically; the tendency of the small businessman to side with big business in most economic and political matters cannot be due entirely to a belief that this is the way to guarantee his economic independence. In instances such as these the individual seems not only not to consider his material interests, but even to go against them. It is as if he were thinking in terms of a larger group identification, as if his point of view were determined more by his need to support this group and to suppress opposite ones than by rational consideration of his own interests. Indeed, it is with a sense of relief today that one is assured that a group conflict is merely a clash of economic interests—that each side is merely out to "do" the other—and not a struggle in which deep-lying emotional drives have been let loose. When it comes to the ways in which people appraise the social world, irrational trends stand out glaringly. One may conceive of a professional man who opposes the immigration of Jewish refugees on the ground that this will increase the competition with which he has to deal and so decrease his income. However undemocratic this may be, it is at least rational in a limited sense. But for this man to go on, as do most people who oppose Jews on occupational grounds, and accept a wide variety of opinions, many of which are contradictory, about Jews in general, and to attribute various ills of the world to them, is plainly illogical. And it is just as illogical to praise all Jews in accordance with a "good" stereotype of them. Hostility against groups that is based upon real frustration, brought about by members of that group, undoubtedly exists, but such frustrating experiences can hardly account for the fact that prejudice is apt to be generalized. Evidence from the present study confirms what has often been indicated: that a man who is hostile toward one minority group is very likely to be hostile against a wide variety of others. There is no conceivable rational basis for such generalization; and, what is more striking, prejudice against, or totally uncritical acceptance of, a particular group often exists in the absence of any experience with members of that group. The objective situation of the individual seems an unlikely source of such irrationality; rather we should seek where psychology has already found the sources of dreams, fantasies, and misinterpretations of the world—that is, in the deep-lying needs of the personality.

Another aspect of the individual's situation which we should expect to affect his ideological receptivity is his membership in social groups—occupational, fraternal, religious, and the like. For historical and sociological reasons, such groups favor and promulgate, whether officially or unofficially, different patterns of ideas. There is reason to believe that individuals, out of their needs to conform and to belong and to believe and through such devices as imitation and conditioning, often take over more or less ready-made the opinions, attitudes, and values that are characteristic of the groups in which they have membership. To the extent that the ideas which prevail in such a group are implicitly or explicitly antidemocratic, the individual group member might be expected to be receptive to propaganda having the same general direction. Accordingly, the present research investigates a variety of group memberships with a view to what general trends of thought—and how much variability—might be found in each.

It is recognized, however, that a correlation between group membership and ideology may be due to different kinds of determination in different individuals. In some cases it might be that the individual merely repeats opinions which are taken for granted in his social milieu and which he has no reason to question; in other cases it might be that the individual has chosen to join a particular group because it stood for ideals with which he was already in sympathy. In modern society, despite enormous commonality in basic culture, it is rare for a person to be subjected to only one pattern of ideas, after he is old enough for ideas to mean something to him. Some selection is usually made, according, it may be supposed, to the needs of his personality. Even when individuals are exposed during their formative years almost exclusively to a single, closely knit pattern of political, economic, social, and religious ideas, it is found that some conform while others rebel, and it seems proper to inquire whether personality factors do not make the difference. The soundest approach, it would seem, is to consider that in the determination of ideology, as in the determination of any behavior, there is a situational factor and a personality factor, and that a careful weighing of the role of each will yield the most accurate prediction.

Situational factors, chiefly economic condition and social group memberships, have been studied intensively in recent researches on opinion and attitude, while the more inward, more individualistic factors have not received the attention they deserve. Beyond this, there is still another reason why the present study places particular emphasis upon the personality. Fascism, in order to be successful as a political movement, must have a mass basis. It must secure not only the frightened submission but the active cooperation of the great majority of the people. Since by its very nature it favors the few at the expense of the many, it cannot possibly demonstrate that it will so improve the situation of most people that their real interests will be served. It must therefore make its major appeal, not to rational self-interest, but to emotional needs—often to the most primitive and irrational wishes and fears. If it be argued that fascist propaganda fools people into believing that their lot will be improved, then the question arises: Why are they so easily fooled? Because, it may be supposed, of their personality structure; because of long-established patterns of hopes and aspirations, fears and anxieties that dispose them to certain beliefs and make them resistant to others. The task of fascist propaganda, in other words, is rendered easier to the degree that antidemocratic potentials already exist in the great mass of people. It may be granted that in Germany economic conflicts and dislocations within the society were such that for this reason alone the triumph of fascism was sooner or later inevitable; but the Nazi leaders did not act as if they believed this to be so; instead they acted as if it were necessary at every moment to take into account the psychology of the people—to activate every ounce of their antidemocratic potential, to compromise with them, to stamp out the slightest spark of rebellion. It seems apparent that any attempt to appraise the chances of a fascist triumph in America must reckon with the potential existing in the character of the people. Here lies not only the susceptibility to antidemocratic propaganda but the most dependable sources of resistance to it.

The present writers believe that it is up to the people to decide whether or not this country goes fascist. It is assumed that knowledge of the nature and extent of antidemocratic potentials will indicate programs for democratic action. These programs should not be limited to devices for manipulating people in such a way that they will behave more democratically, but they should be devoted to increasing the kind of self-awareness and self-determination that makes any kind of manipulation impossible. There is one explanation for the existence of an individual's ideology that has not so far been considered: that it is the view of the world which a reasonable man, with some understanding of the role of such determinants as those discussed above, and with complete access to the necessary facts, will organize for himself. This conception, though it has been left to the last, is of crucial importance for a sound approach to ideology. Without it we should have to share the destructive view, which has gained some acceptance in the modern world, that since all ideologies, all philosophies, derive from nonrational sources there is no basis for saying that one has more merit than another.

But the rational system of an objective and thoughtful man is not a thing apart from personality. Such a system is still motivated. What is distinguishing in its sources is mainly the *kind of personality organization* from which it springs. It might be said that a mature personality (if we may for the moment use this term without defining it) will come closer to achieving a rational system of thought than will an immature one; but a personality is no less dynamic and no less organized for being mature, and the task of describing the structure of this personality is not different in kind from the task of describing any other personality. According to theory, the personality variables which have most to do with determining the objectivity and rationality of an ideology are those which belong to the ego, that part of the personality which appreciates reality, integrates the other parts, and operates with the most conscious awareness.

It is the ego that becomes aware of and takes responsibility for non-rational forces operating within the personality. This is the basis for our belief that the object of knowing what are the psychological determinants of ideology is that men can become more reasonable. It is not supposed, of course, that this will eliminate differences of opinion. The world is sufficiently complex and difficult to know, men have enough real interests that are in conflict with the real interests of other men, there are enough ego-accepted differences in personality to insure that arguments about politics, economics, and religion will never grow dull. Knowledge of the psychological determinants of ideology cannot tell us what is the *truest* ideology; it can only remove some of the barriers in the way of its pursuit.

3. A Methodological Note on the Principle of Cumulation

GUNNAR MYRDAL

Myrdal's An American Dilemma *is the most important book ever written on American race relations. The present selection illustrates one aspect of Myrdal's views about relationships among the many factors that affect prejudice and discrimination. Consider the following hypothetical example of how the principle of cumulation operates: Because Negroes receive poor schooling, it is difficult for them to get good jobs. Having to work at bad jobs, they are kept from exercising as much political influence as they might if they were more prosperous and had more security. In turn, a lack of political influence among Negroes means that school boards elected by*

SOURCE: Gunnar Myrdal, *An American Dilemma* (New York: Harper & Brothers, 1944), pp. 1065–70. Copyright © 1944, 1962, by Harper and Row, Publishers, Inc., and reprinted with their permission.

Gunnar Myrdal is Director of the Institute for International Economic Studies in Stockholm. His most recent book is *Challenge to Affluence*.

primarily white constituencies do not have to devote very much time and effort to improving schools in Negro neighborhoods. The combination of all of these factors then lends support to the views of some white people that Negroes are not only poorly educated, but uneducable as well. However, according to Myrdal, improvement in any one of these factors could lead to improvement in all the others.

In capsule form, the example also illustrates the nature of the "American Dilemma." The United States, the nation that claims to value freedom and equality more than any other, systematically denies them to a tenth of its citizens. Guilt over this disparity between creed and practice thus leads white Americans to rely on their prejudices to rationalize their discriminatory behavior, and to seek mostly that information about Negroes that will reenforce preconceived negative attitudes about them.

Because Myrdal believed that many relevant issues are intertwined, he hesitated to name particular areas as the most strategic points for intervening in the discrimination-prejudice cycle. (See selection 40 for some of his more recent observations.) In contrast, some observers think it is necessary to indicate which factors are primarily causal, and which mere correlates of other processes. In any case, current readers should find Myrdal's perspective valuable on at least two counts. It calls attention to the variety of social forces that must be considered in accounting for discrimination, and it makes clear that these forces are systematically linked to one another.

In social science we have been drawing heavily on the notions and theories of the much farther developed natural sciences, particularly physics. The notion of equilibrium, for instance, has been in all our reasoning for centuries. Actually it is present in most research of the present day, even when it is not formally introduced. In most social research we have restricted our utilization of the equilibrium notion to that simple and static variant of it, the *stable equilibrium*. It is this equilibrium notion which is implicit in the sociological constructions of "maladjustment" and "adjustment" and all their several synonyms or near-synonyms, where equilibrium is thought of as having a virtual reality in determining the direction of change.[a] We propose the utilization of *other equilibrium notions* besides this simplest one. For dynamic analysis of the process of change in social relations, it is highly desirable that we disengage our minds from the stable equilibrium scheme of thinking. The other types of equilibrium notions are often better descriptions of social reality than the stable one.

If we succeed in placing a pencil upright on its end, it is also in equi-

---

[a] These equilibrium concepts have been used also as vehicles for introducing hidden valuations—i.e., bias—into research. . . . Our interest . . . is directed only upon their usefulness as theoretical tools. To explain these other notions it is convenient to think in terms of analogies. The stable equilibrium is like a hanging pendulum, unmoving, and with no tendency to move unless jolted.

librium, but an unstable one, a "labile status" of balancing forces, as we easily find if we touch it. No "adjustment," "adaptation," or "accommodation" toward the original position will follow the application of a push, but only an accelerated movement away from the original state of balance. A third type of equilibrium is present when a pencil is rolling on a plane surface: it may come to rest anywhere. A fourth type is what we might call "created equilibrium," that is, arranging a disordered pile of pencils into a box by intelligent social engineering.

The most important need is to give place in our hypothetical explanatory scheme to a rational recognition of the cumulation of forces. In one branch of social science, economics, these various types of equilibrium notions have lately been used with great advantage. The principle of cumulation has given us, for the first time, something which approaches a real theory of economic dynamics. . . . [We refer] to the theory of the "vicious circle" as a main explanatory scheme for this inquiry into the Negro problem; the scheme reappears in every part of our book. The following brief notes are intended to give an abstract clarification of the theory and a perspective on some of its future potentialities as a method of social research.

In considering the Negro problem in its most abstract aspect, let us construct a much simplified mental model of dynamic social causation. We assume in this model society of our imagination a white majority and a Negro minority. We assume, further, that the interrelation between the two groups is in part determined by a specific degree of "race prejudice" on the side of the whites, directed against the Negroes. We assume the "plane of living" of the Negroes to be considerably lower than that of the whites. We take, as given, a mutual relationship between our two variables, and we assume this relationship to be of such a type that, on the one hand, the Negroes' plane of living is kept down by discrimination from the side of the whites while, on the other hand, the whites' reason for discrimination is partly dependent upon the Negroes' plane of living. The Negroes' poverty, ignorance, superstition, slum dwellings, health deficiencies, dirty appearance, disorderly conduct, bad odor and criminality stimulate and feed the antipathy of the whites for them. We assume, for the sake of simplicity, that society, in our abstract model, is in "balance" initially. By this we mean that conditions are static, that our two variables are exactly checking each other: there is—under these static conditions—just enough prejudice on the part of the whites to keep down the Negro plane of living to that level which maintains the specific degree of prejudice, or the other way around.

If now, in this hypothetically balanced state, for some reason or other, the Negro plane of living should be lowered, this will—other things being equal—in its turn increase white prejudice. Such an increase in white prejudice has the effect of pressing down still further the Negro plane of living, which again will increase prejudice, and so on, by way of mutual interaction between the two variables, *ad infinitum.* A cumulative process is thus set in motion which can have final effects quite out of proportion to the magnitude of the original push. The push might even be withdrawn after a time, and still a permanent change will remain or even the process of change will continue without a new balance in sight. If, instead, the initial change had been such a thing as a gift from a philanthropist to raise the Negro plane of living, a cumulative movement would have started in the other direction, having exactly the same causal mechanism. The vicious circle works both ways.

The Negroes' "plane of living" is, however, a composite entity. Let us, while retaining our major assumptions, approach a more realistic conception by splitting up this quantity into components, assuming that the cumulative principle works also in their causative interrelations. Besides "relative absence of race prejudice on the side of whites," we introduce a number of variables: levels of "Negro employment," "wages," "housing," "nutrition," "clothing," "health," "education," "stability in family relations," "manners," "cleanliness," "orderliness," "trustworthiness," "law observance," "loyalty to society at large," "absence of criminality" and so on. All these variables—according to our hypotheses—cumulate. In other words, we assume that a movement in any of the Negro variables in the direction toward the corresponding white levels will tend to decrease white prejudice. At the same time white prejudice is assumed to be, directly or indirectly, one of the causative factors effective in keeping the levels low for the several Negro variables. It is also our hypothesis that, on the whole, a rise in any single one of the Negro variables will tend to raise all the other Negro variables and thus, indirectly as well as directly, result in a cumulatively enforced effect upon white prejudice. A rise in employment will tend to increase earnings; raise standards of living; and improve health, education, manners and law observance and *vice versa*; a better education is assumed to raise the chances of a higher salaried job, and *vice versa*; and so all the way through our whole system of variables. Each of the secondary changes has its effect on white prejudice.

If, in actual social life, the dynamics of the causal relations between the various factors in the Negro problem should correspond to our hypotheses, then—assuming again, for the sake of simplicity, an initially static state of balanced forces—*any change in any one of these factors, independent of the way in which it is brought about, will, by the aggregate weight of the cumulative effects running back and forth between them all, start the whole system moving* in one direction or the other as the case may be, with a speed depending upon the original push and the functions of causal interrelation within the system.

Our point is not simply that many forces are "working in the same direction." Originally we assumed that there was a balance between these forces, and that the system was static, until we introduced one push coming in

at one point or the other. When the system starts rolling, it is true that
the changes in the forces—though not all the forces themselves—work in
one direction; but this is because the variables are assumed to be inter-
locked in such a causal mechanism that a change of any one causes the
others to change *in the same direction*, with a secondary effect upon the
first variable, and so on.

We may further notice that the "balance" assumed as initial status was
not a stable equilibrium at all—of the type which is tacitly assumed in the
notions of "maladjustment," "adjustment," "accommodation," "social lag"
—and, further, that in our scheme of hypotheses there is not necessarily
assumed to exist any new "balance," or "equilibrium," or "harmony,"
toward which the factors of the system "adjust" or "accommodate." In the
utilization of this theoretical model on problems of actual social reality,
the initial state of labile balance, which we assumed for simplicity in our
demonstration, will, of course, never be found. What we shall have to
study are *processes of systems actually rolling* in the one direction or the
other, systems which are constantly subjected to all sorts of pushes from
outside through all the variables, and which are moving because of the
cumulative effect of all these pushes and the interaction between the
variables.

The individual factors into which we split the Negroes' plane of living
can, of course, be split again, and it is the purpose of scientific analysis
to do so. The causal relations between the sub-factors, and between them
and all other factors, will be assumed to be ruled by the same cumulative
principle. White race prejudice, here assumed as the "cause" of discrimination, is not a solid and static factor. To begin with, it depends upon
discrimination itself. If, for some reason—for example, the demand of the
employer during a war emergency, or the ruling of a trade union—white
workers actually come to work with Negroes as fellow workers, it has been
experienced that prejudice will often adjust to the changed amount of
discrimination. White prejudice itself can be split into a great number of
beliefs and valuations; to a degree, both of these two types of factors are
dependent upon each other . . . and, consequently, are under the rule of
the cumulative principle.

Throughout this treatise on the Negro problem the model of dynamic
causation—and the implied skepticism toward the idea of stable equilibrium—is kept steadily in the back of our mind. A main viewpoint in
our study of every single factor in the Negro problem is thus its interrelation with all other factors and their cumulative effect upon the status
of the Negro. The principle of cumulation allows us to see that there is
sense in the general notion of the "status of the Negro." We should,
indeed, have liked to present in our study a general *index*, year by year
or at least decade by decade, as a quantitative expression of the movement
of the entire system we are studying: the status of the Negro in America.

Such an index would have about the same significance as the general indices of production or prices or any other complex systems of interdependent variables. The index is an average. It should, for the same principal reasons, have to be broken down for regions, classes, and items, and this breaking down would have the same scientific function in an analysis. It would give quantitative precision to the concept of the general status of the Negro—a concept which, because of the cumulative principle, we cannot escape. And it always clarifies our reasoning to be compelled to calculate a quantitative value for a notion we use. Materials for such an index of (relative and absolute) Negro status are, to a great extent, available, and the general theory of the index offers a methodological basis for its construction. But the work of constructing and analyzing a general index of Negro status in America amounts to a major investigation in itself, and we must leave the matter as a proposal for further research.

Our chief task is to analyze the causal interrelation within the system itself as it works under the influence of outside pushes and the momentum of on-going processes within. The system is much more complicated than appears from our abstract representation. To begin with, all factors must be broken down by region, social class, age, sex and so on. As what we are studying is a race relation, the number of combinations increases by multiples for each classification applied. White prejudice, for instance, varies not only with the status of the white man, but also with the Negro's social class and the field of Negro behavior in relation to which race prejudice is active. There are also Negro prejudices in the system.

Each factor has its peculiarities and irregularities. White prejudice, for instance, changes not only as a reaction to actual changes in Negro plane of living, but also to expectations of such changes. The latter reaction may be totally different from the former: a higher plane of living among Negroes, when it is actually achieved, may be expected to effect a *decrease* of white prejudice, but the *expectation* of it for the future might *increase* prejudice, particularly in the South (even if its long-run effects—when it actually comes—will be, as we have assumed, a decrease in prejudice). It is possible, finally, that certain social classes of whites—say poor whites in the South—even in the fairly long-range perspective will react with increased prejudice against the Negro's approaching the white man's status.

The system thus becomes complicated, but the fundamental principle of cumulative causation remains. The scientific ideal is not only to define and analyze the factors, but to give for each one of them a measure of their actual quantitative strength in influencing the other factors, as well as a measure of their ability to be influenced themselves by outside forces. The time element becomes of paramount importance in these formulas. As we have exemplified for the factor of white prejudice, the effects might have different signs in the short and in the long run. Even when this is not the case, the effects will be spread differently along the time axis. A rise of employment, for instance, will almost immediately raise some standards of living, but a change in levels of education or health are slow to be achieved, and their effects back on the other factors are in turn delayed, which slows up the whole process of cumulation. The system regularly develops under a great multitude of different outside pushes, primarily directed against almost every single factor. The actual pushes go in both directions, thus often *turning the system around on its axis as it is rolling.* Ideally, the scientific solution of the Negro problem should thus be given in the form of an interconnected series of quantitative equations, describing the movement of the actual system under various influences. That this complete, quantitative and truly scientific solution is far beyond the horizon does not need to be pointed out. But in principle it is possible to execute, and it remains as the scientific ideal steering our endeavors.

This conception of a great number of interdependent factors, mutually cumulative in their effects, disposes of the idea that there is *one* predominant factor, a "basic factor." This idea—mainly in the form of a vague conception of economic determinism—has been widely accepted in the writings on the Negro problem during the last decade. As we see the methodological problem, this one-factor hypothesis is not only theoretically unclear but is contradicted by easily ascertainable facts and factual relations. As a scientific approach it is narrow.[b]

The theoretical system of dynamic social causation we have selected corresponds more closely to the practical man's common-sense ideas about things than it does to the apprehension of reality met in many scientific writings on the Negro problem. The social scientist tends to rely too much on static notions and *a priori* to give too dominant a role to a "basic factor." The professional philanthropist, the Negro educator, the Negro trade unionist, the leaders of Negro defense organizations like the N.A.A.C.P., the Urban League, or the Interracial Commission, and, indeed, the average well-meaning citizen of both colors, pragmatically applies this same hypothesis.[c] To use once more our parallel from modern economic

---

[b] The usual economic one-factor theory is available in two extreme versions, depending upon the type of political teleology involved: (1) a radical Marxist version, where the expectation is an economic revolution which will change everything and even eradicate race prejudice; (2) a liberalistic version which does not expect an economic revolution and which—as the assumption is that no significant change can be brought about except by tackling the "basic factor," the economic system—is pessimistic about any type of induced change. There are all sorts of intermediary positions and also compromises toward recognizing that factors other than the economic one have some influence. But the one-factor theory always implies a fatalistic tendency and prevents a rational conception of interdependence and cumulative dynamic causation.

[c] The best formulation of our hypothesis available in the literature is, thus, to be found in a book by a practical man writing without scientific pretensions but out of lifelong experiences: "There is a vicious circle in caste. At the outset, the despised group is usually inferior in certain of the accepted standards of the controlling class. Being inferior, members of the degraded caste are denied the privileges and opportunities of their fellows and so are pushed still further down and then are regarded with that much

theory: when the economists during the last two decades abandoned the classical static equilibrium approach and went ahead to construct a dynamic theory of causal interrelations in a process of change, what they actually did was to apply the pragmatic notions of bankers, businessmen, and labor leaders and try to systematize them. This revolutionized economic theory and had great importance for the scientific planning of economic policy. A rational strategy in the Negro problem also assumes a theory of dynamic causation.

4. A Critical Examination of Myrdal's Assumptions

OLIVER CROMWELL COX

Cox's statements about American race relations are almost twenty years old, but they have as much force now as when they first appeared. According to Cox, American racial discrimination is the outcome of a consistent process of economic exploitation. A small white ruling class controls the means of production and the political system as well, manipulating racial prejudice to keep poor whites and Negroes from seeing that their interests are really common, not antagonistic. Government and its false ideology (what Myrdal calls the American Creed) help to maintain the lowly status of the exploited by deluding them into accepting their condition instead of rising against it in revolution.

Cox's emphasis on political power and economic exploitation as the keystones of American racial discrimination contrasts sharply with Myrdal's theoretical moderation and reluctance to single out "prime factors." For

---

less respect, and therefore are more rigorously denied advantages, and so around and around the vicious circle. Even when the movement starts to reverse itself—as it most certainly has in the case of the Negro—there is a desperately long unwinding as a slight increase in good will gives a little greater chance and this leads to a little higher accomplishment and that to increased respect and so slowly upward toward equality of opportunity, of regard, and of status." (Edwin R. Embree, *Brown America* [1931], p. 200.) To this it should only be added that even if the unwinding process is working with time lags so is the opposite movement. In spite of the time lags, the theory of the vicious circle is a cause rather for optimism than for pessimism. The cumulative principle works both ways.

Source: Oliver Cromwell Cox, *Caste, Class, and Race: A Study in Social Dynamics* (Garden City, New York: Doubleday and Company, Inc., 1948; and New York: Monthly Review Press, 1959), pp. 528–38. Copyright, 1948, by Oliver Cromwell Cox, and reprinted with his permission. Unless otherwise noted, all footnotes in this selection refer to the first edition of Myrdal's *An American Dilemma*.

Oliver Cromwell Cox is Professor of Sociology at Lincoln University, Jefferson City, Missouri. Among his other works is *Capitalism and American Leadership*.

instance, Myrdal considers the ban on legitimate cross-race sexual contact as the apex of an American caste system; Cox, however, considers this ban a mere tool for perpetuating power and privilege. By emphasizing racial purity, the ruling group attempts to maintain its distinctiveness without having to diminish social distance between itself and the subordinate group. In addition, by banning interracial marriage it tries to insure that it will not have to consider kinship rights that would call upon it to share property and power with offspring of unions between members of super- and subordinate groups.

Neither Myrdal's nor Cox's theoretical position is ideal. Myrdal's is too diffuse; Cox's, too ready to overlook contrary evidence that it cannot easily explain. Moreover, both men have written ideologies as well as theories, for they have not only attempted to describe and analyze American society, but also tried to show where it ought to go and to indicate the directions it ought to follow in getting there.

THE VICIOUS CIRCLE

Capitalist rationalizations of race relations have recently come face to face with a powerful theory of society and, in order to meet this, the orthodox theorists have become mystics. This evidently had to be so because it is exceedingly terrifying for these scientists to follow to its logical conclusion a realistic explanation of race relations; and yet they must either do this or stultify themselves. Here the social scientist is "on the spot"; he must avoid "the truth" because it is dangerous, regardless of how gracefully he eases up to it. In illustration, Myrdal advises Negroes not to become too radical and to think of many causes as of equal significance with the material factor: "Negro strategy would build on an illusion if it set all its hope on a blitzkrieg directed toward a basic [economic] factor. In the nature of things it must work on the broadest possible front. There is a place for both the radical and the conservative Negro leaders."[1] This, obviously, will lead to a situation in which the ideas of one group of leaders will tend to offset those of another.

Although Myrdal overlays his discussion of race relations with a particularly alien caste belief, his controlling hypothesis has nothing whatever to do with caste. His "theory of the vicious circle"[2] is his controlling idea. This theory is essentially an abstract formulation, inspired by a largely inverted observation of "a vicious circle in caste" by Edwin R. Embree,[3] and rendered "scientific" by the application of certain concepts which Myrdal seems to have used to his satisfaction in his study, *Monetary Equilibrium.*

[1] Gunnar Myrdal, *An American Dilemma* (New York: Harper & Brothers, 1944), p. 794.
[2] Ibid., pp. 75–78, 207–09, and Appendix 3.   [3] Ibid., p. 1069, note.

As we have seen in a previous section, the vicious circle runs as follows: "White prejudice . . . keeps the Negro low in standards of living. . . . This, in turn, gives support to white prejudice. White prejudice and Negro standards thus mutually 'cause' each other." These two variables are interdependent, but neither is consistently dependent; a change in either will affect the other inversely. If we initiate a change in Negro standards, say, by "giving the Negro youth more education," white prejudice will go down; if we change white prejudice, say, by "an increased general knowledge about biology, eradicating false beliefs concerning Negro racial inferiority," then Negro standards will go up.

It is this kind of mystical dance of imponderables which is at the basis of the system of social illusions marbled into Myrdal's discussion. In the first place, Myrdal does not develop a careful definition of race prejudice. He does say, however: "For our purpose [race prejudice] is defined as discrimination by whites against Negroes."[4] But he does not use this definition, in fact we do not see how he can, for race prejudice is a social attitude, an acquired tendency to act; it is not some act or action which is the meaning of discrimination."[5] Myrdal's studied analysis would lead us rather to deduce the following definition of race prejudice: a feeling of bitterness, especially among poor whites, aroused particularly by a standing sexual threat of Negro men to white women. As he sees it, the white man's "prejudice is based upon fundamental attitudes toward sex and personality."

If, according to Myrdal's "rank order of discrimination," the whites are most concerned with sex and the Negroes with economic advancement, his fundamental equilibrium of social forces should be a direct correlation between white prejudice and Negro sexual aggression—not Negro standards, which are clearly basically economic. In this way white prejudice will tend to vanish as Negro men give up their interest in white women; Negro standards will also go up, but only incidentally. If, for instance, Negro men would relinquish their desire to marry white women, "white people" would no longer be prejudiced against Negroes; the latter would be encouraged, say, to vote and campaign for political office and to demand their share of jobs and public funds in the Deep South.[6] To be sure, Myrdal does not

---

[4] Ibid., p. 78.

[5] In another connection Myrdal seems to give a different meaning to the concept: "If for some reason . . . white workers actually came to work with Negroes as fellow workers, it has been experienced that *prejudice* will often adjust to the changed amount of *discrimination*." Ibid., p. 1067. (Italics added.) See also pp. 1141ff.

[6] "Negroes are in desperate need of jobs and bread. . . . The marriage matter [to them] is of rather distant and doubtful interest." Ibid., p. 6. The Negroes, thus goes the logic, want jobs and the white men want to protect their women from Negro men. But white men are rather willing to let Negroes have jobs, while Negro men are not particularly interested in white women. If this is so, if these two admittedly antagonistic groups are vitally interested in different things, why is there antagonism at all? It would seem that men fight only when they are possessed of conflicting interests in the same object.

demonstrate any such proposition. We may put it in still another way: If Negro standards go up and at the same time Negroes increase their interest in white women, then, to be consistent with Myrdal's sexual emphasis, white prejudice must increase. From this it follows that Negro standards are a non-significant variable.

The point which the author seems to have avoided is this: that both race prejudice and Negro standards are consistently dependent variables. They are both produced by the calculated economic interest of the Southern oligarchy. Both prejudice and the Negro's status are dependent functions of the latter interests. In one variation of his theory of the "vicious circle" Myrdal reasons:

> Assuming . . . that we want to reduce the bias in white people's racial beliefs concerning Negroes, our first practical conclusion is that we can effect this result to a degree by *actually improving Negro status.* . . . The impediment in the way of this strategy is . . . that white beliefs . . . are active forces in keeping the Negroes low.[7]

Here beliefs are assumed to be prime movers; they "keep the Negroes low." This is mysticism. If we can "improve Negro status" the reason for the existence of derogatory beliefs about Negroes is, to the extent of the improvement, liquidated. With a rise in the standard of living of Negroes there tends to be merely a concomitant vitiation of the rationalizations for the depressed conditions of Negroes. The belief is an empty, harmless illusion, like beliefs in werewolves or fairies, without the exploitative interest with which it is impregnated. If the economic force could be bridled, the belief would collapse from inanition. There is a vested interest in anti-racial beliefs.

The effective interest is a need for slaves, or peons, or unorganized common laborers—a need for "cheap, docile labor." The latter interest, of course, is involved in a complicated web of feeling established by both immemorial and recent rationalizations. If beliefs, per se, could subjugate a people, the beliefs which Negroes hold about whites should be as effective as those which whites hold about Negroes.

This assumption of Myrdal's, that racial beliefs are primary social forces, leads him to conclude almost pathetically that the "white man's" beliefs are only a "mistake," which he would gladly correct if only he had truthful information. Accordingly our author suggests the following attack upon the beliefs themselves:

> A second line of strategy must be to rectify the ordinary white man's observations of Negro characteristics and inform him of the

[7] Ibid., p. 109. (Italics added.)

specific mistakes he is making in ascribing them wholesale to inborn racial traits. . . . People want to be rational, to be honest and well informed.[8]

Evidently the misapprehension in this presentation inheres in Myrdal's moral approach. He does not recognize consistently that the propagators of the ruling ideas, those whose interest it is to replace debunked beliefs with new ones, are not mistaken at all, and that they should not be thought of merely as people or white people. They are, in fact, a special class of people who fiercely oppose interference with the established set of antagonistic racial beliefs. The racial beliefs have been intentionally built up through propaganda. They are mass psychological instruments facilitating a definite purpose; therefore, they can best be opposed by realistic aggressive propaganda methods.[9] It is, to repeat, consummate naïveté to assume that the ruling class in the South will permit a free, objective discussion of race relations in its schools or public places.[10] Today such a practice can succeed only as a hazardous underground movement.

Furthermore, the author's unstable equilibrium between race prejudice and Negro standards is evidently too simple. For instance, if Negro standards go up because of interference from some outside force, say the Federal Government, the cultivated race prejudice among the poor whites may tend to diminish, but at the same time the hostility of the ruling-class whites may increase. The reason for this is that, because of the interference, the status and problems of Negroes and those of the poor whites may be made more nearly to coincide and thus enhance the possibility of an establishment of a community of interest between these two groups, a process diametrically opposed to the purpose and interests of the white ruling class. Therefore, it becomes incumbent upon the latter class to re-establish its position by bringing into play those very well-known means of reaffirming racial antipathy.

Although Myrdal never permits himself to accept a consistently realistic approach to the study of race relations, he recites as historical fact that which his theory confutes. For instance, the following historical passage says quite clearly that race prejudice is an attitude deliberately built up among the masses by an exploiting class, using acceptable rationalizations derogatory to the Negro race, so that the exploitation of the latter's labor power might be justified.

> The historical literature of this early period . . . records that the improved Negroes—and the captured Indians—originally were kept in much the same status as the white indentured servants. *When*

---

[8] Ibid., p. 109.
[9] This view also holds against certain popular concepts of race prejudice as "superstition" or "myth."
[10] On this point, see Stetson Kennedy, *Southern Exposure*, p. 349.

> *later the Negroes gradually were pushed down into chattel slavery*
> while the white servants were allowed to work off their board, *the*
> *need was felt . . . for some kind of justification above mere eco-*
> *nomic expediency and the might of the strong.* The arguments
> called forth by this need . . . were broadly these: that the Negro
> was a heathen and a barbarian, an outcast among the peoples of
> the earth, a descendant of Noah's son Ham, cursed by God himself
> and doomed to be *a servant* forever on account of an ancient sin.[11]

Now there is no mysticism here—nothing about "sexual drives," "fears,"
"inhibitions," "labile balance," and so on—the historical process is clear.
The exploitative act comes first; the prejudice follows. It explains unequivocally that a powerful white exploiting class, by "the might of the strong"
and for "economic expediency," pushed the Negroes down into chattel
slavery and then, as a justification and facilitation of this, utilized the
means of propaganda, which are ordinarily in its control, to develop racial
antagonism and hate in the white public for the Negroes.[12]

Attacking beliefs by negation is obviously a negative procedure—sometimes even a futile one. In an essay of epoch-making significance, written
in about the year 1800, Henri Grégoire[13] demonstrated, probably as clearly
as ever, that the white man is "making a mistake in ascribing Negro characteristics to inborn racial traits"; yet this assignment is still freshly advocated. As a matter of fact, Count Arthur de Gobineau almost put men
like Grégoire out of existence.[14] In like manner, Dr. W. T. Couch, formerly

---

[11] Op. cit., p. 85. (Italics added.)

[12] It is interesting to observe with what anonymity Myrdal uses such key concepts as
"imported," "captured," "kept," "pushed down," and so on. One would think that the
subject referred to by these terms of action would be of primary concern in the investigation. It is, however, highly impersonalized, and the whole social situation tends to
remain as if it were an act of Nature.

[13] *An Inquiry Concerning the Intellectual and Moral Faculties, and Literature of
Negroes,* trans. by D. B. Warden, Brooklyn, 1810.

[14] After Professor Donald Young had completed his examination of the conditions of
American minority peoples he made the following conclusionary statement: "Action, not
cautious and laborious research, is demanded of those who would lead the populace.
Thus a Chamberlain, a Gobineau, or a Stoddard attracts myriads of followers by a
pseudo-scientific program based on a doctrine of God-given white supremacy . . . while
the very names of Franz Boas, Eugene Pittard, Herbert A. Miller, E. B. Reuter, Friedrich
Hertz, and other scholarly students of the peoples of the world are unknown outside
of a small intellectual circle. 'Give us the solution and let sterile scholars while away
their time with obscure facts which lead but to quibbling books!' is the cry of the
masses." Yet the reason that Gobineau *et al.* have been widely accepted by the white
ruling classes of the world is not that they presented a course of "action" but that they
had the timely ingenuity to contrive a system of plausible logic which justified an accomplished act: the white racial mastery of the world. Explanations and justifications were
desperately needed. For the most part the scholars mentioned have been able only to
point out flaws in the anti-racial arguments; they had already lost their conviction when
they innocently accepted the spurious grounds of discussion which the apologists of racial
exploitation had chosen. They apparently did not recognize that both the racial antagonism and its pseudo-scientific rationalizations are products of a peculiar social system.

editor in chief of probably the most influential Southern press, proceeds to "gobinize" Myrdal.

Couch, in a caustic criticism of Myrdal, referring to him as "silly" and "ignorant," says the white man cannot make concessions to Negroes because these will ultimately lead to Negro men's marrying white men's daughters. "One concession will lead to another, and ultimately to intermarriage."[15] Here the thinking of both authors is bogged down in the slough of sexual passion from which we may not hope for light on race relations. Moreover, in this unrealistic world of beliefs Couch has Myrdal where he wants him; he seems to triumph with such intuitive declarations as: "The assertion of equality is an assertion of values."[16] And, in a characteristically pre-Civil War, slaveholders' contention about the meaning of the Declaration of Independence, he becomes involved with Myrdal's moral orientation. "I believe," says Couch, "*An American Dilemma* was written under gross misapprehensions of what such ideas as equality, freedom, democracy, human rights, have meant, and what they can be made to mean."[17] Thus, without restraint and without enlightenment, the mystics, steeped in metaphysical truck, set upon each other.

A positive program, on the other hand, calls for an attack upon the source of the beliefs, so that it might be divested of its prestige and power to produce and to substitute anti-racial beliefs among the masses. In other words, the problem is that of converting the white masses to an appreciation and realization of the ruling-class function of the beliefs and their effect as instruments in the exploitation of the white as well as of the black masses. Then, not only will the old beliefs lose their efficacy, but also the new ones will die aborning.

A positive program calls for the winning of the white masses over to a different system of thinking—not merely a campaign of scholarly denials of spectacular myths about creation, stages of biological progress, cultural capacity, and so on. Indeed, such negation may even play into the hands of the "racists," for they may not only divert attention from the realities of race relations but also help to spread and implant the myths among the public. However, the effectuation of such a program, the intent of which must be to alienate public support of the aristocracy, will undoubtedly evoke terrific opposition from this class. To be sure, this fact merely demonstrates further the basis of racial antagonism in the South and the correctness of the suggested positive program. At the same time, of course, Negroes must learn that their interest is primarily bound up with that of the white common people in a struggle for power and not essentially in a climb for social status.

At any rate, it is precisely this realization which Dr. Myrdal constantly

---

[15] *What the Negro Wants*, Rayford W. Logan, ed., p. xvi.
[16] Ibid., p. xvii.   [17] Ibid., p. xv.

seeks to circumvent. Accordingly he argues inconsistently that the ruling class in the South is the Negroes' best friend.

> Our hypothesis is similar to the view taken by an older group of Negro writers and by most white writers who have touched this crucial question: that the Negroes' friend—or the one who is least unfriendly—is still rather the upper class of white people, the people with economic and social security who are *truly a "non-competing group."*[18]

The author, by one symptom or another, cannot help showing of what he is really apprehensive: the bringing into consciousness of the masses the identity of the interests of the white and the black workers. In accordance with this attitude he takes a superficial view of the economic order and asks Negroes to go to the labor market and see who is their real enemy. Thus he asserts:

> The aim of [the theory of labor solidarity] is to unify the whole Negro people, not with the white upper class, but with the white working class. . . . The theory of labor solidarity has been taken up as a last solution of the Negro problem, and as such is escapist in nature; its escape character becomes painfully obvious to every member of the school as soon as he leaves abstract reasoning and goes down to the labor market, because there he *meets caste* and has to talk race, even racial solidarity.[19]

As a justificatory illustration of the validity of his principle of "cumulative causation," the summatory interaction of the elements of Negro standards and other social factors, Myrdal says: "The philanthropist, the Negro educator, the Negro trade unionist . . . and, indeed, the average well-meaning citizen of both colors, pragmatically applies the same hypothesis."[20] In reality, however, this is not a confirmation of a sound theory of race relations; it is rather an apology for reformism. Within the existing system of power relationship this is the most that is respectably allowed. Reformism never goes so far as to envisage the real involvement of the exploitative system with racial antagonism. Its extreme aspiration does not go beyond the attainment of freedom for certain black men to participate in the exploitation of the commonalty regardless of the color of the latter. This aspiration is the prospect which the Southern oligarchy with some degree of justification ordinarily refers to as "Negro domination."

---

[18] Op. cit., p. 69. (Italics added.) It is interesting to observe how Dr. Myrdal has finally became almost reactionary in the sense of the incorrigible segregationist, W. T. Couch, who also says: "Nothing is more needed in the South today than rebirth of [Booker Washington's] ideas, restoration of the great leadership that he was giving." Op. cit., p. xxiii.

[19] Myrdal, op. cit., p. 793. (Italics added.)   [20] Ibid., p. 1069.

Then, too, with reformation as an end, the logical "friend" of the Negro leader must necessarily be this same white aristocracy; for he must ultimately become, like the aristocracy, the inevitable economic adversary of the exploited masses; he must become, in other words, a "black Anglo-Saxon." Indeed, assuming bourgeois proclivities, his very appeal to the masses for support in his struggle for "equality" is an unavoidable deception. The reformer seeks to eliminate only the racial aspects of the exploitative system; he compromises with the system which produces the racial antagonism. But the white ruling class cannot willingly accept even this compromise, for it knows that the whole system is doomed if Negroes are permitted to achieve unlimited status as participating exploiters. In such an event there would be no racial scapegoat or red herring to brandish before the confused white commonalty as a means of keeping them and the Negro masses from recognizing the full impact of political-class oppression.

Today "conservative" theories of race relations are not merely denied; they are confronted with a countertheory, the theory that racial antagonism is in fact *political-class* antagonism and that race prejudice is initiated and maintained by labor exploiters. It is not, it would seem clear, that the aristocracy is less antagonistic to the Negroes but that this class uses more respectable weapons against them, which are also infinitely more powerful and effective. As a matter of fact, the poor whites themselves may be thought of as the primary instrument of the ruling class in subjugating the Negroes. The statement attributed to a great financier, "I can pay one half of the working class to kill off the other half," is again in point.

As we have seen, Myrdal does not favor this explanation. He declares that all the Negro's troubles are due to the simple fact that "white people" want to be superior to colored people; or, indeed, merely to the fact that the Negro is colored. His argument follows:

> We hear it said . . . that there is no "race problem" but only a "class problem." The Negro sharecropper is alleged to be destitute not because of his color but because of his class position—and it is pointed out that there are white people who are equally poor. From a practical angle there is a point in this reasoning. But from a theoretical angle it contains escapism in a new form. It also draws too heavily on the idealistic Marxian doctrine of the "class struggle." And it tends to conceal the whole system of special deprivations visited upon the Negro *only because he is not white*.[21]

Throughout the study the author has frequently found it sufficient simply to mention the name of Karl Marx in order to counter views based

[21] Ibid., p. 75. (Italics added.)

upon the determining role of the "material conditions of production" and distribution.[22] After a studied argument in favor of the futility of Negroes adopting a Marxian view of society, he concludes: " 'Even after a revolution the country will be full of crackers' is a reflection I have often met when discussing communism in the Negro community."[23] The least we could say about this is that it is very crude. On this kind of thinking John Stuart Mill is emphatic: "Of all the vulgar modes of escaping from the consideration of the effect of social and moral influences on the human mind, the most vulgar is that of attributing the diversities of conduct and character to inherent natural differences."[24] More especially it expresses the fatalism upon which the whole orthodox school of race relations inevitably rests.

Myrdal, as a confirmed moralist, is not concerned with problems of power but rather with problems of "regenerating the individual" by idealistic preachments. If only the individual could be taught to accept the morality of the Creed, then society would lose its fever of racial pathologies and settle down to a happy existence. However, the point we are trying to make is that, in a feudal system, serfdom is natural and the serf will be treated like a serf regardless of whether the lord is a bishop or a secular noble; in the slavocracy of the South the slave was treated like a slave, whether his master was white or black; in modern capitalism black workers are exploited naturally and race hatred is a natural support of this exploitation. In other words, morality is a function of the social system, and a better system can change both morality and human nature for the better. There will be no more "crackers" or "niggers" after a socialist revolution because the social necessity for these types will have been removed. But

[22] And yet Myrdal has shown himself to be vitally wanting in an understanding of the difference between status rivalry and class struggle. Observe, for instance, the following typical confusion: "Our hypothesis is that in a society where there are broad social classes and, in addition, more minute distinctions and splits in the lower strata, the lower class groups will, to a great extent, take care of keeping each other subdued, thus relieving, to that extent, the higher classes of this otherwise painful task necessary to the monopolization of the power and the advantages.

"It will be observed that this hypothesis is contrary to the Marxian theory of class society. . . . The Marxian scheme assumes that there is an actual solidarity between the *several lower class groups* against the *higher classes*, or, in any case, a potential solidarity. . . . The inevitable result is a 'class struggle' where all poor and disadvantaged groups are united behind the barricades." Ibid., p. 68. (Italics added.) Myrdal thinks that Marx thinks the *upper class* and the *lower class*, mere social illusions, are in conflict. No wonder he seems to conclude that Marx is rather foolish. And he does not trouble himself at all to explain how the "higher classes" exercise the "necessary painful task" of keeping the lower classes subdued when, perchance, the latter stop fighting among themselves and turn their attention to their common enemy. This is, to use the term so frequently employed by Myrdal, "escapism."
[23] Ibid., p. 509.
[24] *Principles of Political Economy*, Vol. 1, p. 390. Long before this John Locke had said quite as much; see *Essay Concerning Human Understanding*.

the vision which the capitalist theorist dreads most is this: that there will be no more capitalists and capitalist exploitation. If we attempt to see race relations realistically, the meaning of the capitalist function is inescapable. At any rate, although Myrdal criticizes Sumner and Park for their inert and fatalistic views of social change, he himself contends that any revolutionary change in the interest of democracy will be futile:

> . . . a national policy will never work by changing only one factor, least of all if attempted suddenly and with great force. In most cases that would either throw the system entirely out of gear or else prove to be a wasteful expenditure of effort which could be reached much further by being spread strategically over various factors in the system and over a period of time.[25]

This is not the place to discuss the theory of revolution, but it must be obvious that the purpose of revolution is not to "throw the system out of gear." It is to overthrow the entire system, to overthrow a ruling class; and the cost of revolution did not frighten the capitalists when it became their lot to overthrow the feudalists.

An American Dilemma, the most exhaustive *survey* of race relations ever undertaken in the United States, is, for the most part, a useful source of data. In detail it presents many ingenious analyses of the materials. But it develops no hypothesis or consistent theory of race relations; and, to the extent that it employs the caste belief in interpretations, it is misleading. Clearly, the use of "the American Creed" as the "value premise" for his study severely limits and narrows Dr. Myrdal's perspective. Even though we should grant some right of the author to limit the discussion of his subject to its moral aspects, he still develops it without insight. He never brings into focus the two great systems of morality currently striving in our civilization for ascendancy, but merely assumes a teleological abstraction of social justice toward which all good men will ultimately gravitate. Moreover, since we can hardly accuse him of being naïve, and since he clearly goes out of his way to avoid the obvious implications of labor exploitation in the South, we cannot help concluding that the work in many respects may have the effect of a powerful piece of propaganda in favor of the status quo. If the "race problem" in the United States is pre-eminently a moral question, it must naturally be resolved by moral means, and this conclusion is precisely the social illusion which the ruling political class has constantly sought to produce. In this connection we are conscious of the author's recognition that "social science is essentially a 'political' science." One thing is certain, at any rate: the work contributes virtually nothing to a clarification of the many existing spurious social

[25] Op. cit., p. 77.

theories of race relations—indeed, on the latter score, Myrdal's contribution is decidedly negative. And for this reason evidently he has been able
to suggest no solution for the dilemma, but, like the fatalists whom he
criticizes, the author relies finally upon time as the great corrector of all evil.

5. Ethnocentrism

ROBIN WILLIAMS

*In this selection, Williams draws a useful distinction between ethno-
centrism and prejudice. An individual can take pride in the accomplishments of his own group without necessarily disparaging the contributions
of others; he can understand why other people value their particular norms
and life-styles at the same time that he retains his commitment to those
of his own group. Indeed, both of these possibilities must be at least partially realized if group relations are to be harmonious in a society that is
at once democratic and pluralistic. On the other hand, there are conditions
under which ethnocentrism is likely to lead to prejudice—where antipathies
are sanctioned by tradition, where there are real or perceived grounds for
believing that one is threatened by members of another group, and where
opportunities for mutual understanding are limited. Williams shows that
these conditions are related, and that no single one is a necessary and
sufficient reason for prejudice to accompany ethnocentrism.*

Ethnocentrism, says William Graham Sumner, is that ". . . view of
things in which one's own group is the center of everything, and all others
are scaled and rated with reference to it."[1] It is a fact that men classify
their fellows in a variety of ways and react to others as members of social
categories. What is the nature of these groups that men form? How do
they form them, and why? What is the nature of ethnocentric feelings,
and how strong are they? The answers to these questions will constitute
the main part of this chapter. We will also consider, in the final pages
of this chapter, whether ethnocentrism necessarily results in prejudice.

SOURCE: Robin Williams, *Strangers Next Door: Ethnic Relations in American
Communities* (Englewood Cliffs, N. J.: Prentice-Hall, Inc., 1964.), pp. 17–29, passim.
Copyright © 1964, reprinted by permission of Prentice-Hall, Inc., Englewood Cliffs, N.J.

Robin Williams is Professor of Sociology at Cornell University. Among his works
are *American Society*; he is also the co-author of *Schools in Transition* and of *What
College Students Think.*

[1] *Folkways* (Boston: Ginn & Company, 1906), p. 13.

The Forming of Groups

The word "group" is used in everyday parlance to refer to anything from a crowd at Yankee Stadium to the members of a family. Although we too may find it convenient to employ the term "group" in our discussion of intergroup relations, it is necessary to understand that there are actually many kinds of groups, which vary from one another in cohesiveness and social significance and which should technically be referred to by some term other than "group." The category of least social importance is the *aggregate*, a collection of human individuals having no relationships among themselves other than those that are intrinsic in occupying geographic space in some proximity. As the distinctiveness, unity, and internal organization of the aggregate increases, we may want to recognize it as a *social category*, then as a *collectivity*, then as a *group*, and finally as a *society*. The social category is exemplified by an occupational grouping or a social class, where there is only a vague sense of membership and very rudimentary capacity for any sort of concerted collective action. A fully developed collectivity, on the other hand, is a *people*, and is characterized by 1) a distinctive culture; 2) tests or criteria of membership; 3) a set of constitutive norms regulating social relations both within the collectivity and with outsiders; 4) an awareness of a distinct identity by both members and nonmembers; 5) obligations of solidarity, such as enforced requirements to help members in need and to resist derogation by outsiders; and 6) a high capacity for continued action by the collectivity on behalf of its members or of itself as a unit. In its most comprehensive development such a collectivity may become a potentially self-sufficient society, able to meet all internal needs from its own resources and to perpetuate itself as a functioning system from generation to generation.

The term "group," then, when used most accurately, refers to a special case of a small-scale collectivity. What traditionally have been called "minority groups" are either social categories or collectivities. However, so long as it is clear from the context what kind of collection of individuals is meant, we will freely use the term "group" (or the compromise term "grouping" when we wish to stress the loose, aggregative quality of some part of the population).

How do aggregates become collectivities? There undoubtedly are several different major sets of processes. One important general sequence, illustrated by the cases of American Negroes and many immigrant populations, is approximately as follows:

1. By reason of any one of many historical circumstances, there is an initial categorization of persons considered to have some important characteristic in common—for example, they are slaves, newcomers, foreigners, or heathens. An identifying set of symbols is found that gives the category high social visibility: skin color, food habits, religious rites.

2. Persons in the category are typically found (or, are believed to be found) in occupations or other social roles that are recognizably different from those typically associated with persons in one or more other social categories: trade, money lending, domestic service, landlordism.

3. As a consequence of their distinctive social roles, persons in the given ethnic category will develop additional relatively distinctive interests, beliefs, values, and specific modes of behavior.

4. These differences will render more distinct, reinforce, and elaborate the initial definition of the social category.

5. As a consequence of all these developments, the like-circumstanced members of the social category will come increasingly to have a sense of common identity, which will tend to increase their within-category interaction and to reduce their contacts with outsiders. This closure of interaction will increase the tendency of outsiders to treat them as a unit, and this tendency, in turn, will enhance the new collectivity's cultural distinctiveness and social separateness.

6. If, however, the collectivity so formed is part of and is economically and politically dependent upon a larger social system, it will not become a completely closed social system. Its members must maintain relationships with members of other collectivities and social categories within the same total society.

7. If some other collectivity, or set of collectivities, is economically and politically dominant, the new subordinate collectivity will be forced to accept the dominant grouping's rules of the game. It will be forced into a largely one-way adaptation to a common set of constitutive norms that will regulate the necessary relations between the two groupings. In other words, the subordinates have to accept some of the culture of the superordinate grouping, especially the basic rules of the game for vital dealings with the members of the dominant collectivity.

GROUPS OF GREATEST SOCIAL SIGNIFICANCE

Although there are numerous social categories that have social importance (such as enlisted men, union workers, women), the groups that are of greatest social significance and those in which students of intergroup relations are most interested are those collectivities that have racial, ethnic, and religious distinctions. It is within the ethnic grouping that all individuals form their first relationships, their deepest dependencies, and the most important bases of emotional ambivalence.

WHY WE ARE ETHNOCENTRIC

All individuals need group belongingness and group anchorage. Without stable relationships to other persons, without some group ties, the individual becomes insecure, anxious, and uncertain of his identity. In order to receive the emotional support of the group (that is, the family group, the neighborhood or school peer group) the individual must heed the opinions of other group members. In the homogeneous family group he learns definite codes for behavior within the group and for behavior towards other groups. The child discovers very early that agreement with group opinions and codes is rewarding. He learns that the teachings of one's parents and close associates are helpful in getting what he wants and avoiding what he does not want. To the extent to which the child finds the instruction of elders and peers reliable for achieving rewarding results, he learns to give credence to their opinions. The child's need is great for relationships of trust that mediate reality to him. And through group attachments and loyalties he learns also of group antipathies and conflicts. He perceives groups, then, as social units in which he can expect security and love or danger and negative emotional experience.

Secure identity as a member of an ingroup is not a free good, contrary to some first appearances, but is only to be had at a price. Often one must have already established credentials of other group memberships and of personal qualities and achievements. Furthermore, maintenance of a clear, full, and secure identity within the ingroup requires conformity to group norms. More exactly, the price of one's group identity is responsible reciprocity with other members, a reciprocity defined by mutually accepted norms.

THE OVERLAPPING OF GROUPS

Particularly in our complex society, most individuals are members of more than one group. The child, aware at first only of his membership in a kinship group, slowly becomes conscious of other memberships. Piaget reports that only at the age of ten to eleven were the children he studied capable of understanding that they could be members of both a locality and a nation, and of understanding what a nation is.[2] By adulthood then, the individual is aware of a plurality of group memberships that help him identify himself. The person is rare in urban America today who feels a clear and strong sense of identification with one and only one grouping or segment of the community and nation. The typical individual is a

[2] J. Piaget and Anne-Marie Weil, "The Development in Children of the Idea of the Homeland and of Relations with Other Countries," *International Social Science Bulletin*, III, No. 3 (Autumn, 1951), 561–78: ". . . the feeling and the very idea of the homeland are by no means the first or even early elements in the child's make-up, but are a relatively late development in the normal child, who does not appear to be drawn inevitably towards patriotic sociocentricity." (p. 562)

member of many ingroups (groups of intimate belonging; "we-groups") and may relate himself to many other reference groups (those that matter to him, and upon whose opinions he relies).

It is difficult to realize fully the enormous significance of alternative group memberships. If the individual can belong to only one group, that group inevitably becomes all-important to him. In it all his satisfactions are found and are controlled and limited. It encompasses and constricts all his experiences. However, totalistic character of group membership diminishes in complex and fluid societies.[3] The growth of alternative possibilities of group membership and group reference depends upon the number and variety of distinctive groupings, but the sheer multiplication of groupings is far from the whole story. Changes in the criteria of membership are accentuated by changes in the functions of groups and by shifts in the alignments among and between groups. The characteristics that actually are statistically typical of a grouping or category at one time cease to be typical later.

．　．　．　．　．

Ethnocentric Feelings

POSITIVE ETHNOCENTRISM

What are the components of the sentiments of ethnocentrism? George Peter Murdock says, "Always the 'we-group' and its codes are exalted, while 'other groups' and their ways are viewed with suspicion, hostility and contempt."[4] It is true that satisfaction with one's own group (Oog) sometimes is accompanied by negative feelings toward other groups, but for the moment let us examine the attitude that ethnocentric groups have toward themselves. The most important are:

1. A belief in the unique value of Oog.
2. Satisfaction with membership in Oog.
3. Solidarity, loyalty, or cooperation with regard to Oog.
4. Preference for association with members of Oog.
5. Belief in the rightness of Oog's relationships with other groups.

The attitudes toward other groups that often accompany the five sentiments just mentioned are:

1. Judging other groups by Oog's standards.
2. Belief that Oog is superior to other groups, in all ways or in some ways.
3. Ignorance of other groups.

---

[3] Of course we recognize that multigroup societies can be engulfed by political totalitarianism, which enforces a new kind of all-encompassing membership.
[4] "Ethnocentrism," *Encyclopedia of the Social Sciences*, V, 613.

4. Lack of interest in other groups.
5. Hostility towards other groups.

NEGATIVE ETHNOCENTRISM

It is not true, as is often assumed, that every group, people, or society considers itself superior in some generalized sense to all others or even to most others. There are many well-documented instances in which positive loyalty to the ingroup goes along with some appreciation of outgroup values and practices. One's own group does provide the norms for judging other groups, and in various particular ways an outgroup may be seen as superior. For instance, a tribe that prides itself upon its skill in the building of boats can recognize that the products of another tribe represent superior craftsmanship. This admission need not result in a general devaluation of Oog; it is negative ethnocentrism only in its admission of specific points of inferiority. One still retains one's ingroup standards and a basic adherence to its values.[5]

Yet, the phenomena of self-hatred and self-deprecation of one's own membership group are common and must be taken into account. History is replete with voluntary exiles, expatriates, outgroup emulators, social climbers, renegades, and traitors. Also, the dominant attitude in a whole people can be one of accepting at least some of the low evaluations of outsiders. Peter A. Munch has given a fascinating account of such attitudes among the inhabitants of the remote island of Tristan da Cahuna.[6] Among the villagers in southern Italy whose amoral familism has been described by Edward C. Banfield, the desire to emigrate, the awareness of poverty, and the deprecation of the local society are evident.[7] Other examples can be found, as in numerous instances of tribal peoples overwhelmed by conquest and subordinated to technologically advanced rulers. But the most important manifestations of negative sentiments toward the individual's own membership group occur in subordinated minority groups that are objects of prejudice and discrimination. [This negative ethnocentrism is discussed further in later sections of Williams' book. Ed.]

Does Positive Ethnocentrism Necessarily Result in Prejudice?

Whether strong negative feelings toward an outgrowup always develop along with positive feelings of ethnocentrism is a question that has been

---

[5] Cf. Marc J. Swartz, "Negative Ethnocentrism," *The Journal of Conflict Resolution*, V, No. 1 (March, 1961), 75–81.

[6] *Sociology of Tristan Da Cahuna* (Oslo, Norway: Det Norske Videnskaps-Akademi I Kommisjon Hos Jacob Dywab, 1945).

[7] *The Moral Basis of a Backward Society* (New York: Free Press of Glencoe, Inc., 1958).

explored in numerous studies. On the one hand we have Mary Ellen Good-man's study of Negro and white children, which showed that racial prefer-ences were associated with hostility in only a minority of cases.[8] On the other hand, William Graham Sumner is usually singled out among Ameri-can sociologists as favoring the idea that ingroup solidarity is related to outgroup hostility. What he says, however, is somewhat ambiguous: "The relationship of comradeship and peace in the we-group and that of hostility toward others-groups are correlative to each other."[9] Sumner was thinking primarily of preliterate groups with relatively clear boundaries in situations in which threat and counterthreat affected the group as a whole. Even so, his statement bears the marks of caution: he says "are correlative" rather than "necessarily occur together." The consensus of studies, however, seems to be that continued interaction between culturally distinctive peoples need not result in conflict. One group may be assimilated by another, or there are even rare examples of sustained contacts between two endoga-mous and ethnocentric peoples with little conflict and little or no assimila-tion of one culture to the other.[10] Such accommodative relations seem to rest upon an economic interdependence that is mutually advantageous and essentially noncompetitive. Much more common, unfortunately, are asym-metrical relations in which cultural differences become signals for discrimi-nating behavior by members of a more powerful collectivity.[11]

Whether or not prejudice results is dependent on such complicated factors as 1) the nature of the social system of which the groups are a part, 2) the extent to which one group is a threat (economically or otherwise) to the other, and 3) the degree of understanding or misunderstanding of one group towards another. [Other significant factors that are discussed in subsequent chapters are the personality structures and dynamics of indi-viduals within the groups. Ed.]

THE NATURE OF THE SOCIAL SYSTEM

When ethnic distinctions have been built into the cultural definitions and the norms of routine behavior in a social system, prejudiced attitudes and discriminatory behavior will be characteristic of normal personalities in that system. The manifestation of prejudice is not necessarily a symptom of unusual psychological needs or of neurotic or psychotic tendencies.

---

[8] Mary Ellen Goodman, *Race Awareness in Young Children* (Cambridge, Mass.: Addi-son-Wesley Publishing Company, Inc., 1952).
[9] *Folkways*, p. 12.
[10] The case usually cited as an example has been described by E. J. Lindgren, "An Example of Culture Contact without Conflict," *American Anthropologist*, XV, No. 5 (October–December, 1938), 605–21. See also: John Gillin, "Race Relations Without Conflict: A Guatemalan Town," *American Journal of Sociology*, LIII, No. 5 (March 1948), 337–43.
[11] Cf. Hilda Kuper, *Indian People in Natal* (Pietermartzburg: University of Natal Press, 1960).

When prejudice is normal in a society its manifestations are found among the respectable members of the population who are most firmly embedded in and committed to the legitimate organizations and conventional behavior characteristic of that social system. (Conversely, as shown by the findings in Southport, low prejudice is found most often among persons who are most likely to be free from the most constrained adherence to the general conventions of the community.) That is, when ethnic differences are the result of deeply rooted historical cleavages, it is usual for prejudice to accompany ethnocentrism.

THREAT

If for any reason two clearly distinguished social categories or collectivities are so situated in a society that their members frequently come into competition, the likelihood is high that negative stereotyping (a common variety of prejudice) will reinforce a sense of difference and that hostile attitudes will tend to restrict interaction and/or cause conflict. Whether the competition is economic, political, sexual, or for prestige, if one group perceives another as a threat, prejudice results. A central implication of Rokeach's extensive résumé of research on dogmatism is that a closed belief system is a consequence of threat.[12] It is implied by this formulation that the greater the threat: (1) the more rigid the belief system that develops in response, (2) the more intense the affects supporting the beliefs, and (3) the more punitive the sanctions against disbelief.

Certain individuals and segments of the population will be so located in the social structure as to be especially likely to attach the meaning of threat, injury, deprivation, or punishment to the presence and behavior of one or more ethnic groups. Concretely, this most often means economic competition. For example, a white union member on strike sees "his" job taken by a Negro; a Protestant businessman believes his profits are reduced by the competition offered by a Jewish merchant. Or the so-called realistic threat may be noneconomic, such as when legislation thought to have been passed at the public behest of Catholic spokesmen confronts the Protestant with legal restrictions on dissemination of birth-control information or materials. Another example might be the Mexican-American father who is deeply concerned with the preservation of customary roles of women and fears the example set for his daughters by Anglo-American schoolmates.

When two ethnocentric groups come into a mutually threatening relationship, the stage for group conflict is fully set.[13] Short of the cycle of threat-hostility-threat that is the classical prelude to group conflict—from gang fights, to riots, to global wars—we can observe a quieter prejudice,

---

[12] Milton Rokeach, *The Open and Closed Mind: Investigations into the Nature of Belief Systems and Personality Systems* (New York: Basic Books, Inc., 1960).
[13] H. M. Blalock, Jr., "A Power Analysis of Racial Discrimination," *Social Forces,* XXXIX, No. 1 (October, 1960), 58.

stabilized in systems of preferential ranking and preferential social access and personal association.

UNDERSTANDING AND MISUNDERSTANDING

The notion that understanding will always lead to the reduction of prejudice and/or the diminution of conflict has limitations that are often overlooked, ignored, or underestimated. Deadly enemies often understand one another all too well. Conversely, some groups manage to live together in a state of uneasy but tolerable accommodation when an accurate and detailed knowledge of each other's real sentiments and intentions would precipitate severe conflict. Understanding will reduce antipathy and the likelihood of conflict only if the groups like or respect what they discover by understanding each other or if one group finds that the threat posed by the other, though real, is not so severe, unalterable, or immediate as previously believed.

When persons feel themselves to be members of a group and identify themselves with that group's corporate views or policies in competition with another group, they necessarily find it difficult to comprehend the other group's position. An ingenious experiment by Blake and Manton[14] suggests that under these conditions a loss in competition leads to hostility both toward impartial judges and toward the winning group, ". . . with feelings expressed that the decision was completely unjustified in the light of the 'evidence.' " Even though the members of the competing groups reported that they understood the competitor's views as well as they understood those of their own group, they, in fact, did not. In all groups, the members knew their own group's position best and were inclined toward distortion in their comprehension of the other group's position.

Misunderstanding another group's beliefs and values. Many observers, noting the relative unimportance of skin color biology—and the failure of scientific studies to produce significant evidence of genetically determined racial differences in intelligence—have been puzzled to observe that many individuals persist in exhibiting prejudice towards those with physical racial characteristics. In studies done by Rokeach it has been revealed that prejudice may not be a result of the fact that the other person is of a different racial category, national origin, or religious group affiliation but a result of the prejudiced person's assuming that the other individual's beliefs and values are incongruent with his own.[15] He found that white students both in the North and in the South prefer a Negro with similar beliefs to a white person with different beliefs. But in most situations

---

[14] Robert R. Blake and Jane Srygley Manton, "Comprehension of Own and of Outgroup Positions under Intergroup Competition," *Journal of Conflict Resolution*, V, No. 3 (September, 1961), 309.
[15] Rokeach, *The Open and Closed Mind.*

many white persons would take it for granted that the Negro person did differ from them in basic ways. Thus misunderstanding or lack of knowledge of the outgroup frequently results in prejudice.

Possibly one can now see why a wide range of concepts and types of data must be dealt with in order to begin to understand the causes and the nature of prejudice. Intergroup behavior involves three great systems of human social action: the culture, the social system, and the personality system. Accordingly, we need to study cultural content—"stereotypes," beliefs, and evaluations; and we need to study personality as related to cultural content and to social interaction. We must analyze interaction both in terms of general patterns of intergroup contact and in terms of specific situations. And even while we deal with each of these sets of factors, we must remember that they all are simultaneously engaged in those person-to-person communications that are conceived by the participants to have an intergroup character.

6. Paternalistic versus Competitive Race Relations: An Ideal-Type Approach

PIERRE L. VAN DEN BERGHE

The following essay draws a distinction between two forms of racial prejudice, the "paternalistic" and the "competitive." The author suggests that the first occurs more frequently in traditionalistic societies with one-crop agricultural economies; the second, in societies with more advanced techniques of production and more complex divisions of labor.

The forms of prejudice are constructed as "ideal-types," that is, as conceptual abstractions emphasizing some common features of empirical phenomena, but not necessarily corresponding to empirical reality in all their specifics. Such types are useful analytical tools, for they call attention to phenomena that may have been overlooked before. In the hands of a skilled builder of typologies, they can also help to indicate whether all the features attributed to a particular social phenomenon are necessarily logically associated with it.

SOURCE: This paper appears for the first time in its present form in this volume. It is reprinted with the permission of the author. The original version appeared in *Social Forces*.

Pierre van den Berghe is Associate Professor of Sociology at the University of Washington. He is the author of *Caneville* and of several other works dealing with the South African scene.

The range of Van den Berghe's essay is broad; he defines different types of prejudice and race relations with materials drawn from societies widely separated in time and space. The paper is long, and its theorizing is abstract. Readers may therefore prefer to read it through for an over-all impression before attempting to grasp all of its details.

Our general contention is that manifestations of racial prejudice have historically polarized around two ideal-types which we shall call *"paternalistic"* and *"competitive."* The choice of labels is always a difficult one. Rather than use arbitrary symbols, and thereby hinder readability, we adopted two words which are in some way descriptive of our two types. Obviously the common sense meanings of the labels do not exhaust the content of the two types.[1]

The Paternalistic Type: Its Characteristics

The paternalistic type is incompatible with a complex manufacturing economy and with large-scale industrial capitalism. The most congenial form of economy is agricultural, pastoral, or handicraft. Mercantile capitalism and a large-scale plantation agriculture geared at the export of staple products (cotton, coffee, rubber, sugar, etc.) are also compatible with the paternalistic type. This type of economy coincides with an "intermediate" level of differentiation in the division of labour. By "intermediate" is meant here a degree of specialization which has gone considerably beyond a "primitive" division of labour based primarily on sex and age criteria, and yet which is not as complex as in the case of large-scale manufacturing industry.

Typically, in this intermediate stage of the division of labour, the mass of the labour force still consists of a fairly unspecialized, servile or quasi-servile peasantry. But there is already considerable differentiation. Handicraft production is in the hands of full-time specialized artisans. Trading is concentrated in the hands of merchant class, though the latter is often not very powerful. A rudimentary professional specialization is present. Warriors, priests, judges, and officials constitute the ruling group. This "intermediate" stage corresponds to what Weber called the "traditional" type of authority and is exemplified by most large-scale pre-modern societies.

---

[1] The labels "paternalistic" and "competitive" will be used in conjunction with the term "prejudice" when the psychological reference is emphasized, and with the term "race relations" when sociological or social system factors are stressed. This paper is a revised version of Chapter Two of my doctoral dissertation: *The Dynamics of Race Relations: An Ideal-Type Case Study of South Africa*, Harvard University, 1959. An earlier version of the theory was presented in my article: "The Dynamics of Racial Prejudice: An Ideal-Type Dichotomy," *Social Forces*, 37, (December, 1958), 138–41.

This stage implies both urbanization and fairly advanced social stratification. In paternalistic interracial situations with which we are concerned, the division of labour is along racial lines. A servile or quasi-servile racial caste (serfs, slaves, indentured labourers, "recruited" labour, *peones*, etc.) performs the heavy manual labour, in particular, the agricultural tasks.[2]

The dominant upper caste confines itself to such occupations as war, the priesthood, the professions, government, supervision of labour, and commerce. The upper caste is, in fact, a ruling aristocracy, usually a small minority of the total population. This ruling caste is fairly homogeneous in social status. Class distinctions within the ruling caste are secondary to the paramount caste distinctions between the racial groups.[3]

A wide and unbreachable gap exists between the castes, as indicated by living standards, income, occupations, education, death rates, etc. There is a horizontal colour bar with no inter-caste mobility. Intra-caste mobility is possible but limited, as there is little status differentiation within the castes. A slave can be manumitted, or gain a privileged position as house servant, skilled craftsman, foreman, etc., but he remains in a subordinate position. Spatial mobility is also limited, serfs are attached to the land, slaves and servants to their masters. Such a non-mobile labour is clearly incompatible with large-scale industry, which requires a flexible allocation of resources.

The form of government found in a paternalistic society is aristocratic or oligarchic. Autocratic authority of Weber's "traditional" type prevails, either in a centralized form as in colonial governments, or in a decentralized "feudal" form. The legal system is on the side of the racial *status quo*. The lower caste has a clearly defined legal status which entails both rights and obligations, though the latter are often more numerous than the former. Nevertheless, the lower caste is protected under law and punished within the framework of the law.

Paternalistis attitudes and stereotypes are well integrated in the value system of the society. Elaborate sets of rationalizations come to the defence of the racial *status quo*, and are subjectively, if not logically, consistent with the basic religious and ethical promises of the society. Examples of such rationalizations are the "white man's burden" theory, the "civilizing

---

[2] In agreement with Dollard, Warner, Myrdal and others, we shall call "caste" a group which satisfies all three of the following criteria: 1) endogamy, 2) membership therein by birth and for life, and 3) a position of superiority or inferiority *vis à vis* other such groups.

[3] Professor Parsons suggested to us an important distinction between social stratification as a product of internal differentiation in the social system and social stratification imposed from the outside. In the latter case, the hierarchy is likely to be rigid. In fact, most caste or quasi-caste systems, such as estates, have their origin in conquest. The greater the disparity in physical characteristics, level of organization, technology, etc., between conqueror and conquered, the greater is the likelihood of a caste system to arise. Of course, a caste system may perpetuate itself long after these differences have been blurred, as exemplified by India.

mission of the West," the "Christianizing of the Heathen," etc. In short, there is no ideological conflict between the existing norms of prejudice and the basic value system of the society.

Racial roles and statuses are sharply defined. An elaborate and rigid etiquette of race relations stabilizes the master-servant relationship. Indeed, etiquette seems to be the primary mechanism of social control to maintain intimacy of contact coupled with status inequality.[4] To borrow Talcott Parsons' pattern variables, roles are based on ascription, particularism, diffuseness, collectivity orientation, and affectivity.

Spacial segregation is minimal because the wide status gap allows close but unequal contact. In other words, spacial distance can be thought of as an alternative mechanism of social control to status distance. Slaves and servants live in close intimacy with their masters, particularly household servants. Although caste endogamy (i.e., prohibition of intermarriage) is rigidly adhered to, miscegenation between upper-caste males and lower-caste females is condoned and frequent. It takes the form of institutionalized concubinage, and is accepted at all class levels within the upper caste. Wealthy masters interbreed freely with their female slaves without any opprobrium or fear of censure. This miscegenation leads to the rise of a group of half-breeds who generally remain in the lower caste but with privileged status. The half-breeds may, by intermarriage among themselves, constitute an intermediate caste of their own. Some half-breeds can and do, of course, become assimilated to the upper caste through "passing," and when interbreeding has been extensive for several generations, the racial caste system may eventually break down. Such complete interbreeding has only rarely taken place wherever physical characteristics of the groups in presence were widely different. The closest approximation to it is the "colour continuum" situation which prevails in Haiti, Mexico, or to a somewhat lesser extent, in Brazil.

Generally speaking, race relations in the paternalistic type are stable. The lower caste is "accommodated" to its inferior status which it may even internalize. What Dollard has called "white folks manner," and Kardiner and Ovesey, the "mark of oppression," are illustrations of such internalized subservient status.[5] To use the Southern United States phraseology, the "old time darky knows his place." The converse of accommodation on the part of the lower caste is paternalism on the part of the upper caste. The upper caste adopts an attitude of benevolent despotism towards members of the lower caste whom it treats as perpetual children. Stereo-

---

[4] Cf. Robert E. Park, *Race and Culture*, Glencoe, Ill.: The Free Press, 1950, p. 183; Bertrand W. Doyle, *The Etiquette of Race Relations in the South*, Chicago: University of Chicago Press, 1937; and Pierre L. van den Berghe, "Distance Mechanisms of Stratification," *Sociology and Social Research*, 44, 1960, pp. 155–164.

[5] John Dollard, *Caste and Class in a Southern Town*, New Haven; Yale University Press, 1937; Abraham Kardiner and Lionel Ovesey, *The Mark of Oppression*, New York; Norton, 1951.

types of members of the lower caste describe them as immature, exuberant, impulsive, uninhibited, lazy, fun-loving, good-humoured, happy-go-lucky. In short, they are inferior but lovable. They ought to be treated sternly and kindly at the same time. Corporal punishment is to be used as one uses it to keep one's own children in line.

This paternalistic prejudice might also be described as "pseudo-tolerance." The slave, or servant, is acceptable "in his place," even "loved" in a condescending way. It should be fairly apparent that this paternalistic "syndrome" bears little relation to "authoritarianism," "high F," etc. The psychological characteristics of the bigot which have come out of research in the United States are, we think, more typical of a competitive situation when the "ethos" of the culture is opposed to prejudice. This is not to say that no "high F's" will be found in a paternalistic situation, but rather that within a paternalistic society the "authoritarian" syndrome will not be a good predictor of racial attitudes, opinions and behaviour. It would also be a misunderstanding of our position to interpret us as saying that psychological variables are not operative in the paternalistic type of prejudice. In fact, we suspect that there might be a corresponding psychological syndrome in the paternalistic type. Roger Bastide, a psychoanalytically oriented social scientist, has suggested that paternalistic master-servant relationships are an extension of the nuclear family situation.[6] He suggests an ambivalent oedipal relationship between master and slave in the plantation situation, and an incest taboo between white mistress and male slaves. We are not equipped to pass judgement on such interpretations. But although our own primary theoretical focus is sociological, we do not deny the operation of psychological factors or the existence of individual differences in the paternalistic situation.

An important note of caution should be added here. The romantic myth of the kindly master who led an existence of genteel leisure on his plantation amidst the happy singing of his slaves, should of course be dismissed. Violence and aggression do occur in the paternalistic type. But they take different forms than in the competitive case. They generally originate from the lower caste, and are not directly and specifically racial in character. Slave rebellions and nationalistic, revivalistic, or messianic movements are typical of the paternalistic type, and indicate a lack of complete integration of the society. Such movements are usually repressed with utmost vigor by the upper caste, because if they are allowed to develop, they tend to lead to a violent and cataclysmic overthrow of the "old regime" as exemplified by the Haitian revolution.

Generally speaking, however, the paternalistic type of prejudice can be said to be "adjustive," "functional," or "integrative" for the social system.

[6] Roger Bastide, *Sociologie et Psychanalyse*, Paris: Presses Universitaires de France, 1950, pp. 241–245.

This statement implies, of course, no value judgement. We simply mean that, barring external influences and other disruptive factors such as industrialization, the more the racial ideology is believed in and practiced in a paternalistic society, the more integrated and stable the social system is. In other words, the more the hierarchial norms have been internalized in the personalities of both upper and lower caste members, the greater the stability of the social system, everything else remaining constant. But this inherent stability of the paternalistic type is accompanied by inherent inflexibility and inadaptability, i.e., when the system is attacked from the outside, as is colonialism today, or when internal developments such as industrialization are incompatible with paternalism, the whole social system collapses altogether, or evolves into a competitive situation.

Examples of the paternalistic type of racial prejudice are the slave plantation regimes of the ante-bellum U. S. South, of the West Indies, of Brazil; the "encomienda" or "hacienda" system in various parts of Spanish America; the colonial regimes of the various European powers in Africa, some of which, such as the former Belgian Congo, have survived in fairly pure form to the recent past. All the preceding examples were taken from Western societies because the cases are more familiar. But paternalism is not limited to Western societies. In Ruanda-Urundi (Central Africa) for example, the Watuzi, a group of pastoralists famous for their tall stature, have imposed their domination over an overwhelming majority of shorter and physically quite distinguishable Bahutu. The latter, who were already tillers of land before the Watuzi conquest, have become the serfs of the Watuzi; the situation is typically paternalistic.

Likewise, paternalism as a type of relationship is not limited to interracial situations as we shall see later.

THE COMPETITIVE TYPE: ITS CHARACTERISTICS

In our ideal-type dichotomy, the competitive type is the polar opposite of the paternalistic type. Generally, the competitive type is found in large-scale manufacturing economy based on industrial capitalism. However, competitive prejudice has existed in pre-industrial societies. The case of the Jews in medieval Europe, though not "racial" according to our definition of the word, was competitive. The problem whether the competitive type is linked with capitalism, as a Marxist might contend, is not easy to settle empirically. Ethnic relations in the Soviet Union and Soviet policies toward the "nationalities" are not easy to investigate. However, the U.S.S.R. has known waves of anti-Semitism indicative of competitive prejudice. At any rate, urbanization seems a prerequisite for a competitive situation, and, empirically, the latter is very much associated with an industrial and capitalistic society.

The division of labour is complex and based on "rational" and "universalistic" criteria as required by a differentiated manufacturing economy. The bulk of the labour force is no longer unskilled, and technical competence and efficiency become paramount criteria of selection. Hence any rigid racial division of labour based on ascription and particularism cannot be maintained without entailing serious economic dysfunctions. Racial criteria of selection are not altogether absent, however. Indeed, they can be operative, due to prejudice, but they can only be maintained at a cost to the efficiency of the system of production and the tendency is toward a breakdown of the industrial colour bar. As a corollary of the above factors, there is much mobility, both social and spacial. Any complex industrial economy based on "organic solidarity" requires a spatially and socially mobile labour force, i.e., one which is responsive to the demand for labour and skills. Again, social mobility is hampered by racial prejudice but only at a cost to the production system, and the tendency is towards *"la carrière ouverte aux talents."*

In typical form, the competitive situation is accompanied by a caste system, but the distance between the castes in education, occupation, income, living standards, death rates, etc., tends to diminish, i.e., the colour bar tends to tilt from a horizontal to a vertical position, though the vertical position has never been fully achieved. Within each colour caste, there is more and more class differentiation. In other words, the status gap *between* castes tends to diminish and the status range *within* the castes tends to increase. With the tilting of the colour bar, an upper-class-lower-caste person may have a higher education, occupation, living standard, etc., than a lower-class-upper-caste person. Hence, there often comes about a "status panic" of lower-class persons from the upper caste, who feel threatened by rising lower-caste members as soon as class status and caste status cease to have a one-to-one correspondence. Though threat to status is probably not the whole story, it goes a long way to account for the higher virulence of competitive prejudice among "poor whites" in the United States, for example.

The dominant caste, in the competitive situation, is usually a majority which has within itself great status and class differences. The upper caste is not a homogenous ruling group as in the paternalistic case. On the contrary, a large segment of the upper caste engages in manual labour, and hence is in direct competition with members of the lower caste. The sheer numerical ratio between the castes makes this situation inevitable. A certain percentage of the population must engage in manual occupations, and only a minority can be "on top."

In some interracial situations where miscegenation has been so extensive as to blur physical distinctions, and where the criteria of group membership are at least partly cultural rather than purely racial, the rigid colour caste system has broken down in part. This has been the case to some extent in most of Latin America. In Mexico, for example, a *mestizo* or *ladino* can be a full-blooded Indian, provided he speaks fluent Spanish and is acculturated to Hispanic ways. But that still does not make him a "Spaniard." Prejudice is still present though it is a mixture of ethnic and racial prejudice, and a quasi-caste system exists, though in much less rigid form than in the United States.

The competitive type is usually accompanied by ideological conflict, at least in a Western, "Christian," "democratic," and "liberal" sort of society. This conflict was the central core of Myrdal's analysis of the U. S. situation.[7] Whether the ideological conflict is simply a "superstructural" reflection of the more basic incompatibility between the production system and prejudice, as the Marxist line of argument would run, is an open question, and one which cannot easily be settled empirically.

The form of government found in a competitive situation is generally a restricted or partial democracy from which the lower caste is excluded by various means, and to a greater or lesser degree. The lower caste has generally no definite legal status. Discriminatory legislation can be passed but usually without explicitly mentioning race as the basis of exclusion. Devious devices such as poll taxes, re-zoning, and the like are used. Extra-legal sanctions against the minority are resorted to, such as lynching in the Southern United States. The law generally is on the side of the general value system of the society and hence opposed to the prejudice norms. In terms of Max Weber's typology, the form of authority found in the competitive type is "rational-legal."

Racial roles and statutes are ill-defined and in a constant state of flux. In terms of Parsons' pattern variables, they are based on achievement, universalism, specificity, self-orientation, and affective neutrality. There is no elaborate etiquette. Rather, members of the lower caste are in constant doubt as to the behaviour expected from them. Conversely, members of the upper caste are in constant difficulty as to how to address educated lower-caste members, for example. The old etiquette is no longer applicable, and no new one has been evolved.

Unequal caste status is constantly assailed by the levelling forces discussed above. Since etiquette has broken down as a mechanism to maintain intimate unequal contacts, spacial segregation is resorted to in order to minimize interracial contacts which threaten to become equal, and which are replete with uneasiness, ambiguity, and tension because of mutual prejudices.[8] Suspicion, hatred, antagonism prevail between the

---

[7] Gunnar Myrdal, *An American Dilemma*, New York: Harper, 1944, pp. 21, 39, 84–89, 460, 614, 899.
[8] If one conceives of spacial distance and social distance as alternative mechanisms of social control in a racial caste situation, certain theoretical considerations follow. Both mechanisms are based on the ascriptive criterion of race, and hence involve a "cost" in

racial groups. Competition, real or imaginary, for status, for jobs, for women, etc., or the threat of competition, poison race relations. Miscegenation is severely condemned and infrequent. If it takes place at all, it will assume the form of transitory or commercialized contacts between the fringe members of both castes (e.g., between poor whites and Negro prostitutes in the United States). Lasting concubinage is not institutionalized. A few cases of intermarriage will occur, at the cost of much disapproval, and usually among fringe groups (artists, bohemians, political radicals, low-class white immigrants, etc.).

Forms of aggression are numerous and originate both from the upper and from the lower caste. The basis of such aggression involves specifically racial issues. Besides the more violent manifestations of prejudice, such as sabotage, bombing, lynchings, race riots and pogroms, other forms of resistance and antagonism are organized mass protests, strikes, passive resistance, etc. The lower caste often seems to turn also to in-group aggression as a response to frustration. Typical of the competitive situation is a recurrent pattern of increase and decrease in prejudice which is in contrast with the relatively stable level of prejudice in the paternalistic case. In the competitive case, prejudice against groups seems to build up to a point of dangerous tension in response to such conditions as rapid influx of lower-caste migrants, unemployment, etc. The slightest incident will then trigger off interracial violence. Such a gradual building up of tension seems to precede most race riots, pogroms, waves of terrorism, and the like.

Naturally, competitive prejudice, irrespective of these cyclical trends, can operate at an average level which is lower in one society than in another (e.g., anti-Semitism is stronger in Germany than in France, but still there has been a Dreyfus affair in France. Anti-Negro prejudice is stronger in the United States than in Brazil, but is far from absent in the latter country).

Stereotypes held about the lower caste are coloured by fear. Lower-caste

---

efficiency, at least in the sense of economic rationality. To quote Linton, "the ascription of status sacrifices the possibility of having certain roles performed superlatively well to the certainty of having them performed passably well." (Cf. Ralph Linton, *The Study of Man*, New York: Appleton-Century, 1936, p. 129). But social distance involves a great measure of functional differentiation insofar as the members of the various castes perform tasks which are largely complementary. Spacial distance, on the contrary, involves a large degree of segmentation without differentiation, insofar as tasks, facilities, and functions are duplicatory rather than complementary. If the above considerations are correct, they may in part account for the greater degree of in-built maladjustment in the competitive type of race relations. An industrial competitive type of society which "needs all the differentiation it can get" can afford the luxury of segmentation even less than a pre-industrial paternalistic society. Yet the tendency is towards spacial segregation as a substitute for social distance. This is one of the inherent paradoxes of the competitive type.

members are held to aggressive, "uppity," insolent, oversexed, dirty. In short, they are despicable and dangerous as well as inferior. Clearly, stereotypes and prejudice are reciprocal. Lower-caste members describe upper-caste members as overbearing, "bullying," brutal, etc.

It appears that competitive prejudice is linked with "authoritarian" personality variables in members of the upper caste. This relationship is probably even closer when the values of total society are opposed to prejudice. In the United States, this aspect of prejudice has been widely studied and the link between competitive prejudice and sexuality, sadism, "anality," etc., has been established. Scape-goating and frustration-aggression are clearly not complete explanations of prejudice even at the psychological level, but the relevance of these psychological mechanisms is beyond question. One may speak of a personality "need," or, as Allport puts it, of the "functional significance" of prejudice for the "high F's."[9] It is still an open question how this relationship between "authoritarianism" and competitive prejudice holds when the values of the society are not openly against prejudice. Fragmentary evidence from the Southern United States suggest, however, that the relationship becomes lesser. In other words, conformity to prejudicial norms in the Southern United States accounts for a good deal of anti-Negro prejudice.[10]

One point stands out clearly from our description of competitive prejudice; it is a highly "maladjusting" or "dysfunctional" phenomenon in an industrial society. Again, no value judgement is implied. Not for a moment would we assert that the paternalistic type is normally "better." By "maladjusting" we mean that the higher the level of competitive prejudice is, the less smoothly the social system will operate. Competitive prejudice, then, is a "luxury" which can only be bought at a price.

The reason for this built-in maladjustive factor in competitive prejudice lies primarily, we think, in the functional prerequisites of an industrial society which conflict with prejudicial norms. Mobility of labour and "rationality" of recruitment based on achievement and universalism are all in conflict with racial prejudice which is ascriptive and particularistic. Competitive prejudice finds itself in the inherently paradoxical position of operating both within a "rational-legal" system and against it.

Some empirical examples of competitive types of prejudice are the anti-Negro prejudice in the United States since the Civil War, the anti-Asiatic prejudice in California, anti-Semitism in Europe and the United States, anti-non-European prejudice in South Africa in recent years, and anti-Negro prejudice in Brazil, at least in the large industrial centers such as São Paulo, Santos, and Rio de Janeiro.

[9] Gordon W. Allport, *The Nature of Prejudice*, Cambridge: Addison-Wesley, 1954, pp. 285–286.
[10] Thomas F. Pettigrew, *Regional Differences in Anti-Negro Prejudice*, Harvard University, Unpublished Thesis, 1956.

THE TWO TYPES OF PREJUDICE:
A SUMMARY AND ANALYTICAL SCHEMA

Such a broad description of the two types of prejudice as we have presented is rather unmanageable for analytical purposes. We shall now attempt to isolate the main variables, classify them for purposes of analysis, and present a schema contrasting the two types side by side to insure that they do indeed constitute polar opposites and differ on the same dimensions.

We propose to classify the main variables of analysis into "dependent," "independent," and "social control" variables. Since these terms call to mind the experimental model, we should immediately emphasize that we are using them, for lack of better words, only in an analogical manner, not in a strict experimental sense. As variables interact, the words "dependent" and "independent" are interchangeable. In the present context, they are only meant to clarify the starting point of our analysis, and to disentangle somewhat the relationship between variables.

We shall call "dependent variables" those that are directly concerned with race relations and prejudice, such as stereotypes, patterns of segregation, psychological syndromes, etc. They are the variables which we shall attempt to "predict" *ex post facto* from the "independent variables." The latter are broader social structure variables, i.e., the social framework within which prejudice expresses itself. They are the type of economy, the division of labour, the social stratification, etc. Lest we be accused of economic, sociological, or some other form of determinism, we must again emphasize that the primacy we give to these "independent" variables is strictly heuristic, and in no way precludes reciprocal causation.

A third set of variables we shall call "social control" variables, though we depart again from the strict experimental model. By "social control" we mean here deliberate attempts to modify, restore, or preserve an existent set of social conditions. This set of variables includes primarily governmental action in its executive, legislative, and judicial forms.

Here, then, follows the schema:

A. *"Independent" Variables*

	PATERNALISTIC	COMPETITIVE
1. Economy	Non-manufacturing, agricultural, pastoral, handicraft; mercantile capitalism; plantation economy.	Typically manufacturing, but not necessarily so. Large-scale industrial capitalism.

	PATERNALISTIC	COMPETITIVE
2. Division of Labour	Simple ("primitive") or intermediate (as in pre-industrial large-scale societies). Division of labour along racial lines. Wide income gap between racial groups.	Complex (manufacturing) according to "rational" universalistic criteria. Narrow gap in wages. No longer strictly racial.
3. Mobility	Little mobility either vertical or horizontal (slaves, servants, or serfs "attached" in space).	Much mobility both vertical and horizontal (required by industrial economy).
4. Social Stratification	Caste system with horizontal colour bar. Aristocracy vs. servile caste with wide gap in living standards (as indexed by income, education, death and birth rates). Homogeneous upper caste.	Caste system but with tendency for colour bar to "tilt" to vertical position. Complex stratification into classes within castes. Narrower gaps *between* castes and greater range *within* castes.
5. Numerical Ratio	Dominant group a small minority.	Dominant group a majority.
6. Value Conflict	Integrated value system. No ideological conflict.	Conflict at least in Western, "Christian," "democratic," "liberal" type of society.

B. "Dependent" Variables

1. Race Relations	Accommodation. Everyone in his place and "knows it." Paternalism. Benevolent despotism.	Antagonism. Suspicion, hatred. Competitiveness (real or imaginary).
2. Roles and Statuses	Sharply defined roles and statuses based on ascription, particularism diffuseness, collectivity orientation, affectivity. Unequal status unthreatened.	Ill-defined and based on achievement, universalism, specificity, self-orientation, affective neutrality. Unequal status threatened.
3. Etiquette	Elaborate and definite.	Simple and indefinite.

	PATERNALISTIC	COMPETITIVE
4. Forms of Aggression	Generally from lower caste: slave rebellions, nationalistic, revivalistic or messianistic movements. Not directly racial. "Righteous" punishment from the master.	Both from upper and lower caste. More frequent and directly racial: riots, lynchings, pogroms. Passive resistance, sabotage, organized mass protests.
5. Miscegenation	Condoned and frequent between upper-caste males and lower-caste females. Institutionalized concubinage.	Severely condemned and infrequent.
6. Segregation	Little of it. Status gap allows close but unequal contact.	Much of it. Narrowing of status gap makes for increase of spacial gap.
7. Psychological Syndrome	Internalized subservient status. No personality "need" for prejudice. No "high F." "Pseudo-tolerance."	"Need" for prejudice. "High F." Linked with sexuality, sadism, frustration. Scapegoating.
8. Stereotypes of Lower Caste	Childish, immature, exuberant, uninhibited, lazy, impulsive, fun-loving, good-humored. Inferior but lovable.	Aggressive, uppity, insolent, oversexed, dirty. Inferior, despicable, and dangerous.
9. Intensity of Prejudice	Fairly constant.	Variable, and sensitive to provocative situations.

C. "Social Control" Variables

1. Form of Government	Aristocratic, oligarchic, autocratic. Either centralized or "feudal." Colonial.	Restricted or partial democracy.
2. Legal System	Lower caste has separate legal status. Law on side of racial *status quo*. Weber's "traditional" type of authority.	Lower caste has no separate legal status. Resort to extralegal sanctions. Weber's "rational-legal" type of authority.

The Two Types of Prejudice in Relation to Other Theoretical Schemes

We have already indicated explicitly our borrowings from Parsons and from Weber. Weber's traditional type of authority tends to coincide with our paternalistic type of prejudice whereas his "rational-legal" type of authority both coincides and conflicts with competitive prejudice. Weber's third type of authority, the charismatic one, is unstable and rarely found in a pure state. Insofar as charisma is revolutionary and unstable, it is incompatible with our paternalistic type. An example of competitve prejudice under a system which had strong charismatic elements is anti-Semitism under National Socialism in Germany. But anti-Semitism was already present in the rational-legal Germany of pre-Hitler days. Hence, charisma and the competitive type are not incompatible, but the relationship is not a necessary one.

In our use of Parsons' pattern-variables, we have seen that they polarized along our two types. The pattern-variables are conceived of by Parsons as being *independently* variable, however. That such is the case in many of the possible applications of the scheme, we shall not dispute. But in application to racial roles, there does not seem to be independent variation.

Our dichotomy is obviously related to some of the classical distinctions in sociology. Our competitive type coincides largely with the type of social solidarity which Durkheim called "organic." However, the reverse relationship between paternalism and mechanical solidarity does not hold. Most cases of paternalistic prejudice are found in a functionally differentiated, though pre-industrial, society with a division of labour which we have termed "intermediate." Such a level of differentiation in the division of labour already contains strong "organic" elements, and no longer represents a primitive "mechanical" level of solidarity, at least not in anywhere near a pure state.

Redfield's "folk" *versus* "urban" distinction likewise bears only a partial relationship to our own typology. Although the competitive type is associated with urbanism, and although paternalism is compatible with a "folk" society, the paternalistic situation is also found in urban societies. As regards Toennies *Gemeinschaft-Gesellschaft* dichotomy, the correspondence to our two types is perhaps closer. The paternalistic type has many *Gemeinschaft* characteristics and a *Gesellschaft* society is most compatible with the competitive type.

Subject to the reservations mentioned above we may schematize the relationship between our dichotomy and the distinctions reviewed above as follows:

	PATERNALISTIC TYPE	COMPETITIVE TYPE
Max Weber's types of authority	Traditional	Rational-legal (occasionally: charismatic)
Parsons' pattern-variables	Ascription, particularism, affectivity, collective orientation, diffuseness.	Achievement, universalism, affective neutrality, self-orientation, specificity.
Durkheim's forms of solidarity	Mechanical-organic mixture	Organic
Toennies	*Gemeinschaft*	*Gesellschaft*
Redfield	Folk or urban	Urban

Applicability of the Paternalistic-Competitive Distinction and the Problem of "Mixed Types"

We must first answer the question: Is our scheme synchronic or diachronic? The answer is that it is both. Historically, at least in Western societies since the first period of overseas expansion in the fifteenth century, the general tendency has been away from the paternalistic type and toward competitive prejudice. In that sense, then, our scheme is diachronic and evolutionary. But each of the two types can also be viewed as an existing situation in a given society. There is no *necessary* evolution from one type to the other. A competitive situation can prevail without having been preceded by a paternalistic one, as with Jews in medieval Europe; conversely, a paternalistic system can endure, barring disruptive factors, without leading to the competitive type, as between Watuzi and Bahutu in Ruanda-Urundi until the eve of independence.

There is another sense in which our scheme is to be regarded as synchronic. The two types of prejudice can co-exist within different segments of the same society, and toward different groups. One example comes to mind to illustrate this point, though it is not a case of racial prejudice. In medieval Europe, the prejudice against Jews in the cities was competitive, while the feudal lord-serf relationship in the rural areas was paternalistic.

We have already hinted that our scheme was applicable cross-culturally to non-Western societies. The argument that racial prejudice is a recent development limited to Western societies, and intended to rationalize the economic exploitation of subject peoples is only a half-truth. True, the pseudo-scientific theories of racial differences have attained their most thorough elaboration in the Western world with the writings of Gobineau and the popularization of social Darwinism. That such theories provided convenient justifications for the exploitation of "native" labour and slaves in the European colonies is likewise incontrovertible. But the exploitation preceded the development of the theories, and a simplistic view that the theories were devised with the Machiavellian purpose of justifying the colonial system is untenable. The main point, however, is that racial prejudice is much older than Gobineau, and not limited to the Western world. Whenever phenotypical differences have existed between groups of people, racial prejudice seems to have arisen. The Bantu groups of central Africa regard the pygmies who live among them as intermediate between chimpanzees and men. The Japanese express contempt for the bearded Ainu of Hokkaido. The Chinese expressed bewilderment at the sight of the first Europeans who landed in their country, and compared the Europeans to monkeys because of their hairiness. In India, there is considerable evidence that the caste system originated in racial differences between Aryan conquerors and Dravidians, though, of course, race alone does not account for the florescence of caste. In short, physically distinguishing characteristics are generally seized upon to perpetuate group differences, and establish the superiority of one group over the other.

Not only does our scheme apply to non-Western societies. It also applies *mutatis mutandis* to forms of prejudice other than racial. The competitive ethnic and religious prejudice against Jews in Europe and the United States is an example of non-racial prejudice. Similarly, the paternalistic syndrome can be found in a wide variety of contexts: between the factory owner and his workers; between the company or ship commander and his men. In this study, however, we shall limit ourselves to specifically racial prejudice.[11]

The problem of "mixed types" is crucial in any ideal-type scheme. As ideal-types are logical constructs, it is important not to reify them. The fact that no empirical situation coincides exactly with one of the types does not invalidate a typology. But, as in any scientific theory, heuristic usefulness is a paramount consideration. A distinction should be made here between schemes that are constructed in terms of a continuum between two or more poles and schemes based on what we may call a "true typology." The first sort of scheme admits of all intermediate posi-

---

[11] This limitation of our subject matter is heuristic rather than substantive. We do not believe that racial prejudice is fundamentally different from the other forms of prejudice. We conceive rather of racial prejudice as a special case of a more general phenomenon. But the relative permanency of physical charactristics makes for a more rigid definition of groups, and for more clear-cut and enduring situations than in other forms of prejudice. For these reasons, racial prejudice is particularly well suited to scientific inquiry.

tions on the continuum; even a normal distribution where most cases are found in the middle of the continuum, and none at the extremes, is compatible with this sort of scheme.

A true typology, in the restricted sense in which we use that term, implies an empirical polarization of cases around the extremes, and qualitative rather than quantitative differences. "Mixed cases" must be inherently unstable and tend to move towards one of the ideal-types. We believe that our dichotomy satisfies this condition. Societies have moved from the paternalistic to the competitive type of prejudice and hence must have gone through a "mixed" stage. But the social system as a whole tends to continue to evolve until the competitive situation is rather closely approximated. It cannot remain in a stable intermediate position between the polar opposites. Mixed types at the total society level of analysis can only be transitory. But there is another sense in which "mixed types" can occur. Sub-systems within the society can belong in different types as in the case of medieval Europe mentioned earlier. Different groups within the same society can be the object of different types of prejudice. Also, in the case of a society in transition, different segments of the total society (e.g., rural *versus* urban) can be in different stages in the process of evolution. The isolated rural areas will tend to remain paternalistic longer than the industrial centers, for example. All these possibilities can make the overall characterization of a total society a complex matter. But again, this does not invalidate the criterion of polarization. It is only a question of defining the boundaries of the social system or sub-system under analysis.

II. EXAMPLES OF
ETHNIC AND RACIAL
SUBCULTURAL VARIATION

7. The Welcome Heritage

JUDITH KRAMER AND
SEYMOUR LEVENTMAN

Contemporary theorists of social stratification have begun to emphasize that an individual's over-all rank in a given stratification system is a composite of the ranks of his various statuses—e.g., ethnic, occupational, financial, and educational. Kramer and Leventman examine several aspects of status placement among American Jews. Their treatment of class and life-style is similar to that of Max Weber, who used the first to refer to occupational and financial rank, and the second to refer to rank as based on canons of taste and honorific aspects of prestige. Among American Jews, as this selection points out, trends toward status consistency are apparently emerging now, as the third generation attempts to bolster with its life-style the higher economic status that was won by the second generation. In time, as high-status Jews become less distinguishable from their non-Jewish

SOURCE: Judith R. Kramer and Seymour Leventman, *Children of the Gilded Ghetto* (New Haven: Yale University Press, 1961.), pp. 141–50. Copyright © 1961 by Yale University. Reprinted by permission of Yale University Press.

Judith Kramer is Assistant Professor of Sociology at Brooklyn College. *Seymour Leventman* is Assistant Professor of Sociology at the University of Pennsylvania.

counterparts, the low ethnic status formerly ascribed to Jews will also rise. Indeed, many Jewish religious spokesmen are concerned about threats to the survival of American-Jewish communal and religious identity because they believe that these processes are already occurring and that inter-marriage is bound to accompany them.

Several observers of the Jewish scene have suggested that aspirations have changed from second to third generation. The fathers had the ambition to build successful businesses and professional practices, the sons only the ambition to inherit them. In wanting to be like everyone else, the third-generation Jew wants also to feel that he doesn't have to strive unduly for success. He prefers to believe that he doesn't have to prove anything to anybody by earning an ever increasing income, and he is wary of offending his well-adjusted neighbors by any display of aggressive ambition. Like everyone else he knows, he wants comfort and security for himself and his family, and time in which to enjoy the income he does earn. He concentrates on spending his money and finding out what it can do for him rather than on enlarging his income. This permits him to avoid incurring the hostility of his non-Jewish peers.

The decline of economic tensions in the third generation offers evidence that many of the economic problems of the minority situation were solved effectively by the second generation. In large part, however, the lowered economic sights simply reflect the broader changes in goals among the younger generation of all Americans. Brogan observes a general reassessment of values among Americans. "One [new type of value decision] is the decision for leisure rather than for ever-expanding income. The man continually striving loses the chance for leisure. His very recreations are driven by a passion to 'succeed.' " Taking for granted the advantages an older generation struggled to acquire is hardly unique to young Jews. "Few self-made men can resist the temptation to give their sons 'advantages' that they didn't have and these advantages often include an education that alienates the son from his father's simple world." Young Jews and non-Jews alike want the comforts of life without having to pay the high price of overwork. They assume they will come into possession of these comforts as a result of a job they will have no difficulty in obtaining (especially if it's in a family business).

Although the values of the third generation are certainly part of a general climate of opinion favoring "peace of mind" over "success," they also reflect changes taking place within the Jewish community. Kurt Lewin argued that it was the tensions of marginality characteristic of second-generation Jews which served to generate their intense strivings for success; a decline in such tensions produces diminished ambition. The tensions of the third generation have been eased in important ways.

The men of the third generation are, after all, not "marginal men."

Because of their acceptable middle-class American background with its mild version of Judaism, they do not experience their Jewishness as a source of much conflict. Since in many respects they feel more accepted by non-Jews than their fathers, they have little cause for self-hatred or embittered striving for membership in the non-Jewish world. With the problems of survival and success solved by earlier generations, the third generation rarely experiences the degree of tension necessary for the ambition of its fathers. Even Marjorie Morningstar could not fail to take note of the new Philistine of her generation, the young Jew who "wants to be a writer or a forest ranger or a composer or anything except what his father is, because he's ashamed of his father being a Jew, or because he thinks he's too sensitive for business or law, or whatever the damned Freudian reason may be —and he winds up in his father's business just the same. . . ."

What members of the younger generation are concerned with is the cultivation of appropriate styles of life. Education has helped to nurture their interest in this area. Even more than money, they want time to consume and to engage in the proper leisure-time activities. "Today's heroes don't lust for big riches, but they are positively greedy for the good life." The consummate dedication of the second generation to business left little time for dabbling in status symbols. The third generation wants to "enjoy life" in a way its fathers did not.

> I won't kill myself for a buck. There's more to living than just money. I'm more concerned with the way I want to live.
>
> I like my way of life now. I won't cut out activities I like just to earn another buck.
>
> I make enough to get along—I don't want more money—and the heart attack that goes with it.
>
> I don't know what the goal would be for making more money. . . . There's no goal in just making money. You only know what your goals are when you're doing what you want.

These are the voices of men whose fathers devoted twelve hours a day to work and the other twelve to worry. Their sons see no point in having money you can't enjoy, and they reject the "materialistic" preoccupation of the fathers. They take for granted, however, a "suitable" income and assume they will continue to earn an adequate living. To be concerned with material gain, however, smacks of "money grubbing," a peculiarly Jewish vice in the stereotypes of American society.

Although few are looking for wealth, 39 per cent anticipate increased incomes. Motivation for economic improvement derives from a desire to provide appropriate standards of living for their families.

> I want to provide adequately for my family and have as much as others have in comforts.

> I want more income since I'm not yet up to the standard of living I'd like to achieve.

These ambitions are eminently reasonable for young men starting out in careers whose income potential increases with time. Although they will not "grub for money," they expect to make enough in the near future to afford the style of life they want. Only 5 per cent express some dedication to the pursuit of their professional interests, regardless of the possibilities of success, financial or otherwise.

The secure aura of economic well-being is enhanced by the fact that few have been handicapped by their Jewishness. Fifty-two per cent feel that being Jewish had no influence whatsoever on their occupational choice. Another 43 per cent feel that being Jewish influenced them to enter a profession, to be self-employed or in public service, and/or to strive for achievement (whether intellectual or financial). Influences of this sort are not considered restrictive. On the contrary, it is still desirable to be motivated to enter a profession, even if the source of such motivation is one's "Jewishness." Even those who chose self-employment because they thought Jews couldn't get ahead any other way do not feel impeded by this. They reason as follows:

> I wanted to be self-employed because of the problem of anti-Semitism impeding advancement.

> Being Jewish led me to be a self-employed professional. As a Jewish employee in North City, I couldn't have advanced very far. Jewish businesses are all family businesses and I had no way of getting into them.

North City has had an especially virulent tradition of discriminatory employment which has influenced even members of the younger generation to work for themselves. Nevertheless, they have no cause for complaint. Even in North City, an increasing number of young Jews claim,

> I like working for the company. I have security there and I don't feel the need to be self-employed.

Being Jewish is no longer an economic problem to the third generation. Only 17 per cent feel that their religious identity has either restricted their occupational choice, limiting them to fewer and less desirable occupations, or impeded their opportunities for advancement within their chosen fields. Not many of this generation encounter job discrimination; few even apply for positions in local industries reputed to be discriminatory. Some of the older members of the third generation were counselled out of certain fields when they were making their career decisions because of the difficulty of finding employment for Jews.

> I didn't go into the scientific field (chemical research) for fear of not being employed in the big industries that do the research. I felt I had to be an independent professional to get ahead and law seemed to permit mobility.

> I wanted to be an engineer originally, but I worried about discrimination since Jews are not hired. Even as a self-employed professional, being Jewish affects you since you get mostly Jewish clients and patients.

The salaried professions are increasingly open to Jews as the demand for highly trained personnel grows. But those seeking lower-middle-class white-collar positions without any particular skill or training to offer still run up against discrimination. In this sample, however, there are few men with only high school education. One respondent, looking for a job as an insurance salesman found that,

> Being Jewish makes it difficult when you don't have real training. If you have special training, being Jewish doesn't matter.

It is easier for a Jew to sell his "skills" on the job market than his "personality." Consequently, he has more access to jobs requiring professional training or technical expertise than to jobs involving executive managerial capacities.

The members of the third-generation sample are a highly educated and disproportionately professional group for whom economic discrimination has rarely been a problem. Complacent in their security, few feel they must be self-employed to insure their source of livelihood. Most respondents are convinced that being Jewish will in no way limit their opportunities for advancement or restrict the number of their business contacts or clients. Some even find their religious identity an asset; there are people who, for example, prefer Jewish professionals because "they're better."

Although the third generation has experienced few occupational restrictions as Jews, it does recognize some occupations as "more Jewish" than others. Perhaps as a result of this awareness, members of the sample have steered away from "Jewish" occupations which lack more general status in the community. Most frequently mentioned as typically "Jewish" occupations are the independent professions (e.g., law and medicine) and retail proprietorships. Factory worker and corporation executive positions are the occupations considered "least Jewish," i.e., respondents believe fewer Jews are found in them than in the others.

The "Jewishness" of an occupation affects its standing in the wider community. In 1953, the North City Junior Chamber of Commerce published a list of "One Hundred Young Men Selected by the Committee for North City's Future." The list, composed mostly of businessmen and such professionals as clergymen, professors, lawyers, and doctors, suggests the type of Jew held in general esteem. Seven Jews were among the chosen and none, except the rabbi of a high-ranking Conservative congregation (whose modern Ivy League approach to religion qualifies him as a representative young clergyman), was in an occupation traditionally associated with Jews in North City. Two were symphony musicians in no way connected with the local Jewish community, one a newspaper columnist. The others included a research chemist, a municipal judge, and a president of a long established manufacturing firm. There are richer Jews in the city, but these six were distinguished by their occupations, which are not the characteristically marginal occupations of an ethnic group.

The immigrant and working-class status of the first generation created tensions to which its sons responded with a fierce drive for success. The second generation was more likely to advance in class than status, but was able to bestow upon its sons all the advantages of economic security, including a college education. The third generation receives its comfortable heritage with some reservations. Although members of this generation have no conscientious objection to the profit they derive from the economic gains of their fathers, they are critical of the "materialistic" values of the older generation. They permit themselves the illusion that interest in money is a peculiar monopoly of Jews, of which they want no part (except in dollars and cents).

The achievement of the second generation brought with it problems requiring resolution by the next generation. The literary voice of the younger generation asks petulantly whether "upper-middle-class Jewish life is different and worse than upper-middle-class life in general" or just different. Heroines of recent Jewish novels insist upon falling in love with unsuitable young men who represent a different way of life from that of their fathers—a way of life that precludes financial success. Young Jews are less concerned with the accumulation of wealth than with the cultivation of appropriate styles of life. Many a bewildered second-generation father has wondered why, if his college educated son is so smart, he isn't rich.

The "materialistic" values and the marginal nature of the occupations of the second generation are a source of tension for its sons. Yet despite any qualms they may have about making money, those of the third generation who are heir to successful family businesses rarely refuse them.

They appease an occasionally troublesome conscience by spending their money in different and less "Jewish" ways than their fathers. Those without the "burden" of a family business use advanced education as a key to open the doors of a variety of new occupations. Entry into these occupations is one of the important tension resolutions of the third generation, whose life situation is, in part, a response to the demands of a national economy for increasing levels of expertness among its citizens.

Not all members of the third generation have either the means of access to these new occupations or the motivation. The family business still represents greater security and ease. Nevertheless, these new occupations furnish an escape from social uniqueness for a growing number of young Jews. The occupations are not identifiable as "Jewish" and their status in the general community is high. The impetus for the occupational redistribution of the third generation derives, in part, from the characteristic discrepancy between class and status in the second generation. Entrance into traditionally non-Jewish occupations thus by-passes the tensions inherent in marginal occupations, which are low in status, however profitable they may be.

In sum, we find that members of the third generation have not merely accepted the more successful economic resolutions of their fathers, they have improved upon them. They have achieved considerable occupational mobility and are well satisfied with themselves. Being Jewish has rarely hindered the attainment of their occupational goals, although they are aware of the economic discrimination practiced in North City. They are excluded from the local executive world of "organization men," but they have entered through the back door as salaried professionals and technical experts.

It is quite clear then that the third generation accepts the economic world of its fathers, at least in so far as it is a comfortable world. Here there is no wholesale over-throwing of the goals of the second generation, although accumulation of wealth is exchanged for time to spend it. One generation earns the money, and the next learns how to spend it appropriately. The economic mobility begun by the second generation is extended by its sons, who make their gains in occupational status.

8. Achievement, Culture, and Personality: The Case of the Japanese Americans

WILLIAM CAUDILL AND
GEORGE DE VOS

American and Japanese culture both place a premium on achievement, on the capacity to defer immediate gratification for the sake of greater long-term rewards, and on devoting close attention to practical detail. These parallel values help to explain why individuals raised in Japanese-American communities are often well adapted to American educational and vocational demands. By inculcating the oncoming generation with motivations congruent with American needs and opportunities, first-generation Japanese-Americans made good use of parts of their traditional culture to aid the social mobility of their children.

Differential rates of upward mobility within various ethnic groups primarily reflect differences in group standards, and not a differential distribution of native talents. The standards of some groups—along with the Japanese, American Jews and Greeks are notable examples—are better suited than others for teaching an individual group member the steps he must take in order to get ahead through his own efforts. Therefore, although American folklore holds that success is and should be the result of individual effort and ability, it is important to see that not all individuals find themselves in situations in which they learn effective ways of bringing their capacities to bear.

The burden of this paper is that much further study of the cultural variable in achievement is needed in terms of understanding: (1) the achievement goals that are emphasized in the value system of the specific culture from which the subjects are drawn; (2) the processes by which these goals are implemented in the interpersonal behavior of individuals in the family, the peer group, the school, on the job, and in leisure time activities; and (3) the range and most frequent types of individual personality adjustment to these goals within the context of the specific culture, rather than a consideration of personality traits solely as an independent

SOURCE: *American Anthropologist*, 58, 1956, pp. 1102–25, passim., and with footnotes omitted. Reprinted by permission of the editor and the authors.

William Caudill is Chief of the Laboratory for Socio-Environmental Studies, National Institutes of Mental Health. He is the author of *The Psychiatric Hospital as a Small Society*. *George De Vos* is Associate Professor, School of Social Work, University of California at Berkeley.

variable. The methods used in the research reported below were both quantitative analysis of data on the groups in question, and intensive clinical analysis of testing, interview, and psychotherapeutic data on specific individuals.

THE ACHIEVEMENT ORIENTATION OF
JAPANESE AMERICANS IN CHICAGO

Between 1943 and 1946, approximately 20,000 Japanese Americans arrived in Chicago from relocation camps set up by the federal government when all persons of Japanese ancestry were evacuated from the Pacific Coast shortly after the United States entered World War II. Roughly a third were Issei—first generation immigrants who came to America during the early part of the century; the other two-thirds were Nisei—second generation, who are American citizen children of the Issei. The cultural and personality adjustment of this group to life in Chicago was studied for three years (1947–1950) by an interdisciplinary team from the University of Chicago. Although the problem of achievement was not a central focus of the research, the data serve to point up the success of the Japanese Americans in this regard, and to show the necessity of a thorough consideration of cultural factors in the further study of achievement.

In terms of the usual sociological or anthropological approach, there are many reasons why the 342 Japanese American families represented in the Chicago research, or the Japanese American group in general, should experience great difficulty in achievement in the United States. Traditionally, Japanese culture, social structure, values, and religion are thought of as alien to those of America. Moreover, the Issei had a background of rural, peasant, subsistence farming, and came to the United States with only temporary settlement in mind. Most important of all, the Japanese are a racially visible group to race-conscious Americans.

Yet the data show that by 1947 the Nisei, almost as a group, held white collar and skilled trade jobs within the general employment market of the city. White employers and fellow employees accepted the Nisei and were enthusiastic in their praise of them. The median level of education for the Nisei in Chicago was, as it had been on the Pacific Coast, beyond high school graduation. Almost all who did not go on to college took vocational training in order to become secretaries, laboratory technicians, beauty operators, or skilled workers. It must be noted, however, that the Issei had a surprisingly high level of education for immigrants—a median of 10 years. . . .

The Japanese Americans first found housing in some of the least desirable sections of Chicago. However, they disliked living in these sections and many families soon moved into predominantly white upper-lower and lower-middle class neighborhoods. The Japanese Americans were accepted in these areas. Neighbors and landlords liked them because they improved the property, paid their rent promptly, and were quiet and courteous. In their clothing and general appearance the Nisei were almost stereotypes of the American middle class. This was particularly true for the women, who invariably appeared well-groomed, in conservative but chic dresses, blouses always snow white, nylons, and high heels. In their attitudes and aspirations the Nisei were oriented toward careers, white collar work, or small businesses. They wanted little to do with factory jobs. They saw in unions a block to rapid advancement through individual achievement. In their social life the Nisei tended to stay within their own group. While they interacted freely with their white fellow workers on the job and in casual social intercourse at lunch, they had not yet achieved close intimate social contact with the white middle class they emulated. Yet they had achieved more in the space of four years in Chicago than other ethnic groups who had long been in the city, and who appear far less handicapped by racial and cultural differences.

Since occupation (as well as education) is a major avenue to achievement in America, it is worthwhile to look in a little more detail at the Japanese American data in this respect. The jobs the Japanese Americans were first able to obtain in the city were menial, unskilled, and poorly paid. Very shortly they left such jobs for semi-skilled factory and service work at which the Issei stayed, while the Nisei, having higher aspirations, moved on rapidly to better employment. By 1947, the Japanese Americans showed [an] occupational distribution . . . where . . . 19 percent of the Issei and 60 percent of the Nisei fall in the categories of skilled workers, white collar workers, small business owners, or managerial and professional jobs.

. . . . .

It must be remembered that the sample had been in the city for only a few years, and that the Nisei are young—clustering between 20 and 30 years of age—and have not yet reached their occupational peak.

Alan Jacobson and Lee Rainwater investigated employers' evaluations of their Japanese American employees from 79 firms. These were owned by white business men, within the general economic and industrial structure of the city, and drew their employees from the general employment market. Firms owned by Japanese Americans were excluded, as were such organizations as social agencies, which might be expected to be somewhat more liberal in their employment policies. Better than two-thirds of the employers were very positive in their evaluations of Japanese Americans as workers; they considered them to be as good as the best employees they had ever had. The remaining one-third of the employers considered Japanese Americans to be no better and no worse than their average employees. An occasional negative evaluation usually took the form of criticizing the Nisei for being too ambitious and wanting to move on to a better job too quickly. In general, Japanese Americans were praised for their technical abilities such as speed and efficiency, and for their character traits of honesty, punctuality, willingness to work overtime, general moral standards, personal appearance, and so forth. They were also praised for the way they got along with other workers in informal relations. Japanese Americans had been up-graded in job and salary in 46 of the 79 firms, and in five others in salary alone. Seventeen Nisei were promoted to jobs which gave them authority over white workers.

Why was this so? How was it possible for the children of an immigrant group to succeed as well as the Nisei have in Chicago in approximating the American middle class way of life, when the culture of their parents seems to diverge in so many respects from the American pattern?

Certainly relocation was a factor. No matter how well the Nisei were prepared in attitudes, behavior, and education for living a middle class life, it seems unlikely that they would have been able to do so on the Pacific Coast because of anti-Oriental prejudice. Also, the Japanese Americans on the Coast had formed tight, self-contained communities controlled by parental authority and strong social sanctions, from which it was difficult for the Nisei to break free. Secondly, Chicago had had a Japanese population of only 390 persons, and had no social techniques for dealing with this group. Thirdly, with the scarcity of labor during the war, the highly trained Nisei were in a relatively favorable position in terms of the employment market.

These reasons may help to explain why the Nisei got their jobs, but will not satisfactorily explain why they were able to keep them and to please their employers and fellow workers.

A major hypothesis used as an orientation to our research was: there seems to be a significant compatibility (but by no means identity) between the value systems found in the culture of Japan and the value systems found in American middle class culture. This compatibility of values gives rise to a similarity in the psychological adaptive mechanisms which are most commonly used by individuals in the two societies as they go about the business of living.

It is necessary to be aware that the hypothesis does not say that the social structure, customs, or religion of the two societies are similar. They are not, and Japan and the American middle class differ greatly in these respects. But the hypothesis does say that it is often overlooked that the Japanese and American middle class cultures share the values of politeness, respect for authority and parental wishes, duty to community, diligence, cleanliness and neatness, emphasis on personal achievement of long-range goals, importance of keeping up appearances, and others. Equally, the hypothesis does not say that the basic personality or character structure of Japanese and middle class American individuals is similar; but it does say that, for example, both Japanese and middle class Americans characteristically utilize the adaptive mechanism of being highly sensitive to cues coming from the external world as to how they should act, and that they also adapt themselves to many situations by suppression of their real emotional feelings, particularly desires for physical aggressiveness.

Given this sort of relationship between the two cultures, when they meet under conditions favorable for acculturation (as in Chicago) Japanese Americans, acting in terms of their Japanese values and personality, will behave in ways that are favorably evaluated by middle class Americans. Nevertheless, because the values and adaptive mechanisms are only compatible (and not identical), and because the social structures and personalities of the two groups are different, there are many points of conflict as well as agreement for the Nisei individual attempting to achieve in American middle class life. Certain points of conflict are made all the more poignant by the fact that the points of agreement are sufficiently strong to hold out much promise to the individual that he will succeed.

. . . . .

From the foregoing, it appears that much more than a surface evaluation of behavior is necessary for the understanding of achievement. Japanese American and white middle class behavior looks very much the same in many areas of life, but the psychological motivations underlying such behavior may occur within quite different cultural matrices. The following sections of this paper will present material illustrating this problem, as well as the further problem of individual differences in achievement within the Japanese American group itself.

CULTURAL VALUES AND PSYCHOLOGICAL
MECHANISMS IN THE ACHIEVEMENT ORIENTATION
OF JAPANESE AMERICANS

. . . . .

In general, the over-all results of the research on Japanese Americans in Chicago seem to bear out the hypothesis that the values and adaptive mechanisms of the Japanese Americans and lower middle class are highly compatible, while the upper lower class diverges from both these groups and presents a different psychological adjustment. Where Japanese American values differ in emphasis by comparison with middle class values, these differences are not of such a nature as to draw unfavorable comment from the middle class. Indeed, the differences would probably be considered praiseworthy by the middle class, if a little extreme, as in the extent of duty to one's parents, and the need to be of benefit to society.

The Issei place a high value on the attainment of such long-range goals as higher education, professional success, and the building of a spotless reputation in the community. These goals the Issei have passed on to their children, and the Issei willingly help the Nisei to achieve them because it is the unquestioned expectation of the Issei that their children will in turn fulfill their obligations to their parents. It is this "unquestioned expectation" that is the source of greatest conflict for the Nisei, who feel deeply their obligations to their parents but who also are striving for integration into American middle class life.

What appears to have occurred in the case of the Japanese Americans is that the Nisei, while utilizing to a considerable extent a Japanese set of values and adaptive mechanisms, were able in their prewar life on the Pacific Coast to act in ways that drew favorable comment and recognition from their white middle class peers and made them admirable pupils in the eyes of their middle class teachers. This situation repeated itself in Chicago, and personnel managers and fellow workers also found the Nisei to be admirable employees. What has happened here is that the peers, teachers, employers, and fellow workers of the Nisei have projected their own values onto the neat, well-dressed, and efficient Nisei in whom they saw mirrored many of their own ideals.

Because of this situation, the Nisei tend to be favorably evaluated by the American middle class, not only as individuals but as a group. Hence in Chicago, where they are removed from the high level of discrimination to be found on the Pacific Coast, the Nisei can be thought of as an entire group which is mobile toward, and attempting to achieve in, the American middle class. They are tremendously helped in this process by the praise both of their parents and of the white middle class; conversely, they are thrown into conflict over their inability to participate as fully as they would like in the middle class way of life, and at the same time fulfill their Japanese obligations to their parents.

A simile is useful in pointing up the similarities and differences between Japanese American and white middle class achievement orientations: the ultimate destinations or goals of individuals in the two groups tend to be very similar; but Japanese Americans go toward these destinations along straight narrow streets lined with crowds of people who observe their every step, while middle class persons go toward the same destinations along wider streets having more room for maneuvering, and lined only with small groups of people who, while watching them, do not observe their every movement. In psychoanalytic terminology, this means that the Japanese Americans have an ego structure that is very sensitive and vulnerable to stimuli coming from the outer world, and a superego structure that depends greatly upon external sanction. This tends to be true of middle class Americans as well, but not nearly to such an extent. For example, individuals in both groups are interested in acquiring money in amounts sufficient to be translated in the achievement of social class prestige; however, every move of a Japanese American toward amassing money is carefully watched, and the way he does it and the ultimate use he makes of it in benefiting the community are equal in importance to the financial success itself. This is less true of the American middle class, where an individual can make his money in a great variety of ways and, so long as these are not downright dishonest, the ways are sanctioned because of the end product— the financial success.

The Japanese Americans provide us, then, with the case of a group who, despite racial visibility and a culture traditionally thought of as alien, achieved a remarkable adjustment to middle class American life because certain compatibilities in the value systems of the immigrant and host cultures operated strongly enough to override the more obvious difficulties.

The foregoing summary should by no means be taken to imply that all Japanese Americans will meet with success in the achievement of their goals. What is meant is that, because of the compatibility between Japanese and American middle class cultures, individual Nisei probably have a better chance of succeeding than individuals from other ethnic groups where the underlying cultural patterns are less in harmony with those of the American middle class.

INDIVIDUAL INTEGRATIONS OF
THE ACHIEVEMENT VALUE

Through the analysis of individual cases by means of both psychological test data and psychoanalytic interviews, it is possible to show how very similar values and adaptive mechanisms are variously integrated in the personality structures of individual Nisei. There are, however, certain types of adjustment that are more favored by the culture, and these provide modal points in the total range. All that is desired here is to show, through the responses of three individuals briefly considered, how essentially the same values and broad ways of adjusting to life are differentially combined so that one individual is more likely to succeed in the achievement of his goals than another.

All three of the following Nisei stress, in their TAT stories, the positive achievement value of determination to get an education and to succeed in a career; likewise, all three see that in order to achieve these goals they must adapt themselves by working hard and foregoing immediate gratifications. This similarity in orientation is set, in the first case, within a relatively flexible personality structure in which energies are in part directed into achievement because of, rather than in spite of, certain apparently unresolved emotional problems. In the second case, the over-all picture is one of successful achievement within a pattern of rigid conformity. There are many neurotic conflicts evident in the third case that prevent the satisfactory expression of the need felt by the individual for achievement.

The first example is that of a 29-year-old married Nisei man with two small children. He had two years in college, and is now doing well in a responsible white collar job where he is continually meeting the general public. In his work adjustment he seems to have been able to reconcile whatever problems have arisen in a positive nonhostile manner. From the TAT and interview data it appears that he has not rebelled against Japanese values nor, on the other hand, has he lost his individuality and self-assertion in over-conformity. His is one of the very few Nisei TAT records that indicates a sense of humor, an ability to laugh at himself occassionally.

In the area of long-range goals this Nisei man is strongly self-motivated. As do all Nisei who are positively striving in this area, this man experiences some conflict with his parents, but he is able overtly to handle the conflict satisfactorily. For example, the daughter in his story to picture 2 goes ahead and makes her own decisions, then talks it over with her mother who temporarily is displeased but later reconciled, and the daughter is able to leave the family without guilt and with feelings of warmth toward her parents. In almost all of his stories, this man is able to have his characters be self-assertive but at the same time desirous of talking things out with family members or other older people whose advice they respect. He sees himself as very fond of his parents and wants to visit them as a pleasure rather than just as a duty.

Like most Nisei, this man does not like to have his personal emotions on display for others to see. He is much less sensitive about this, however, than other Nisei.

The adjustment outline above gives evidence of a great many positive qualities—the self-assertion, the flexibility, the seeking for and acceptance of advice without seeming hostility, and the ability to build one's own life and still retain pleasant, respectful ties with one's parents.

The Rorschach picture, however, is somewhat at variance with the impression gained from the attitudes and values presented in the TAT stories. There are signs of what would be considered serious underlying emotional maladjustment in a clinical record (a preoccupation with oral-sadistic fantasies, and indications that authority figures are seen as very threatening). The achievement drive to this individual, however, is so pronounced and so invested with energy that these underlying conflicts do not greatly debilitate his functioning. On the contrary, ambition becomes an avenue through which some of these conflicts are discharged. As already indicated, the average Nisei record is characterized by a strong drive toward organizing the Rorschach cards into integrated responses. This individual exemplifies this trend by producing 13 over-all responses, many of them of a rather complex nature (a W% of 76 compared with the mean of 35 for Nisei generally and 20 for the Normal sample). He pushes himself very hard.

This individual does not use ego constrictive defenses. While sensitive to social norms, he is not stereotyped. His is an open, rich record with both inner and outer controls of a complex nature utilized in the integration of his personality. However, he does show egocentric tendencies which are only partially offset by a readiness to respond to others with anxiety and compliance.

The greatest difficulty appears in this individual's impulsive life. In spite of what appears to be a relaxed attitude toward people on the TAT, the Rorschach suggests that deeply felt relationships toward people are productive of considerable anxiety. He shows an underlying hostility to both male and female figures (in his perception of humans on the cards, they are distorted into witches or animals engaged in human activity). He is consciously aware of his inner tensions, as indicated by his response to color (the red symbolizing hell, blast furnaces, and sunsets hidden behind clouds). It is as if he were sitting on a volcano. His skill in organizing demonstrates the utility of an achievement drive as a safety valve enabling this individual to function adequately. The skill with which he handles the TAT cards with little indication of these underlying tensions demonstrates the value of combining projective evidence dealing with several levels of consciousness in gaining a total impression of an individual. This individual has been able to integrate himself quite well on a conscious level in terms of what are usually considered mature social attitudes. However, the Rorschach adds a note of caution about assuming that all is as well at deeper levels of his personality.

There is another and more frequent type of fairly successful Nisei adjustment which involves a much more rigid conformity to parental standards, and less conscious flexibility and ease in meeting problems. An example of this second kind of adjustment is that of a 23-year-old, single Nisei man who is completing his medical training in Chicago while his family are in California on a farm. In an interview this Nisei man frequently referred to the strictness of his parents when he was young, how his behavior was always compared unfavorably with that of an older brother, and how most of his social life centered around the Buddhist Church where his father was always on committees and hence able to observe his son's activities. When asked how he had decided to become a physician, he said, "My mother decided for me, she thought it would be a good idea."

In the projective material there is no warmth in this Nisei man's TAT stories about his parents. The adaptive mechanism is to comply completely with the parental demands, to internalize the parents' goals and to suppress all personal individuality. Only through such a stereotyped conforming adjustment does the subject feel secure.

With this sort of conforming adjustment this Nisei man is able to strive realistically for long-range goals, but the striving is unimaginative and over-conventional. His values are the same in many areas of life as the values of the well-adjusted Nisei discussed earlier, but in his life they appear as philosophical clichés. The subject, however, is not aware that his behavior appears over-conventional, as he sincerely believes in it and it is his main source of strength. In his story to picture 1 there is competition and then identification with the father; there is also the necessity of being of benefit to society; and there is realistic recognition of the work necessary to attain father's goal.

In this man, the Rorschach analysis is in almost direct agreement with that drawn from the TAT. Whereas the first case demonstrated the utilization of achievement as an outlet for energies of a pathological as well as a healthy nature, this individual presents a picture of persistence, tenacity, and conformity in the face of severe anxiety that tends to block and immobilize his actions. The severity of his emotional blocking is well brought out by examining his time of first response to the Rorschach cards. He averaged over 95 seconds before giving a response. On two cards (VIII and IX) he took over four minutes before he was able to give a response. During all the time he was trying, he gave no indication that he considered rejecting the card. He was able to maintain a fairly systematic approach to the cards in spite of these constrictive tendencies. He showed no originality or imaginativeness, but rather a plodding persistence.

The anxiety aroused in this man by affective stimuli is countered on the Rorschach by anatomical-vocational responses indicating how his concentration on work and achievement is used to avoid difficulties with the spontaneous expression of emotions. There are indications on the Rorschach also that in spite of his rigid conscientiousness he has managed to preserve a retreat within himself so that, although he is not a particularly insightful individual, he is on fairly good terms with his impulse life. He is therefore capable of a certain level of understanding in his relationship with others, although he may be awkward in establishing contact.

In general, this is an individual who has to overcome considerable blocking and constriction in working out his drive toward achievement.

It is more difficult for Nisei women who aspire to a professional career to be successfully adjusted than it is for those Nisei women who are housewives or office workers. This can be illustrated by the case of one of the psychoanalytic patients—a 25-year-old, single Nisei woman who is a university-trained professional worker. The TAT material reveals the lack of real satisfaction afforded this subject in her striving for education and a career. The conflict with her parents is shown in her story to picture 1.

> 1. NF25. This boy doesn't seem to want to play on the violin, way he's looking at the violin. And the expression on his face seems to be that of, what is it? Not rebellion but, uh, well, the feeling that he doesn't want to do it. Doesn't want to play the violin but someone like his mother has made him take lessons and is trying to make him practice. He probably feels quite (long pause) resentful of his mother's forcing him to do it against his

will. He'll probably (long pause) refuse to do it at all, or else he'll play it so badly he won't have to take lessons any more.

In this story, the demands made by the mother touch off an emotional conflict for the subject, and at first the defense of being outwardly aggressive is considered—"refuse to do it at all." This defense is abandoned, probably in part because the subject's internalization of Japanese values makes her say "not rebellion but . . . ." The defense finally utilized is one of negativistic compliance, suppression of hostility, and a turning inward of aggression.

The subject's story to picture 3BM shows that her parental conflicts are carried over into her relations with other people, including her employers, so that in her own words she "no longer is able to distinguish between people." The Japanese value that rebellion against one's parents is also a rebellion against the whole structure of society is shown here, along with values of correct speech, close attention to personal appearance, and careful observation of the proprieties.

> 3BM. NF25. Well, a young fellow who wanted very much to do something and then was told that he couldn't by his parents and he was very broken hearted about it and he is crying. I don't think he'll say or do anything externally to show how he feels toward his parents but he will carry a deep resentment towards them inside himself and probably show his hostility through devious means such as refusing to carry out an order or refusing to obey his parents when a request has been made. [What happens to him?] He becomes a delinquent and he's referred to juvenile court. He carries resentment and so becomes bad for mother and child and society. He becomes careless in his speech, his attire, his contacts with other people, and transfers this resentment towards his parents to society and no longer is able to distinguish between people.

The lack of adequate satisfaction of this woman's basic dependency needs causes her to have poor and nonrealistic interpersonal relations. She has developed an unconscious defense of using practical and intellectual interests as an approach to people (her employers, friends, etc.) from whom she actually wants nurturant affection. The people respond practically and intellectually to her, she resists and resents this, and the relationship bogs down. Another major defense for this Nisei woman lies in withdrawal from problems and situations that precipitate emotional conflict. Early in the course of therapy (the fourth hour) she said, "I keep rejecting people . . . I feel rejected and I reject them. It has something to do with my always having to fight with my mother and my family. I can't fight any more. I just withdraw instead of expressing things—withdraw completely from the situation."

The Rorschach analysis of this case brings out the interference of neurotic inhibition with need for achievement. This subject was in therapy, and was not a case in our representative sample. In comparison with the total sample of Nisei, her Rorschach record shows some interesting similarities and differences. Her most notable difference from the representative sample is her difficulty in producing a whole response. She manages to produce only one W out of 34 responses. This result suggests a neurotic difficulty in externalizing her desire for achievement. A second discrepancy, from both clinical norms and those of the Nisei group, that reinforces the impression of neurosis is the imbalance in the ratio between human and animal movement responses. Contrary to the usual picture, she has a predominance of animal movement which, along with certain features of the content, suggests definite immaturity. She also shows the tendency toward a high number of space responses that is characteristic of many Nisei. Analysis suggests that this indication of rebelliousness is on a rather immature level and may be related to the neurotic maintenance of certain impulsive and childish ways of meeting problems in daily life. There are indications in the record, however, that this rebelliousness may remain covert, as her Rorschach manifests considerable underlying passivity and dependence on others. She is more apt to modify her ideas than to assert herself openly, in spite of a critical undercurrent in her personality.

As positive characteristics, she has a strong sense of the popular and the expected, and has an ego with a great deal of strength and resiliency. Also, the over-all affective tone of her responses is more positive and optimistic than one would usually expect in an individual seeking therapeutic help. Although there is a certain tendency to force or formalize her emotions, she probably can, with help, respond positively to friendliness in others. An attempt to push herself intellectually beyond her capacity in order to meet internalized social demands may develop into a serious source of conflict.

In general, the picture presented in this Rorschach record is one of neurotic incapacitation, without the personality constriction of the second record, or the more severe underlying disturbance of the first record. Of the three, this record shows the most direct interference with achievement itself. In this it is different from the usual Nisei record with regard to the variables considered in relation to achievement.

As a summary of this case, and an indication of how the analyses of the projective data (done before therapy had commenced) fit with the clinical material, it is useful to quote part of a tentative formulation written by Dr. Babcock after 85 hours of therapy:

> "The patient's problems center around her extreme dependency and helplessness which result from her early emotional deprivations, and her defenses against her hostility which are totally un-

acceptable to her family. Much of her hostility arises because of the failure of her emotional environment to provide for her any support adequate to meet her infantile impulses and needs of which she was ashamed and frightened. Intelligent and capable of considerable independent thinking, she has been in great conflict because of the discrepancy between her ideals for herself (one should be independent, achieve high status, be successful in the eyes of the public, and never show any negative attitudes) and her abilities to obtain in a concrete form any of her ideals. . . .

"She talked a great deal of her job in which she was very interested, but whenever something was hard for her at work, she would deny the reality setting of the situation. If a certain service seemed needed, and she thought her employer would not permit it, she would rebel in her feeling, but fail to take up the problem with her employer. Instead she would physically avoid the employer, and in many other withdrawing and stubbornly denying ways circumvent the problem. . . ."

These three records demonstrate the complexity on a psychological level of the structuring of certain similar culturally induced attitudes toward achievement. Although the overt attitudes and aims of these three individuals were quite similar, they were embedded in differing over-all personality structures. Such differences in total personality have a great deal to do with how an individual attempts to actualize his desires for achievement and the degree to which he meets with success in achieving his goals.[1]

9. Tradition and Change in Italo-American Family Structure

HERBERT GANS

Differences among ethnic subcultures in American society tend to become less prominent as higher proportions of group members rise from working-class to middle-class status. Nevertheless, traditional ways of life and patterns of social organization often persist in the predominantly working-

SOURCE: Reprinted with permission of The Free Press from Herbert Gans, *The Urban Villagers*, pp. 209–17. Copyright © 1962 by The Free Press of Glencoe, a Division of The Macmillan Company.

Herbert Gans is Associate Professor of Sociology, Teachers' College, Columbia University. He has published widely in the fields of urban sociology and urban planning.

[1] Details of this project and a fuller exposition of the data may be found in William Caudill's discussion, "Japanese-American Personality and Acculturation," *Genetic Psychology Monograph* 45: 3–102.

class ethnic enclaves of major cities. On the one hand, these traditions tend to reenforce ethnic identity, leading the minority group member to define his standards and seek his rewards in his "own" community. On the other, in conjunction with whatever antipathies prevail toward his group outside of his community, they limit his opportunities for occupational advancement and channels for self-expression.

People who wish to participate more fully in the dominant sectors of American life, but who simultaneously feel bound to honor ethnic obligations, often find their situation stressful. An important reason for this is that ties of ethnic loyalty are formed in families and expressed in norms that emphasize kinship solidarity. It is therefore often guilt-provoking to consider leaving the group behind and striking out for oneself.

Gans' study of a large Italian community in Boston's West End, since displaced by an urban renewal project, shows how older and more traditional Italian family patterns continue to influence other areas of Italo-American culture, even as family structure itself changes as the result of American experience.

A comparison of the lives of the West Enders with those of the immigrants suggests a number of other changes. For the West Enders, life is much less of a struggle than it was for their parents. There are more jobs, more secure ones, and better paid as well. As economic conditions improve, the ethos which Banfield calls amoral familism has begun to recede in importance. Most West Enders, for example, no longer need to fear their neighbors and unrelated people as a threat to their own existence. These "others" are no longer competitors for a small number of scarce jobs, but people with whom one can associate. Consequently, social life and mutual aid are not entirely restricted to the family circle; West Enders can and do make friends more easily than their ancestors.[1]

Nor is the outside world as threatening as it was to immigrants. The second generation is not barred from it by language, and it can maneuver in the outside world if absolutely necessary. As a result, the attitude toward caretakers, the law, city government, and other phases of the outside world is no longer based on total incomprehension and fear.

The processes by which these generational changes came to be were of course not always painless. In too many cases, the family circle and other immigrant institutions could not cope with acculturation, poverty, and the

[1] A number of other changes between Italians and Italian-Americans are described as part of a larger study of drinking patterns in G. Lolli, E. Serianni, G. Golder, and P. Luzzatto-Fegiz, *Alcohol in Italian Culture,* New York: The Free Press of Glencoe and Yale Center of Alcohol Studies, 1958. This study notes, for example, that Italian-Americans go to church more than Italians (p. 22); that they report drinking for social reasons, rather than for their health (pp. 68–69); that they get drunk more often (p. 85); and that unlike Italians they get drunk in the presence of the opposite sex (p. 88).

other degradations forced on the newcomers and their children by the outside world. Some turned to delinquency, crime, and violence to resolve their difficulties; others were beset by individual and family breakdowns. Although these problems affected only a minority of the population, they too are a part of the transition from immigrant to second-generation status.

The Slowness of Change: The Basis of the Peer Group Society

Some aspects of a group's way of life change more rapidly than others. Moreover, the observer's perception of change is affected by his own perspective, by the indices he uses, and by his own value judgments about the desirability of change per se.

These considerations affect any attempt to summarize the comparison of the West Enders to the generations that preceded them. Clearly, there has been considerable change in the standard of living, and in certain patterns of culture. At the same time, however, the many parallels between Southern Italian society and the West Enders suggest that many basic features of the way of life have not changed. The old social structure has remained intact.

What accounts for the stability of the social structure in the face of what would seem to be a rather drastic change in environment? The static, poverty-stricken, and highly stratified rural society of Southern Italy bears little resemblance to the frequently changing, more prosperous, and comparatively open society of urban-industrial Boston. *A brief review of the three generations may suggest the answer: the environment has not really changed as drastically as it appears.* This review will also make it possible to outline more clearly the basis of the peer group society as a response to the opportunities and deprivations in the environment.

The Italians who came to America were not farmers or peasants, but town-dwelling farm laborers who worked for absentee owners and managers. Although there was some evidence of the existence of a clanlike extended family, the occupational role of the farm laborer made it impossible for the extended family to function as a unit. The farm laborer, who was paid in wages that barely supported even his wife and children, could exist only in a nuclear family household.

Since people lived under conditions of extreme poverty, and in a static social system from which escape—other than by emigration—was impossible, the overriding goal was the survival of the nuclear family. Moreover, as marriages were contracted to advance—or at least not to retrogress— the economic and social position of the families involved, they had to be arranged. Consequently, husband and wife were usually not as close as in partnerships based on love. Since children had to go to work at the earliest opportunity, they were raised to adult status as quickly as possible, which was accomplished by treating them as small adults from an early age.

The nuclear family is neither entirely self-sufficient nor independent; nor can it satisfy all the needs of daily life. It is particularly handicapped in dealing with emergencies. Consequently, other institutions must be available. But when every family was involved in a struggle to survive— as was the case with the Southern Italian farm laborer—few people could be called on for aid, or trusted to give it when their own families were equally in need. Nor could they be treated as friends and companions, for they might take advantage of this relationship to help themselves in the fight for survival. Moreover, in order to attract friends, one had to be able to make a good impression. This required a dwelling unit to which people could be invited without shame, money to pay the costs of entertaining, and a considerable amount of trust over a long period of time. As one of Covello's respondents put it: "Friends are a luxury we cannot afford." Community agencies, were they churches, schools, or welfare agencies, could not be trusted because they were controlled by the employer. It made no difference when they had been founded for beneficial purposes; they were rejected by their intended clients as a matter of pride.

Under such conditions, relatives were the only source of group life and mutual aid. Being tied to each other by what were felt to be irrevocable ties of blood, they could face each other without putting on appearances, without feelings of shame, and without suspicion that the relationship would be exploited. In a society where no one could afford to trust anyone else, relatives had to trust each other. Moreover, when survival depended on the ability to work strenuously for long hours, older people were at a disadvantage. Possessing no special skills or traditional knowledge not also available to younger people, they had little influence in the group once they had become too old to support themselves. In addition, since relatives had to double as friends, people naturally gravitated to family members with whom they had the most in common. Consequently, they were drawn to peers.

The Southern Italian farm laborers lived not simply in poverty, but in poverty in the midst of a visibly higher standard of living enjoyed by the artisans, the middle class, and the gentry. In some areas they resorted to strikes and to class conflict; in others, to emigration.[2] But until these solutions were possible, most farm laborers lived in a state of extreme relative deprivation, a state made even more painful because of the close proximity of more fortunate people. In such circumstances, the restriction of aspirations was emotionally a most functional solution—at least in the short

[2] John S. MacDonald and Lea D. MacDonald, "Migration Versus Non-Migration: A Typology of Responses to Poverty," paper read at the 1961 meetings of the American Sociological Society.

range—since it prevented the development of frustrations, which were frequently harder to endure than physical deprivation. Parental lack of interest in education, detachment from the larger community, and unwillingness to fight the exploiting powers—all were practical solutions in a society in which mobility was so restricted that there was no reason to expect benefits from schooling, and where the oversupply of labor made it possible to starve out rebellious individuals. While these solutions were harsh and denying, they also reduced stress, and made life as bearable as possible. Since the achievement of object-goals was certain to be frustrated, children were reared to reject them. The development of empathy was also discouraged; too great a sensitivity to the problems of other people would have been hard to endure.

Many of the conditions that gave rise to this way of life accompanied the Southern Italians in their move to America. In Italy, they had labored from sunrise to sunset on the farms of landowners; in America, they worked long hours as laborers for factory owners or contractors. Moreover, since they did not gravitate to the highly mechanized and rationalized assembly line jobs, the nature of their work did not change radically either. Many worked with the earth—pick and shovel in hand—in both countries, although in America, they brought forth construction projects rather than farm products. In Italy, they had lived in densely built-up and overcrowded small towns, barren of vegetation; in America, they moved into equally overcrowded and barren tenement neighborhoods. Indeed, their trip across the ocean took them only from rural towns to urban villages.

Most of these parallels continued into the adulthood of the second generation. Not until World War II, in fact, and the subsequent prosperity of the postwar era, did their economic position differ radically from that of their forebears. Even then, many West Enders have been dogged by unemployment, layoffs, and other forms of economic insecurity. Since they —as well as their parents—have often been employed in marginal industries, they also have felt themselves to be exploited occupationally. Moreover, like their ancestors, they have been beset by serious illness, premature death, infant mortality, and by other of the sudden and unpredictable tragedies that so frequently hit low-income people.

Many other parallels exist between Southern Italy and Boston. The immigrants who settled in Boston found a society stratified not only by class but also by ethnic background and religion. In fact, in Boston—more so perhaps than in other cities—they encountered a hereditary aristocracy that at the time of the Italian influx still held considerable social, economic, and political power. Since then, its place has been taken by the Irish and by other groups, all of them culturally different from the Southern Italians. In short, the world outside the home was and still is dominated by people different in class and culture, by outsiders to be suspected and rejected.

Thus, the environment that the immigrants and the West Enders have encountered in America has differed in degree rather than in kind; it is less hostile and depriving, of course, but it is otherwise still the same. There have been no radical changes in the position of the working class vis-à-vis other classes, or in the position of minority ethnic groups vis-à-vis the majority. As a result, there have been as yet no strong pressures or incentives among the West Enders for any radical change in the basic social structure with which they respond to the environment.

FROM SECOND TO THIRD GENERATION: SIGNS OF CHANGE[3]

In addition to the changes that have already taken place between the past and present generations, other changes are only now developing. Noticeable among a few West Enders today, they are likely to become more prevalent in the next generation. These changes are the result of processes in the larger society that are creating new opportunities for West Enders. They also will make it more difficult to maintain some of the traditional ways of life.

The major source of opportunities is occupational. A few West Enders are now beginning to move into white-collar technical jobs, actually the modern equivalents of skilled factory work. They are also beginning to enter service occupations, notably in sales, in which their ability for self-display and for competitive group activity is helpful.[4]

The third generation will be able to respond to the new occupational opportunities partly because their parents believe in the need for education as a means of obtaining job security. Parents also can now afford to keep children in school at least until high school graduation. Whether or not the third generation actually will take up these opportunities will depend, of course, on their willingness to stay in school, and to learn what is necessary to compete for stable and secure jobs. I assume that an increasing number of third-generation adolescents will remain in school.

New occupational and educational attainments are likely to have repercussions on the structure of the family, and on the peer group society generally. For one thing, they will create more social and cultural differences between people. This, in turn, will affect the family circle, for rela-

---

[3] This section is speculative, since it deals with a generation only now reaching adulthood. It is based on observations of West Enders, a few ex-West Enders who had left before redevelopment, and on additional observations made among a handful of Italian families in a suburban community near Philadelphia which I studied after I concluded my field work in the West End.

[4] Whether these opportunities will be available to the third generation in as plentiful amounts as I am suggesting depends on the consequences of automation on the labor market in the coming decades.

tives who have responded to the widening opportunities may begin to find that they have less in common, and are no longer compatible in their interests. At the same time, since people have fewer children than in previous generations, the number of potential family circle members will be reduced. Consequently, the family circle may be somewhat harder to maintain than in the second generation.

Although someday these trends may even decimate the circle, other changes are likely to attract new recruits. I have already noted that as unrelated people cease to be competitors in the struggle for survival, they can become allies in the search for companionship. Indeed, the desire for companionship combined with the decreasing number of compatible kin can mean that friends and neighbors will begin to play a more important role in the social life of the peer group society.

Meanwhile, other changes are taking place in the nuclear family unit. The decimation of the family circle by differential mobility is one step in a larger social process that brings nuclear family members into a more intimate dependence on each other. For while friends can replace relatives in a number of functions, rarely do they help each other as fully or are they as close as people bound by blood ties. Other changes are reinforcing the cohesion of the nuclear family. With the disappearance of arranged marriages, husband and wife are emotionally closer to each other than were their parents and grandparents. Moreover, the nature of the educational process—both in and out of the classroom—is such that husbands and wives now grow up with a more similar background than was true in previous generations. By and large, both sexes are exposed to the same subjects in school. In addition, they are taught by the school, and by American culture generally, that the man may participate in child-rearing and household duties and in sparetime activities with his wife with no reflection on his masculinity. Given the increasing influence of the wife, and the larger number of common bonds between the marriage partners, the segregation of roles now existing in the family is likely to decrease.

Moreover, as the economic functions of the child have disappeared completely, the child's need to become an adult as rapidly as possible has disappeared also. Indeed, as relatives become less close, parents are likely to discover that the child can help to draw husband and wife together. Thus will begin the shift from the adult-centered family to the child-centered one, and the eventual development of the kind of nuclear family structure now prevalent in America.

Also, relations between parents and children are likely to become closer. With fewer ethnic differences between the second and third generation than existed between the first and second, parents will feel more capable of advising their children. This could result in increased family conflict, if only because questions which were never raised before between parents and children will now be thought of as proper subjects of discussion.

Family conflict also may be engendered by the fact that children will make greater demands on their parents, not only for goods but also for freedom to participate in children's and teenagers' activities.

Such a family is also likely to increase its participation in the outside world. Reduced suspicion and a decrease in cultural differences will make it less necessary for the next generation to reject the outside world as strongly as did the second. With more economic security, installment buying will seem less risky, and changing tastes will attract people to the consumer products and services that are now rejected. Already, the desire for modernity has made itself felt among some pioneering West Enders. And while the postwar suburbs have attracted only a few, they are likely to seem less frightening to the next generation. Indeed, it is probable that young mothers who look askance on the life of the street and wish closer supervision over their children's activities will find the attractions of suburban life most advantageous, even should their husbands not share this enthusiasm or their urgency about the children. Even now, the bright and sometimes garish pleasures of California and Florida are luring some West End vacationers, and will do so increasingly in the next generation. I remember how intensely a West End mother in her early twenties spoke of her plan to move to California, if only she could persuade her husband to give up his ties in Boston.

By virtue of the women's greater receptivity to education, and their premarital employment in the white-collar world, they are likely to take the lead in the process of change. The husbands may resist their pressure, and will probably be more reluctant to give up the old ways, especially since these were designed—intentionally or not—to maximize their freedoms and privileges. But because the wife remains subordinate to the husband in most families, because she is thoroughly indoctrinated in her homemaker role, and because she is hesitant about leaving the house to go to work, she may be unable to implement many of the changes of which she dreams. Her traditional role could act as a brake on her aspirations and perhaps as an accelerator on her frustrations.

Moreover, the social forms of the outside world will continue to be less attractive than its products, for the unwillingness and inability to concern oneself with object-oriented ways of behaving is likely to remain, among women as well as men. Churches and formal organizations, civic associations, government agencies, and politicians—all will probably be suspect even in the next generation, and participation in such activities is likely to be notably less among people of Italian background than among others.

Most of the people who will be making these changes are routine-seekers. As life becomes more secure, they no longer need—or want—to live for the gratifications of the moment. Not only is the search for adventurous episodes losing its urgency, but the drawbacks of action-seeking now loom larger than they did before. The lulls between episodes, the depression that sometimes accompanies the waiting, and the negative consequences of action-seeking now make it seem much less desirable. The availability of more predictable forms of gratification within the family and the peer group also takes something away from the pleasures of successful action-seeking. Its attractiveness as a way of life is thus being reduced, especially after adolescence. The parental desire to have children grow up respectably encourages this development, as does the increasing influence of women, who are the more earnest advocates of routine-seeking.

Yet parental desires are not always achieved, and, indeed, parental behavior may contradict them. Thus, some third-generation people will pursue action as fervently as did their ancestors. But increasingly, they will be those people who have grown up in idiosyncratic or pathological surroundings. Therefore the search for action will be a consequence of distinctive—and increasingly deviant—childhood experiences, rather than a prevalent way of life that stems from the economic and social insecurity of an entire group.

10. The Formation of Social Attitudes

DANIEL THOMPSON

The following selection shows how individual case analysis can illuminate interconnections between personality and social structure. It also shows how close study can reveal new ways of organizing data in order to reveal how the subjects of an investigation view their own world. Finally, it provides a colorful and searching introduction to the study of key patterns of social organization in an urban Negro community in the Deep South. (Selection 26 is set in the same city.)

The article briefly surveys the middle class and its interest in respectability and achievement; the matriarchy, with its antipathy toward men and its strong cross-generational ties between mothers and daughters; the gang, with its emphasis on physical demonstrations of masculinity; and the nuclear family, with its extremely high valuation of ties of loyalty to the home and its members. A discussion of marginality among those unable to establish satisfying ties with any of these groups concludes the paper.

SOURCE: *American Journal of Orthopsychiatry*, 31, 1962, pp. 74–85. Copyright by the American Orthopsychiatric Association, Inc. Reprinted by permission of the Association and of the author.

Daniel C. Thompson is Professor of Sociology and Dean of the Social Division at Dillard University. He is the author of *The Negro Leadership Class*.

During the middle 1930's American sociologists began to develop a serious interest in social stratification. Since then they have made extensive use of two interpretive variables, "social class" and "color caste." These two variables have been used in attempts to account scientifically for differences in the manners, morals, opinions, beliefs and attitudes which are characteristic of various communities, ethnic groups, races, and other social segments in American society.†

One of the most definitive studies of social stratification is *Children of Bondage* by Allison Davis and John Dollard. That study was designed to explain the "personality development of Negro youth in the urban South." Not only do Davis and Dollard assume that "social class" and "color caste" impose certain conditions under which the socialization of Negro children takes place, but they further assume that all Negroes are more or less positively identified with members of their social class within the "color caste" system.

The research for the "Children of Bondage" study was done in 1937–38. The conclusions are based upon extensive information gathered about 197 Negro children representing all social classes in the urban South. At that time these children were between the ages of 12 and 16.

On the basis of their findings the authors made intensive interpretations of the various social attitudes manifested by the youngsters they studied and came to the conclusion that they are usually "class types," and predicted that these attitudes would persist into adulthood.

In 1953 an interdisciplinary team at the Urban Life Research Institute of Tulane University began a systematic follow-up study of the "Children of Bondage" subjects. We were particularly interested to find out the extent to which Davis and Dollard's predictions regarding the basic attitudes of their subjects were valid.

From the beginning of our study we were impressed with the rigid scientific method Davis and Dollard applied at every stage of their research. At the end of our follow-up study we were particularly impressed with the large number of valid predictions they made concerning the attitudes of the now adult subjects. There were significant points, however, where their predictions missed the mark. Since we could find no significant flaws in their application of the scientific method, we reasoned that basic errors in their predictions likely stemmed from certain basic assumptions underlying their research.

Since their major hypotheses and predictions stem from the assumptions inherent in "social class" and "color caste" theories, we were led almost immediately to an examination of these concepts as they were used in the

† Data used in this paper are taken from two main sources: Allison Davis and John Dollard, *Children of Bondage* (Washington, D.C.: America Council on Education, 1940); and John Rohrer et al., *The Eighth Generation* (New York: Harper, 1960).

"Children of Bondage" study. Both of these concepts divided society into such large segments that they forced the researcher to generalize regarding the several very different social worlds constituting a given social class. Thus, for instance, we found that all Negroes are generally intellectually aware of "class" differences and "caste" restrictions, yet these are most often remote psychological realities, except for those who have been socialized in a middle-class environment. For most others it is necessary to discover much more precisely the outlines of their social environments than is usually done by social scientists who use "class" and "caste" as interpretive variables.

Underlying our interpretation is the assumption that all individuals are primarily identified with some limited distinct social segment. We labeled that segment the individual's "social world." As a rule, an individual's "social world" is a much smaller psychological reality than "social class" or "color caste." The fact is, our analysis of social classes in the Negro urban community revealed that they include several distinct "social worlds" where the way of life is significantly diverse. Thus, each of the subjects studied was positively identified with some "social world" and tended to reject other persons or groups which they classify psychologically as "outsiders." Consequently, we became convinced that attitudes developed during childhood are much more characteristic of these more limited "social worlds" than they are of "class" or "caste." As a result, some of our subjects reserved their bitterest denunciation for individuals who might objectively be classified in their own social class, but who actually belonged to some different "social world" within their particular social class.

The significant "social worlds" we discovered in Negro society in New Orleans are the middle class, the matriarchy, the gang, the nuclear family and marginality. The basic attitudes characteristic of individuals in each of these "social worlds" can be accounted for in terms of the ethnocentrism manifested therein.

THE MIDDLE CLASS

When education, occupation, and style of life are used as criteria for differentiating one social class from another, 3 of our 20 representative subjects cleanly classify as middle-class. (This is likely to be about the same proportion as might be found in Negro society generally.) For these subjects the middle class is a psychologically real social world in which the socialization process is designed to instill in them "proper" attitudes toward the self, others, race, sex, family and achievement.

Our middle-class subjects think of themselves as representatives of the American Creed. They regard themselves as definitely superior to the masses and resent being classified in any situation with lower-class people. They are also critical of the few upper-class Negroes in the community whom they delight in referring to as snobbish, selfish, and undemocratic.

All of the middle-class subjects are keenly aware of racial segregation and bitterly resent the "evils" inherent in it. They view segregation as "a threat to their ideology of achievement, equality, and progress, and their common reaction can only be a denial of the valuation placed upon race and color." Therefore, as we would expect, their denunciation of racial discrimination, though varying in intensity from one to the other, is always done in terms of a cardinal middle-class value, namely, that it tends to prevent able, ambitious Negroes from achieving the degree of individual success of which they are capable and deserving. One subject, for example, emphatically expressed an attitude toward racial segregation which seems to be shared by middle-class Negroes generally. She described several incidents involving segregation in order to make the central point that "segregation is stupid," and reasoned that "white people who indulge in it are ignorant and undemocratic"—therefore, by implication, inferior themselves.

There is ample evidence that this primary attitude toward segregation is a result of their socialization which articulated the ideology that success comes to those who are intelligent, ambitious, industrious, virtuous and patient. And anyone, white or Negro, who tries to prevent the orderly functioning of this formula is "stupid," "undemocratic," and hence, to be despised. It is not surprising, then, that our middle-class subjects express about as much hostility toward lower-class "immoral Negroes who hinder the progress of the race" as they do toward "ignorant white people who believe that all Negroes are alike, and who don't want to see a Negro get ahead of them."

Respectability is most highly valued by middle-class Negroes. Consequently, the socialization of our middle-class subjects included strict training in regard to "proper" sex behavior. The major image of sexual respectability for these subjects during their adolescent years was at least one parent. Among the supporting symbols were teachers, classmates, and relatives, as well as other respected "leaders" in community affairs with whom they came in contact.

As a result of their moral training, each of our middle-class subjects expressed strong resentment of people who do not adhere to strict moral standards. One subject repeatedly denounced his brother and his sister who violated middle-class sex codes. Another had a complete break with her close relatives, even denying the existence of a criminal brother, because they did not adhere to her conception of respectability. And the third divorced two lower-class husbands because of infidelity.

During adolescence all of the middle-class subjects resented authority, yet all were fortunate in having some significant adult available whom they respected during this period of struggle to establish an ego identity.

Their need for success was manifested early in life as they achieved prestige and distinction in their peer groups. They continued to strive for success both in school and in the community. Thus, despite handicaps and disappointments, all managed to finish college and are now apparently on the way to success in their business or professional life.

All of our middle-class subjects had some ambivalence toward skin color. On the one hand, having internalized the basic values in American culture, they tend to associate light skin with achievement. On the other hand, since skin color is not in itself an "achievement" to value, it is a contradiction to their "success" ideology.

The ambivalence they have toward skin color is brought out by statements made to interviewers at various times. All expressed negative attitudes toward Negroes at one time or another. But they were careful to use class, not racial symbols, in doing so. One subject accused Negroes of not being able to acquire and hold property. Another felt that Negroes would enjoy greater civil rights and privileges if they were not so "undependable and immoral." The third middle-class subject went into a long discussion to prove that "Negroes are their own worst enemy."

They also indicated identification with Negroes. Sometimes it was in a denunciation of some aspect of the doctrine of white supremacy. One of the darker subjects spoke about the beauty of one of her close relatives who was quite dark. At another time she, like the others, expressed a positive attitude toward some distinctly Negro person. They made complimentary statements about physical appearance, professional competence, and intelligence of dark-skinned Negroes. At times such statements were so deliberate that interviewers got the impression that they were spontaneously denying the value they placed upon light skin.

Despite the ambivalence our middle-class subjects manifested in regard to skin color, there is no definitive evidence that they have deep feelings of "self-hate" as Abram Kardiner reported in *The Mark of Oppression*.

THE MATRIARCHY

The matriarchy is the oldest and most persistent family structure in the Negro community. It had its origin during the slave period, when Negroes were not legally regarded as persons and therefore could not enter into any legal contract such as marriage. It is true that certain white slave masters, motivated by religious principles, insisted that their slaves should be "married" before living together as "man" and "wife." Nevertheless, such an arrangement, despite some ceremony which might be performed by the slave master or his minister, was not legally binding on the parties concerned. Slave traders or planters who were in the market for slaves did not allow this pseudolegal arrangement to prevent them from trafficking in slaves if it promised to be profitable. Even the most religious slave masters have been known to separate "husband" and "wife" when they deemed it economically wise.

Since the mother is considered more necessary to the physical well-being of the child than the father, slave masters traditionally allowed young children to remain with the mother, who might have a series of "husbands" sold from her during the course of a lifetime. Consequently, insofar as the slave family was concerned, it was the mother, not the father, who represented love, stability and authority.

Three of our subjects may be classified as primarily identified with the matriarchy. Perhaps the most significant thing about the "social world" of the matriarchy is its inner solidarity. This solidarity is manifested in at least two ways: 1) a high degree of cooperation among females, and 2) the way in which males are regarded as "enemies."

There is some indication that the matriarchy can be found in one form or another on all social class levels. As we will see in our discussion of "social marginality," some middle-class families are so dominated by the mothers that there is little real function or authority left for the father. However, our subjects whose primary identification is with the matriarchy are all lower-class.

Those whose primary identification is with the matriarchal family still regard femaleness as a symbol of love, stability and authority, such as it symbolized during the slave period. There is then, between mother and daughter, a deep sense of mutual dependency. Since the lower-class matriarchal family must always strive for economic security, much of this interdependency between mother and daughter is economically based. There is ample evidence, however, that this dependency goes much deeper than mutual economic security. Socially, daughters depend upon their mother's advice and counsel, and on a psychological level, the relation between mother and daughter is invested with strong emotional feelings. One subject expressed her primary identity in this way: "I am my mother's daughter."

Girls reared in a "social world" dominated by the mother regard themselves primarily as *women*, and all other roles are secondary. Their identification with the mother is so strong that their husbands, children, friends and careers may be sacrificed for what is alleged to be her welfare. This overwhelming identification with the mother colors all their social attitudes.

Men are held in very low esteem by the matriarchs. They habitually refer to men as irresponsible, sexually aggressive and brutal. One matriarch said, "All men are dogs." In our interview materials we found ample evidence that hers was not a unique attitude.

Since matriarchs regard all men as irresponsible and immoral, it is hardly possible for them to internalize middle-class sex attitudes such as loyalty and faithfulness. To them a "boy friend" or husband should be exploited since he is not expected to be faithful, and may desert at any time. Therefore, it is logical to get everything possible out of him while he is still available. Sex, then, is an important means for getting something out of men. The woman who doesn't is being "made a fool of." One dominant grandmother expressed this attitude when she retorted, "What is love? I tell my girls: 'Don't hear what no man say, but see how much he got.'"

To those socialized in the matriarchy the outside world is of little concern unless it threatens the inner solidarity of the female world that gives security. Thus, they have almost no affiliations except those in which a sisterly relationship is characteristic, and even these are temporary and superficial.

None are particularly devout though all attend church occasionally. To some, church affiliation is important because elaborate funerals are highly valued. One matriarch expressed this attitude. She said, "I will always be grateful to my pastor and support the church because he made my mother's funeral the talk of the town." And she added, "You never know when you might need the church."

None belonged to, or supported, organizations whose main purpose is racial uplift, such as the National Association for the Advancement of Colored People. Yet all expressed some degree of dissatisfaction with racial segregation. Unlike the middle-class subjects who oppose segregation because it tends to frustrate their success ideology, the matriarchs oppose segregation primarily because it makes them liable to be exploited economically and sexually. Basically, segregation tends to undermine the authority they are accustomed to exerting over the masculine aspect of their environment. In this connection one subject was expressly bitter because "white men like to take advantage of Negro women."

There was little evidence of "self-hate" among the matriarchs. One was jealous of a light-skinned half sister, but simply because this sister seemed to be preferred by the mother. Another wished that she were able to "pass" for white, not because she particularly admired white skin, but because it would then be possible for her to get jobs which are not now available to Negro women. (Actually, all of our subjects who had attempted to pass for white or even daydreamed about being white gave this as their only reason.)

There is no evidence of the ambition to succeed among the matriarchs as is true of the middle class. They may sacrifice to get an education, or prepare for a vocation, but there is no concept of "calling" involved. Instead, they are motivated by mundane, practical considerations. A typical expression of this was made by one of the subjects. "After I got through high school, I wanted to become a nurse because a nurse can make more money than most other Negro women."

Boys in the matriarchy must either conform to what might be called "female patterns" (become "sissies") or renounce the home and identify with the gang and become "men."

The Gang

The culture of the gang can only be understood in relation to the matriarchy. And just as the matriarchy is primarily organized around some dominant female, and all attitudes are colored by identity with what might be referred to as the "female principle" in society, the gang is centered around exclusive "masculine" interests and articulates the "male principle" in society. It is inevitable, then, that the matriarchy and the gang should regard each other as "natural enemies" because each is emphatic in its allegiance to mutually exclusive ideologies.

Unlike the matriarchy, where members are bound together by mutual affection, membership in the gang is highly individualistic and each boy must "prove" himself a "man" before he is accepted. The main theme in the ethos of the gang is "Prove yourself a man. Don't be a sissy. Don't be a woman." Thus, the generalized enemy of the gang is the "female principle" in society. This "principle" seems to be symbolized by women, refined men, laws, morals, religion, education and the striving for success and respectability.

Manhood is defined in terms of independence, secretiveness, aggressiveness, and sexual prowess. Thus to be a "man" means to renounce entirely the "female principle" in society. It involves fear of women, scorn for middle-class standards, and hatred of authority.

The social life of the gang revolves around strictly masculine activities. It includes such things as drinking, gambling, "playing the dozens" (a behavior pattern which best exemplifies the completeness with which the "female principle" in society is rejected), sports, and telling stories about the outwitting of authorities and the exploitation of women.

It is obvious that the "masculine principle" with which the gang member identifies provides no basis for the establishment of stable family life. All ties developed in this "social world" are necessarily temporary and loose. Rarely did we find a gang member who had substantial friendships, or heterosexual unions, for more than a few months in duration.

Like the matriarchs, gang members have almost no interest in community affairs unless they present some threat to their way of life. None belonged to, or supported, any community or "uplift" organization. They are aware of racial segregation and on occasions complain bitterly about discrimination. They are touchy around white people and deeply resent being "pushed around." All related incidents to illustrate how they defended themselves against white "aggressors." One young man offered to fight his employer for "hollering" at him. Another boasted of the time he "told off" a prison guard who "crossed" him, even though he knew he would be severely punished for doing so.

The touchiness which gang members manifest concerning race does not stem from the fact that discrimination violates some conception of justice in which they believe. Rather, their resentment of white people stems from a natural source—white authority is a challenge to their masculinity. Thus, in one way or another, the gang members find ways of expressing their hatred of white people who treat them like inferiors or "women."

There is no rigid determinancy attached to gang affiliation. Some do become successful in business and the professions. This is true of two of our gang subjects who were fortunate in having a strong ego ideal available during their early adolescent years, when they were struggling for a socially acceptable self-identity. There is evidence, however, that once the boy develops a self-identity based upon the "masculine principle" so fundamental in gang culture, his attitude toward "male" and "female" does not change.

The Nuclear Family

The nuclear family may be found on all social class levels in Negro society. It is most characteristic, however, among Negroes who may be classified as upper-lower or lower-middle-class.

Six of our representative subjects were primarily identified with their nuclear families. So strong is the ethnocentrism of this family-type that individual members regard their family roles such as father, mother, daughter, son, and so on, as central in their lives, and all other roles are secondary. It is from this primary self-conception that all attitudes expressed by the subjects are colored, or even determined.

The strong "we" feeling repeatedly expressed by members of the nuclear family tends to limit their concern for "outside" persons or issues unless they threaten to intrude upon their private domestic life, or may contribute something to the family welfare. Thus, a father and mother may be stable church members if they feel, for instance, that somehow this affiliation may contribute to the upbringing of their children. Also a father may attend labor union meetings regularly, and even concern himself with union politics, if such participation is deemed important in regard to his own economic security. A mother may become a responsible member of the PTA if she feels that such activities may result in the academic welfare of her children. In other words, there is no evidence that members of the nuclear family are ever motivated to give their time or money to support any cause that does not directly affect their inner circle. Thus, none of our subjects whose primary self-identity is that of family member belongs to any Negro "uplift" organization, or manifests any active interest in political affairs. The fact is that it is difficult for them to conceive of anyone's doing so unless some family end is to be achieved. When one subject was asked why he did not support the NAACP, he remarked matter-of-factly that "those who run the NAACP do so because it is their job. That's their job. My job is carrying mail." Another subject gave only one reason for voting for a controversial political candidate who ran for an important political office: "He promised to give old people more pension money. My mother is getting old."

Characteristically these subjects manifested strong family pride. Some kept written genealogies in family Bibles where important events in the lives of family members are recorded in detail. Others delighted in giving long detailed accounts of the adventures and achievements of relatives. In all of these homes there are albums of family pictures which the subjects voluntarily displayed with pride for the interviewers.

We did not find any significant evidence of "race hate" among our family subjects. One subject did show a keen admiration for light skin color. Of course, he is light-skinned himself, and thinks of himself as a "creole." However, he married a girl who is considerably darker than he.

During his adolescence, another young man daydreamed about having affairs with white girls. Now, as an adult, he never expresses any such wish, nor did he report having had any such affairs. He, too, married a dark brown-skinned girl.

These and other attitudes concerning skin color were analyzed, and we concluded that, on the whole, members of the nuclear family tended to prefer the skin color most characteristic of their own family. They tended to depreciate any skin color distinct from their own, whether it was some variation found among Negroes or that typical of Caucasians.

All of the subjects who identified with the nuclear family expressed some attitude toward racial segregation. Their opinions differed widely. One subject was reared among white children, and idealized a white baseball coach with whose children he played. He later named several of his sons after both white and Negro baseball players. He realizes that racial discrimination exists, and he considers it an evil, yet he expressed no bitterness about it. He was always careful to point out that "there are good and bad white people. There are also good and bad Negro people."

Some simply deny that a race problem exists. On one occasion when a subject was asked to express herself regarding racial discrimination, she almost got angry because she felt that the interviewer expected her to express dislike for white people. In effect she said very emphatically: "I don't dislike white people, I don't feel discriminated against."

Another subject, a former GI, likes to relate the negative experiences he has had with white persons, and expressed strong hostility toward them, and even fantasied about means Negroes might use to kill large numbers of white people at one time. He became frightened with his own ideas and hastened to add that Negroes would never do this because they realize that "all men are brothers," and wish that white people felt the same way.

All of the racial attitudes expressed by our subjects who were socialized in the nuclear family had one important element in common: They think of racial segregation and discrimination as a personal, individual phenomenon rather than the inevitable outcome of an impersonal social system. They interpreted all incidents involving discrimination as the doings of evil individuals. They defined race relations as relations between individuals in a face-to-face situation, such as is characteristic of family members. Discrimination was seldom or never discussed in terms of economics, political and social ideologies.

Fundamentally their conception of "good" race relations was expressed succinctly by one of the subjects who was the only Negro in a white outfit during World War II. When asked how he got along with his white buddies, he replied, "They treated me like a brother."

A definite double standard of sex morality prevails in the nuclear family. Normatively sex behavior is regarded as "proper" only between husband and wife. However, no great emphasis is placed upon morality as such. Yet when some member of the nuclear family deviates from sexual norms other members have no compunction about questioning such behavior. This aspect of family control may be the primary reason why there is no reported illegitimacy among our family-centered subjects. Young people marry early and are encouraged to have children. The men expect the women to maintain high moral standards, yet they may admit openly that they have extramarital relationships.

Insofar as social mobility is concerned, the nuclear family in the Negro community looms large in importance. Although we hardly expect children from such families to become revolutionists or reformers, a relatively large number of outstanding Negro leaders come from such a family background. Even our lower-class family-centered subjects manifested occupational ambitions and a determination to "get ahead in life." Regardless of social class position, those whose self-identity stems from family relationships manifested social values which we have defined as middle-class. One sociologist referred to Negroes socialized in such families as "Black Puritans."

MARGINALITY

Four of our representative subjects have failed to develop a satisfactory self-identity. This is evidently due to the fact that during the "identity-crisis" period of adolescence they were subject to strong conflicting psychological "pulls" from two diverse social worlds. Basic values in each of the different social worlds contradict or deny certain basic values in the other. An adolescent, then, socialized in a situation where two (or more) mutually exclusive sets of social values are forcefully presented, must necessarily develop an attitude of selection and rejection in order to develop any satisfactory ego identity.

The main problem the adolescent faces in the process of selecting and rejecting social values is the need to select, first of all, some norm or criterion according to which certain social values may be accepted or rejected with a minimum of frustration. Each distinct social world provides such a criterion.

The adolescent socialized in either of the ethnocentric social worlds discussed above is indoctrinated with the accepted criterion to be used in the process of selecting and rejecting social values. Furthermore, significant adults in his social world are always available to give social and psychic support when needed.

Our "marginal" subjects have had, and are still having, dramatic struggles in their attempts to create for themselves a consistent social world and self-identity. Presented, as they were during adolescence, with at least two contradictory sets of basic social values, they generally attempt to resolve this dilemma in one of two ways:

1. Some spend their lives in a vain effort to synthesize certain social values that are basically inconsistent. For example, one of our subjects who was socialized in the matriarchy has not been able to completely identify either as a "daughter," as the term implies in the matriarchy, or "wife," as the term implies in the middle class. She wanted very much to be a wife, but she was unable to give up being a daughter. And so she tried to force each of her two respective husbands to live with her in her mother's home, where she could be both daughter and wife at the same time. As is characteristic of the matriarchy, this attempt at synthesis failed.

The basic thing to remember about those who attempt to synthesize contradictory social values learned from different social worlds is the fact that they carry on this struggle because rejecting any basic value characteristic of a social world in which one is socialized is likely to be psychologically painful and result in feelings of guilt.

2. Some who have no socially approved criterion for choosing between conflicting sets of social values develop a highly organized Bohemian philosophy of life designed to legitimatize the gratification of their narcissistic needs. Consequently the criterion for selecting among social values is "It is pleasing to me." When intellectualized, this attitude toward social values, as expressed by some of our subjects, becomes a kind of "principle." One subject justified his aggressive, ganglike behavior in a middle-class situation by this excited defense: "What you are asking me to do is to give up my principles, and that is all that I live by. . . . You are asking me to sell out." Our subjects who have been unable to develop a satisfactory self-identity

differed widely in the attitudes they expressed concerning certain common social values. One subject who remains marginal between gang culture and middle-class culture finds any one conception of self painful and frustrating. Consequently, when participating in middle-class culture, and accepted as middle-class, he soon becomes uncomfortable and launches into a compulsive defense of his gang-oriented social values. Likewise, when he achieves recognition as a professional gambler "on the 'Ramp'" (a well-known center for gang activities) he will soon begin attempts to establish a middle-class identity by eloquently relating his noteworthy academic achievements (he holds a Master's degree in a highly respected field from one of America's top universities) and boasting about his upper-class "social contacts."

Another of these subjects frequently passed for white. Yet when she was accepted as white by those with whom she came in contact, she would deliberately and abruptly establish her Negro identity. Once she worked in a plant that employed only white girls on a certain job. For the first few days she was anxious about being detected. After a while she was satisfied that she had established a Caucasian identity. Soon she became uncomfortable in that role and set about the re-establishment of her Negro identity. She did this by having an obviously Negro male escort her from the plant each evening. She did this knowing full well that she would lose the job she enjoyed.

One of the marginal subjects is still struggling to synthesize diverse social values drawn from three of the social worlds in which she participated during her adolescence: the nuclear family, the middle class, and the matriarchy. It happened in this way. Her parents died during the early years of her adolescence. She went, eventually, to live with a matriarchal aunt, who sent her to a private graded school that was a symbol of middle-class values. Lacking the superior intelligence of some of our other marginal subjects, she has not spun for herself a neat narcissistic philosophic covering to veil her inconsistent social values. Therefore she was described by one of her interviewers as a "social chameleon" who tended to express attitudes that are basically inconsistent. Hence, she manifests the matriarchal fear and distrust of men, but rationalizes this attitude in terms of middle-class morality. She emphathizes with members of her family, but they are not a source of pride to her as is true of those socialized in the nuclear family. Instead she judges them meticulously according to rigid middle-class standards and hates them because they do not measure up.

Unlike those socialized in a given social world, and identified with a primary social role that colors all of their attitudes, the socially marginal personality has no clearly defined social roles. All roles are, in effect, secondary. Thus, as we observed, if someone structures the situation in terms of color they react to color; if in terms of class they reveal convenient class attitudes; and if it is morality they express themselves in terms of morality. The most important characteristic of the attitudes they express is the fact that they are not logically consistent and are expressed outside of any well-defined frame of reference.

Two of our subjects consistently manifested hate for accepted traditional rules and regulations. The young woman stated that "nothing makes me as unhappy as people who accept rules and regulations as though they came from God." The young man in this category is best described as an iconoclast. For example, he has a wide knowledge of classical literature and drama, but delights only in writing where nontraditional ideas are being presented. He automatically identifies with the "outsider," the martyr, the iconoclast and the rebel in history. He takes great delight, for instance, in pointing out the alleged immorality of Popes, the insincerity of white liberals, and the dishonesty of our most respected Negro leaders. Though he aspires to establish himself in a middle-class profession and enjoys the association of middle-class people, he joined a carnival club where the culture of African people is caricatured in a major parade. Over the years this parade has been repeatedly denounced by middle-class people. Not only did the subject join this club, but he wrote a history of the club in which he lauded the "contributions" it makes to the cultural life of the community.

Summary

The social attitudes held by the subjects included in *The Eighth Generation* are much more closely related to the self-identities they developed as active participants in a specific social world than they are to a generalized social class or "color caste." The ethos of each social world delineated in this paper articulates a cardinal social value that tends to color, even determine, the basic social attitudes of the individuals socialized in it. For the small, more or less well-organized middle class it is "respectability" (however defined). For the matriarchy it is security, as provided by a cohesive female society. For the gang it is the protection of "masculinity" that symbolizes escape from a "treacherous" female world. For the nuclear family it is family solidarity based upon mutual affection and loyalty. And for the "marginals," who have not achieved a satisfactory self-identity, it is independence that stems from a narcissistic interpretation of their role in society. Consequently, the attitude of a given subject held regarding the self, other, skin color, sex, religion, race, family and achievement is due largely to the degree that he has achieved identity with some distinct social world.

11. The Puerto Ricans in New York

NATHAN GLAZER AND
DANIEL PATRICK MOYNIHAN

The central theme of Glazer and Moynihan's Beyond the Melting Pot *is
that American ethnic groups, far from being assimilated into a dominant
common American culture, maintain significant aspects of their own cultural identity for generations—even after many group members have
attained middle-class status, thus creating the impression that assimilation
has occurred. In New York City, two groups stand out as being quite far
removed from the probability that the majority of their members will
soon move into the middle class. One, the Negroes, faces the obstacle of
racial discrimination, and must overcome the hurdle of lacking a long-
standing traditon emphasizing the paramount importance of acquiring
academic and vocational skills of a reasonably high order. The second,
the Puerto Ricans, suffers less from racial discrimination, but faces a
language barrier and a culture quite different from the one it knew in
Puerto Rico. This selection concentrates on some of the difficulties Puerto
Ricans encounter. As such, it is not representative either of Glazer and
Moynihan's over-all perspective or of the Puerto Ricans of New York, for
space limitations have made it impossible to include other sections dealing
with the progress that Puerto Ricans have been able to make in the last
twenty years despite their handicaps.*

LOWER INCOME

The way we talk about poverty and misery today almost determines
how we interpret it: our rhetoric explains that society is at fault. It is interesting to look back at the great study of poverty conducted by Charles Booth
in London toward the end of the nineteenth century. Booth in a rather
unimaginative and matter-of-fact way went through the whole population
of London, looking for those who were poor and miserable and finding
out the reasons why. The huge mass of poverty in London 60 to 70 years
ago contained remarkably few able-bodied men, who were healthy, who
had some modicum of education, who had some skill, and who were not
mentally unbalanced.

SOURCE: Nathan Glazer and Daniel Patrick Moynihan, *Beyond the Melting Pot*
(Cambridge: M.I.T. Press, 1963), pp. 121–29 (footnotes omitted). Copyright © 1963
by the Massachusetts Institute of Technology and the President and Fellows of Harvard
College. Reprinted by permission of the M.I.T. Press.

Nathan Glazer is Professor of Sociology at the University of California at Berkeley. He is one of the co-authors of *The Lonely Crowd*, and author of *American
Judaism. Daniel Patrick Moynihan* has been Assistant Secretary of Labor since 1963.

This rather obvious conclusion is nevertheless one that seems to play little role in present-day discussions of poverty. It does not explain every-thing—the proportion of unemployed *does* go up and down in response to conditions that have nothing to do with the qualities of individuals. But for any individual, and for any group made up of individuals, such factors as education, health, and skill are very important in determining income; and for a society as a whole the level of health, education, and skill is not only related to income but probably related to the level of employment too.

We have spoken up to this point of the successful and the adjusted among the Puerto Rican migrants. It takes no discerning eye to see that there is a sea of misery among the newcomers.

As to its extent: Puerto Rican median family income was considerably lower than even nonwhite median family income—$3,811 as against $4,437 —in 1960. This was 63 per cent of the median income for all New York families. Unemployment among the Puerto Ricans seems to be consistently higher than among nonwhites and whites. The census of 1950 showed, for men, 7 per cent of the non-Puerto Rican whites, 12 per cent of the Negroes, and 17 per cent of the Puerto Ricans unemployed; for women, 5 per cent of the non-Puerto Rican whites, 8.5 per cent of the Negroes, and 11 per cent of Puerto Ricans. A random sample of New York City households in 1952 showed 13 per cent of the Puerto Ricans unemployed, 6 per cent of nonwhites, 4 per cent of the non-Puerto Rican whites. In 1960, 5 per cent of all New York males, 6.9 per cent of nonwhite males, and 9.9 per cent of all Puerto Rican males were unemployed.

In explaining misery among the Puerto Ricans, the high birth rate must be taken into account. While the birth rate among Puerto Ricans in the United States does not reach the heights of that in St. Croix, it was esti-mated in 1950 at 43 per thousand. The nonwhite birth rate was 29 per thousand, the white birth rate 17 per thousand. By 1960 the crude birth rate had declined slightly, to 40 per thousand, but it was still twice the continental birth rate, and half again as much as the nonwhite birth rate.

These are crude figures, affected by the fact that so many of the Puerto Ricans are in the childbearing ages, so few of them are aged (in 1950 of 605,000 New Yorkers over 65, only 5,000 were Puerto Rican; and it was estimated that of 865,000 over 65 in 1960, only 18,000 would be Puerto Rican). But even making adjustment for this factor of a dispropor-tionate number of young people, the Puerto Rican birth rate is remarkably high. Puerto Ricans begin bearing children younger, and bear more of them. The 1950 analysis showed that for women between 15 and 19 the Puerto Rican rate was about five times the continental white rate (the Negro rate for this age group was almost as high); for women 20 to 24 it was almost twice the white rate, and a third higher than the Negro birth rate. The early arrival of children and the large numbers of children mean that a family income that in 1950 was slightly less than that earned by Negroes must support more people.

We see the strain in a number of ways. For example, there have been a number of studies of adjusted Puerto Rican families, families that are not on relief, that are not broken, that do not have any severe problems. It is interesting to note how many of these families have only one or two children. The job at $50 a week, which manages to support such a small family in an apartment in the Bronx and which, compared with the $12 a week income that was left behind on the island, represents real advancement, is completely inadequate to support five children or more. All problems tend to pile up. The bigger family may not get into a good apartment or a housing project. The crowding in a small apartment may mean more illness and poor management of children.

One sees the impact of the large families in welfare statistics. Once again, the same $50 a week that means bare self-sufficiency with one child (and it may mean more, for a child or two can be left with a neighbor or a relative and thus permit the mother to add to family income) means the need to go to welfare for supplementation with a large family. One-half of all the families in the city receiving supplementation from the Department of Welfare are Puerto Rican. One-quarter of all the Puerto Rican children in the city are on some form of assistance. About one-seventh of all Puerto Ricans are on public assistance.

It requires special reasons to explain an incapacity to support oneself in New York. Some of these reasons are to be found in age, some in disablement. Puerto Ricans make no significant contribution of the aged and disabled to the welfare load. They do however contribute one-half of the home-relief cases and one-third of the aid-to-dependent-children cases. And when one reads that more than half of the home relief cases consist of six persons or more, one discovers that the special misfortune that consigns so many Puerto Ricans to the relief rolls is their large number of children.

Health also plays a special role. The Puerto Rican is not happy about going on relief; no one is, but one must be aware that the prevailing degree of poverty coexists with a high value placed on the maintenance of dignity and self-respect. There is no shame in a woman with children and without a husband to support her going on relief; that is understandable. But there is a good deal of shame in a man being forced to go on relief. If however he suffers from an understandable and acceptable misfortune—he has had an accident, he is in ill-health and cannot work—then there is no shame in requiring public assistance. Now as a matter of fact there seems to be a higher degree of illness among Puerto Ricans. Many arrive with ills, many acquire them in the strain of transition.

. . . . .

Everything may contribute to breaking the circle of dependency: more education, more training, fewer children, fewer illnesses, better housing, dedicated people who are interested in you, etc., etc. Sometimes at the bottom of the scale things are too far gone for anything to break the circle. Here are the "multiproblem" families, afflicted simultaneously by a variety of miseries—a child who is a drug-addict, another who is delinquent, a father who is psychologically or physically unable to work, or perhaps is not there. Here are the families so vividly described in Julius Horwitz's *The Inhabitants*, a novel by a man who has worked as an investigator for the welfare department. (Eight thousand employees are required to service the 300,000 people in the case load of the welfare department of the city.) Perhaps the worst misfortune of this bottom layer in New York is the need to deal with large numbers of harried city employees who have no contact with each other, or, in truth, with their clients, except for the specific malfunction which brought them into action. The schoolteacher or principal can do nothing about what goes on at home; the welfare investigator's role must be simply one of testing whether the family is qualified; the probation officer is supposed to keep in touch with his case, not the case's family, and can do nothing if the home in which the probationer lives is located in a tenement that is a center for drug addiction or thievery; the housing project employee (if the family is lucky enough to be in one) is concerned with financial eligibility, the payment of rent, and the maintenance of the physical property; the hospital hands out drugs and treatment, and so on and so on. And social workers and others now and then set up a joint project to see if out of the welter of bureaucratic confusion there can be fashioned an instrument that responds to families and individuals as full human beings.

The Puerto Rican has entered the city in the age of the welfare state. Here and there are to be found the settlement houses of an earlier period, in which a fuller and richer concern for the individual was manifested by devoted people from the prosperous classes. The job of such social workers today is largely to humanize and coordinate, often through arousing the people of a neighborhood to bring pressure on public authorities, the various agencies on which the poor are so dependent. But there are few such agencies and social workers who can stand outside the system and see what is wrong with it, and within each Puerto Rican community there flourish individuals—"interpreters"—who accompany the unfortunates on their round of the city agencies, and who claim to be more skillful in finding their way through the maze of regulations and requirements.

In New York City one of the greatest misfortunes of the unfortunates who cannot help themselves is the enormous difficulty of managing one of the most complex and ingrown bureaucracies in the world. An equal misfortune is the housing situation, which consigns those without sufficient resources and without energy to the frightful one-room furnished dwellings carved out of brownstones and apartment houses principally on the West Side of Manhattan. There are better living quarters, at cheaper rents, in the Bronx and Brooklyn. But when one is overwhelmed by so many misfortunes, the energy to take the subway to look for an unfurnished apartment, to get together the few sticks of furniture and the minimal kitchen equipment (the welfare department will pay), is often literally beyond the capacity of many families. And so they migrate dully from one of these awful dwellings to another scarcely better a few blocks away. On these lower levels, what are needed are rehabilitation programs on a scale that scarcely anyone dares propose. It may cost no more than what the many agencies now spend, but the difficulties of breaking through the encrusted barriers that assign functions to each agency are simply too great for a new and more effective arrangement.

Meanwhile, one generation on relief gives rise to another. One-quarter of the Puerto Rican children in the city are on public assistance. The culture of public welfare, which Horwitz has so brilliantly described, is as relevant for the future of Puerto Ricans in the city as the culture of Puerto Rico.

During the fifties, despite all this, there was not an exceptionally high rate of delinquency among Puerto Rican children. But it takes a while to adapt to a new culture, and one may reasonably expect that the "Americanization" of the Puerto Ricans under conditions we have described will lead to somewhat higher rates of delinquency and crime in the future. Today, a good deal of Puerto Rican crime consists of crimes of passion involving members of the community, but once again, it is not unreasonable to expect that in the future more and more of this violence will be turned outward. Rates of admission to mental hospitals are higher than they are on the island, or for New Yorkers in general. And the Midtown study of mental health showed a remarkably high rate of impairment for the Puerto Ricans in the East Midtown area. This is not one of the typical areas of Puerto Rican settlement; the authors suggest that this group, isolated from the main body of new migrants, may be under greater strain than Puerto Ricans in more characteristically Puerto Rican parts of the city, yet the findings are consistent with other findings on rates of illness. The migration it seems has hit New York Puerto Ricans very hard. For some reason, the rate of suicide seems to be less than it is on the island. It may have risen since this study was made in the late forties.

THE NEXT GENERATION:
FAMILY, SCHOOL, NEIGHBORHOOD

What kind of experiences do the children meet in their families, schools, neighborhoods? How are they growing up?

A typical pattern of migration of families with children is for the father to migrate alone, stay with relatives and friends, find a job and living quarters, and then gradually bring over the rest of the family. Many families are consequently divided between Puerto Rico and New York, and when they are united, if ever, they show wide differences in degree of knowledge of English, assimilation, and the like. A second pattern of migration involves a woman with children—her husband has deserted her, or she has decided to leave home and go to New York, where jobs are plentiful, where the government is reputed to be "for the women and the children," and where relief is plentiful.

The Puerto Rican mother works here much more often than she does in Puerto Rico, but women still tend, if at all possible, to stay home to take care of the children. Fewer of them work than do Negro mothers.

The question then is what kind of care the children get from these mothers, many of whom have been married since what we could consider childhood. In Puerto Rico, despite rapid urbanization and industrialization, and many consequent social changes, it is perfectly clear how one raises children. The boys are praised for their manliness, taught to be proper males, and aside from requiring them to be respectful to their fathers (whether or not these still live with their mothers) are left to raise themselves. In radically different fashion, the girls are carefully watched, warned to keep their virginity—without which a proper marriage is inconceivable—and relatively early escape from this restrictive stifling atmosphere into marriage and motherhood.

But in New York both traditional patterns raise serious problems. If the boys are left to themselves, they find bad friends, may take to drugs, will learn to be disrespectful and disobedient. And even if a boy survives the streets morally, how is he to survive them physically, with cars and trucks whizzing by, and tough Negro and Italian boys ready to beat him up under slight provocation? If the girls are guarded, are raised in the house as proper girls should be, they become resentful at a treatment that their classmates and friends are not subjected to. In addition, guarding in Puerto Rico means to keep an eye on one's daughters in a community where everyone was known and you knew everyone. Here, since the streets are dangerous, it means keeping the girl literally in the house. And if the house is a furnished room or apartment, tiny and overcrowded, it seems cruel and heartless to do so (yet many Puerto Rican parents do).

The radical boy-girl disjunction does not work in New York City. To the mind of the migrant parent the social agencies and settlement houses are no great help and often seem nests of sin. To the social worker or young minister working in the slums the dancing and other co-educational activities seem to be inducting young boys and girls into proper American behavior patterns, to be teaching them how to relate to each other in ways that are not purely sexual and exploitative, and perhaps in a measure they do accomplish this. To the Puerto Rican (and often Negro) parents what goes on seems simply shocking invitations to premature pregnancy. Very often then the children who go to the centers and the church activities are the ones from the most disorganized families, where the effort to raise them in proper fashion has been given up, and they are allowed to run wild!

In this confusing situation there are two possibilities. One is to give up. There is a widespread belief among migrant parents that the government prevents disciplining of children, but this seems to be in part a rationalization for the difficulty of making the adjustment to the great freedom of American children, for the Puerto Rican Commonwealth protects children as much as New York City does. The parents feel inadequate at handling the children (and one can sympathize with such feelings in a teen-age mother) and explain the inadequacy by the government's responsibility for the children. Another sign of giving up is the frequency with which Puerto Rican parents express the desire that their children should be sent away someplace where they may learn discipline, manners, and respect.

But a more typical reaction to this confusing new situation is a tightening of the screws, not only on the girls but on the boys too. Many cases of disturbed Puerto Rican boys that come to the attention of social agencies are cases of anxious concern by parents, overprotection, exaggerated fear of the streets—their physical and moral dangers. What is exaggeration or what is realism in thinking of the New York streets is a difficult question. The Puerto Rican mother is not as well disciplined as the native American mother who, in her desire to see her child become independent, can steel herself to forget the dangers her children face in such a simple act as coming home from school. The overprotection of the boys is often a response, social workers feel, to dissatisfaction with the marital relationship. The pattern is of course a common and widespread one, and there is nothing especially Puerto Rican about it.

The screws will also be tightened on the girls. Even without a tighter discipline against the greater dangers, the same discipline here as in Puerto Rico is going to be felt as a serious deprivation. One also faces the change in the age of marriage. Half the girls in Puerto Rico will be married by 19 and freed from the stern parental supervision. But there is no place in Puerto Rican cultural and family patterns for the older working girls who will not get married at such young ages here, and who are expected to scurry home from work as fast as they did from school. When one social worker suggested to a Puerto Rican girl who was working that she get away from the traditionally strict supervision of her father by moving into a residence, the girl was shocked. "She seems to think that in Puerto Rico they would consider any girl who moves away from her family into a residence as someone who goes into a house of prostitution."

Then another problem is created by the inevitable shift from the extended family in Puerto Rico to the smaller one in New York. The Puerto Rican mother expects to have someone around to relieve her in the care of her children—there will be a mother, a sister, an aunt, a *comadre*, and she will be living with her or close enough to be helpful. In New York this traditional pattern will often be found, but it is much more difficult to maintain. It cannot be arranged, for example, to have mother or sister move next door in the same housing project. Children become much more of a bother, much more of a strain. One is expected to take care of them completely on one's own, and without help. An anthropologist who has studied this matter feels that the more traditional Puerto Rican family in New York does a better job raising its children than the nuclear family of man and woman, for in the latter the mother is likely to feel resentment and strain.

The changing city no longer provides the neighborhood that is exclusive to one ethnic group. And the city administration insists that in the low-rent housing under its management the groups be mixed as much as possible (20 per cent of the city's low-cost housing is now occupied by Puerto Ricans, and about a seventh of the Puerto Rican population now lives in them). And so the models for new conduct in rearing one's children vary; there are Negro, Jewish, and Italian models of child rearing and child discipline, as well as the American models of the welfare workers and the settlement houses, and a variety of subvariants in each. What degree of discipline, what kind of punishment and rewards, what expectations should one have from one's children—the Puerto Rican mother is at a loss in deciding the right course.

We speak of the Puerto Rican mother, because on her falls the main task of child rearing, in part because so many of them manage homes without males present, or with males who take no particular responsibility for the children; and because in the traditional Puerto Rican home the father expects, aside from his demand for respect and obedience, to have little to do with the children. He also considers it beneath his dignity to participate in the management of the home, and considers it his prerogative to be off by himself whenever he wishes to be. But of course his traditional position is seriously challenged in America. Not only can the mother get relief and throw him out, not only can she get a job that pays as well as his does (she can often do this in Puerto Rico, too, today), but society does not prevent her from following an independent course. The women, many of the men grumble, are "spoiled" here; the women, on the other hand, will often express preference for a man raised in America who does not expect the same self-effacement from them. Nor are the courts or the police or the social workers sympathetic to the position of a traditional Puerto Rican male standing upon his dignity. His world often falls apart—this is why there is so often a descent into incapacity and into mental or physical illness.

And then there is the role of the school in the lives of the children. Even the least-schooled migrant knows the value of education; Puerto Ricans universally would like to see their children well educated, and hope they will be professionals. But school is often a frustrating experience. The shift to a new language has been peculiarly difficult for the Puerto Ricans. We can only speculate about the reasons why Jews and even Italians, coming into the city at roughly the same ages, with much less formal knowledge of English, should have made a rather better linguistic adjustment. Certainly the schools did much less to ease their path. Of course in the years of the heaviest Jewish and Italian migration the school-leaving age was much lower, children often began working at 12, and the problems that the schools must today face (which are severer with the older children) were reduced. In other words, the children who could not learn English forty years ago got out before their problems became too noticeable. But we can only guess at the differences—no one seems to have gone back to see what the schools did when whole districts were filled with Yiddish-speaking and Italian-speaking children.

Probably no public school system has spent as much money and devoted as much effort to the problem of a group of minority children as the New York public school system has devoted to the Puerto Ricans. There are now hundreds of special personnel to deal with parents, to help teachers, to deal with special problems of students. The magnitude of the problems is barely communicated by figures. "On October 31, 1958," reports the Board of Education, "of the 558,741 children in our elementary schools, there were 56,296 children of Puerto Rican ancestry whose lack of ability to speak or understand English represented a considerable handicap to learning."

The numbers alone are enormous; there is the additional problem of the rapid movement of the newcomers. On the West Side of Manhattan, one of the major sections of entry for new migrants, the turnover in an area containing sixteen schools was 92 per cent; which means that each year the school confronts what is in effect a completely new student body.

It is probably particularly difficult for the adolescent boys to adjust to this situation. The pattern of maintenance of male self-dignity makes it embarrassing to speak English with an accent. Dr. Berle believes it is easier for adolescent girls who have not had this emphasis in their upbringing to adapt to the English language school. (Perhaps the Jewish tradition of self-ridicule—dignity there is only for the old—stands them in good stead in new situations. One is astonished at the willingness of Jewish storekeepers to speak a most corrupt Spanish to deal with their Puerto Rican clientele: in contrast to their customers they are shameless.)

Meanwhile, there is a good deal of school-leaving at the earliest possible age, and relatively small proportions today go into the academic high schools. The register for New York City schools in October 1960 showed that 18 per cent of the elementary school students, 17 per cent of the junior high school students, and only 8 per cent of the high school students were Puerto Ricans. The proportion in the academic high schools was 5 per cent.

The other side of the coin is an impressive amount of activity by young, educated Puerto Ricans to raise the level of concern for education. For example, Puerto Rican social workers, professionals, and teachers have set up an organization, *Aspira*, devoted to working with students and their parents so that they will take all possible advantage of educational opportunities. It runs workshops in which plans to get through high school or into or through college are worked out, it gives lectures on professional opportunities, looks for money for scholarships, reaches parents and community organizations. The young Puerto Rican leaders also run an interesting annual youth conference that gives a revealing insight into the concerns and struggles of the young people. This group clearly sees Puerto Ricans as following in the path of the earlier ethnic groups that preceded it, and speaks of them as models of emulation rather than as targets for attack. Its identification is with the Jews or Italians of forty years ago, rather than with the Negroes of today. It has a rather hopeful outlook, which emphasizes the group's potential for achievement more than the prejudice and discrimination it meets. One can only hope that this buoyant outlook will be better sustained by life in the city. It is a note in tune with the gentleness and gaiety of the Puerto Ricans themselves.

12. Exposure to Child-Rearing Experts among Negro and White Mothers[*]

ZENA SMITH BLAU

Dependence on child-rearing experts has been particularly marked in the United States. It is one indication of the extent to which American nuclear families have become independent units, relatively divorced from traditions

* This study was supported in part by National Institute of Mental Health, Public Health Service Research Grant 07316–01, and in part by a grant from the University of Illinois Graduate College Research Board. I also wish to acknowledge the assistance of Arlene Krieger and former Dean Emily C. Cardew, of the University of Illinois College of Nursing, and the advice of James A. Davis, Jacob J. Feldman, and Harold Levy, of the National Opinion Research Center during early phases of the research.
    SOURCE: *American Journal of Sociology*, 64, 1964, pp. 596–608, passim. Copyright © 1964 by The University of Chicago. Reprinted by permission of The University of Chicago Press.
    Zena Smith Blau is Assistant Professor of Sociology at the University of Illinois College of Nursing.

and residence patterns that bind generations and collateral kin in the family systems of many other societies. Blau's paper shows that among both white and Negro mothers, more members of the middle than of the working class had read Dr. Benjamin Spock's enormously popular book, Baby and Child Care. However, even white working-class mothers were more likely than Negro middle-class mothers to have read it. The author thinks her findings reflect the relatively small size of the Negro middle class; she supports her interpretation by referring to materials drawn from upwardly and downwardly mobile mothers. She reasons that because of Negroes' lack of past opportunities for upward mobility, the present Negro middle class can provide only a few role models for those Negro mothers who are currently moving into it. As a result, there is a gap between white and Negro preferences for sources of advice about child-rearing, even where Negro and white mothers have about the same social class position. Processes like these help to explain why it takes longer than a generation for a group to move from a marginal position into the cultural mainstream. (See also selection 9.)

The writings of experts bearing on diverse realms of behavior, transmitted by the mass media, constitute a major mechanism for the diffusion of new information and ideas in contemporary societies. As yet, however, we have achieved little systematic understanding of the social processes by which exposure to this source of innovation comes about, or about the related problem of the processes that lead to the adoption of the ideas advocated.

. . . . .

[Katz, Levin, and Hamilton][1] suggest some of the ways in which social structures may condition the diffusion process. Their idea that social structure implies, among other things, the existence of boundaries which differentiate "the frequency and character of social relations"[2] and thus constitute barriers to diffusion comes very close to the central problem with which the present paper deals—the analysis of selected structural attributes of class-color groups and how they facilitate or hinder the exposure of their members to the writings of a body of experts in the realm of child-rearing. More specifically, the substantive problem is to provide a structural interpretation of a pattern of differences between Negro and white middle- and working-class mothers in their exposure to the writings of child-rearing experts, in their attendance at child-care classes, and in their attitudes toward experts.

Child-rearing studies have repeatedly shown that the class position and educational level of mothers condition their exposure to diverse sources of

[1] Elihu Katz, Martin L. Levin, and Herbert Hamilton, "Traditions of Research on the Diffusion of Innovation," *American Sociological Review*, XXVIII (April, 1963), 248.
[2] *Ibid.*, p. 247.

formal and informal information and advice.[3] Although these findings were based, for the most part, on samples of white women, there was every reason to believe that they would apply as well to Negro women of similar class position and educational level.

Indeed, color differences in the realm of child-rearing had largely ceased to be a matter of specific research interest after Davis and Havighurst reported, in a pioneering study published in 1946, that they found few differences in the child-rearing practices of Negro and white mothers who occupied similar class positions.[4] Although their study did not deal with the problem of exposure to experts' writings it seems to have been assumed by the researchers who followed them that the pattern of findings would extend to this kind of behavior as well. However, in the last decade several studies of class differences in the child-rearing patterns of white mothers have reported findings which contradict those of Davis and Havighurst.[5] Whatever the reason for these discrepancies, they suggest the need for taking a new look at the problem of class-color differences in child-rearing, and especially for bringing to bear on this question some of the new modes of sociological analysis that have been developed since the appearance of the early Chicago study.

The study of which the present paper is a part does not replicate the content of the Davis and Havighurst study, but it has a similar sample design.[6] A quota sample of 224 mothers, selected on the basis of race, class position,[7] and parity, was interviewed during the period of confinement on the maternity floors of three large, centrally located hospitals in Chicago

---

[3] See, e.g., Martha Sturm White, "Social Class, Child Rearing Practices, and Child Behavior," *American Sociological Review*, XXII (December, 1957), 704–12; Melvin L. Kohn, "Social Class and Parent-Child Relationships: An Interpretation," *American Journal of Sociology*, LXVIII (January, 1963), 471–80; and esp. Urie Bronfenbrenner, "Socialization and Social Class through Time and Space," in Eleanor E. Maccoby, Theodore M. Newcomb, and Eugene L. Hartley (eds.), *Readings in Social Psychology* (New York: Henry Holt & Co., 1958), pp. 400–425, which presents a review of many child-rearing studies and a provocative discussion of how reading the experts may promote changes in child-rearing.

[4] Allison Davis and Robert J. Havighurst, "Social Class and Color Differences in Child Rearing," *American Sociological Review*, XI (1946), 698–710.

[5] E.g., Robert R. Sears, Eleanor E. Maccoby, and Harry Levin, *Patterns of Child Rearing* (Evanston, Ill.: Row, Peterson & Co., 1957), and White, *op. cit.*; for an interpretation of these inconsistencies see Bronfenbrenner, *op. cit.*

[6] The original design called for fifty cases each of middle-class and working-class white and Negro mothers, one third having had only one child and the rest having had more than one. However, we could not locate as many Negro middle-class mothers as planned (although we remained in the field longer in an attempt to do so), and decided instead to obtain more interviews with women in the other three class-color categories in order to prevent undue shrinkage of the sample. Conclusions based on so small a sample, particularly of Negro middle-class mothers, are admittedly tentative and are presented merely as hypotheses which still need to be tested on a more adequate sample.

[7] The index of class position is based on husband's occupation. Respondents whose husbands are engaged in non-manual occupations are classified as middle class, and those whose husbands are in manual occupations are defined as working class.

during 1961–62. One section of the interview schedule contained a series of questions about the extent and nature of respondents' exposure to various mass media and to child-rearing content in these sources. Some of these data are presented in the analysis that follows.

Exposure to Child-Rearing Literature

An index of the extent of exposure to child-rearing literature was obtained by combining the scores assigned to answers to three questions: the frequency with which respondents read child-rearing articles (1) in their daily newspapers and (2) magazines, and (3) whether they have read Dr. Benjamin Spock's book, *Baby and Child Care*.[8] "High" exposure (a score of 3 or 4) signifies regular readership of child-rearing articles in at least one of the mass media, and of Spock's book. "Medium" exposure (a score of 1 or 2) indicates regular readership of such articles in at least one of the mass media, or only of Dr. Spock's book; and "low" exposure (a score of 0) indicates that a respondent has not read Spock and does not ordinarily read child-rearing articles.[9] . . . The extent of exposure to child-rearing literature is influenced by both the class position and color of mothers. White mothers expose themselves more to this kind of literature than Negro mothers, both in the middle and in the working class, and exposure is more prevalent in the middle class than in the working class, independent of skin color. In other words, the woman with no regular exposure to child-rearing literature is highly exceptional in the white middle class, considerably less so in the Negro middle class and white working class, but in a majority in the Negro working class.[10]

[8] The individual questions were cross-tabulated and scored in the following way: a score of 1 each was given if a respondent regularly read child-rearing articles in a daily newspaper or in any magazine mentioned, and a score of 2 was given to those who had read Dr. Spock's book, on the assumption that the latter covers at least as wide a range of content and has at least as much impact as the other two sources taken together. Respondents were also asked about their exposure to the well-known pamphlet, *Infant Care*, published by the U.S. Children's Bureau, but so few had read it (33 respondents) that it was not included in the exposure index. Two open-ended questions concerning other sources read by respondents yielded even fewer returns.

[9] No value judgment that mothers ought to read child-rearing literature is implied here, nor are any a priori assumptions made about the impact of this literature on the child-rearing practices of mothers variously located in the social structure. The latter problem will be dealt with in a forthcoming paper.

[10] The Negro-white differences in exposure to child-rearing content are not due to differences in extent of exposure per se to newspapers and magazines. Analysis of scores on a mass-media exposure index, based on the frequency of newspaper and magazine reading, indicates that the exposure of respondents varies primarily with class position and only slightly with color. Thus the proportions of respondents who read both a newspaper and a magazine regularly, or one regularly and the other occasionally, are 82 per cent among whites and 79 per cent among Negroes in the middle class and 59 per cent and 54 per cent, respectively, in the working class. Also of interest is our

The difference between Negro and white mothers in *extent* of exposure to child-rearing content stems in part from the difference between them in the *kind* of media to which they expose themselves, specifically their use of Dr. Spock's book. Separate analysis of the proportions who have read this book shows that among white middle-class mothers the overwhelming majority (77 per cent) have read the book, but in the Negro middle class the proportion is strikingly smaller (32 per cent); indeed it is lower than in the white working class (48 per cent). The smallest proportion of Spock readers is found among Negro working-class mothers (12 per cent).[11]

It is well known, of course, that book readership is more widespread in the middle class than in the working class, particularly among the better educated. Higher education, in turn, is more widespread among whites than among Negroes in the middle class. For example, among middle-class respondents in our study only 8 per cent of the whites but 37 per cent of the Negroes have not completed high school, and 69 per cent and 21 per cent, respectively, have had some college education. In the working class, on the other hand, the level of education of white and Negro mothers is virtually identical. Fifty-five per cent in each color group have not completed high school; and 9 per cent and 8 per cent, respectively, have had some college education. But the differences in exposure to Dr. Spock's book between Negroes and whites persist, for the most part, even when educational background of respondents is controlled. . . . at each educational level in both classes the proportion of mothers who have read Spock is higher among whites than among Negroes, although in the middle class the size of the differences between the two color groups diminishes considerably as educational level rises. In the working class, the difference in readership between Negroes and whites is greatest among high-school graduates. It can also be seen that, while each of the three variables—class, color, and educational level—independently affects exposure to Spock's book, the magnitude of differences between Negro and white mothers in most cases is greater than between mothers of comparable educational background in the two classes, or between respondents at different educational levels within the same class. It is noteworthy that in the middle class the differences in the proportions of Negro and white mothers who

---

finding that none of the Negro respondents exposes herself *exclusively* to Negro publications. Only five respondents read the *Chicago Defender*, the local daily Negro newspaper (which, incidentally, does not carry a column on child care) and all these also read at least one of the four daily Chicago newspapers.

[11] Respondents were first asked whether they had ever heard of Dr. Spock's book. The proportions who had never heard of the book were only 5 per cent in the white middle class, but 37 per cent in both the Negro middle class and the white working class, and 65 per cent in the Negro working class. It is interesting that, although identical proportions of white working-class and Negro middle-class women knew about the book, fewer in the latter group had read it.

have read Spock diminish considerably as educational level increases. But in the working class the largest difference between Negro and white mothers occurs among the high-school graduates, because the proportion of white mothers who have read Spock is as high in this group as among those with some college education, whereas among Negro mothers this proportion is considerably higher among the college-educated than among high school graduates. In other words, readership of this source of child-rearing information varies more with education among Negro than among white mothers. But it is apparent that educational differences do not account for the large variance between the two color groups with respect to readership of Spock's book.[12]

．　．　．　．　．

ATTITUDES TOWARD EXPERTS

The question arises whether the pattern of differences between Negro and white mothers in their exposure to formal sources of information may simply reflect different evaluations on their part of the importance of expert advice in the realm of child care and child-rearing. One might expect that the greater exposure of white mothers, particularly those in the middle class, to various sources of information reflects a belief on their part that they can thereby enhance the effectiveness of their behavior in the maternal role, while Negro women may expose themselves less to such sources because they are less inclined to share this opinion. The data, however, contradict this assumption.

Respondents were asked: "Some mothers feel it's important to find out what the exeprts (like doctors, psychologists, etc.) have to say about raising children while others don't think that is necessary. What do you think?" Responses were classified as generally favorable (e.g., "experts have more knowledge or experience"), unfavorable (e.g., "I don't believe in raising children by the book" or "mothers know best"), or ambivalent (e.g., "it does not hurt to get their ideas, but I'll use my own judgment"). . . . contrary to expectation, . . . favorable attitudes toward child-rearing experts are expressed more frequently by Negro mothers in both the middle and the working class. Negative sentiments, on the other hand, occur slightly more often among whites. Ambivalent attitudes are more frequent among middle-class women, both white and Negro, than among those in the working class.

That Negro women express favorable attitudes toward child-rearing experts more often than white women, regardless of class position, but

---

[12] Similar differences occur between Negro and white respondents of like class position and educational background on the composite index of exposure. . . .

typically expose themselves less to such informational sources seems contradictory and might even be dismissed as simply another instance of the known tendency of respondents in low-prestige groups to express agreement more readily, regardless of item content, in the interview situation.[13] But some recent evidence of a similar order suggests another explanation, which turns out to be more fruitful for understanding the dynamic interplay of attitudes and behavior toward experts among mothers in different social contexts.

In a recent National Opinion Research Center study of public attitudes toward medical care, Feldman found that people who have more contact with physicians are also more critical of them than those with less contact.[14] More recently, in a study of attitudes toward fluoridation in a Massachusetts community, Gamson and Schuman reported that respondents who accord physicians high-prestige rankings in comparison with other professionals also express hostile sentiments toward them more frequently than those who give them lower rankings.[15] One explanation for this ambivalence suggested by the authors is that "the very standards that lead to high prestige may cause physicians to be judged against criteria that are exceedingly difficult to meet. The stronger a respondent feels about the importance of such standards the more he is likely to accord prestige to physicians as against other occupations but to judge physicians severely by these same standards."[16]

By the same token, white mothers may be more prone than Negro mothers to express ambivalence toward child-rearing experts precisely because they depend more on them for guidance, as indicated by the fact that they expose themselves more to the writings of experts. Indeed, a comparison of mothers' attitudes toward experts according to mothers' exposure scores in each of the four class-color groups lends support to this interpretation (see Table 1). It shows that in each class-color group, the proportion who express ambivalence toward experts is greater among respondents who have high- or medium-exposure scores than among those with low-exposure scores. The original differences . . . between Negro and white mothers virtually disappear in the middle class, and become smaller in the working class, among respondents who expose themselves to experts' writings.

Among those with low exposure to this literature, on the contrary, the differences in ambivalence and particularly in negativism between white

[13] See, e.g., Gerhard E. Lenski and John C. Leggett, "Caste, Class, and Deference in the Research Interview," *American Journal of Sociology*, LXV (March, 1960), 463–67.
[14] Jacob J. Feldman, "What Americans Think about Their Medical Care," American Statistical Association, Proceedings of the Social Statistics Section Meeting (December, 1958).
[15] William A. Gamson and Howard Schuman, "Some Undercurrents in the Prestige of Physicians," *American Journal of Sociology*, LXVIII (January, 1963), 463–70.
[16] *Ibid.*, p. 469.

Table 1: *Per Cent Ambivalent and Per Cent Unfavorable toward Experts, by Exposure Score, Class, and Color*

	MIDDLE CLASS		WORKING CLASS	
Exposure	White	Negro	White	Negro
Per cent of total with medium and high scores	87	68	63	44
	PER CENT AMBIVALENT			
Low	18(11)	0 (6)	10(21)	0(37)
Medium and high	24(72)	23(13)	14(35)	10(29)
	PER CENT UNFAVORABLE			
Low	55(11)	17 (6)	43(21)	33(37)
Medium and high	28(72)	23(13)	26(35)	21(29)

and Negro women become *more* pronounced. Unfavorable sentiments are voiced more often by mothers who do not read the experts in three of the four groups—all except the middle-class Negroes. But among mothers with low exposure negative attitudes are expressed considerably more often by whites, particularly in the middle class, than by Negroes. This suggests that the woman who does not "read the experts" but is located in a social milieu where this practice is prevalent feels called upon to justify her deviance by denigrating experts. Thus, in the white middle class where the pattern of reading child-rearing literature is most prevalent, women with low-exposure scores are most often negative toward experts.[17] In the white working class where this pattern is less widespread women with low exposure scores exhibit negative attitudes correspondingly less often. Exposure to experts' writings is least prevalent among Negro mothers in the working class. Consequently, Negro women who do not read this literature do not feel constrained to rationalize their indifference to expert opinion by denying its value. This difference in social context may well explain why Negro women with lower exposure scores express hostility toward experts considerably less often than their white counterparts.

CLASS MOBILITY AND COLOR DIFFERENCES

The pattern of high exposure to the writings of child-rearing experts is more prevalent among white middle-class mothers than among Negro

[17] The proportion of mothers in the Negro middle class who express negative sentiments is lower than in the white middle class, as expected. But contrary to expectation, it is also lower than in the other strata.

middle-class mothers with a similar amount of formal education . . .[18] In fact, even white working-class women who have not completed high school have high-exposure scores nearly as often as women with more education in the Negro middle class. Differences in the constitution of the middle classes and the working classes in the two color groups, and their implications for acculturation to middle-class modes of behavior, may help to explain the differences noted above.

Reliance on experts' writings is part of a larger complex of orientations and modes of behavior that differentiate the child-rearing patterns of middle-class mothers from those in the working class in white society.[19] We would therefore expect to find this pattern more prevalent among women of middle-class origin than among those of working-class origin who have moved into the middle class.[20] . . . high exposure is in fact considerably more frequent among the stationary members of the white middle class (59 per cent) than among the upwardly mobile (32 per cent). Her newly won middle-class status does not automatically lead a woman to emulate the less visible forms of behavior that prevail among her established class peers. The acculturation process in this realm of behavior, as in others, requires opportunities for association with established members of the middle class in the course of which social pressure can be exerted upon the new members to adopt middle-class ways. Since the stationary members constitute the majority in the white middle class, such social opportunities would seem to be readily available to the upwardly mobile woman. And the fact that the tenure of the stationary members in the middle class has been of longer duration and that they are apt to be better educated further enhances their ability to influence the incoming members

[18] The sample contains four cases of Negro middle-class mothers who have had some college education. Only one of them has a high-exposure score compared to 58 per cent among *white* middle-class respondents who have attended college.

[19] That this practice is in fact more prevalent in the white middle than working class has been shown by a number of studies besides this one. See, e.g., White, *op. cit.*, and Kohn, *op. cit.* The latter study also contains a suggestive interpretation of these observed patterns of differences as reflections of differences in the value systems that prevail among the two strata.

[20] Class origin is defined by father's occupation when the respondent was sixteen years old. Respondents are classified as stationary members of the middle class if their fathers and husbands are in non-manual occupations, and as upwardly mobile members if their father did manual work but their husband does non-manual work. In the working class, downwardly mobile respondents are those whose fathers did non-manual work but whose husbands are manual workers, and stationary respondents are those whose fathers and husbands are manual workers. There is some variation in the age composition of these groups. Thus, the proportion over twenty-five years old in the white middle class is 58 per cent among stationary respondents and 45 per cent among the upward mobiles; in the white working class this proportion is 30 per cent among stationary respondents and 27 per cent among downward mobiles; and among Negroes it is 24 per cent among the upward mobiles and 44 per cent among stationary working-class respondents. However, the pattern of differences in exposure . . . persists even when age is controlled (except that there are too few cases of older upwardly mobile Negroes to make meaningful comparisons).

of their group. Thus, the pattern of reliance on experts could be expected to spread by degrees among the upwardly mobile as they acquire longer tenure in their new position, resulting in closer conformity to the behavior of their stationary peers.

A comparison of the exposure scores of upwardly mobile white women with those of similar origin who have remained in the working class constitutes a crude test of this hypothesis. Although there is little difference in high exposure, the proportion with some exposure (high or medium) is considerably greater among the upwardly mobile (89 per cent) than among stationary members of the working class (55 per cent), which indicates that the former have assimilated the middle-class pattern to some degree—although not to the full extent, since *high* exposure is less widespread among them than among the stationary members of the middle class. Thus, the data lend support to our hypothesis concerning the acculturation effects that accompany upward mobility into the white middle class.

The constitution of the Negro middle class differs sharply from that of the white middle class, and therein may lie the explanation, at least to some degree, of the differences in the extent to which their members expose themselves to child-rearing literature. Owing to the long history of pervasive economic and social discrimination against Negroes in our society the size of the established Negro middle class has traditionally been much smaller than its white counterpart, both in absolute and in relative terms. Since World War II, however, employment opportunities for Negroes in non-manual occupations have increased with a corresponding increase in the numbers who have recently moved from the working class into the middle class.[21] Indeed, in our sample fully 90 per cent of the middle-class Negro women come from working-class backgrounds, in contrast to 35 per cent in the white middle class. Owing to their insignificant number,[22] the stationary members of the Negro middle class are not in a position to exert any appreciable effect on the behavior of the upwardly mobile members of their class. And since the barriers of segregation allow for little, if any, informal association between members of the two color groups the upwardly mobile Negro woman is also cut off from the influence exerted by stationary members of the white middle class.

As a result, the acculturation of Negro upwardly mobile women to the modes of behavior that prevail in the middle class is likely to proceed at

[21] This is not meant to imply, of course, that the size of the Negro middle class approaches that of the white middle class, even relative to the total Negro population, but only that the proportion of the Negro middle class with working-class origins is larger than the corresponding proportion in the white middle class. The analysis assumes that this is true for the Chicago population at large as well as for our sample, which is admittedly small and not representative.

[22] The tiny number of stationary middle-class Negroes (2) and of downwardly mobile working-class Negroes (1) in our sample makes impossible some comparisons corresponding to those in the white group and results in some unavoidable gaps in the analysis.

a slower pace than in the case of upwardly mobile whites, and this is exemplified by the differences between them in the extent of their exposure to the writings of child-rearing experts. . . . In contrast to only one-tenth of the upwardly mobile whites, over one-third of the upwardly mobile Negroes have low exposure to this kind of literature.[23]

Analysis of the composition of the white working class also helps explain why even in this stratum exposure to experts' writings is more widespread than in the Negro middle class, despite the fact that the latter contains a larger proportion of better educated women. Although the large majority (79 per cent) of white working-class respondents are stationary members of their stratum, the rest (21 per cent) were reared in the middle class and subsequently moved down into the working class. A comparison of the exposure scores of the downwardly mobile and stationary members of the white working class . . . shows that a higher proportion (91 per cent) of the former have high or medium scores than of the latter (55 per cent). And it is the presence of this downwardly mobile contingent that largely accounts for the greater prevalence of high exposure in the white working class than in the Negro middle class. For in the latter group the proportion with low-exposure scores (35 per cent) is less than among the stationary members of the white working class (45 per cent). But downwardly mobile white working-class mothers expose themselves considerably more to experts' writings than upwardly mobile Negro middle-class women, an indication that former social ties with her middle-class family and friends are maintained to some extent by the downwardly mobile woman who thereby remains subject to middle-class influences to a greater degree than the upwardly mobile Negro middle-class woman. But the data also suggest that the impact of middle-class influence on downwardly mobile women has waned, since only 36 per cent of them have high exposure to child-rearing literature in contrast to 59 per cent of their former class peers, those who have retained their middle-class status.

However, although the downwardly mobile white mother shows evidence of being negatively influenced by her association with her new class peers, she may also act, to some degree, as a carrier of middle-class patterns of behavior to the stationary members of the working class with whom she develops social ties. For the stationary members of the white working class expose themselves more to child-rearing literature than stationary members of the Negro working class, despite the fact that the educational level of the members of the two strata is similar. But in the Negro working class in our sample there are virtually no downwardly mobile respondents (2 per cent) and consequently here the chances of exposure to middle-class social influences are most limited.

---

[23] When age is controlled this difference becomes even more pronounced among younger women (under twenty-six): only 27 per cent of the upwardly mobile whites compared to 77 per cent of the upwardly mobile Negroes have low-exposure scores.

SUMMARY AND CONCLUSIONS

Exposure to informational sources in the realm of child-rearing was shown to be more widespread among white than among Negro mothers, regardless of class position. This pattern of Negro-white differences persists even when respondents' educational level is taken into account. But Negro women tend to express favorable sentiments toward child-rearing experts more often than white women, despite the fact that they expose themselves less to their writings. Simultaneous analysis of these two variables revealed that in all four class-color groups women with high or medium exposure were more prone to express ambivalence toward experts than those with little or no exposure. But an interesting pattern of differences was observed in the incidence of negative attitudes between the two color groups: among women with low exposure, whites were more often negative toward experts than Negroes, but no such differences were noted among women with higher exposure. This suggests that the prevalence of a pattern of behavior in a group conditions the relationship between behavior and attitudes among its individual members. Where reading child-rearing literature is a widespread practice, as it is among white mothers, the very prevalence of this pattern within the group operates as a pressure toward conformity upon the individual. In this *social* context, *not* to read the experts constitutes a deviant act, and women who do not conform to the pattern of exposure feel constrained to justify their deviance by denigrating experts. But in a group where this practice is rare, as is the case among Negro mothers, the woman who does not read the experts is under no social or psychological pressure to provide rationalizations for her abstinence.

Analysis of the differences in the proportions of stationary and upwardly mobile members in the two middle classes helps to explain why the pattern of reading child-rearing literature is less widespread among Negro women, even the better educated Negroes, than among whites. The existence of a stationary majority in the white stratum creates numerous opportunities for upwardly mobile women to become exposed to middle-class modes of behavior such as "reading the experts." And association with these better educated, more prestigeful members in their stratum constitutes the source of social pressure through which new members become acculturated to these middle-class ways. In contrast, the Negro middle class contains an overwhelming majority of upwardly mobile members. Thus the new member has fewer opportunities than her white counterpart for exposure to, and assimilation of, middle-class modes of behavior within her own color group, and the barriers of segregation forestall her exposure to these influences through association with the stationary members of the white middle class. Indeed, even white working-class mothers may have a better chance of exposure to middle-class influences through their association with the downwardly mobile members of their stratum. But the Negro working-class mother is removed from even this source of influence, since there are virtually no downwardly mobile women in her stratum.

That economic discrimination and social segregation are major impediments to the acculturation of the Negro masses to urban middle-class culture is well known. Our analysis helps to specify *how* these practices operate to delay this process even among middle-class, better educated Negroes. Cognizant as we all are of the existence of a dual stratification system, we tend to think of the Negro and white class systems as similar though separate. Our findings suggest that there may be a number of structural differences between them that differentiate not only the rate with which middle-class norms diffuse among their members but also the amount of strain that accompanies the acculturation process. These differences in social structure mediate the effects that upward mobility and higher education exert on the attitudes and behavior of their individual members, not only in the realm of child-rearing, but probably in other realms of behavior as well. In other words, although the existence of a dual stratification system constitutes a grave social liability to a society that espouses democratic values, it constitutes an opportunity, while it persists, for the social scientist to make systematic comparisons between two class systems within a common cultural framework and thereby to gain a better understanding of how specific structural variables, present to a different degree in the two class systems, condition the diffusion of various kinds of norms, practices, and innovations among the members similarily situated within them. By the same token, it would undoubtedly prove fruitful to study the impact of desegregation on these processes by comparing their effects on Negroes who have gained opportunities for informal association with their white counterparts and on those similarly located in their class system for whom such opportunities still do not exist.

13. Race, Ethnicity, and the Achievement Syndrome*

BERNARD C. ROSEN

The paper that follows starts with the premise that various ethnic groups who migrated to the northeastern United States from abroad and from other sections of this country still differ in their motivations, values, and aspirations. Originating when the groups had different life-situations, these differences came to be expressed in each group's traditions and child-rearing techniques. Rosen shows how social class and ethnicity affect achievement motivation, independence training, achievement value-orientations, and aspiration levels among the following groups: French-Canadians, Greeks, Italians, Jews, Negroes, and white Protestants. Using both personality and cultural data, and controlling for the effects of differential class placement, Rosen helps to explain why these groups have not been equally successful in accomplishing upward mobility after several generations in the Northeast.

The upward mobility rates of many racial and ethnic groups in America have been markedly dissimilar when compared with one another and with some white Protestant groups. For example, among the "new immigration" groups which settled primarily in the Northeast, the Greeks and Jews have attained middle class status more rapidly than most of their fellow immigrants. In general, ethnic groups with Roman Catholic affiliation have moved up less rapidly than non-Catholic groups. And the vertical mobility of Negroes, even in the less repressive environment of the industrial Northeast, has been relatively slow.[1]

The reasons offered to explain these differences vary with the group in

* The writer wishes to express his appreciation to David C. McClelland for his generous support and advice. The contributions of Marian Winterbottom for her work in scoring the TAT protocols, Shirley Rosen for her help in evaluating ethnographic material and in statistical computational work, and James Sakoda for his assistance on statistical procedures are gratefully acknowledged. Roy D'Andrade and June Schmelzer also helped with statistical work.

[1] Cf. W. L. Warner and L. Srole, *The Social Systems of American Ethnic Groups*, New Haven: Yale University Press, 1945; F. L. Strodtbeck, "Jewish and Italian Immigration and Subsequent Status Mobility," in D. McClelland, A. Baldwin, U. Bronfenbrenner and F. Strodtbeck, *Talent and Society*, Princeton: Van Nostrand, 1958; M. Davie, *World Migration*, New York: Macmillan, 1936.

SOURCE: *American Sociological Review*, 24, 1959, pp. 47–60. Reprinted with the permission of the author and The American Sociological Association.

Bernard C. Rosen is Professor of Sociology at the University of Nebraska. He has published extensively in the area of cross-cultural studies of achievement orientation and motivation.

question. Thus, differences in group mobility rates have sometimes been interpreted as a function of the immigrant's possession of certain skills which were valuable in a burgeoning industrial society. In this connection, there is some evidence that many Jews came to America with occupational skills better suited to urban living than did their fellow immigrants. Social mobility seems also to be related to the ability of ethnic and racial groups to organize effectively to protect and promote their interests. Both the Greeks and the Jews were quicker to develop effective community organizations than were other immigrants who had not previously faced the problem of adapting as minority groups. For the Jews, this situation grew out of their experiences with an often hostile gentile world; for the Greeks, out of their persecutions by the Turks. The repressiveness of the social structure or the willingness of the dominant groups to permit others to share in the fruits of a rich, expanding economy has also been given as an explanation of differential group mobility. This argument has merit in the case of Negroes, but it is less valid in a comparison of the Jews with Southern Italians or French-Canadians. Finally, it has been suggested that groups with experiences in small town or urban environments were more likely to possess the cultural values appropriate to achievement in American society than were ethnic and racial groups whose cultures had been formed in rural, peasant surroundings. Here, again, it has been noted that many Jews and a small but influential number of Levantine Greeks had come from small towns or cities, while most of the Roman Catholic immigrants from Eastern and Southern Europe (and Southern Negroes before their migration to the North) came from rural communities.[2]

As valid as these explanations may be—and we believe they have merit—they overlook one important factor: *the individual's psychological and cultural orientation towards achievement;* by which we mean his psychological need to excel, his desire to enter the competitive race for social status, and his initial possession of or willingness to adopt the high valuation placed upon personal achievement and success which foreign observers from Tocqueville to Laski have considered an important factor in the remarkable mobility of individuals in American society.

Three components of this achievement orientation are particularly relevant for any study of social mobility. The first is a psychological factor,

---

[2] Cf. N. Glazer, "The American Jew and the Attainment of Middle-Class Rank: Some Trends and Explanations," in M. Sklare, editor, *The Jews: Social Patterns of an American Group,* Glencoe, Ill.: Free Press, 1958; W. L. Warner and L. Srole, *op. cit.;* T. Burgess, *Greeks in America,* Boston: Sherman, French, 1913; T. Saloutos, "The Greeks in the U. S.," *The South Atlantic Quarterly,* 4 (January, 1945), pp. 69–82; T. Kalijarvi, "French-Canadians in the United States," *Annals, American Academy of Political and Social Science* (September, 1942); F. L. Strodtbeck, "Family Interactions, Values and Achievement," in D. McClelland, *et al., op. cit.;* G. Myrdal, *An American Dilemma,* New York: Harper, 1944.

achievement motivation, which provides the internal impetus to excel in situations involving standards of excellence. The second and third components are cultural factors, one consisting of certain *value orientations* which implement achievement-motivated behavior, the other of culturally influenced *educational-vocational aspiration levels*. All three factors may affect status achievement; one moving the individual to excel, the others organizing and directing his behavior towards high status goals. This motive-value-aspiration complex has been called the *Achievement Syndrome*.[3]

It is the basic hypothesis of this study that many racial and ethnic groups were not, and are not now, alike in their orientation toward achievement, particularly as it is expressed in the striving for status through social mobility, and that this difference in orientation has been an important factor contributing to the dissimilarities in their social mobility rates. Specifically, this paper examines the achievement motivation, values, and aspirations of members of six racial and ethnic groups. Four of these are "new immigration" ethnic groups with similar periods of residence in this country who faced approximately the same economic circumstances upon arrival: the French-Canadians, Southern Italians, Greeks, and East European Jews. The fifth is the Negro group in the Northeast, the section's largest "racial" division. The last, and in some ways the most heterogeneous, is the native-born white Protestant group. Contributing to the fact that these six groups have not been equally mobile, we suggest, are differences in the three components of the achievement syndrome: their incidence is highest among Jews, Greeks, and white Protestants, lower among Southern Italians and French-Canadians, and lowest among Negroes.

RESEARCH PROCEDURE

The data were collected from a purposive sample of 954 subjects residing in 62 communities in four Northeastern states: 51 in Connecticut, seven in New York, three in New Jersey, and one in Massachusetts. The subjects are 427 pairs of mothers and their sons; 62 pairs are French-Canadians, 74 are Italians, 47 are Greeks, 57 are Jews, 65 are Negroes, and 122 are white Protestants. Most subjects were located through the aid of local religious, ethnic, or service organizations, or through their residence in neighborhoods believed to be occupied by certain groups. The subject's group membership was determined ultimately by asking the mothers in personal interviews to designate their religion and land of national origin. The interviewers, all of whom were upper-classmen enrolled in two sociology classes, were instructed to draw respondents from various social

[3] B. C. Rosen, "The Achievement Syndrome: A Psychocultural Dimension of Social Stratification," *The American Sociological Review*, 21 (April, 1956), pp. 203–211.

strata.[4] The respondent's social class position was determined by a modified version of Hollingshead's Index of Social Position, which uses occupation and education of the main wage-earner, usually the father, as the principal criteria of status. Respondents were classified according to this index into one of five social classes, from the highest status group (Class I) to the lowest (Class V).[5] Most of the mothers and all of the sons are native-born, the sons ranging in age from eight to 14 years (the mean age is about 11 years). There are no significant age differences between the various groups.

Two research instruments were a projective test to measure achievement motivation and a personal interview to obtain information on achievement value orientations and related phenomena. Achievement motivation has been defined by McClelland and his associates as a redintegration of affect aroused by cues in situations involving standards of excellence. Such standards usually are imparted to the individual by his parents, who impart the understanding that they expect him to perform well in relation to these standards of excellence, rewarding him for successful endeavor and punishing him for failure. In time he comes to have similar expectations of himself when exposed to situations involving standards of excellence and re-experiences the affect associated with his earlier efforts to meet these standards. The behavior of people with high achievement motivation is characterized by persistent striving and general competitiveness.

Using a Thematic Apperception Test, McClelland and his associates have developed a method of measuring the achievement motive that involves identifying and counting the frequency with which imagery about evaluated performance in competition with a standard of excellence appears in the thoughts of a person when he tells a brief story under time pressure. This imagery now can be identified objectively and reliably. The test assumes that the more the individual shows indications of connections between evaluated performance and affect in his fantasy, the greater the degree to which achievement motivation is part of his personality.[6] This projective test, which involves showing the subject four ambiguous pictures and asking him to tell a story about each, was given privately and individually to the sons in their homes. Their imaginative responses to the pictures were scored by two judges; the Pearson product moment correlation between the two scorings was .86, an estimate of reliability similar to those reported in earlier studies using this measure.

Following the boys' testing, their mothers were interviewed privately.

[4] The interviewers were trained by the writer; efforts were made to control for interviewer biases. It should be remembered that the sample is not random at any point in the selection process. Hence, the reader is cautioned to regard the data presented here as tentative and suggestive.

[5] A. B. Hollingshead and F. C. Redlich, "Social Stratification and Psychiatric Disorders," *American Sociological Review*, 18 (April, 1953), pp. 163–169.

[6] D. C. McClelland, J. Atkinson, R. Clark, and E. Lowell, *The Achievement Motive*, New York: Appleton-Century-Crofts, 1953.

The interview guide included several standardized questions designed to indicate the mother's achievement value orientations, her educational and vocational aspirations for her son, and the degree to which she had trained him to be independent.

FINDINGS AND INTERPRETATION

ACHIEVEMENT MOTIVATION

Empirical studies have shown that achievement motivation is generated by (at least) two kinds of socialization practices: (1) *achievement training*, in which the parents, by imposing standards of excellence upon tasks, by setting high goals for their child, and by indicating their high evaluation of his competence to do a task well, communicate to him that they expect evidences of high achievement; (2) *independence training*, in which the parents indicate to the child that they expect him to be self-reliant and, at the same time, grant him relative autonomy in decision-making situations where he is given both freedom of action and responsibility for success or failure. Essentially, achievement training is concerned with getting the child to *do things well*, while independence training seeks to teach him to do things *on his own*. Although both kinds often occur together and each contributes to the development of achievement motivation, achievement training is the more important of the two.[7]

Two bodies of information—ethnographic studies of the "old world" or non-American culture and recent empirical investigations of the training practices used by Americans of various ethnic backgrounds—strongly indicate that the six groups examined here, in the past and to some extent today, differ with respect to the degree to which their members typically emphasize achievement and independence training. Ethnic differences in these matters were first studied by McClelland, who noted that the linkage between independence training and achievement motivation established by recent empirical studies suggests an interesting parallel with Weber's classic description of the characterological consequences of the Protestant Reformation. Weber reasoned, first, concerning salvation, that an important aspect of the Protestant theological position was the shift from reliance on an institution (the Church) to a greater reliance upon self; it seemed reasonable to assume that Protestant parents who prepared their children for increased self-reliance in religious matters would also tend to stress the necessity for the child to be self-reliant in other aspects of his life. Secondly,

[7] M. Winterbottom, "The Relation of Need for Achievement to Learning Experiences in Independence and Mastery," in J. Atkinson, editor, *Motives in Fantasy, Action and Society*, Princeton: Van Nostrand, 1958; B. C. Rosen, "The Psychosocial Origins of Achievement Motivation," mimeographed progress report to the National Institute of Mental Health, 1957.

Weber's description of the personality types produced by the Reformation is strikingly similar to the picture of the person with high achievement motivation; for example, the hard-working, thrifty Protestant working girl, the Protestant entrepreneur who "gets nothing out of his wealth for himself except the irrational sense of having done his job well."[8]

The hypothesis deduced from these observations was put to the test by McClelland, who questioned white Protestant, Irish-Catholic, Italian-Catholic, and Jewish mothers about their independence training practices. He found that Protestants and Jews favored earlier independence training than Irish and Italian Catholics.[9] These findings are supported and enlarged upon by data derived from questioning the 427 mothers in this study about their training practices. The mothers were asked, "At what age do you expect your son to do the following things?" and to note the appropriate items from the following list (taken from the Winterbottom index of training in independence and mastery):[10]

1. To be willing to try things on his own without depending on his mother for help.
2. To be active and energetic in climbing, jumping, and sports.
3. To try hard things for himself without asking for help.
4. To be able to lead other children and assert himself in children's groups.
5. To make his own friends among children of his own age.
6. To do well in school on his own.
7. To have interests and hobbies of his own. To be able to entertain himself.
8. To do well in competition with other children. To try hard to come out on top in games and sports.
9. To make decisions like choosing his own clothes or deciding to spend his money by himself.

An index of independence training was derived by summing the ages for each item and taking the mean figure. The data in Table 1 show that

[8] D. C. McClelland, "Some Social Consequences of Achievement Motivation," in M. R. Jones, editor, *Nebraska Symposium on Motivation, 1955*, Lincoln: University of Nebraska Press, 1955.

[9] D. C. McClelland, A. Rindlisbacher, and R. C. deCharms, "Religious and Other Sources of Parental Attitudes Towards Independence Training," in D. C. McClelland, editor, *Studies in Motivation*, New York: Appleton-Century-Crofts, 1955.

[10] Winterbottom, *op. cit.* Though primarily a measure of independence training, two items in this index—items 6 and 8—are considered measures of mastery training, a concept akin to our notion of achievement training. The failure to disentangle independence training from mastery (achievement) training has been responsible for some confusion in earlier studies of the origins of achievement motivation. (For an analysis of this confusion, see Rosen, "The Psychosocial Origins of Achievement Motivation," *op. cit.*) The two components were kept in the index in order to maintain comparability between this study and the earlier work on ethnic groups by McClelland reported above.

the Jews expect earliest evidence of self-reliance from their children (mean age 6.83 years), followed by the Protestants (6.87), Negroes (7.23), Greeks (7.67), French-Canadians (7.99), and Italians (8.03). Both primary sources of variation—ethnicity and social class—are significant at the .01 level.

Table 1: *Mean Age of Independence Training by Ethnicity and Social Class*

	SOCIAL CLASS *				
Ethnicity	I-II-III	IV	V	$\bar{x}$	N
French-Canadian	8.00	7.69	8.08	7.99	62
Italian	6.79	7.89	8.47	8.03	74
Greek	6.33	8.14	7.52	7.67	47
Jew	6.37	7.29	6.90	6.83	57
Negro	6.64	6.98	7.39	7.23	65
Protestant	5.82	7.44	7.03	6.87	122
$\bar{x}$	6.31	7.64	7.59		

Ethnicity: $F = 8.55 \quad P < .01$
Social Class: $F = 21.48 \quad P < .001$
Ethnicity $\times$ Class: $F = 6.25 \quad P < .01$

* The three-class breakdown was used in an earlier phase of the analysis. An examination of the means of cells using a four-class breakdown revealed no change in pattern and did not warrant new computations.

Data on the relative emphasis which racial and ethnic groups place upon achievement *training* (that is, imposing standards of excellence upon tasks, setting high goals for the child to achieve, and communicating to him a feeling that his parents evaluate highly his task-competence) are much more difficult to obtain. Achievement training as such, in fact, is rarely treated in studies of ethnic socialization practices. Hence, inferences about achievement training were drawn primarily from ethnographic and historical materials, which are usually more informative about achievement as such than about relevant socialization practices.

The groups about which the most is known concerning achievement training, perhaps, are the Protestants, the Jews, and, to a lesser extent, the Greeks. These groups traditionally have stressed excellence and achievement. In the case of the Protestants, this tradition can be located in the Puritan Ethic with its concept of work as a "calling" and the exhortation that a job be done well. Of course, not all Protestants would be equally comfortable with this tradition; it is much more applicable, for example, to Presbyterians and Quakers than to Methodists and Baptists. Nonetheless, the generally longer residence of Protestants in this country makes it probable that they would tend to share the American belief that children should be encouraged to develop their talents and to set high goals, possibly a bit beyond their reach. The observation that Jews stress achievement training is commonplace. Zyborowski and Herzog note the strong tendency among *shtetyl* Jews to expect and to reward evidences of achievement even among very young children. The image of the Jewish mother as eager for her son to excel in competition and to set ever higher goals for himself is a familiar one in the literature of Jewish family life.[11] Careful attention to standards of excellence in the Greek home is stressed by the parents: children know that a task which is shabbily performed will have to be re-done. In this country, the Greek is exhorted to be "a credit to his group." Failure to meet group norms is quickly perceived and where possible punished; while achievement receives the approbation of the entire Greek community.

Among the Southern Italians (the overwhelming majority of American-Italians are of Southern Italian extraction), French-Canadians, and Negroes the tradition seems to be quite different. More often than not they came from agrarian societies or regions in which opportunities for achievement were strictly curtailed by the social structure and where habits of resignation and fatalism in the face of social and environmental frustrations were psychologically functional. Under such conditions children were not typically exhorted to be achievers or urged to set their sights very high. Of course, children were expected to perform tasks, as they are in most societies, but such tasks were usually farm or self-caretaking chores, from which the notion of competition with standards of excellence is not excluded, but is not ordinarily stressed. As for communicating to the child a sense of confidence in his competence to do a task well, there is some evidence that in the father-dominant Italian and French-Canadian families, pronounced concern with the child's ability might be perceived as a threat to the father.[12]

On the whole, the data indicate that Protestants, Jews, and Greeks place a greater emphasis on independence and achievement training than Southern Italians and French-Canadians. The data on the Negroes are conflicting: they often train children relatively early in self-reliance, but there is little evidence of much stress upon achievement training. No doubt the socialization practices of these groups have been modified somewhat by the acculturating influences of American society since their arrival in the

---

[11] M. Zborowski and E. Herzog, *Life Is With People*, New York: International University Press, 1952.

[12] P. H. Williams, *South Italian Folkways in Europe and America*, New Haven: Yale University Press, 1938; H. Miner, *St. Dennis: A French-Canadian Parish*, Chicago: University of Chicago Press, 1939.

Northeast.[13] But ethnic cultures tend to survive even in the face of strong obliterating forces, and we believe that earlier differences between groups persist—a position supported by the present data on self-reliance training. Hence, the hypothesis that the racial and ethnic groups considered here differ with respect to achievement motivation. We predicted that, on the average, achievement motivation scores would be highest among the Jews, Greeks, and white Protestants, lower among the Italians and French-Canadians, and lowest among the Negroes. Table 2 shows that the data support these predictions, indicated by the following mean scores: Greeks 10.80, Jews 10.53, Protestants 10.11, Italians 9.65, French-Canadians 8.82, and Negroes 8.40.

Table 2:   Mean Achievement Motivation Scores by Ethnicity and Social Class

Ethnicity	SOCIAL CLASS					
	I-II	III	IV	V	$\bar{x}$	N
French-Canadian	10.00	10.64	8.78	7.75	8.82	62
Italian	8.86	12.81	7.54	10.20	9.65	74
Greek	9.17	12.13	10.40	8.75	10.80	47
Jew	10.05	10.41	10.94	11.20	10.53	57
Negro	11.36	9.00	8.23	6.72	8.40	65
Protestant	11.71	10.94	9.39	7.31	10.11	122
$\bar{x}$	10.55	11.26	9.01	8.32		

Ethnicity: $F = 1.23$ $P > .05$
Social Class: $F = 5.30$ $P < .005$
Ethnicity $\times$ Class: $F = 1.32$ $P > .05$

A series of "t" tests of significance between means (a one-tail test was used in cases where the direction of the difference had been predicted) was computed. The differences between Greeks, Jews, and Protestants are not statistically significant. The Italian score is significantly lower ($P < .05$) than the score for the Greeks, but not for the Jews and Protestants. The largest differences are between the French-Canadians and Negroes on the one hand and the remaining groups on the other: the French-Canadian mean score is significantly lower ($P < .01$) than those of all other groups

[13] It does not necessarily follow that the impact of American culture has reduced the differences between groups. An argument can be made that for some groups life in America has accentuated differences by allowing certain characteristics of the groups to develop. We have in mind particularly the Greeks and Jews whose need to excel could find little avenue for expression through status striving in Europe.

except Italians and Negroes; the mean score for all Negroes is significantly lower (P < .01) than the scores for all other groups except French-Canadians. A "Roman Catholic" score was obtained by combining Italian and French-Canadian scores, and scores for all non-Negro groups were combined to form a "White" score. The differences between group means were tested for significance (by a one-tail "t" test) and it was found that the "Catholic" score is significantly lower than the scores for Protestants, Greek Orthodox, and Jews (P < .01). The Negro mean score is significantly lower than the combined score of all white groups (P < .002).

A comparison of ethnic-racial differences does not tell the whole story. There are also significant differences between the social classes. In fact, analysis of Table 2 indicates that social class accounts for more of the variance than ethnicity: the F ratio for ethnicity is 1.23 (P > .05), for class 5.30 (P < .005). The small number of cases in Classes I and II greatly increases the within-group variance; when these two classes are combined with Class III the variance is decreased and the F ratio for ethnicity increases sharply to 2.13 (P < .06). Social class, however, remains more significantly related to achievement motivation than ethnicity. This finding is especially important in this study since the proportion of subjects in each class varies for the ethnic groups. There are relatively more middle class than lower class subjects among the Jews, Greeks, and Protestants than among Italians, French-Canadians, and Negroes. To control for social class it was necessary to examine the differences between cells as well as between columns and rows. A series of "t" tests of differences between the means of cells revealed that for the most part the earlier pattern established for total ethnic means persists, although in some instances the differences between groups are decreased, in others increased, and in a few cases the direction of the differences is reversed. Neither ethnicity nor social class alone is sufficient to predict an individual's score; both appear to contribute something to the variance between groups, but on the whole social class is a better predictor than ethnicity. Generally, a high status person from an ethnic group with a low mean achievement motivation score is more likely to have a high score than a low status person from a group with a high mean score. Thus, the mean score for Class I-II Negroes is higher than the score for Class IV-V white Protestants: the score for the former is 11.36, for the latter, 7.31; a "t" test revealed that the difference between these two means is significant at the .05 level, using a two-tail test. This relatively high score for Class I-II Negroes, the third highest for any cell in the table, indicates, perhaps, the strong motivation necessary for a Negro to achieve middle class status in a hostile environment. Generally, the scores for each group decrease as the class level declines, except for the Jews whose scores are inversely related to social status—a finding for which we can offer no explanation.

ACHIEVEMENT VALUE ORIENTATIONS

Achievement motivation is one part of the achievement syndrome; an equally important component is the achievement value orientation. Value orientations are defined as meaningful and affectively charged modes of organizing behavior—principles that guide human conduct. They establish criteria which influence the individual's preference and goals. Achievement values and achievement motivation, while related, represent genuinely different components of the achievement syndrome, not only conceptually but also in their origins and, as we have shown elsewhere, in their social correlates.[14] Value orientations, because of their conceptual content, are probably acquired in that stage of the child's cultural training when verbal communication of a fairly complex nature is possible. Achievement motivation or the need to excel, on the other hand, has its origins in parent-child interaction beginning early in the child's life when many of these relations are likely to be emotional and unverbalized. Analytically, then, the learning of achievement oriented values can be independent of the acquisition of the achievement motive, although empirically they often occur together.

Achievement values affect social mobility in that they focus the individual's attention on status improvement and help to shape his behavior so that achievement motivation can be translated into successful action. The achievement motive by itself is not a sufficient condition of social mobility: it provides internal impetus to excel, but it does not impel the individual to take the steps necessary for status achievement. Such steps in our society involve, among other things, a preparedness to plan, work hard, make sacrifices, and be physically mobile. Whether or not the individual will understand their importance and accept them will depend in part upon his values.

Three sets of values (a modification of Kluckhohn's scheme[15]) were identified as elements of the achievement syndrome,[16] as follows:

> 1. *Activistic-Passivistic Orientation* concerns the extent to which the culture of a group encourages the individual to believe in the possibility of his manipulating the physical and social environment to his advantage. An activistic culture encourages the individual to believe that it is both possible and necessary for him to improve his status, whereas a passivistic culture promotes the acceptance of the notion that individual efforts to achieve mobility are relatively futile.

[14] Rosen, "The Achievement Syndrome," *op. cit.*, pp. 208–210.
[15] F. Kluckhohn, "Dominant and Substitute Profiles of Cultural Orientations," *Social Forces*, 28 (May, 1950), pp. 376–393.
[16] For the most part, the value orientations examined in this study, their description, and the items used to index them, are identical with those which appear in Rosen, "The Achievement Syndrome," *op. cit.*

2. *Individualistic-Collectivistic Orientation* refers to the extent to which the individual is expected to subordinate his needs to the group. This study is specifically concerned with the degree to which the society expects the individual to maintain close physical proximity to his family of orientation, even at the risk of limiting vocational opportunities; and the degree to which the society emphasizes group incentives rather than personal rewards. The collectivistic society places a greater stress than the individualistic on group ties and group incentives.

3. *Present-Future Orientation* concerns the society's attitude toward time and its impact upon behavior. A present oriented society stresses the merit of living in the present, emphasizing immediate gratifications; a future oriented society encourages the belief that planning and present sacrifices are worthwhile, or morally obligatory, in order to insure future gains.

Examination of ethnographic and historical materials on the cultures of the six ethnic groups revealed important differences in value orientation—differences antedating their arrival in the Northeast. The cultures of white Protestants, Jews, and Greeks stand out as considerably more individualistic, activistic, and future-oriented than those of the Southern Italians, French-Canadians, and Negroes. Several forces—religious, economic, and national—seem to have long influenced the Protestants in this direction, including, first, the Puritan Ethic with its stress upon individualism and work; then the impact of the liberal economic ethic (Weber's "Spirit of Capitalism") emphasizing competitive activity and achievement; and finally, the challenge of the frontier, with its consequent growth of a national feeling of optimism and manifest destiny. All of these factors tended very early to create a highly activistic, individualistic, future-oriented culture—the picture of American culture held by foreign observers since Tocqueville.[17]

The Jews, who for centuries had lived in more or less hostile environments, have learned that it is not only possible to manipulate their environment to insure survival but even to prosper in it. Jewish tradition stresses the possibility of the individual rationally mastering his world. Man is not helpless against the forces of nature or of his fellow man; God will provide, but only if man does his share. Like Protestantism, Judaism is an intensely individualistic religion and the Jews an intensely individualistic people. While the family was close knit, it was the entire *shtetyl* which was regarded as the inclusive social unit; and in neither case was loyalty to the group considered threatened by physical mobility. The Jews typically have

[17] For a history of the development of the liberal economic ethic and its manifestation on the American scene, see J. H. Randall, *The Making of the Modern Mind*, Boston: Houghton Mifflin, 1926; J. K. Galbraith, *The Affluent Society*, Boston: Houghton Mifflin, 1958.

urged their children to leave home if in so doing they faced better opportunities. *Shtetyl* society, from which the vast majority of American Jewry
is descended, vigorously stressed the importance of planning and working
for the future. A *shtetyl* cultural tradition was that parents save for many
years, often at great sacrifice to themselves, in order to improve their son's
vocational opportunities or to provide a daughter with a dowry.[18]

In some respects, Greek and Jewish cultures were strikingly similar at
the turn of the century. The ethos of the town and city permeated the
Greek more than most other Mediterranean cultures, although only a
small proportion of the population was engaged in trade—with the important exception of the Levantine Greeks, who were largely merchants. The
image of the Greek in the Eastern Mediterranean area was that of an
individualistic, foresighted, competitive trader. Early observers of the Greek
in America were impressed by his activistic, future-oriented behavior. E. A.
Ross, a rather unfriendly observer, wrote as early as 1914 that "the saving,
commercial Greek climbs. From curb to stand, from stand to store, from
little store to big store, and from there to branch stores in other cities—
such are the stages in his upward path."[19]

Though separated by thousands of miles, French-Canadian and Southern
Italian cultures were similar in many respects. Both were primarily peasant
cultures, strongly influenced by the Roman Catholic Church. Neither could
be described as activistic, individualistic, or future-oriented. In Southern
Italian society the closed-class system and grinding poverty fostered a tradition of resignation—a belief that the individual had little control over his
life situation and a stress upon the role of fate (*Destino*) in determining
success. The living conditions of French-Canadians, although less harsh,
were sufficiently severe to sharply limit the individual's sense of mastery
over his situation. In neither group was there a strong feeling that the
individual could drastically improve his lot; for both groups the future was
essentially unpredictable, even capricious. Extended family ties were very
strong in both groups: there is the Southern Italian saying, "the family
against all others"; the French-Canadian farmer in need of help will
travel many miles to hire a kinsman rather than an otherwise convenient
neighbor.[20]

Ironically, although Negroes are usually Protestant (however, not ordinarily of the Calvinistic type) and have been exposed to the liberal economic ethic longer than most of the other groups considered here, their

---

[18] Zyborowski and Herzog, *op. cit.*; B. C. Rosen, "Cultural Factors in Achievement,"
mimeographed, 1952; Strodtbeck, "Family Interactions, Values and Achievement,"
op. cit.

[19] Quoted in Saloutos, *op. cit.*, p. 71. The writer is indebted to J. Gregoropoulos, a
native of Athens, for many helpful comments on European and American Greek
communities.

[20] Miner, *op. cit.* See also Williams, *op. cit.*; Strodtbeck, "Family Interactions, Values
and Achievement," *op. cit.*

culture, it seems, is least likely to accent achievement values. The Negro's history as a slave and depressed farm worker, and the sharp discrepancy between his experiences and the American Creed, would appear to work against the internalization of the achievement values of the dominant white group. Typically, the Negro life-situation does not encourage the belief that one can manipulate his environment or the conviction that one can improve his condition very much by planning and hard work.[21] Generally, family ties have not been strong among Negroes, although traditionally the mother was an especially important figure and ties between her and her children, particularly sons, may still be very strong.[22]

Another and more direct way of studying ethnic values is to talk with group members themselves; thus our personal interviews with the mothers. (Their sons in many cases were too young to give meaningful answers.) They were asked whether they agreed or disagreed with the following statements, listed here under the appropriate value orientation categories.

(1) *Activistic-Passivistic Orientation.*
   Item 1. "All a man should want out of life in the way of a career is a secure, not too difficult job, with enough pay to afford a nice car and eventually a home of his own."
   Item 2. "When a man is born the success he is going to have is already in the cards, so he might just as well accept it and not fight against it."
   Item 3. "The secret of happiness is not expecting too much out of life and being content with what comes your way."

(2) *Individualistic-Collectivistic Orientation.*
   Item 4. "Nothing is worth the sacrifice of moving away from one's parents."
   Item 5. "The best kind of job to have is one where you are part of an organization all working together even if you don't get individual credit." [23]

(3) *Present-Future Orientation.*
   Item 6. "Planning only makes a person unhappy since your plans hardly ever work out anyway."

[21] We recognize that to infer a group's values from its life-situation and then to use these values to explain an aspect of that situation is to reason circularly. However, the temporal sequence between values and mobility has a chicken-egg quality which is difficult to avoid because values and life-situation interact. To some extent, knowledge of ethnic cultures prior to their arrival in the United States helps to establish the priority of values to mobility. In the case of the Negroes, however, relatively little is known about their several cultures before their transportation to this country.

[22] E. F. Frazier, *The Negro Family in the United States*, Chicago: University of Chicago Press, 1939; see also Frazier's *The Negro in the United States*, New York: Macmillan, 1957, especially Chapters 13 and 24.

[23] Of course, if Whyte is correct about the growth of the organization man and the importance of the "social ethic," agreement with this statement may indicate an asset rather than a handicap to social mobility. See W. H. Whyte, Jr., *The Organization Man*, New York: Simon and Schuster, 1957.

Item 7. "Nowadays with world conditions the way they are the wise person lives for today and lets tomorrow take care of itself."

Responses indicating an activistic, future-oriented, individualistic point of view (the answer "disagree" to these items) reflect values, we believe, most likely to facilitate achievement and social mobility. These items were used to form a value index, and a score was derived for each subject by giving a point for each achievement-oriented response. In examining the mothers' scores two assumptions were made: (1) that they tend to transmit their values to their sons, and (2) that the present differences between groups are indicative of at least equal, and perhaps even greater, differences in the past.

The ethnographic and historical materials led us to expect higher value scores for Jews, white Protestants, and Greeks than for Italians, French-Canadians, and Negroes. In large measure, these expectations were confirmed. Table 3 shows that Jews have the highest mean score (5.54), followed closely by Protestants (5.16), Greeks (5.08), and Negroes (surprisingly) (5.03). The Italians' score (4.17) is almost a point lower, and the French-Canadian score (3.68) is the lowest for any group. The scores for Jews, Protestants, and Greeks do not significantly differ when the two-tail test is used (we were not able to predict the direction of the differences), but they are all significantly higher than the scores for Italians and French-Canadians. When Italian and French-Canadian scores are combined to form a "Roman Catholic" score, the latter is significantly lower ($P < .001$) than the scores for Jews, Protestants, or Greeks.

The prediction for the Negroes proved to be entirely wrong. Their mean score (5.03) is significantly higher ($P < .001$) than the scores for Italians

Table 3: Mean Value Scores by Ethnicity and Social Class

	SOCIAL CLASS					
Ethnicity	I-II	III	IV	V	$\bar{x}$	N
French-Canadian	4.00	4.21	4.60	2.46	3.68	62
Italian	5.86	4.00	3.96	3.40	4.17	74
Greek	6.33	5.52	4.80	3.25	5.08	47
Jew	5.94	5.47	5.41	4.80	5.54	57
Negro	6.00	5.00	4.90	4.67	5.03	65
Protestant	5.86	5.50	4.97	3.54	5.16	122
$\bar{x}$	5.91	5.08	4.78	3.49		

Ethnicity: $F = 11.62$ $P < .001$
Social Class: $F = 33.80$ $P < .001$
Ethnicity $\times$ Class: $F = 2.43$ $P < .01$

and French-Canadians. Nor is the Negro score significantly different from those for Protestants and Greeks, although it is significantly lower than the Jewish score ($P < .05$) when the one-tail test is used. The skeptic may regard the relatively high Negro value score as merely lip-service to the liberal economic ethic, but it may in fact reflect, and to some extent be responsible for, the economic gains of Negroes in recent years.[24]

Social class also is significantly related to achievement values and accounts for more of the variance than ethnicity: the F ratio for class is 33.80 ($P < .001$) for ethnicity 11.62 ($P < .001$). Almost without exception, the mean score for each ethnic group is reduced with each decline in status. *Social class, however, does not wash out the differences between ethnic groups.* A series of "t" tests between cells across each social class reveals that Greek, Jewish, and Protestant scores remain significantly higher than Italian and French-Canadian scores. Negro scores also remain among the highest across each social class. Ethnicity and social class interact and each contributes something to the differences between groups: the individual with high social status who also belongs to an ethnic group which stresses achievement values is far more likely to have a high value score than an individual with low status and membership in a group in which achievement is not emphasized. For example, the Class I-II Greek score is 6.33 as compared with the Class V French-Canadian score of 2.46—the difference between them is significant at the .001 level. On the other hand, the score for Class I-II Italians, an ethnic group in which achievement values are not stressed, is 5.86 as compared with 3.25 for Class V Greeks—the difference between them is significant at the .001 level. Neither variable, then, is sufficient to predict an individual's score; and for some groups social class seems to be the more significant factor, for others ethnicity appears to play the greater role. Thus, for Jews and Negroes the mean scores remain relatively high for each social class; in fact, Class V Jews and Negroes have larger mean scores than many French-Canadians and Italians of higher social status.

ASPIRATION LEVELS

Achievement motivation and values influence social mobility by affecting the individual's need to excel and his willingness to plan and work hard. But they do not determine the areas in which such excellence and effort take place. Achievement motivation and values can be expressed, as they often are, through many kinds of behavior that are not conducive to social mobility in our society, for example, deviant, recreational, or religious behavior. Unless the individual aims for high vocational goals and prepares

---

[24] The relatively high value score for Negroes supports our contention that achievement motivation and achievement values are genuinely different components of the achievement syndrome. It will be remembered that the Negroes had the lowest mean motivation score. If achievement motivation and values are conceptually and empirically identical, there should be no difference between the two sets of scores.

himself appropriately, his achievement motivation and values will not pull him up the social ladder. Increasingly, lengthy formal education, often including college and post-graduate study, is needed for movement into prestigeful and lucrative jobs. An educational aspiration level which precludes college training may seriously affect the individual's chances for social mobility.

Their cultures, even before the arrival of the ethnic groups in the Northeast, were markedly different in orientation towards education.[25] The Protestants' stress upon formal education, if only as a means of furthering one's career, is well known. Traditionally, Jews have placed a very high value on educational and intellectual attainment; learning in the *shtetyl* society gave the individual prestige, authority, a chance for a better marriage. Contrariwise, for Southern Italians, school was an upper class institution, not an avenue for social advancement for their children, booklearning was remote from everyday experience, and intellectualism often regarded with distrust. French-Canadians, although not hostile to education and learning, were disinclined to educate their sons beyond the elementary level. Daughters needed more education as preparation for jobs in the event they did not marry, but sons were destined to be farmers or factory workers, in the parents' view, with the exception at times of one son who would be encouraged to become a priest. Greeks—generally no better educated than Italians or French-Canadians—on the whole were much more favorably disposed towards learning, in large part because of their intense nationalistic identification with the cultural glories of ancient Greece.[26] This identification was strengthened by the relatively hostile reception Greeks met on their arrival in this country, and is in part responsible for the rapid development of private schools supported by the Greek community and devoted to the teaching of Greek culture—an interesting parallel to the Hebrew School among American Jews. Finally, Negroes, who might be expected to share the prevalent American emphasis upon education, face the painfully apparent fact that positions open to educated Negroes are scarce. This fact means that most Negroes, in all likelihood, do not consider high educational aspirations realistic. And the heavy drop-out in high school suggests that the curtailment of educational aspirations begins very early.

To test whether and to what degree these differences between groups persist, the mothers were asked: "How far do you *intend* for your son to

---

[25] For a comparison of ethnic group education and vocational aspirations, see R. M. Williams, Jr., *American Society*, New York: Knopf, 1951, Chapter 8; F. J. Woods, *Cultural Values of American Ethnic Groups*, New York: Harper, 1956, Chapters 5 and 7.

[26] Attempts by Mussolini to create a similar bond between his people and ancient Rome, or even the more recent Renaissance, were unsuccessful. French-Canadians for the most part have long refused to be impressed by the "secular" achievement of European anti-clerical French society.

go to school?" It was hoped that the term *intend* would structure the question so that the reply would indicate, not merely a mother's pious wish, but also an expression of will to do something about her son's schooling. The data show that 96 per cent of the Jewish, 88 per cent of the Protestant, 85 per cent of the Greek, 83 per cent of the Negro (much higher than was anticipated), 64 per cent of the Italian, and 56 per cent of the French-Canadian mothers said that they expected their sons to go to college. The aspirations of Jews, Protestants, Greeks, and Negroes are not significantly different from one another, but they are significantly higher than the aspirations of Italians and French-Canadians ($P < .05$).

Social class, once more, is significantly related to educational aspiration. When class is controlled the differences between ethnic groups are diminished—particularly at the Class I-II-III levels—but they are not erased: Jews, Protestants, Greeks, and Negroes tend to have aspirations similar to one another and higher than those of Italians and French-Canadians for each social class. The differences are greatest at the lower class levels: at Class V, 85 per cent of the Protestants, 80 per cent of the Jews, and 78 per cent of the Negroes intend for their sons to go to college as compared with 63 per cent of the Greeks, 50 per cent of the Italians, and 29 per cent of the French-Canadians.

The individual, to be socially mobile, must aspire to the occupations which society esteems and rewards highly. An individual, strongly motivated to excel and willing to plan and work hard, who sets his heart on being the best barber will probably be less vertically mobile than an equally endowed person who aspires to become the best surgeon. Moreover, the individual who aspires to a high status occupation is likely to expend more energy in competitive striving—and in so doing improve his chances for social mobility—than someone whose occupational choice demands relatively little from him.

Since many of the boys in this study were too young to appraise occupations realistically, we sought to obtain a measure of ethnic group vocational aspiration by questioning the mothers about their aspirations for their sons, once again assuming that they would tend to communicate their views of status levels and their expectations for their sons. Ten occupations were chosen which can be ranked by social status; seven of our ten occupations (marked below by asterisks) were selected from the N.O.R.C. ranking.[27] The occupations, originally presented in alphabetical order, are given here in the order of status: Lawyer*, Druggist, Jewelry Store Owner, Machinist*, Bank Teller, Insurance Agent*, Bookkeeper*,

---

[27] National Opinion Research Center, "Jobs and Occupations: A Popular Evaluation," *Opinion News*, 9 (September 1, 1947). We substituted store salesman for store clerk and bus driver for streetcar motorman. The position of the three occupations which did not appear in the N.O.R.C. survey are ranked according to their similarity to occupations in the survey.

Mail Carrier*, Department Store Salesman*, and Bus Driver*. The mothers were asked: "If things worked out so that your son were in the following occupations, would you be satisfied or dissatisfied?" To obtain aspiration scores for each mother, her responses were treated in three ways:

1. The number of times the mother answered "satisfied" to the ten occupations was summed to give a single score. In effect this meant giving each occupation a weight of one. Since the subject must inevitably select lower status occupations as she increases her number of choices, the higher the summed score, the lower the aspiration level. The basic limitation of this method is that it is impossible to know from the summed score whether the occupations chosen are of low or high status.

2. To correct for this, a second index was derived by assigning weights to the seven occupations taken from the N.O.R.C. study according to their position in the rank order. Thus the highest status position, lawyer, was given a rank weight of 1.0 and the lowest a weight of 6.5 (store salesman and bus driver were tied for last place). Here again, the higher the score, the lower the aspiration level.

3. A third method of weighting the occupations was devised by taking the percentage of the entire sample of mothers who said that they would be satisfied with a particular occupation, and using the reciprocal of each percentage as the weight for that occupation. (The reciprocal was first multiplied by one thousand to eliminate decimals.) The mothers ranked the occupations somewhat differently than the N.O.R.C. ranking (assigning a higher status to bookkeeper and insurance agent and lower status to machinist and mail carrier). The assumption here is that the higher the percentage who answered "satisfied," the higher the status of the occupation. A score for each mother was obtained by summing the reciprocal weights for each occupation chosen. With this method, the highest status occupation is lawyer (score of 11.0), the lowest bus driver (48.0). All ten occupations were used in this index. The higher the subject's score, the lower her aspiration level.

Although these indexes differ somewhat, they provide very similar data on ethnic group vocational aspirations. Table 4 shows the same rank ordering of groups for all three indexes, in descending order as follows: Jews, Greeks, Protestants, Italians, French-Canadians, and Negroes. A series of "t" tests of differences between group mean scores revealed differences and similarities much like those found for achievement motivation. Thus the Jews, Greeks, and Protestants show significantly higher mean scores (that is, they tend to be satisfied with fewer occupations and indicate satisfaction with only the higher status positions) than the Roman Catholic Italians and French-Canadians.[28] The mean score for Jews is significantly higher

[28] Similar Jewish-Italian differences are reported in F. L. Strodtbeck, M. McDonald, and B. C. Rosen, "Evaluation of Occupations: A Reflection of Jewish and Italian Mobility Differences," *American Sociological Review*, 22 (October, 1957), pp. 546–553.

*Table 4:   Mean Scores and Rank Position of Six Ethnic Groups Using Three Indexes of Vocational Aspiration * *

	INDEX OF VOCATIONAL ASPIRATION			
Ethnicity	Number Satisfied	Rank Weight	Reciprocal Weight	N
French-Canadian	6.60(5)	14.43(5)	119.90(5)	62
Italian	5.96(4)	12.66(4)	104.55(4)	74
Greek	4.70(2)	7.78(2)	73.51(2)	47
Jew	3.51(1)	6.02(1)	59.48(1)	57
Negro	6.95(6)	16.18(6)	138.74(6)	65
Protestant	5.28(3)	10.12(3)	88.19(3)	122

* Rank positions are shown by figures in parentheses.

than the scores for Protestants and Greeks, but there are no significant differences between Greeks and Protestants, or between Italians and French-Canadians. The mean score for Negroes is significantly lower than the scores for all other groups except French-Canadians. In examining the aspirations of Negroes it should be remembered that most of these occupations are considered highly desirable by many Negroes, given their severely limited occupational opportunities, so that their aspiration level may appear low only by "white" standards. There are, however, these problems: are the Negro mothers (83 per cent) in earnest in saying that they intend for their sons to go to college? And, if so, how is this to be reconciled with their low vocational aspirations?

Social class, too, is significantly and directly related to vocational aspiration—a familiar finding—*but it is not as significant as ethnicity.* Analysis of variance of data for each of the three indexes reveals that ethnicity accounts for more of the variance than social class. For example, when the number of occupations with which the mother would be satisfied for her son is used as an index of vocational aspiration, the F ratio for ethnicity is 12.41 ($P < .001$) as compared with a ratio of 9.92 for social class ($P < .001$). The same pattern holds for data derived from the other two indexes. Although ethnicity and class interact, each contributing to the differences between groups, the effects of class are more apparent at the middle class (Classes I-II-III) than at the working and lower class (Classes IV-V) levels.

As the question was worded in this study, in one sense it is misleading to speak of the "height" of vocational aspirations. For all groups have "high" aspirations in that most mothers are content to have their sons achieve a high status. The basic difference between groups is in the "floor," so to speak, which they place on their aspirations. For example, at least 80 per cent of the mothers of each ethnic group said that they would be satisfied to have their sons be lawyers, but only two per cent of the Greeks and seven per cent of the Jews were content to have their sons become bus drivers, as compared with 26 per cent of the French-Canadians and 43 per cent of the Negroes. Again, 12 per cent of the Jewish, 22 per cent of the Protestant, and 29 per cent of the Greek mothers said they would be satisfied to have their sons become department store salesmen, as compared with 48 per cent of the Italians, 51 per cent of the Negro, and 52 per cent of the French-Canadian mothers.

Summary

This paper examines differences in motivation, values, and aspirations of six racial and ethnic groups which may explain in part their dissimilar social mobility rates. Analysis of ethnographic and attitudinal and personality data suggests that these groups differed, and to some extent still differ, in their orientation toward achievement. The data show that the groups place different emphases upon independence and achievement training in the rearing of children. As a consequence, achievement motivation is more characteristic of Greeks, Jews, and white Protestants than of Italians, French-Canadians, and Negroes. The data also indicate that Jews, Greeks, and Protestants are more likely to possess achievement values and higher educational and vocational aspirations than Italians and French-Canadians. The values and educational aspirations of the Negroes are higher than expected, being comparable to those of Jews, Greeks, and white Protestants, and higher than those of the Italians and French-Canadians. Vocational aspirations of Negroes, however, are the lowest of any group in the sample. Social class and ethnicity interact in influencing motivation, values, and aspirations; neither can predict an individual's score. Ethnic differences persist when social class is controlled, but some of the differences between ethnic groups in motivations, values, and aspirations are probably also a function of their class composition.

14. Group Involvement, Religious Orientations, and Economic Behavior

GERHARD LENSKI

Strictly speaking, the next selection does not deal with ethnic patterns as much as with religious and racial ones, but it appears here because it is so relevant to a classic area of sociological interest. Max Weber's The Protestant Ethic and the Spirit of Capitalism *has been one of the most influential works in all of sociology. Its thesis is that as certain beliefs of ascetic Protestantism underwent secularization in the seventeenth and eighteenth centuries, such convictions came to favor the growth and development of capitalism. Weber did not doubt that existing economic systems influenced men's religious and moral perspectives, but he also wanted to demonstrate that the causal association could run in either direction. Here, Lenski examines some of Weber's assumptions, as well as those of some of his critics, in the light of data gathered in midtwentieth-century Detroit. Lenski's findings lend support to Weber's thesis, but sharpen it, too. Social-class position as well as religion affects the economic outlooks of members of different religious groups. Then, these different economic outlooks, together with differences in the ways Detroit Catholics and Protestants define their child-rearing tasks (not reported in the present selection), help to explain why the Protestants have had higher rates of upward mobility.*

Group Involvement and Economic Behavior

ASSOCIATIONAL INVOLVEMENT

One question is immediately raised by our findings concerning differences in economic thought and action among the several socio-religious groups. Have *the churches* contributed to these differences, or are they the result of other influences? Are the churches as irrelevant and uninfluential in the economic realm as many people think, or do they play a role in shaping and molding economic attitudes, values, beliefs, and behavior?

SOURCE: Gerhard Lenski, *The Religious Factor* (New York: Doubleday and Co., Inc., 1961), pp. 115–33 (selected footnotes and tables omitted). Copyright © 1961 by Gerhard Lenski. Reprinted by permission of Doubleday and Company, Inc.

Gerhard Lenski is Professor of Sociology at the University of North Carolina. Well known for his work on status crystallization, he is also a co-author of *Principles of Sociology*.

154

This is not an easy question to answer, but as a first step we shall compare those members of each of the groups who were *more* actively involved in their church with others in the same group who were *less* actively involved.[1] If the churches do contribute to these differences between socioreligious groups, we would expect that the greater the degree to which white Protestants are involved in their churches, the more likely they will be to display the individualistic, competitive, rationalistic patterns of thought and action identified with the Protestant Ethic and with the middle class. Similarly, we would expect that the more Catholics and Negro Protestants are involved in their churches, the more they will display the collectivistic, security-oriented, anti-entrepreneurial working-class patterns of thought and action. If, however, the churches are irrelevant and have no effect on economic behavior and attitudes, we would expect to find no noticeable differences between those members of a given group who attend their church regularly, and those who do not, when other relevant factors are controlled.

Economic Success and Associational Involvement In examining the relationship between involvement in the churches and vertical mobility, we found that upwardly mobile men (i.e., middle-class sons of working-class or farmer fathers) were more likely to be regular church attenders than non-mobile men, in both the middle and working classes. Among white Protestants 38 per cent of the upwardly mobile men (N=19) were regular church attenders compared with 31 per cent of the non-mobile middle-class men (N=16) and 16 per cent of the non-mobile working-class men (N=62). Among Catholics 78 per cent of the upwardly mobile (N=27), 76 per cent of the non-mobile middle class (N=17), and 58 per cent of the non-mobile working class (N=52) reported regular church attendance.

While these figures suggest that church attendance may be conducive to upward mobility we cannot ignore the possibility that active involvement in the churches may be a *consequence*, rather than a *cause*, of vertical mobility. The high level of involvement among the upwardly mobile may simply represent conformity, or even overconformity, to middle-class norms.

In an effort to resolve this problem, we examined the relationship between vertical mobility and the religious situation in the home in which these respondents were raised. This was possible since we had gathered data on the religious commitments of respondents' parents (Q. 36 and 38) as well as on the respondents themselves.

When we compared white Protestants raised in working-class families in which both parents were highly religious with those raised in working-class families in which this was not true, we found a notable difference in the

---

[1] Unfortunately, owing to the small number of Jewish respondents, such comparisons were not possible in this group.

percentage who had risen to the middle class.[2] Among the 43 children of devout working-class or farm parents, 51 per cent had risen to the ranks of the middle class. By contrast, only 31 per cent of the 102 children of other working-class and farm parents had been as successful.

When we divided these respondents by sex and by class background (working class vs. farm), the same pattern emerged in *all four* subsamples. The pattern was more pronounced among women than among men.[3] The class background of respondents apparently had no effect on the relationship.

Not only were the children of devout Protestant parents more likely to be upwardly mobile, they were also somewhat less likely to be downwardly mobile. Of the 16 children of devout parents in business or the professions, 38 per cent were downwardly mobile, compared with 47 per cent of the 15 children of less devout parents. While this difference is too small to be statistically significant, it is worthy of note in view of the evidence on upward mobility.

These data strongly indicate that the relationship of the individual white Protestant to his church *antedates* upward *mobility*. Thus, while it is plausible to argue that this relationship is merely due to the attraction which church membership and activity have for the successful middle-class Protestant, the causal relationship seems to operate more often in the opposite direction. This is not to deny that to some degree there is a two-way flow of influence. As a result of modern research, social theorists are becoming more aware of the fact that in human affairs influence normally operates on *two-way* streets with some traffic moving in each direction. Hence, positive correlations between variables frequently reflect mutual reinforcement rather than a simple relationship where one variable is the cause and the the other the effect. However, this is not to say that the flow of traffic on all streets is equally heavy in both directions. On the contrary, quite often most of the traffic moves in one direction. In the present instance our data indicate that a high degree of involvement in the white Protestant churches more often stimulates upward mobility than the other way round.

In the case of Catholics the situation seems quite different. Using the same mode of analysis, we found that 31 per cent of the sons and daughters of devout Catholic workers and farmers had been upwardly mobile (N=84). Of the children of less devout Catholic workers and farmers, 39 per cent had been upwardly mobile (N=38). In short, there was either no relationship, or a negative relationship between the commitment of Catholics to

---

[2] The parents of a respondent were classified as highly religious if (a) the respondent reported attending worship services every week and if he further stated that *both* his mother and father were at least as religious as he, or (b) if the respondent reported that he attended worship services less than once a week but at least once a month, and that *both* of his parents were *more* religious than he.

[3] Among men there was a percentage difference of 13 points; among women it was 29 points.

their church and the economic success of their children. Once again this pattern was more pronounced among women than among men.[4]

When the sons and daughters of Catholic professional men and businessmen were studied, it was found that those raised in devout families were somewhat more likely to be downwardly mobile than those raised in less devout families (64 vs. 50 per cent). Since there were only 14 persons in each of these categories, the difference was too small to be statistically significant, though noteworthy because of its similarity to our other findings.

On the basis of these data it appears that involvement in the Catholic Church does not have the same consequences as involvement in the white Protestant churches. At best it seems to be irrelevant to mobility, and at worst, something of a hindrance. The relationship between upward mobility and *current* church attendance among Catholics therefore appears to be a result of the influence of mobility on attendance rather than the reverse, as appears to be the case among white Protestants. The fact that upwardly mobile sons and daughters of working-class and farm parents are more faithful in their attendance at Mass seems to reflect conformity, or overconformity, to the standards of their new social peers rather than the influence of childhood socialization.

Other Types of Economic Behavior These conclusions were reinforced by our analysis of the relationship between associational involvement and economic attitudes, beliefs, values, and behavior of other types. On the overwhelming majority of the questions asked, white Protestants who were active in the churches were more likely to take a stand consonant with the spirit of capitalism than were marginal members of the group. Among middle-class Protestants, this pattern was observed in 12 out of 14 questions where comparisons were possible; among members of the working class, the pattern was observed on 14 out of 17 questions.[5]

The situation among Catholics proved to be quite different. Our data indicate that involvement in the Catholic Church is *not* conducive to commitment to the spirit of capitalism. There is either no relationship, or perhaps even a slight negative relationship. Comparisons among middle-class Catholics were possible on 14 questions, and on only 6 did the active churchgoers express views consonant with the spirit of capitalism more often than the marginal members. Among working-class Catholics this same pattern was observed in only 5 out of 13 comparisons.[6]

---

[4] Among men there was a difference of 3 percentage points; among women 14 points.
[5] The reason for the difference between the classes in the number of questions was that several of the items were asked only of union members and there were not enough middle-class union members to make comparisons possible.
[6] It was not possible to make three of the comparisons made among white Protestant workers because there were so few Catholic workingmen who were *both* inactive in the church and also union members.

On 12 questions our sample included enough active and inactive members of both socio-religious groups in both classes for uniform comparisons to be made. Table 1 gives some indication of the average magnitude of the differences involved. At both class levels there is a steady progression from the active Catholics to the active Protestants, with the percentage of responses consonant with the spirit of capitalism steadily increasing. White Protestants who are active in the churches are nearly half again as likely to take stands consistent with the spirit of capitalism as those active in the Catholic Church.

Table 1: Mean Percentage of Responses on 12 Items Consonant with the Spirit of Capitalism,* by Socio-religious Group, Degree of Associational Involvement, and Class

Socio-religious Group:	MIDDLE CLASS		WORKING CLASS	
Degree of associational involvement	Per Cent	N	Per Cent	N
White Protestant: active	53	43	40	33
White Protestant: marginal	45	74	35	116
White Catholic: marginal	40	17	31	35
White Catholic: active	38	74	29	101

* The items included are: (1) positive attitude toward work; (2) disagreement with majority of CIO members on controversial issues; (3) agreement with majority of businessmen on controversial issues; (4) believe workingmen's sons chances of advancement good; (5) believe ability more important than family connections; (6) believe God loves those who strive; (7) now self-employed; (8) ever self-employed; (9) disapproves of installment buying; (10) keeps budget; (11) gives multiple reasons for saving; (12) has long-range goals for saving.

It is not practicable to examine in detail each of the patterns of response for both socio-religious groups at both class levels for all of the many items. However, there are some differences among the items which deserve special attention. In the first place, involvement in the white Protestant churches is quite clearly associated with some measure of hostility toward the labor unions. For example, 34 per cent of the Protestant male workers who rarely if ever attend church (N=64) reported being strongly interested in the unions in the 1957 survey, but only 17 per cent of the irregular churchgoers (N=23) and 4 per cent of the most active churchgoing workers (N=25) shared this interest. In the 1952 survey 55 per cent of the active churchgoing Protestant members of the working class (N=20) believed that most members of the CIO would disagree with them on controversial political issues, but only 35 per cent of the irregular participants from this group (N=20) and 28 per cent of the marginal members who rarely attended (N=50) shared this view. Finally, in the 1958 survey we found that none of the active, middle-class, Protestant men (N=16) had joined a union, but 19 per cent of the marginal members of the group had (N=31).

A second area of noteworthy differences involves self-employment. Whereas 31 per cent of the active, middle-class, white Protestant men (N=16) were self-employed, this was true of only 6 per cent of the marginal members (N=31). In the working class the difference was much smaller, the comparable figures being 8 and 5 per cent (Ns=12 and 57). Also noteworthy is the fact that marginal members of the white Protestant churches were much more likely to have shifted out of self-employed positions into the ranks of those hired by others. Whereas 62 per cent of those active middle-class, white Protestant males who had ever been self-employed were still self-employed at the time of the interview in 1958, the same was true of only 19 per cent of the marginal members of the group. Among members of the working class the comparable figures were 30 and 22 per cent.

Involvement in the white Protestant churches was also strongly associated with the belief that ability is more important than family connections in getting ahead, with agreement with businessmen in controversial economic and political issues, and, among working-class people, with a critical view of installment buying.

There were, however, two important questions which produced *no* evidence that involvement in the white Protestant churches strengthened commitment to behavior patterns usually associated with the spirit of capitalism. First, we found no evidence that involvement in the white Protestant churches intensifies aspirations for advancement.[7] When respondents were asked to choose between chances for advancement, high income, economic security, and other items, marginal members of the group were as much concerned with advancement as the more active members. This is consistent with our earlier finding that there are no appreciable differences between Protestants and Catholics in this respect.

Second, and more surprising, we found no evidence that involvement in the churches increases the frequency of positive attitudes toward work on the part of men. On the contrary, those who were marginal to the churches seemed a bit more likely to hold a positive attitude toward work than were those who were more active. This again suggests that the Protestant churches have allowed the doctrine of the calling to be neglected.[8]

As Table 1 indicates, differences between marginal and active Catholics were generally small. A few, however, were large enough to deserve com-

---

[7] At least this was true when men and women were combined. For men alone a small relationship was observed with 29 per cent of those active in the churches ranking a chance for advancement ahead of all other criteria, compared with 23 per cent of the marginal members of the group.

[8] Contrary to this finding, Westoff found a positive relationship between commitment to work and involvement in the Protestant churches. This was especially evident among men in the working class. He found no such relation among Catholic men. . . .

ment. At both class levels active Catholics were more likely to believe that God prefers to see men strive to get ahead rather than rest content with what they have. This indicates that involvement in the Catholic Church does not reduce aspirations. Active working-class Catholics were also more likely than marginal members to rank chances for advancement higher in their hierarchy of job-related values. Finally, active working-class Catholics were much less often critical of installment buying than were marginal members, and active working-class Catholic males were much less likely to have a positive attitude toward work than were marginal males. Over-all, there were not many substantial differences, and most of them occurred when the active Catholics were *less* committed than marginal Catholics to standards associated with the spirit of capitalism.

One of the more surprising findings in this area concerned the Negro Protestant churches and their relationship to the spirit of capitalism. We had expected that involvement in the Negro Protestant churches would be *negatively* linked with commitment to the spirit of capitalism, since the group as a whole lacked a strong commitment. However, such was not the case. Those who were active in the Negro Protestant churches were *more* likely to express views consonant with this spirit than were marginal members. On 10 out of 15 questions this relationship was observed. On the 12 items used in Table 1, 30 percent of the responses given by the active, working-class churchgoers were consistent with the capitalist spirit, but the same proved true of only 24 per cent of the responses of the marginal members.

A comparison of these figures with the corresponding figures for *working-class* white Catholics and Protestants is extremely interesting. Active Negro Protestant churchgoers actually show a higher frequency of responses compatible with a capitalist orientation than active Catholics. Furthermore, the difference between active and marginal members within the Negro Protestant group is greater than the difference within the white Protestant group, indicating that the Negro Protestant churches exercise an even stronger influence than the white Protestant churches. If Negro Protestants in Detroit do not generally exhibit as strong a commitment to the spirit of capitalism as members of other groups, this is not because of the influence of the churches—it is *in spite of* their influence.

These findings are especially significant in view of the very different social situation of the Negro and white Protestant groups. If we were to adopt the position of the economic determinists, we would inevitably predict that Catholics would occupy a position intermediate between that of white and Negro Protestants so far as economic thought and action are concerned, since both historically and currently the economic situation of American Catholics has been intermediate between that of Negro and white Protestants. Our findings indicate, however, that the common elements of the Protestant tradition shared by these latter groups constitute a very real factor in the situation. Despite the marked economic differences which still divide white Catholic and Negro Protestant workers, the two groups are currently quite similar in their basic economic values. This suggests that if and when the objective differences in economic status are reduced, Negro Protestants will come to resemble white Protestants in economic beliefs, values, attitudes, and actions more closely than Catholics because of the influence of their churches.

COMMUNAL INVOLVEMENT

When we examined the interrelations between vertical mobility and the involvement of white Protestants and Catholics in their subcommunities, we found that a *high* degree of communal involvement was consistently linked with a *low* rate of vertical mobility. Those who were highly involved in their socio-religious subcommunities were less likely *either* to have risen *or* to have fallen in the class system than were those who were more marginal to the group. This pattern was especially marked for Catholics.

Among Catholic sons and daughters of workingmen and farmers, only 22 per cent of those who were highly involved in their subcommunity at the time of the 1958 survey (N=67) had risen to middle-class status. By contrast, 38 per cent of those who were less highly involved (N=97) had been upwardly mobile. Among Catholic sons and daughters of middle-class fathers, only 21 per cent of those highly involved in their subcommunity (N=14) had fallen to the ranks of the working class, as against 36 per cent of those who were less involved (N=39).

Among white Protestant sons and daughters of workingmen and farmers, 34 per cent of those highly involved in their sub-community (N=61) had risen to middle-class status. The corresponding figure for the less highly involved (N=153) was 37 per cent. Among white Protestant sons and daughters of middle-class fathers the comparable figures for downward mobility were 22 and 34 per cent (Ns=18 and 32).

These figures again pose the difficult problem of causality: is a high rate of vertical mobility a *cause* or a *consequence* of the separation of individuals from their socio-religious subcommunity? Unfortunately, this time our data do not permit us to settle this important question. On logical grounds it seems possible that a high rate of mobility may be both cause and consequence of such separation, but one can build a somewhat stronger case for the thesis that mobility causes a weakening of communal ties than for the opposite thesis.

On one point, however, the findings seem clear. When considering vertical mobility the *differences* between the two subcommunities are much less important than their *similarities*. In other words, it is the relationship of the individual to *some* subcommunity, rather than his relationship to a *specific* subcommunity which is important. This is especially true when we are considering probabilities of downward mobility. It seems to matter little whether an individual is highly involved in the Catholic or the white Protestant subcommunity, as long as he is highly involved in some subcommunity.

When the relations between degree of communal involvement and other aspects of economic behavior were examined, no differences of any magnitude could be found in either the white Protestant or Catholic groups.[9] This suggests that the churches, rather than the subcommunities, are the primary source of the differences in economic behavior between these two major groups.

RELIGIOUS ORIENTATIONS AND ECONOMIC BEHAVIOR

When the relationships between religious orientations and economic behavior were examined, evidence indicated that devotionalism is linked with upward mobility and also with many of the patterns of thought and action associated with the spirit of capitalism. This was not true, however, in the case of doctrinal orthodoxy. Our data indicate that this type of religious orientation was not linked either with upward mobility, or with most of the elements associated with the spirit of capitalism.

DEVOTIONALISM

Among white Protestant and Catholic sons and daughters of workingmen and farmers, 37 per cent of those who ranked high in terms of devotionalism had been upwardly mobile (N=134), compared with 31 per cent of those who ranked low (N=232). At the same time, of the respondents raised in *middle-class* families, only 29 per cent of those who ranked high in terms of devotionalism were *downwardly* mobile (N=42), compared with 33 per cent of those who ranked low (N=58). In other words, those ranking high in terms of devotionalism were slightly more successful than those ranking low. This pattern was observed despite the fact that Catholics were somewhat more numerous among those ranking high. Hence there is no reason to believe that this relationship is an artifact of our earlier finding that Catholics are generally less mobile than Protestants.

Noteworthy differences were also observed when other aspects of economic behavior were examined. The largest of these differences appeared in connection with the attitudes toward work of middle-class males. Those

---

[9] Among middle-class white Protestants, those who were highly involved in the white Protestant subcommunity gave responses 45 per cent of which were in conformity with the standards of the spirit of capitalism compared with 42 per cent conformity among those less highly involved. Among working-class white Protestants the comparable figures were 32 and 30 per cent, for middle-class Catholics 37 and 35 per cent, and for working-class Catholics 29 and 28 per cent. The questions involved here differ slightly from those which served as the basis for Table 1, since we had no data on communal involvement for any survey except that conducted in 1958.

ranking high in terms of devotionalism (both white Protestants and Catholics) were twice as likely to express a positive attitude toward work as those ranking low (41 vs. 21 per cent: Ns=27 and 58). Those ranking high were also noted for their criticisms of installment buying, their tendency to save for long-range goals, and their use of budgets. There were, however, no differences to speak of with respect to aspirations for advancement, record of self-employment, or number of reasons given for believing saving important. On the question of whether God prefers to see men strive to advance themselves or be content with what they have, those ranking high in terms of our measure of devotionalism were a bit more likely to believe that God prefers to see men be content.

DOCTRINAL ORTHODOXY

By contrast with our finding concerning the relationship between mobility and devotionalism, we found that the *less* orthodox white Protestants and Catholics were somewhat more likely to have risen in the class system than those who were *more* orthodox. However, the difference was small and could well be due to sampling error. What is important in this instance is the fact that doctrinal orthodoxy and devotionalism are clearly something more than two interchangeable indices of "religiosity." Men's religious commitments clearly take different forms, even within a given group, and these variations seem linked with variations in secular behavior. Especially intriguing is the evidence that *these commitments, or orientations, seem able to transcend group loyalties and thus produce similarities in behavior among members of different groups who share a common orientation.*

On most of our measures of economic behavior and attitudes we could find no difference linked with variations in degree of orthodoxy. There was, however, one notable exception. This involved men's attitudes toward work. Here a strong relationship was observed. Among white Catholics and Protestants, those who were not so orthodox were twice as likely to express a positive attitude toward work as the more orthodox (33 vs. 16 per cent: Ns=66 and 60). In this area the contrast between doctrinal orthodoxy and devotionalism was extremely pronounced, with the two orientations seeming to pull men strongly in opposite directions.

THE PROBLEM OF CAUSATION

These findings, especially those involving the relationships between devotionalism and economic behavior, again pose the difficult problem of causation. Which is cause, and which effect?

Economic determinists always have a ready answer to such questions. However, our earlier findings concerning the relationship between vertical mobility and socio-religious group membership make one skeptical of the fundamental tenets of their theory. Furthermore, all of the differences in economic behavior associated with differential commitment to these two religious orientations are differences which we established *with the class positions of respondents held constant*. In other words, if people committed to the devotional orientation are more often advocates of the spirit of capitalism, this cannot be explained simply on the grounds that they are more often members of the middle class while those who lack this commitment are more often members of the working class.

On the basis of our data we cannot assert positively that the religious orientations to which a man is exposed, and to which he becomes committed, actually influence his actions in the economic field. Nevertheless our findings create a strong suspicion that this is in fact the case. If religious ideas and beliefs have any impact at all on economic behavior, it seems reasonable to suppose that the differences in ideas and beliefs associated with the various religious orientations are not without consequences. This is a subject which deserves far more attention than it has yet received.[10]

ECONOMIC DETERMINISM RE-EXAMINED

On the basis of the evidence presented in this chapter it seems safe to conclude that religion makes a difference in the behavior of men in the realm of economic activity. We should not exaggerate the magnitude of this influence, but neither should it be minimized. If there is any single variable which might be regarded as a key factor influencing economic behavior, this is surely class position. Therefore it is significant that, on the whole, differences between *socio-religious groups*, with class controlled, are not much smaller than differences between *classes*, with socio-religious group controlled.

As we have seen, religion makes a difference in several respects. Not only are there differences among the several socio-religious groups, but important differences also frequently exist *within* each group, depending upon the degree and type of religious involvement of the individual and the type, or types, of religious orientation which he has adopted. As a general rule, *commitment to the spirit of capitalism*:

1. is especially frequent among white Protestants and Jews;
2. is much less frequent among Catholics and Negro Protestants, even when position in the class system is held constant;

[10] From the beginning of this study, the examination of the influence of religious orientations on secular institutions has been secondary to our concern with the role of socio-religious groups in daily life. Thus in both the design and analysis of the data it has not been possible to explore this area as fully as it deserves. In future research in this area it is to be hoped that a systematic effort will be made to determine the types of religious orientations dominant in the childhood experience of individuals, since only when one has established the anteriority of religious orientations can one handle adequately the important problem of causality.

3. is positively linked with regularity of church attendance among Protestants, both Negro and white;

4. is negatively correlated with communal involvement both among white Protestants and Catholics;

5. is linked with a high level of devotionalism in all three of the larger socio-religious groups: Catholic, white Protestant, and Negro Protestant;

6. stands in no consistent relationship to degree of doctrinal orthodoxy.

To assert that religion is a factor influencing the economic attitudes and actions of men raises ultimately the question of *why* this should be so. Two major schools of thought present themselves at this point. On the one hand (as we noted earlier) there are those who look for an explanation in terms of factors *external* to the religious groups, such as their location in the class structure. By contrast, the second school focuses on the attributes of the religious groups themselves, especially their theology, and seeks to find the explanation there.

The critical difference between these two schools of thought lies in their basic premises. Members of the first school assume that all systems of thought are mere epiphenomena, shaped and molded by economic forces in particular, and social conditions in general. Members of the second school assume that ideas are something more than this. They believe that the origin and subsequent development of ideas are governed to some degree by their own immanent principles, and to attempt to treat social conditions as the sole cause and explanation of systems of thought is to be guilty of the fallacy of reductionism.

The data obtained in this study do not permit us to prove or disprove either of these theories, but they do shed some light on the problem, and therefore it may be well to reconsider the issues in the light of our evidence.

Much of the evidence turned up in this study fits in well with the theory that social conditions determine systems of thought. For instance, it seems more than coincidence that white Protestants are the most likely to express commitment to the spirit of capitalism, followed by white Catholics and Negro Protestants in that order. This constellation of values which we have labeled "the spirit of capitalism" might well have been called "the middle-class ethic," or perhaps even "the upper-middle-class ethic." In other words, our data indicate that members of an economically advantaged group think and act in a manner appropriate to members of an economically advantaged group, and conversely, members of a disadvantaged group, such as the Negro Protestants, think and act in a manner appropriate to their social situation.

Admittedly, working-class white Protestants tend to think and act like middle-class people almost as often as middle-class Catholics. However, this may be explained on the grounds that a man's behavior is conditioned as much by the social situation of the group to which he belongs as by his own personal situation. For example, many of the attitudes and actions of *middle-class* Catholics in our society represent *working-class* responses to life because of the historic position of the Catholic group as a whole in American society. Historically, the overwhelming majority of Catholics have been members of the working class. Even more important, throughout American history the majority of *leaders* in the Catholic group have been persons raised in the working class. By contrast, the white Protestant group has always had a higher percentage of members in the middle class. Even though the majority of white Protestants may not have been raised in the middle class, the majority of their leaders probably have since leaders are normally recruited from higher status levels than other members of the group.

The marked differences in economic behavior between white and Negro Protestants might also be cited as strong evidence to support the first thesis described above: that the social conditions in which a group finds itself, rather than its theology, determine the economic attitudes and actions of its members. The theological positions of these two groups are not very different, yet there are marked differences in the economic behavior of their members. Similarities in theology obviously cannot account for differences in economic behavior.

While one cannot deny that there are real and important links between the social situation of individuals and groups and their economic behavior, this is not to say that these differences in social situation are the whole (or even the chief) explanation for the differences in economic behavior. Far too many difficulties present themselves for one to accept such a view.

To begin with, if such a view is valid, why should there be a relationship between degree of devotionalism and commitment to the spirit of capitalism when the social situations of individuals are held constant? Yet within the limitations set by the size of the sample with which we are working, this seems to be the case. When we hold constant the class position both of individuals and of the socio-religious group to which they belong, differences persist between those who are strongly devotionalistic and those who are not.

A second finding which raises difficulties for the strict "environmentalist" view is that commitment to the spirit of capitalism varies with degree of involvement in Protestant churches, *both* Negro and white. If it varied with associational involvement in the white Protestant churches only, one might argue that associational involvement was a subtle measure of the individual's involvement in an organization dominated by members of the middle class—and therefore only a measure of his exposure to middle-class values. But this is clearly not the case where involvement in the Negro churches is concerned. Since the Negro churches are overwhelmingly made up of working-class people, one would expect involvement in these churches to reinforce *working-class* values, according to any logical derivation from environmentalist theories. As Marx pointed out more than a century ago, class consciousness is stimulated by interaction among persons whose position in the class structure is comparable. Yet we found that such interaction as occurs among members of the working class within the context of the Negro Protestant churches in Detroit facilitates and stimulates identification with economic values long linked with the *middle class.*

A third finding which raises difficulties for the environmentalist position is the remarkable similarity in economic values between the Negro Protestant and white Catholic members of the working class. As we have already noted, the Negro Protestants are disproportionately concentrated in the lower half of the working class when judged by income and occupation. White Catholics are much more evenly distributed. . . . Furthermore if one considers the economic situation of *the group* rather than that of *the individual*, the differences become even more pronounced: a much larger percentage of the members of the Catholic group are members of the middle class. Even so, Negro Protestants differ very little from Catholics in the frequency with which they express commitment to the spirit of capitalism. In fact, when comparisons are limited to the active churchgoers among the working-class members of the two groups, Negro Protestants rank somewhat ahead of white Catholics in this respect. While the differences between Negro and white Protestants may reflect the influence of social conditions on economic values, the similarities between Negro Protestants and white Catholics seem to indicate that economic values are shaped by something more than economic conditions alone.

Yet another difficulty which confronts the environmentalist is that of accounting for the phenomenal success of the Jewish group and their strong commitment to most elements of the capitalist spirit. Starting as poor immigrants fifty or seventy-five years ago, the members of this group have advanced to the point where they are in Detroit, and probably throughout the country as a whole, the most properous of the major socio-religious groups. They have far outdistanced the Catholics who came to this country a generation or two earlier, and have even moved ahead of the white Protestants who originally dominated the positions of privilege in this country.

We cannot account for these successes merely by saying that the Jews were a minority group subject to discrimination and therefore challenged to work harder than other groups. Other minorities have been confronted with similar situations without responding in this fashion. One may invoke their urban background in Europe as a factor contributing to their success. Without denying its influence, we are led to ask why urban experience has not had a greater effect on the Catholics in this country. The great majority of Catholic immigrants settled in urban centers while the Protestants have been heavily concentrated in the rural areas. Yet three generations of urban experience seem to have done little to stimulate Catholic commitment to the spirit of capitalism. In fact, in many respects Catholic commitment to this system of values seems higher among first- and second-generation immigrants (more often of rural background) than among members of the third generation (typically of urban background). In brief, the urban experience of the Jews in Europe would seem at best a necessary cause, but never a sufficient cause for their economic behavior.

In view of the evidence available both from this study and elsewhere it appears that the strict environmentalist position, which explains economic behavior solely in terms of the social situation of the individual and the group, is untenable. This is not to deny that social conditions, and especially those of an economic nature, are powerful forces influencing such behavior. However, other factors also exercise a significant influence. Notable among these are the belief systems, or ideologies, to which men subscribe: phenomena whose existence seems limited, but not determined, by the social conditions to which their originators and subsequent proponents are exposed. [A subsequent chapter considers these matters at greater length.—Ed.]

15. Ethnic Membership
and Urban Voting

EDWARD C. BANFIELD AND
JAMES Q. WILSON

Ethnic differences play a large part in the politics of America's cities. In New York City, for example, both parties attempt to present "balanced tickets," usually with a Protestant, a Catholic, and a Jew as candidates for major offices. (Perhaps before long the pattern will also include a Negro.) The following selection represents a portion of an attempt by two political scientists to demonstrate the importance of ethnic ties to urban political behavior, and to explain why different ethnic groups have different views of the political process. Minority bloc voting involves a diffuse sense of ethnic loyalty and pride, and the assumption that one's interests will be

SOURCE: Edward C. Banfield and James Q. Wilson, City Politics (Cambridge: Harvard University Press, 1963), pp. 38–44, 229–31. Copyright © 1963 by the President and Fellows of Harvard College. Reprinted by permission of the publishers.

Edward C. Banfield is Professor of Government at Harvard University and is the author of, among other works, The Moral Basis of a Backward Community. James Q. Wilson is Associate Professor of Government at the University of Chicago and the author of Negro Politics.

best served by a member of his own group. Such considerations frequently override what reformers, perhaps unaware of the large part self-interest plays in their own attitudes, would like to call their desires for "clean, efficient, and orderly" government in the hands of the most competent prospective office-holders.

Ethnic and Racial Groups

Ethnic and racial differences have been, and still are, basic to much of the conflict in the city. Here it will be convenient to speak of three such lines of cleavage: that between native Protestant and all others, that among the various nationality groups of foreign stock, and that between the Negro and all others.

Although the largest waves of immigration ended long ago, some cities, such as New York and Boston, still have, as Table 1 indicates, a sizable number of persons of foreign stock. Other cities, such as Dallas, have scarcely been touched by immigration at all.

Table 1: *Cities Over 500,000 Population Ranked by the Percentage of Persons Foreign-Born or with At Least One Foreign-Born Parent, 1960*

Rank	City	Percent	Rank	City	Percent
1	New York	48.6	12	Philadelphia	29.1
2	Boston	45.5	13	San Antonio	24.0
3	San Francisco	43.5	14	San Diego	21.5
4	Chicago	35.9	15	Baltimore	14.8
5	Buffalo	35.4	16	St. Louis	14.1
6	Los Angeles	32.6	17	Washington	12.6
7	Detroit	32.2	18	Cincinnati	12.0
8	Seattle	31.4	19	Houston	9.7
9	Cleveland	30.9	20	New Orleans	8.6
10	Pittsburgh	30.3	21	Dallas	6.9
11	Milwaukee	30.0			

Source: 1960 Census. The term "foreign-born" does not, of course, include Puerto Ricans.

Until the latter part of the last century, native Protestant industrialists and businessmen ran most cities. Then, in the Northern cities, when the tide of immigration swelled, the newly arrived ethnic groups began to challenge the natives for political control. For a time there was a sharp conflict, but in most cities the natives soon retired from the scene, or, more precisely, they transferred their activity from one sector of the scene to another.

In Boston, for example, the Irish were able to command a majority beginning about 1890 and the native Protestants thereafter ran the city from the state house. Boston's police commissioner was appointed by the governor and so was its licensing board; a finance commission, also appointed by the governor, was set up to make continuing investigations of the city's affairs and was given the power of subpoena. Much of the interference of the legislatures in the affairs of other large cities at this time and afterward reflected the same cleavage between the outnumbered native Protestants and what Mayor James M. Curley of Boston used to call the "newer races."

In a good many cities, where several new ethnic groups competed for control, the old native Protestant elite might conceivably have retained its control by serving—as the Irish so often have—as a neutral force on which all elements of the ethnic struggle could agree. But the elite was incapacitated for this role by its distaste for the political culture of the new immigrant, a distaste that it did not try to conceal. As Peter and Alice Rossi have shown in an unpublished paper on "Bay City," Massachusetts, local politics, which was a source of prestige for the local industrialists until the immigrants became numerous, was "dirty business" afterwards. Accordingly, the old elite turned from elective office and took up instead the control of a relatively new set of institutions, the community service organizations. The local hospital, Red Cross chapter, Community Chest, and Family Welfare Society became the arenas in which the "old families," who of course now asserted that there was no prestige in public office, carried on their public activities.[1]

One can see today in many places elements of informal government that have been produced by this cleavage between the "old family" Protestants and the "newer races." A study in 1947 indicated that in "Jonesville," Illinois, the Rotary Club was handpicking the members of the school board.[2] The interviewer was told: "This school board around here has been looked upon as the private property of the Rotary Club for about twenty-five years. The fact is, the school board has been kind of a closed corporation. . . . The boys decide who they want to run. The fact is, they invite them to run." For at least fifteen years prior to 1947, all members of the "Jonesville" school board were Protestant Republicans; only twice in that period did candidates for the board face any opposition.

The Rossis, who are sociologists, in their report on "Bay City" interpret the change in the character of the old elite's public service as a redirection of its drive for status and recognition. Unwilling to play the status game in the same set with the immigrant, the old elite (according to the Rossis)

---

[1] Peter H. and Alice S. Rossi, "An Historical Perspective on Local Politics," paper delivered at the 1956 meeting of the American Sociological Association (mimeo).
[2] Joseph Rosenstein, "Small-Town Party Politics," unpublished dissertation, Department of Sociology, University of Chicago, 1950.

set up its own game and in effect said that henceforth that was to be *the* game.

We prefer a different explanation. The native middle-class Protestant inherited from his Anglo-Saxon ancestors a political ethos very different from that which the new immigrants brought with them. The ethos of the native could not mix with that of the immigrant, and therefore the natives, who were in the minority, retired to a sphere in which they could conduct public affairs in the manner their culture prescribed.

Richard Hofstadter described the difference of ethos very well in *The Age of Reform:*

> Out of the clash between the needs of the immigrants and the sentiments of the natives there emerged two thoroughly different systems of political ethics. . . . One, founded upon the indigenous Yankee-Protestant political traditions, and upon middle class life, assumed and demanded the constant, disinterested activity of the citizen in public affairs, argued that political life ought to be run, to a greater degree than it was, in accordance with general principles and abstract laws apart from and superior to personal needs, and expressed a common feeling that government should be in good part an effort to moralize the lives of individuals while economic life should be intimately related to the stimulation and development of individual character. The other system, founded upon the European background of the immigrants, upon their unfamiliarity with independent political action, their familiarity with hierarchy and authority, and upon the urgent needs that so often grew out of their migration, took for granted that the political life of the individual would arise out of family needs, interpreted political and civic relations chiefly in terms of personal obligations, and placed strong personal loyalties above allegiance to abstract codes of law or morals.[3]

The Anglo-Saxon Protestant middle-class style of politics, with its emphasis upon the obligation of the individual to participate in public affairs and to seek the good of the community "as a whole" (which implies, among other things, the necessity of honesty, impartiality, and efficiency) was fundamentally incompatible with the immigrants' style of politics, which took no account of the community.

The native elite withdrew to the community service organizations because these constituted the only sphere in which their political style could prevail. The boards of these organizations were self-perpetuating, they could not be "crashed" by "outsiders." Because of the nature of their political ethos, Protestants and Jews have been in the vanguard of every fight for municipal reform. In Worcester, Massachusetts, for example, according to Robert Binstock:

[3] Richard Hofstadter, *The Age of Reform* (New York: Alfred A. Knopf, 1955), p. 9.

Yankees are the cultural, business, and social leaders—in short, "the first families of Worcester." They are not numerous enough to control the governmental apparatus of the city, yet by forming an alliance with the Scandinavians, they manage to place two representatives on the City Council. The influence of the Yankee within the city government is limited, but participation in a strong and active citizens association, the CEA, enables this group to enlarge its role in the political process.

The Jews, more often than not, are political allies of the Yankees and Scandinavians. . . .[4]

Conflict as between one immigrant ethnic group and another has tended to be over "recognition"—the prestige that accrues to a nationality group when one of its members is elected to public office. Since in the nature of the case there cannot be enough recognition to go around (if all were equally recognized, none would be recognized at all), the question of which groups are to get it must inevitably lead to conflict. The avidity of the "newer" ethnic groups to see their kind in office has been, and still is, of great importance, both as a motive force in the political system and because of certain incidental effects.

When one recalls the contempt with which "micks," "wops," and "polacks" were once—and to some extent still are—treated by some other Americans, no further explanation of the appeal of ethnic "recognition" is needed. But an additional reason is that ethnic politics, like sports, enter- tainment, and crime, provided a route of social mobility to people who were to a large extent excluded from power in business and industry. Mayor Daley of Chicago was born behind the stockyards. John E. Powers, the president of the Massachusetts Senate, began life as a clam digger.

One would expect that as the "newer" ethnic groups became assimilated to the middle class, they would become assimilated to the Anglo-Saxon Protestant political ethos as well, and that their interest in ethnic politics would decline accordingly. This seems to be happening, but at different rates among different groups. Jews, particularly those in the reform tradi- tion, seem to acquire the Protestant political ethos very readily.[5] It is inter- esting that the Jews have not sought ethnic "recognition" in city politics to

---

[4] Robert H. Binstock, *A Report on Politics in Worcester, Mass.* (Cambridge, Mass.: Joint Center for Urban Studies, 1961, mimeo), part V, p. 2.
[5] Compare the findings of Edgar Litt: "Jewish Ethno-Religious Involvement and Political Liberalism," *Social Forces*, May 1961, pp. 328–332; "Ethnic Status and Political Perspectives," *Midwest Journal of Political Science*, August 1961, pp. 276–283; and "Status, Ethnicity, and Patterns of Jewish Voting Behavior in Baltimore," *Jewish Social Studies*, July 1960, pp. 159–164. Litt argues that the basis of Jewish identification with the Democratic party varies with socio-economic status: upper-class Jews are Demo- cratic because they see the party as an instrument of "social justice" on national and international issues; lower-class Jews are Democratic because they see it as a source of material benefits and economic welfare. These findings are broadly consistent with our argument about political ethos.

the extent that other groups have. It may be that they have never doubted their worth as a group, and therefore have not felt any need for public reassurance. More likely, however, their political ethos is such that a politics of ethnic appeal strikes them, as it does the Anglo-Saxon Protestant, as uninteresting and even immoral.

Other ethnic groups also seem to be taking on the middle-class political ethos, but to be doing it more slowly. Third-generation Poles, for example, usually show a decided preference for Polish candidates, and third-generation Italians usually prefer Italian candidates. Middle-class Irish Catholics who seem entirely to have shed the mentality that caused the immigrant to vote on the basis of personal loyalty to a ward politician are nevertheless rarely found in the ranks of the civic reformers; these are almost all Protestants and Jews.

Where the taste for ethnic recognition persists, it is for a special kind of recognition, however. The candidate must not be *too* Polish, *too* Italian, or *too* Irish in the old style. The following description of Jewish candidates in Worcester suggests the trend:

> Israel Katz, like Casdin, is a Jewish Democrat now serving his fourth term on the Worcester City Council. Although he is much more identifiably Jewish than Casdin, he gets little ethnic support at the polls; there is a lack of rapport between him and the Jewish voter. The voter apparently wants to transcend many features of his ethnic identification and therefore rejects candidates who fit the stereotype of the Jew too well. Casdin is an assimilated Jew in Ivy-League clothes; Katz, by contrast, is old world rather than new, clannish rather than civic-minded, and penny-pinching rather than liberal. Non-Jews call Katz a "character," Casdin a "leader." It is not too much to say that the Jews, like other minorities, want a flattering, not an unflattering, mirror held up to them.[6]

Apparently, nowadays, the nationality-minded voter prefers candidates who represent the ethnic group but at the same time display the attributes of the generally admired Anglo-Saxon model. The perfect candidate, then, is of Jewish, Polish, Italian, or Irish extraction and has the speech, dress, manner, and the public virtues—honesty, impartiality, and devotion to the public interest—of the upper-class Anglo-Saxon.

The cleavage between white and Negro is pervasive in city politics. Until World War II, few Northern cities had many Negroes. As we have already seen, the Negro population of most Northern cities now is growing at a very rapid rate, partly from natural increase and partly from migration from the rural South. The new arrivals go into the Negro slum, which

[6] Binstock, part II, pp. 33–34.

almost everywhere is the oldest part of the central city, where housing has
been swept by successive waves of low-status and low-income migrants.
For many years restrictive covenants, written into deeds and prohibiting
sale of property to Negroes, made it difficult or impossible for Negroes to
buy in districts that were not already Negro; their districts therefore
became more and more crowded. But after 1948, when the Supreme Court
declared such covenants to be unenforceable in the courts, the Negro community began to spread more rapidly.[7]

In many Northern cities, the question of where Negroes are to live lies
behind almost every proposal for civic action. Will locating a major
highway here prevent them from "invading" that white neighborhood?
And where will those Negroes who are displaced by an urban renewal
project resettle? If a school or a hospital is placed here or there, will it
bring Negroes to the neighborhood? And if it does, will the neighborhood
eventually "tip" and become all Negro?

Many whites have fled to the suburbs to get away from the Negroes.
One reason why many suburbanites want to remain politically separate
from the central city is that they think this will make it easier for them
to resist "invasion" by Negroes.

In all this, upper-class Negroes exhibit much the same attitude as do
whites. Everything that we have said of the reaction of whites to Negroes
can also be said of the reaction of upper-class Negroes to lower-class
ones.

· · · · ·

Socio-economic and Ethnic Status

As is well known, there is generally a correlation between the party voted
for and the income, education, religion, and ethnic origin of the voter.
Sample surveys and election studies focused on state and national contests
have amply demonstrated that, for example, lower-income Negroes or
Catholics with little schooling are far more likely to vote Democratic than
upper-income, college-educated, Anglo-Saxon Protestants.[8] We have no

---

[7] *Shelley v. Kraemer*, 334 U.S. 1 (1948).
[8] Studies of class, ethnicity, and voting include the following: Bernard Berelson, *et al.*,
Voting (Chicago: University of Chicago Press, 1954); Angus Campbell *et al.*, *The
American Voter* (New York: John Wiley & Sons, 1960); V. O. Key, Jr., *Public Opinion
and American Democracy* (New York: Alfred A. Knopf, 1961); Seymour M. Lipset *et al.*,
"The Psychology of Voting: An Analysis of Political Behavior," in Gardner Lindsey
(ed.), *Handbook of Social Psychology* (Cambridge, Mass.: Addison-Wesley, 1954), II,
1124–1175; Samuel Lubell, *The Future of American Politics* (New York: Doubleday
Anchor Books, 1956); Paul F. Lazarsfeld *et al.*, *The People's Choice* (New York: Duell,
Sloan & Pearce, 1944); Angus Campbell *et al.*, *The Voter Decides* (Evanston, Ill.:
Row, Peterson, 1954).

reason to believe that these findings do not hold generally true in partisan city elections as well.

Differences in income, education, and ethnicity are all closely associated with differences in social class. Sometimes, of course, class is *defined* in terms of income and education. But even if it is defined in terms of position in a deference hierarchy or participation in a subculture (i.e., the sharing of certain standards of taste and certain modes of behavior), it is usually closely related to the characteristics listed.

The relationship between class and political attitudes seems to vary somewhat with the size of the city. V. O. Key, Jr., finds, for example, that "blue collar" and "white collar" workers differ most in their attitudes toward certain policy issues in large metropolitan areas and differ least in smaller cities (with populations between ten and fifty thousand).[9] In almost every case, blue-collar (i.e., working-class) attitudes became more similar to white-collar (middle-class) attitudes in the smaller communities. Two other researchers found that laborers in small Michigan cities were less likely to vote Democratic than were laborers in large cities.[10] A study of Elmira, New York, suggested that workers there showed "less political solidarity and more political ambivalence" than workers generally, in part because the community norms were favorable to middle-class business groups and thus reinforced middle-class attitudes and weakened working-class attitudes.[11]

All of these characteristics tend to be empirically associated: for example, the voters with low incomes tend also to have little education, to include a high proportion of foreign-born and nonwhites, and to vote for Democratic candidates. One would like to "factor out" the causal significance of each separate element in this mixture, so as to be able to say, for example, "If education, ethnic origin, and party affiliation are all held constant and if income is varied, the effect on the vote will be thus and so"; but this is often very difficult.

The importance in voting behavior of ethnic identifications varies a good deal with the ethnic and class status of the voter. Usually it is impossible to disentangle this influence from others, like party affiliation, but occasionally a situation arises in which some light is shed on the subject. For example, from the data in Table 2 one can make a rough assessment of the importance which ethnic attachments had to the Boston electorate in 1962. The table shows how certain ethnically different precincts chose among ethnically different candidates in the state and national elections.

[9] Key, *Public Opinion and American Democracy*, pp. 116–118.
[10] Nicholas A. Masters and Deil S. Wright, "Trends and Variations in the Two-Party Vote: The Case of Michigan," *American Political Science Review*, December 1958, pp. 1078–1090, esp. p. 1088.
[11] Berelson *et al.*, *Voting*, pp. 56–57.

Table 2: Voting in Selected "Ethnic" Precincts in Boston, 1962

Candidate's ethnic and party identification	PERCENTAGE DIVISION OF VOTE IN FIVE PRECINCTS COMPOSED PREDOMINANTLY OF:				
	Middle-Class Italians	Lower-Class Italians	Middle-Class Yankees	Lower-Class Irish	Lower-Class Negroes
FOR U.S. SENATOR					
Irish Democrat (Kennedy)	77	74	28	87	76
Yankee Republican (Lodge)	23	26	72	13	24
FOR GOVERNOR					
Yankee Democrat (Peabody)	47	32	36	81	52
Italian Republican (Volpe)	53	68	64	19	48
FOR STATE AT-TORNEY-GENERAL					
Irish Democrat (Kelly)	56	63	17	85	11
Negro Republican (Brooke)	44	37	83	15	89

It would be easy to "over-interpret" these figures; for one thing, although the parties are notoriously weak in Boston, party loyalty rather than ethnic loyalty accounts for some of the differences; moreover, one cannot be certain that voters did not vote *against* ethnic groups rather than *for* them (some of the lower-class Irish, for example, may have voted for Kelly, not because he was Irish but because his opponent was a Negro). Nevertheless, the figures show, we think, that in the absence of strong party organization, ethnic attachments may be of considerable importance, especially among lower-class voters. For example, the lower-income Italian precinct, deserting the Democratic party, voted more heavily for the Italian Republican running for governor than did the middle-income Italian precinct; this comports with our general hypothesis that as voters rise in socio-economic status they attach less value to ethnic considerations, which are part of the immigrant political ethos.

The size and concentration of a particular ethnic group (or, for that matter, of certain social classes) in a city seems to affect voting turnout. This is often called the "bandwagon effect." Where, for example, Italians, Negroes, Poles, or laborers are a sizable percentage of the total population and where they live in close proximity to one another, turnout is greater than when they are fewer in number or less concentrated.[12]

[12] Herbert Tingsten, *Political Behavior* (London: P. S. King, 1937), pp. 126–127; Lane, *Political Life*, p. 262; James K. Pollock, *Voting Behavior: A Case Study* (Ann Arbor: University of Michigan Press, 1941), p. 12.

The large city, by concentrating the population, provides a necessary (but not sufficient) condition for ethnic political activity. The various nationality and racial groups are sufficiently large that they believe they have some reasonable chance of affecting the outcome of elections; there are enough members of the group to feel a sense of group solidarity and to support their own political leaders and institutions; and they are sufficiently set apart from other groups to stimulate a sense of competition and even conflict.

16. Crime: A Queer Ladder
of Social Mobility

D A N I E L   B E L L

When other paths to success have been closed, politics and athletics have provided alternative ways for members of minority groups to rise to positions of eminence and wealth. In contrast to these two areas, which are not disapproved of even though they often seem unconventional as sources of careers for most middle-class people, crime is clearly a deviant activity. Yet crime has served some of the same purposes, providing careers and advancement to those who had the requisite skills and appropriate motivations. Bell's discussion shows how control of organized crime shifted from members of one ethnic group to those of another over time— from the Jews, to the Irish, to the Italians—as groups that had once been prominent in crime generally became better able to achieve success through more widely approved means.

THE JEWS . . . THE IRISH . . . THE ITALIANS

The Italian community has achieved wealth and political influence much later and in a harder way than previous immigrant groups. Early Jewish wealth, that of the German Jews of the late nineteenth century, was made largely in banking and merchandising. To that extent, the dominant group in the Jewish community was outside of, and independent of, the urban

SOURCE: Reprinted with permission of The Free Press from Daniel Bell, "Crime as an American Way of Life," in his *The End of Ideology*, pp. 141–48 of the Collier Books edition (footnotes omitted). Copyright © 1960 by The Free Press, a Corporation.
    Daniel Bell is Professor of Sociology at Columbia University. He is the editor of *The New American Right*.

political machines. Later Jewish wealth, among the East European immigrants, was built in the garment trades, though with some involvement with the Jewish gangster, who was typically an industrial racketeer (Arnold Rothstein, Lepke and Gurrah, etc.). Among Jewish lawyers, a small minority, such as the "Tammany lawyer" (like the protagonist of Sam Ornitz's *Haunch, Paunch and Jowl*), rose through politics and occasionally touched the fringes of crime. Most of the Jewish lawyers, by and large the communal leaders, climbed rapidly, however, in the opportunities that established and legitimate Jewish wealth provided. Irish immigrant wealth in the northern urban centers, concentrated largely in construction, trucking, and the waterfront, has, to a substantial extent, been wealth accumulated in and through political alliance, e.g., favoritism in city contracts.

Control of the politics of the city thus has been crucial for the continuance of Irish political wealth. This alliance of Irish immigrant wealth and politics has been reciprocal; many noted Irish political figures lent their names as important window-dressing for business corporations (Al Smith, for example, who helped form the U.S. Trucking Corporation, whose executive head for many years was William J. McCormack, the alleged "Mr. Big" of the New York waterfront), while Irish businessmen have lent their wealth to further the careers of Irish politicians. Irish mobsters have rarely achieved status in the Irish community, but have served as integral arms of the politicians, as strong-arm men on election day.

The Italians found the more obvious big-city paths from rags to riches pre-empted. In part this was due to the character of the early Italian immigrant. Most of them were unskilled and from rural stock. Jacob Riis could remark in the nineties, "the Italian comes in at the bottom and stays there." These dispossessed agricultural laborers found jobs as ditch-diggers, on the railroads as section hands, along the docks, in the service occupations, as shoemakers, barbers, garment workers, and stayed there. Many were fleeced by the "padrone" system; a few achieved wealth from truck farming, wine growing, and marketing produce, but this "marginal wealth" was not the source of coherent and stable political power.

Significantly, although the number of Italians in the United States is about a third as high as the number of Irish, and of the thirty million Catholic communicants in the United States, about half are of Irish decent and a sixth of Italian, there is not one Italian bishop among the hundred Catholic bishops in this country or one Italian archbishop among the 21 archbishops. The Irish have a virtual monopoly. This is a factor related to the politics of the American church; but the condition also is possible because there is not significant or sufficient wealth among Italian Americans to force some parity.

The children of the immigrants, the second and third generation, became wise in the ways of the urban slums. Excluded from the political ladder—in the early thirties there were almost no Italians on the city payroll in top jobs, nor in books of the period can one find discussion of Italian political leaders—and finding few open routes to wealth, some turned to illicit ways. In the children's court statistics of the 1930's, the largest group of delinquents were the Italian; nor were there any Italian communal or social agencies to cope with these problems. Yet it was, oddly enough, the quondam racketeer, seeking to become respectable, who provided one of the major supports for the drive to win a political voice for Italians in the power structure of the urban political machines.

This rise of the Italian political bloc was connected, at least in the major northern urban centers, with another important development which tended to make the traditional relation between the politician and the protected or tolerated illicit operator more close than it had been in the past. This is the fact that the urban political machines had to evolve new forms of fund-raising, since the big business contributions, which once went heavily into municipal politics, now—with the shift in the locus of power—go largely into national affairs. (The ensuing corruption in national politics, as recent Congressional investigations show, is no petty matter; the scruples of businessmen do not seem much superior to those of the gamblers.) One way that urban political machines raised their money resembled that of the large corporations which are no longer dependent on Wall Street: by self-financing—that is, by "taxing" the large number of municipal employees who bargain collectively with City Hall for their wage increases. So the firemen's union contributed money to O'Dwyer's campaign.

A second method was taxing the gamblers. The classic example, as *Life* reported, was Jersey City, where a top lieutenant of the Hague machine spent his full time screening applicants for unofficial bookmaking licenses. If found acceptable, the applicant was given a "location," usually the house or store of a loyal precinct worker, who kicked into the machine treasury a high proportion of the large rent exacted. The one thousand bookies and their one thousand landlords in Jersey City formed the hard core of the political machine that sweated and bled to get out the votes for Hague.

A third source for the financing of these machines was the new, and often illegally earned, Italian wealth. This is well illustrated by the career of Costello and his emergence as a political power in New York. Here the ruling motive has been the search for an entree—for oneself and one's ethnic group—into the ruling circles of the big city.

Frank Costello made his money originally in bootlegging. After repeal, his big break came when Huey Long, desperate for ready cash to fight the old-line political machines, invited Costello to install slot machines in Louisiana. Costello did, and he flourished. Together with Dandy Phil Kastel, he also opened the Beverly Club, an elegant gambling establishment just outside New Orleans, at which have appeared some of the top entertainers in America. Subsequently, Costello invested his money in New

York real estate (including 79 Wall Street, which he later sold), the Copacabana night club, and a leading brand of Scotch whiskey.

Costello's political opportunity came when a money-hungry Tammany, starved by lack of patronage from Roosevelt and LaGuardia, turned to him for financial support. The Italian community in New York has for years nursed a grievance against the Irish and, to a lesser extent, the Jewish political groups for monopolizing political power. They complained about the lack of judicial jobs, the small number—usually one—of Italian congressmen, the lack of representation on the state tickets. But the Italians lacked the means to make their ambition a reality. Although they formed a large voting bloc, there was rarely sufficient wealth to finance political clubs. Italian immigrants, largely poor peasants from southern Italy and Sicily, lacked the mercantile experience of the Jews and the political experience gained in the seventy-five-year history of Irish immigration.

During the Prohibition years, the Italian racketeers had made certain political contacts in order to gain protection. Costello, always the compromiser and fixer rather than the muscle-man, was the first to establish relations with Jimmy Hines, the powerful leader of the West Side in Tammany Hall. But his rival, Lucky Luciano, suspicious of the Irish and seeking more direct power, backed and elected Al Marinelli for district leader of the Lower West Side. Marinelli in 1932 was the only Italian leader inside Tammany Hall. Later, he was joined by Dr. Paul Sarubbi, a partner of gangster Johnny Torrio in a large, legitimate liquor concern. Certainly, Costello and Luciano represented no "unified" move by the Italians as a whole for power: within the Italian community there are as many divisions as in any other group. What is significant is that different Italians, for different reasons and in various fashions, were achieving influence for the first time. Marinelli became county clerk of New York and a leading power in Tammany. In 1937, after being blasted by Tom Dewey, then running for district attorney, as a "political ally of thieves . . . and big-shot racketeers," Marinelli was removed from office by Governor Lehman. The subsequent conviction by Dewey of Luciano and Hines, and the election of LaGuardia, left most of the Tammany clubs financially weak and foundering. This was the moment Costello made his move. In a few years, by judicious financing, he controlled a block of "Italian" leaders in the Hall—as well as some Irish on the upper West Side and some Jewish leaders on the East Side—and was able to influence the selection of a number of Italian judges. The most notable incident, revealed by a wire tap on Costello's phone, was the "Thank you, Francisco" call in 1943 by Supreme Court judge nominee Thomas Aurelio, who gave Costello full credit for his nomination.

It was not only Tammany that was eager to accept campaign contributions from newly rich Italians, even though some of these *nouveaux riches* had "arrived" through bootlegging and gambling. Fiorello LaGuardia, the wiliest mind that melting-pot politics has ever produced, understood in the early thirties where much of his covert support came from. (So, too, did Vito Marcantonio, an apt pupil of the master: Marcantonio has consistently made deals with the Italian leaders of Tammany Hall—in 1943 he supported Aurelio and refused to repudiate him even when the Democratic party formally did.) Joe Adonis, who had built a political following during the late twenties, when he ran a popular speakeasy, aided LaGuardia financially to a considerable extent in 1933. "The Democrats haven't recognized the Italians," Adonis told a friend. "There is no reason for the Italians to support anybody but LaGuardia; the Jews have played ball with the Democrats and haven't gotten much out of it. They know it now. They will vote for LaGuardia. So will the Italians."

Adonis played his cards shrewdly. He supported LaGuardia, but also a number of Democrats for local and judicial posts, and became a power in the Brooklyn area. His restaurant was frequented by Kenny Sutherland, the Coney Island Democratic leader; Irwin Steingut, the Democratic minority leader in Albany; Anthony DiGiovanni, later a councilman; William O'Dwyer; and Jim Moran. But, in 1937, Adonis made the mistake of supporting Royal Copeland against LaGuardia, and the irate Fiorello finally drove Adonis out of New York.

LaGuardia later turned his ire against Costello, too. Yet Costello survived and reached the peak of his influence in 1942, when he was instrumental in electing Michael Kennedy leader of Tammany Hall. Despite the Aurelio fiasco, which brought Costello into notoriety, he still had sufficient power in the Hall to swing votes for Hugo Rogers as Tammany leader in 1948. In those years many a Tammany leader came hat-in-hand to Costello's apartment or sought him out on the golf links to obtain the nomination for a judicial post.

During this period, other Italian political leaders were also coming to the fore. Generoso Pope, whose Colonial Sand and Stone Company began to prosper through political contacts, became an important political figure, especially when his purchase of the two largest Italian-language dailies (later merged into one), and of a radio station, gave him almost a monopoly of channels to Italian-speaking opinion of the city. Through Generoso Pope, and through Costello, the Italians became a major political force in New York.

That the urban machines, largely Democratic, have financed their heavy campaign costs in this fashion rather than having to turn to the "moneyed interests" explains in some part why these machines were able, in part, to support the New and Fair Deals without suffering the pressures they might have been subjected to had their source of money supply been the business groups. Although he has never publicly revealed his political convictions, it is likely that Frank Costello was a fervent admirer of Franklin D. Roosevelt and his efforts to aid the common man. The basic measures of the New Deal, which most Americans today agree were necessary for the public good, would not have been possible without the support of the "corrupt" big-city machines.

THE "NEW" MONEY—AND THE OLD

There is little question that men of Italian origin appeared in most of the leading roles in the high drama of gambling and mobs, just as twenty years ago the children of East European Jews were the most prominent figures in organized crime, and before that individuals of Irish descent were similarly prominent. To some extent statistical accident and the tendency of newspapers to emphasize the few sensational figures gives a greater illusion about the domination of illicit activities by a single ethnic group than all the facts warrant. In many cities, particularly in the South and on the West Coast, the mob and gambling fraternity consisted of many other groups, and often, predominantly, of native white Protestants. Yet it is clear that in the major northern urban centers there was distinct ethnic sequence in the modes of obtaining illicit wealth and that, uniquely in the case of the recent Italian elements, the former bootleggers and gamblers provided considerable leverage for the growth of political influence as well. A substantial number of Italian judges sitting on the bench in New York today are indebted in one fashion or another to Costello; so too are many Italian district leaders—as well as some Jewish and Irish politicians. And the motive in establishing Italian political prestige in New York was generous rather than scheming for personal advantage. For Costello it was largely a case of ethnic pride. As in earlier American eras, organized illegality became a stepladder of social ascent.

To the world at large, the news and pictures of Frank Sinatra, for example, mingling with former Italian mobsters could come somewhat as a shock. Yet, to Sinatra, and to many Italians, these were men who had grown up in their neighborhoods and who were, in some instances, bywords in the community for their helpfulness and their charities. The early Italian gangsters were hoodlums—rough, unlettered, and young (Al Capone was only twenty-nine at the height of his power). Those who survived learned to adapt. By now they are men of middle age or older. They learned to dress conservatively. Their homes are in respectable suburbs. They sent their children to good schools and sought to avoid publicity. Costello even went to a psychiatrist in his efforts to overcome a painful feeling of inferiority in the world of manners.

As happens with all "new" money in American society, the rough and ready contractors, the construction people, trucking entrepreneurs, as well as racketeers, polished up their manners and sought recognition and respectability in their own ethnic as well as in the general community.

The "shanty" Irish became the "lace curtain" Irish, and then moved out for wider recognition. Sometimes acceptance came first in established "American" society, and this was a certificate for later recognition by the ethnic community, a process well illustrated by the belated acceptance in established Negro society of such figures as Sugar Ray Robinson and Joe Louis, as well as leading popular entertainers.

Yet, after all, the foundation of many a distinguished older American fortune was laid by sharp practices and morally reprehensible methods. The pioneers of American capitalism were not graduated from Harvard's School of Business Administration. The early settlers and founding fathers, as well as those who "won the West" and built up cattle, mining, and other fortunes, often did so by shady speculations and a not inconsiderable amount of violence. They ignored, circumvented, or stretched the law when it stood in the way of America's destiny and their own—or were themselves the law when it served their purposes. This has not prevented them and their descendants from feeling proper moral outrage when, under the changed circumstances of the crowded urban environments, latecomers pursued equally ruthless tactics.

III. THE SCOPE AND QUALITY OF RACIAL AND ETHNIC ATTITUDES

17. Negro-Jewish Prejudice: Authoritarianism and Some Social Variables as Correlates

RICHARD L. SIMPSON

Relatively few studies have examined attitudes of members of two minority groups toward one another. Fewer still have attempted to combine that examination with an inquiry into the interaction between personality variables and ethnic group membership. Simpson's study has this dual aim. In carrying out his study of mutual and reciprocal prejudices among Negroes and Jews, he found that some variables are closely associated with prejudice in both groups—a punitive outlook, "conventional" religiosity, social isolation. Other variables have more prominent effects in one group than in the other—such as education among the Jewish respondents, and sex among the Negro ones.

SOURCE: *Social Problems*, Vol. 7, No. 2, 1959, pp. 138–46 (footnotes and tables omitted). Reprinted by permission of the author and of the Society for the Study of Social Problems.

Richard L. Simpson is Associate Professor of Sociology at the University of North Carolina. He is the author of *Attendants in American Mental Hospitals*, and co-editor of *Social Organization and Behavior* (with Ida Harper Simpson).

Since the publication of the classic study by Adorno et al.,[1] numerous researchers have confirmed their finding that authoritarianism is associated with ethnic prejudice. Most studies, however, have focused on the attitudes of the majority group (white non-Jewish) subjects. This paper will report tests of five hypotheses designed to discover whether authoritarianism is associated with anti-Semitism among Negroes and with anti-Negro prejudice among Jews. Findings will also be presented showing the relationships between prejudice and certain social variables among Negroes and Jews.

METHOD

Staff members of the Cornell University Intergroup Relations Project interviewed, in the summer of 1949, 150 Negroes and 150 Jews randomly selected from the Negro and Jewish populations aged 21 and older in a north-eastern city of about 60 thousand population. Included in the interview schedule were the following questions, which were used to measure prejudice:

TENSION QUESTIONS

(a) "On the whole, would you say you like or dislike (Negroes, Jews)?" If dislike: "Are your feelings about (Negroes, Jews) very strong, pretty strong, or not strong at all?"

(b) "As you see it, are (Negroes, Jews) today demanding more than they have a right to or not?" If yes: "Does this make you pretty angry, a little angry, or don't you feel strongly?"

(c) "Do you think that (Negroes, Jews) today are trying to push in where they are not wanted?" If yes: "Does this bother you a great deal, a little, or hardly at all?"

SOCIAL DISTANCE QUESTIONS

"Do you think you would ever find it a little distasteful:

(a) to eat at the same table with a (Negro, Jew)?"
(b) to dance with a (Negro, Jew)?"
(c) to go to a party and find that most of the people are (Negroes, Jews)?"
(d) to have a (Negro, Jew) marry someone in your family?"

STEREOTYPE QUESTION

Asked of Jews: Agree or disagree: "Generally, speaking, Negroes are lazy and ignorant."

Asked of Negroes: Agree or disagree: "Although some Jews are honest, in general Jews are dishonest in their business dealings."

---

[1] *The Authoritarian Personality*, New York, Harper, 1950.

To construct a measure of prejudice, respondents were assigned separate scores on the tension, social distance, and stereotype questions and these three scores were combined into an over-all prejudice score. In assigning tension scores, on each tension question the most unprejudiced response counted zero, the most prejudiced (an unfavorable response about which the subject felt very strongly) counted two, and any other response counted one. In assigning social distance scores, each affirmative response counted one and each negative response zero. On the stereotype questions, respondents were simply classified according to whether they agreed, disagreed, or gave "don't know" answers to the questions. It was found that the tension scores, social distance scores, and stereotype answers were sufficiently intercorrelated to make feasible a combination of the three into an overall prejudice score, in the following way. Respondents were divided into high-prejudice and low-prejudice groups as nearly equal in size as possible on the basis of their tension scores; the high-prejudice respondents were given two points, the low-prejudice respondents, zero. The same procedure was followed with the social distance scores, each respondent receiving two or zero points. On the stereotype questions, agreement with the stereotype gave a score of two, "don't know" one, and disagreement zero. Adding these scores, all respondents were assigned over-all prejudice scores ranging from zero to six. Seventy-five Negroes had scores from zero to three and were designated "low-prejudice Negroes." The remaining 75 Negroes, with scores from four to six, were designated "high-prejudice Negroes." Seventy-seven Jews with scores zero to two were designated "low-prejudice Jews" and 73 with scores three to six were designated "high-prejudice Jews." All further analysis of the data was based on this classification of respondents as high- and low-prejudice Negroes and Jews.

Various questionnaire items were used as indicators of different aspects of authoritarianism. These items will be presented in connection with the specific hypotheses to which they relate.

FINDINGS: AUTHORITARIANISM AND PREJUDICE

Tests of five hypotheses derived from the general theory that authoritarianism is associated with prejudice among Negroes and Jews will be presented. . . .

Hypothesis 1. People with a punitive, disciplinarian outlook tend to be highly prejudiced. Two questions were used to measure punitiveness:

(a) Agree or disagree: "The most important thing to teach children is to obey *every* order their parents give *without question* even if they think the parents are wrong."
(b) Agree or disagree: "Prison is too good for sex criminals. They should be publicly whipped or worse."

According to our hypothesis, agreement with these statements should be associated with prejudice, and this was found to be the case. Of the Negroes who agreed with both statements—designated high in punitiveness . . . —67 per cent were in the high-prejudice group, as compared with 39 per cent of those who agreed with only one statement or neither. A Chi-square test of this finding shows a probability less than .01. Among the Jews, 63 per cent of those who agreed with one or both statements but only 38 per cent of those who disagreed with both were high in prejudice. A Chi-square test shows a probability less than .01.

These data on both Negroes and Jews support Hypothesis 1.

Hypothesis 2. People who view life as a harsh, competitive struggle tend to be highly prejudiced. On the basis of three questions, each respondent was assigned a score which measured the extent to which he subscribed to a viewpoint labeled the "jungle philosophy." One who adheres to this philosophy, according to our hypothesis, carries a rich vein of hostility which finds an outlet in ethnic prejudice. The three questions, and the way in which they were scored in assigning "jungle philosophy scores," are as follows:

(a) "Some say you can't be too careful in your dealings with others, while others say that most people can be trusted. From your experience, which would you agree with more?" ("Can't be too careful" gets one point for jungle philosophy score.)
(b) Agree or disagree: "I have to struggle for everything I get in life." ("Agree" gets one point.)
(c) "How often do you find yourself bitter about the way things have turned out for you? Would you say often, sometimes, or hardly ever?" ("Often" or "sometimes" gets one point.)

Negroes averaged considerably higher in jungle philosophy than Jews. The 68 Negroes who scored three were classified high in jungle philosophy, as were the 48 Jews who scored either two or three.

The hypothesized relationship between jungle philosophy and prejudice was found to exist among both Negroes and Jews, but neither finding was significant at the .05 level on a Chi-square test. Therefore Hypothesis 2 cannot be accepted as confirmed, although the relationships found were in the hypothesized direction.

Hypothesis 3. Intrapunitive people tend to be relatively unprejudiced. Intrapunitive people were defined as those who agreed with the statement, "When things go wrong, I usually find that it's my own fault." The hypothesized relationship between intrapunitiveness and low prejudice was found in both ethnic groups, and the probabilities of obtaining Chi-squares as large as those obtained were less than .02 for the Negroes and less than .01 for the Jews. These findings support Hypothesis 3.

Hypothesis 4. Conventionally religious people tend to be highly preju-

diced. This hypothesis is derived from the finding by Adorno et al.[2] that the authoritarian is highly conventional in his social attitudes and behavior, using conventional beliefs as an emotional anchor to cling to in an uncertain and dangerous world.

Negroes' frequency of church attendance was used to measure their conventional religiousness. . . . Negroes high in religious attendance—those who reported attending services most Sundays or every Sunday—were, as predicted, more likely to be highly prejudiced than were the infrequent attenders or non-attenders. A Chi-square test shows a probability less than .01.

Among the Jews, however, respondents high in religious attendance— those who reported attending both High Holy Day and Sabbath services —were not significantly more prejudiced than those who reported attending services on High Holy Days only or not at all.

In a further effort to see whether conventional religiousness might be associated with anti-Negro prejudice among Jews, the Jews were classified according to whether they belonged to the Orthodox Synagogue, the Reform Temple, or neither. As predicted, Synagogue members tended to be more prejudiced than Temple members, and Jews who did not belong to either congregation were the least prejudiced of all, though this finding was not significant at the .05 level on a Chi-square test.

In a further test of the relation between religiousness and prejudice among Jews, Temple and Synagogue members were classified according to whether they believed that Jews should observe most, only some, or hardly any Jewish customs such as dietary laws. Synagogue members who believed in following most Jewish customs, and Temple members who believed in following most or some customs, were designated high in conventional religiousness. The hypothesized relationship between religiousness and prejudice was found, with Chi-square tests showing probabilities less than .01 and .04 for Synagogue and Temple members respectively. When the high-religious and low-religious categories of Synagogue and Temple members were combined to produce a single high-or-low-religious dichotomy for all Jews who belonged to either congregation, 62 per cent of the highly religious Jews but only 37 per cent of the less religious Jews were in the high-prejudice group. For this tabulation, a Chi-square test shows a probability less than .01.

Thus the data on both Negroes and Jews are consistent with Hypothesis 4.

Hypothesis 5. Status-strivers tend to be highly prejudiced. Studies of authoritarianism have found that status, like power, is very important to the authoritarian individual. From this we would expect status-striving to

[2] *Ibid.*

be associated with prejudice, and a number of studies have confirmed this expectation.

In the present study, two questions were used to measure the extent of status-striving:

(a) "Do you think a person's aim in life should be to constantly try to get ahead in his work, or do you think if he has a job he likes he should settle down and be contented?"
(b) "Do you think a person should keep trying to get into a better class of people socially, or should he stick pretty much to the social friends he grew up with?"

. . . Respondents are classified according to whether they gave status-striving responses to both questions (high status-strivers), to one but not both (medium), or to neither (low). The results among the Negroes were the *opposite* of our prediction. Negroes high in status-striving were the least prejudiced, and Negroes low in status-striving were the most prejudiced. The differences were large (28 per cent vs. 60 per cent highly prejudiced) and significant at the .04 level on a Chi-square test. Among the Jews, there was no consistent relationship in either direction between status-striving and prejudice.

Hypothesis 5 therefore cannot be accepted. The substantially different results obtained among Negroes and among Jews suggest that additional research would be needed to clarify the relationships between status-striving and differing degrees of prejudice.

Findings: Social Correlates of Prejudice

Statistical findings showing the association of social characteristics with prejudice . . . include the test of one hypothesis regarding social isolation and prejudice, and findings regarding sex, education, and age as correlates of prejudice.

Hypothesis 6. Social isolates tend to be highly prejudiced. The reasoning behind this hypothesis is that people who feel socially inadequate will tend to avoid extensive social contacts, and will use ethnic prejudice as an unconscious ego-bolstering device. Alternatively, one might reason that people who are denied social contact with others will come to feel inadequate and will therefore use ethnic prejudice as an ego-support. Two questions were used to measure social isolation:

(a) "Do you have a bunch of close friends who visit back and forth in each other's homes?"
(b) "Do you belong to any organizations, not counting church?"

The prediction, that people who had no close friends and who belonged to no organizations would be the most prejudiced, was borne out at the .02 level of significance or better for both questions among both Negroes and Jews.

Sex, Education, Age, and Prejudice   We began with no hypotheses regarding sex, education, and age as correlates of prejudice, although we expected to find the greatest amount of prejudice among the older and less educated respondents. The findings were not what we expected, and we have no satisfactory explanation for them. They are presented simply as data, in the hope that future research will clarify the relationships found.

Among Negroes, no consistent or significant relationship was found between either age or education and anti-Semitism. . . . Negro women, however, were strikingly more prejudiced than Negro men. More than two-thirds of the Negro women, but only a fourth of the Negro men, were in the high-prejudice half of the Negro sample. No other variable, with the exception of the educational level among Jews, showed so high an association with prejudice. Further tabulation controlling on other variables . . . failed to explain the differences between Negro men and Negro women.

Among the Jews, education was very strongly related to prejudice. College-educated Jews were less than half as likely as those without college education to be highly prejudiced. Since it is well known that the younger people in all ethnic groups are remaining in school longer than their elders did, we felt that the negative association between education and prejudice among the Jews might be explainable on the basis of their age. To examine this possibility, the high and low prejudice groups of Jews were classified by both age and education. When this was done, it was found that age differences in prejudice were not the explanation for the educational differences, but instead differences between educational levels provided the explanation for what would otherwise have appeared to be differences in prejudice between age groups. (The younger but less educated Jews, who tended to be low in prejudice, were an exception to this generalization.)

Jewish men and Jewish women did not differ significantly in prejudice. . . . Thus we find, paradoxically, that age and education were related to prejudice among Jews but not among Negroes, while sex was related to prejudice among Negroes but not among Jews.

Summary and Discussion

The data lend support to four of the five hypotheses relating prejudice to aspects of authoritarianism, and to the hypothesis that social isolation is associated with prejudice. The discussion below will be confined to the one authoritarianism hypothesis which did not work out as expected and the findings regarding sex, education, and age as correlates of prejudice.

Status-Striving The hypothesis that status-strivers are highly prejudiced was derived from the authoritarian personality hypothesis; status-striving is generally held to be a characteristic of the authoritarian personality. This hypothesis, as we have seen, was not borne out. Status-striving showed no significant relationship to prejudice among Jews, and was *negatively* related to anti-Semitism among Negroes.

We are frankly unable to suggest any explanation for the negative finding about status-striving and prejudice among Jews. It would make sense to hypothesize that *moderate* status-striving is correlated with lack of prejudice and extreme striving or extreme nonstriving is correlated with high prejudice, on the ground that the emotionally secure individual in our culture will be a moderate striver and will be relatively unprejudiced. Our finding, however, while not statistically significant, suggests that the moderate strivers among Jews may be the *most* prejudiced. For this we have no explanation.

Among the Negroes, a plausible explanation for the negative association between status-striving and prejudice can be ventured, subject to future test. It may be that anti-Semitism among Negroes is a function of emotional insecurity, not merely of the authoritarian defense against insecurity. It may also be that among Negroes, the nonstrivers are the least emotionally secure; they are people who do not strive because they have lost hope. This suggestion is consistent with the lack of relationship between striving and prejudice among the Jews. Jews, unlike Negroes, have comparatively little difficulty in improving their social position if they are determined to do so.

Prejudice among Men and Women We know of no reason to expect Jewish men and women to differ in anti-Negro prejudice; therefore our finding that they did not differ in our sample does not seem to require explanation. We are left, however, with the finding that Negro women were much more anti-Semitic than were Negro men.

Williams* hypothesizes that contacts between members of two groups will reduce prejudice if the persons interact "as functional equals, on a common task jointly accepted as worthwhile." Contact between members of different groups, where one is subordinate to the other, is more likely to intensify any stereotypes and hostilities which exist. It seems likely that Negro women interact with whites as equals less often than Negro men do. Negro women work as domestic servants under the command of white

---

* Robin M. Williams, Jr., *The Reduction of Intergroup Tensions*, Social Science Bulletin No. 57 (New York: Social Science Research Council, 1947), p. 69.

women, or in menial capacities as kitchen workers, cleaning women, and the like in business organizations. If they do not work for white employers, they stay at home and have virtually no contact with whites except in secondary relationships such as shopping. Negro men, on the other hand, are much more likely to work with white men as equals; or if they occupy subordinate positions, they often engage in the banter and give-and-take which are more characteristic of male than of female informal group life; consider, for example, the joking and horseplay of workers at service stations, white and Negro, North and South. These facts, coupled with Williams' hypothesis, may help to explain the greater anti-Semitism found among the women in our Negro sample. It is also likely that some Negro women in our sample worked as domestics for Jewish housewives, thus adding a specifically Jewish component to whatever anti-white feelings they may have had.

Education, Age, and Prejudice   Among Negroes, neither education nor age was significantly related to prejudice. Among Jews, however, the youthful and the college-educated showed the least prejudice. A plausible explanation for this finding lies in the realm of inter-ethnic contacts. Jews of the younger generation, and virtually all college-educated Jews, have had extensive contacts with Gentiles. Older, less educated Jews are more likely to have confined their social participation to limited circles of Jewish friends and relatives, where Jewish ethnocentrism and stereotyped ideas about the Goyim—including Negroes—prevail.

These interpretations are of course sheer speculation, but the findings regarding social correlates of prejudice are so striking that they seem to call for further research. All findings, including the tests of hypotheses, should be interpreted with caution. They are based on a single survey in one city; and the validity of interview items as indicators of deep-seated psychodynamic patterns may be open to question and has not been established in the present instance. Moreover, the number of cases was too small to permit a number of cross-tabulations which might have helped to clarify some of the relationships found.

18. The Mutual Images and Expectations of Anglo-Americans and Mexican-Americans

OZZIE G. SIMMONS

Simmons' paper resembles Simpson's in its comparison of attitudes of two ethnic groups toward one another; however, Simmons' focus and method are different. Rather than presenting quantitative data, he perspicaciously describes group members' feelings and beliefs, and shows how they relate to the groups' cultures and relative social statuses. The dominant Anglo-Americans think that Mexicans are inferior, incapable, or unmotivated to improve themselves. The Mexican-Americans, especially those in the middle class, call attention to the hypocrisy implied in the Anglo definition of the situation, and see no reason why they should not try to retain enough of their own traditional culture to have the best of both worlds. Simmons clearly reveals that an important reason why neither group understands the other is that both have their perceptions rooted in different basic values.

A number of psychological and sociological studies have treated ethnic and racial stereotypes as they appear publicly in the mass media and also as held privately by individuals.[1] The present paper is based on data collected for a study of a number of aspects of the relations between Anglo-Americans and Mexican-Americans in a South Texas community, and is concerned with the principal assumptions and expectations that Anglo- and Mexican-Americans hold of one another; how they see each other; the extent to which these pictures are realistic; and the implications of their intergroup relations and cultural differences for the fulfillment of their mutual expectations.[2]

[1] See John Harding, Bernard Kutner, Harold Proshansky, and Isidor Chein, "Prejudice and Ethnic Relations," in Gardner Lindzey (ed.), *Handbook of Social Psychology* (Cambridge, Addison-Wesley Publishing Company, 1954), vol. 2, pp. 1021–1061; and Otto Klineberg, *Tensions Affecting International Understanding*, New York, Social Science Research Council, 1950, Bulletin 62.

[2] The term "Anglo-American," as is common in the Southwest, refers to all residents of Border City who do not identify themselves as Spanish-speaking and of Mexican descent. The Anglo-Americans of Border City have emigrated there from all parts of the United States and represent a wide variety of regional and ethnic backgrounds. The

SOURCE: *Daedalus*, Vol. 90, No. 2, 1961, pp. 286–99. Reprinted by permission of the author, *Daedalus*, and the American Academy of Arts and Sciences.

Ozzie G. Simmons is Professor of Sociology and Director of the Institute of Behavioral Science at the University of Colorado. He is the co-author of *The Mental Patient Comes Home* and of numerous papers on public health, medical sociology, and cross-cultural illness behavior.

The Community

The community studied (here called "Border City") is in South Texas, about 250 miles south of San Antonio. Driving south from San Antonio, one passes over vast expanses of brushland and grazing country, then suddenly comes upon acres of citrus groves, farmlands rich with vegetables and cotton, and long rows of palm trees. This is the "Magic Valley," an oasis in the semidesert region of South Texas. The Missouri Pacific Railroad (paralleled by Highway 83, locally called "The longest street in the world") bisects twelve major towns and cities of the Lower Rio Grande Valley between Brownsville, near the Gulf of Mexico, and Rio Grande City, 103 miles to the west.

Border City is neither the largest nor the smallest of these cities, and is physically and culturally much like the rest. Its first building was constructed in 1905. By 1920 it had 5,331 inhabitants, and at the time of our study these had increased to an estimated 17,500. The completion of the St. Louis, Brownsville, and Mexico Railroad in 1904 considerably facilitated Anglo-American immigration to the Valley. Before this the Valley had been inhabited largely by Mexican ranchers, who maintained large haciendas in the traditional Mexican style based on peonage. Most of these haciendas are now divided into large or small tracts that are owned by Anglo-Americans, who obtained them through purchase or less legitimate means. The position of the old Mexican-American landowning families has steadily deteriorated, and today these families, with a few exceptions, are completely overshadowed by the Anglo-Americans, who have taken over their social and economic position in the community.

The Anglo-American immigration into the Valley was paralleled by that of the Mexicans from across the border, who were attracted by the seemingly greater opportunities for farm labor created by the introduction of irrigation and the subsequent agricultural expansion. Actually, there had been a small but steady flow of Mexican immigration into South Texas that long antedated the Anglo-American immigration.[3] At present, Mexican-Americans probably constitute about two-fifths of the total population of the Valley.

terms "Mexican-American" and "Mexican," as used here, refer to all residents of Border City who are Spanish-speaking and of Mexican descent. The term "Spanish-speaking" is perhaps less objectionable to many people, but for present purposes is even less specific than Mexican or Mexican-American, since it also refers to ethnic groups that would have no sense of identification with the group under consideration here.

[3] For the historical background of the Valley, see Frank C. Pierce, *A Brief History of the Lower Rio Grande Valley*, Menasha, George Banta Publishing Company, 1917; Paul S. Taylor, *An American-Mexican Frontier*, Chapel Hill, University of North Carolina Press, 1934; and Florence J. Scott, *Historical Heritage of the Lower Rio Grande*, San Antonio, The Naylor Company, 1937.

In Border City, Mexican-Americans comprise about 56 percent of the population. The southwestern part of the city, adjoining and sometimes infiltrating the business and industrial areas, is variously referred to as "Mexiquita," "Mexican-town," and "Little Mexico" by the city's Anglo-Americans, and as the *colonia* by the Mexican-Americans. With few exceptions, the *colonia* is inhabited only by Mexican-Americans, most of whom live in close proximity to one another in indifferently constructed houses on tiny lots. The north side of the city, which lies across the railroad tracks, is inhabited almost completely by Anglo-Americans. Its appearance is in sharp contrast to that of the *colonia* in that it is strictly residential and displays much better housing.

In the occupational hierarchy of Border City, the top level (the growers, packers, canners, businessmen, and professionals) is overwhelmingly Anglo-American. In the middle group (the white-collar occupations) Mexicans are prominent only where their bilingualism makes them useful, for example, as clerks and salesmen. The bottom level (farm laborers, shed and cannery workers, and domestic servants) is overwhelmingly Mexican-American.

These conditions result from a number of factors, some quite distinct from the reception accorded Mexican-Americans by Anglo-Americans. Many Mexican-Americans are still recent immigrants and are thus relatively unfamiliar with Anglo-American culture and urban living, or else persist in their tendency to live apart and maintain their own institutions whenever possible. Among their disadvantages, however, the negative attitudes and discriminatory practices of the Anglo-American group must be counted. It is only fair to say, with the late Ruth Tuck, that much of what Mexican-Americans have suffered at Anglo-American hands has not been perpetrated deliberately but through indifference, that it has been done not with the fist but with the elbow.[4] The average social and economic status of the Mexican-American group has been improving, and many are moving upward. This is partly owing to increasing acceptance by the Anglo-American group, but chiefly to the efforts of the Mexican-Americans themselves.

ANGLO-AMERICAN ASSUMPTIONS AND EXPECTATIONS

Robert Lynd writes of the dualism in the principal asumptions that guide Americans in conducting their everyday life and identifies the attempt to "live by contrasting rules of the game" as a characteristic aspect of our culture.[5] This pattern of moral compromise, symptomatic of what is likely to be only vaguely a conscious moral conflict, is evident in Anglo-American assumptions and expectations with regard to Mexican-Americans, which

[4] Ruth D. Tuck, *Not with the Fist*, New York, Harcourt Brace and Company, 1946.
[5] Robert S. Lynd, *Knowledge for What?* Princeton, Princeton University Press, 1948.

appear both in the moral principles that define what intergroup relations ought to be, and in the popular notions held by Anglo-Americans as to what Mexican-Americans are "really" like. In the first case there is a response to the "American creed," which embodies ideals of the essential dignity of the individual and of certain inalienable rights to freedom, justice, and equal opportunity. Accordingly, Anglo-Americans believe that Mexican-Americans must be accorded full acceptance and equal status in the larger society. When their orientation to these ideals is uppermost, Anglo-Americans believe that the assimilation of Mexican-Americans is only a matter of time, contingent solely on the full incorporation of Anglo-American values and ways of life.

These expectations regarding the assimilation of the Mexican are most clearly expressed in the notion of the "high type" of Mexican. It is based on three criteria: occupational achievement and wealth (the Anglo-American's own principal criteria of status) and command of Anglo-American ways. Mexican-Americans who can so qualify are acceptable for membership in the service clubs and a few other Anglo-American organizations and for limited social intercourse. They may even intermarry without being penalized or ostracized. Both in their achievements in business and agriculture and in wealth, they compare favorably with middle-class Anglo-Americans, and they manifest a high command of the latter's ways. This view of the "high type" of Mexican reflects the Anglo-American assumption that Mexicans are assimilable; it does not necessarily insure a full acceptance of even the "high type" of Mexican or that his acceptance will be consistent.

The assumption that Mexican-Americans will be ultimately assimilated was not uniformly shared by all the Anglo-Americans who were our informants in Border City. Regardless of whether they expressed adherence to this ideal, however, most Anglo-Americans expressed the contrasting assumption that Mexican-Americans are essentially inferior. Thus the same people may hold assumptions and expectations that are contradictory, although expressed at different times and in different situations. As in the case of their adherence to the ideal of assimilability, not all Anglo-Americans hold the same assumptions and expectations with respect to the inferiority of Mexican-Americans; and even those who agree vary in the intensity of their beliefs. Some do not believe in the Mexican's inferiority at all; some are relatively moderate or skeptical, while others express extreme views with considerable emotional intensity.

Despite this variation, the Anglo-Americans' principal assumptions and expectations emphasize the Mexicans' presumed inferiority. In its most characteristic pattern, such inferiority is held to be self-evident. As one Anglo-American woman put it, "Mexicans are inferior because they are so typically and naturally Mexican." Since they are so obviously inferior, their present subordinate status is appropriate and is really their own fault. There is a ready identification between Mexicans and menial labor, buttressed by an image of the Mexican worker as improvident, undependable, irresponsible, childlike, and indolent. If Mexicans are fit for only the humblest labor, there is nothing abnormal about the fact that most Mexican workers are at the bottom of the occupational pyramid, and the fact that most Mexicans are unskilled workers is sufficient proof that they belong in that category.

Associated with the assumption of Mexican inferiority is that of the homogeneity of this group—that is, all Mexicans are alike. Anglo-Americans may classify Mexicans as being of "high type" and "low type" and at the same time maintain that "a Mexican is a Mexican." Both notions serve a purpose, depending on the situation. The assumption that all Mexicans are alike buttresses the assumption of inferiority by making it convenient to ignore the fact of the existence of a substantial number of Mexican-Americans who represent all levels of business and professional achievement. Such people are considered exceptions to the rule.

ANGLO-AMERICAN IMAGES OF MEXICAN-AMERICANS

To employ Gordon Allport's definition, a stereotype is an exaggerated belief associated with a category, and its function is to justify conduct in relation to that category.[6] Some of the Anglo-American images of the Mexican have no ascertainable basis in fact, while others have at least a kernel of truth. Although some components of these images derive from behavior patterns that are characteristic of some Mexican-Americans in some situations, few if any of the popular generalizations about them are valid as stated, and none is demonstrably true of all. Some of the images of Mexican-Americans are specific to a particular area of intergroup relations, such as the image of the Mexican-American's attributes as a worker. Another is specific to politics and describes Mexicans as ready to give their votes to whoever will pay for them or provide free barbecues and beer.[7] Let us consider a few of the stereotypical beliefs that are widely used on general principles to justify Anglo-American practices of exclusion and subordination.

One such general belief accuses Mexican-Americans of being unclean. The examples given of this supposed characteristic most frequently refer

[6] Gordon W. Allport, *The Nature of Prejudice*, Cambridge, Addison-Wesley Publishing Company, 1954.
[7] For an analysis of Mexican-American value orientations and behavior in the occupational and political spheres, see Ozzie G. Simmons, Anglo-Americans and Mexican-Americans in South Texas: A Study in Dominant-Subordinate Group Relations (unpublished doctoral dissertation, Harvard University, 1952).

to a lack of personal cleanliness and environmental hygiene and to a high incidence of skin ailments ascribed to a lack of hygenic practices. Indeed, there are few immigrant groups, regardless of their ethnic background, to whom this defect has not been attributed by the host society, as well as others prominent in stereotypes of the Mexican. It has often been observed that for middle-class Americans cleanliness is not simply a matter of keeping clean but is also an index to the morals and virtues of the individual. It is largely true that Mexicans tend to be much more casual in hygienic practices than Anglo-Americans. Moreover, their labor in the field, the packing sheds, and the towns is rarely clean work, and it is possible that many Anglo-Americans base their conclusions on what they observe in such situations. There is no evidence of a higher incidence of skin ailments among Mexicans than among Anglo-Americans. The belief that Mexicans are unclean is useful for rationalizing the Anglo-American practice of excluding Mexicans from any situation that involves close or allegedly close contact with Anglo-Americans, as in residence, and the common use of swimming pools and other recreational facilities.

Drunkenness and criminality are a pair of traits that have appeared regularly in the stereotypes applied to immigrant groups. They have a prominent place in Anglo-American images of Mexicans. If Mexicans are inveterate drunkards and have criminal tendencies, a justification is provided for excluding them from full participation in the life of the community. It is true that drinking is a popular activity among Mexican-Americans and that total abstinence is rare, except among some Protestant Mexican-Americans. Drinking varies, however, from the occasional consumption of a bottle of beer to the heavy drinking of more potent beverages, so that the frequency of drinking and drunkenness is far from being evenly distributed among Mexican-Americans. Actually, this pattern is equally applicable to the Anglo-American group. The ample patronage of bars in the Anglo-American part of Border City, and the drinking behavior exhibited by Anglo-Americans when they cross the river to Mexico indicate that Mexicans have no monopoly on drinking or drunkenness. It is true that the number of arrests for drunkenness in Border City is greater among Mexicans, but this is probably because Mexicans are more vulnerable to arrest. The court records in Border City show little difference in the contributions made to delinquency and crime by Anglo- and Mexican-Americans.

Another cluster of images in the Anglo-American stereotype portrays Mexican-Americans as deceitful and of a "low" morality, as mysterious, unpredictable, and hostile to Anglo-Americans. It is quite possible that Mexicans resort to a number of devices in their relations with Anglo-Americans, particularly in relations with employers, to compensate for their disadvantages, which may be construed by Anglo-Americans as evidence of deceitfulness. The whole nature of the dominant-subordinate relationship does not make for frankness on the part of Mexicans or encourage them to face up directly to Anglo-Americans in most intergroup contacts. As to the charge of immorality, one need only recognize the strong sense of loyalty and obligation that Mexicans feel in their familial and interpersonal relations to know that the charge is baseless. The claim that Mexicans are mysterious and deceitful may in part reflect Anglo-American reactions to actual differences in culture and personality, but like the other beliefs considered here, is highly exaggerated. The imputation of hostility to Mexicans, which is manifested in a reluctance to enter the *colonia*, particularly at night, may have its kernel of truth, but appears to be largely a projection of the Anglo-American's own feelings.

All three of these images can serve to justify exclusion and discrimination: if Mexicans are deceitful and immoral, they do not have to be accorded equal status and justice; if they are mysterious and unpredictable, there is no point in treating them as one would a fellow Anglo-American; and if they are hostile and dangerous, it is best that they live apart in colonies of their own.

Not all Anglo-American images of the Mexican are unfavorable. Among those usually meant to be complimentary are the beliefs that all Mexicans are musical and always ready for a fiesta, that they are very "romantic" rather than "realistic" (which may have unfavorable overtones as well), and that they love flowers and can grow them under the most adverse conditions. Although each of these beliefs may have a modicum of truth, it may be noted that they tend to reinforce Anglo-American images of Mexicans as childlike and irresponsible, and thus they support the notion that Mexicans are capable only of subordinate status.

MEXICAN-AMERICAN ASSUMPTIONS,
EXPECTATIONS, AND IMAGES

Mexican-Americans are as likely to hold contradictory assumptions and distorted images as are Anglo-Americans. Their principal assumptions, however, must reflect those of Anglo-Americans—that is, Mexicans must take into account the Anglo-Americans' conflict as to their potential equality and present inferiority, since they are the object of such imputations. Similarly, their images of Anglo-Americans are not derived wholly independently, but to some extent must reflect their own subordinate status. Consequently, their stereotypes of Anglo-Americans are much less elaborate, in part because Mexicans feel no need of justifying the present intergroup relation, in part because the very nature of their dependent position forces them to view the relation more realistically than Anglo-Americans do. For the same reasons, they need not hold to their beliefs about Anglo-Americans with the rigidity and intensity so often characteristic of the latter.

Any discussion of these assumptions and expectations requires some mention of the class distinctions within the Mexican-American group.[8] Its middle class, though small as compared with the lower class, is powerful within the group and performs the critical role of intermediary in negotiations with the Anglo-American group. Middle-class status is based on education and occupation, family background, readiness to serve the interests of the group, on wealth, and the degree of acculturation, or command of Anglo-American ways. Anglo-Americans recognize Mexican class distinctions (although not very accurately) in their notions of the "high type" and "low type" of Mexicans.

In general, lower-class Mexicans do not regard the disabilities of their status as being nearly as severe as do middle-class Mexican-Americans. This is primarily a reflection of the insulation between the Anglo-American world and that of the Mexican lower class. Most Mexicans, regardless of class, are keenly aware of Anglo-American attitudes and practices with regard to their group, but lower-class Mexicans do not conceive of participation in the larger society as necessary nor do they regard Anglo-American practices of exclusion as affecting them directly. Their principal reaction has been to maintain their isolation, and thus they have not been particularly concerned with improving their status by acquiring Anglo-American ways, a course more characteristic of the middle-class Mexican.

Mexican-American assumptions and expectations regarding Anglo-Americans must be qualified, then, as being more characteristic of middle- than of lower-class Mexican-Americans. Mexicans, like Anglo-Americans, are subject to conflicts in their ideals, not only because of irrational thinking on their part but also because of Anglo-American inconsistencies between ideal and practice. As for ideals expressing democratic values, Mexican expectations are for obvious reasons the counterpart of the Anglo-Americans'—that Mexican-Americans should be accorded full acceptance and equal opportunity. They feel a considerable ambivalence, however, as to the Anglo-American expectation that the only way to achieve this goal is by a full incorporation of Anglo-American values and ways of life, for this implies the ultimate loss of their cultural identity as Mexicans. On the one hand, they favor the acquisition of Anglo-American culture and the eventual remaking of the Mexican in the Anglo-American image; but on the other hand, they are not so sure that Anglo-American acceptance is worth such a price. When they are concerned with this dilemma, Mexicans advocate a fusion with Anglo-American culture in which the "best" of the Mexican ways, as they view it, would be retained along with the incorpora-

---

[8] See *ibid.*, for a discussion of the Anglo-American and Mexican class structures.

tion of the "best" of the Anglo-American ways, rather than a one-sided exchange in which all that is distinctively Mexican would be lost.

A few examples will illustrate the point of view expressed in the phrase, "the best of both ways." A premium is placed on speaking good, unaccented English, but the retention of good Spanish is valued just as highly as "a mark of culture that should not be abandoned." Similarly, there is an emphasis on the incorporation of behavior patterns that are considered characteristically Anglo-American and that will promote "getting ahead," but not to the point at which the drive for power and wealth would become completely dominant, as is believed to be the case with Anglo-Americans.

Mexican ambivalence about becoming Anglo-American or achieving a fusion of the "best" of both cultures is compounded by their ambivalence about another issue, that of equality versus inferiority. That Anglo-Americans are dominant in the society and seem to monopolize its accomplishments and rewards leads Mexicans at times to draw the same conclusion that Anglo-Americans do, namely that Mexicans are inferior. This questioning of their own sense of worth exists in all classes of the Mexican-American group, although with varying intensity, and plays a substantial part in every adjustment to intergroup relations. There is a pronounced tendency to concede the superiority of Anglo-American ways and consequently to define Mexican ways as undesirable, inferior, and disreputable. The tendency to believe in his own inferiority is counterbalanced, however, by the Mexican's fierce racial pride, which sets the tone of Mexican demands and strivings for equal status, even though these may slip into feelings of inferiority.

The images Mexicans have of Anglo-Americans may not be so elaborate or so emotionally charged as the images that Anglo-Americans have of Mexicans, but they are nevertheless stereotypes, over-generalized, and exaggerated, although used primarily for defensive rather than justificatory purposes. Mexican images of Anglo-Americans are sometimes favorable, particularly when they identify such traits as initiative, ambition, and industriousness as being peculiarly Anglo-American. Unfavorable images are prominent, however, and, although they may be hostile, they never impute inferiority to Anglo-Americans. Most of the Mexican stereotypes evaluate Anglo-Americans on the basis of their attitudes toward Mexican-Americans. For example, one such classification provides a two-fold typology. The first type, the "majority," includes those who are cold, unkind, mercenary, and exploitative. The second type, the "minority," consists of those who are friendly, warm, just, and unprejudiced. For the most part, Mexican images of Anglo-Americans reflect the latter's patterns of exclusion and assumptions of superiority, as experienced by Mexican-Americans. Thus Anglo-Americans are pictured as stolid, phlegmatic, cold-hearted, and distant. They are also said to be braggarts, conceited, inconstant, and insincere.

INTERGROUP RELATIONS, MUTUAL EXPECTATIONS,
AND CULTURAL DIFFERENCES

A number of students of intergroup relations assert that research in this area has yet to demonstrate any relation between stereotypical beliefs and intergroup behavior; indeed, some insist that under certain conditions ethnic attitudes and discrimination can vary independently.[9] Arnold M. Rose, for example, concludes that "from a heuristic standpoint it may be desirable to assume that patterns of intergroup relations, on the one hand, and attitudes of prejudice and stereotyping, on the other hand, are fairly unrelated phenomena although they have reciprocal influences on each other . . ."[10] In the present study, no systematic attempt was made to investigate the relation between the stereotypical beliefs of particular individuals and their actual intergroup behavior; but the study did yield much evidence that both images which justify group separatism and separateness itself are characteristic aspects of intergroup relations in Border City. One of the principal findings is that in those situations in which contact between Anglo-Americans and Mexicans is voluntary (such as residence, education, recreation, religious worship, and social intercourse) the characteristic pattern is separateness rather than common participation. Wherever intergroup contact is necessary, as in occupational activities and the performance of commercial and professional services, it is held to the minimum sufficient to accomplish the purpose of the contact.[11] The extent of this separateness is not constant for all members of the two groups, since it tends to be less severe between Anglo-Americans and those Mexicans they define as of a "high type." Nevertheless, the evidence reveals a high degree of compatibility between beliefs and practices in Border City's intergroup relations, although the data have nothing to offer for the identification of direct relationships.

In any case, the separateness that characterizes intergroup relations cannot be attributed solely to the exclusion practices of the Anglo-American group. Mexicans have tended to remain separate by choice as well as by necessity. Like many other ethnic groups, they have often found this the easier course, since they need not strain to learn another language or to change their ways and manners. The isolation practices of the Mexican

---

[9] Robert K. Merton, "Discrimination and the American Creed," in R. M. MacIver (ed.), *Discrimination and National Welfare* (New York, Harper and Brothers, 1949), pp. 99–128; John Harding, Bernard Kutner, Harold Proshansky, and Isidor Chein, *op. cit.*; Arnold M. Rose, "Intergroup Relations vs. Prejudice: Pertinent Theory for the Study of Social Change," *Social Problems*, 1956, 4: 173–176; Robin M. Williams, Jr., "Racial and Cultural Relations," in Joseph B. Gittler (ed.), *Review of Sociology: Analysis of a Decade* (New York, John Wiley and Sons, 1957), pp. 423–464.
[10] Rose, *op. cit.*   [11] Simmons, *op. cit.*

group are as relevant to an understanding of intergroup relations as are the exclusion practices of the Anglo-Americans.

This should not, however, obscure the fact that to a wide extent the majority of Mexican-Americans share the patterns of living of Anglo-American society; many of their ways are already identical. Regardless of the degree of their insulation from the larger society, the demands of life in the United States have required basic modifications of the Mexicans' cultural tradition. In material culture, Mexicans are hardly to be distinguished from Anglo-Americans, and there have been basic changes in medical beliefs and practices and in the customs regarding godparenthood. Mexicans have acquired English in varying degrees, and their Spanish has become noticeably Anglicized. Although the original organization of the family has persisted, major changes have occurred in patterns of traditional authority, as well as in child training and courtship practices. Still, it is the exceedingly rare Mexican-American, no matter how acculturated he may be to the dominant society, who does not in some degree retain the more subtle characteristics of his Mexican heritage, particularly in his conception of time and in other fundamental value orientations, as well as in his modes of participation in interpersonal relations.[12] Many of the most acculturated Mexican-Americans have attempted to exemplify what they regard as "the best of both ways." They have become largely Anglo-American in their way of living, but they still retain fluent Spanish and a knowledge of their traditional culture, and they maintain an identification with their own heritage while participating in Anglo-American culture. Nevertheless, this sort of achievement still seems a long way off for many Mexican-Americans who regard it as desirable.

A predominant Anglo-American expectation is that the Mexicans will be eventually assimilated into the larger society; but this is contingent upon Mexicans' becoming just like Anglo-Americans. The Mexican counterpart to this expectation is only partially complementary. Mexicans want to be full members of the larger society, but they do not want to give up their cultural heritage. There is even less complementarity of expectation with regard to the present conduct of intergroup relations. Anglo-Americans believe they are justified in withholding equal access to the rewards of full acceptance as long as Mexicans remain "different," particularly since they interpret the differences (both those which have some basis in reality and those which have none) as evidence of inferiority. Mexicans, on the other

---

[12] For cultural differences and similarities between Anglo-Americans and Mexicans, see Simmons, *op. cit.*; Tuck, *op. cit.*; Lyle Saunders, *Cultural Difference and Medical Care,* New York, Russell Sage Foundation, 1954; Munro S. Edmonson, *Los Manitos: A Study of Institutional Values* (New Orleans, Middle American Research Institute, Tulane University, 1957, Publication 25), pp. 1–72; and Margaret Clark, *Health in the Mexican-American Culture,* Berkeley, University of California Press, 1959.

hand, while not always certain that they are not inferior, clearly want equal opportunity and full acceptance now, not in some dim future, and they do not believe that their differences (either presumed or real) from Anglo-Americans offer any justification for the denial of opportunity and acceptance. Moreover, they do not find that acculturation is rewarded in any clear and regular way by progressive acceptance.

It is probable that both Anglo-Americans and Mexicans will have to modify their beliefs and practices if they are to realize more nearly their expectations of each other. Mutual stereotyping, as well as the exclusion practices of Anglo-Americans and the isolation practices of Mexicans, maintains the separateness of the two groups, and separateness is a massive barrier to the realization of their expectations. The process of acculturation is presently going on among Mexican-Americans and will continue, regardless of whether changes in Anglo-Mexican relations occur. Unless Mexican-Americans can validate their increasing command of Anglo-American ways by a free participation in the larger society, however, such acculturation is not likely to accelerate its present leisurely pace, nor will it lead to eventual assimilation. The *colonia* is a relatively safe place in which new cultural acquisitions may be tried out, and thus it has its positive functions; but by the same token it is only in intergroup contacts with Anglo-Americans that acculturation is validated, that the Mexican's level of acculturation is tested, and that the distance he must yet travel to assimilation is measured.[13]

Conclusions

There are major inconsistencies in the assumptions that Anglo-Americans and Mexican-Americans hold about one another. Anglo-Americans assume that Mexican-Americans are their potential, if not actual, peers, but at the same time assume they are their inferiors. The beliefs that presumably demonstrate the Mexican-Americans' inferiority tend to place them outside the accepted moral order and framework of Anglo-American society by attributing to them undesirable characteristics that make it "reasonable" to treat them differently from their fellow Anglo-Americans. Thus the negative images provide not only a rationalized definition of the intergroup relation that makes it palatable for Anglo-Americans, but also a substantial support for maintaining the relation as it is. The assumptions of Mexican-Americans about Anglo-Americans are similarly inconsistent, and their images of Anglo-Americans are predominantly negative, although these are primarily defensive rather than justificatory. The mutual expectations of the two groups contrast sharply with the ideal of a complementarity of

[13] See Leonard Broom and John I. Kitsuse, "The Validation of Acculturation: A Condition to Ethnic Assimilation," *American Anthropologist*, 1955, 57: 44–48.

expectations, in that Anglo-Americans expect Mexicans to become just like themselves, if they are to be accorded equal status in the larger society, whereas Mexican-Americans want full acceptance, regardless of the extent to which they give up their own ways and acquire those of the dominant group.

Anglo-Americans and Mexicans may decide to stay apart because they are different, but cultural differences provide no moral justification for one group to deny to the other equal opportunity and the rewards of the larger society. If the full acceptance of Mexicans by Anglo-Americans is contingent upon the disappearance of cultural differences, it will not be accorded in the foreseeable future. In our American society, we have often seriously underestimated the strength and tenacity of early cultural conditioning. We have expected newcomers to change their customs and values to conform to American ways as quickly as possible, without an adequate appreciation of the strains imposed by this process. An understanding of the nature of culture and of its interrelations with personality can make us more realistic about the rate at which cultural change can proceed and about the gains and costs for the individual who is subject to the experiences of acculturation. In viewing cultural differences primarily as disabilities, we neglect their positive aspects. Mexican-American culture represents the most constructive and effective means Mexican-Americans have yet been able to develop for coping with their changed natural and social environment. They will further exchange old ways for new only if these appear to be more meaningful and rewarding than the old, and then only if they are given full opportunity to acquire the new ways and to use them.

19. An Anglo-Saxon Core Group

AUGUST B. HOLLINGSHEAD AND

FREDRICK C. REDLICH

A minority group in only a numerical sense, old and well-established Anglo-Saxon families rank at or near the top of the status-hierarchy of many small and medium-sized American cities. Because of their wealth, power, and prestige, groups such as the one described here have frequently served

SOURCE: August B. Hollingshead and Fredrick C. Redlich, *Social Class and Mental Illness* (New York: John Wiley and Sons, 1958), pp. 68–79. Copyright © 1958 by John Wiley and Sons, Inc. Reprinted with the permission of the publisher.

August B. Hollingshead is Professor of Sociology at Yale University. One of his best-known books is *Elmtown's Youth.* Fredrick C. Redlich is Professor of Psychiatry at the Yale Medical School.

*as models for the aspirations of many upwardly mobile members of mi-
nority groups. The selection indicates some of the ways that the core group
in New Haven, Connecticut, attempts to maintain its position by controlling exclusiveness and capitalizing on ascribed status criteria that are
available to only a relatively few others. The group looks down on minority
group members, branding even the successful ones as mere "arrivistes." Its
tight control over intimate social interaction, especially its restriction of
marriage to status equals in New Haven or some other city, helps to keep
minority members at a distance and limits their access to informal sources
of power and influence.*

*Some observers believe that such elite groups can perform an important
purpose for American society if their wealth and security, which enable
them to provide well-trained and responsible leaders, are coupled with a
strong sense of noblesse oblige. Others however, holding what is probably
the more prevalent view among American sociologists, believe that any
restriction of the mobility of other members of the society restricts and
ultimately threatens the entire democratic process.*

When persons or families are arranged on the ordinal scales included
in the Index of Social Position, namely, place of residence, education, and
occupation, and their positions on these scales are compared with other
cultural items, such as the newspapers they read or the television programs
they view, their positions on the Index are correlated significantly with
their behavior in regard to most items. Persons who possess particular
patterns of consumption, taste, attitudes, and other identifiable sociocultural characteristics that are correlated with the three factors built into
the Index of Social Position are the constituent units in the population
aggregates which we identify as "social classes." In short, classes, as delineated by the Index of Social Position, are characterized by distinct subcultures. The principal constellation of cultural traits associated with each
class will be traced in the ensuing sections of this chapter. The rich details
of the subculture for each class are based upon a series of studies Hollingshead and his students have made in the last decade supplemented by data
collected for this study.

The specific subcultural traits more or less common to the members of
a class are learned through participation in the behavior system peculiar
to it. The identification of persons with other persons who share similar
cultural values, attitudes, beliefs, and customs produces group solidarity as
well as group differences. Persons in a particular class learn almost unconsciously, in the course of their lives, a subtle series of cues which enable
them to recognize one another and to identify even strangers as equals or
unequals; cues shown by persons in other classes are shared as well. Those
who are marked by out-group stigmata are viewed with suspicion, if not
with hostility or denegation. Differences in patterns of subcultural traits,

and the recognition of them by members of the community, set each class off from the others.

SOCIAL MOBILITY

Social mobility involves a change in the class status of individuals during the course of their lives. The class position occupied by an individual's parental family during his childhood and early adolescence is the base line against which mobility may be measured. Viewed theoretically, an individual either goes through life occupying the class position he inherited from his parental family, or he acquires a different class status through the instrumentality of his own activities. An individual who does not change his class is viewed as being intergenerationally *stable*. An individual who changes his class position is *mobile*. A person who achieves a class status higher than that of his parental family is defined as being *upward mobile*. A person who fails to hold the status occupied by the parental generation and acquires a class position lower than his parents' in the status structure is identified as being *downward mobile*. Generally speaking, upward mobility in the American social structure is approved behavior and downward mobility is unapproved behavior. Mobile behavior is learned in the course of an individual's life, but the details of how mobility or stability are acquired are far from being clear.

The principal requisites for achieving upward mobility are skill, education, and knowledge, particularly in males, and physical beauty, charm, and talent in females. The particular choice of goals of upward mobile persons—power, wealth, or fame—depends on specific values of the individuals concerned.

Class I

STATUS AWARENESS

Each respondent in the control sample was asked a series of questions designed to elicit his awareness of status. The first question asked was: "Do you think classes exist in the community?" The second was: "What things determine one's class?" Each respondent made his own decision as to his belief in classes and the criteria that placed a person in a class. After responses were recorded from these questions, the interviewer asked, "To what class would you say you belong?" The interviewer then read slowly eight choices: "upper," "upper-middle," "middle," "lower-middle," "working," "lower," "do not know," and "I do not believe in classes." The direct questions on "class" brought into focus incongruity between a person's response to a question involving values in the publicly professed dimensions of the culture, particularly if it involves democratic beliefs, and his actions in situations involving in-group codes. A class I matron, who was startled by the questions but who identified herself as "upper" class, provided insight into this facet of the social ethic with the acid comment, "One does not speak of classes; they are felt." In spite of such incongruities, over 98 percent of the class I respondents think there are "social classes" in the community: 37 percent identify with the "upper" class, 56 percent classify themselves as "upper-middle" class, and 5 percent as "lower-middle" class. The remaining 2 percent do not believe in classes.

Whereas class status brings its members into contact with one another in many functional relationships in the maintenance of the community's general social life, ethnic and religious differences segment the 3.4 percent of the community's population placed in class I (by the Index of Social Position) into internally organized, almost self-contained, social worlds. A *core group*, composed of pacesetting, commonly recognized "old families," enjoys the highest prestige and power positions in the status system. Revolving around it are satellite groups composed of persons who have "arrived" recently in the business and professional worlds and, in the words of an *arriviste*,* "Yale professors who try to play the game on $10,000 a year." Although there are distinct differences in the ability of different groups to "play the game," all groups respect and, in many ways, emulate those who sometimes satirically are referred to by members of fringe groups as "proper New Haveners." "Proper New Haveners" are truly "at the summit" of local "society." Members of these families have been at the summit for two, three, and more generations, and some have been in the "nuclear group" since colonial times.

Fifty-three percent of the adults in this class are stable through two and more generations and 47 percent are upward mobile from their parental families. Stable members of the core group possess a complex subculture which aspirants must acquire before they are admitted into the group. Those who are accorded "accepted" status are the "gatekeepers"; they decide which "new people" are invited into their exclusive organizations. Conversely, the gatekeepers "drop the black ball" on those they do not approve.

ECONOMIC ORIENTATION

Executives and professional men head class I families. Those in business are major office holders, such as on boards of trustees, presidents, vice-presidents, secretaries, and treasurers in the larger industries, construction and transportation companies, stores, banks, brokerage houses, and utilities. Two thirds of the men in the professions are in independent practice—lawyers, physicians, engineers, architects, and certified public accountants;

---

* By *"arrivistes"* we mean persons who are upward mobile, who have achieved class I positions through their own efforts rather than by inheritance, usually in the current generation. The connotation of unscrupulousness usually associated with the word does not apply in these discussions.

the other one third are salaried—professors, clergymen, and engineers for the most part. A few executives receive from $40,000 to $50,000 a year, but more earn from $20,000 to $30,000. The modal range for mature free professionals is from $20,00 to $25,000 per year. However, the median reported family income, where the male head is the only one gainfully employed, is $10,000. This median is conditioned in large part by the presence of Yale University and its large, comparatively low-paid faculty, as well as the presence of young professionals, widows, and retired people in the sample. In the 8 percent of the households where a wife is engaged in business or a profession, the median income is $15,025 a year.

Families in the core group are, on the whole, wealthy, but there are large differences in their economic positions. A few families are multi-millionaires; other families may possess only a quarter- to a half-million dollars. The wealth of the core group has been inherited by two, three, and more generations, whereas that of the *arrivistes* has been acquired during the present or previous generation. Inherited wealth is accorded a higher social value within the core group than "made money." Several generations of inherited wealth attests to the genuineness of the patina on the family's pecuniary escutcheon. A family which possessed the ability to make money in the first place, and to hold it and add to it through the generations, has demonstrated its "true" worth.

A cardinal principle in established families is that capital funds should not be squandered. Each generation should live on income only and add to capital by conservative management. Squandering of capital funds results in the next generation's being faced with the problem of earning its living. An inherited income assures a high standard of living without undue effort of a family head to support his family of procreation. Men are expected to look after their inheritances and those of their wives, but estate managers may be employed and trust departments of large banks relied upon for counsel, if not actual management of securities, trusts, and properties. A man should have an occupation or a profession, although he may not rely too heavily upon it for income. Income from inherited wealth supplemented by income from salaries and fees earned by the male head is the most general pattern.

Persons with private incomes are careful to see that the dollar sign is muted on their possessions and on the things they do. The dollar sign and interest in the dollar sign are stigmata of newly rich strivers. Individuals who accumulate wealth view money as *the* requisite of high social position; those who have inherited wealth look to other things as the sine qua non of position. The core group is not ostensibly interested in money, but a substantial income is necessary to their way of life. This point was brought to our attention sharply by an elderly member of a distinguished family who, in response to a question on income, reported with indignation, "We have it."

ETHNIC ORIGIN

Persons able to pass the core group's test of financial means are faced with a more crucial barrier—the lineage test. Lineage is used to protect the group from "social climbers" who are attempting to reach "the summit" on the basis of personal achievement. The upward mobile nuclear family with the right ethnic background is the most serious threat to privileged position, and they are a target for the group's hostile and biting remarks. For example, a man in the core group was discussing local families and their estates when the interviewer commented on the purchase of an estate by an *arriviste* of mixed Irish and Yankee descent in the respondent's neighborhood. The respondent, who was interviewed in his office, straightened in his chair, tapped the desk with a forefinger, and stated emphatically, "Money does not count up there (a hill in a suburb covered with estates). Family background, who you are—these are the things that count." This man overlooks the simple fact that these families could not live on their estates without wealth. An *arriviste* may manage to purchase an estate "on the hill" and be isolated from the social life of the families who accept one another as equals. The question of who one is, ethnically, places acceptance in the group in a different dimension of the social structure from economic competence. A person is able to do something about his role and function in the economic system, but he is powerless in the ethnic dimension of his life. Here he is dependent upon his ancestors.

The core group ascribes a different and lower status to persons from disapproved ethnic backgrounds—Jews, Irish, Italians, Greeks, Poles, and others from southern and eastern Europe. Core group members tend to lump these national origin groups together; all are undesirable. An industrial leader, when asked why New Haven has such a diverse population, stated, "I should say largely it was an overflow of great tidal waves of these races—Italians, Irish, Jews, Germans, and so on—reaching New York and sliding on to the next place. These races are very gregarious, and they are coaxed easily by a roll of money." A prominent core group matron thought that the "Italians just swarmed into this area. It seemed to be the happy hunting ground. New Haven has become an Italian colony. It's amazing." Another emphasized, "The Poles and Italians gave us our vicious gangs." A prominent attorney accused the "Jewish traders" of "gobbling up fine old companies in trouble" and continuing "their Sheeney ways."

Chronologically, wealth comes first; then one's family background is discovered, and the importance of wealth is pushed into the background. The number of generations a family has been prominent *and* resident in the community is important to the elderly arbiters of power and status. This point was well put by a distinguished matriarch while we were discussing the importance of some families in the life of the city over a number of generations. Such a family was named as an illustration. The respondent closed her eyes, thought for a few moments, and resumed the discussion with, "The ———— are not really old New Haveners. They first settled in Saybrook (a pioneer settlement on the Connecticut coast) in the 1640s, but the family did not move to New Haven until 1772."

The core group is composed of extended families who trace their ancestry directly to the colonial period and then to England, Scotland, the Netherlands, or to French Huguenot refugees. These well-known "old Yankees" represent 59 percent of this stratum. Persons of Irish descent, who through the years have accumulated wealth and established family positions but have maintained their identifications with the Roman Catholic Church, are a group apart and compose 11 percent of this class. Descendants of other immigrant stocks—German (6 percent), Scandinavian (2 percent), and Italian (9 percent)—who are accumulating wealth through business enterprise and successful professional practices, represent other subgroups. Jews (13 percent) represent a separate hierarchy from the Gentile groups. German-Jewish families as a rule occupy higher prestige positions in the Jewish segment of class I than Jews of Polish and Russian descent.

RELIGIOUS AFFILIATION

Ethnic origins and religious affiliations are highly correlated. Viewed overall, the three major religious groups are divided as follows: Protestants—61 percent, Roman Catholics—24 percent, Jews—13 percent, and mixed or no affiliation—2 percent. Within the Protestant group, 61 percent of the families are Congregationalists, 17 percent are Episcopalians, 7 percent are Lutherans, 5 percent are Baptists, 2 percent are Methodists, and other denominations comprise the remaining 7 percent. In each religious group—Protestant, Catholic, and Jewish—the membership is concentrated in a small number of congregations. For example, there are 24 Congregational churches in the community, but over 93 percent of the core group members belong to three of these churches. Episcopalians are clustered in 2 of 19 parishes in the area, and Roman Catholics are concentrated in 4 parishes. Among Jews, the greatest clustering is in the Reformed Congregation. As Russian and Polish Jews have moved upward in the class structure, they have left the Orthodox and Conservative congregations and affiliated with the Reformed Temple founded by German Jews who came to the community a century ago. As these *arrivistes* have become affiliated with the Temple, the descendants of its Germanic founders have tended to withdraw from its affairs except for important ritualistic occasions and high holy days.

Although 98 percent of the respondents claim affiliation with three religions, from 8 to 33 percent are not members of any specific congregation and do not attend services. For practical purposes, these people are "unchurched." Approximately 25 percent of Protestant men and women and 38 percent of Jewish men and women have no congregational ties; only 15 percent of the Roman Catholic men and 8 percent of the women are in this category. These people probably had nominal connections with their claimed denominations at one time in their lives, but currently they are outside the religious participation pattern. The percentage of "unchurched" persons is significantly higher in class I in comparison with the other strata. The "unchurched" men and women in each major religion are upward mobile in significantly larger numbers than those who are stable socially. However, a considerable number of upward mobile persons function actively in selected churches and thereby aid their mobility strivings in a positive way.

Religious identification rather than affiliation and active participation is a salient factor in the organization of this stratum's social life. If a person is identified as a Jew, most Gentile doors are closed to him; moreover if he is a Roman Catholic, lines are drawn around him in Protestant circles, but not so openly. Conversely, Jews and Roman Catholics react in negative ways to Protestants. The three parallel hierarchies of Protestant, Catholic, and Jew, around which the social life of the community, at all levels, is organized, have crystallized in class I with signal force. A core group member made this very clear when he stated, in response to a question about his relationships with Jews, "We have business dealings with them. I sometimes sit next to an eminent Hebrew at a business luncheon." When asked if Hebrews were ever invited into his home, he bristled and said coldly, "In my living room there is never a Hebrew, no matter how eminent he is in professional or business life. Hebrews know."

A distinguished member of a prominent Jewish family described in detail how his family has been discriminated against in its attempts to be accepted into "restricted" clubs and associations. With particular reference to having the "black ball dropped" on his application for membership in a beach club, he remarked with feeling, "My ass is not good enough to sit on their sand."

A housewife whose husband changed his name legally from an easily recognizable Polish-Jewish one to a distinguished New England Yankee one about thirty years ago in the hope that it would enable him, in her words, "to cross over," told how this move failed. They then joined the Temple and became leaders in the Jewish community. She feels strongly that her religion is her "social gospel" but it does not help her make contact with the "white Protestants" who are "the privileged group in New Haven society."

A male member of the "privileged group" who was nominally a Congregationalist but attended church on Easter, Christmas, and only a few other times, did not think religion was too important in his way of life. He commented, "The churches are becoming women's and children's organizations, and, outside of paying the bills, the men don't seem to have much control."

EDUCATION

Class I is the most highly educated segment of the population. The median years of school completed by the male heads of families is 17.6. The median for the wives is 14.4 years. One wife in five has the same amount of education as her husband; 43 percent of the husbands have had at least four years more education than their wives, but only 7 percent of the wives have had at least one more year of education than their husbands. The distinct difference in the amount of education between husbands and wives is an outstanding characteristic of this class.

Formal schooling, after the eighth grade, normally is received in a private institution patterned after the English public school. Secondary education in a public school is frowned upon by all segments of the core group; many in this stratum refuse to send their children to the public schools from the earliest years. The core group families send their sons to distinguished New England boarding schools where they spend from four to six years preparing for an Ivy League College. Daughters are sent to well-known boarding schools to prepare them for entrance into a select women's college. Families who cannot afford to send their children to boarding schools enter them in one of the accepted single-sex day schools in the community.

The country day and boarding schools are staffed by an elite corps of headmasters and headmistresses of approved Yankee lineages and Protestant faiths, from "upper class" families, who were educated in the aristocratic-value system and are dedicated to preserving and transmitting it. They may close the educational gates to persons who cannot pass both the means and lineage tests, but other criteria are used to justify such actions. They attempt to hire teachers with backgrounds similar to theirs; as this is difficult today, their staffs tend to be made up of upward mobile individuals who have identified with the core group's value system.

Private secondary schooling is preparatory, if not a requisite, to entrance into a one-sex "name" college. The "big three," Yale, Harvard, and Princeton, are the dominant preference for men. The smaller men's colleges occupy secondary positions in the local value hierarchy—Amherst, Williams, Dartmouth, Brown, and Wesleyan. Women should be sent to Smith, Vassar, Wellesley, Bryn Mawr, Mount Holyoke, or Radcliffe to be acceptable in the social world under discussion. Coeducational private colleges such as Swarthmore or Oberlin are respectable but do not carry prestige. Attendance at a state university marks a man or a woman as an *arriviste*; the state university graduate is at best a "fringer" in the elite groups. The vast majority of the upward mobile family heads, whether from old American stock or ethnic groups, were trained in whole or in part at state universities, but they generally do everything within their means to see that their children attend private secondary schools and name colleges.

Lessons to teach the individual how to act in various social situations and how to use leisure time in approved ways are extremely important in the way of life of this stratum. Professional functionaries who sell their skills and talents to class I families run classes for ballroom dancing, tennis, golf, sailing, music, and so on. Several years of formal training in leisure time pursuits prepare the young person for the core group's way of life, as well as the parallel one prevailing among the fringe groups.

FAMILY CONSTELLATION

The nuclear group of husband, wife, and dependent children constitutes the primary family and common household unit. This group normally passes through a family cycle which begins with marriage, extends through the childbearing and child-rearing years, and ends in old age through the death of one of the parental pair. Each marriage brings into being a new family cycle. Upon the birth of their first child, the nuclear pair becomes a family of procreation, but for the child this family of origin is his family of orientation. Thus, each individual who marries and rears children has a family of orientation and a family of procreation.

Each nuclear family is related to a number of other nuclear families by consanguinal and affinal ties. Also, each family in the kin group occupies a position in the status system which may be the same or different from the others. The differences are produced by the mobility of some families. This movement of the individual nuclear family in the status system, while it is approved and often lauded as "the American way," has important effects on kin group relations.

One's ancestors and relatives count for more in the core group than what one has achieved in one's own lifetime. Background is stressed most heavily when it comes to the crucial question of whom a member may marry. One of the perennial problems of the established family is the control of the marriage choices of its young men. Young women can be controlled more easily because of the more sheltered life they lead and their more passive role in courtship. The relative passivity of the female, coupled with sex exploitation of females from lower social positions by high level males that sometimes leads to marriage, results in a significant number of old maids in established families. Strong emphasis on family background leads to the selection of marriage mates from within the old-family group in an exceptionally high percentage of cases and, if not from the old-family group, then from the new-family segment of this stratum. The degree of kinship solidarity, combined with intraclass marriages, results in comparative stability in the class, in the extended kin group, and in the nuclear family within it.

The core group family is basically an extended kin group, solidified by lineage and a heritage of common experience in the communal setting. A complicated network of consanguinal and affinal ties unites nuclear families of orientation and procreation into an in-group that rallies when its position is threatened by the behavior of one of its members, particularly where out-marriage is involved; this principle will be illustrated later. The nuclear family is viewed as only a part of a broader kin group that includes the consanguinal descendants of a known ancestral pair, plus kin brought into the group by marriage. Divorce is avoided if possible; when it occurs the entire family looks upon it as a disgrace, if not a scandal. The solidarity of the kin group is markedly successful in keeping divorce to a minimum. The ratio of widows and widowers to divorced persons is 27 to 1. This is the highest ratio in the population.

An important factor in the established family's ability to maintain its position through several generations is its economic security. Usually a number of different nuclear families within a kin group are supported, in part at least, by income from a family estate held in trust. Also, because of the practice of intramarriage within the core group, it is not unusual for a family to be the beneficiary of two or more estates held in trust. For example, one extended family group is the beneficiary of a trust established a century ago that yields something over $300,000 annually after taxes. This income is divided among 37 different nuclear families descended from the founder, 28 of whom live in the home community; 23 of these families are beneficiaries of one other trust fund, and 14 receive income from two or more other trust funds. These different nuclear families regard themselves as part of the "Scott" family; moreover, they are so regarded by other established families, as well as by persons lower in the status system who know something of the details of the family history.

The Scott family has maintained its social position for more than two centuries by a combination of property ownership, educational, legal, and political leadership, and control of marriages. Its members are proud that it has never had a non-Protestant marriage in seven generations; only five divorces have been traced, but these are not mentioned; one desertion has been hinted but not confirmed.

The family tradition of Protestant intermarriages had a severe test in recent years. A son of one nuclear family, who had spent four years in the Armed Forces in World War II, asked a class II Catholic girl to marry him. The engagement was announced by the girl's family to the consternation of the Scott family, who immediately brought pressure on the boy to "break off the affair." After several months of family and class pressure against the marriage, the young man "saw his error" and broke the engagement. A year later he married a family-approved girl from one of the other "old" families in the city. Today he is an officer in his wife's family's firm, and his father has built him a fine suburban home.

This case illustrates a number of characteristics typical of the established core group family. It is stable, extended, tends to pull together when its position is threatened—in this instance by an out-marriage—exerts powerful controls on its members to ensure that their behavior conforms to family and class codes, and provides for its members economically by trust funds and appropriate positions.

The *arriviste* family is characterized most decisively by phenomenal economic or professional success during a short interval of time. Its meteoric rise in the social system is normally the personal triumph of the nuclear head of the family. If the head is a businessman, he is busy making a "million bucks"; the family purchases the symbols associated with the wealthy American family: a large house, fine furniture, big automobiles, and expensive clothes. The new tycoon knows the power of money in the market place, and he often attempts to buy high position in the status system. In a professional family, the head is intent on making a "name" in his profession and acquiring some wealth. His family follows the same general pattern of purchasing the outward symbols of success but in a more modest fashion. The new family is able to meet the means test, but not the lineage test of the established families. Consequently, it is generally systematically excluded from membership in the cliques and associations of greatest prestige. This is resented especially by the wife and children, but less often by the tycoon or professional man.

The new family is unstable in comparison with the established family. It lacks the security of accepted position at the top of the local status system—a position that will come only with time; it cannot be purchased. The stabilizing influence exerted by an extended family group, as well as friends, on the deviant individual is absent. Then too, the adults in the new family are self-directing, full of initiative, believe in the freedom of the individual, and rely upon themselves rather than upon a kin group. (Many upwardly mobile individuals break with their kin groups to aid their mobility.) The result is, speaking broadly, conspicuous expenditure, insecurity, and family instability. Thus, we find divorces, broken homes, and other symptoms of disorganization in a significantly large number of new families. The ratio of widows and widowers to divorced persons is only 5 to 1; this is significantly lower than in the core group. In like manner, the percentage of children under 17 years of age living in broken homes is decidedly higher in the new families (18 percent versus 3.4 percent). Because new families are so conspicuous in their consumption and behavior, they become, in the judgment of the general population, symbolic of "upper class" actions and values to the resentment of established families who generally frown upon such behavior.

20. Status Concern, Authoritarianism, and Anti-Semitism

WALTER C. KAUFMAN

How prejudice is expressed frequently depends upon how prospectively prejudiced people assess their social situation. The person who encounters real or imagined threats to his status is more likely than a secure person to claim that minority group members are inferior to himself. If many members of a dominant majority feel this way, minority group members can find that their prospects for social acceptance have been blocked. In response, they sometimes establish their own organizations, paralleling those of the rejecting dominant group.

The following study shows that status concern was more closely associated with undergraduates' expressions of anti-Semitic attitudes than were authoritarian predispositions. It is not difficult to understand why middle-class Jews who were assumed to have high aspirations might have seemed threatening to non-Jewish students who were uncertain about their own future prospects. In comparison, members of an upper-class group like the one described in selection 19, because they were in a better position to protect their particularly privileged status, would probably find Jewish ambitiousness less threatening, and would select other characteristics they assumed were typical of Jews as a basis for antipathy and for maintaining social distance.

Research based on *The Authoritarian Personality* has been one of the most fashionable areas of recent social-psychological investigation. Yet it might well be concluded that the resulting *Continuities in Social Research* has shown this line of investigation to be at a point of discontinuity rather than continuity. The methodological critique by Hyman and Sheatsley has served to point out all too clearly the limitations in the applicability of the measures employed, particularly the F scale, which purports to measure "Fascist" or "authoritarian" tendencies. Furthermore, the relationship of the obtained scales to the underlying theory is tenuous at best.

Thus the hope that the California research would validate a genetic "dynamic" approach to the explanation of prejudice has not been fulfilled. Yet most of our attempts to explain such phenomena on a social-psychological or sociological level have been in terms of some theory of person-

SOURCE: *American Journal of Sociology*, 62, 1957, pp. 379–82. Copyright © 1962 by the University of Chicago. Reprinted by permission of the University of Chicago Press.

At the time of writing this selection, *Walter C. Kaufman* was with the Social Science Institute of Washington University, St. Louis.

ality, on the one hand, or on a historical-descriptive level, on the other. There appears to be deficient validation of such explanations, as well as defects in the testing of more limited or alternative relationships— "middle," if not "low, range" theory. It is the latter problem to which this paper is addressed.

One promising approach is in way of social stratification and mobility. Unfortunately, although there has been a considerable amount of writing and research on them, relatively little has been focused on the correlates of status and mobility and very little on their relationship to the problem of prejudice. Yet even in *The Authoritarian Personality*, frequent reference is made to the presumed relationship between aspects of social status and prejudice. Thus Frenkel-Brunswik, in her summary of the interview results of the California studies, describes the high scorer on the F scale as tending to use status as the primary criterion in appraising people and to evaluate others according as they appear to be a threat to his own standing.

In his set of propositions dealing with intergroup tensions, Robin Williams points out the high value put upon mobility in American society and the concomitant relation of prejudice to changes in and threats to status. Greenblum and Pearlin, in their re-analysis of the Elmira survey, examined father-son occupational mobility, restricted to changes between manual and non-manual occupations. In this case, both the upwardly and the downwardly mobile were more prejudiced than the non-mobile. These findings were interpreted as showing that prejudice is a function of the insecurity of marginal (mobile) status groups. The study also showed that a "middle-class" identification of manual workers, whether downwardly mobile or not, was associated with more highly prejudiced responses.

Bettelheim and Janowitz, in their study of veterans, found occupational mobility, particularly rapid downward mobility, significantly related to prejudice. No direct relationships between actual occupational and income status and prejudice were found. The lack of relationship between "objective" measures of status (income, father's occupation) and prejudice was also found in the California studies. However, the admittedly questionable validity of the information obtained, as well as the limitations of the sample, must be taken into consideration.

One of the few instances of a simultaneous test of several dimensions as related to prejudice is Srole's study relating anomie, authoritarianism, and prejudice, and the replication by Roberts and Rokeach. Both Srole's study and the replication found significant interrelationships among the three scales employed. In the former, for all but the college-educated sample, partial correlation analysis showed anomie to be the more important variable, the influence of authoritarianism on prejudice becoming negligible. This finding was not supported by the replication, in which each variable was held to be an equally important correlate of prejudice. Each study employed measures of status: education in the former, education and income in the latter. Both studies, using broader samples than the California researchers, found high status, particularly as measured by education, negatively correlated with authoritarianism and prejudice. Rokeach and Roberts found that, upon partialing, these correlations did not affect the relationships among anomie, authoritarianism, and prejudice.

In most of these previous studies attitudes about status and mobility are inferred from variations in mobility and concomitant variation in prejudiced attitudes. In the present study the focus of attention was on the direct measurement of attitudes to status and mobility or status concern. Status concern may here be defined as the value placed on symbols of status and on the attainment of higher status. Specifically, it was hypothesized that the greater the concern with status, the greater the prejudice, in this case defined by a measure of anti-Semitism.

One of the aims of the present study was the construction of an attitude scale to measure concern with status. The following items were employed in the final questionnaire (the six-choice pattern of agreement and disagreement of the California scales was applied to each of the items):

1. The extent of a man's ambition to better himself is a pretty good indication of his character.
2. In order to merit the respect of others, a person should show the desire to better himself.
3. One of the things you should consider in choosing your friends is whether they can help you make your way in the world.
4. Ambition is the most important factor in determining success in life.
5. One should always try to live in a highly respectable residential area, even though it entails sacrifices.
6. Before joining any civic or political association, it is usually important to find out whether it has the backing of people who have achieved a respected social position.
7. Possession of proper social etiquette is usually the mark of a desirable person.
8. The raising of one's social position is one of the more important goals in life.
9. It is worth considerable effort to assure one's self of a good name with the right kind of people.
10. An ambitious person can almost always achieve his goals.

Pretests showed that these items, hereafter to be called the "SC scale," did not meet the 90 per cent reproducibility criterion for a Guttman scale. Inspection of the responses showed what might be termed a "quasi-scalable" pattern, in that no systematic error patterns were evident. The differences between means of high and low scorers were significant at the

.01 level for each item, and the split-half reliability, corrected for double-length, was .78. Thus, although not strictly unidimensional, the SC scale does appear to have a reasonably consistent focus.

The other scales employed were a set of fifteen items from the previously mentioned F scale and the A-S scale, measuring anti-Semitism. The correlation between the fifteen-item F scale and the original 30-item scale was .95. Hyman and Sheatsley criticize the intercorrelations built into the California scales by the similarity of items, and, although no attempts were made to enhance correlations by manipulation of items, it is probable that this criticism also applies to some unknown extent in the present study. Finally, it must be pointed out that the SC scale here presented partakes of another characteristic of the other scales, namely, that the attitudes tested are primarily platitudes.

The limitations of sampling and consequently of general applicability pointed out by Hyman and Sheatsley likewise apply to the present sample. For one thing, as Hatt demonstrated, patterns of ethnic attitudes vary by the social class of respondents. The sample in this study was 213 non-Jewish college undergraduates, a "middle-class" population comparable to most subjects in the California studies.

The highest correlation obtained in the present study is a correlation of .71 between the SC and F scales. The correlation between status concern and anti-Semitism is .66, which is significantly higher at the .01 level of confidence than the correlation of .53 between authoritarianism and anti-Semitism.* The latter correlation is identical with the unweighted mean correlation between the F and A-S scales found in the California study.

An analysis of the partial correlations sheds further light on the interrelationships of the variables. All correlations become lower, but two of the correlations remain significant at the .01 level. In each case, with the third variable held constant, the correlation between the SC and F scales is .57, the correlation between the SC and A-S scales is .48, but the correlation between the F and A-S scales drops to a non-significant .12.

Corroborating findings from other restricted samples, father's income, occupation, and education were not significantly related to scores on the A-S scale.

To summarize: concern with status is more closely related to anti-Semitism than is authoritarianism, and the relationship between authoritarianism and anti-Semitism may be largely explained by their mutual relationship to concern with status. That concern with status is the dominant dimension is supported by most of the previously cited findings

---

* $F = 10.99$, $p < .01$. For the test applied cf. P. O. Johnson, *Statistical Methods in Research* (New York: Prentice-Hall, Inc., 1949), p. 54. The use of the F scale in addition to the SC scale in a multiple correlation does not increase the amount of A-S variance explained. An analysis of the B weights leads to the same conclusion, as shown by the partial correlation.

relating mobility and attitudes toward status to prejudice and revives the doubts about the significance of authoritarianism voiced by Srole. Some possible interpretations may be offered, although no definitive answers can be given on the basis of the findings here presented.

The first, and in many ways the most discouraging, explanation of the correlations is the platitudinousness common to attitude scales. Perhaps nothing more is being measured than a tendency toward clichés. The recurrent negative correlations between education and prejudice, authoritarianism, and anomie might be used to support the argument of variation in degrees of sophistication. However, the fact that high intercorrelations persist among the pertinent scales, even when education is held constant or the sample is relatively homogeneous, casts some doubt on this explanation.

Attitude studies such as the present one are not well adapted to test the relationship of general traits of "personality" to specific attitudes, such as prejudice. The fact that a specifically defined dimension, concern with status, is more closely related to prejudice than is the universal trait of personality called "authoritarianism" does not automatically rule out personality as a factor. It may merely indicate that the shortest road to scientific significance is not by indirection, such as characterizes the miscellany of items on the F scale. The high correlation between the SC and F scales and the drastic reduction in the correlation between authoritarianism and anti-Semitism, when concern with status is held constant, lead to the conjecture that the F scale measures in a diffuse way the sort of attitude measured more specifically by the SC scale. Instead of a reflection of personality, the common element among these scales could very well be the function of an ideology of status achievement and maintenance.

If concern with status is indeed as important as contemporary sociologists think and as these findings indicate, there remains the problem of the inconclusive nature of research employing "objective" indicators of status and mobility. Presumably, attitudes such as those measured here are a function of the operation of social stratification as experienced by the respondents, but a closer empirical and theoretical connection needs to be made. Part of the problem probably arises from the relatively crude categorical measures of status commonly employed, which are far removed from the actual experience of the respondents, whereas attitude measurements are more directly interpretable as individual characteristics. It is in the bridging of this gap that research findings such as those presented here will assume greater theoretical relevance.

21. What Whites Think of Negroes

WILLIAM BRINK AND LOUIS HARRIS

The following selection is more important as a source of basic information than as an example of theoretical sophistication. It is included in this volume because it provides an overview of the feelings of a nationwide probability sample of white Americans toward Negroes. Among other findings, note the widespread prevalance of stereotyped judgments: Two-thirds of American whites agree that Negroes laugh a lot; three-fifths believe that Negroes smell different. Nearly two of five think that Negroes have less native intelligence.

About half of white Americans claim they would object to having Negroes as next-door neighbors. Nine out of ten would object to having a teenage daughter date a Negro, a finding that obviously reflects the caste-like ban on equal-status interaction between Negro males and white females. Even in the white group generally most sympathetic to Negroes, made up of people who have actually had social contact with Negroes, 80 per cent share the same objection.

Findings of this kind do more than satisfy curiosity about how "most people" feel about issues that interest us. They are also useful in warning us of the pitfalls of using ourselves and our closest associates as the measure of all things. For a more personal treatment of some of these matters, see selection 23.

The Negro's attitude toward the white man is fundamentally simple: it is based on the desire for equality. But when the white man in America looks at the Negro he is torn by a conflict between his emotions and his intellect. His intellect tells him that the Negro has indeed suffered years of discrimination, directly contradicting the American creed of equality for all. But his emotions make him feel uneasy at the prospect of such equality for the Negro.

Newsweek conducted a special survey of whites to determine the extent of the gulf between the two races and the likelihood of bridging it. This poll confirmed many of the suspicions of Negroes about the negative feelings of whites—perhaps beyond even what many Negroes imagine.

In the course of interviews lasting over two hours each, some more than three, whites were asked how they felt about contact with Negroes and

SOURCE: William Brink and Louis Harris, *The Negro Revolution in America,* (New York: Simon and Schuster, Inc., 1963), pp. 138–54, passim. Copyright © 1963 by Newsweek, Inc. Reprinted by permission of Simon and Schuster, Inc.

William Brink is a journalist staff member of *Newsweek* who has concentrated on civil rights in the last several years. Louis Harris is a political analyst who heads the public opinion polling agency, Louis Harris Associates.

why. This question released a stream of uninhibited feeling about Negroes as people. The violent emotionalism of many comments was striking. A retired clerk from Inverness, Florida, declared, "They stink. In cafeterias here you go around and collect your food. Then niggers paw over your food and then you have to give them a tip to carry your tray. Big old dirty black paws pawing your food, then you've got to eat it." A 57-year-old hospital employee in Mobile, Alabama, said, "I couldn't stomach it if I thought I was eating after or beside a diseased Negro—which 90 per cent of them are. All this will lead to is social mixing. Their own kind don't keep a clean place."

The outpour was by no means limited to whites of the Deep South. . . . A 56-year-old maintenance man for the Detroit, Michigan, highway department told this story: "There was a good Negro living around here and my little boy shook hands with him and then he turned his hand over and looked at it and the Negro said, 'It won't rub off on you.' I never forgot that. It's the idea of rubbing up against them. It won't rub off but it dont' feel right, either."

. . . A young repairman in East Springfield, Massachusetts, said, "I feel as though I can't trust them. I think they'll start a fight. I might pick up some type of disease." . . .

This wall of white emotion is the real enemy of the Negro revolution. The survey explored in detail the components of prejudice, both North and South. In addition, it sought to discover whether prejudice diminished with social contact.

A series of ten stereotypes about Negroes was set before the white people, who were then asked which statements they agreed with and which they rejected. The following table reports the results from the nationwide cross-

White Stereotypes about Negroes

Agree with statement:	Nationwide %	South %	Previous Social Contact Group %
Negroes laugh a lot	68	81	79
Negroes tend to have less ambition	66	81	56
Negroes smell different	60	78	50
Negroes have looser morals	55	80	39
Negroes keep untidy homes	46	57	31
Negroes want to live off the handout	41	61	26
Negroes have less native intelligence	39	60	23
Negroes breed crime	35	46	21
Negroes are inferior to whites	31	51	15
Negroes care less for the family	31	49	22

section, from the South and from a special group of those who had had social contact with Negroes. This last group, 25 per cent of the total, proved throughout the survey to be the most sympathetic to the Negro and his cause.

While the white South accepts these stereotypes to a greater degree, it would be a vast error to conclude that the North is much different. Even those whites who have had social contact with Negroes share many of these feelings—some of them without even realizing it.

. . . . .

If views such as these comprised the total white attitude toward Negroes, then the only logical conclusion to draw would be that America is on the threshold of a bloody race war. But whites hold a whole roster of other beliefs that are in direct conflict with their emotions about Negroes as people. One is that Negroes have rights as citizens which must be guaranteed under the laws of the United States. Whites were asked about some of the Negro's demands:

The White View of Negro Rights

Approve:	Nationwide %	South %
Voting in elections	93	88
Unrestricted use of buses and trains	88	75
Job opportunities	88	80
Decent housing	82	76

The most startling figures in this table are those that reflect Southern attitudes. Even in the South, a large majority of whites feel Negroes should be guaranteed these rights. What is more, sizable majorities of whites feel that further legislation is needed from Congress to strengthen Negro rights. On this question, however, Southern whites disagree sharply with white people elsewhere:

White Support for Civil-Rights Legislation

Approve:	Nationwide %	South %
Federal vote-enforcement law	57	31
Federal Fair Employment Practices law	62	40
Kennedy civil-rights bill	63	31
Public-accommodations bill	66	29

Comparison of these two tables reveals an interesting anomaly: 88 per cent of the white Southerners believe that Negroes have the right to vote, but only 31 per cent favor legislation backing up that right. There is a similar though less striking contrast on the subject of jobs. Legislation seems to be the sticking point; all whites are more ready to approve other forms of Federal intervention for equal rights. The [next] table . . . shows how they stand on the role played by the government since 1954.

. . . . . .

Whites Assess Federal Action

Approve:	Nationwide %	South %
Eisenhower use of troops in Little Rock, Ark.	71	44
Kennedy use of troops at Oxford, Miss.	65	37
The original Supreme Court decision	64	35
Over-all role of Federal government in civil rights	64	35
Over-all role of Federal courts in civil rights	60	33

How do whites rationalize this acceptance of equality under the law with the personal aversions to Negroes so many of them apparently feel? Timing plays a part. By better than a 2 to 1 margin, whites feel that Negroes are moving too fast in their revolution. . . .

By a 64–36 per cent count, whites feel Negroes are asking for more than they can possibly absorb. . . . The methods of the revolution are just as disturbing to whites as its tempo. While Negroes feel demonstrations have been vital and effective most whites feel that the demonstrations have hurt the Negro cause. "A lot of it is show-off," thought a retired man in Palmyra, Pennsylvania. "They want to be seen, make a lot of noise." A 65-year-old widow from Macon, Georgia, made a judgment about the demonstration in her town: "I think locally it has hurt. They look like they are wild people out of the jungle and this is the way all Negroes are inside." . . .

When asked in detail about the methods of the Negro revolution, whites went on record as 2 to 1 in opposition to the lunch-counter sit-ins, 4 to 3 against Negro willingness to go to jail voluntarily for their cause, 5 to 3 against picketing of stores and over 10 to 1 against the "lie-downs" in front of trucks on construction sites. However, by slim margins, whites do accept the general idea of demonstrating and think that the Negroes are justified in having conducted the march on Washington.

. . . . . .

These very demonstrations appear to have driven home the whole point of the Negro protest. But the majority view of whites was clearly that the Negroes were pressing too hard, asking for too much. Whites have remarkably clear understanding of Negro demands. The following table, drawn from volunteered comments, shows what whites think Negroes want:

What Whites Think Negroes Want

	Whites Nationwide %
Equal treatment	41
Better jobs	14
Better education	11
Make America aware of their problem	8
Better housing	7
Dignity, respect, status	6
Publicity for the problem	6
Representation in government	5
Be able to go anywhere, do anything	2

There is a remarkable parallel between what whites think Negroes want and what Negroes themselves said they want.

Furthermore, there is widespread recognition among whites that Negroes are discriminated against. Fully 71 per cent of all whites in the country and even a majority of 56 per cent in the South acknowledge this fact. By better than 3 to 2, white people feel Negroes do not have job opportunities equal to whites. By a somewhat closer margin whites also believe Negro children receive an inferior education. And by almost 3 to 1, whites believe Negro housing is not nearly so good as that for whites.

. . . . .

In fact, when whites were asked how they thought it must feel to be discriminated against as a Negro, they bristled with indignation and even outrage at the thought of being treated like Negroes. "I think it would be hard on the morale." . . . "When we get some little minor snub, we are so upset. Imagine how it would be to live with discrimination all your life. It would take a mighty strong person to try to improve yourself." . . . "It must be horrible. If it were me, there would be a terrible rage inside me. It would make me a mean, spiteful person and I'd be ready to do battle at any moment. I'd also treat anyone who suppressed me as dirt if I got the chance." . . .

If whites are thus able to understand in human terms just what it means to be a Negro in America, how far are they willing to go toward integration? This is obviously a key question, and in large part American history of the next ten years will be written by the answer. The survey investigated the limits of white viability, from willingness to work side by side with a Negro to allowing a teen-age daughter to date a Negro boy:

White Feeling about Contact with Negroes

Would object to:	Nationwide %	South %	Previous Social Contact Group %
Working next to a Negro on the job	17	31	8
Sitting next to a Negro at a lunch counter	20	50	4
Sitting next to a Negro on a bus	20	47	5
Sitting next to a Negro in a movie theater	23	54	6
Own children going to school with Negroes	23	55	9
Using same restroom as Negroes	24	56	9
Trying on same suit or dress that Negro had tried on in clothing store	32	57	16
Having own child bring Negro friend home to supper	41	76	16
Having Negro family as next-door neighbors	51	74	26
Close friend or relative marrying a Negro	84	91	70
Own teen-age daughter dating a Negro	90	97	80

It is immediately apparent from these results that the vast majority of white America is prepared to accept a great deal more contact with Negroes than has taken place up to now. The degree of Southern viability may come as a surprise. Nationwide, in view of the revulsion expressed by many earlier in this chapter, the over-all results testify to white willingness—grudging though it may be—to accommodate. But white America is not at all ready for social integration to the extent of dating and intermarriage. Even among those who have had social contact with Negroes, 70 per cent would object to a close friend or relative marrying a Negro and 80 per cent would be worried if their teen-age daughter dated a Negro. Some whites rationalized segregation in this area as former President Harry S. Truman once did—all the way back to the Bible.

These results also indicate the likely areas of accommodation for the immediate future as well as the areas of sharp conflict.

Equal employment, which is also the number-one priority for Negroes, seems ripe for a breakthrough. Nearly nine out of every ten whites—including eight out of every ten Southerners—feel that Negroes have the right to equal jobs. What is more, as another question in the poll revealed, a majority all over the country do not fear that Negroes will take their jobs away. Significantly, a solid majority (62 per cent) of whites favor a Federal law enforcing an end to discrimination on the job. However, white people are equally adamant that there should *not* be a strict 10 per cent quota for Negroes in job hiring (rejected by over 4 to 1) or that Negroes should actually be given job preference over whites (turned down by a staggering 31 to 1 margin).

Part of the reason for whites' willingness to go along with an end to job discrimination is the highly positive experience of white people who have associated with Negroes on the job:

> "You are there to get a job done, not to socialize. I don't mind working with them." . . .

> "I've worked with colored girls. They were really on the ball, with good sense and efficient. Clean and neat, too." . . .

> "They were wonderful to me. I worked as a teacher and they were teachers. Because I was a substitute, I found them much better and kinder than many white teachers." . . .

>   .   .   .   .   .

> "It is just like working with any other man. Heck, he's entitled to work." . . .

>   .   .   .   .   .

Education is another major area in which there appears to be a considerable amount of white willingness to go along with the Negro revolution, although the South registers a loud and determined "no" on this score. Better than seven out of ten whites would not mind their own children going to integrated schools, and an equal number reject the notion that the education of white children would suffer if both races go to school together. Finally, in reply to another question in the poll, fully three-quarters of all white people in America said they believed that school integration is inevitable. In fact, 57 per cent of the white South share this view.

  .   .   .   .   .

Whites may be receptive to the idea of integrated education, but they are not amenable to the next step, which is probably the only path to integrated schooling: whites and Negroes living in the same neighborhoods.

While 59 per cent of all whites in the country feel that integrated housing is on the way, 50 per cent say they would be upset if it happened where they live. However, those who now live in integrated neighborhoods report by better than 5 to 1 that they are not bothered by having Negroes live near them. This result should ease some of the fear that explosions are bound to occur in white neighborhoods now undergoing an influx of Negroes.

... A widow in San Jose, California, harked back to what she thought of Negroes as people: "Negroes are their own worst enemy. [If they move in] the people that are for them will get disgusted and turn away." A housewife in Mobile, Alabama, agreed: "They are not capable of the general upkeep, maintenance and improvement of any home. This is why they are living in shacks."

To some whites, the idea of Negroes moving into their neighborhood evoked fighting words, such as those of a woman in Burnham, Texas: "It ain't gonna happen right here. Maybe the edge of town. Nobody ain't gonna sell 'em no lots so as they can build. I tell you, nigger settlement here just ain't gonna be like whites."

But if one half of the white people, North and South, would be upset by integrated housing, the other half say they would not. For example, a 68-year-old laborer in St. Louis said simply, "They have the right to go anywhere they want to go." And a 51-year-old housewife in Hillsboro, Oregon, added, "They have earned people's respect and those who can afford the better homes are the nicer class, too." ...

Does the oft-expressed revulsion of whites to Negroes, and their apparent resistance to accommodation, mean that the Negro's social revolt will end in a bloody clash? To some extent the very history of the United States argues differently. Time and again the American people have adapted to changing times, changing customs—and changing neighbors. This has happened with successive waves of immigration by the Irish, the Poles, the Italians and others.

Of course, there are obvious differences in the situation of the Negroes ... to argue against such optimism. Their color is different. A bitter war was fought in their name. They have been here far longer without achieving equality. And there are more of them to intensify conflict. But numbers can be a double-edged sword; for ultimate effectiveness in a democracy, numbers have counted in the past.

Furthermore, while some of the whites' emotions have vitiated their intellectual acceptance of equality for Negroes, other feelings are working in a different way. Many whites reported that their ministers were preaching that it is morally wrong to discriminate. According to the poll, whites feel by a 2 to 1 margin that the whole question of Negro rights is a moral issue. ...

22. Negro Conceptions of White People in a Northeastern City

PAUL A. MC DANIEL AND
NICHOLAS BABCHUK

Like the previous selection, this one displays neither an incisive analysis nor a particularly impressive research design. However, it carefully illustrates some beliefs about white people that are prevalent among Negroes who live in a large city in upstate New York, and it compares their beliefs to those of Negroes who live in a southern city. Not surprisingly, the paper indicates that as compared to middle- and upper-class Negroes, those in the lower class are more hostile toward whites, and believe that whites are more hostile toward them. Many findings here seem like reflections of findings reported in the previous selection. Over three-quarters of the Negroes interviewed agreed that white people felt superior to Negroes; more than four-fifths of them thought that white people under-estimated Negroes' abilities; and over two-thirds thought that white people did not care to be among Negroes.

Less directly, the study shows that willingness to engage in stereotyped thinking is not a characteristic restricted to majority group members. Minority-group membership by itself does not guarantee wisdom or a balanced perspective about intergroup relations.

This study duplicates for a northeastern city an earlier study of Negro conceptions of white people.[1] It is concerned with the extent, uniformity, direction, and intensity of these conceptions among Negroes. The present inquiry is essentially and deliberately different in one major respect from

---

[1] Tilman C. Cothran, "Negro Conceptions of White People," *American Journal of Sociology*, LVI (1951), 458–67. The Southern community in which this study was conducted was New Orleans. Hereafter the city in Cothran's study will be referred to as "Southern City" and that in the present study as "Northeastern City."

Negro stereotypes of white Americans are similar in many respects to the stereotypes of Negroes held by whites. See Allison Davis, Burleigh B. Gardner, and Mary R. Gardner, *Deep South* (Chicago, 1941), pp. 15–58. There are many parallels between the views of whites toward Negroes as expressed in *Deep South* and the image held by a majority of persons in Plainville (an all-white community) concerning "back hill people," categorized as "people who live like animals." This latter group was considered to be apart from the community structure in Plainville in much the same way as Negroes are considered to be apart by white persons in other communities; almost identical statements were made by the superordinate persons describing those considered subordinate, even though in *Deep South* the community was interracial and in Plainville

SOURCE: *Phylon*: The Atlanta University Review of Race and Culture, Vol. 21, No. 1 (Spring, 1960), pp. 7–19 (footnotes and tables omitted). Reprinted by permission of the editor of *Phylon*.

Nicholas Babchuk is Professor of Sociology at the University of Nebraska.

the one after which it was modeled: In the original study Cothran used a sample drawn from a large metropolitan community in the deep South, whereas the present study employs a sample from a different geographical area. This fact, difference in location, is of central importance; it is viewed as constituting an important variable in the conceptions that Negroes have of whites. It should also be noted that the present community has a very small proportion of Negroes (less than 3 percent).

This study attempted to discover the extent to which the Northern Negroes differed from those in the Southern sample in the favorableness or unfavorableness of their conceptions of white people. A major hypothesis and one related to Cothran's findings was that the Negro's conception of the white group would be significantly related to his social class. In testing a similar hypothesis, Cothran used thirty stereotyped conceptions in interviews with 174 Negro subjects who represented three social-class groups These thirty conceptions had been those found by Cothran to be most frequently mentioned by 341 Negroes questioned, using an open-ended interviewing technique, on stereotypes of whites. This same set of conceptions was used in Northeastern City with a sample of 100 Negroes sixteen years of age and over who were asked first, whether they recognized the conceptions, and second, what attitudes they held in regard to the conceptions. Cothran's data showed the middle-class Negro to be more favorable in his conceptions of white people than either the lower or upper-class Negro. This finding was pivotal in the design of the present inquiry.

The sample of 100 Negroes in Northeastern City was selected so as to represent different social classes as designated by educational achievement and occupation (upper class, 25 respondents; middle class, 45 respondents; and lower class, 30 respondents). In addition, the sample was evenly divided between men and women and represented a wide age range.

UNIVERSE OF CONCEPTIONS

A vast majority of the 100 respondents in Northeastern City was familiar with most of the stereotypes with which they were confronted. Thus, the respondents in the present study were in agreement with those in the South with regard to the universality of the conceptions. . . .

---

all residents were white. See James West, *Plainville, U.S.A.* (New York, 1945), pp. 115–41. In a case from another society, it is suggested that the Ladino views the Indian in much the same way as the Negro is viewed by the white in the United States. Cf. Melvin V. Tumin, *Caste and Class in a Peasant Society* (Princeton, 1952), pp. 234–49. That stereotypes held by whites of Negroes and mulattoes in Brazil are widespread and comparable to the ones held by many whites of Negroes in the United States is suggested by Roger Bastide and Pierre Van Den Berghe, "Stereotypes, Norms and Interracial Behavior in Sao Paulo, Brazil," *American Sociological Review*, XXII, No. 6 (December, 1957), 687–94.

In this study, the lower-class Negro showed the greatest familiarity with the conceptions, the middle class the least familiarity. The upper class, however, showed the lowest percentage of recognition on any single item: Only 40 percent were familiar with the conception that "White people are not very brave." This particular conception proved to be the least known by the sample as a whole. The conceptions most generally recognized were "White people feel superior to Negroes" (98 percent), "White people stick together better than Negroes" (98 percent), "White people judge Negroes by the worst type" (97 percent), "White people try to keep the Negro down" (97 percent), "White people are very businesslike" (94 percent), "White people underestimate the Negro's ability" (91 percent), "Poor whites have more prejudice" (91 percent), and "White people have superior intellectual ability" (91 percent). The most widely known stereotyped conceptions in Southern City were, in general, the most widely known in Northeastern City irrespective of social class. Regional determinants were therefore not important with regard to whether the conceptions were familiar.

UNIFORMITY AND DIRECTION OF THE CONCEPTIONS

"Uniformity" was defined as the extent to which an individual's response was in accord with the response of others and "direction" was defined as favorableness or unfavorableness of responses. Agreement was analyzed from the proportion of individual responses falling in one of five categories ranging from "strongly agree" to "strongly disagree." . . . There was considerable similarity between the respondents in the two populations. The pattern initially discovered in Southern City prevailed, i.e., the lower-class group was uniformly more unfavorable in its conception of white people than the middle and upper-class groups. In Northeastern City, however, the respondents in all three social classes were not as likely to be neutral in their views.

THE DIRECTION OF NEGRO CONCEPTIONS OF WHITE PEOPLE

While the results were, in general, similar for the two samples, there were several sharp differences in individual conceptions between the two populations compared as a whole. Also, in several instances, two of the social-class groups showed agreement on a conception but there was disagreement in the third social-class group. To illustrate, the Northeastern City sample was more likely to disagree with the statement "White people do not trust

Negro leaders" than was the Southern City sample. On the other hand, while there was considerable consensus between the upper and middle-class groups in both cities on the conception "White people are easily fooled by 'Uncle Tomism,'" there were substantial differences in the collective views of the lower-class groups. A consideration of the group responses in both cities to each of the conceptions follows.

Upper-class respondents in Northeastern City were much less likely to feel that "White people are very neat and clean" than were the middle-class and lower-class respondents. (The difference in the views between the upper and lower-class persons was statistically significant.) However, in Southern City, upper-class persons were more favorable to the conception than were middle and lower-class persons. Thus, in both cities the differences in views of the upper and lower classes were statistically significant but in opposite directions. The data on Northeastern City suggest that the upper-class Negro has extensive contacts with white persons of all social classes, a fact which might account for the difference in the above conception. Only further research could offer a reliable explanation, however.

There was uniformity in the responses of all social classes in Northeastern City to the conception "White people feel superior to Negroes." Fewer of the middle-class respondents, however, felt that white people feel superior to Negroes; differences in the percentage of favorable responses to the conceptions in the middle-class group as compared with upper and lower-class responses proved to be significant. Upper and lower-class persons in Northeastern City held a more favorable view of the conception than did persons in these two classes in the South. This suggests that Negroes are more inclined to feel that they are treated "more democratically" in the North than in the South.

The lower-class groups in the two communities were in close agreement on the conception "White people are insincere in religion." Almost one-third were favorable, another third neutral, and the remaining unfavorable. Sixty-four percent of the upper-class group as compared with 29 percent of the lower-class group in Northeastern City were favorable to the conception; this difference was statistically significant. A majority of the upper and middle-class sample in the North were inclined to feel that white people were sincere in religion, but the Negroes from all social classes in the South were disposed to feel that whites were insincere in religion. This may be a function of greater contact between the higher-class Negroes and whites in the North. It is also plausible that the religious observances and church affiliations of the middle and upper-class Negroes are more nearly comparable to those of the whites in the North than in the South.

The upper and lower-class Negroes in Southern City were more inclined to believe that "White people distrust Negro leaders" than were these in

Northeastern City. Fewer middle-class Negroes in the North, however, responded in a comparable manner; they were more likely to view the conception less favorably than the sample in the South. In Northeastern City the upper-class Negro did exercise a modicum of leadership and hence might feel that white people did not distrust Negro leaders. Middle-class persons are less likely to exercise leadership and this may result in the fact that their view was less favorable than that of the upper-class group. It is not clear why the lower-class view was so favorable to white people in regard to the conception of Negro leaders. The fact that Negro leaders in Northeastern City were accorded recognition in the community might have influenced the view expressed by the lower-class group.

Most of the respondents felt that the conception "White people judge Negroes by the worst type" characterized the thinking of whites. The response of Negroes to this conception was comparable in the two communities. The belief was widely held that most whites look upon Negroes as a group. When a Negro manifests "undesirable" behavior, his actions are generalized by the whites to Negroes as a group, and when a Negro's behavior is exemplary, it is discounted as atypical.

In Northeastern City, upper and middle-class Negroes were more unfavorable in their belief that "White people have superior mechanical ability" than lower-class Negroes. The difference in the views expressed between the middle and lower-class respondents proved to be statistically significant. In both samples there was over-all agreement that whites do not have superior mechanical ability. It was more widely expressed by the Northern community.

The direction of the responses to the conception "White people do not care to be among Negroes" was comparable in the two cities. A greater number of middle and lower-class Negroes in the Northern community felt this way. The lower-class Negro group in the North especially held this view; 93 percent registered unfavorable responses. In Northeastern City (as is characteristic of most Northern cities) the lower-class Negro was permitted to live only in the most undesirable quarters of the city, a fact which undoubtedly contributed to his sentiments.

There was greater variation in the responses to the conception "White people are easily fooled by the 'Uncle Tom' type of Negro" in Southern City than in Northeastern City. In the South, there was statistically significant difference in the responses of the lower and middle-class groups; there was considerable uniformity in the responses of the three class groups in the North.

Sixty-four percent of the upper-class Negroes in the North did not subscribe to the conception "White people have low morals." The lower-class group held the most hostile views. While there appeared to be little difference in the responses to the conception in the two lower-class groups in the North and South, there were considerable differences in the views expressed by the upper-class groups. Upper-class persons in the South were more likely to impute lower morals to white people.

Both populations felt that "White people underestimate the Negro's ability." As Cothran suggested, the Negro's conception of the way the white feels about Negroes differs greatly from the way in which the Negro conceives himself.

Approximately one out of every two Negroes in the middle and upper classes in both communities did not agree that "In general, white people hate Negroes." On the other hand, 68 percent of the lower-class Negro group in the South and 64 percent in the North believed that, in general, Negroes were hated by whites. The differences between the lower-class proportions and the two upper-class proportions in both cities were statistically significant.

While the upper-class Negro group in the South, as well as both middle and lower-class groups in the North and South, held the conception "White people are very ambitious," the upper-class Negro group in Northeastern City did not. These data, once again, indicate that the experiences of the upper-class Negroes as between the two communities were substantially different.

Most of the Negroes were not inclined to believe that "White people have superior intellectual ability." In Southern and Northeastern City, both the upper and middle-class did not agree with the conception. Yet 37 percent of the lower-class Negroes in Southern City and 36 percent in Northeastern City thought that white people did possess superior intellectual ability.

The respondents in both communities were inclined to feel that "White people try to keep Negroes down," although the Northern Negro group were slightly less unfavorable to this conception. These differences may be related to the greater opportunities for Negroes which exist in the North.

The Northern group were less likely to agree with the conception "White people are very shrewd" than the group in the South. Only one in three upper-class Negroes in the North agreed with the conception. Lower-class Negroes were most in agreement with it (74 percent in the South, 64 percent in the North). The fact that lower-class Negroes are more likely than others of their race to be exploited by whites would bear, of course, on the differences between classes on this conception.

"White people are good singers and dancers" was viewed favorably by approximately one-third of all the respondents. In the lower-class Southern City groups, however, only two in ten held a favorable conception. Upper and middle-class Negroes in both cities were more likely to hold the opinion that many white people are good singers and dancers. In Northeastern City, many persons expressed the opinion that some white persons were good singers but not good dancers and vice versa.

Upper and lower-class Negroes were divided on the conception "White people are not very brave," especially in the North. Three out of four upper-class Negroes in the North felt that whites were brave, whereas only three of ten in the lower-class Northern sample felt that way. This difference was statistically significant. The middle-class groups in both communities were inclined to agree with the lower-class groups. So did the upper-class group in the South.

About eight out of ten Negroes in both communities expressed the belief that "White people are very businesslike." But, in the Northern community, a greater proportion of persons expressed this view. The greatest difference in view point was within the middle-class group (South 73 percent, North 89 percent).

The belief that "White people stick together better than Negroes" was also widely held in both cities. The sample of upper and middle-class Negroes in Northeastern City indicated slightly less belief than did that in Southern City; the views of the lower-class Negroes, as expressed in percentages, were identical in the two cities. Persons in both the North and South were likely to perceive this conception as relating to racial issues.

The concept "White people are deceitful and tricky" was widely held by Negroes in both communities. Sharper differences between social classes were found in the Northern community. Less than one in two upper-class Negroes in the North shared this conviction but more than nine out of ten lower-class persons did so. This difference was statistically significant. Notable was the fact that a larger proportion of lower-class Negroes in the North felt whites to be tricky and deceitful than of the lower-class group in the South.

Responses to the conception "In general, Jews are more sympathetic toward the Negro than other whites" were similar in the two samples. While a greater proportion of the Northern Negroes held an unfavorable view, the difference between regions was not very large.

All three social classes in Northeastern City were favorably disposed to the notion that "White men are more considerate of white women." They were not, however, as favorably disposed to the view as were the Southern group.

The Northern lower-class Negroes were most likely to hold the conception that "White liberals give lip service." The difference in the view held by the Northern upper-class group and lower-class group proved to be statistically significant. Cothran notes that the Negro finds it difficult to believe the sincerity of "liberal" whites toward Negroes in the South where there is a one-party system emphasizing local and regional patriotism. "Liberal" whites are furthermore condemned for their outspoken interest in the application of democracy abroad and their silence on the application of democracy at home. The data suggested that Negroes in the Northern group were also not convinced of the sincerity of the Northern "liberal" even though he might champion the Negro's cause in all realms. The responses of the Negroes to the conception that "The white liberal is not sincere" were similar in the two regions. Upper-class Negroes were more disposed to believe that white "liberals" were sincere, lower-class Negroes that white "liberals" were not sincere. In general, Negroes in the North and South were skeptical of the role played by the white "liberal."

Of the three social classes in the South, the middle one was most in agreement with the conception "White women are more affectionate than Negro women." Middle-class Negroes in the North were somewhat more in agreement with this conception than the other Negroes in the North. In the upper and lower-classes in both cities, one in two respondents disagreed with the conception.

DISCUSSION

In Northeastern City, the upper class was consistently the most favorable in its view of the white group as indicated through their favorable and neutral responses to the twenty-six stereotyped conceptions. The lower-class group was the most unfavorable.

The three social-class groups in the North were less neutral in responding to the stereotyped conceptions than the persons in the South. Consequently, there were more favorable and unfavorable responses to the conceptions in the North. A similar relationship prevailed when the samples were compared along class lines. The Northern middle-class sample was especially more unfavorable in its view of the whites when compared to the Southern middle-class group.

There was considerable consensus among respondents on thirteen stereotyped conceptions irrespective of region or social-class background. These conceptions were: "White people underestimate the Negro's ability," "White people feel superior to Negroes," "White people judge all Negroes by the worst type," "White people have superior intellectual ability," "White people have superior mechanical ability," "White people stick together better than Negroes," "White people try to keep the Negro down," "White people do not care to be among Negroes," "White people are deceitful and tricky," "White liberals give lip service," "White people are very businesslike," "White men are more considerate of white women," and "In general, Jews are more sympathetic toward Negroes than other whites." The present inquiry shows that the stereotyped conceptions of all types are found and strongly held by Negroes in the North. The greater hostility of the lower-class group in the Northern city is consistent with the often expressed view that the lowest-class Negro groups are most hostile toward whites.

Intensity of the Conceptions

Intensity of the conceptions was measured through a self-rating technique suggested by Lickert. Weights of one to five points were assigned to the five kinds of responses (very unfavorable, favorable, etc.) made by a subject in evaluating the stereotyped conception. In this scheme, five point weights connoted the very favorable view, four points the favorable view, three points a neutral response, and so forth. In this way it was possible to ascertain the maximum possible favorable score, neutral scores, etc., for any sized sample for each of the conceptions as well as for all of the conceptions taken as a whole. Actual scores were computed and compared with the maximum possible score and the possible neutral score as an index of the intensity of the conceptions held by the three classes in Northeastern City. These scores were compared with the ones obtained in Southern City.

. . . The intensity of the conceptions held by the three classes in Northeastern City followed the same pattern revealed in Southern City. The differences in the intensity scores for the middle and lower-class groups were statistically significant in both communities. In the comparison among the social classes of the two cities, the Northern lower-class sample was most intensely unfavorable. On the other hand, the other two classes were less intensely unfavorable than their counterparts; all three classes in both cities, however, held predominantly unfavorable conceptions.

. . . Of . . . twenty-six conceptions, the three classes in the two communities were as a group in agreement with each other on only three conceptions indicating a favorableness in the stereotyped conception held. These were "White men are more considerate of white women," "White people stick together better than Negroes," and "White people are very businesslike." The data suggest that the "sticking together" of white people was favorably viewed as a trait which should be emulated by Negroes as a group. Both samples were also favorably disposed toward the view that "White people are very shrewd," with the exception of the upper-class group in the North. All other conceptions elicited unfavorable responses from the two samples considered as a whole.

Conclusion

A sample of one hundred Negroes representing three social classes as designated through occupation and education in a Northern community was confronted with stereotyped conceptions of white people, conceptions which had been found to be widely known among a Negro sample in the South. These conceptions were found to be equally well known in the North. Furthermore, the sample in the North was less likely to respond neutrally to the stereotyped conception of whites. There was considerable consensus between the samples in the two communities with regard to the degree of uniformity in the responses; in most instances the direction of the responses was unfavorable. The lower-class groups in both communities were more intensely unfavorable than either the middle or upper-class groups. This was especially true of the lower-class group in the North. The upper and middle-class groups in the Northern community were somewhat less intensely unfavorable than the classes in the South. Essentially, the same pattern of responses was manifest in the two populations, suggesting considerable universality and agreement in the stereotyped conceptions of white people held by Negroes.

23. My Negro Problem—and Ours

NORMAN PODHORETZ

Soon after Podhoretz' article appeared, it provoked a storm of controversy in the "Letters" section of Commentary. *Many readers praised the article for its honesty; many others criticized it for its remnants of prejudice and for what they took to be Podhoretz' unwillingness to grant that Negroes had a right to define their own place in American society. The article demonstrates how prejudice can develop out of what seemed to be ordinary daily experience at some earlier time. It also shows how difficult it can be to erase emotionally tinged impressions that subtly but firmly become part of a perceptual set at quite an early age. These points could not have been made so clearly if Podhoretz had not tried to work through his feelings, and if he had not been ready to indicate publicly that in his own case prejudice could be overcome even if it could not be wiped out.*

Two ideas puzzled me deeply as a child growing up in Brooklyn during the 1930's in what today would be called an integrated neighborhood. One of them was that all Jews were rich; the other was that all Negroes were persecuted. These ideas had appeared in print; therefore they must be true. My own experience and the evidence of my senses told me they were not true, but that only confirmed what a day-dreaming boy in the provinces—for the lower-class neighborhoods of New York belong as surely to the provinces as any rural town in North Dakota—discovers very early:

SOURCE: *Commentary*, 35 (February, 1963) pp. 93–101. Copyright © 1963 by The American Jewish Committee. Reprinted by permission of the editors and of the author.

Norman Podhoretz is the editor of Commentary.

his experience is unreal and the evidence of his senses is not to be trusted. Yet even a boy with a head full of fantasies incongruously synthesized out of Hollywood movies and English novels cannot altogether deny the reality of his own experience—especially when there is so much deprivation in that experience. Nor can he altogether gainsay the evidence of his own senses —especially such evidence of the senses as comes from being repeatedly beaten up, robbed, and in general hated, terrorized, and humiliated.

And so for a long time I was puzzled to think that Jews were supposed to be rich and the only Jews I knew were poor, and that Negroes were supposed to be persecuted when it was the Negroes who were doing the only persecuting I knew about—and doing it, moreover, to *me*. During the early years of the war, when my older sister joined a left-wing youth organization, I remember my astonishment at hearing her passionately denounce my father for thinking that Jews were worse off than Negroes. To me, at the age of twelve, it seemed very clear that Negroes were better off than Jews—indeed, than *all* whites. A city boy's world is contained within three or four square blocks, and in my world it was the whites, the Italians and Jews, who feared the Negroes, not the other way around. The Negroes were tougher than we were, more ruthless, and on the whole they were better athletes. What could it mean, then, to say that they were badly off and that we were more fortunate? Yet my sister's opinions, like print, were sacred, and when she told me about exploitation and economic forces I believed her. I believed her, but I was still afraid of Negroes. And I still hated them with all my heart.

It had not always been so—that much I can recall from early childhood. When did it start, this fear and this hatred? There was a kindergarten in the local public school, and given the character of the neighborhood, at least half of the children in my class must have been Negroes. Yet I have no memory of being aware of color differences at that age, and I know from observing my own children that they attribute no significance to such differences even when they begin noticing them. I think there was a day— first grade? second grade?—when my best friend Carl hit me on the way home from school and announced that he wouldn't play with me any more because I had killed Jesus. When I ran home to my mother crying for an explanation, she told me not to pay any attention to such foolishness, and then in Yiddish she cursed the *goyim* and the *schwartzes*, the *schwartzes* and the *goyim*. Carl, it turned out, was a *schwartze*, and so was added a third to the categories into which people were mysteriously divided.

Sometimes I wonder whether this is a true memory at all. It is blazingly vivid, but perhaps it never happened: can anyone really remember back to the age of six? There is no uncertainty in my mind, however, about the years that followed. Carl and I hardly ever spoke, though we met in school every day up through the eighth or ninth grade. There would be embarrassed moments of catching his eye or of his catching mine—for whatever it was that had attracted us to one another as very small children remained alive in spite of the fantastic barrier of hostility that had grown up between us, suddenly and out of nowhere. Nevertheless, friendship would have been impossible, and even if it had been possible, it would have been unthinkable. About that, there was nothing anyone could do by the time we were eight years old.

Item The orphanage across the street is torn down, a city housing project begins to rise in its place, and on the marvelous vacant lot next to the old orphanage they are building a playground. Much excitement and anticipation as Opening Day draws near. Mayor LaGuardia himself comes to dedicate this great gesture of public benevolence. He speaks of neighborliness and borrowing cups of sugar, and of the playground he says that children of all races, colors, and creeds will learn to live together in harmony. A week later, some of us are swatting flies on the playground's inadequate little ball field. A gang of Negro kids, pretty much our own age, enter from the other side and order us out of the park. We refuse, proudly and indignantly, with superb masculine fervor. There is a fight, they win, and we retreat, half whimpering, half with bravado. My first nauseating experience of cowardice. And my first appalled realization that there are people in the world who do not seem to be afraid of anything, who act as though they have nothing to lose. Thereafter the playground becomes a battleground, sometimes quiet, sometimes the scene of athletic competition between Them and Us. But rocks are thrown as often as baseballs. Gradually we abandon the place and use the streets instead. The streets are safer, though we do not admit this to ourselves. We are not, after all, sissies —that most dreaded epithet of an American boyhood.

Item I am standing alone in front of the building in which I live. It is late afternoon and getting dark. That day in school the teacher had asked a surly Negro boy named Quentin a question he was unable to answer. As usual I had waved my arm eagerly ("Be a good boy, get good marks, be smart, go to college, become a doctor") and, the right answer bursting from my lips, I was held up lovingly by the teacher as an example to the class. I had seen Quentin's face—a very dark, very cruel, very Oriental-looking face—harden, and there has been enough threat in his eyes to make me run all the way home for fear that he might catch me outside.

Now, standing idly in front of my own house, I see him approaching from the project accompanied by his little brother who is carrying a baseball bat and wearing a grin of malicious anticipation. As in a nightmare, I am trapped. The surroundings are secure and familiar, but terror is suddenly present and there is no one around to help. I am locked to the spot. I will not cry out or run away like a sissy, and I stand there, my heart wild, my throat clogged. He walks up, hurls the familiar epithet

("Hey, mo'f——r"), and to my surprise only pushes me. It is a violent push, but not a punch. A push is not as serious as a punch. Maybe I can still back out without entirely losing my dignity. Maybe I can still say. "Hey, c'mon Quentin, whaddya wanna do *that* for. I dint do nothin' to *you*," and walk away, not too rapidly. Instead, before I can stop myself, I push him back—a token gesture—and I say, "Cut that out, I don't wanna fight, I ain't got nothin' to fight about." As I turn to walk back into the building, the corner of my eye catches the motion of the bat his little brother has handed him. I try to duck, but the bat crashes colored lights into my head.

The next thing I know, my mother and sister are standing over me, both of them hysterical. My sister—she who was later to join the "progressive" youth organization—is shouting for the police and screaming imprecations at those dirty little black bastards. They take me upstairs, the doctor comes, the police come. I tell them that the boy who did it was a stranger, that he had been trying to get money from me. They do not believe me, but I am too scared to give them Quentin's name. When I return to school a few days later, Quentin avoids my eyes. He knows that I have not squealed, and he is ashamed. I try to feel proud, but in my heart I know that it was fear of what his friends might do to me that had kept me silent, and not the code of the street.

Item   There is an athletic meet in which the whole of our junior high school is participating. I am in one of the seventh-grade rapid-advance classes, and "segregation" has now set in with a vengeance. In the last three or four years of the elementary school from which we have just graduated, each grade had been divided into three classes, according to "intelligence." (In the earlier grades the divisions had either been arbitrary or else unrecognized by us as having anything to do with brains.) These divisions by IQ, or however it was arranged, had resulted in a preponderance of Jews in the "1" classes and a corresponding preponderance of Negroes in the "3's," with the Italians split unevenly along the spectrum. At least a few Negroes had always made the "1's," just as there had always been a few Jewish kids among the "3's" and more among the "2's" (where Italians dominated). But the junior high's rapid-advance class of which I am now a member is overwhelmingly Jewish and entirely white— except for a shy lonely Negro girl with light skin and reddish hair.

The athletic meet takes place in a city-owned stadium far from the school. It is an important event to which a whole day is given over. The winners are to get those precious little medallions stamped with the New York City emblem that can be screwed into a belt and that prove the wearer to be a distinguished personage. I am a fast runner, and so I am assigned the position of anchor man on my class's team in the relay race. There are three other seventh-grade teams in the race, two of them all Negro, as ours is all white. One of the all-Negro teams is very tall—their anchor man waiting silently next to me on the line looks years older than I am, and I do not recognize him. He is the first to get the baton and crosses the finishing line in a walk. Our team comes in second, but a few minutes later we are declared the winners, for it has been discovered that the anchor man on the first-place team is not a member of the class. We are awarded the medallions, and the following day our home-room teacher makes a speech about how proud she is of us for being superior athletes as well as superior students. We want to believe that we deserve the praise, but we know that we could not have won even if the other class had not cheated.

That afternoon, walking home, I am waylaid and surrounded by five Negroes, among whom is the anchor man of the disqualified team. "Gimme my medal, mo'f——r," he grunts. I do not have it with me and I tell him so. "Anyway, it ain't yours," I say foolishly. He calls me a liar on both counts and pushes me up against the wall on which we sometimes play handball. "Gimme my mo'f——n' medal," he says again. I repeat that I have left it home. "Le's search the li'l mo'f——r," one of them suggests, "he prolly got it *hid* in his mo'f——n' *pants*." My panic is now unmanageable. (How many times had I been surrounded like this and asked in soft tones, "Len' me a nickle, boy." How many times had I been called a liar for pleading poverty and pushed around, or searched, or beaten up, unless there happened to be someone in the marauding gang like Carl who liked me across that enormous divide of hatred and who would therefore say, "Aaah, c'mon, le's git someone else, *this* boy ain't got no money on 'im.") I scream at them through tears of rage and self-contempt, "Keep your f——n' filthy lousy black hands offa me! I swear I'll get the cops." This is all they need to hear, and the five of them set upon me. They bang me around, mostly in the stomach and on the arms and shoulders, and when several adults loitering near the candy store down the block notice what is going on and begin to shout, they run off and away.

I do not tell my parents about the incident. My team-mates, who have also been waylaid, each by a gang led by his opposite number from the disqualified team, have had their medallions taken from them, and they never squeal either. For days, I walk home in terror, expecting to be caught again, but nothing happens. The medallion is put away into a drawer, never to be worn by anyone.

Obviously experiences like these have always been a common feature of childhood life in working-class and immigrant neighborhoods, and Negroes do not necessarily figure in them. Wherever, and in whatever combination, they have lived together in the cities, kids of different groups have been at war, beating up and being beaten up: micks against kikes against wops against spicks against polacks. And even relatively homogeneous areas have not been spared the warring of the young: one block against another, one gang (called in my day, in a pathetic effort at gentility, an "S.A.C.," or social-athletic club) against another. But the Negro-white conflict had—and no doubt still has—a special intensity and was conducted with a ferocity unmatched by intramural white battling.

In my own neighborhood, a good deal of animosity existed between the Italian kids (most of whose parents were immigrants from Sicily) and the Jewish kids (who came largely from East European immigrant families). Yet everyone had friends, sometimes close friends, in the other "camp," and we often visited one another's strange-smelling houses, if not for meals, then for glasses of milk, and occasionally for some special event like a wedding or a wake. If it happened that we divided into warring factions and did battle, it would invariably be half-hearted and soon patched up. Our parents, to be sure, had nothing to do with one another and were mutually suspicious and hostile. But we, the kids, who all spoke Yiddish or Italian at home, were Americans, or New Yorkers, or Brooklyn boys: we shared a culture, the culture of the street, and at least for a while this culture proved to be more powerful than the opposing cultures of the home.

Why, *why* should it have been so different as between the Negroes and us? How was it borne in upon us so early, white and black alike, that we were enemies beyond any possibility of reconciliation? Why did we hate one another so?

I suppose if I tried, I could answer those questions more or less adequately from the perspective of what I have since learned. I could draw upon James Baldwin—what better witness is there?—to describe the sense of entrapment that poisons the soul of the Negro with hatred for the white man whom he knows to be his jailer. In the other side, if I wanted to understand how the white man comes to hate the Negro, I could call upon the psychologists who have spoken of the guilt that white Americans feel toward Negroes and that turns into hatred for lack of acknowledging itself as guilt. These are plausible answers and certainly there is truth in them. Yet when I think back upon my own experience of the Negro and his of me, I find myself troubled and puzzled, much as I was as a child when I heard that all Jews were rich and all Negroes persecuted. How could the Negroes in my neighborhood have regarded the whites across the street and around the corner as jailers? On the whole, the whites were not so poor as the Negroes, but they were quite poor enough, and the years were years of Depression. As for white hatred of the Negro, how could guilt have had anything to do with it? What share had these Italian and Jewish immigrants in the enslavement of the Negro? What share had they—down-trodden people themselves breaking their own necks to eke out a living—in the exploitation of the Negro?

No, I cannot believe that we hated each other back there in Brooklyn because they thought of us as jailers and we felt guilty toward them. But does it matter, given the fact that we all went through an unrepresentative confrontation? I think it matters profoundly, for if we managed the job of hating each other so well without benefit of the aids to hatred that are supposedly at the root of this madness everywhere else, it must mean that the madness is not yet properly understood. I am far from pretending that I understand it, but I would insist that no view of the problem will begin to approach the truth unless it can account for a case like the one I have been trying to describe. Are the elements of any such view available to us?

At least two, I would say, are. One of them is a point we frequently come upon in the work of James Baldwin, and the other is a related point always stressed by psychologists who have studied the mechanisms of prejudice. Baldwin tells us that one of the reasons Negroes hate the white man is that the white man refuses to *look* at him: the Negro knows that in white eyes all Negroes are alike; they are faceless and therefore not altogether human. The psychologists, in their turn, tell us that the white man hates the Negro because he tends to project those wild impulses that he fears in himself onto an alien group which he then punishes with his contempt. What Baldwin does *not* tell us, however, is that the principle of facelessness is a two-way street and can operate in both directions with no difficulty at all. Thus, in my neighborhood in Brooklyn, I was as faceless to the Negroes as they were to me, and if they hated me because I never looked at them, I must also have hated them for never looking at *me*. To the Negroes, my white skin was enough to define me as the enemy, and in a war it is only the uniform that counts and not the person.

So with the mechanism of projection that the psychologists talk about: it too works in both directions at once. There is no question that the psychologists are right about what the Negro represents symbolically to the white man. For me as a child the life lived on the other side of the playground and down the block on Ralph Avenue seemed the very embodiment of the values of the street—free, independent, reckless, brave, masculine, erotic. I put the word "erotic" last, though it is usually stressed above all others, because in fact it came last, in consciousness as in importance. What mainly counted for me about Negro kids of my own age was that they were "bad boys." There were plenty of bad boys among the whites— this was, after all, a neighborhood with a long tradition of crime as a career open to aspiring talents—but the Negroes were *really* bad, bad in a way that beckoned to one, and made one feel inadequate. We all went home every day for a lunch of spinach-and-potatoes; *they* roamed around during lunch hour, munching on candy bars. In winter *we* had to wear itchy woolen hats and mittens and cumbersome galoshes; *they* were bare-headed and loose as they pleased. We rarely played hookey, or got into serious trouble in school, for all our street-corner bravado; *they* were defiant, forever staying out (to do what delicious things?), forever making disturbances in class and in the halls, forever being sent to the principal and returning uncowed. But most important of all, they were *tough*; beautifully, enviably tough, not giving a damn for anyone or anything. To hell with the teacher, the truant officer, the cop; to hell with the whole of the adult world that held *us* in its grip and that we never had the courage to rebel against except sporadically and in petty ways.

This is what I saw and envied and feared in the Negro: this is what finally made him faceless to me, though some of it, of course, was actually there. (The psychologists also tell us that the alien group which becomes the object of a projection will tend to respond by trying to live up to what is expected of them.) But what, on his side, did the Negro see in me that made me faceless to *him?* Did he envy me my lunches of spinach-and-potatoes and my itchy woolen caps and my prudent behavior in the face of authority, as I envied him his noon-time candy bars and his bare head in winter and his magnificent rebelliousness? Did those lunches and caps spell for him the prospect of power and riches in the future? Did they mean that there were possibilities open to me that were denied to him? Very likely they did. But if so, one also supposes that he feared the impulses within himself toward submission to authority no less powerfully than I feared the impulses in myself toward defiance. If I represented the jailer to him, it was not because I was oppressing him or keeping him down: it was because I symbolized for him the dangerous and probably pointless temptation toward greater repression, just as he symbolized for me the equally perilous tug toward greater freedom. I personally was to be rewarded for this repression with a new and better life in the future, but how many of my friends paid an even higher price and were given only gall in return.

We have it on the authority of James Baldwin that all Negroes hate whites. I am trying to suggest that on their side all whites—all American whites, that is—are sick in their feelings about Negroes. There are Negroes, no doubt, who would say that Baldwin is wrong, but I suspect them of being less honest than he is, just as I suspect whites of self-deception who tell me they have no special feeling toward Negroes. Special feelings about color are a contagion to which white Americans seem susceptible even when there is nothing in their background to account for the susceptibility. Thus everywhere we look today in the North, we find the curious phenomenon of white middle-class liberals with no previous personal experience of Negroes—people to whom Negroes have always been faceless in virtue rather than faceless in vice—discovering that their abstract commitment to the cause of Negro rights will not stand the test of a direct confrontation. We find such people fleeing in droves to the suburbs as the Negro population in the inner city grows; and when they stay in the city we find them sending their children to private school rather than to the "integrated" public school in the neighborhood. We find them resisting the demand that gerrymandered school districts be re-zoned for the purpose of overcoming de facto segregation; we find them judiciously considering whether the Negroes (for their own good, of course) are not perhaps pushing too hard; we find them clucking their tongues over Negro militancy; we find them speculating on the question of whether there may not, after all, be something in the theory that the races are biologically different; we find them saying that it will take a very long time for Negroes to achieve full equality, no matter what anyone does; we find them deploring the rise of black nationalism and expressing the solemn hope that the leaders of the Negro community will discover ways of containing the impatience and incipient violence within the Negro ghettos.[1]

But that is by no means the whole story; there is also the phenomenon of what Kenneth Rexroth once called "crow-jimism." There are the broken-down white boys like Vivaldo Moore in Baldwin's *Another Country* who go to Harlem in search of sex or simply to brush up against something that looks like primitive vitality, and who are so often punished by the Negroes they meet for crimes that they would have been the last ever to commit and of which they themselves have been as sorry victims as any of the Negroes who take it out on them. There are the writers and intellectuals and artists who romanticize Negroes and pander to them, assuming a guilt that is not properly theirs. And there are all the white liberals who permit Negroes to blackmail them into adopting a double standard of moral judgment, and who lend themselves—again assuming the responsibility for crimes they never committed—to cunning and contemptuous exploitation by Negroes they employ or try to befriend.

And what about me? What kind of feelings do I have about Negroes today? What happened to me, from Brooklyn, who grew up fearing and envying and hating Negroes? Now that Brooklyn is behind me, do I fear them and envy them and hate them still? The answer is yes, but not in the same proportions and certainly not in the same way. I now live on the upper west side of Manhattan, where there are many Negroes and many Puerto Ricans, and there are nights when I experience the old apprehensiveness again, and there are streets that I avoid when I am walking in the dark, as there were streets that I avoided when I was a child. I find that I am not afraid of Puerto Ricans, but I cannot restrain my nervousness whenever I pass a group of Negroes standing in front of a bar or sauntering down the street. I know now, as I did not know when I was a child, that power is on my side, that the police are working for me and not for them. And knowing this I feel ashamed and guilty, like the good liberal I have grown up to be. Yet the twinges of fear and the resentment they bring and the self-contempt they arouse are not to be gainsaid.

But envy? Why envy? And hatred? Why hatred? Here again the intensities have lessened and everything has been complicated and qualified by the guilts and the resulting over-compensations that are the heritage

---

[1] For an account of developments like these, see "The White Liberal's Retreat" by Murray Friedman in the January 1963 *Atlantic Monthly*.

of the enlightened middle-class world of which I am now a member. Yet just as in childhood I envied Negroes for what seemed to me their superior masculinity, so I envy them today for what seems to me their superior physical grace and beauty. I have come to value physical grace very highly, and I am now capable of aching with all my being when I watch a Negro couple on the dance floor, or a Negro playing baseball or basketball. They are on the kind of terms with their own bodies that I should like to be on with mine, and for that precious quality they seem blessed to me.

The hatred I still feel for Negroes is the hardest of all the old feelings to face or admit, and it is the most hidden and the most overlarded by the conscious attitudes into which I have succeeded in willing myself. It no longer has, as for me it once did, any cause or justification (except, perhaps, that I am constantly being denied my right to an honest expression of the things I earned the right as a child to feel). How, then, do I know that this hatred has never entirely disappeared? I know it from the insane rage that can stir in me at the thought of Negro anti-Semitism; I know it from the disgusting prurience that can stir in me at the sight of a mixed couple; and I know it from the violence that can stir in me whenever I encounter that special brand of paranoid touchiness to which many Negroes are prone.

This, then, is where I am; it is not exactly where I think all other white liberals are, but it cannot be so very far away either. And it is because I am convinced that we white Americans are—for whatever reason, it no longer matters—so twisted and sick in our feelings about Negroes that I despair of the present push toward integration. If the pace of progress were not a factor here, there would perhaps be no cause for despair: time and the law and even the international political situation are on the side of the Negroes, and ultimately, therefore, victory—of a sort, anyway—must come. But from everything we have learned from observers who ought to know, pace has become as important to the Negroes as substance. They want equality and they want it *now*, and the white world is yielding to their demand only as much and as fast as it is absolutely being compelled to do. The Negroes know this in the most concrete terms imaginable, and it is thus becoming increasingly difficult to buy them off with rhetoric and promises and pious assurances of support. And so within the Negro community we find more and more people declaring—as Harold R. Isaacs recently put it in these pages[2]—that they want *out*: people who say that integration will never come, or that it will take a hundred or a thousand years to come, or that it will come at too high a price in suffering and struggle for the pallid and sodden life of the American middle class that at the very best it may bring.

[2] "Integration and the Negro Mood," December 1962.

The most numerous, influential, and dangerous movement that has grown out of Negro despair with the goal of integration is, of course, the Black Muslims. This movement, whatever else we may say about it, must be credited with one enduring achievement: it inspired James Baldwin to write an essay[3] which deserves to be placed among the classics of our language. Everything Baldwin has ever been trying to tell us is distilled here into a statement of overwhelming persuasiveness and prophetic magnificence. Baldwin's message is and always has been simple. It is this: "Color is not a human or personal reality; it is a political reality." And Baldwin's demand is correspondingly simple: color must be forgotten, lest we all be smited with a vengeance "that does not really depend on, and cannot really be executed by, any person or organization, and that cannot be prevented by any police force or army: historical vengeance, a cosmic vengeance based on the law that we recognize when we say, 'Whatever goes up must come down.'" The Black Muslims Baldwin portrays as a sign and a warning to the intransigent white world. They come to proclaim how deep is the Negro's disaffection with the white world and all its works, and Baldwin implies that no American Negro can fail to respond somewhere in his being to their message: that the white man is the devil, that Allah has doomed him to destruction, and that the black man is about to inherit the earth. Baldwin of course knows that this nightmare inversion of the racism from which the black man has suffered can neither win nor even point to the neighborhood in which victory might be located. For in his view the neighborhood of victory lies in exactly the opposite direction: the transcendence of color through love.

Yet the tragic fact is that love is not the answer to hate—not in the world of politics, at any rate. Color is indeed a political rather than a human or a personal reality and if politics (which is to say power) has made it into a human and a personal reality, then only politics (which is to say power) can unmake it once again. But the way of politics is slow and bitter, and as impatience on the one side is matched by a setting of the jaw on the other, we move closer and closer to an explosion and blood may yet run in the streets.

Will this madness in which we are all caught never find a resting-place? Is there never to be an end to it? In thinking about the Jews I have often wondered whether their survival as a distinct group was worth one hair on the head of a single infant. Did the Jews have to survive so that six million innocent people should one day be burned in the ovens of Auschwitz? It is a terrible question and no one, not God himself, could ever answer it to my satisfaction. And when I think about the Negroes in America and about the image of integration as a state in which the Negroes

[3] Originally published last November in the *New Yorker* under the title "Letter From a Region in My Mind," it has just been reprinted (along with a new introduction) by Dial Press under the title *The Fire Next Time* (128 pp., $3.50).

would take their rightful place as another of the protected minorities in a pluralistic society, I wonder whether they really believe in their hearts that such a state can actually be attained, and if so *why* they should wish to survive as a distinct group. I think I know why the Jews once wished to survive (though I am less certain as to why we still do): they not only believed that God has given them no choice, but they were tied to a memory of past glory and a dream of imminent redemption. What does the American Negro have that might correspond to this? His past is a stigma, his color is a stigma, and his vision of the future is the hope of erasing the stigma by making color irrelevant, by making it disappear as a fact of consciousness.

I share this hope, but I cannot see how it will ever be realized unless color does *in fact* disappear: and that means not integration, it means assimilation, it means—let the brutal word come out—miscegenation. The Black Muslims, like their racists counterparts in the white world, accuse the "so-called Negro leaders" of secretly pursuing miscegenation as a goal. The racists are wrong, but I wish they were right, for I believe that the wholesale merging of the two races is the most desirable alternative for everyone concerned. I am not claiming that this alternative can be pursued programmatically or that it is immediately feasible as a solution; obviously there are even greater barriers to its achievement than to the achievement of integration. What I am saying, however, is that in my opinion the Negro problem can be solved in this country in no other way.

I have told the story of my own twisted feelings about Negroes here, and of how they conflict with the moral convictions I have since developed, in order to assert that such feelings must be acknowledged as honestly as possible so that they can be controlled and ultimately disregarded in favor of the convictions. It is *wrong* for a man to suffer because of the color of his skin. Beside that clichéd proposition of liberal thought, what argument can stand and be respected? If the arguments are the arguments of feeling, they must be made to yield; and one's own soul is not the worst place to begin working a huge social transformation. Not so long ago, it used to be asked of white liberals, "Would you like your sister to marry one?" When I was a boy and my sister was still unmarried, I would certainly have said no to that question. But now I am a man, my sister is already married, and I have daughters. If I were to be asked today whether I would like a daughter of mine "to marry one," I would have to answer: "No, I wouldn't *like* it at all. I would rail and rave and rant and tear my hair. And then I hope I would have the courage to curse myself for raving and ranting, and to give her my blessing. How dare I withhold it at the behest of the child I once was and against the man I now have a duty to be?"

24. Negro Reactions to Minority Group Status

ROBERT B. JOHNSON

Johnson's paper is notable for its clarification of Negroes' central concerns about themselves and about their relations with white people in a city in upstate New York. Johnson orders these concerns along five continua that he calls Hostility-Friendliness, Insulation-Integration, Lassitude-Militance, Avoidance-Whiteward Mobility, and Self-hatred-Race Pride. The paper also shows how differences in social background affect the ways that individuals assess their current situations. For example, older southern-born Negroes tend to be more passive but also more bitter than others about Negro-white relations. Near the end of the paper, the author synthesizes some of his earlier observations by constructing "social types" to represent combinations of positions on the various attitude continua. The reader should not concretize these types, but should remind himself that they are abstractions from the data. Otherwise, he may find that he is dealing in stereotypes, although on a more sophisticated level than usually occurs in cases of categorical prejudgment.

INTRODUCTION

In the current international crisis of conflicting group attitudes, sentiments and loyalties, Americans are fortunate in having available to them a vast amount of academic and empirical literature derived from studies of minority group relations in world society. Most of these studies have dealt with (a) the position of minorities in the social structure; (b) the clarification of thinking on the subject of race, and on the relation of race and culture; (c) the psychological, sociological, and economic analyses of the nature of race prejudice and discrimination; and (d) the discussion of techniques for the reduction of intergroup tension and the improvement of the socio-economic position of minorities.

The present article is an attempt to contribute to a fifth area of interest; the differential reaction of American Negroes to their minority group status.

SOURCE: This paper appears for the first time in its present form in this volume. It is reprinted with the permission of the author and of Milton Barron. The original version appeared in Milton Barron (ed.), *American Minorities* (New York: Alfred A. Knopf, Inc., 1957).

Robert B. Johnson is Chairman of the Division of Social Science at Wilberforce University. He has published many articles in the field of minority and intergroup relations.

It is the outgrowth of an intensive three-year investigation in a single small city, using as a setting the general community as well as the rest of the American Negro world. In this part of the study, the research techniques of participant-observation and of the cross-sectional survey method have been combined to determine how the American Negro in this community feels and reacts toward his minority status.

We are generally familiar with the current credo of the American Negro as expressed by Negro leaders, organizations, and publications on the national level. This credo implies the desirability of concerted movement toward two goals: (a) the promotion of the general American drive toward the "More Perfect Union," and (b) the improvement of the Negro's status within the framework of the democratic creed. Militancy is urged, self-hatred is decried, interest in international events is encouraged, friendliness and goodwill toward whites are advocated with notable exception. In addition, a seemingly contradictory but actually realistic dual value is implied: (a) the desirability of strengthening Negro group identification and race pride, and (b) the desirability of struggling for full integration into American society.

On a local community level, it is evident that the extent of adherence to the national Negro Creed will be conditioned by the regional location of the community, the size of the Negro community and of the general community, and the extent to which the community is accessible to the media of communication that promote this national creed. Hence, this intensive community-wide examination of intergroup contacts, attitudes, and social relations selected, as part of its scope, the relationship of the national Negro credo to Negro attitudes in a specific locus.

THE COMMUNITY SETTING

The study was made in a middle-sized, middle-Atlantic community of 60,000 persons, which we shall call "Hometown." It is a predominantly industrial community, boasting twelve locally-owned and twelve absentee-owned relatively small industries and one large industrial plant with 7000 employees. The city was selected on the basis of these criteria: (a) its economic and industrial organization was relatively representative of most middle-sized American cities; (b) it was not a "boom town" nor was it "dominated" by large nearby cities, large industries, or educational institutions; (c) it had a fair distribution of ethnic groups. The Negro and Jewish communities were of approximately equal size, each comprising close to three percent of the city's population. Roughly, six percent of the community members were of Italian-American descent. In addition, the community contained several Irish, Russian-Ukranian, and Polish families.

After compiling relevant data on the history, demography, and ecology, economic organization, and social structure of the community, and after making "quickie" surveys in six similar cities, the research group devised a questionnaire which was administered to 529 adult "NAM's" (native American white gentiles), 150 Jews, 150 Negroes, and 150 persons of Italian ancestry. The questionnaire contained an exhaustive inventory of contacts between majority and minority group members, an inventory of personality traits (authoritarianism, "Jungle" outlook, frustration, and indices of psychoneurosis) and an intensive inventory of the elements of prejudice— hostility, antipathy, scapegoating, social distance, and stereotyped thinking.

When the majority group was asked about the Negro community, it soon became evident that most majority group members had (a) very little contact with Negroes, and (b) a great deal of prejudice against them. Half of the majority group members in the community had *no* contact with *any* minority group member (Negro, Jew, or Italian) in any of the four areas investigated—job, neighborhood, organization, or informal social group.

Respondents were asked about actual and hypothetical contacts with Negroes in these four areas. Fourteen percent stated that there were Negroes living within a block or two of their home, 13 percent reported contact with a Negro fellow worker or employee on their job, 10 percent belonged to organizations with Negro members (half of these were unions or veteran's organizations), and none of the respondents interviewed reported any Negroes in their informal social group. Attitudes toward Negroes in these four areas are shown in Table 1.

Table 1: *Attitudes toward Associations with Negroes*

Those who had Negroes:	Respondent "Feels Different" (%)	Others "Feel Different" (%)
In their club (52)	10	23
On their job (67)	17	33
In their neighborhood (74)	27	46
In their social group (0)	—	—

Attitudes of those who contacted no Negroes in these areas are shown in Table 2.

It may be consistently shown that respondents reacted more favorably to the actual presence of Negroes in these four areas than they responded to the *hypothetical* possibility of Negroes in those areas, and also that in every single case, the respondent was more likely to say that *others* would object than to admit that *he* the respondent would object.

Table 2: Attitudes toward Possible Associations with Negroes

Suppose a Negro wanted to come into:	Respondent Would Object (%)	Others Would Object (%)
Your club (205)	43	68
Your work group (226)	33	47
Your neighborhood (448)	60	86
Your social group (293)	77	93

When presented with a social-distance scale (known as the "distaste-fuls"), Hometown white persons answered as follows:

I would find it distasteful:
1. To eat with a Negro 49%
2. To dance with a Negro 82%
3. To go to a party and find that most of the people there are Negro 80%
4. To have a Negro marry somebody in my family .. 99%

When presented with a modified version of the "Chicago Tension Barometer," 20% of Hometown residents said that they disliked Negroes; 22% thought that Negroes are demanding more than they have a right to (and 26% of these said that this made them feel "pretty angry"); 41% felt that Negroes were pushing in where they were not wanted (of these, 23% averred that it bothered them a good deal). In addition, 42% agreed with the stereotyped statement that, "generally speaking, Negroes are lazy and ignorant."

Accompanying these prejudices are the patterns of racial discrimination against the Negro and the configuration of operating policies and pro-cedures by which Negroes are admitted to or barred from various institu-tional and organizational community structures. The most noticeable form of discrimination was in the area of public facilities. Although New York has strong anti-discrimination laws, a survey of 150 Negro adults yielded the names of 37 restaurants, 26 taverns and bars, 6 hotels, 5 night clubs, and 5 other places of recreation where they thought Negroes might not be welcome. When asked about specific incidents of discrimination, 28% of the 150 Negroes cited cases of differential treatment in public facilities that had recently happened to *them*.

In addition to the factors of prejudice and discrimination against the Negro, a third factor contributes to his isolation from the general life of the community. Woven into the speech of many Americans are elements of the *"language of prejudice,"* derogatory remarks, jokes, slurs, and epi-thets that are insulting to the Negro. The content of interracial contacts is frequently (and negatively) loaded and charged with affect by the white person's careless or non-insighted employment of these elements.

However, there are variations in Negro reactions to white breaches of the *Northern* "Etiquette of Race Relations." Some Negroes take these things harder than others; some would resent them in an outsider and ignore them in a friend; some employ them when talking to other Negroes, some with a low degree of racial identification would pay them no mind. To test the reactions of a variety of Negroes in Hometown, a few elements of the "language of prejudice,"—the "testimonial," the anti-Jewish rapport device, the "slip," and the epithet—were selected and included in a questionnaire. A cross-section of 150 adult Negro respondents were asked: "Which of these things make you angry, which just annoy you, and which doesn't bother you at all?" The response is shown in Table 3.

Table 3: Negro Response to White "Language of Prejudice"

	Makes Me Angry (%)	Annoys Me (%)	Doesn't Bother Me (%)
When a white person tells you how much he likes Negroes ("testimonial")	9	32	59
When a white person tells you how much he dislikes some other minority like the Jew (faulty rapport device)	26	36	38
When a white person forgets or "slips" and uses the word "darky" (the "slip")	57	26	17
When a white person uses the word "nigger" (the intentional epithet)	74	15	11

In addition, 44 percent of the Negroes reported that they felt uncomfortable when a white person told them: "You're as good as I am," whereas only 23 percent reported a positive reaction. When asked about deterrents to greater contact with white people, two-thirds mentioned one or more barriers. Of these 50 percent agreed that "I expect the white person to make a 'slip' and say something wrong about Negroes." Even among the Negro youth 43 percent agreed with the extreme statement: "When I am around whites, I am *always* expecting someone to make a 'slip' and say something bad about Negroes."

Violent negative reaction to the epithet was further documented by the Negro youths. At the end of a battery of questions about their white best friend, they were asked: "If your white *best* friend 'slipped,' called you a nigger, what would you do?" The response was explosive. Only six youths said they would assume the white friend didn't mean it, 13 percent said they would ignore it, or do nothing, 2 percent said they would sympathize, 23 percent said they would make a vigorous verbal protest ("wise him up," "tell him to watch his tongue," "I'd resent it and tell him so in strong words."). Twenty-four percent mentioned physical violence ("Slap her face, but good," "I think I would find myself fighting," "I would dip my fist into his mouth," "give him a black eye," "Sock him in the teeth."). Only one charitable-hearted thirteen-year-old girl said, "I would forgive."

The varied interrelationships of these three factors: the patterns of prejudice, the patterns of discrimination, and the elements of the "language of prejudice" constitute the "Gestalt" that confronts the Hometown Negro. The expectation of prejudice in most whites, the fear of a rebuff or ambiguously embarrassing discrimination, the tense wait for the almost inevitable "language of prejudice," including what one Negro called the possibility of being "*stabbed* with the word nigger," produces in the Hometown Negro a pattern of avoidance and defensive insulation, prompting the frequent white statement that "the Negroes prefer to be by themselves."

Hence, though the Negro community shows several types of internal differentiation, based on length of residence, socio-economic level, extent and type of social participation, etc., it is a socially isolated community and there are several evidences of it. Questionnaire evidence shows not only that contacts with whites are quite limited in quantity and in depth, but also that Negroes viewed many issues more as part of a psychological community of 1200 members than as part of a Hometown community of 60,000. For example, when asked the question: "If you were asked to put yourself and your family into one of these classes, which would you say you are in; the upper class, the middle class, the working class, or the lower class?" 2 percent of the 150 Negro adults said *upper* class, because their standard of comparison was the working-class Negro community rather than the predominantly middle-class general community. Meanwhile, only 6 percent of Jews, and 3 percent of "NAM's" and Italian Americans put themselves in this category.

Casual statements of community members also reflected the isolated social world. The statement "It's all over town" generally meant "all over the Negro community" and even this takes in only the solid core of the Negro community, and not its indefinite periphery. "The prettiest girl in town," or "the meanest man in town" referred not to Hometown but to its Negro community. The term "we" usually turned out, under probe, to refer to Hometown Negroes or to Negroes throughout the country, rather than to Hometown in general. At one time, the observer was reassured by a lifetime resident that he could feel free to discuss confidential subjects over the telephone, since the only people who would possibly be listening on the party line were white people who were so removed from the Negro's life that it didn't matter what *they* heard.

The Negro's Race Attitude Components

A general survey of the Negro's reaction to his minority status suggests these facts: The historical position and past southern experience of the Hometown Negro strongly affect his present relations with whites; the Hometown Negro community is socially almost completely isolated from the general community; the Hometown Negro feels strongly identified with the national Negro community and much less identified with the Hometown community; the Hometown Negro maintains a high level of consciousness on intergroup relations; a good deal of confusions, status dilemma and bitterness is produced by the Hometown Negro's uncertainty of his position in interracial situations; a number of the face-gaining and face-losing attributes in the Negro community are connected with ingroup-outgroup relations; the undefined nature of many interracial contacts, and the fear of insult or rebuff from outsiders erect strong barriers to interracial communication; the attitude of the Hometown Negro toward other minorities and toward himself are strongly conditioned by the majority definition of minority groups; the integration of the Negro into general community life is most likely when a new in-group definition is created, transcending racial lines.

Yet complete unanimity in the Negro community seems to exist only in realization of minority status, expectation of white prejudice, and reactions to racial epithets. Even within the realm of racial attitudes, there is a vast difference of opinion within the community depending on (a) personality factors, (b) regional origin and length of residence, (c) current contacts and experiences with whites, (d) exposure to the media of Negro life and Negro protest, (e) exposure to "significant others" who mold opinion on race as well as other issues, (f) social position and social mobility, (g) conforming to the role that the community has created for the individual, and (h) success or failure in the enactment of that role. The Negro's reaction to his minority status may be described (in addition to differential reactions to the "language of prejudice") in terms of five main continua:

1. Hostility————friendliness   (attitude toward larger community)
2. Insulation————integration   (involvement in larger community)
3. Lassitude————militancy   (orientation toward own group's position in larger community)
4. Avoidance————"whiteward mobility"   (behavior toward larger community)
5. Self-hatred————Race Pride   (attitude toward own group)

These five continua cannot be separated within the individual personality, but rather, hang together in a configuration of "creeds." For example, the hostile person is also likely to be insulated; the lassitudinous person is most likely to practice avoidance. However, they may be discussed separately.

HOSTILITY AND FRIENDLINESS

It is certain that every Hometown Negro has encountered evidences of white prejudice, or differential treatment from whites. In addition to his own experiences, he may feel *vicariously* the experiences of other Negroes, transmitted through the endless racial conversations, and through the militant Negro press which seldom hesitates to present in graphic detail the inequities, discriminations, and atrocities perpetrated on Negroes throughout the country. Consequently, at one time or another, every Negro has experienced the emotion of hostility toward whites. This hostility is usually only sporadic and occasional, rising under stress, and receding under pressure of a favorable interracial contact or under the necessity of turning attention to other things. However, in several cases, this hostility is generally resting near the surface, and is tapped in our questionnaire through reactions to the following questions, based on the responses of 150 adult Negroes:

> "I would like to get even with the white man for some of the things he has done to Negroes." (25% agree)

> "No matter how nicely he treats a Negro, a white man doesn't really mean it." (26% agree)

> "Sometimes I hate white people." (33%)

In general, Negro hostility is more prevalent among the less educated, among the Southern-born, the youths and adults under 45, the female, the isolated, and the Negroes whose interracial contact was minimal. Often, this hostility is deflected at specific groups, particularly the foreign-born, who are resented as having greater privilege on their first day in America than the Negro.

Hostility in the Hometown Negro community was most closely related to place of birth. Lifetime residents were least hostile, and the Southern-born were most hostile. As C. S. Johnson states:

> There is considerable amount of racial discrimination in the North, but it is a common observation that the Negroes who discuss these discriminatory practices most frankly are those who originally came from the South . . . Buried racial antagonisms can easily be called to the surface, however, in a variety of overt expressions with or without strong provocation. Migrants from the South in particular

who have stored away memories of deep-cutting offenses discreetly tolerated in the South, may reveal undue aggressiveness in the areas of open competition.

Table 4:   *The Greater Hostility of Southern Negroes*

	Born in Hometown (%)	Born in Other Northern City (%)	Born in South; came Here from Other Northern City (%)	Came from South (%)
Number of cases	28 (19%)	39 (26%)	34 (24%)	47 (31%)
Percent who agree that:				
I would like to get even with the white man for some of the things he has done to Negroes	18	13	32	37
No matter how nicely he treats a Negro, a white man doesn't really mean it	4	24	27	42
Sometimes I hate white people	12	41	33	42

INSULATION AND INTEGRATION

Minority group reactions have often been described in terms of a cycle: first, an absorption of majority group attitudes toward the subject's minority group and a consequent development of self-hate feelings toward his group; second, an attempt to integrate into the majority group; third, a rebuff from the majority group and a subsequent development of feelings of hostility, avoidance, and defensive insulation. According to Everret Stonequist's description of the "Marginal Man," a fourth process is possible; the development of in-group identification, pride, and militancy.

There is evidence that Hometown's Negro youths may follow a cycle similar to this description. At any rate, the life history of almost every Negro's reaction to minority status will include a variety of rebuffs ending in a general withdrawal and isolation from the stresses of interracial contacts. This withdrawal results in a syndrome of attitudes that characterize what we call the "insulated personality." The insulate is characterized by his endorsement of the following statements:

"I would find it a little 'distasteful' to go to a party and find that most of the people there were white." (21% agree)

"Negroes should live around their own people." (27% agree)

"If I had a choice between an all-Negro club and a mixed club,
I would join the all-Negro club." (50% agree)

Like the hostile personality, the insulate is likely to be Southern-born,
less educated, relatively non-participant, and usually a female. The insulate
is also likely to be older than the non-insulate. In addition, the insulation
responses tend to cluster together, or "scale"; that is, any person who would
find it distasteful to go to a party and find that most of the people are
white will also agree that Negroes should live around their own people,
and prefer an all-Negro club to a mixed club.

In reference to background characteristics, the most significant variables
that will condition the Negro's attitude toward insulation are his education
and his regional origin. Here educational level is divided between those
who had some high school education or better (only two of the 150 had
college training) and those who had a grammar school education, or less.
Regional origin was defined by whether the respondent was Northern-born
or Southern-born. Results are given in Table 5.

Table 5: Negro Attitudes According to Education and Regional Origin

	Better-Educated Northern Born (33%)	Better-Educated Southern Born (19%)	Less-Educated Northern Born (15%)	Less-Educated Southern Born (35%)
Percent who agree that:				
Negroes should live around their own people	12	21	23	47
I would prefer an all-Negro club to a mixed club	31	43	59	69
I do not think it is all right for a Negro to marry a white person	29	21	50	49
I would find it distasteful to go to a party and find that most of the people are white	12	11	14	37

LASSITUDE AND MILITANCY

The Negro community is also divided on the necessity and possibility of
militant action to improve the status of Negroes. Myrdal has stated:

> [The protest] attitude is not so uncommon as one would think,
> even among Negroes of humble status. But with the individual
> Negro there is always a tendency for protest to become bent into

defeatism. Negroes on all class levels give vent to this feeling of defeatism in expressions such as "niggers ain't got a thing," "We're the underdogs," "Negroes can't win," "there is just no hope for Negroes," "why bother?"

This cannot be said publicly though. The protest motive does not allow it. No Negro leader could preach it. No Negro newspaper could print it. It must be denied eagerly and persistently. But privately it can be said and it is said.

This ambivalence about lassitude and militancy is frequently present in the Hometown Negro. On the other hand, it is status-losing for him to publicly articulate statements of defeatism about the Negro's position, except in an intimate circle of friends. On the other hand, disparagement of the Negro and joking references to the Negro's incapacity is sometimes acceptable and is often the subject of much banter and levity. Even the Race Leader sometimes pauses from his denouncement of prejudiced whites and directs amused or angry criticism at the Negro community, provided no whites are present. At an NAACP meeting, the chairman of its membership campaign shouted, to great roars of answering laughter: "I get sick of working for people with no thanks and no help. I asked one man to join the NAACP and he told me: "You know what—that thing ain't legal."

Thirty-five percent of Hometown Negroes, and 51 percent of the even less effective Negro youths agreed with the statement: "I don't worry about the race problem since I can't do anything about it." When asked what they would do if refused service in a Hometown restaurant, 60 percent of the adults said they would leave without saying anything, 12 percent said they would protest to the manager, 13 percent said they would try to sue, 8 percent would report it to the NAACP, and 7 percent gave other answers. As one middle-aged Negro hotel waiter said: "I'd turn around and come on out. Didn't have no business in there in the first place."

AVOIDANCE AND "WHITEWARD MOBILITY"

Most Negroes tend to avoid the ambiguous interracial contacts that abound in Northern cities. Sixty-four percent of Negro adults agreed that "Negroes shouldn't go into business establishments where they think they are not wanted." The 100 Negro youths were also asked a battery of avoidance questions, and showed a similar tendency. Ten percent of the youths agreed that "I keep away from white people as much as I can"; 29 percent agreed that "it is best to stay away from white people, then you will avoid all embarrassing situations," 57 percent agreed that Negroes shouldn't go into business establishments where they think they're not wanted," and 77 percent agreed that "if a business place refuses to serve me, I think I should leave without causing any trouble."

Comparison of adult and youth responses on avoidance show that these avoidance techniques are acquired at an early age, are retained with little alteration throughout life, and are most frequently practiced by older adults. Avoidance techniques are sometimes passed on from parents and other adults to youths, but are often acquired as a result of bitter experience, as these comments from recent migrants show:

> "When I go in a place, they all look at me so funny . . . everybody gets quiet. So I just stay home."

> "This town ain't supposed to be Jim Crow. They told me before that we could go in there (a tavern). Me and my wife went and the man met us at the door and told us colored people couldn't get served. I just said 'thank you' and left. I figured that if he didn't want you, didn't any of 'em want you. You can't go in any of these places here."

> "I go in a place just as quiet and well dressed as I can be. When I get refused, it hurts me . . . it hurts me to my soul. So I don't go anymore."

On the other hand, 38 percent of Negro adults and 39% of youths agreed that "I would prefer to live in a neighborhood where there are not many Negroes"; 46 percent of adults and 62 percent of youths said they would prefer a mixed social club to an all-Negro club. Statements like "I would like to know more white people than I know now," "Colored and white people should try to mix together more often," and "I wouldn't mind having white people in my social group" were dropped from the youth questionnaire after the first 25 interviews because everybody agreed with them.

SELF-HATE AND RACE PRIDE

The nature of self-hatred has been clearly expressed by the late social psychologist Kurt Lewin:

> There seems to exist in every underprivileged group a tendency to accept the values of the more privileged group in a given society. The member of the underprivileged group therefore becomes excessively sensitive to everything within his own group that does not conform to these values, because it makes him feel that he belongs to a group whose standards are lower. Such feelings against one's own group conflict with the natural tendency of the individual in favor of it. The result is a typically ambivalent attitude on the part of members of an underprivileged group toward their own group.[1]

[1] Kurt Lewin, *Resolving Social Conflicts*, Harper and Brothers, 1948.

The Negroes of Hometown are caught in this cross-pressure between the high value placed on race pride and group identification of the national Negro creed, and the disparaging view of the Negro which they have absorbed from the general community. The tendency to disparage the in-group was strongly shown by Negro youths in response to questioning (Table 6).

Table 6: Negro Disparagement of Negroes

Statement	Percent Who Agree
Negroes blame whites for their position, but it is really their own fault.	50
Negroes will never get ahead, because when one is succeeding, the others pull him down.	41
Negroes are always shouting about their rights, and have nothing to offer.	28

On the other hand, it is status-losing to admit to others or even to one's self that one has no race pride or strong group identification. Most respondents said they were proud to be Negro and hopefully pointed to the Negro's past, his progress, and to current Negro heroes like Ralph Bunche, Jackie Robinson, and Marian Anderson as the basis of their pride. Only 28 percent of Negro youths said they would rather work for a white person than a Negro; 23 percent agreed that "Sometimes I wish I were anything but a Negro," 9 percent agreed that they would rather play with white kids than with Negro kids, and only 5 percent agreed that "If I could be born again, I would like to be born white." When asked what group they would like most to be born into, 82 percent maintained that they would like most to be born Negro, 26 percent mentioned "Spanish," 17 percent mentioned "Mexican," and 17 percent said "French." Only 8 percent indicated "white American" as the group they would like most to be born into, whereas 46 percent stoutly mentioned "white American" as the group they would like *least* to be born into.

Efforts to work up a spirit of pride often conflicted with the obvious disadvantages of minority group status, as shown in these ambivalent statements:

> "I'm proud to be a Negro, but it's an ordeal and a struggle. You have a hard time to get anywhere. In view of the treatment, I wouldn't 'pick to scuffle.'"

> "Lots of people are worse off than we are. Negroes are advancing faster than any other race."

"I'm proud of being a Negro—no use wishing—I've got to bear with it and make the best of what comes."

One 78-year-old Negro woman summed it up by saying:

"Being a Negro is no disgrace, but it sure is an inconvenience."

A SOCIAL TYPOLOGY

In a study of Negroes in Chicago, Samuel Strong adopted the method of empirical typology to reflect the nature of race relations in a large metropolis. Strong says:

> The assumption is that socially isolated minority groups, resenting their exclusion from the larger society, develop their own universe of discourse which is likely to express many reactions usually withheld in conventional communication with the out-group. Under such conditions indigenous social types arise and are referred to in the everyday language of the group in a distinctive way that reveals their connotation. By isolating empirically the significant social types recognized by a minority group and studying the various characterizations attributed to them, it is possible to ascertain the meaning they have in the life of the community.[2]

Social types may be discovered by sheer observation or by interviewing of insightful community participants. However, a more systematic method of discovering and describing social types is by selecting and combining the most relevant variables that bear on the subject. In the case of the Hometown Negro, the three most relevant variables that determine his reaction to minority group status are (a) his hostility or friendliness toward the larger community, (b) his belief in the desirability of insulation from or integration into the larger community, and (c) the extent to which his orientation to his own group's position is lassitudinous or militant. In selecting these variables, we had to look into history for a precedent.

Human minorities are almost as old as the dawn of mankind, and historically, minorities have always been divided into different camps according to their reaction to minority status. In Biblical times, we are told, the Jews were not as of one mind, any more than any other minority. Two thousand years ago, they were divided into four groups on the basis of their reactions to dominance—Sadducees, Pharisees, Essenes, and Zealots.

The Sadducees were the aristocrats who wished to see the Jews a nation among nations. They were sympathetic to the culture of the Romans and

[2] Samuel Strong, "Negro-White Relations as Reflected in Social Types," *American Journal of Sociology*, July, 1946, p. 23.

the Greeks and were disposed to assimilate it. The Pharisees were strictly religious. They wanted to make Judea an isolated religious commonwealth removed as far as possible from the contention of the heathen, and they were scrupulous in their observance of religious customs, traditions, and rules. The Essenes went further even than this in their determination to separate themselves from the contamination of the world. Whereas the Pharisees, driven by circumstances, were forced to participate in political affairs, the Essenes withdrew further and further into the wilderness and the region of the Dead Sea. The Zealots were militant in their protest. Like the Pharisees, they looked forward to complete independence from Rome; however, they came to despair of a divine deliverer, grew tired of exercising faith and patience, and eventually resorted to arms and revolution.[3]

Louis Wirth presents a typology of minorities derived from an analysis of the major goals toward which the ideas, the sentiments, and the actions of minority groups are directed.[4] The Wirth typology bears a striking resemblance to the Biblical typology; the Sadducees are similar to Wirth's assimilationist minority; the Pharisees remind us of Wirth's pluralists; the Essenes correspond to Wirth's secessionists, and the Zealots resemble Wirth's militant minority.

Although the study of Hometown's Negroes did not begin with this focus, the social typology that gradually emerged from it bore resemblance to the typologies presented above. Since the main focus of the Hometown research was intergroup relations certain individuals in the Negro community attained special significance for our study because of the role they played in Negro-white relations. It soon became apparent that as far as race relations were concerned, there were discreet "types" in the Negro community who were expected by the community to play certain roles in interracial elements of community life. Some of the more articulate community members were asked to formulate the racial types in Hometown and other communities. Combining this community articulation with the observer's impressions, it was possible to designate four social types in the Negro community, which we have designated as (a) The "Race Men," (b) the "Whitewardly Mobiles," (c) the "Uncle Toms" and (d) the "Hostiles."

1. *The Race Men* are generally the spearheads of militant race leadership in these smaller communities. They have achieved a measure of personality adjustment on racial matters, but see the world through race-colored glasses and interpret most events in their racial context—how they will affect the Negro. They strongly distrust whites, have a life history of frictional inter-

---

[3] Brewton Berry, *Race Relations*, Houghton Mifflin Company, 1951, p. 411.
[4] Louis Wirth, "The Problem of Minority Groups," in Ralph Linton. *The Science of Man in a World Crisis*, Columbia University Press, 1945, pp. 347–364.

racial experiences about which they are very bitter, and they are uncompromisingly militant and hostile toward whites in general. The Race Man is bitter not only at whites but also at more accommodating Negro leadership, at the indifferent Negro masses who won't support him, at the more disorganized areas of Negro life, and at all persons who are able or qualified to help in the struggle for Negro rights, but refuse to do so.

However, he is able to completely waive the hostility towards the outgroup when he encounters whites who are willing to help the Negro through militant action. He is favorably disposed toward all liberal elements in the community who are willing to help him—unions, political groups, Jews, and many organizations that the general community regards as left-wing. The credo of the Race Man may be summed up thusly:

> The white man has been depriving us for years; profiting off our labor and taking our women. He can't be trusted; he will smile in your face and then stab you in the back. I will fight him at every opportunity and make him accord our people their rights. If I encounter discrimination I will fight back through the courts, through picketing, through boycott, by any legal means available. "Our people" take too much of this discrimination lying down. We should stick together, give each other a boost, and fight the white man until he gives us our rights.

2. *The "Whitewardly Mobiles"* (researcher's term) are usually of higher socio-economic status, but have an almost minimal identification with the Negro community and a low degree of group identification. They idealize all things white and disparage all things Negro. They have strong self-hate feelings, and they resent being classified with the Negro community in general. They are upwardly mobile but must strain toward integration into white middle-class life since they are already near the top of the Negro status hierarchy. Because of their obsequious and ingratiating behavior toward whites, they are often despised and disparaged by Negroes with stronger in-group ties and loyalties. On the surface, their hostilities are turned back toward the Negro group, and whatever hostility they bear toward whites is deeply buried, except under stress. They are in the extremely small proportion of the Negro community (5 to 10 percent) who admit that they would rather be white than Negro and would rather associate with whites than with other Negroes. Such admissions are so "face-losing" that they must be uttered in secret, if at all.

3. *The "Uncle Toms"* are such a familiar part of Negro community life in America that the term is now being employed in the general community to describe an ingratiator and a "sellout." This is the term most frequently recognized and used by Negroes, and is probably the worst epithet that one Negro can hurl at another. Arnold Rose has stated:

Especially since the time of the Washington-Dubois controversy, Negroes have been somewhat divided in their ideas as to what they should do about different aspects of the Negro problem. The major division today is between those who would be aggressive in the Negro protest and those who would compromise. The former call the latter "Uncle Toms" and "handker-chief-heads," while the latter call the former "radicals" and "hotheads." It is a serious charge in the Negro community today to call a person an "Uncle Tom." [5]

On the local community level, whether it be deep South or extreme North, the "Uncle Tom" is characterized as a person who "sells out" the Negro race; grins, clowns, and ingratiates in the presence of whites; tells the gossip and secrets of the Negro community to whites; and places self-advancement and white favors ahead of allegiance and loyalty to the Negro community.

The person designated by the community as an "Uncle Tom" usually tries to rationalize his behavior by explaining that the whites are fine and generous and that the Negroes themselves are responsible for the prejudice and discrimination that exists. However, the social pressures in the Negro community are so strong in this current era of growing group identification that it is now difficult for any person to practice "Uncle Tom" behavior and still be accorded respect from the Negro community.

4. The *"Hostiles"* are not frequently found in these smaller northern communities although they abound and are well recognized in the South. Recall Richard Wright's statement in *Black Boy*.

> Having grown older and taller, I now associated with older boys, and I had to pay for my admittance into their company by subscribing to certain racial sentiments. The touchstone of fraternity was my feeling toward white people, how much hostility I had toward them, what degree of value and honor I assigned to race. None of this was premeditated but sprang spontaneously out of the talk of black boys who met at the crossroads.[6]

In the Hometown community, a Negro who was articulately and violently hostile would not be supported by the community in quite the same manner; he would more likely be thought "queer" or "soreheaded." However, a few are known. One 25-year-old referred the researcher to one of his friends, saying:

> He hates a white man's guts. If he hears that a man was killed somewhere, he'll ask, "White or colored?" If twenty white men

[5] Arnold Rose, *The Negro Morale*, University of Minnesota Press, 1949, p. 79.
[6] Richard Wright, *Black Boy*, Harper and Brothers, 1937, p. 23.

got killed somewhere, he'll say, "Good. Should have been two hundred." He loves to read in the papers about some white man getting killed. He is the only guy in this town who *really* don't like a "paddy" (white man). My father don't like 'em either. But what you gonna do? You got to like 'em. They got all the money—they control the wealth. We'd look mighty funny not liking "paddies." We'd starve to death.

Interviews with "hostile" Negroes show that they usually have a basis for their hostility, rooted in a bitter past experience. However, the fact that many less hostile Negroes (even "Uncle Toms" and "Whitewardly Mobiles") have had equally bitter experiences suggests that the violent hostility toward whites may be the outgrowth of a larger personality problem.

In terms of approval or disapproval of these four special types, the Negro community was asked: "How do people in this town feel about this kind of person: would you say they strongly approve, mildly approve, mildly disapprove, or strongly disapprove?" Their answers are given in Table 7.

Table 7: Negro Attitudes toward Social Types

	Race Man (%)	Whitewardly Mobile (%)	Uncle Tom (%)	Hostile (%)
Strongly approve	45	12	9	7
Mildly approve	39	23	5	7
Don't care either way	2	12	12	23
Mildly disapprove	3	17	15	25
Strongly disapprove	2	22	45	24
I don't know	9	17	14	14
Percent that recognized this type	70	60	47	32

The results of this cross-sectional inventory of social types suggest that the Negro community is aware of these types, is willing to identify them, and has a clear-cut perception of Negro community approval or disapproval, depending on the service that each social type performs for the Negro race.

SUMMARY—THE OLD AND NEW NEGRO CREEDS

The empirical social types from the Hometown research are similar to the other two typologies in that all are based on the two most crucial variables that determine the reaction of a minority group; hostility—non-hostility; and insulation—and desire for integration. The correspondence of these three typologies according to the two variables might be diagrammed as shown.

	HOSTILE	NON-HOSTILE	TYPOLOGY
	Essenes	Pharisees	Biblical
Insulates	Secessionists	Pluralists	Wirth
	Hostiles	Uncle Toms	Hometown
	Zealots	Sadducees	Biblical
Integrates	Militants	Assimilationists	Wirth
	Race Men	Whitewardly Mobiles	Hometown

This scheme is only partly adequate in explaining the reactions of the total minority community of Hometown. Most members of the Negro community do not fit easily into any of these types. The social types of Hometown are deviant cases and are noticeable and outstanding in the community because they are not typical. Actually, the community is divided into two opposed configurations of attitude which we may call the "Old Negro Creed" and the "New Negro Creed" with the social types falling somewhere in between. A more accurate diagram of the Negro community might be obtained by adding the variable of lassitude—militancy.

	HOSTILE		NON-HOSTILE	
	Lassitudinous	Militant	Lassitudinous	Militant
Insulated	The "Old Negro Creedists"	The "Hostiles"	The "Uncle Toms"	"Pluralists"
	(Secessionists)		(Pluralists)	
Integration-alist	"Grumblers"	The "Race Men"	The "Whitewardly Mobiles"	The "New Negro Creedists"
	(Militants)		(Assimilationists)	

Note here that the characteristic racial attitude of the "Race Man" is directly opposed to that of the "Uncle Tom," the "Hostile" is the opposite of the "Whitewardly Mobile," and the old and new Negro creeds are diametrically opposed to each other. Since the vast majority of community members in the cross-sectional survey fall into either the old or the new Negro creed, we may summarize by describing the two creeds as follows:

1. THE OLD NEGRO CREED
   (LASSITUDINOUS HOSTILE INSULATES)

The people who endorse this creed are generally likely to be older, less educated, of lower socio-economic status, Southern-born, less participant in either all-Negro or interracial activities. They are likely to endorse all the items of lassistude, hostility, insulation, self-hatred, avoidance, and "angry" reactions to the "language of prejudice." They are likely to have fewer interracial contacts than the rest of the community, likely to avoid or withdraw from interracial contacts, likely to feel "uncomfortable" in most interracial situations, and likely to have a high number of "distastefuls." They are strongly opposed to racial intermarriage. Their hostility is also directed towards the foreign-born, though not toward Jews. They are likely to admire any Negro who fights vigorously for the rights of Negroes in preference to the Negro leader who concentrates on general community improvements, but they express inability, disinterest, or lack of qualification to fight the race's battle themselves.

2. THE NEW NEGRO CREED
   (MILITANT FRIENDLY INTEGRATES)

Community members who endorse this creed are likely to be younger, better educated, of higher socio-economic status, and Northern-born (exception—the educated Southern-born). They have almost no "distasteful" reactions, express a belief in militancy, and maintain an attitude of friendliness toward whites in general. They have a large number of favorable interracial contacts and are interested in joining interracial clubs and promoting more tranquil contacts between the races. They have few discomforts in interracial situations, and have a more temperate reaction to the language of prejudice, i.e., they are more likely to be annoyed than angry.

They are likely to deplore the incendiary aspects of the Negro press or the all-out, violent crusades of the "Race Man," but on the other hand, they have a high degree of racial optimism and are committed to an unwavering race pride and support of militant endeavor. They believe strongly in the possibility and desirability of an integrated society in which the Negro is accorded equal rights which are reinforced by law. They hold complete integration as their goal, have a somewhat more permissive attitude toward intermarriage, and regard the struggles of the Negro as part of a general drive toward "The More Perfect Union."

Thus, the new Negro creed which is continually reiterated by Negro leaders, organizations, and publications on a national level finds a definite counterpart in the Hometown community, and, to varying degrees, in all Negro communities throughout the American land.

IV. SOUTHERN AND NORTHERN PATTERNS OF RACIAL SEPARATION AND SUBORDINATION

25. The Deep South, Past and Present

REMBERT W. PATRICK

In this essay, a southern historian dispels a number of assumptions about southern history that have frequently been employed as myths to justify racist ideology and regional resistance to change. For example, linking white supremacy with reverence for "the southern way of life" has been an especially effective way of glorifying prejudice and rationalizing segregation. Like many southerners, Patrick has a warm feeling for his region, but this does not prevent him from criticizing it. As an historian, and perhaps as a southern white person as well, he takes a long view, surveying the Deep South with a scholar's detached perspective. Contrast his detachment with the urgency of the next two selections which attempt, although in quite different ways, to indicate Negro southerners' immediate personal involvement in southern racial patterns.

Source: Robert Highsaw, ed., *The Deep South in Transformation*, (University, Ala.: University of Alabama Press, 1964), pp. 111–34. Copyright © 1964 by the University of Alabama. Reprinted with the permission of the University of Alabama Press.

Rembert W. Patrick is Julien C. Yonge Graduate Research Professor of History at the University of Florida. He has written *Jefferson Davis and His Cabinet*.

Every survey of the South begins with a question. Answering that question—what is the South?—is the imperative task of the historian or the scholar in any other discipline. Those who attempt to account for the distinctiveness of the South seek answers in causation which range from definable climate to indefinable mystique. Inevitably these investigators reach common conclusions, namely, that a unified, monolithic South is a myth and that there are many "Souths" instead of just one South.

Even more difficult than delineating the Old South is defining the modern South. Today, the contrasts between Miami and Bonifay, Florida, are as marked as the differences between New York City and Centreville, Alabama. Whatever the historical period considered, "South" is more realistic than South. In speech and writing, however, there is a region of the United States known as the South.

Although describing a part of this mythical South is less difficult than identifying the whole, there is no satisfactory answer to the question: "What is the Deep South?" Physical similarity offers one explanation of the Deep South. Most of its land is low and flat, watered by abundant rainfall, and drained by a network of rivers which flow into the Atlantic or the Gulf of Mexico. Each of its six states* borders on the sea, four of them on the Gulf, and a fifth, Georgia, has an outlet to the Gulf by the Chattahoochee-Flint-Apalachicola waterway; three of the states have long coastlines on the Atlantic Ocean. The summers often seem interminable, the heat unendurable. The winters are mild; the humidity is high but the days of sunshine are numerous. On the average the growing season for crops lasts for nine months. On the other hand, there are notable variations in physical characteristics. The Appalachian highlands of the northern area have a maximum altitude of 3,500 feet in South Carolina, rise to 4,784 in Georgia, and descend gradually until they disappear in Mississippi. The rolling hills of the Piedmont extend south to the 325 foot high Iron Mountain of peninsular Florida. There are waterpower sites in some areas, minerals in others, and oil deposits in still others. Natural lakes, swamps, and bayous dot the landscape. Winter temperatures range from subzero to forty degrees above zero.

Physically the region is one of similarities and contrasts, but geography has not determined the civilization of the Deep South. According to Rupert B. Vance, history has given the South its distinctive characteristics, and his statement is more applicable to the Deep South than to the entire region. Nothwithstanding a dedication to the status quo in many aspects of their culture, white and colored southerners have lived and are living in a changing South. Variation in the use of natural resources, technological development in agriculture and industry, and alteration in philosophy have repeatedly modified the culture of a people.

* Alabama, Florida, Georgia, Louisiana, Mississippi, and South Carolina.

The Deep South has unique historical features. The flags of five governments have flown over the region—Spain, France, England, the United States, and the unrecognized Confederate States of America. Prior to the Civil War the six states of the Deep South concentrated on the production of staple money crops—cotton, sugar cane, and rice. These states were the most rural of all the so-called sovereign states of the Union. In 1860 Louisiana's 26 per cent urban population was percentage-wise ten times larger than Mississippi's 2.6 per cent. In whole numbers the rural population of the other four states was: Alabama, 95; Florida, 95; Georgia, 93; and South Carolina, 93. In racial composition these states ranged from 60 per cent Negro in South Carolina to 44 per cent in Georgia, and the total population of the six states was 50.4 per cent white and 49.6 per cent Negro.

These Deep South states were the first ones to withdraw from the Union. Before the arrival of Texans at Montgomery, delegates of these revolutionary states had established a provisional southern government and selected a president and a vice president. Throughout the Confederacy, sons of the Deep South occupied most of the executive offices of the rebel government. The presidency, vice presidency, and half of the cabinet positions were monopolized by sons of the Deep South. In addition cabinet members Robert Toombs, Leroy Pope Walker, and Thomas Hill Watts came from the region.

After the Civil War white citizens of these states were less willing than other southerners to accept the cultural implications of military defeat. The "Black Codes" of Mississippi, South Carolina, Louisiana, and Florida rigorously and unreasonably proscribed the freedmen to a second class citizenship. When checked by a legal government, supported by a majority of the voters, the white minority used lawlessness and economic intimidation to defeat democratic processes. Flagrant illegalities forced federal action and extended Congressional Reconstruction in Florida, Louisiana, and South Carolina to 1877.

Once in control of their state governments, white conservatives relied on fraud to negate the vote of the Negro and white opposition. With the passage of time, the nation abandoned the Negro, leaving him to the care of his former master who established a caste system and devised constitutional provisions and state laws acceptable to a United States Supreme Court whose justices were more interested in upholding property rights than in protecting human rights. The Deep South not only led its region in the passage of Jim Crow legislation but also in mob action to insure white supremacy. Perhaps because they doubted the efficacy of laws and courts to sublimate the Negro, these southerners blackened their region's reputation with lynchings and other extra-legal actions. Furthermore, most Americans associated the Deep South with peonage and the chain gang as well as poverty, disease, and ignorance. Politicians Theodore Bilbo,

Cole L. Blease, Tom Heflin, and "Cotton Ed" Smith became symbols of the bigotry and racism of southerners. Although the Ku Klux Klan was a national disgrace, the stronghold of this organization was the Deep South. In the twentieth century, whenever possible white southerners gave no more than surface compliance to Supreme Court decrees relating to racial matters.

Maintaining white supremacy either by slavery or the caste system has been a consistent policy, but in other respects the Deep South has experienced revolutions. Tractors have replaced mules, cultivators have conquered hoes, and diversified agriculture has won over the single crop economy. Industry and services have relegated agriculture to a secondary status. Hookworm, malaria, and other debilitating diseases have been almost eradicated. Increased productivity has brought balanced diets, comfortable houses, and good clothing for most of the people. Such heavy blows have been dealt illiteracy that this critical problem of yesteryear requires less attention today than do adequate facilities for high school and college students.

In 1960 the city instead of the farm was characteristic of the Deep South. Only Mississippi with 63 per cent and South Carolina with 59 per cent rural inhabitants were agrarian. Seventy-three per cent of Floridians, 63 per cent of Louisianans, 54 per cent of Alabamians, and 55 per cent Georgians resided in cities. Florida's urban population was 5 per cent higher than the national average. Between 1950 and 1960 Mississippi lost 214,000 rural residents while gaining 213,000 urban ones. Urban communities in South Carolina attracted 203,000 people compared with 62,000 for rural places. Within a century the population of the Deep South shifted from 90 per cent rural to more than 50 per cent urban.

The recency of this change has political significance. Florida became urban in the 1930's, Louisiana in the 1940's, and Alabama and Georgia in the 1950's. The majority of southern urbanites are less than a generation removed from a farm environment. Although living in cities, these people retain rural attitudes; a mere scratch will disclose the farm base under their city veneer. As yet they do not realize that their interests and needs differ from those of their rural cousins. Compared to the financial status of their progenitors, southern urbanites enjoy affluence. As a result of this sudden increase in their standard of living, and of the quickness of the population shift from country to city, these people support conservative politicians who give lip service to laissez-faire economic principles while pushing government aid to business and placing the burden of taxation on the common man. City people have not attained sufficient unity to force their legislators to give them equitable representation in state assemblies or in the United States House of Representatives.

In racial composition the Deep South has also experienced revolutionary change. The nearly 50 per cent Negro population of 1860 was reduced to

29 per cent a century later, when in density the Negro population ranged from 42 per cent in Mississippi to 18 per cent in Florida. Although the Negroes were not the majority in any Deep South state, their numbers were unevenly distributed within every state. Hence, they constituted a majority in some counties. In 1960, 32 per cent of the almost 19,000,000 Negro citizens of the nation resided in the Deep South. The number of Negroes in the region and the determination of white southerners to dominate them has always been the most potent factor in making the Deep South a unique region.

Among modern romanticists are many rabid segregationists who, judged by their speeches and writings, believe American civilization attained its apex before the Civil War. Their conception of the Old South is a blending of myth, romance, and fact. History forces them to admit that only two states of the Deep South belonged to that select circle of states which united to establish the United States of America, but in their opinion later political units created by the federal government attained sovereignty upon admission into the Union. According to these romanticists the south-land was peopled by cavaliers of England whose descendants dotted the Deep South with white-columned mansions. Living in these were a cultured, hospitable people, burdened only with the care of childlike, contented slaves. The racially superior white man uplifted the inferior Negro, who worked under a benign master and enjoyed the most comprehensive social security system ever devised by man. From the joint production of happy slaves and responsible managers, the master class gave the laborer the necessities of life and used the remainder in a gracious living, known as the "southern way of life." Instead of racial conflict there was harmony and mutual respect, with every person knowing and keeping his ordained place in society. If the white man contributed little to the creative arts, he enjoyed the best in literature and excelled in the forensic and political arts.

What are the facts? There were at least five social classes in the Deep South: the free Negro, the slave, the poor white trash, the yeoman, and the planter-aristocrat. In origin most of the white people were the descendants of poor European immigrants. The ancestors of the Deep South southerners were so poor that they could not pay their passage to America. Like the first Negro immigrants they were indentured servants who agreed to serve a predetermined number of years in return for transportation across the Atlantic. Freedom and opportunity were the inducements given to white and Negro alike, but these rewards for faithful service soon became the exclusive right of white people. Because of the color of his skin the Negro's term of service was lengthened to life and his child's inheritance was slavery. There was no disgrace in being the sons of white indentured servants; on the contrary, the advancement of these people testified to their ambition and industry, and to the opportunities in America. Whatever the desire for freedom, whatever the ability and industry possessed by the Negro, these were suppressed by the laws of the white majority. Consequently, the two largest social classes that settled and developed the Deep South were the Negro slave and the yeoman white, the latter having opportunity and the former being denied it by law.

The economic and social order of the Deep South was complex for a primarily agrarian society. Most numerous were the slaves while the free Negroes composed the smallest class. There were many gradations in occupation and social position within these classes. Among the slaves were domestic servants and skilled artisans, foremen and fieldhands; the free Negroes ranged from wealthy, slaveowning planters to poverty-stricken, unskilled laborers. In 1860 more than 250,000 "free persons of color" resided in the entire South; but less than 37,000 of these lived in the Deep South, almost 30,000 of whom were in Louisiana and South Carolina. Only 932 Negroes in Florida and 773 in Mississippi were allowed a second class citizenship, the lot of all free Negroes in the United States.

Numbers can only be estimated for the white classes of the Deep South. The demarcation line between the poor whites and the yeoman and the yeoman and the planter-aristocrat cannot be determined. Although the farmer and the planter loomed largest in the yeoman and planter-aristocrat classes, the designations are semantical nomenclature. According to the 1860 census, the planters of Louisiana outnumbered those of any other Deep South state, but there were more clerks than planters in the pelican state. The 907 barkeepers of Louisiana and the 201 of Alabama are indicative of the hundreds of non-farmers included in the yeoman class. Doctors, lawyers, professors, hotel keepers, merchants, and bankers as well as large land and slaveowners belonged to the planter-aristocracy. Certainly the non-slaveowning yeomen were numerically the largest white class in the Deep South and the poor whites the smallest.

The ownership of slaves and acres, however, was the goal of ambitious men. In popular opinion these evidences of wealth somehow endowed their possessors with an aura of culture and political acumen. Did they? There were educated aristocrats in the Deep South and wealthy illiterates; there was a gracious society and a crude society, depending upon the individuals involved. There were benign masters and cruel ones; there were strong bonds of affection between slaves and masters as well as deep-rooted hatreds. Always the white people had a gnawing fear that the slave would rebel against his legally enforced status. This fear expressed itself in many ways: by the deletion in newspapers of every reference to the fighting ability of Negroes, by the repressive laws passed after slave uprisings, by the use of religion both to frighten the Negro and offer him eternal rewards, and by the patrol system to keep the slaves under control. While astute owners appealed to the loyalty and pride of their slaves, or gave their laborers gifts and leisure to stimulate effort, the institution of slavery was perpetuated by law and lash. It stripped human dignity from almost half of the people and debased many of the others.

If the peculiar social and economic systems of the Deep South had produced a golden age of literature and fine arts, modern man would have some reason to justify their existence. But the best tribute to the enlightened southerners is to say that they were the consumers instead of creators of the arts. The residents of two states participated in and contributed to the revolutionary and early national periods of the United States, the golden ages of the South. Despite the novels of William Gilmore Simms and the poems of Paul Hamilton Hayne, the literary production of Deep South southerners can be dismissed except for the earthy humor of Augustus B. Longstreet and Joseph G. Baldwin. Unfortunately many modern Negroes reject the outstanding achievement of that age: the pleadings in spirituals and folksongs of a people yearning for freedom.

Knowledgeable apologists for the cultural desert which was the Deep South emphasize the region's short life span. They make a point that is frequently overlooked. "Old South" often implies a long existence, but in reality the antebellum Deep South endured for only one generation. In the eighteenth century fortunes were made in rice and indigo on the coastal lands of South Carolina and Georgia, but the cotton and sugar kingdoms of the Deep South belonged to the third through the sixth decade of the nineteenth century. Louisiana had been a state forty-nine years before it seceded and Florida was in the Union for less than sixteen years. The span of time requisite for creativeness in the arts was, therefore, largely the figment of imagination. In the fluid society of the Deep South, human energy was mainly utilized in acquiring property and the social status associated with wealth.

The economic backgrounds of prominent southerners support this contention. Jefferson Davis came from yeoman stock. Vice president of the Confederacy, Alexander H. Stephens, and three cabinet members, Judah P. Benjamin, Christopher G. Memminger, and Stephen R. Mallory, rose from poverty or orphanhood to economic affluence. William Gilmore Simms was poor until his second wife's father provided him security, and John C. Calhoun was aided by perceptive South Carolinians. If the skin of the ambitious man were white and if he had ability, the doors of Deep South mansions were open to him.

To retain his status he had to conform to the ideological tenets of the master class. Southern womanhood had to be praised, and, if necessary, defended. Following the preaching of orthodox ministers was essential. To question the literal interpretation of the Bible, or to doubt God's endorsement of slavery, endangered one's earthly and celestial home. Above all a responsible member of society was obligated not only to uphold the institution of slavery but also to detail its virtues.

Deep South southerners possessed admirable characteristics but their prowess as public speakers and statesmen is a myth. Years before secession, orators had run out of ideas. Their voices were good, their gestures were pleasing, and their speeches were embellished with quotations from classical literature, but in content reason yielded to emotion and invective. By their own words southerners admitted their political ineffectiveness. In a single paragraph they lauded themselves or their ancestors for political leadership and condemned a federal government which favored the North and discriminated against the South. John C. Calhoun had a rare ability to describe and analyze a problem, but little talent for solving it. When his theory of nullification proved unacceptable, the Deep South turned to state sovereignty and secession. Extraneous argument and meaningless theories glossed the essential reason for disunion, the defense of an antiquated way of life based on slavery. In an age of nationalism and freedom, southern politicians demonstrated their lack of prescience by adhering to provincialism and defending human bondage.

Secession was the most costly political blunder in American history. It brought on a war which cost the lives of 600,000 men and left other thousands wounded in body and mind. Billions of dollars worth of property was destroyed. The advocates of state sovereignty endured more centralization under their own Confederate government than they had dreamed possible under federal rule. However beneficial nationally, emancipation confiscated most of the accumulated capital of southerners. Failure in battle broke the spirit and wrecked the economy of the Deep South.

The unexpected leniency of the victor quickly revived southerners and gave them hope of winning the peace. They accepted reunion, the original northern purpose of the war, in good faith, but neither admitted war guilt nor completely repudiated the idea of state sovereignty. Although some legislators held that the Thirteenth Amendment made redundant the outlawing of slavery in state constitutions, southerners recognized that slavery belonged to history. They were unwilling, however, to give freedmen equality under law. Sometimes referred to as the third objective of the Civil War, equality was more the product of peace than of the battlefield. The legislators of Mississippi and South Carolina, therefore, were amazed by northern reaction to their "Black Codes."

In a rare demonstration of political awareness, Mississippians repealed the more obnoxious provisions of their code, but Floridians reflected the real southern sentiment by defying northern opinion. Before the Florida legislators began consideration of a black code, they were fully cognizant of the northern attitude. Despite this fact, the legislature accepted a report which praised slavery as the best economic institution devised by man, criticized the institution only for its failure to regulate properly the sex activities of Negroes, and proceeded to enact a series of discriminatory laws. Florida's action was indicative of southern resurgence and a determination both to resist the demands of "do-gooders" and to give the freedmen no more than a second class citizenship.

Probing the reasons for the fiasco which was Reconstruction has been an interesting pastime. Perhaps the emotionalism of the postwar era prevented a reasoned approach to difficult problems. Even without the conquered's defiance of the conqueror, or without an uncompromising, politically inept man in the White House, Congress may have repudiated presidential reconstruction and assumed control. The historian, however, is confronted with the facts of presidential reconstruction, congressional reconstruction, and the southern determination to maintain white supremacy.

Certainly the reconstruction era cries for more study. The myths surrounding it, especially those associated with the Deep South, should be separated from actuality. Southerners have legitimate reason for condemning a political indecision which gave them hope for reprieve in presidential reconstruction and then attempted to enforce the principle of first class citizenship regardless of race under congressional reconstruction. Undoubtedly, the southern Republic governments were corrupt. The desire of Deep South southerners to establish and maintain white supremacy cannot be denied. The political base of Deep South Republican governments was the Negro voter.

After recognizing these facts, without passing judgment on them, the investigator runs into myths. The first of these is the reputed harshness of congressional reconstruction. The fact is that never in history have the defeated in a civil war received so light a sentence as did southerners in 1867. Under congressional reconstruction not a single man was executed or imprisoned for rebellion, and not an acre of land or a penny's worth of other property belonging to the vanquished was confiscated. The second myth claims that thirty or more per cent of southerners were disenfranchised. In fact only those who could not take the iron-clad oath were denied the franchise in selecting delegates to constitutional conventions and in recording their acceptance or rejection of the proposed constitutions. Either Negro constitution-makers or Negro voters refused to deny the franchise to their white brothers. The Fourteenth Amendment prevented many former confederates from holding state and federal office, but did not interfere with the voting privilege of these people. A third myth describes a southern society as inverted with the bottom rail placed on top. In no Deep South state, even South Carolina with its Negro majority in the legislature, did the freedmen control the government. Politically, economically, and socially the white people retained primacy over the Negroes. A fourth myth indicts the freedmen for their lawlessness, but in reality conservative white men resorted to nihilism to subjugate the freedmen.

Southerners who condemn the past World War I Ku Klux Klan and praise the klan and other terrorist organizations of the post Civil War period handle truth lightly. Except for a few years of juvenile antics, the klan was a vicious organization. Even the pro-southern historian E. Merton Coulter has declared that the klan "left a heritage which was to bedevil and disgrace the South thereafter, as mobs took the law into their own hands and engaged in barbarous lynchings—unjustified under any code of civilized rule." Furthermore, the claim that terrorism speeded the restoration of white political supremacy in the Deep South is questionable. Lawlessness necessitated federal action to protect citizens from assault. In my opinion, the illegal activities of klan members and like-minded terrorists extended the life of Republican governments in the Deep South.

These illustrations point out some of the mythology surrounding the southern phase of Reconstruction without detailing other realities. The post Civil War period was an age of national as well as local corruption. No Deep South government swindled its taxpayers of as much money as the Tweed Ring grabbed from residents of New York City. In the South the Negro's ill-gotten gain was miniscule in comparison with that of the white carpetbagger, white scalawag, or white conservative. Historians should give more attention than they have to ideological changes which multiplied the services of state and local governments and consequently required the collection of more taxes and the expenditure of larger sums of money. And the achievements of Deep South Republican regimes should not be overlooked: the excellence of state constitutions, the widening of political democracy, economic and social reforms, and educational progress. Instead of being the terminal date of Reconstruction, 1877 more accurately marks the beginning of the southern-dominated phase of that misunderstood era.

During the fifteen years following the Civil War the Deep South gained political power in the United States House of Representatives. In 1860 the region's six states sent twenty-eight men to the House or 11.5 per cent of its total. Despite enlargement of the Union by the admission of five states and the phenomenal increase of population in frontier areas, in 1880 the Deep South had forty men or over 12 per cent of the members of the House. A literal application of Section 2 of the Fourteenth Amendment would have reduced representation from the Deep South, but by 1880 southerners were winning a part of the peace.

A combination of factors gave the South partial victory. The northern people tired of the seemingly eternal Negro question. Accepting social Darwinism, they judged and condemned the former slave who had not utilized freedom to prove himself a superman. Needing southern votes in the Congress, northern industrialists and politicians sacrificed Negro rights for material wealth. Newspaper and magazine editors welcomed the articles of writers who sympathized with the misjudged and downtrodden South. A mythical Old South floated cloud-like from the past to cover the ills of the New South. Public opinion supported white southerners, not the colored ones; and swayed by that opinion, the Supreme Court rendered decisions which made possible legal discrimination.

At the same time a resurgent imperialism turned nations toward the undeveloped regions of the world. Industrialist and intellectual, politician and patriot accepted the white southerner's contention that there were inferior and superior races. Exporting his superior civilization to the racially inferior peoples of Africa and Asia became the white man's burden. In the twentieth century senators and representatives who voted millions of dollars to kill islanders in the Philippines could only shed crocodile tears for Deep South Negroes. The caste system was condoned in the South and imitated in the North. In racial affairs southerners enjoyed the pleasant midstream waters of American history.

In domestic and foreign affairs, many twentieth century southerners were stalwart advocates of progressive measures. During the New Freedom of President Wilson and the New Deal of President Roosevelt, Deep South congressmen gave essential votes for legislation to better or to bolster the capitalistic system of the United States. The Federal Reserve System, credit for farmers, federal aid to education, relief measures, the Tennessee Valley Authority, social security, wage and hour laws are some of the domestic acts, now proven worthwhile by experience, which southerners supported. In foreign affairs, they foresaw that Imperial and Hitler's Germany threatened the world balance of power. Southerners voted for reciprocal trade agreements and aided in changing the Monroe Doctrine from a unilateral policy of the United States to a multilateral policy of the American republics. They welcomed a plan for the peaceable solution of international problems through the United Nations and supported every move to assail or contain communism. Before the court of public opinion a strong case can be made for the progressivism of the Deep South.

Within their territorial boundaries, these states attacked critical problems with statesmanship. The needs of citizens living in an increasingly complex society were recognized by giving local and state governments regulatory and service powers. Even a listing of reforms, an enumeration of material and ideological advances, would tax the patience of listener and reader. These innovations limited capricious and predatory individualism, but, in result, they helped to give Deep South residents a higher standard of living and more opportunity than they or their ancestors had ever enjoyed.

In human relations some southerners worked to ease the burden placed upon Negroes. Hands were shaken; last names were used and Miss, Mr., or Mrs. placed before them; efforts were made to pronounce Negro correctly; and the first letter of that word was capitalized. These were not unimportant concessions by white southerners with deep-rooted prejudices. Various forms of discourtesy were and still are the psychological weapons of racial discrimination. Like Thomas Jefferson did in the wisdom of age, liberal southerners realized that environment, not heredity, was the principal reason for the lowly station of the Negro. Still they shuddered at "Uncle Tomism" without acknowledging their part in forcing the Negro into a degrading obeisance. They took care of "their Negroes," excused their faults and protected them from their would-be tormentors, but seldom treated them with the dignity desired by human beings. Southerners eased throbbing consciences by imitating the Christ-approved act of the Good Samaritan, never admitting that the teachings of Jesus encompassed both relieving the sufferer and attacking the cause of his distress.

As the twentieth century advanced, the opportunities and rights of Deep South Negroes increased. Though remaining relatively inferior, Negro schools gave educational advantages to youths and teaching positions to adults. By serving their own people, many Negroes achieved financial success in business and the professions. During the New Deal and subsequent years the Negro shared in the national economic betterment. His buying power forced sales-conscious white merchants to treat him with some respect.

Deep South southerners and outsiders were responsible for elevating the Negro. While many southerners protested against outside criticism of or interference with their local institutions, the Supreme Court rendered decisions because southern officials refused to give equal protection under the law to a minority under their jurisdiction. Local and state governments of the Deep South responded in different ways to court orders: some complied, but others used subterfuge to delay enforcement or contravene the intent of court decrees. In some places Negroes served on juries, rode on integrated interstate carriers, registered and voted; in other localities hastily enacted laws, variation in interpretation of laws, police power, and prejudiced courts were relied on to maintain the caste system.

Following the *Brown* v. *Board of Education* decision in 1954, white southern opposition against outside interference erupted. The do-nothingism of the national administration, as well as the failure of middle-class southerners to support law and order, allowed the lawless and the legal "befuddler" to control the Deep South. Unfortunately the national spotlight focused on the wielders of bats and clubs, who attempted to maintain segregation by force, and on the dramatic acts of governors, who were no more successful in preventing token integration in educational institutions than a ruler of ancient times was in commanding tidal waters to be still.

As degrading as were these demonstrations, the most serious indictment of Deep South leaders was their intellectual paucity. In defense of caste they resorted to Old South reasonings for the continuation of slavery. Southern politicians resurrected nullification, the most colossal political failure of the Old South's most famous political scientist. No southern state other than his own supported John C. Calhoun's idea; even in South Carolina opponents of the "nullies" raised American flags and armed themselves to resist the nullifiers. Yet twentieth century southerners relied on this discredited idea to maintain racial discrimination. After failing, they returned to the successful methods employed by their post Reconstruction ancestors: interpreting laws in one way for white people and in another for Negroes, using the police power of the majority to cow the minority, and depending on juries to give more consideration to the color of skin than to evidence.

It would be foolhardy to predict the Deep South's future on the basis of its past. History belongs more to the humanities than to the exact sciences. Historians cannot be truly objective for their sphere is humanity —men and women with fears, prejudices, superstitions, and expectations. The interpretations of historians are conditioned by environment, and truth, however sought after, is illusive. The conscientious historian can do no more than detail and interpret ancestral successes and failures and apply intelligence in suggesting future actions.

On these bases one foresees tremendous possibilities for the Deep South. The region is endowed with a pleasant climate, bountiful resources, and a favorable location. It has the human resources requisite to remarkable achievement. The economic achievements of one generation have demonstrated the region's potential. But with regard to freedom, the Deep South remains the nation's number one problem. If it can shed narrow provincialism, liberate itself from retarding prejudices and superstitions, create a society in which the exchange of ideas is encouraged and equality under law is recognized as the right of every citizen, living in the Deep South will challenge the best minds of our nation. Unusual courage will be required to paddle out of brackish intellectual waters into the mainstream of history.

The magnificent Marten ten Hoor Hall on the University of Alabama campus is indicative of the quest of concerned citizens for excellence. The South needs physical facilities, but it requires also intellectual freedom at its educational institutions. From these halls should go free men who will stop the human loss suffered by the Deep South. For generations, outstanding native sons have migrated to other regions which offered them greater freedom and more opportunity than their own states.

In comparison with Birmingham, Atlanta exemplifies the potential of a relatively free Deep South city. Every year tens of thousands of Georgia's white and Negro agrarians move to Atlanta. Despite this influx, Atlanta's unemployment rate remains below the national average and the city's annual growth in population, economic indicators, and intellectual achievements are envied by other southern urban communities. In contrast, ambitious rural Alabamians by-pass segregated Birmingham, and the city is almost stagnant. Atlanta attracts the brightest members of a rising generation while Birmingham apparently repels them; integration in Atlanta symbolizes a free society, segregation in Birmingham symbolizes a closed one. The contrast between the two cities suggests that freedom in the Deep South could result in retaining its best human resources and attracting desirable people from other states.

To accomplish this reversal in migratory habits, Deep South business and professional men must recognize and assume their responsibilities. To single out ministers is unfair, but by profession they represent the ideal in human relations. Yet when a ministerial association of a Deep South city demands that every public event, football games included, be opened with prayer, but refuses to meet and eat with the Negro ministerial association, thousands of southerners lose their respect for organized religion. The minister who replies with "no comment" to reporters requesting his reaction to the refusal by an usher of his church to seat a Negro and a rector who cancels a religious service on being forewarned of plans to integrate it sears the souls of our brightest young people.

The right of merchant and industrialist to a fair profit is not questioned by American capitalist society. However, those people who define free enterprise in laissez-faire terms, or attempt to make private business of today as sacrosanct as the religious orthodoxy of yesteryear, perpetrate frauds. Unless they locate their enterprises on some unclaimed atoll, the hotel-keeper and restaurant owner of today is subject to numerous regulations. In American cities, owners of private enterprises admit the public nature of their businesses by complying with sanitary and fire ordinances, wage and hour laws, and many other governmental requirements. A national law requiring firms to serve all customers regardless of race would no more strangle free enterprise in the Deep South than state laws similar to it have interfered with private business in a majority of the American states. On the contrary, it would protect the Deep South businessman who welcomes all customers from the predatory tactics of his prejudiced competitor.

To establish a social climate conducive to progress, southerners must disown the "hate Washington" campaign of reactionaries. Individuals working in cooperation with federal and state governments have given our generation its high standard of living. The economies of mass production created big business just as community needs fostered big governments. While the federal government is more powerful today than ever before, so also are state and city governments. Ours is an age of big business and big government.

The Deep South politician who refers to his sovereign state utters nonsense. No politician is so ignorant as to attribute sovereignty to Alabama or Florida or Mississippi for any reason other than to befuddle his listeners. He knows full well that the primacy of the nation has been established by public opinion, war, and court decision. The honest politician who cannot live under the laws of the United States will lead his misguided followers in revolution and suffer the penalties prescribed for treason.

All regions of the nation have resorted to the legitimate doctrine of states' rights to protect peculiar interests. But in the Deep South, states' rights have become synonymous with the desire of a white majority to perpetuate a caste system. Thus a minority within the nation becomes a majority within a state and, while demanding its minority rights, uses its majority status to deny equality under the law to a minority in a state. The use of states' rights to destroy fundamental American principles is not a legitimate exercise of local power.

Evidence of the rabid segregationist's "hate Washington" campaign are billboards which urge the impeachment of Chief Justice Earl Warren. But why stop with Warren? The "separate but equal" issue was under consideration before he became a member of the Court. *Brown* v. *Board of Education* was the unanimous ruling of nine justices and has been unanimously supported by the four members appointed to the Court since 1954. Instead of deserving criticism, the Supreme Court merits commendation for strengthening our basic rights.

The Court also deserves plaudits for another decision which will have far-reaching effects. In the 1960's most Americans possessed two essentials of representative government, universal adult suffrage and free elections. But state legislatures refused to provide equitable reapportionment. By ordering this done, the Supreme Court has given the rapidly increasing urban population of the Deep South the opportunity for a larger role in state and national affairs.

With power and age urbanites may repeal discriminatory acts and insist on fair interpretation of laws. If they do, a minority within a Deep South state will be shorn of its power to undermine an economic program of the majority. Floridians receive a large percentage of their income from the expenditures of tourists. Millions of dollars have been spent to advertise the state's attractiveness, but in 1964 at St. Augustine the use of cattle prods and snarling dogs against people who aspired to first class citizenship did untold damage to the tourist trade. Economists classify this trade as a growth industry, and the Deep South's potential in it is tremendous, but that potential will never be realized as long as racial discrimination exists within its borders.

Southern politicians should consider their role in history as they uphold states' rights for unjust reasons and at the same time boast of their prowess in obtaining federal grants for their constituents. Today's historian studies slavery for two reasons: to condemn it and to examine a historical fact. Tomorrow's historian will study the caste system for two reasons: to condemn it and to examine a historical fact. Yesteryear's coarse, vulgar anti-Negro demagogues have been replaced by suave Deep South politicians who mouth pious words and seek to deny or delay equal citizenship to Negroes. These politicians become gray-haired and distinguished in appearance, follow the prejudiced rabble to win or retain political office, and will win no higher place in history than automatic listing in *Who's Who in America.*

In his essay for a recent book, *We Dissent,* Paul Green declared that "the Old South was an error in history and the Civil War was the horror resulting from that error. . . ." He saw "no salvation to be got now from digging in the sodden dunghill of the Old South and the Civil War. Let's forget them," he advised, "or if we must remember, then remember them for what they were, for their sins and errors, and so keep before us the stern warning of their failures, their perversions, and their death as we work on toward the days of humanity's triumph and a life ahead." These statements came from one who has deep affection for his South.

Critics of this essay may point out omissions, especially those which could have dwelled on the accomplishments of the Deep South and the charm of its people. And they will be on solid ground. With hopeful heart this South Carolinian transplanted in Florida has criticized more than he has praised the land he likes and people he loves. A golden age beckons the Deep South. Every southerner can enter it by supporting basic American principles and perpetuating worthwhile regional tradition.

26. Black Like Me

JOHN HOWARD GRIFFIN

While white people can understand what it means to be a Negro in American society, it is much more difficult for them to share the experience and feelings of a Negro who must encounter white hostility and disparagement. The author of the following selection darkened his skin and traveled in the Deep South in an attempt to approximate this experience. Although his report is obviously affected by his not having been socialized into a Negro's role from early childhood, his presentation of the difference between his actual status as a white writer and his "as-if" status as a Negro traveler is dramatic and effective.

SOURCE: John Howard Griffin, *Black Like Me* (Boston: Houghton Mifflin Co., 1960), pp. 14–28 of the paperback edition. Copyright © 1960, 1961 by John Howard Griffin. Reprinted by permission of Houghton Mifflin Co.

John Howard Griffin is a novelist and essayist.

NOVEMBER 7

I had my last visit with the doctor in the morning. The treatment had not worked as rapidly or completely as we had hoped, but I had a dark undercoating of pigment which I could touch up perfectly with stain. We decided I must shave my head, since I had no curl. The dosage was established and the darkness would increase as time passed. From there, I was on my own.

The doctor showed much doubt and perhaps regret that he had ever cooperated with me in this transformation. Again he gave me many firm warnings and told me to get in touch with him any time of the day or night if I got into trouble. As I left his office, he shook my hand and said gravely, "Now you go into oblivion."

A cold spell had hit New Orleans, so that lying under the lamp that day was a comfortable experience. I decided to shave my head that evening and begin my journey.

In the afternoon, my host looked at me with friendly alarm. "I don't know what you're up to," he said, "but I'm worried."

I told him not to be and suggested I would probably leave sometime that night. He said he had a meeting, but would cancel it. I asked him not to. "I don't want you here when I go," I said.

"What are you going to do—be a Puerto Rican or something?" he asked.

"Something like that," I said. "There may be ramifications. I'd rather you didn't know anything about it. I don't want you involved."

He left around five. I fixed myself a bite of supper and drank many cups of coffee, putting off the moment when I would shave my head, grind in the stain and walk out into the New Orleans night as a Negro.

I telephoned home, but no one answered. My nerves simmered with dread. Finally I began to cut my hair and shave my head. It took hours and many razor blades before my pate felt smooth to my hand. The house settled into silence around me. Occasionally, I heard the trolley car rattle past as the night grew late. I applied coat after coat of stain, wiping each coat off. Then I showered to wash off all the excess. I did not look into the mirror until I finished dressing and had packed my duffel bags.

Turning off all the lights, I went into the bathroom and closed the door. I stood in the darkness before the mirror, my hand on the light switch. I forced myself to flick it on.

In the flood of light against white tile, the face and shoulders of a stranger—a fierce, bald, very dark Negro—glared at me from the glass. He in no way resembled me.

The transformation was total and shocking. I had expected to see myself disguised, but this was something else. I was imprisoned in the flesh of an utter stranger, an unsympathetic one with whom I felt no kinship. All traces of the John Griffin I had been were wiped from existence. Even the senses underwent a change so profound it filled me with distress. I looked into the mirror and saw reflected nothing of the white John Griffin's past. No, the reflections led back to Africa, back to the shanty and the ghetto, back to the fruitless struggles against the mark of blackness. Suddenly, almost with no mental preparation, no advance hint, it became clear and permeated my whole being. My inclination was to fight against it. I had gone too far. I knew now that there is no such thing as a disguised white man, when the black won't rub off. The black man is wholly a Negro, regardless of what he once may have been. I was a newly created Negro who must go out that door and live in a world unfamiliar to me.

The completeness of this transformation appalled me. It was unlike anything I had imagined. I became two men, the observing one and the one who panicked, who felt Negroid even into the depths of his entrails.

I felt the beginnings of great loneliness, not because I was a Negro but because the man I had been, the self I knew, was hidden in the flesh of another. If I returned home to my wife and children they would not know me. They would open the door and stare blankly at me. My children would want to know who is this large, bald Negro. If I walked up to friends, I knew I would see no flicker of recognition in their eyes.

I had tampered with the mystery of existence and I had lost the sense of my own being. This is what devastated me. The Griffin that was had become invisible.

The worst of it was that I could feel no companionship with this new person. I did not like the way he looked. Perhaps, I thought, this was only the shock of a first reaction. But the thing was done and there was no possibility of turning back. For a few weeks I must be this aging, bald Negro; I must walk through a land hostile to my color, hostile to my skin.

How did one start? The night lay out there waiting. A thousand questions presented themselves. The strangeness of my situation struck me anew—I was a man born old at midnight into a new life. How does such a man act? Where does he go to find food, water, a bed?

The phone rang and I felt my nerves convulse. I answered and told the caller my host was out for the evening. Again the strangeness, the secret awareness that the person on the other end did not know he talked with a Negro. Downstairs, I heard the soft chiming of the old clock. I knew it was midnight though I did not count. It was time to go.

With enormous self-consciousness I stepped from the house into the darkness. No one was in sight. I walked to the corner and stood under a street lamp, waiting for the trolley.

I heard footsteps. From the shadows, the figure of a white man emerged. He came and stood beside me. It was all new. Should I nod and say "Good evening," or simply ignore him? He stared intently at me. I stood like a statue, wondering if he would speak, would question me.

Though the night was cold, sweat dampened my body. This also was new. It was the first time this adult Negro had ever perspired. I thought it vaguely illuminating that the Negro Griffin's sweat felt exactly the same to his body as the white Griffin's. As I had suspected they would be, my discoveries were naïve ones, like those of a child.

The streetcar, with pale light pouring from its windows, rumbled to a stop. I remembered to let the white man on first. He paid his fare and walked to an empty seat, ignoring me. I felt my first triumph. He had not questioned me. The ticket-taker on the streetcar nodded affably when I paid my fare. Though streetcars are not segregated in New Orleans, I took a seat near the back. Negroes there glanced at me without the slightest suspicion or interest. I began to feel more confident. I asked one of them where I could find a good hotel. He said the Butler on Rampart Street was as good as any, and told me what bus to take from downtown.

I got off and began walking along Canal Street in the heart of town, carrying one small duffel bag in each hand. I passed the same taverns and amusement places where the hawkers had solicited me on previous evenings. They were busy, urging white men to come in and see the girls. The same smells of smoke and liquor and dampness poured out through half-open doors. Tonight they did not solicit me. Tonight they looked at me but did not see me.

I went into a drugstore that I had patronized every day since my arrival. I walked to the cigarette counter where the same girl I had talked with every day waited on me.

"Package of Picayunes, please," I said in response to her blank look.

She handed them to me, took my bill and gave me change with no sign of recognition, none of the banter of previous days.

Again my reaction was that of a child. I was aware that the street smells, and the drugstore odors of perfume and arnica, were exactly the same to the Negro as they had been to the white. Only this time I could not go to the soda fountain and order a limeade or ask for a glass of water.

I caught the bus to South Rampart Street. Except for the taverns, the street was deserted when I arrived at the Butler Hotel. A man behind the counter was making a barbecue sandwich for a woman customer. He said he'd find me a room as soon as he finished. I took a seat at one of the tables and waited.

A large, pleasant-faced Negro walked in and sat at the counter. He grinned at me and said: "Man, you really got your top shaved, didn't you?"

"Yeah, doesn't it look all right?"

"Man, it's slick. Makes you look real good." He said he understood the gals were really going for bald-headed men. "They say that's a sure sign of being high-sexed." I let him think I'd shaved my head for that reason. We talked easily. I asked him if this were the best hotel in the area. He said the Sunset Hotel down the street might be a little better.

I picked up my bags and walked toward the door.

"See you around, Slick," he called after me.

An orange neon sign guided me to the Sunset Hotel, which is located next to a bar. The drab little lobby was empty. I waited a moment at the desk and then rang a call bell. A man, obviously awakened from sleep, came down the hall in his undershirt, buttoning on trousers. He said I would have to pay in advance and that he didn't allow men to take girls up to the rooms. I paid the $2.85 and he led me up narrow, creaking stairs to the second floor. I stood behind him as he opened the door to my room and saw over his shoulder the desolate, windowless cubicle. I almost backed out, but realized I could probably find nothing better.

We entered and I saw that the room was clean.

"The bathroom's down the hall," he said. I locked the door after him and sat down on the bed to the loud twang of springs. A deep gloom spread through me, heightened by noise of talk, laughter and juke-box jazz from the bar downstairs. My room was scarcely larger than the double bed. An open transom above the door into the hall provided the only ventilation. The air, mingled with that of other rooms, was not fresh. In addition to the bed, I had a tiny gas stove and a broken-down bed stand. On it were two thin hand towels, a half bar of Ivory soap.

It was past one now. The light was so feeble I could hardly see to write. With no windows I felt boxed in, suffocating.

I turned off my light and tried to sleep, but the noise was too much. Light through the open transom fell on the ceiling fan, casting distorted shadows of the four motionless blades against the opposite wall.

A dog barked nearby, and his bark grew louder as another tune from the juke box blasted up through my linoleum floor. I could not shake the almost desperate sadness all this evoked, and I marveled that sounds could so degrade the spirit.

I slipped into my pants and walked barefoot down the narrow, dim-lit hall to the door with a crudely lettered sign reading MEN. When I stepped in, the hollow roar of water beating against the wall of a metal shower filled the room, along with an odor of cold sweat and soap. One man was in the shower. Another, a large, black-skinned man, sat naked on the floor awaiting his turn at the shower. He leaned back against the wall with his legs stretched out in front of him. Despite his state of undress, he had an air of dignity. Our eyes met and he nodded his polite greeting.

"It's getting cold, isn't it?" he said.

"It sure is."

"You talking to me?" the man in the shower called out above the thrumming.

"No—there's another gentleman here."

"I won't be much longer."

"Take your time—he don't want to shower."

I noted the bathroom was clean, though the fixtures were antique and rust-stained.

"Have you got a stove in your room?" the man on the floor asked. We looked at one another and there was kindness in his search for conversation.

"Yes, but I haven't turned it on."

"You *didn't* want to take a shower, did you?" he asked.

"No—it's too cold. You must be freezing on that bare floor, with no clothes on."

His brown eyes lost some of their gravity. "It's been so hot here recently. It feels kind of good to be cold."

I stepped over to the corner washbasin to rinse my hands.

"You can't use that," he said quickly. "That water'll run out on the floor." I looked beneath, as he indicated, and saw it had no drainpipe.

He reached beside him and flicked back the wet canvas shower curtain. "Hey, how about stepping back and letting this gentleman wash his hands?"

"That's all right, I can wait," I said.

"Go ahead," he nodded.

"Sure—come on," the man in the shower said. He turned the water down to a dribble. In the shower's obscurity, all I could see was a black shadow and gleaming white teeth. I stepped over the other's outstretched legs and washed quickly, using the soap the man in the shower thrust into my hands. When I had finished, I thanked him.

"That's all right. Glad to do it," he said, turning the water on full strength again.

The man on the floor handed up his towel for me to dry my hands. Under the dim light in the tiny room without windows, I realized I was having my first prolonged contact as a Negro with other Negroes. Its drama lay in its lack of drama, in its quietness, in the courtesies we felt impelled to extend to one another. I wondered if the world outside were so bad for us that we had to counter it among ourselves by salving one another with kindness.

"Do you want a cigarette?" I asked.

"Please sir—I believe I will." He leaned his heavy body forward to accept one. His black flesh picked up dull highlights from the bare globe overhead. I fished in my pants pocket for matches, and lighted our cigarettes. We talked local politics. I told him I was new in town and knew nothing about them. He refrained from asking questions, but explained that Mayor Morrison had a good reputation for fairness and the Negroes were hoping he would get elected governor. I sensed the conversation made little difference, that for a few moments we were safe from the world and we were loath to break the communication and go back to our rooms. It gave us warmth and pleasure, though we talked formally and showed one another great respect. Not once did he ask my name or where I came from.

When the man in the shower finished and stepped out dripping, the larger man hoisted himself up from the floor, tossed his cigarette into the toilet bowl and got into the shower. I told them good night and returned to my room, less lonely, and warmed by the brief contact with others like me who felt the need to be reassured that an eye could show something besides suspicion or hate.

NOVEMBER 8

The dark room. The streak of pale light through the transom. I woke to it several times, thinking it a long night. Then it occurred to me that there were no windows, that it might well be day outside.

I dressed, took my bags and walked down the steps. The sun glared brilliantly on Rampart Street. Traffic rushed past the lobby window.

"You coming back tonight, Mr. Griffin?" the man at the desk asked pleasantly.

"I'm not sure."

"You can leave your bags here if you wish."

"Thanks—I need what's in them," I said.

"Did you sleep all right?"

"Yes—fine. What time is it?"

"Little past eleven thirty."

"Damn. I think I did sleep."

The world looked blurred through the window and I waited for my eyes to accustom themselves to sunlight. I wondered what I should do, where I should go. I had a few changes of shirts, handkerchiefs and underwear in my duffel, about $200 in travelers checks and $20 in cash. In addition I had my medicines and a month's supply of the pigmentation capsules.

I stepped out into the street and began to walk in search of food.

No one noticed me. The street was full of Negroes. I ambled along, looking in store windows. White proprietors who cater exclusively to Negro trade stood in doorways and solicited us.

"Step right in—nice special in shoes today."

"Come in just a minute—no obligation—like to show you these new hats."

Their voices wheedled and they smiled in counterfeit.

It was the ghetto. I had seen them before from the high altitude of one who could look down and pity. Now I belonged here and the view was different. A first glance told it all. Here it was pennies and clutter and spittle on the curb. Here people walked fast to juggle the dimes, to make a deal, to find cheap liver or a tomato that was overripe. Here was the indefinable stink of despair. Here modesty was the luxury. People struggled for it. I saw it as I passed, looking for food. A young, slick-haired man screamed loud obscenities to an older woman on the sidewalk. She laughed and threw them back in his face. They raged. Others passed them, hearing, looking down, pursing lips, struggling not to notice.

Here sensuality was escape, proof of manhood for people who could prove it no other way. Here at noon, jazz blared from juke boxes and dark holes issued forth the cool odors of beer, wine and flesh into the sunlight. Here hips drew the eye and flirted with the eye and caused the eye to lust or laugh. It was better to look at hips than at the ghetto. Here I saw a young man, who carried in his body the substance of the saint, stagger, glass-eyed, unconscious from the dark hole, sit down on the curb and vomit between his feet.

"Man, he can't hold his a-tall," someone said.

I saw the sun caught in sweaty black wrinkles at the back of his neck as his head flopped forward.

"You okay?" I asked, bending over him.

He nodded listlessly.

"Yeah, shit, he's just gassed," someone said. "He's okay."

An odor of Creole cooking led me to a café at the corner. It was a small but cheerful room, painted baby blue. Tables were set with red-checked cloths. Except for a man at the counter, who nodded as I entered, I was the only customer. A pleasant young Negro woman took my order and fixed my breakfast: eggs, grits, bread and coffee—forty-nine cents— no butter and no napkin.

The man at the counter turned toward me and smiled, as though he wanted to talk. I had made it a rule to talk as little as possible at first. He noticed my bags and asked me if I were here looking for work. I told him I was and asked him if there were any better part of town where I could get a room.

"Ain't this awful?" He grimaced, coming over to my table.

"You live down here?"

"Yeah." He closed his eyes wearily. Light from the door struck gray in his temples.

"The Y over on Dryades is about the best place. It's clean and there's a nice bunch of fellows there," he said.

He asked me what kind of work I did and I told him I was a writer.

He told me that he often took the bus into the better parts of town where the whites lived, "just to get away from this place. I just walk in the streets and look at the houses . . . anything, just to get somewhere where it's decent . . . to get a smell of clean air."

"I know . . ." I sympathized.

I invited him to have a cup of coffee. He told me about the town, places where I might go to find jobs.

"Is there a Catholic church around here?" I asked after a while.

"Yeah—just a couple of blocks over on Dryades."

"Where's the nearest rest room?" I asked.

"Well, man, now just what do you want to do—piss or pray?" he chuckled. Though we talked quietly, the waitress heard, and her high chortle was quickly muffled in the kitchen.

"I guess it doesn't hurt for a man to do both once in a while," I said.

"You're so right," he laughed, shaking his head from side to side. "You're so right, sir. Lordy, Lordy . . . if you stick around this town, you'll find out you're going to end up doing most of your praying for a place to piss. It's not easy, I'm telling you. You can go in some of the stores around here, but you've almost got to buy something before you can ask them to let you use the toilet. Some of the taverns got places. You can go over to the train station or the bus station—places like that. You just have to locate them. And there's not many of them for us. Best thing's just to stick close to home. Otherwise sometimes you'll find you've got to walk halfway across town to find a place."

When I left him I caught the bus into town, choosing a seat halfway to the rear. As we neared Canal, the car began to fill with whites. Unless they could find a place to themselves or beside another white, they stood in the aisle.

A middle-aged woman with stringy gray hair stood near my seat. She wore a clean but faded print house dress that was hoisted to one side as she clung to an overhead pendant support. Her face looked tired and I felt uncomfortable. As she staggered with the bus's movement my lack of gallantry tormented me. I half rose from my seat to give it to her, but Negroes behind me frowned disapproval. I realized I was "going against the race" and the subtle tug-of-war became instantly clear. If the whites would not sit with us, let them stand. When they became tired enough or uncomfortable enough, they would eventually take seats beside us and soon see that it was not so poisonous after all. But to give them your seat was to let them win. I slumped back under the intensity of their stares.

But my movement had attracted the white woman's attention. For an instant our eyes met. I felt sympathy for her, and thought I detected sympathy in her glance. The exchange blurred the barriers of race (so new to me) long enough for me to smile and vaguely indicate the empty seat beside me, letting her know she was welcome to accept it.

Her blue eyes, so pale before, sharpened and she spat out, "What're you looking at me like *that* for?"

I felt myself flush. Other white passengers craned to look at me. The silent onrush of hostility frightened me.

"I'm sorry," I said, staring at my knees. "I'm not from here." The pattern of her skirt turned abruptly as she faced the front.

"They're getting sassier every day," she said loudly. Another woman agreed and the two fell into conversation.

My flesh prickled with shame, for I knew the Negroes rightly resented me for attracting such unfavorable attention. I sat the way I had seen them do, sphynxlike, pretending unawareness. Gradually people lost interest. Hostility drained to boredom. The poor woman chattered on, reluctant apparently to lose the spotlight.

I learned a strange thing—that in a jumble of unintelligible talk, the word "nigger" leaps out with electric clarity. You always hear it and always it stings. And always it casts the person using it into a category of brute ignorance. I thought with some amusement that if these two women only knew what they were revealing about themselves to every Negro on that bus, they would have been outraged.

I left the bus on Canal Street. Other Negroes aboard eyed me not with anger, as I had expected, but rather with astonishment that any black man could be so stupid.

For an hour, I roamed aimlessly through streets at the edge of the French Quarter. Always crowds and always the sun. On Derbigny Street I had coffee in a small Negro café called the Two Sisters Restaurant. A large poster on the wall caught my attention:

DESEGREGATE THE BUSES WITH THIS 7 POINT PROGRAM:
1. Pray for guidance.
2. Be courteous and friendly.
3. Be neat and clean.
4. Avoid loud talk.
5. Do not argue.
6. Report incidents immediately.
7. Overcome evil with good.
   Sponsored by Interdenominational
   Ministerial Alliance
       Rev. A. L. Davis, Pres.
       Rev. J. E. Poindexter, Secretary

I walked to the same shoeshine stand in the French Quarter that I had been visiting as a white man. My friend Sterling Williams sat on an empty box on the sidewalk. He looked up without a hint of recognition.

"Shine?"

"I believe so," I said and climbed up on the stand.

He hoisted his heavy body on his crutch and hobbled over to begin the work. I wore shoes of an unusual cut. He had shined them many times and I felt he should certainly recognize them.

"Well, it's another fine day," he said.

"Sure is."

I felt brisk strokes of his brush across the toe of my shoe.

"You're new in town, aren't you?"

I looked down on the back of his head. Gray hair kinked below the rim of a sea-captain cap of black canvas.

"Yeah—just been here a few days," I said.

"I thought I hadn't seen you around the quarter before," he said pleasantly. "You'll find New Orleans a nice place."

"Seems pretty nice. The people are polite."

"Oh . . . sure. If a man just goes on about his business and doesn't pay any attention to them, they won't bother you. I don't mean any bowing or scraping—just, you know, show you got some dignity." He raised his glance to my face and smiled wisely.

"I see what you mean," I said.

He had almost finished shining the shoes before I asked, "Is there something familiar about these shoes?"

"Yeah—I been shining some for a white man—"

"A fellow named Griffin?"

"Yeah." He straightened up. "Do you know him?"

"I am him."

He stared dumfounded. I reminded him of various subjects we had discussed on former visits. Finally convinced, he slapped my leg with glee and lowered his head. His shoulders shook with laughter.

"Well, I'm truly a son-of-a-bitch . . . how did you ever?"

I explained briefly. His heavy face shone with delight at what I had done and delight that I should confide it to him. He promised perfect discretion and enthusiastically began coaching me; but in a guarded voice, glancing always about to make sure no one could overhear.

I asked him if I could stay and help him shine shoes for a few days. He said the stand really belonged to his partner, who was out trying to locate some peanuts to sell to the winos of the quarter. We'd have to ask him, but he was sure it would be all right. "But you're way too well dressed for a shine boy."

We sat on boxes beside the stand. I asked him to check me carefully and tell me anything I did wrong.

"You just watch me and listen how I talk. You'll catch on. Say," he said excitedly, "you got to do something about those hands."

Sunlight fell on them, causing the hairs to glint against the black skin.

"Oh Lord," I groaned. "What'll I do?"

"You got to shave them," he said, holding up his large fist to show his own hand had no hairs. "You got a razor?"

"Yes."

"Hurry up, now, before somebody sees you." He became agitated and protective. "Down that alleyway there—clear to the end. You'll find a rest room. You can shave there right quick."

I grabbed my bag as he watched in agony to see that the way was clear. The shoe stand was in skid row—a street of ancient buildings with cheap rooming houses and bars.

I hurried to the alley and walked down it into the gloom of a cluttered courtyard. A few Negroes, who could not enter the white bar, were served from the back. They stood around or sat at wooden tables drinking. I saw a sign that read GENTLEMEN and was almost at the door when several voices shouted.

"Hey! You can't go in there. Hey!"

I turned back toward them, astonished that even among skid row derelict joints they had "separate facilities."

"Where do I go?" I asked.

"Clean on back there to the back," a large drunk Negro said, pointing with a wild swinging gesture that almost made him lose his balance.

I went another fifty feet down the alley and stepped into the wooden structure. It was oddly clean. I latched the door with a hook that scarcely held, smeared shaving cream on the backs of my hands and shaved without water.

Sterling nodded approval when I returned. He relaxed and smiled, the way one would after averting a terrible danger. His entire attitude of connivance was superbly exaggerated.

"Now, there's not a hitch to you, my friend," he said. "Nobody'd ever guess."

An odd thing happened. Within a short time he lapsed into familiarity, forgetting I was once white. He began to use the "we" form and to discuss "our situation." The illusion of my "Negro-ness" took over so completely that I fell into the same pattern of talking and thinking. It was my first intimate glimpse. We were Negroes and our concern was the white man and how to get along with him; how to hold our own and raise ourselves in his esteem without for one moment letting him think he had any God-given rights that we did not also have.

27. Voting in Mississippi

UNITED STATES COMMISSION
ON CIVIL RIGHTS

Of all areas of the country, the state of Mississippi has been the most reluctant to change established patterns of segregation and discrimination. In James Silver's term, it has been a "closed society," devoting itself to the perpetuation of white supremacy, employing intimidation and misinformation among both whites and Negroes in order to maintain a tight caste distinction between the races. Many of Mississippi's techniques for avoiding change in traditional racial patterns have occurred in other southern areas. Nevertheless, the gap between whites and Negroes is so great in Mississippi that the state cannot even be regarded as typical of the entire Deep South.

At present, and frequently in response to problems uncovered by local Negro protest organizations, federal government action has become extensive enough to suggest the possibility that in several decades today's reports on Mississippi will be more important as historical documents than as descriptions of affairs still current there. For the present, it is worthwhile to note that material of the kind in this selection was instrumental in framing and passing the Voting Rights Act of 1965.

ECONOMIC DEPENDENCE AND FEAR OF ECONOMIC REPRISAL

Since its organization in 1957 the Commission has received numerous reports from Mississippi of economic intimidation and reprisal in connection with registration and voting. At the hearing the Chairman of the Mississippi Advisory Committee to the Commission reported:

> Many other witnesses appearing before the advisory committee testified that those seeking to register to vote have been fired from their jobs, have had their loans called in, and their credit cut off, have been forced to leave their homes, and, in many cases, have been subjected to acts of physical violence.[1]

Even before the hearing had closed, the Commission received a complaint that during the preceding two weeks three Negro residents of Carroll

[1] T. 18. ["T," in footnotes throughout this selection, refers to testimony in the volume *Hearings before the United States Commission on Civil Rights, Volume I, Voting* (Washington, D.C.: Government Printing Office, 1965). Ed.]

SOURCE: *Voting in Mississippi,* A Report of the United States Commission on Civil Rights (Washington, D.C., May, 1965), pp. 31–39, 59–61.

County had been discharged from employment following their attempt to register.[2] While it is often difficult to determine whether a discharge or other economic sanction has been imposed in reprisal for registration,[3] Commission investigation revealed that charges of such reprisal are widely circulated and that large numbers of Mississippi Negroes fear the economic consequences of an attempt to register and vote. This belief was reflected in the testimony given by Aaron Henry, a leader of the NAACP in Mississippi:

> Any step which will bring a Negro into the public view, in an effort to register to vote, will increase the likelihood that an employer, or a creditor, or landlord will deprive him of the economic necessities of life.
>
> This problem is amplified manyfold by the extreme degree of poverty which exists among the Negro communities of Mississippi. To take an economic risk in Mississippi is to risk life itself.[4]

ECONOMIC DEPENDENCE AND LOW INCOME

Fears of economic reprisal are rooted in the economic dependence of Negroes on whites in Mississippi. Most Negroes look to whites for employment, for loans, for credit to purchase food, seed and fertilizer, for use of farm equipment, or for a monthly welfare check.

The pattern of dependence appears particularly strong where Negroes are employed in agriculture. In the counties studied by the Commission between 60 and 85 percent of the Negroes were so employed.[5] In 1959 about 35 percent of Mississippi's total Negro employment was in agriculture, while the comparable figure for white agricultural employment was about 13 percent.[6] Approximately 60 percent of the Negro farmers worked as tenants, most of them on land owned by whites.[7] Most of these tenants are classified as "croppers." Croppers differ from other farm tenants in that they are subject to close supervision by the landlord or his agent and are dependent upon them for work animals or tractor power.[8]

---

[2] U.S. Commission on Civil Rights, Complaint File No. 5099.

[3] In a few cases, such as the arrest of Mrs. Alene Hunter a few minutes after she returned from attempting to register, the circumstances demonstrate that the action was taken in reprisal for the attempt. . . . In other cases investigated by the Commission Staff, such as the discharge from public employment of a cook whose son had been involved in civil rights activity (Commission Staff Report on Sunflower County dated December 3, 1964), the link between the economic sanction and the assertion of the right to vote is less clear.

[4] T. 157.

[5] T. 27, 52, 93, 110, 122.

[6] *Hearings in Jackson, Miss. Before the U.S. Commission on Civil Rights*, Feb. 16–20, 1965, Vol. II (in preparation), *Economic Status of Negroes in Mississippi* (hereinafter cited as *Economic Status*).

[7] *1959 Agriculture Census*, Vol. I, pt. 33, table 17 at 34–35; *1954 Agriculture Census*, Mississippi, Vol. III, pt. I, table 2 at 416.

[8] *1959 Agriculture Census*, Vol. I, pt. 33 at XXIII.

Witnesses at the hearing from predominantly agricultural counties testified that the fear of economic reprisal prevented Negroes from attempting to register or vote. In Issaquena County Negro farmers were reportedly "afraid to go [register] and get cut off their welfare and get thrown off the farms and everything else. . . ."[9]

A witness from Humphreys County testified that Negroes were afraid to come forward and register. Asked why, he replied, "They're afraid they'll lose their jobs, afraid of not getting money. . . ." [10]

A Negro witness from Carroll County, who attempted unsuccessfully to persuade Negroes to register, testified that Negroes told him that they would be denied credit if they made the attempt.[11]

A witness from Tallahatchie County reported that Negroes were afraid of "economic squeezes." [12] Another believed that economic reprisal was the reason law enforcement officers photographed registration applicants:

> Well, I thought [the photographing] meant just about what it did mean, that they take your picture and if you had any credit with anybody they probably give them a picture to let them know you were up there and they probably cut out your credit. . . .[13]

The fears generated by dependence have been sharpened by extreme poverty. In 1959 the median income of Negro men in Mississippi was $984 a year, and of Negro women, $596 a year. White men in Mississippi earned more than three times as much as Negro men, and white women earned more than twice as much as Negro women. In 1959 more than 70 percent of occupied Negro rural housing was classed by the Bureau of Census as deteriorated or dilapidated—which means that the structures were becoming, or had become, unfit for human habitation. More than three-quarters of rural Negro homes were without plumbing.[14]

In the counties studied by the Commission, median yearly income for Negro families ranged from $885 in Carroll County to slightly more than $1,600 in Washington County. The range for white families in the same counties was $2,500 in Carroll to $5,600 in Washington.[15] In the Delta Negroes cut and chop cotton in the late spring and early summer at $3 per ten-hour day.[16] In the fall they pick cotton for approximately $4 per ten-hour day.[17] The near destitution of many Negroes makes any economic reprisal a major disaster.

The poverty of Mississippi Negroes also affects their ability to comply

---

[9] T. 28.   [10] T. 59.   [11] T. 96.   [12] T. 129.   [13] T. 139.
[14] *Economic Status.*   [15] T. 27, 52, 93, 110, 122, 148, 191.
[16] United States Bureau of Employment Security, *In Season Farm Labor Reports*, No. ES 223 (June 15, 1964); T. 31.
[17] This is based on a "piece" wage of $2.50 per hundred pounds of cotton. A farm laborer can pick an average of 160 pounds of cotton a day. United States Bureau of Employment Security, *In Season Farm Labor Reports*, No. ES 223 (September 30, 1964).

with Mississippi voting laws. A Negro desiring to qualify to vote for the first time must pay $4 in poll taxes.[18] At the wage rates prevailing in the Delta, many Negroes would need a day or more of labor to earn this amount. Payment of the tax for each adult would constitute a significant expenditure for a family whose yearly income is less than $1,000.

Under Title I of the 1964 Civil Rights Act an applicant for registration is entitled upon written demand to receive a copy of any literacy test.[19] Witnesses testified that the registrar of Issaquena County charged $2.50 for such copies [20] and the registrar of Humphreys County testified that he charged $1.50.[21] While the 1964 Act does not specify that no charge should be made, the imposition of fees in these counties has inhibited the exercise of a right conferred by Congress.

TEACHERS

Economic dependence and fear of economic reprisal are not confined to Negroes in the lowest economic status. Frequently Negroes with relatively good economic positions or with superior education are those who feel most vulnerable to the white community. School teachers and public employees with incomes well above the Negro median rely on white officials for their employment. In short, Negroes with the most to lose may be among the first to be deterred from registration or voting by the fear of economic consequences.

Among the best educated and best paid Negroes in Mississippi are the public school teachers. Prior to its recent investigation in Mississippi, the Commission had received reports that in some counties Negro teachers had failed to attempt to register because of fear of economic reprisal.

At the hearing the Commission heard testimony from the Executive Secretary of the all-Negro Mississippi Teachers Association. He stated that Negro teachers in Mississippi failed to register or vote because "they are afraid that they will lose their jobs. Their principal has been informed by their superintendent of education . . . if you try to register in this system, you won't have a job next year." He further stated that in his opinion teachers in many Mississippi counties were justified in this fear. He emphasized that all superintendents of education in Mississippi were white.[22]

Two other witnesses, both of whom had taught school for many years in Mississippi, told the Commission that they knew of no Negro teachers registered to vote in their respective counties. One witness, a retired teacher, testified that he was the only teacher registered to vote in Carroll County. In the 1950's he had attempted unsuccessfully to convince other

[18] A $2 poll tax must be paid for the two years preceding the election. Miss. Const. art. 12, §§ 241, 243.
[19] 42 U.S.C.A. § 1971 (a)(2)(C)(1964).   [20] T. 31, 36, 41, 46.   [21] T. 74.
[22] Testimony of L. P. Alexander, T. 216, 218.

Negro school teachers to register. When asked why his efforts had failed, he replied:

> My opinion is they were afraid of their job. In the first place some of the teachers in the school went to the courthouse and paid their poll tax. The superintendent . . . heard of it and called them in and let them know if they are going to register for voting they wouldn't have a job, and consequently everybody had to back up.[23]

Another retired teacher, who had taught school for 35 years in Tallahatchie County, testified she knew of no other Negro teacher in her county who was registered to vote. She became a registered voter only after she retired from teaching and began receiving social security payments.[24]

To determine the extent to which Negroes were inhibited from registering or voting the Commission contracted with the National Opinion Research Center of the University of Chicago for a survey of political participation by Negro teachers in Mississippi. Professor James W. Prothro of the University of North Carolina, an expert in the field of Negro voting, was retained as a consultant.[25] Four counties with differing rates of registration were designated for the survey. A sample of teachers in each county was selected and the teachers were interviewed by professional interviewers from the National Opinion Research Center during December 1964 and January 1965. The persons interviewed were given assurances of anonymity; for this reason the names of the counties are not given in this report. Table I shows the number of teachers in each sample and the number of completed interviews.

Of those teachers who were interviewed, the number registered varied

Table I: Negro Teachers in Sample

County	Teachers in County	Number in Sample	Number Contacted	Completed Interviews
W	225	63	48	46
X	169	41	29	26
Y	74	54	47	40
Z	73	56	50	19 [a]

[a] The small number of completed interviews in County Z was due to the fact that most teachers in this county refused to be interviewed. The significance of this is discussed [below].

[23] T. 95–96.   [24] T. 143.

[25] The discussion which follows is drawn from Professor Prothro's report. T. 242–55.

from 73.9 percent in County W to zero percent in County Z. Table II shows the percentages registered.

Table II: Registration of Negro Teachers in Four Mississippi Counties *(in percent)*

	W	X	Y	Z
Registered	73.9	42.3	2.5	0
Not registered	26.1	57.7	97.5	100
Total	100	100	100	100
(Number)	(46)	(26)	(40)	(19)

The findings of the report indicate that in counties where few teachers had registered there were also few attempts to register. Table III shows the frequency of registration attempts among nonregistered teachers.

Table III: Frequency of Attempted Registration among Nonregistered Negro Teachers *(in percent)*

	W	X	Y	Z
Attempted	8.3	40.0	2.6	0
Not attempted	91.7	60.0	97.4	100
Total	100	100	100	100
(Number)	(12)	(15)	(39)	(19)

Thus, in County Z not a single Negro teacher was registered or had attempted to register.

Lack of interest in voting is the usual cause of low registration. The survey was designed to determine the extent to which this was so in Mississippi. The interviewers questioned respondents as to their interest in politics, their desire to vote, and their feelings about the significance of voting. The responses to these questions were correlated with registration or attempted registration to determine whether those expressing greater political interest were registering in greater numbers. The report shows that, although there were differences in motivation to participate in politics, a significant proportion of teachers in all four counties displayed a high degree of interest.

When questioned about their interest in the 1964 Presidential Election, almost all respondents in Counties W, X, and Y, and about two-thirds of the respondents in County Z (none of whom were registered) expressed strong interest. In correlating the expression of interest in the election with the respondent's registration, the pattern varied significantly. In County W, over 75 percent of those expressing strong interest were registered; in County X less than half with strong interest were registered; in County Y only one of the 37 with strong interest was registered; and in County Z none of the eleven with strong interest was registered.

A similar pattern appeared in other tests of political interest, such as the respondent's desire to vote. In fact, it was found that in some areas of inquiry in County Y (2.5 percent teacher registration), expressions of political interest were higher than in any of the other counties. Even in County Z (no teachers registered), a majority expressed significant political interest.

Professor Prothro's report states that teachers in all four counties overwhelmingly believed that the presence of a Negro electorate or a larger Negro electorate would make a difference in the Negro way of life in the county.

Table IV: Do You Feel It Would Make a Difference If Negroes (More Negroes) Registered and Voted In This County? (in percent)

	W	X	Y	Z
Yes	88.6	92.0	87.5	50.0
No	6.8	8.0	7.5	38.9
Don't know	4.6		5.0	11.1
Total	100	100	100	100
(Number)	(44)	(25)	(40)	(18)

Some felt that the presence of a Negro electorate would result in greater political freedom; others believed it would lead to fairer law enforcement; and some looked to a greater responsiveness by officials to the needs of the Negro community. One teacher in County Z merely stated, "Maybe we would feel better about things like just talking with you."

The disparity between expressions of political interest and registration or attempted registration, particularly in Counties Y and Z, indicated that interest was not the controlling factor in registration. Registration generally increases with the education of the class under consideration. Studies in other Southern States had shown that 80 percent of Negroes with college degrees were registered to vote. The lack of registration among the teachers interviewed, all of whom had college degrees, was therefore striking.

Professor Prothro reached the conclusion that fear, principally fear of losing a job, was the major factor preventing Negro teachers from attempting to register to vote.

This fear was strongest among Negro teachers in County Z. Professor Prothro found that 79 percent of those interviewed in County Z, where none were registered or had attempted to register, expressed fear in the course of the interview. Most of these teachers stated that they would lose their jobs if they attempted to register. The fear in County Z was so pronounced that a general feeling persisted among Negro teachers that it was not safe to discuss civil rights among themselves. One teacher, when asked if she discussed politics with other teachers, stated, "I don't dare talk to my coworkers." Another teacher, when asked if he had attended any meetings where voter registration was discussed, said that "with the situation in this county you know better than to do so." Another, when asked if she ever persuaded Negroes to register, asserted: "I am a teacher. If I want my job I know better than to do that." Fear of discussion was expressed by another teacher who stated that voter registration was not discussed because the "walls have ears."

One teachers related an incident which gave credence to the fear of open discussion:

> We discussed it [Negro voter registration] in a very general manner at a meeting, and before we could get settled at home the phone was ringing and there was some explaining to do. I guess I better not go into it anymore. You know I would rather you did not write what I am saying—we have to be careful. . . .

Another teacher, asked if it would make a difference in their way of life in the county if more Negroes could register and vote, stated, "Well, one thing—they could speak up . . . Talk up instead of being afraid. . . . Now listen, please understand, I don't want you to even say I talk with you—we must be careful."

A majority of the teachers approached in County Z (31 out of 50) refused to grant an interview. Most of those refusing offered no explanation, but about a third offered the comment that granting an interview could jeopardize their jobs. Those who commented explained that their school principal had instructed them not to discuss civil rights with anyone and that this order had emanated from the county school superintendent. The issuance of the order and the high degree of compliance by teachers is itself a significant indication of the lack of political freedom in this county.

Fear was also found among Negro teachers in County Y, where 75 percent of those interviewed stated they were afraid when asked why they had not attempted to register. Most of these teachers expressed fear they would lose their jobs. For example, one teacher said, "We have our reasons [for not trying to register]. . . . We want to keep our jobs. We have to work. All I know how to do is teach." Another woman, who was extremely apprehensive about the interview, was asked if she ever encouraged Negroes to register. She described her attitude:

> I've always felt it was important, but at the same time I felt it is right for someone else to do these things first. . . . People who can't actually be hurt financially or lose their jobs because of this sort of thing. I think in our position as school teachers that would be the first thing to happen.

Some teachers stated they were afraid of being subjected to physical violence as well as the possibility of job loss. One teacher said, "I have heard talk . . . you might be ganged up on . . . if they catch you by yourself they will jump you . . . beat you up." Another, when asked if he believed he would ever vote in the county, gave the following answer:

> Not unless we get some help . . . outside pressure . . . protection. . . . If I decide to vote I go down there and they might bomb my house. If I registered they might do anything. I don't trust the law officials. I trust them about as much as I trust a mad dog.

Others mentioned specific incidents of violence or the publicity of a registration attempt as reasons for failure to attempt to register.

The situation in County Y seems to be changing. One teacher successfully registered in January 1965 without any difficulty.[26] Several of those interviewed reported that they had heard of a recent change in policy which would permit them to register. Two teachers said that such a change was announced by a Negro school principal at a recent teachers' meeting. Professor Prothro concluded that despite some improvement there was still extreme uncertainty among Negro teachers in County Y about voter registration.

In County X 42 percent of the teachers were registered. Some of the registered teachers stated they had experienced no difficulty after registering, and 40 percent (6 of 15) of the unregistered teachers had made the attempt.[27] Fear did not play as prominent a role in this county as it did in Counties Y and Z. Of the nine unregistered teachers who had made no effort to register, only one felt that fear played a part in his failure to try. The others stated that lack of interest was their reason for not registering. In the course of the questioning, however, a majority of all those interviewed expressed some fear. These expressions included fear of job loss

[26] The Commission has been advised by resident Negroes in County Y that since the survey was conducted several teachers have successfully registered.
[27] A major complaint among those interviewed was directed at the registration test, which many teachers believed was not fairly administered. The fact that 40 percent of the unregistered teachers, all of whom were college graduates, failed the test (one teacher did not meet the residency requirement) indicates that the registration test is a major obstacle to voter registration in County X.

and violence, although fear of job loss was not considered as likely as in Counties Y and Z.

Professor Prothro found a "startling contrast in County W from the other counties investigated." About 74 percent of those interviewed were registered; there was a virtual absence of fear and few complaints were directed at the administration of the registration test. Lack of interest was a major factor preventing teachers from registering to vote. The teachers were proud of the political freedom in County W and many expressed an awareness that County W differed significantly from other parts of Mississippi.

The low income and economic dependence of most Negroes in Mississippi has given rise to widespread fears that registration or voting will result in reprisals. These fears are intensified because Negroes in rural counties who attempt to register cannot hope to remain anonymous. Any doubt that applicants will be identified has been removed by the legal requirement that their names be published in local newspapers and by practices such as the photographing of Negro applicants by public officials. In this climate a single incident of reprisal may be sufficient to deter many potential registrants. Thus, many Negroes believe with Aaron Henry that:

> For many people an attempt to register would result in their not having any money to buy milk for the baby, no money to buy food for the family, and no money to pay the rent for the roof over their heads.[28]

Fears of economic reprisal are not confined to Negroes with the lowest incomes. In some areas of Mississippi Negro teachers want to register and vote but fail to do so because they fear they will lose their jobs. The intimidation of Negro teachers is particularly significant because in the absence of any large group of Negro lawyers, doctors, accountants, or technicians in Mississippi, teachers account for a disproportionately large segment of the group which most often provides community leadership. Moreover, teachers have a professional obligation to communicate to young people an interest in political participation and a sense of civic duty. When teachers themselves fail to participate, they set an example for those they teach.

FINDINGS

PRELIMINARY STATEMENT

The 15th amendment to the United States Constitution commands that no citizen shall be deprived of the right to vote by reason of race or color.

[28] T. 156.

This requirement of the Constitution which is binding in every State has, in substance, been repudiated and denied in Mississippi. Since 1875 Negroes in Mississippi have been systematically excluded from the franchise by legislative enactment, fraud and violence.

For many years the Federal Government failed to take any action to enforce the 15th amendment in Mississippi or in other Southern States where similar practices existed. But since 1957 Congress has acted three times in an effort to eliminate discrimination in voting, and the Civil Rights Division of the Department of Justice has vigorously exercised the authority conferred by Congressional enactment.

In Mississippi these efforts have proved largely unavailing and few Negroes have been registered to vote. The barriers of unjust tests and discriminatory administration have remained all but insurmountable while a deep-seated fear of economic or physical reprisal has acted as a significant deterrent for Negroes who would otherwise wish to register.

Legislation is now pending in Congress which will go far to solve these problems by eliminating the tests and by authorizing the appointment of Federal examiners to register voters. Since 1959 the Commission has recommended such legislation as the only solution and its recent experience in Mississippi which is reflected in this report has confirmed this view.

At the same time the Commission has received evidence of the beginning of a change of attitude in Mississippi towards Federal law. At the hearing, Governor Paul Johnson appeared before the Commission and stated that Mississippi would obey the Civil Rights Act of 1964 "as the law of the land." The Mississippi Economic Council, the State chamber of commerce, issued a statement urging, among other things, "that registration and voting laws, should be administered fairly and impartially for all." Similar statements have been made more recently by other groups.

The Commission is gratified by this evidence of acceptance of the requirements of the Constitution. In this state of affairs, it is worth emphasizing that there is nothing in existing or pending Federal Legislation which will in any way detract or interfere with local efforts to eliminate discrimination. While the pending voting bill, if enacted, may result in the appointment of Federal examiners in Mississippi, it would not prevent State officials from registering voters. The State in fact could do much to undo past acts of discrimination by taking affirmative action to encourage citizens to register and vote. State officials might consider, for example, the adoption of procedures, already utilized in a number of other states, to facilitate registration by providing local or precinct registration units or even door-to-door canvassing. They might further consider positive steps to assure Negro teachers that registration and voting will not result in the loss of their jobs.

Under the leadership of President Johnson, the Federal Government is now making a new and full commitment to assure all citizens the right to vote. If this commitment is enacted into law and the law is implemented vigorously, Negro Mississippians may finally enjoy the right to participate in the processes of self government. If the State of Mississippi joins in this commitment and assumes its share of the responsibility, places now suffering the consequences of racial strife can become communities of understanding and progress in which all citizens have a stake.

FINDINGS

1. The State of Mississippi, for the purpose of preventing registration by Negroes, has enacted over the past 75 years a series of laws establishing a constitutional interpretation test, and other tests for registration, and has vested broad discretion in county registrars to administer these requirements. The stringency of these tests was increased at a time when most whites were already registered and few Negroes were registered.

2. Registration records indicate that county registrars in a large number of Mississippi counties have discriminated against Negroes in the administration of these tests primarily by (a) giving Negroes more difficult constitutional sections to interpret than whites; (b) disqualifying Negroes for insufficiencies in the completion of the application form or in the interpretation of the selected constitutional section when comparable or greater insufficiencies failed to disqualify white applicants; and, (c) affording assistance to white applicants but not to Negroes.

3. The Mississippi poll tax was established and made a qualification for voting for the purpose of preventing the exercise of the franchise by Negroes. In some counties local officials have refused to accept payment of the poll tax from Negroes, or have encouraged white electors to pay such tax and have failed to encourage, or have discouraged, Negroes from doing so. The poll tax was adopted on the belief that Negroes as a class would find it more difficult to pay than whites as a class. In 1890, when the poll tax was adopted, this belief was justified and it remains so today. In light of actual economic conditions, the payment of a poll tax is a significantly heavier burden for most Negroes than it is for most whites.

4. Negro applicants for registration, Negroes seeking to vote, and civil rights workers have been harassed and intimidated by local officials in connection with registration and voting activities. On occasion such persons have suffered violence from private persons.

5. Negro applicants for registration, Negroes seeking to vote, and civil rights workers have, on occasion, suffered acts of economic intimidation and reprisal in connection with registration and voting, both from public officials and from private persons.

6. There is widespread fear in many Negro communities that an attempt to register or vote would result in economic or physical reprisals. Such fears

have been increased by the provisions of Mississippi law which require newspaper publication of the name and address of any applicant, and by the practice of requiring the applicant to return to the office of the registrar to determine whether he has passed the test. Fear of reprisal is a major factor inhibiting attmpts by Negroes to register or vote. In counties where fear is great, Negroes will not attempt to register in significant numbers without assistance or encouragement.

7. Most Negro Mississippians now of voting age have been educated in segregated public schools which were and still are inadequate and greatly inferior to public schools provided for white children. Public education of Negroes has been so poor and so inferior to the education afforded whites that any test of skill taught in the public schools is inherently unfair as a prerequisite to voting.

8. Existing Federal remedies have not proved adequate to eliminate discrimination and to prevent reprisals for voting. Law suits against registrars have proved too slow and too cumbersome a device to remedy discrimination. Recent judicial approaches promise more speedy relief but are still inadequate in that the registration machinery will remain in the hands of State officials who have demonstrated an unwillingness to enforce Federal law. Law suits aimed at acts of reprisal have been filed in only a few cases and do not appear to have provided an effective remedy.

9. As a result of the foregoing, it is estimated that in Mississippi less than 7 percent of the Negro voting age population but more than 70 percent of the white voting age population are registered to vote. Mississippi has by far the lowest rate of Negro registration of any State in the South and has shown virtually no increase in such registration as the result of the enactment of Federal legislation designed to eliminate discrimination in voting.

28. The Negro as an Immigrant Group: Recent Trends in Racial and Ethnic Segregation in Chicago*

KARL E. TAEUBER AND
ALMA F. TAEUBER

Over two and a half million Negroes left the South between 1940 and 1960. World War II opened up new employment opportunities, and then the pattern of migration continued, prompted by the declining need for a large labor force in southern agriculture. Most Negro migrants moved to northern and western cities, into areas already established as Negro districts. Large numbers of whites left the central cities during the same period, but the Negro communities were not formed anew in different areas. (New York City's Bedford-Stuyvesant district is an exception, although it is also a densely populated Negro ghetto.) The older ones simply kept expanding, though not enough to decrease the density of population in major Negro neighborhoods. In Chicago, the setting for the next selection, the Negro population increased over 200 per cent between 1940 and 1960, rising to 890,000 people, or 24 per cent of the city's total population. The Taeubers' work documents and makes more specific the reasonably apparent observation that the predominant pattern of growth in urban Negro communities has been the maintenance and expansion of ghetto areas.

During the last half of the nineteenth century and the early decades of the twentieth, millions of immigrants from Europe entered the United States. Many of these immigrants settled initially in ethnic colonies in large northern cities and found jobs as unskilled laborers in burgeoning mass-production industries. With the onset of World War I in Europe, and with the passage of restrictive legislation in the United States in the early 1920's, the period of massive overseas migration came to an end. At the

* Paper No. 15 in the series, "Comparative Urban Research," was issued from the Population Research and Training Center, University of Chicago, under a grant from the Ford Foundation. A preliminary version of this paper was read at the 1962 annual meetings of the American Statistical Association. We appreciate the reactions of Stanley Lieberson, Judah Matras, and Margaret G. Reid to that version.

SOURCE: *American Journal of Sociology*, 69, 1964, 374–82. Copyright © 1964 by the University of Chicago. Reprinted by permission of the University of Chicago Press.

Karl E. Taeuber is Assistant Professor of Sociology at the University of Wisconsin. He and *Alma F. Taeuber* have collaborated on several papers in the area of comparative demography and ecology.

same time, however, there developed a large-scale migration of Negroes
from the South to the same large northern industrial cities. Like the immigrants from abroad, the Negro migrants to northern cities filled the lowest
occupational niches and rapidly developed highly segregated patterns of
residence within the central cities.

In view of many obvious similarities between the Negro migrants and
the various immigrant groups preceding them, it has been suggested that
northern urban Negroes are but the latest of the immigrant groups, undergoing much the same processes of adaptation to city life and of assimilation
into the general social structure as the European groups preceding them.[1]
The persistence of Negroes as a residentially segregated and underprivileged
group at the lowest levels of socioeconomic status, however, is frequently
interpreted in terms of distinctive aspects of the Negro experience, particularly their historical position in American society.[2]

The question of whether or not a northern urban Negro population can
fruitfully be viewed as an immigrant population, comparable to European
immigrant populations of earlier decades with respect to the nature and
speed of assimilation, will be explored on the basis of data permitting
analysis of recent trends in racial and ethnic segregation in Chicago.

The process by which various immigrant groups have been absorbed into
American society are complex and have been studied from a variety of
viewpoints. Unfortunately there is no sociological consensus on a definition
of assimilation and there is nothing approaching a definitive study of the
processes of assimilation for any one immigrant group. It is beyond the
scope of our task here to attempt to provide such a definition. We feel
that a distinctively sociological approach to the topic must view assimilation as a process of dispersion of members of the group throughout the
social structure. Cultural and psychological processes, we feel, should not
be incorporated into a sociological definition, although their relationship
to institutional dispersion should, of course, be retained as one focus of
research on assimilation.

For our purposes, it will suffice to have a working definition of the
process of assimilation considerably less sophisticated than that required
for a general sociological theory. Accepting the view that both immigrant
groups and Negro migrants originally settled in segregated patterns in
central areas of cities and ranked very low in terms of socioeconomic
measures, assimilation then consisted in large part of a process of social
and economic advancement on the part of the original members of the

[1] Philip M. Hauser, "On the Impact of Urbanism on Social Organization, Human
Nature and the Political Order," *Confluence*, VII (Spring, 1958), 65. Elsewhere Hauser
has expressed a more cautious view, emphasizing the lack of definitive knowledge; see
his *Population Perspectives* (New Brunswick, N.J.: Rutgers University Press, 1960),
p. 129.
[2] D. J. Bogue, "Chicago's Growing Population Problem," *Commerce*, LIX (July, 1962),
31.

group and their descendants, along with a decreasing residential concentration in ethnic colonies. Our concern with diminishing residential segregation as a necessary concomitant of the assimilation process derives from Myrdal's discussion of the "mechanical" importance of residential segregation in facilitating other forms of segregation and discrimination, and Hawley's discussion of the impact of spatial patterns on race relations.[3] Our concern with socioeconomic advance reflects the initially low status of the groups with which we are concerned, whereas a more general treatment would need to reckon with the unusually high status of some immigrant stocks, as well as with other aspects of social status and institutional disperson than those for which we have data.

The data in Table 1 illustrate for selected immigrant groups the patterns of socioeconomic advance and residential dispersion from highly segregated ethnic colonies. For each of the larger ethnic groups, data for 1950 show the average standing on three measures of socioeconomic status, standardized for age, of the first generation (the foreign-born white, FBW) and the second generation (native white of foreign or mixed parentage, NWFMP). The nationality groups are split into "old," "new," and "newer" groups in an extension of the traditional system. On the average, comparing within the first or within the second generation, the "old" immigrant groups are the best off on these measures, the "new" groups are intermediate, and the "newer" groups are the worst off. It cannot be determined from these data to what extent the old immigrants are better off by virtue of their longer average length of residence in the United States, or to what extent they may have been better off at their time of immigration than the newer immigrants were at the time of their move.

Comparisons between the first and second generations might appear to be a more direct means for assessing the extent of socioeconomic advance, particularly since the emphasis in the literature on assimilation is on intergenerational processes rather than simply on processes of upward mobility through time in the status of the original immigrants. Comparisons of corresponding status measures for the first and second generations in Table 1 reveal, in general, the expected pattern of intergenerational advance. Data such as these, however, do not refer directly to a specific set of immigrant parents and their native-born children and must be interpreted with great caution.[4] For instance, it would be unwarranted on the basis of these data to assume that descendants of German immigrants are not as well off as their parents in terms of education. It is more credible

---

[3] Gunnar Myrdal, *An American Dilemma* (New York: Harper & Bros., 1944), I, 618; Amos H. Hawley, "Dispersion versus Segregation: Apropos of a Solution of Race Problems," *Papers of the Michigan Academy of Science, Arts, and Letters*, XXX (1944), 667–74.

[4] For an enumeration of some of the difficulties see C. A. Price and J. Zubrzycki, "The Use of Inter-marriage Statistics as an Index of Assimilation," *Population Studies*, XVI (July, 1962), 58–69.

that recent immigrants from Germany, under our immigration laws, include a large proportion of persons of high socioeconomic status.

Measures of the changing residential patterns of the immigrant groups are given in columns 7–9 of Table 1. The measure, an index of residential segregation between the total foreign stock (FBW + NWFMP) of each nationality and the total native whites of native parentage (NWNP), assumes a value of 100 for maximum residential segregation and a value of 0 if the residential distributions are identical.[5] The indexes were computed from the distribution of each group among the seventy-five community areas of the city of Chicago for 1930 (the last previous census year that included information on the total foreign stock) and 1960. The degree of residential segregation from the native population is highest for the "newer" immigrants and lowest for the "old" immigrants. Between 1930 and 1960, most of the ethnic groups became less segregated from the native population. Only for England, Ireland, and Sweden did the indexes fail to decline, and these were already at relatively low levels.[6]

This general approach to the measurement or assimilation of immigrant groups has been pursued for a number of cities and longer time periods by Lieberson. He found a remarkably persistent and consistent association through time between residential desegregation of an ethnic group and increasing socioeconomic similarity to native whites, and cross-sectionally between the position of each group as compared to others on measures of residential segregation and its relative levels on status measures.[7]

The index of residential segregation between Negroes and NWNP for 1930 was 84, and for 1960, 82. These values are higher than any of those for specific immigrant stocks. Furthermore, each of the immigrant stocks was highly segregated from Negroes in 1930 and 1960. There is relatively little intermixture of Negro residences with those of any group of whites. Even the "newer" immigrant groups, the Puerto Ricans and Mexicans, are not joining or replacing Negroes in established Negro areas but are moving into separate ethnic colonies of their own at the periphery of Negro areas. Negroes clearly occupy a distinctive position as the most residentially segregated of the principal migrant groups. The separation of Negroes from all groups of whites is sharper than any of the patterns of residential segregation between ethnic groups or between socioeconomic groups within the

[5] The index of residential segregation is an index of dissimilarity between the residential distributions of each group. For further discussion, see Otis Dudley Duncan and Beverly Duncan, "A Methodological Analysis of Segregation Indexes," *American Sociological Review*, XX (April, 1955), 210–17.

[6] For a more detailed discussion of these patterns, using data for 1930 and 1950, see Otis Dudley Duncan and Stanley Lieberson, "Ethnic Segregation and Assimilation," *American Journal of Sociology*, LXIV (January, 1959), 364–74.

[7] Stanley Lieberson, *Ethnic Patterns in American Cities* (New York: Free Press of Glencoe, 1963).

Table 1: Selected Characteristics (Age-Standardized) of Foreign-Born and
Native Ethnic Populations in 1950, and Indexes of Residential Segregation
of Selected Groups of Foreign Stock from Native Whites of Native Parentage,
1930 and 1960, Chicago *

| | PER CENT HIGH-SCHOOL GRADUATES (MALES AGE 25 AND OVER) | | PER CENT WITH INCOME ABOVE $3,000 (PERSONS WITH INCOME) | | PER CENT WITH WHITE-COLLAR JOBS (EMPLOYED MALES) | | INDEX OF RESIDENTIAL SEGREGATION (COMPARED WITH NWNP) | | |
COUNTRY OF ORIGIN	FBW	NWFMP	FBW	NWFMP	FBW	NWFMP	1930	1960	Change
"Old" immigrant groups:									
England and Wales	45	50	53	58	49	51	11	18	+ 7
Ireland	24	47	47	56	22	47	23	31	+ 8
Norway	31	47	54	57	24	51	44	37	− 7
Sweden	25	48	59	60	23	51	26	30	+ 4
Germany	37	34	53	55	34	42	22	19	− 3
"New" immigrant groups:									
Austria	29	40	54	57	33	44	30	16	−14
Czechoslovakia	25	33	44	54	22	36	59	37	−22
Italy	15	27	47	53	24	37	52	32	−20
Poland	18	25	42	49	25	30	63	38	−25
U.S.S.R.	35	60	60	69	59	74	51	44	− 7
"Newer" immigrant groups:									
Mexico	14	16	38	29	8	13	71	54	−17
Puerto Rico †	13	29	16	37	22	36	†	67	†

* Data for 1930 and 1950 refer to foreign white stock (foreign-born plus native of foreign or mixed parentage); data for 1960 refer to total foreign stock. Abbreviations used are FBW for foreign-born white, NWFMP for native white of foreign or mixed parentage, and NWNP for native white of native parentage. The three socioeconomic characteristics refer to the Standard Metropolitan Area population, while the segregation indexes are based on community areas within the city. Age-standardization was by the direct method, using age groups 25–44 and 45 and over, with the Standard Metropolitan Area age composition as a standard.
† Socioeconomic characteristics for Puerto Rican population refer to total United States; Puerto Rican population by community areas for Chicago available for 1960 only.

SOURCE: Characteristics from U.S. Bureau of the Census, U.S. Census of Population: 1950, Vol. IV, Special Reports, Pt. 3, chap. A, "Nativity and Parentage," and chap. D, "Puerto Ricans in Continental United States." Distributions of population by community areas for 1930 and 1960 from data on file at Chicago Community Inventory, University of Chicago.

white population.[8] Apparently this pattern has developed during the last few decades. Lieberson has demonstrated that, although prior to the great Negro migrations of World War I there were instances of immigrant stocks being more segregated from native whites than were Negroes, since 1920 there has been a general tendency for Negro residential segregation to be highest.[9]

Data pertaining specifically to the comparison between whites and non-whites (97 per cent of Chicago's non-whites are Negroes) on measures of socioeconomic status and of residential segregation are presented in Table 2. For each of four measures reflecting socioeconomic status, there was improvement in the status of the non-white population between 1940 and 1960. (For whites, improving status would be more clearly evident if the data referred to the entire metropolitan area rather than just the city of Chicago.) The indexes of residential segregation between whites and Negroes, in the top panel of the table, show minor fluctuations around an extremely high level and give no indication of the decline anticipated on the basis of the socioeconomic advancement of the Negro population. That this is not an atypical finding is indicated by reference to other data showing a long term historical trend toward increasing residential segregation between whites and non-whites. Increasing racial residential segregation was evident in most large cities of the United States between 1940 and 1950, while during the 1950's southern cities continued to increase in segregation and northern cities generally registered modest declines.[10]

In broad perspective, the historical trend toward improving socioeconomic status of immigrant groups has gone hand in hand with decreasing residential segregation. In contrast, Negro residential segregation from whites has increased steadily over past decades until it has reached universally high levels in cities throughout the United States, despite advances in the socioeconomic status of Negroes.

We have been unable to locate any data permitting a comparison between Negroes long resident in Chicago, or born and raised in the North, and Negroes with lesser periods of residence in the city. Thus we are not able to make even the crude intergenerational comparisons for Negroes that are possible for the immigrant groups. The only analysis of this type possible with census data is a comparison between recent migrants and the rest of the population, and the only published data are residential distributions, with no socioeconomic characteristics. For 1960, with the seventy-five community areas of Chicago as units, the index of residential

[8] For a discussion of class residential segregation in Chicago see Otis Dudley Duncan and Beverly Duncan, "Residential Distribution and Occupational Stratification," *American Journal of Sociology*, LX (March, 1955), 493–503.

[9] Lieberson, *op. cit.*, pp. 120–32.

[10] Karl E. Taeuber, "Negro Residential Segregation, 1940–1960: Changing Trends in the Large Cities of the United States" (paper read at the Annual Meetings of the American Sociological Association, 1962).

Table 2: *Selected Socioeconomic Characteristics (Unstandardized) of Whites and Non-Whites, Chicago, 1940, 1950, and 1960*

Characteristic	Non-White	White
Residential segregation index, whites vs. Negroes:*		
1930	85	
1940	85	
1950	79	
1960	83	
Per cent high school graduates, ages 25+:		
1940	16	25
1950	25	37
1960	29	37
Per cent white collar, male:		
1940	17	40
1950	17	41
1960	21	40
Per cent home-owners:		
1940	7	26
1950	12	33
1960	16	39
Per cent multiple-person households with 1.01 or more persons per room:		
1940	41	17
1950	46	14
1960	34	10

* These values differ slightly from those cited in the text for Negroes as compared to native whites of native parentage.

SOURCE: Data for 1940 from the 1940 Census Tract Bulletin for Chicago; for 1950 from Philip M. Hauser and Evelyn M. Kitagawa (eds.), *Local Community Fact Book for Chicago, 1950* (Chicago: Chicago Community Inventory, 1953); and for 1960 from the 1960 Census Tract Bulletin for Chicago.

segregation between non-whites resident in the metropolitan area five years or more and native whites of native parents is 80.5. Comparing non-whites with less than five years' residence in the metropolitan area and NWNP, the index was 81.0. Comparing the recent in-migrants with the non-whites who were resident in the metropolitan area five years or more, the index was 13. Thus the recent non-white in-migrants are distributed differently from the rest of the non-white population, but each group is highly segregated from the native whites. Unfortunately, these results cannot be readily interpreted in terms of the general assimilation and dispersion processes under consideration. Possibly there are trends toward socioeconomic advancement and residential dispersion on the part of "second generation" Negroes in Chicago that are confounded in the data for the total Negro population.

Decreasing residential concentration of immigrant groups occurred despite the efforts of many nationality organizations to maintain the ethnic colonies.[11] Few Negro organizations have been as explicitly segregationist. In some immigrant groups, many members were dispersing from the ethnic colonies even while large-scale immigration of that group was still under way. For every immigrant group, diminishing residential segregation has been evident since the cessation of large-scale immigration. For Negroes, however, residential segregation has increased since the first period of large-scale in-migration to northern cities, and this increase in residential segregation continued during the late 1920's and 1930's when the volume of migration was at a low level. These observations tend to discredit the argument that a major barrier to residential dispersion of the Negro population of Chicago is its continuing rapid increase. However, the size of the Negro population and the magnitude of its annual increase are larger than for any single ethnic group in the past, and comparisons with smaller groups are not completely convincing. That rapid increase of Negro population does not necessarily lead to increasing residential segregation was demonstrated directly in the intercity comparative study previously cited. There was no definite relationship between increase in Negro population and increase in the value of the segregation index. Indeed, during the 1950–60 decade, there appeared to be a slight relationship in the opposite direction.[12]

More significant in accounting for the divergent trends in residential segregation may be the different urban contexts in which the immigrant and Negro populations found themselves. Comparing the residential locations of Italian-born and Polish-born in Chicago in 1899 and in 1920, Wallace observed:

> it can be seen that the areas of greatest dispersion, low proportion, and presumably of "second" settlement for many immigrants were those which were not settled at all in 1899.
>
> The implication of this fact is that the so-called "assimilation" process was not reflected by the geographic dispersion of the immigrant populations into "cosmopolitan American areas." The dispersal was more directly related to an increase in housing alternatives as the city grew at the periphery.[13]

[11] David A. Wallace, "Residential Concentration of Negroes in Chicago" (unpublished Ph.D. dissertation, Harvard University, 1953).
[12] Taeuber, *op. cit.*   [13] Wallace, *op. cit.*, p. 205.

By the time the Negro concentrations were forming near the central areas of Chicago, the city was built up and the urbanized area extended well beyond the present boundaries. Residential alternatives at a price Negroes could afford and located sufficiently close in to permit inexpensive commuting were no longer available.

It has been suggested that considerable time is required for Negroes to make the transition from a "primitive folk culture" to "urbanism as a way of life."[14] Several types of data indicate that large and increasing proportions of the Negro urban population are city-born and raised. For instance, there is a rapidly decreasing color differential in the percentage of the Chicago population born in the state of Illinois. In 1960, 44 per cent of the native-born, non-white residents of Chicago were born in Illinois, as contrasted to 66 per cent of the white population.[15] National estimates for 1958 showed that of all males aged 45–64 living in metropolitan places of 500,000 or more population, 65 per cent of the non-whites, as compared to 77 per cent of the whites, had lived in this size city for twenty years or longer.[16] Estimates of the components of growth of the non-white population of Chicago indicate that between 1950 and 1960 natural increase was as important as net in-migration, and that natural increase will in the future account for rapidly increasing proportions of the growth of the non-white population.[17]

Unfortunately there is inadequate knowledge of the specific length of time under specified conditions for the required cultural transformation to occur. Wallace's observations indicate a significant degree of dispersal over time among first-generation immigrants. Such processes are more often conceived as primarily intergenerational. That many of the "first generation" Negro migrants to northern cities have lived there for twenty years or more and that in the younger adult ages there are sizable numbers of "second generation" urban Negroes suggest that there has been ample time for any necessary adjustment to urban living, at least for large proportions of the Negro population. It is also clear that if northern Negroes remain inadequately educated for urban living and fail to participate fully in the urban economy, the "primitive folk culture" of the South can less and less be assigned responsibility, and northern cities will be suffering from the neglect of their own human resources.

[14] Philip M. Hauser, "The Challenge of Metropolitan Growth," *Urban Land*, XVII (December, 1958), 5.
[15] Data from U.S. Bureau of the Census, *U.S. Census of Population, 1960: General Social and Economic Characteristics, Illinois*. Final Report PC(1)–15C, Tables 72 and 77.
[16] Karl E. Taeuber, "Duration-of-Residence Analysis of Internal Migration in the United States," *Milbank Memorial Fund Quarterly*, XXXIX (January, 1961), Table 3.
[17] D. J. Bogue and D. P. Dandekar, *Population Trends and Prospects for the Chicago–Northwestern Indiana Consolidated Metropolitan Area: 1960 to 1990* (Chicago: Population Research and Training Center, University of Chicago, 1962).

The "visibility" of Negroes due to skin color and other features which make the large majority of second-, third-, and later-generation descendants readily identifiable as Negroes is often cited as a basic factor in accounting for the distinctive position of Negroes in our society. It is exceedingly difficult to assess the significance of visibility. There is no other group that is strictly comparable to Negroes regarding every factor except visibility. It is not completely irrelevant, however, to note that non-white skin color, by itself, is not an insurmountable handicap in our society. The socio-economic status of the Japanese population of Chicago in 1950 substantially exceeded that of the Negro population; and their residential segregation from whites, although high, was considerably lower than that between Negroes and whites.[18] Unfortunately there are no trend data available on the characteristics of the Japanese in Chicago. A more appropriate Japanese population for comparison, however, is the much larger one in the San Francisco area. A recent study there affirmed that "ethnic colonies of Japanese are gone or rapidly going" and documented their rapid socioeconomic advance.[19]

In the traditional immigrant pattern, the more recent immigrants displaced the older groups at the bottom socioeconomic levels. How do the Negroes compare with the other "newer" immigrant groups, the Mexicans and the Puerto Ricans? The limited data now available suggest that the Negroes may soon be left alone at the bottom of the social and economic scale. We have already noted (from data in Table 1) that the "newer" groups were, in 1950, of very low status compared to the other immigrant groups, and that their residential segregation from the native whites of native percentage was the highest of all the immigrant groups. For 1960, data on distribution within Chicago of persons born in Puerto Rico are available separately from data on those persons born in the United States of Puerto Rican parentage. Thus it is possible to compute indexes of residential segregation for first- and second-generation Puerto Ricans. For Chicago in 1960, these index values were 68.4 for the first generation and 64.9 for the second generation, indicating that residential dispersion has already begun for the Puerto Ricans. This difference actually understates the amount of dispersion, since the second generation consists in large proportion of children still living with their first-generation parents.

Selected socioeconomic measures for the Puerto Rican and the non-white populations of Chicago in 1960 are shown in Table 3. On every measure, the Puerto Rican population is less well off—it is less educated, has lower

---

[18] Although the maximum value of the residential segregation index is less than 100 for ethnic groups of small size, this is not sufficient to vitiate the Negro-Japanese comparison.

[19] Harry H. L. Kitano, "Housing of Japanese-Americans in the San Francisco Bay Area," in Nathan Glazer and Davis McEntire (eds.), *Studies in Housing and Minority Groups* (Berkeley: University of California Press, 1960), p. 184.

income, is more crowded, is less likely to own homes, is less well housed, and lives in older buildings. Yet the index of residential segregation (computed with respect to NWNP) for Puerto Ricans is 67 as compared with 82 for Negroes.

Table 3: Selected Socioeconomic Characteristics (Unstandardized) of Puerto Ricans and Non-Whites, Chicago, 1960

Characteristic	Non-White	Puerto Rican
Residential segregation vs. whites	83	67
Per cent high school graduates, total	29	11
Median family income	$4,742	$4,161
Per cent families earning <$3,000	28	27
Per cent families earning >$10,000	9	4
Per cent home-owners	16	6
Per cent substandard dwellings	26	33
Per cent 1.01 or more persons per room	34	52
Per cent housing units built since 1940	12	6
Median gross rent	$88	$79
Median number of rooms	3.9	3.7
Median number of persons	3.0	4.0

SOURCE: Data are from the 1960 Census Tract Bulletin for Chicago.

Up to now we have been making comparisons between Negroes and immigrant groups, demonstrating that residential dispersion has not accompanied socioeconomic advance by Negroes in the way that it did for immigrant groups. Economic status and expenditure for housing, however, are clearly correlated, and there is also a correlation between economic status and residential segregation. By virtue of variations in the type, age, and quality of housing, and in the patterns of residential choice by persons of varying socioeconomic status, the subareas of a city are differentiated in terms of the average status of their residents. Since Negroes are of much lower average status than whites, they would be expected to be disproportionately represented in low-status residential areas. In fact, an extreme position regarding the relationships between patterns of socioeconomic residential segregation and racial residential segregation would attribute all of the latter to the former. Such a position is sometimes offered as a counterargument to charges of racial discrimination against the real estate business. To the extent that this position is correct, it might be expected that future economic advances on the part of the Negro population should be translated into decreased residential segregation.

The task of partialing out a component of racial segregation due to economic factors involves some difficult methodological problems, and no

method is entirely satisfactory.[20] Our approach utilizes indirect standardization of available census data. Let us delineate the status of a residential
area in terms of, say, the income distribution of its residents. Specifically,
consider for each community area of Chicago the number of families with
incomes below $1,000, from $1,000–1,999, from $2,000–2,999, and so forth.
For the city as a whole in 1960, 44 per cent of all families with an income
below $1,000 were non-white, as were 44 percent of families with incomes
from $1,000–1,999, and 40 per cent of families with incomes from $2,000–
2,999. For each community area, we can apply these city-wide percentages
to the observed income distribution to obtain the number of non-white
families expected if income alone determined the residential locations of
whites and non-whites.

By the method of indirect standardization just outlined, we obtain an
expected number of non-white and white families for each of the seventy-
five community areas. We can then compute an index of residential segregation between expected numbers of non-white and white families. This
index can be regarded as the amount of racial residential segregation
attributable to patterns of residential differentiation of income groups.
For 1950, the index of residential segregation between the numbers of
whites and non-whites expected on the basis of income was 11, as compared with the actual segregation index of 79. As a rough measure, then,
we can attribute 11/79, or 14 per cent, of the observed racial residential
segregation in Chicago in 1950 to income differentials between whites and
non-whites. For 1960, the corresponding values are 10 for the expected
index, 83 for the observed index, and 12 per cent for the racial segregation
attributable to income differentials.

In a recent study of the relationships between housing consumption and
income, Reid has demonstrated many pitfalls in the uncritical use of
income distributions in the analysis of housing patterns.[21] We have therefore repeated the above analyses, using distributions by major occupational
groups and distributions by educational attainment. For 1960, the index
of residential segregation computed from the numbers of whites and non-
whites expected on the basis of patterns of occupational differentiation is
9, and that expected on the basis of patterns of educational differentiation
is 3. The results using income distributions are thus supported by the
results from other measures of socioeconomic status, and the conclusion
seems clear that patterns of socioeconomic differentiation of residential
areas can account for only a small proportion of observed racial residential
segregation.

Reid demonstrated that differences between whites and non-whites

---

[20] A general discussion of this problem can be found in the section on explanation of
areal variation in Otis Dudley Duncan, Ray P. Cuzzort, and Beverly Duncan, *Statistical
Geography* (Glencoe, Ill.: Free Press, 1961).
[21] Margaret G. Reid, *Housing and Income* (Chicago: University of Chicago Press, 1962).

in observed patterns of housing consumption are largely attributable to income differentials between whites and non-whites. Our analysis suggests that residential segregation cannot be attributed to these differentials. Apparently the economic structure of the housing market for whites is similar to that for non-whites, even though non-whites are excluded from a large share of the housing supply for which their economic circumstances would allow them to compete.

The judicious conclusion from our review of a variety of pieces of data is that we simply do not yet know enough about immigrant assimilation processes and any corresponding processes among Negro migrants to northern cities to be able to compare the two. We believe that this very lack of knowledge makes questionable any attempt to reason from presumed patterns of assimilation among immigrants in the past to current racial problems in northern cities. Furthermore, such evidence as we could compile indicates that it is more likely to be misleading than instructive to make such comparisons.

Our definition of assimilation as involving socioeconomic advancement and residential dispersion is simple, and greater differences between groups would appear were a more complex definition adopted. Restriction of portions of the analysis to the city of Chicago had little effect on the measures for non-whites, but probably led to an understatement of the degree of assimilation of the immigrant stocks insofar as higher-status members of these groups have moved to the suburbs. The segregation indexes probably overstate somewhat the residential isolation of small groups, such as particular immigrant stocks, as compared with large groups such as total native whites of native parents. Taking account of any of these limitations in our data would tend to increase the differences between Negroes and immigrant groups. Even so, our data showed that second-generation persons from several countries are of higher socioeconomic status than the total native whites of native parentage. Relatively few Negroes in Chicago have white-collar jobs or incomes above the median level for whites, and yet there are large numbers of adult Negroes who were born in the city. Basic differences between the Negroes and the immigrant groups seems to us implicit in the failure of residential desegregation to occur for Negroes while it has continued for the immigrant groups.

In view of the fundamental impact of residential segregation on extra-legal segregation of schools, hospitals, parks, stores, and numerous other facilities, the failure of residential dispersion to occur strikes us as an especially serious social problem. Socioeconomic advance and residential dispersion occurred simultaneously for the various immigrant groups. It is apparent that the continued residential segregation of the Negro population is an impediment to the continued "assimilation" of Negroes into full and equal participation in the economy and the society at large.

29. Report From a Spanish Harlem "Fortress"

RICHARD HAMMER

To the commuter or tourist briefly passing through, a slum-like ghetto often seems simply an unpleasant sort of place in which to live. Seeing one, the resident of a more comfortable area may feel some relief because he has been able to place his own family in a cleaner, safer, and more acceptable sort of community. But to a ghetto resident, apparent signs of physical decay and visible indications of human failure are symbols of systematic social deprivation. Many ghetto residents feel trapped and hostile, angry at the profit others make from their cheap labor, discouraged because there seems so little hope that those who hold power will use it in any way that might effectively ameliorate the lot of the ghetto as a community and of the individuals who live in it. For more detailed information on Spanish Harlem and some of its deprivations, see selection 11.

The people will tell you that his block is a fortress: Its walls are invisible; they are inside the mind, built by the people who live on the block and by society outside. But the walls are as real as if they were made of mortar and stone; they keep 3,000 people locked up inside, afraid, and they keep most outsiders away, afraid.

The block is in the middle of Spanish Harlem, a section of New York that runs roughly from 96th Street to 118th Street between Fifth Avenue and Park Avenue. As events constantly make clear, the area is seething. To the outsider, it is a strange and unfamiliar and often frightening world —one he can never know on his own and one he can understand only partially even with the most expert help.

Recently I met a young man, 18 years old, for whom Spanish Harlem is home. He was born on the block on which he lives and has spent his entire life on it, in the same small apartment he now shares with his mother, widowed for 10 years, three brothers, three sisters and three other relatives. From all outward signs, Hiram Gonzales (this is not his name) could be a typical 18-year old from his block. He has grown up in its poverty and faced discrimination all his life because his skin is dark and he is recognizably of Puerto Rican descent. Twice he has dropped out of high school,

Source: *The New York Times Magazine,* January 5, 1964, pp. 22, 32, 34, 37, 39. Copyright © 1964 by the New York Times Company. Reprinted by permission of the author and the publisher.

Richard Hammer, editor-writer for the *New York Times Sunday Magazine,* has written extensively on matters of racial and ethnic relations for publications here and abroad.

once from vocational high school in Brooklyn and later from an academic high school in Manhattan.

But Hiram is articulate beyond his education and background, made so by self-education and by an innate brightness and intelligence, and he has thought long and hard about what it is like to grow up and live in Spanish Harlem. He also has a goal and the talent and determination to realize it; he wants to be a professional photographer and he is driven by a desire to return to school and then go on to college. And he has the sensitivity to see into and beneath the sights and sounds and texture of the life around him.

For several nights, we sat together and talked. At first, he was hesitant and wary, looking for something in the interviews other than interest in him and his problems. "To tell you the truth, man," he said later, "I dislike white men because I feel all the injustice that I, my family, my mother, my friends . . . you know, that all of us have gone through." Later, as respect and trust grew, Hiram led me through his world.

"When you walk through my block," he said, "probably the first thing you realize is that there are a lot of people on the streets all the time, from early in the morning to late at night. You'll see that the buildings are old, almost falling apart, but a lot of people have hung curtains in the windows.

"If you are an observing person, you'll notice prostitutes waiting for guys with money, most of them white men from downtown. You'll see drug addicts just moving nowhere; you'll see dope peddlers practically passing the stuff right out in the open. You'll see incidents of theft, you'll just walk along and see them. You'll see a lot of things that are wrong by moral standards and by the moral laws of the rest of society.

"But, man, ever since I was a little kid, this was my block, the block of the fellows who live in it. It was our property and we govern it and we make our own laws and no outsider or no people who don't live in the block can tell us what to do. There are a lot of people who come up and they try to tell us. But, man, they don't understand, they're living in some kind of dream.

"Their standards and ideas don't belong on this block. Because we've been made to feel like we're different, like we don't fit, like we don't belong any place but on our own crummy little block. And there's nobody up here who's going to listen until the white man lets us become a part of his society outside, and I don't mean just a couple of guys who are really exceptional, who've got a lot of brains, but I mean everybody who can make it."

One of the things the rest of society has to understand, Hiram thought, was that the people on his block are not different or strange. "To live on my block," he said, "is to live anywhere where there are a lot of people who are poor and who don't have any place else to go. There's a lot of pain and a lot of sorrow, but underneath there's also a lot of glory and happiness and love. Sure, there are a lot of problems on my block, and maybe more problems than a lot of other places. And everybody on the block knows that you think we brought all the problems with us. Well, man, we didn't. The problems were all here before the people came, or anyway, the things that made the problems. For every unjust act done by the people in my neighborhood, there was an unjust act, directly or indirectly done to these people by society."

By indirect, Hiram meant the often unthinking attitudes of whites. "There was this white woman from downtown," he said, "who sometimes came into the neighborhood to help my mother when she was sick. One day, this woman said to me, 'Now, I don't have anything against the Irish or the Italians, but I just don't like most Negroes and I don't like most Puerto Ricans.'

"Now, man, even though she was helping us when we needed help, I got damn mad. 'Now just a minute,' I said to her, 'how many Puerto Ricans or Negroes do you know? How many do you associate with? Where do you come off saying something like that?'

" 'Well, she told me, 'I see lots of Negro and Puerto Rican boys hanging on the street corners who look tough, and I'm afraid of them.'

" 'You go out to Bedford-Stuyvesant and you'll see plenty of white boys hanging on the street corners who are just as tough; you go anywhere where people have to live in this kind of filth and you'll see the same damn thing. When you and your kind first came here, you weren't any better.' "

Later, Hiram said, "You know, I'd like to move all the people from Scarsdale, N. Y., right into my block, into the same apartments where some of them have to pay maybe $70 for a couple of crummy little rooms for 10 or 11 people and have to share a bathroom in the hall with the door falling off. Let them live in a place where somebody throws a tire in the furnace and stinks out the place and then the cops come along and tell you that it's nothing and laugh when they're telling you.

"I'll tell you, I think they'd make just as much of a mess as we do, maybe more, because we're used to it, we're used to dodging those weak spots in the floors and not leaning on the wall because it will fall in.

"I don't think those people from Scarsdale could take it. In Scarsdale, the first things the kids learn are how to read and write; that's taken for granted. In my neighborhood, the first things the kids learn are how to fight and steal and not take any crap from anyone. We grow up knowing about narcotics, I mean we don't even remember when we didn't know about them, and everybody just takes that for granted.

"In my block, there are five places where you can buy marijuana cigarettes and I know, even though he's never said anything, that my little brother who's 14 knows where most of them are, that he's known for a long time."

I suggested that nobody forces the kids to use narcotics. "Of course, nobody comes up to us and says, "Man, here's some pot, you *got* to take a drag; man, here's some horse, you *got* to shoot.' But, man, these little kids look at the teen-agers who are using, and they *look* bigger, and, man, they can laugh and forget everything that's around. So, the little kids think, 'That's a tough man; he's great.' And then they see the pushers and racketeers in their $50 shoes and $100 suits, driving a big car, and they think, 'Man, he's tough; he's into some money and he's doing good.' So, when the pusher talks, they listen."

Hiram told me that by the time the boys on the block get to be 20 probably 95 per cent of them have tried some kinds of drugs and about 40 per cent of them are hooked.

"We aren't fooling ourselves," he said, "when we try drugs. We know what can happen. When I was 13, I saw somebody die of heroin. I went up to the roof of the house next door . . . I think it was to fly my kite . . . anyway, when I came out the door I nearly fell over these addicts who were sort of sitting around in the hallway next to the door. They saw I was only a kid, so they kept right on shooting.

"All of a sudden, I heard a lot of rumbling and this one guy leaped out through the door and started running and turning and jumping all over the roof. Man, he still had the niddle sticking in his arm. His friends, and they were still half asleep, sort of staggered out and grabbed him and held him down until he was quiet; then they started walking him back and forth to keep him awake. After a while, they sent me downstairs to get some milk, and more people began coming up to try to help. But nobody could do nothing, and by the time the ambulance got there, he was dead."

Most of the young people in Spanish Harlem are bitter and disillusioned. They sit on the stoops because there isn't anything else most of them can do, and they play cards and they joke. "Our goal is to have a good time, to keep having fun so we don't have to think," said Hiram. "You know what we're doing? We think we're sending the world on its own way while we go on ours. But we know, and, man, that's the trouble, we know that we can't send the world away, that we're part of the world and the world is looking down at us and snarling and laughing at us."

Isn't there, I asked, a desire to get out of the block and into that world to stop that sneering?

"Man, when I was a kid, I used to have dreams that maybe I'd be a scientist and discover all kinds of things. But they were only dreams; when I woke up, there wasn't anything real about them, there couldn't be anything real about them. I've never seen a scientist; I don't understand anything about them; there aren't any scientists, or anybody else who has a big job, on my block so I haven't got the least idea of what they're like. It's hard to even picture them mentally. These things are so far above us they aren't real. They're like a cloud that looks solid until you grab into it and find it falls apart in your hands."

The boys on the block feel that even with an education they have no hope of realizing any dreams. "I know guys with a diploma who start looking for jobs. You know what they can get? A stockboy or a delivery boy or something like that, but not something where they feel they can move ahead.

"I've got a friend who wants to be a mathematician and he's a real smart guy. But when he graduated from high school, an academic one, too, not a lousy vocational one like most of us dropped out of, he went looking for a job so he could make the money to go to college. Nobody had nothing for him. Finally, he answered an ad for a lousy bus boy's job in a crummy cafeteria.

You know what they told him? They told him that he had too much education, that they were afraid he would quit. Now this kid would have worked like hell because he needed the money; but he couldn't even get that crummy job, a job any fink who didn't even know how to read could handle."

So most of the boys just sit. They are convinced that if they went back to school, it would not assure them of a decent job; besides, they are disenchanted with the schools themselves. "When I reached sixth grade, I couldn't read," said Hiram. "The teachers, most of them didn't give a damn."

The school, instead of revealing the world, merely mirrored the world the young people from the block already knew. "But when I was in seventh grade, I went to a Catholic school for a year. They put a kind of wrench in my mind and opened it a crack and I began to see that there was a world outside my block. Man, that school cared, about me and about everybody, and they wanted to teach and they wanted me to learn.

"Then I went back to public school because, man, the work just got too hard and I wasn't ready for it. In public school, the only thing the teachers wanted was quiet. If they thought we didn't want to learn, they'd sit there smoking and reading and if you got out of line, sometimes they'd curse at you: 'You little spic, sit down.' "

But in that school Hiram's horizons were broadened by one teacher of a subject he hated, English. "One day, the teacher came in and played us 'The Three Penny Opera,' and there was something about this 'Mack the Knife' character that really hit us. We asked him to play it over and over, and the next day he brought in 'West Side Story,' and every day he played us records for a while. Then he began to read to us. He read 'The Old Man and the Sea,' 'The Most Dangerous Game,' and lots of others.

"Now, man, we weren't angels after that; we still carried on, maybe even more because we were getting some freedom, but when that man asked for silence, he got it, and when he began to suggest things, they began to move."

While there were some who managed to get an education, Hiram explained that they paid a terrible price for it. They had to be the teacher's pet, and this put them at the mercy of their fellows, who were not slow to deal out fitting punishment. For most, however, "this was the white man's education, taught the way the white man wanted it taught, without giving it any meaning for us. It was routine, do this and do that, and today we try to escape routine all the time. And it was using things from the white man's world which didn't mean anything to us or things that were so completely against everything we knew that we laughed at them. They even had books telling us what great guys the cops are.

"Now look, man, I know that most cops are just doing their jobs and trying to protect people most of the time. But I've grown up admiring people, I mean *admiring*, who would fight back at cops; to some extent, I still admire them. Why, I think that if right now, right this minute, a cop walked into this room and told me to do something, I don't think I'd do it, just because he was a cop."

This is the way Hiram and his friends see the law. "In my neighborhood, the cops feel that they're superior to the people, and, man, they let us know they think they're better than us. They walk into our homes and look around and tell us to open up, and we're afraid, and I mean afraid, to do anything or say anything. We just do what the cops say.

"And they'll come walking down the street and see us sitting on the stoop, and you know what they do? They come up to us asking us who we're going to rape next and what job we're planning to pull, and then they tell us to get moving. Man, it can be our stoop, right in front of our house, with our mothers watching out the windows, and the cops are cursing and, man, even demanding that we show them identification."

Another group of "outsiders," youth board and social workers, also rank low in the opinion of the block, Hiram said. "They're all around the neighborhood and most of them are rat fink types. They act like they think that we're not human. They think they've got all there is and all they've got to do is convert us to think and do what they think and do. Then, everything will be just great. But, man, these jerks pop up in the morning with their little briefcases and they cut out for their homes a hell of a way away around 5 or 6 at night, and that's it. If you ever are nuts enough to go to one of them, they hand you the old crap, 'Now, son, you shouldn't feel that way.'

"Now, look, I don't think these guys mean any harm. I think the least thing they want is to do any harm. But harm comes in many forms."

So Hiram and the people on the block have come to distrust those who arrive with good words and offers of help. They feel that they have only themselves to depend on, that only within their group is there reliability.

"As bad as things are here," Hiram said, "in my lifetime I have seen more good things on this block than I have seen bad. On my block, people help each other and most of them do the right things, for themselves and for everybody. Man, I have seen thieves help other guys; I have seen guys who have to rob for a living, and I mean really rob because they don't have any other way, I have seen them give their money to make another guy a little happier.

"I have seen an addict—and this guy was nearly crying for a fix and practically running across the street to get one—stop and shove his last $3 in the shirt pocket of another guy who was married and had a lot of kids but who couldn't find a job and didn't have any money. And this junkie went walking away, kicking himself and cursing, 'Now, why the hell did I do that?'

"Now, man, this may not sound like much, but that one incident, for me, could equal 50 unjust things, because it shows that these people do have concern about each other, even though it may be hard for them to show it or express it or maybe even to understand it."

The people on the block are not unconscious of the horror and the filth and destitution around them. They know that it is bad and, at times, they talk of leaving it, though few ever do. But now, today, most of them are afraid. They are afraid because their block is going; all around, new housing projects have risen and this is almost the last block to remain unchanged. It will not remain so for long, and the people know it. Hiram said that most of them would not be able to get into the new projects; some because they wouldn't be able to afford the rents, some because they have an addict or a criminal in the family and the rules of projects forbid such tenants.

"The people are going to have to move, like up to the Bronx, and the landlords know that these people are going to need houses, so instead of $50 they'll make it $70 or $100 an apartment; they're already doing it.

"Man, this is the end of my block," said Hiram. "This is something that we all evade; like, this has been going on for five years. All the other blocks have been going, and this has been in my mind, in everybody's mind, but I haven't really given it any thought, but it scares me. I fear it. But wherever, any place, there is poverty and minorities like us, you will find another block like this one, with all the same horrors that we have. Maybe that's where we will have to go. Forget it, man, let me live in this rathole that I have now, that I know, instead of some other new rathole that I don't know."

30. Class, Race, and Urban Renewal

ROBERT C. WEAVER

Although the next selection appeared prior to a good deal of recent federal action in the field of housing, it is still a cogent statement of interconnections among population patterns, racial differences, political developments, and prestige and economic interests. For example, as Negro communities expand, they tend to spill over into areas that were previously all-white. White residents then leave these central city areas, moving to the suburbs. And following them frequently are other white people who leave their former neighborhoods with increasing rapidity after a racial "tipping point" has been reached. These white migrants feel that their property interests and social status have been threatened by the influx of Negroes, and often insist, without stopping to realize that their neighborhoods were already in decline, that Negroes have no respect for and do not know how to care for property. There are other less obvious implications of these population movements. Renewal projects centered in a city's worst residential areas displace higher proportions of Negroes than of whites; plans for integrated public housing projects in white districts meet resistance from white political and community leaders; the political character of the central city changes as Negroes come to represent a greater proportion of its voting population.

A noteworthy aspect of Weaver's article is its emphasis on how public schools fit in with these developments. Urban Negro leaders are becoming increasingly insistent that de facto segregation, or racial imbalance, be alleviated. They believe that Negroes will be able to obtain better public education only through substantial integration—because white people do care about the schools that white children attend. They also believe that it is an important educational experience for white and Negro children to attend school together. In addition, more widespread integration that did not concentrate Negro students in particular schools would demonstrate to white parents that their children's schools would neither be "taken over" by Negroes nor decline drastically in quality because of increasing numbers of previously poorly educated Negro children.

In some cities, white leaders have responded to Negro pressures for a more equitable racial balance by attempting to uphold the sanctity of "the neighborhood school." This concept, of course, fits neatly into patterns

Source: *Land Economics*, 36, 1960, pp. 235–51. Reprinted by permission of the editor and the publisher. Portions of this selection appeared in Dr. Weaver's *Urban Complex* (1964), published by Doubleday & Company, who have also granted permission to reprint.

Robert C. Weaver, author of *Negro Labor* and of *The Urban Complex*, is Secretary of the (U.S.) Department of Housing and Urban Development.

of sentiment in neighborhoods already organized on class or ethnic lines, where residents are likely to feel that "their" schools belong to district residents, and not to the population of the city as a whole. In Boston in particular, the voting for members of the School Committee has clearly reflected both white reluctance and Negro eagerness to put an end to de facto segregation in the public schools.

It is an impressive credit to Weaver that his article anticipated such developments and, as it turns out, helped to account for them before they occurred.

INTRODUCTION

Urban renewal has opened Pandora's Box in several fields. It has occasioned a fresh look at slums; it has given rise to renewed discussion of racial balance in neighborhoods; it has inspired new thought and approaches relative to the racial and class composition of schools in the central city; and of course it has intensified research in the fields of housing, city planning, and municipal government.

Since one of the principal objectives of urban renewal is to attract more middle-class families back into the central city and slow down the exodus of middle-class families from the inlying areas, much of the current discussion about color and class is oriented around these goals. There is, however, a tendency to treat current problems as though they were unique and devoid of historical precedents. Actually, this is not only untrue but dangerously misleading. As Oscar Handlin has most recently pointed out, the flight of older, middle-class families from proximity to the latest newcomers is as old as immigration. What is unique is not the human behavior but the physical limits of the city and the multiplicity of local governments.[1]

Since in many American cities a principal wave of low-income migrants is composed of readily identifiable members of color minorities, there is a tendency to identify the problem as one of race alone.[2] This is inaccurate and unfortunate. Cities which have few non-white migrants are experiencing the same problems[3]—a fact suggesting that this is a class as well as a color phenomenon. Should further proof of this be required, the experiences of Chicago, Cleveland, Detroit, Cincinnati, and a score of other

[1] Oscar Handlin, *The Newcomers* (Cambridge, Massachusetts: Harvard University Press, 1959), pp. 14–16, 30–5.
[2] See especially Morton Grodzins, *The Metropolitan Area as a Racial Problem* (Pittsburgh, Pennsylvania: University of Pittsburgh Press, 1958); and "Metropolitan Segregation," *Scientific American*, October 1957, pp. 33–41.
[3] Robert C. Weaver, "Non-White Population Movements and Urban Ghettos," *Phylon*, Third Quarter (Fall), 1959, pp. 235–8.

cities with Appalachian Mountain whites will provide convincing documentation.[4]

Identification of the decline of central cities with the encroachment of non-whites (and in a few places Puerto Ricans) upon established middle-class neighborhoods reflects our consciousness of color. It does more. Such superficial analysis weakens our capacity to deal effectively with the problems of our cities. The color and class aspects of these problems are frequently intertwined but neither should be ignored. Any workable program must recognize both and learn to deal with each.

On the other hand, it would be sheer sophistry to deny that, under existing demographic and ecological changes, long-standing racial attitudes, and the current economic forces which operate in the housing market, the arrival of increasing numbers of non-white families may, and often does, lead to the departure of previous middle-class whites.[5] This long recognized phenomenon has recently been expressed in terms of a "tipping point" theory, which says that there is in any neighborhood a point at which whites will move out when the proportion of non-whites reaches a certain size.[6]

Many factors are involved in the desertion of a neighborhood. First there is the economic climate. In a period of general prosperity transition is accelerated; the same occurs in a loose housing market. The location of the neighborhood involved is important, too. Factors tending to stabilize middle-class occupancy include proximity to, and identification with, institutional facilities, such as in the area around a university or college or around long-established religious facilities.

Access of minority and low-income families to a formerly white middle-class neighborhood is not always a consequence of whites' desertion of an area in the face of the encroachment of new user groups. Often it results from vacancies caused by the movement of earlier residents and failure of other middle-class whites to replace the former occupants. The cause of the desertion of such neighborhoods is usually the attractiveness of other areas: they may be suburban subdivisions or, as in the case of the East Side of Manhattan, a new prestige location in the central city. Once the vacancy rate becomes high, as it did in New York City's West Side,

---

[4] For an interesting account of the Chicago experience, see Albert N. Votaw, "The Hillbillies Invade Chicago," *Harpers*, February 1958, pp. 64–7.

[5] For an excellent account of this process, even when the in-coming Negroes were middle-class, see Albert J. Mayer, "Russell Woods: Change Without Conflict," in Nathan Glazer and Davis McEntire, ed., *Studies in Housing and Minority Groups* (Berkeley, California: University of California Press, 1960) pp. 198–220. There are, however, in this article and Nathan Glazer's Introduction to the volume, unsupported assertions about the absence of racial prejudice on the part of the former Jewish residents.

[6] Morton Grodzins, *op. cit.*, pp. 6–7. While the author of this concept is probably over-pessimistic due to his involvement with Chicago's experience, his is a useful idea.

owners and property managers are happy to substitute new user groups rather than suffer greater losses.

The Impact of Newcomers
on the Housing Market

From early days, middle-class Americans have wanted distance between themselves and the newcomer; that desire has been actuated by two recent developments—the rise of prestige-laden, single-class, homogeneous suburban areas and the identification of color with a large number of low-income migrants. The recent concern of Americans with the quality of education has, of course, occasioned increasing emphasis upon good schools.

As long as there was ample space within the city limits and no effective modes of rapid transportation, most of the outward movement of middle-class families occurred within the city proper. The streetcar, automobile, and bus changed the situation, opening for housing development large areas of virgin land removed from the central city. The fact that estates of the wealthy were already located on such lands augmented their appeal to medium-income groups intent on upward social mobility. Real estate operators, developers, and land speculators, readily joined the commuting railroad lines in selling the exclusiveness of these developments.[7] This was the stage when the great impetus to Negro migration occurred during World War I. Low-income colored Americans from the South poured into many Northern cities, replacing, as the new source of unskilled and semi-skilled labor, the earlier European immigrants who were no longer available during and after the hostility. Not only were the newcomers mostly poor and ill-prepared for urban life, but they were also dark-skinned. As the readily-identified descendants of slaves, they had the least amount of social prestige of any ethnic group. Race and color joined class in rendering them forbidden neighbors.

Middle-class whites, led by the real estate fraternity, frequently resorted to racial housing covenants and zoning to contain non-whites in a restricted area. Low-income whites, only slightly less undesirable in the eyes of the middle-class, sometimes used intimidation, violence, and threats to assert their Americanism. On the part of the former, this was a manifestation of class as well as racial prejudice; on the part of the latter it was primarily racial. Yet lower-class whites and Negroes frequently shared the same residential areas and faced the same disabilities of poor neighborhoods. Class was often more important than color in neighborhoods which failed

---

[7] For an excellent description of this process, see Charles Abrams, *Forbidden Neighbors* (New York: Harper and Bros., 1955) Chapter XII.

to offer prestige or adequate protection and public services to any residents, regardless of race.[8] The early governmental policy of segregation in public housing subsequently served to accentuate color consciousness in low-cost housing at the same time that it reflected the strategic role of authority in establishing racial patterns.

World War II brought in a new stream of Negro, Mexican-American, and Puerto Rican migrants to the urban North and West. It also brought greater residential segregation. This too represented, first, resistance to the expansion of land space available to non-whites and, most recently, abandonment of segments of the central cities to them. Several factors played an important part in this. The federal government through the Federal Housing Administration had facilitated phenomenal expansion of suburban construction, and low down-payments and a longer period for mortgages had made a large part of this available to middle- and lower middle-income families. At the same time FHA accepted the concept of homogeneous neighborhoods and until 1947 the instrument of the racial restrictive housing covenants.[9] Higher incomes during the war enabled a vast number of families to accumulate down payments and sustained prosperity facilitated their meeting monthly carrying charges. At the same time government housing policy made home ownership more attractive than rental[10] and practically all new construction was in lily-white suburbs.

Not only was it possible for the upper-middle class to desert the central city but many of lesser means—if they were white—could follow suit. Even the low-income white family could hope for homogeneity—either in the suburbs with a little more money or perhaps in the grey areas of the core city if the expansion of non-whites was contained. Racially homogeneous neighborhoods had achieved a new prestige and this was increasingly apparent in slums and blighted areas where residents sought to emulate dominant racial attitudes.

Rapid movement of whites to the suburbs was but a part of the population trend. For example, over 7,000,000 persons entered the suburbs between 1940 and 1950. While a large volume of long-term residents left the cities, an even larger number of individuals moved from non-urban areas directly to the suburbs. Meanwhile a much smaller number of whites moved into than moved out of central cities while many non-whites

[8] Findings of recent research challenge the oft-repeated assertion that the source as well as the center of anti-Negro prejudice and discrimination in this country is in the lower socio-economic classes. See Robert K. Merton, "Discrimination and the National Creed," in R. M. MacIver, ed., *Discrimination and National Welfare* (New York: Harper and Bros., 1949), p. 111; and National Committee on Segregation in the Nation's Capital, *Segregation in Washington* (Chicago, Illinois: The Committee, 1948), p. 38.

[9] R. C. Weaver, *The Negro Ghetto* (New York: Harcourt, Brace & Co., 1948), pp. 71–3, 152–3.

[10] Louis Winnick, *Rental Housing: Opportunities for Private Investment* (New York: McGraw-Hill Book Company, 1958), Chapter 3.

entered the in-lying areas. "The process of losing one net migrant to the suburbs actually was the end result of a larger process whereby for each two non-white persons moving into the central city about three white persons moved out."[11]

These movements have brought interesting changes in the housing market. Throughout the North and West, non-whites have acquired a much larger number of housing units and frequently a more diversified and a better quality of housing. In the process they have expanded into many areas which were formerly all white. The Chicago experience of 1940–50 suggests the human components of this development. Those who initiated the movement were long-term rather than newer residents, resulting in no significant changes in socioeconomic characteristics;[12] and the first arrivals had had to "pay a premium rental, which they are able to finance only by using residential space very intensively, e.g., by doubling up families in the household or by including relatives or lodgers in the household."[13]

While it is true that only in a quite general sense has succession in Chicago followed a pattern of radial expansion of the Negro community outward from the center of the city, it is significant that:

> . . . within both the Negro and the white community, high-status groups tend to share residential areas and to be residentially segregated from low-status groups. Apparently, the selective forces which produce differentiation of residential areas in the urban community operate in somewhat the same way upon the Negro and the white population. This is also in line with the finding that patterns of interarea differentiation with respect to physical characteristics of the area and social and economic characteristics of the residents tend to be maintained under the impact of succession from white to Negro occupancy.[14]

These developments in Chicago, which are fairly typical of larger northern industrial centers, reflect the interaction of many events. Such expansion of housing accommodations for Negroes as took place was facilitated largely by the decline in the white population. It reflected a growing demand for shelter on the part of an expanding non-white population in which a significant number were able to pay higher rents and prices for housing and it enabled some whites to sell profitably and buy new suburban houses. Even where sales were not profitable the availability of Negro purchasers and renters greatly accelerated the liquidation of property

[11] Donald J. Bogue, *Components of Population Change, 1940–50* (Miami, Ohio: Miami University, 1957), p. 34.
[12] Otis Dudley and Beverly Duncan, *The Negro Population of Chicago*, (Chicago, Illinois: The University of Chicago Press, 1957), pp. 125, 191, 206, 223, 225.
[13] *Ibid.*, p. 236.   [14] *Ibid.*, p. 298.

in the central city and the acquisition of new homes elsewhere on the part of previous residents in the core areas. To a degree, this greater effective demand for housing on the part of non-whites sustained property values in many parts of the central city and accelerated the purchase of new homes by whites who were replaced by non-whites, many of whom paid higher prices than could otherwise have been secured.

Had there been less racial segregation in the suburbs, a larger number of non-whites would have joined whites in moving from the central cities to the suburbs and going directly to them rather than to the central cities. Even in the face of a most effective color bar, about one-third of a million Negroes did join whites in the 1940–50 trek to the suburbs. Most of those involved were in the South but there was a pronounced desire of northern middle-class Negroes to escape from central cities,[15] and there are indications that some of the colored migrants to the North avoided the central city and moved directly to older Negro settlements elsewhere. This seems to have occurred in the industrial cities of New Jersey and the larger cities in New York's Westchester County.

One upshot of residential segregation has been to contain most Negro middle-class families in the core cities.[16] Another, and much more serious consequence for the cities has been the concentration of demand for housing on the part of the growing middle-class Negroes on certain city areas. This too has often sustained property values but it has tended to accelerate the exodus of middle-class whites. Were middle-class Negroes able to compete freely in the total market, their volume in most neighborhoods would have been so slight as to have occasioned little concern. There would have been much less premium payment incident to initial non-white occupancy and white owners would have had less economic incentive to forsake attractive neighborhoods and homes. Even the real estate operators would have had slight impetus to engineer flight of middle-class whites since the principal source of effective demand—the middle-class Negro purchaser—would be more discriminating and less available for any one neighborhood.[17]

---

[15] Handlin, *op. cit.*, pp. 125–31.

[16] Actually, this is due to factors other than residential segregation, but it is primarily a consequence of the color line: see Weaver, "The Effect of Anti-Discrimination Legislation upon the FHA- and VA-Insured Housing Market in New York State," *Land Economics*, November 1955, pp. 305–7.

[17] There can be no better illustration of the confusion between emotion and economics than the implications of this analysis. Without a color line, housing in certain areas of the central city would probably have fallen in value. This would have been accounted for in economic terms—architectural obsolescence, loss of neighborhood prestige, age of structure, competition of more desirable facilities and neighborhood location, and resulting weakness in demand for the affected housing. Under conditions of color concepts the experience in these areas is cited (and rightfully) as evidence that non-white occupancy does not necessarily adversely influence property values. See, Luigi Laurenti, *Property Values and Race* (Berkeley, California: University of California Press, 1960).

For the process described above to have taken place, there would have had to have been a much larger volume of low-priced housing available to non-whites in metropolitan areas. Without such a supply the sheer pressure of numbers occasioned the growth of non-white areas of concentration. In some instances this involved expansion of one or several major Negro ghettos, engulfing surrounding housing regardless of its price or suitability. In other instances it involved the development of new pockets of non-white residential concentration. Invariably, it occasioned overcrowding, undesirably high densities, and blight.

However, in a situation where the supply of low-cost housing available to non-whites is limited, the entrance of middle-income, non-white families into a neighborhood and its subsequent desertion by whites has benefited the mass of colored home-seekers. For, had there been less turnover, there would have been less filtration. This, in turn, would have delayed the improvement in the quality of housing occupied by non-whites. In the present situation of enforced residential segregation in many segments of the housing market, rapid racial transition of desirable housing in parts of the central city has made a larger amount of physically good housing available to non-whites. It has also resulted in more intensive and often socially undesirable occupancy patterns in the areas recently accessible to non-whites and it has made it difficult to sustain the middle-class characteristics of the affected areas, even when higher-income non-whites have attempted to do so. Relatively high vacancy rates, as in Philadelphia and Cleveland, have accelerated racial transition in certain neighborhoods with the result of substantial upgrading in the quality of the occupied housing stock and instability in some middle-class housing areas.

Modern cities can absorb a large supply of low-income migrants without subjecting the newcomers to economic exploitation and greatly augmenting slums and blight only by building more low-rent housing on open sites, solving the problem of rehabilitation without excessive costs and providing a free housing market. The central city has a stake in open occupancy throughout the metropolitan area because it is necessary in order that the market may operate most efficiently. Under conditions of open occupancy a much smaller number of areas of middle-class housing need be threatened by inundation by non-whites and it is possible to make the most effective use of the existing supply of housing—particularly the low-rent sector.[18]

[18] This is the economic rationale for open-occupancy (fair housing) legislation. As in all non-discriminatory legislation, enactment of a law is but a first step. To be effective, such laws need implementation—and that not only involves enforcement but also positive action on the part of minority groups. Thus the Philadelphia Commission on Human Relations is encouraging Negroes to seek homes in all-white neighborhoods, saying: "To break the stubborn pattern of segregated housing many Negro citizens must have the courage to live in 'new' neighborhoods." *The New York Times*, March 6, 1960, p. 49.

Efforts to Attract Middle-Class Families
to the Central City

It is against this background that urban renewal programs' efforts to attract and maintain middle-class families in the central city must operate. Regardless of any social, political, or moral considerations, the economics of the situation require concern for retention of white middle-class families in central cities because their numbers far exceed those among non-whites.[19] In any given locality the problem has three manifestations: creation of new areas in which middle-class families will establish stable communities, rehabilitation or partial renewal of areas which will attract and hold middle-class families, and the arresting or preventing the desertion of middle-class families from existing areas of residence.

In the larger cities of the South new, segregated middle-class Negro communities have been developed. This has been possible for several reasons. In some instances it results from annexation of new areas by the central city after informal agreements have been made concerning the color identification of land. Atlanta is a prime example,[20] New Orleans has had somewhat similar experience.[21] In cities like Charlotte, Greensboro, and Winston-Salem, North Carolina, and Austin, Texas, availability of vacant land contiguous to, or in the path of, existing centers of Negro concentration has afforded sites for new, segregated FHA-insured housing. In Houston, Texas, where availability of good housing has made the owning of attractive homes an important source of status among Negroes, there has been an appreciable amount of new construction and a significant

[19] "What the city needs is a core of upper-middle-class people to support its theatres and museums, its shops and its restaurants—even a Bohemia of sorts can be of help. For it is the people who like living in the city who make it an attraction to the visitors who don't. It is the city dwellers who support its style; without them there is nothing to come downtown *to*." William H. Whyte, Jr., "Are Cities Un-American?" *Fortune*, September 1957, pp. 124–25. Despite significant recent improvement in the economic status of non-whites and a significant increase in the number of middle-class Negroes in urban areas, the number of the latter is not now able, nor does it have a potential in the near future to provide a large or affluent enough population to perform the functions outlined above by Whyte.
[20] Robert A. Thompson, Hylan Lewis and Davis McEntire, "Atlanta and Birmingham: A Comparative Study in Negro Housing," Glazer and McEntire ed., *Studies in Housing and Minority Groups* (Berkeley, California: University of California Press, 1960), pp. 22–40; and "Civil Rights Official Lauds Atlanta's Gentleman's Agreement," *House and Home*, May 1959, p. 91. For a discussion of the implications of the use of new, segregated middle-class Negro housing in the South, see R. C. Weaver, "Southern Comfort: A Possible Misapplication of Federal Funds," *Journal of Intergroup Relations*, Fall 1960.
[21] Forrest E. LaViolette, "The Negro in New Orleans," Glazer and McEntire, *op. cit.*, pp. 124–30; also "Minority Housing," *House and Home*, April 1955, pp. 146–7.

source of excellent middle-class housing in a good neighborhood available to Negroes during the last decade.

Clearly, by creation of new segregated areas in most of these cities and restriction of Negro encroachments upon middle-class white neighborhoods to a few locations in others, the impact of the non-white market has had but limited effect upon the desertion of the central city by middle-class whites. In Houston, where there seems to have been a rather loose housing market,[22] Negro expansion into one good neighborhood served to sustain values and thereby accelerated movement of the older residents to the suburbs. However, some of those who sold to Negroes may have replaced other central city whites moving to the suburbs and thereby supported property values elsewhere in the central city.

In northern cities the establishment of all-Negro suburbs is usually impossible. This is due to the spatial distribution of non-whites[23] and rejection of segregated patterns by non-whites in the North.[24] The latter fact is, of course, supported by legislation: a score of northern states and cities have non-discrimination housing laws, and racial discrimination in urban renewal areas is banned in several states and many cities. In all of these and other cities, the capacity and willingness of Negroes to pay for better housing in middle-class neighborhoods has increased significantly during the last decade at the same time that the low-income non-white population has grown appreciably. Indeed, the growth of non-white urban populations has been much greater in border and northern cities than in their southern counterparts. Thus the pressure of Negroes for more housing has had greater impact in the North than in the South. Also, it has had less outlet via expansion into new, vacant areas. The consequence is that

---

[22] Jack E. Dodson, "Minority Group Housing in Two Texas Cities," Glazer and McEntire, *op. cit.*, pp. 101–9.

[23] See R. C. Weaver, *The Negro Ghetto*, pp. 91, 138, 154–6.

[24] "In certain ways, the North presents more problems for upper-income Negroes than the South, for here the problem is not only to get good housing—and if Atlanta can supply a Negro market for extensive Negro subdivisions, unquestionably this can also be done in northern cities—but to get good *unsegregated* housing." Glazer, "Introduction," Glazer and McEntire, *op. cit.*, p. 6. Of course, where there is the base of a Negro settlement which originally housed domestics, as on the North Shore of Chicago's suburbs or in cities and towns of Westchester County and Long Island or clusters of industrial workers in suburban towns and cities, growing Negro populations—mostly in ghettos—are developing in northern suburbs. Also, a small number of upper middle-income Negroes have bought homes outside areas of non-white concentration. Current developments suggest that, were the suburbs open to Negroes, they would attract a large segment of the still relatively small number of middle-income non-whites. At the same time, concentration of industry in fringe areas has already attracted a significant number of non-white workers. Many are now commuting from the core areas, but there are indications of a desire for, and a trend to, suburban living on their part. Competent studies suggest that there will be an outward movement of Negroes and Puerto Ricans in the New York City Metropolitan area in response to job opportunities. (Edgar M. Hoover and Raymond Vernon, *Anatomy of a Metropolis* (Cambridge, Massachusetts: Harvard University Press, 1959), pp. 212–13.

Negroes have expanded to a much greater degree into areas formerly occupied by whites in northern than in southern cities.

Efforts to attract and retain middle-class families in the central urban centers of the North and border states must recognize the pressure for housing occasioned by a growing Negro population. Some of these cities also face the arrival of large numbers of Appalachian Mountain whites, Puerto Ricans, and Mexicans. Since the Negro presents problems of class as well as color, concentration upon his impact is fruitful. Glazer, while minimizing the problem of the dark-skinned Puerto Ricans and Mexican-Americans, has set forth the peculiar disabilities of the Negro in American society:

> . . . it may seem far-fetched to consider the implications of a social situation in which Mexicans, Puerto Ricans, and Negroes show roughly the same social constitution as the rest of us. However, in the case of the Negroes such large middle-class groups are already developing. They will change greatly the whole character of anti-Negro prejudice in America. But—and this is the point of this last observation—the Negroes will still be a long way from taking up the status in American society of assimilated European ethnic groups. The Mexicans and Puerto Ricans, because of their physical characteristics, will find it easier to achieve this status.[25]

Survival of healthy, central cities requires recognition and solution of this problem. First, there needs to be an acceleration of the size of the middle-class among non-whites. Second, this will be achieved in large measure in proportion to the degree that the middle-class Negro is accepted as his immigrant prototype was accepted.[26] Third, unless the achievement of American norms of success on the part of Negroes is rewarded, as it has been among others who started at the bottom of the economic and social scale, there will be a loss of motivation (already apparent among Negroes) with consequences which are inimical to the economic, political, and cultural health of the central city. Fourth, such results would be tragic for the nation—and western democracy—in the world of the cold war and the emergence of Asian and African nationalism.

Northern cities, if they are to maintain a sound economic base, must strive to adjust to continuing in-migration of low-income Negroes, Puerto Ricans, Appalachian whites, and Mexicans. A first step in this direction is to understand the nature of cities and the historical precedents. A second step is to face up to the unique problems of the present migrant groups. These can be summarized in a single statement: All of certain ethnic groups, because of their physical identification are assumed to be a threat

[25] Nathan Glazer, *op. cit.*, pp. 11–12. For a more realistic discussion of the Puerto Rican, see Handlin, *op. cit.*, pp. 59–60.
[26] Oscar Handlin, *op. cit.*, pp. 78–80, 100, 103, 117–19.

to a middle-class neighborhood, regardless of the individual's or the family's income, education, or behavior. Centuries of slavery, generations of color discrimination, repeated instances of economic disadvantage via perpetuation of a color line, and a liberal amount of guilt have perpetuated color concepts. These are most apparent and effective in situations involving areas of living and schools.

Most liberals and many social scientists advocate heterogeneous neighborhoods. The majority of them would favor a community of homes in which low-, medium-, and upper-income groups lived; as a minimum, they would mix low- and medium-income people. Some have equally strong feelings about racial heterogeneity, affirming that in the modern world it behooves us in the United States to learn and demonstrate how a multiracial society can live together under democracy. Recently an outstanding land economist has dissented, questioning the innate superiority of multi-income neighborhoods.[27] In this paper no attempt will be made to pass moral, social, or political judgments on this issue; rather, the problem will be treated from the point of view of the survival of central cities. Our orientation will be primarily economic, recognizing that enforced racial residential segregation is under attack and in the process of change in the nation.

From this point of view, it must be recognized that the middle class in America is keenly conscious of the threat of lower-class encroachments. As was pointed out above this has long been a national characteristic, perhaps an inevitable consequence of a socially mobile people who are status-conscious. During the last quarter of a century, it has become more acute. This leads to the conclusion that many middle-class families will not long voluntarily remain in an area which they believe threatened by lower-class engulfment; few will migrate to such areas. The second fact that has to be

---

[27] "It is not clear why economically heterogeneous neighborhoods are innately superior to the homogeneous. We do not really know whether economically diverse groups truly mix or merely live side by side. And casual observation indicates that many exclusively high-income or middle-income neighborhoods seem to have withstood neighborhood decline extremely well while many economically-mixed neighborhoods have proven quite vulnerable. The social gains of mixture and the social losses from homogeneity have yet to be demonstrated." (Louis Winnick, *Facts and Fictions in Urban Renewal*, p. 12. Mimeographed: a speech delivered before the Forum of the Philadelphia Housing Association, January 28, 1960). Most planners, however, believe that there are such social gains. A recent forum composed of citizens and professionals who met to consider what neighborhoods should be like "pleaded for variety—variety of housing types . . . available at a variety of prices and rentals so that a varied neighborhood population could result, all races, young and old, rich and poor, and people falling between these extremes." Ironically enough, zoning as currently practiced was considered a chief deterrent to such mixture. (Howard W. Hallman, "Citizens and Professionals Reconsider the Neighborhood," *Journal of the American Institute of Planners*, August 1959, p. 123). For a somewhat similar point of view, see Arthur L. Grey, Jr., "Los Angeles: Urban Prototype," *Land Economics*, August 1959, pp. 237–8.)

recognized is that the white middle class fears neighborhood deterioration on the entry of non-whites—an attitude that has partial roots in the history of decline in city services, lax enforcement of housing codes, and over-crowding in areas inhabited by non-whites. Actually, the degree of this fear is often a function of the speed and intensity of non-white penetra-tion, although it is today an almost immediate reaction upon the first evidence of non-white entry.[28] Most white middle-class families will not long remain in a neighborhood where they are a racial minority. Should they fear this eventuality, they usually act so as to assure its fruition. On the other hand, there are many evidences of whites' accepting a few Negro neighbors, particularly if they are of comparable economic and social status.[29]

The Impact of Urban Renewal

Urban renewal activity concerned with attracting and holding middle-class households in the central city must be geared to creating neighborhoods which offer good schools, a reasonable degree of cleanliness, protection from violence, and physical attractiveness. They need not be single-class neighborhoods,[30] but there is a limit—a class tipping point—to which they can at the present be heterogeneous from a class point of view. Similarly, they can absorb some minority group families of middle-class attributes

[28] This is a most complex phenomenon. Its manifestation varies from city to city, from time to time, and from area to area within a given city. For example, in the color-conscious Washington, D. C. of the present writer's youth, whites did not hesitate to enter Brookland (a suburb of the central city) despite the presence of a few middle-class Negro families. (R. C. Weaver, *The Negro Ghetto*, pp. 290–91.) As Negro incomes rose in the District of Columbia, an increasing number of middle-class colored families moved into Brookland but, until World War II, it remained a racially mixed area. By 1952, non-whites had penetrated adjoining Woodridge and Michigan Park, areas of white middle-class occupancy. The official organ of the Rhode Island Avenue Citizens' Association exhorted whites to remain in Woodridge. (Weaver, "Relative Status of the Housing of Negroes in the United States," *Journal of Negro Education*, Summer 1953, pp. 351–52). But the combined force of the pent-up non-white demand for good housing and the lure of the suburbs in surrounding Maryland and Virginia for whites was too much. Today Brookland is largely Negro, Woodridge and Michigan Park house many non-white families, and Brookland's Negroes are no longer almost exclusively middle-class. The new prestige area for Washington's middle-class Negro families is in the far Northwest, where a relatively few reside among white neighbors.
[29] See Gus Turberville, "The Negro Population of Duluth, Minnesota, 1950," *Sociology and Social Research*, March-April, 1952, pp. 231–38; Arnold M. Rose, Frank J. Atelsek and Laurence R. MacDonald, "Neighborhood Reactions to Isolated Negro Residents; An Alternative to Invasion and Succession," *American Sociological Review*, October 1953; Davis McEntire, "A Study of Racial Attitudes in Neighborhoods Infiltrated by Non-Whites," *Bay Area Real Estate Report* (San Francisco), Second Quarter 1955, pp. 126–29.
[30] Those who insist on this will probably move to the suburbs anyway.

as well as some of lower-incomes.[31] The class and racial mix will vary from new urban redevelopment sites, partial redevelopment and rehabilitation efforts, and conservation areas. The greatest flexibility is in the newly reconstructed redevelopment areas—if for no other reason because new areas and new houses have a snob appeal in themselves.

Proximity to an established blighted non-white slum complicates or deters white occupancy in redevelopment projects. Either large-scale demolition, or extra value for the housing dollar, or both are required to offset this circumstance. Chicago illustrates well this situation. The New York Life Insurance Company financed and constructed Lake Meadows, a large redevelopment, medium-cost rental project in the heart of what had been some of the worst of the city's Negro slums. Although it announced open occupancy from the start and, despite the scope of the redevelopment and its inherent desirable location in relation to downtown and in proximity to city-wide health and educational institutions, the attractive new facilities failed to appeal to a large number of white tenants.[32] Intensive efforts and tangible evidences of a new neighborhood achieved 20 percent white occupancy and, currently, 25 percent of the tenants are white.

Prairie Shores was subsequently constructed on the site of a former Negro slum and on the edge of the Negro ghetto. But it was adjacent to Lake Meadows and the upgrading of the neighborhood was well under way. Indeed, the promotion of Prairie Shores describes it as "an entirely new community immediately adjacent to the Michael Reese Hospital campus." In the words of its developer—who incidentally evidenced his commitment to the project by selling his house in the suburbs and moving into Prairie Shores—"people just recognized a hell of a good buy when they saw it." The nature of this buy is indicated by the fact that apartments rented for an average of $33 a room as against $45 to $65 for comparable new accommodations elsewhere in the city. And the first 342 units in the initial structure of this five-building development rented quickly. Seventy-seven percent of the occupants were white but most households were childless and none had children of high school age.[33] As of May 1960, two buildings in Prairie Shores had been completed. Both were fully rented and leases were being signed on a third which will be ready for occupancy in

---

[31] For an analysis of the experience of builders of interracial private developments during the last decade, see Eunice and George Grier, *Privately Developed Interracial Housing* (Berkeley, California: University of California Press, 1960).

[32] Lake Meadows is located on a 100-acre site and rented initially from $30 per room per month—about a quarter less than comparable accommodations elsewhere in the city. The first building of slightly less than 600 units attracted only about three percent white tenants. Subsequent special efforts appreciably increased white participation. (Eunice and George Grier, *op. cit.*, pp. 106–7).

[33] "Open Occupancy Builder Lands 77% White Tenants," *House and Home*, March 1959, p. 76.

in late summer. The racial mix remained about 80 percent white and, while few families with school-age children were in occupancy, there were many with pre-school children.

With rare exceptions a small island of medium-cost redevelopment housing in a sea of non-white slums will not attract whites. This was the experience of the attractive—but not relatively competitively-priced—Longwood Redevelopment in Cleveland. An exception was the reasonably priced (single-family, sales house) and slow moving redevelopment project in Richmond, California.[34] On the other hand, redevelopment in an area which is fairly large and marked for total treatment can attract middle-class whites when a minority of non-whites are housed in it. This has been demonstrated in architecturally attractive Capitol Park Apartments of the Southwest Redevelopment in Washington, D. C., and in the Gratiot Redevelopment in Detroit. Both of these are fairly high-rent and that fact alone has greatly limited non-white participation.

Partial redevelopment and rehabilitation present more difficult problems. In the first place, frequently the old neighborhood which is the symbol of the threat of lower-class and minority families is not destroyed. Even if a new type of area is planned the physical evidences of the old remain. Where, as in the area around the University of Chicago, there is a sizeable amount of good housing and an enduring institutional base, the possibilities of success are enhanced. The urban renewal plan for the West Side of New York,[35] which also involved spot clearance and a great amount of rehabilitation, is also favorably located. On the north is a large middle-income redevelopment project partially occupied and nearing completion, on the east an attractive predominantly upper middle-class residential strip on Central Park West, on the south a middle-class strip on 86th Street, and on the west a traffic artery.

In the Chicago and New York projects there has been great controversy as to how much public housing will be provided. In both instances the amount has been limited so that low-income families will be a definite minority of those in the areas. New York's West Side will also have a sizeable amount of lower medium-rent facilities or reasonably priced cooperatives, but most of the shelter will be priced so as to attract middle-income households. There is no question that both the New York and the Chicago neighborhoods will be predominantly middle class. Both will have some nonwhite, low-income families and some non-white, middle-income households. But they will be predominantly middle- and upper-income white communities.

[34] "Pilot Project Survives FHA Red Tape, Starts Blighted Area on Road Back," *House and Home*, February 1959, p. 59.
[35] *Urban Renewal* (New York: New York City Planning Commission, undated) and *West Side Urban Renewal Area* (New York: Urban Renewal Board, 1959).

Since conservation areas are subjected to the least amount of physical change, they share characteristics with most of the standard areas of existing housing. While the structures in such areas of the old city may be imposing in size and appearance, frequently they are architecturally obsolete. This may occasion new property uses—rooming houses, conversions to apartments of varying degrees of adequacy, or other forms of multi-family occupancy. Seldom are they suited for small families and their utilization by low-income households usually involves undesirable economic and social consequences.

In some instances the location of conversion areas (in terms of proximity to present concentrations of non-white families) inspires acute fear of minority inundation on the part of present residents. Thus, the possibility of panic selling is real and immediate upon the entrance of non-whites. There is another complicating factor. Present residents of these areas have not elected to live with non-white neighbors. The latter have come in after the neighborhood has been established as a racially homogeneous one. Thus there may be a feeling on the part of old residents that they had lost the opportunity to exercise freedom of choice in selecting non-white neighbors. In this regard they differ from those who move into a new or existing bi-racial community.[36] The physical attributes of conservation areas and the process of change involved in establishing racial mixture complicate the process in such neighborhoods.

Thus conservation areas present perplexing problems to those who would attract and hold middle-class whites in the central city. At the outset it must be recognized that many parts of the core city are destined to be occupied by non-whites. Under present conditions they will provide the almost sole supply of housing for Negroes and other non-whites who seek better shelter and are achiveing or have achieved sufficiently high earnings to pay for it. In addition, if the past is any indication of the future, many areas of this type will, should they lie in the path of the geographic expansion of existing racial ghettos, be occupied by house-hungry lower-income non-whites.

The degree to which low-income minority families enter these areas depends upon several things. If there is an alternative supply of good housing which better fits the family needs and pocketbooks of non-whites, the process will be delayed. If housing and occupancy standards are

[36] Henry G. Stetler, *Racial Integration in Private Residential Neighborhoods in Connecticut* (Hartford, Connecticut: Connecticut Commission on Civil Rights, 1957) pp. 72–5. Of course, as has been observed, when one buys or rents in any neighborhood, one has no vested right in its composition. This was emphatically delineated by the 1948 decision of the Supreme Court which outlawed judicial enforcement of race restrictive housing covenants and in the rise of nondiscrimination housing legislation. As a practical matter, however, many people do react to what they consider their freedom of choice in this regard and nothing in the law prevents families from moving away from neighbors they do not like.

enforced—a thing that is unlikely unless there is an alternative supply [37] —this too will slow up racial displacement. And of course the extent to which the central city becomes more attractive to whites will lessen the availability of such housing to non-whites. At the same time, however, the volume of migration of non-whites to urban centers will be a major factor in determining the demand for housing on their part. Finally, in proportion as we continue to concentrate upon clearing slums inhabited by non-whites the process of racial displacement will take place elsewhere in the city.

In recent years there has been a series of attempts on the part of middle-class neighborhoods to stay the departure of whites with the arrival of colored residents. To date, most if not all of these have been delaying tactics at best.[38] Perhaps if such efforts were a part of an over-all program involving new open-occupancy construction, action for spreading the non-white demand over a larger area of the central city, prevention of the engineering of panic selling by real estate operators, better enforcement of housing and occupancy codes and effective action to open the suburbs to non-whites, such programs might succeed in maintaining the bi-racial character of some well-located and attractive neighborhoods.[39]

THE ROLE OF GOOD SCHOOLS

Up to this point little has been said of family composition and its implications for middle-class residence in the central city. Most of the urban renewal projects mentioned are designed for small families and the most

---

[37] "For many years a high-class residential enclave around the University of Chicago, Hyde Park-Kenwood began developing pockets of slums, then found itself turning from a white to a Negro neighborhood. Concerted community action, with citizen participation on a scale perhaps unmatched in the nation, has done much to slow the drift toward blight. Moreover, the neighborhoods set out to do so on a deliberate interracial basis. . . . Leaders of the effort found out how to make the city government help them enforce decent living standards. But continuing Negro pressure for more housing raised doubts as to whether this unique and pioneering effort could succeed in the face of overwhelming odds. . . . By the end of 1955 physical conversion of apartments into cell-like slum structures . . . had been stopped cold. . . . But conversion by use— moving three or four families into one apartment—had not been stopped." (Martin Millspaugh and Gurney Breckenfeld, *The Human Side of Urban Renewal* (Baltimore, Maryland: Flight-Blight Inc., 1958), pp. 91 and 105–6.)
[38] *Loc. cit.* See also Mayer, *op. cit.*
[39] The same analysis applies to the use of quotas as a means of effecting and perpetuating interracial neighborhoods. Aside from the troublesome questions of their violation of fair housing laws, they do not offer permanent barriers against the economic pressure of a concentration of non-white demand on one or a few locations. (For a description of the case for quotas, see Oscar Cohen, "The Benign Quotas in Housing," *Phylon*, First Quarter (Spring) 1960, pp. 20–29.) My analysis suggests that benign housing quotas are as temporary a means of stabilizing bi-racial areas as race restrictive housing covenants were to do the opposite. For a discussion of the latter point, see Weaver, *The Negro Ghetto*, Ch. XIII.

successful of them house few young people of school age. A recent analysis of the demand for renewal and redeveloped housing in downtown Phila-delphia eliminates families with children as a source of occupants, sug-gesting that such families would gravitate to "the massive sections of slums and deterioration that lie beyond the central core."[40] There they would look for single-family houses or garden-type apartments.

Obviously, the needs and requirements of upper- and middle-income families without children are quite different from those who have young-sters. For the latter, schools are important. Among those of large incomes (and to some degree among the less prosperous) the possibility of using private schools may cause little concern for public educational facilities. In many northern cities parochial schools serve a similar purpose.[41]

Most knowledgeable observers consider schools a basic factor in attract-ing or holding middle-class families in the central city.[42] Indeed in the Russel Woods area of Detroit, concern for education of children seemed to be the most important element motivating liberal families to leave their desirable homes.[43] This too is often as much of a class as a racial phenomenon. In Cleveland, for example, middle-class Negroes entered the comfortable homes in the outlying Glenville section of the central city after World War II. More recently, as large numbers of low-income non-whites have entered the area, some of the earlier Negro residents have moved a second time, entering the more exclusive and prestige-laden Shaker Heights section. Many of those involved explain their action on the basis of the superior schools in the latter location. On the other hand, in Russel Woods and elsewhere, the existence of synagogues and other institutions related to Jewish life and religion was a strong factor in holding the white residents. Provision of similar facilities in the suburbs facilitated subse-quent departure of many of these families.[44]

One student of the racial aspects of housing has proposed abandonment of the rule requiring children to attend a neighborhood public school and provision of special facilities for the middle-class oriented families. Thus, heterogeneity in residential patterns would be purchased at the cost of

[40] Chester Rapkin and William G. Grigsby, *Residential Renewal in the Urban Core* (Philadelphia, Pennsylvania: University of Pennsylvania Press, 1960), p. 118.
[41] "A significantly high percentage of purchasers in nonhomogeneous 'mixed' areas have been found to be families who, if they had school-age children, were sending them to relatively homogeneous (Roman Catholic) schools." (*The Demand for Housing in the Eastwick Redevelopment Area*, Interim Report, June 1956, Table XXIV, p. 42 (Phila-delphia) cited by John W. Dyckman, "Comment on Glazer's School Proposals," *Journal of the American Institute of Planners*, November, 1959, footnote 2, p. 197.)
[42] "Studies . . . provide confirmation for the general hypothesis that in certain large northern cities, choice of school is at least as sensitive as choice of residence to the pull of 'homogeneity,' and for some may play an important part in residential choice." (Dyckman, "Comment on Glazer's School Proposals," *op. cit.*, p. 197).
[43] Albert J. Mayer, "Russel Woods: Change Without Conflict," *op. cit.*, pp. 215–16, 219.
[44] *Ibid.*, pp. 212, 216, 219.

homogeneity in public schools.[45] It has been pointed out that special schools of the type suggested might well fail to preserve or facilitate heterogeneity in residential patterns, reinforcing "islands of upper-income white occupancy in an ethnic sea of educational proletarianization." [46] In light of the growing political power of non-whites in northern urban areas such a consequence would sow the seeds of its own destruction—and that of urban renewal in the process.

Public schools are a symbol and an instrument of democracy. While their programs can and should be tailored to meet the needs of students, the whole trend in the nation, as dramatized by the Supreme Court decision of May 1954, is away from racial segregation. This of course is not to say that every child receives the same training but it does call for no arbitrary assignment to schools on basis of color or class. It is compatible with an open system which, within a given school, assigns pupils to educational programs which meet their needs, provided that the system is fluid and based upon some universally applied criteria for assignment. The latter must be a reflection of ability and not social status. The track system now in operation in Washington, D. C. is one which seems to meet these requirements.

But there is still another requirement. It is a system which avoids the implications or consequences of separate identification by tracks. This has been accomplished in one school on the West Coast where there are several curricula for students of differing aptitudes. However, all students of a given grade have a common homeroom or common homerooms, regardless of differences in educational programs. Such arrangement is not only productive of identification with a common institution for all but it is also compatible with the concept of a democratic public school.[47]

Just as most middle-class families, if they have an alternative, will not long remain in a neighborhood where they are a minority so they will not long send their children to a school where they are a minority. Middle-class whites with children will remain in the central city in large numbers only if they have access to a middle-class oriented, educationally satisfactory public school or can afford private or parochial schools. The degree of possible class and racial mix in a neighborhood is lessened, therefore, when school-age children are involved. It can be conceived however that as the number of stable bi-racial neighborhoods increases, tolerance for this type of living will grow. In light of the importance of prestige considerations in the selection of housing, it may well be that this process will be accelerated through the creation of attractive, newly

---

[45] Nathan Glazer, "The School as an Instrument in Planning," *Journal of the American Institute of Planners*, November 1959, pp. 191–6.
[46] J. W. Dyckman, "Comment on Glazer's School Proposals," *op. cit.*, p. 196.
[47] See James B. Conant, *The American High School Today*, New York: McGraw-Hill Book Company, 1959, p. 74.

constructed, racially mixed neighborhoods in the central city. The efficacy of the latter will be minimized as long as the suburbs remain essentially racially homogeneous.

Public schools in the central city cannot compete with their suburban prototypes on terms of the latter. The city public schools can never match the snob appeal of many suburban ones. Seldom can they assure the same degree of class or racial homogeneity nor can they equal the spaciousness of the surrounding campus. But they can be good schools. Indeed if they are specialized high schools concentrating on specific fields, they can be better schools. This is demonstrated by certain technical schools, fashion schools, and performing arts high schools in New York City. Emphasis must be upon high scholastic standards, adequate discipline in the school, and exploitation of the opportunities for cultural enrichment which urban life offers. While these potentialities will not be given a chance to flower if middle-class white parents feel that low-income and minority group children are to be a large element in the student body, they are possible of achievement in a city school which is not homogeneous. Proof of this is the effort prestige private schools have made for years to attract and enroll children of poorer parents and from non-white households. The administrations and parents of many of these schools lament the fact that such enrollment is not larger.

At the same time the central city public school has a unique character to sell—a degree of class and racial heterogeneity which will teach young people to live with other children of varying backgrounds.[48] Many middle-class families are acutely aware of the importance of this in a democracy; in the world today it has even more pressing international implications. Unfortunately, realization of its desirability is far from accepting situations in which there is heterogeneity.[49] This is due largely to fear that some class and racial mixture will lead to an inevitable lowering of academic and discipline standards and an ultimate minority status for white children in the school. It is also manifestation of apprehension lest there may be loss of social status in living in a predominantly non-white neighborhood or having one's children in a school with large Negro enrollment. If, however, the public school is geared primarily to the educational goals of middle-class-families, it can and will attract and hold many middle-class white children even though some lower-income and middle-class minority pupils are included.

[48] *Ibid.*, pp. 75–6.
[49] The inclination of liberal, middle-class white families to offer lip-service to the desirability of racial heterogeneity in schools results in some peculiar situations. Frequently, in an effort to establish the form of bi-racial student bodies, a few non-whites are either admitted or actively sought. This is most prevalent in private schools and the minority group students are "special" in more ways than the obvious. While potential guilt of liberal whites may be assuaged, the non-white symbol of integration may suffer from a forced and artificial gesture.

Another attraction which the school in the central city can have is to afford a richer and more meaningful education. This suggests delineation and exploitation of the educational advantages of the central city. The many cultural institutions located in the central city—its theatres, museums, concerts, and the like—are great assets. The school program should utilize fully and dramatically these facilities of the central city.

With all of this, there will be fear and apprehension on the part of middle-class parents. Over the long run, this can be met only as the living standards, opportunities, and assimilation of those least advantaged in the city are increased. Here too the public schools have a basic but not an exclusive role. In those areas where the schools serve large numbers of migrant, low-income, and minority families, programs need to be developed to accelerate their adjustment to urban life. Included among these are activities for remedial work, the discovery and nurture of talent, curriculum enrichment, reaching parents and involving them in community problems related to schools, and the preparation of teachers who understand the cultural problems involved.

All of these programs and activities will hold only some of the middle-class families now in the central cities. They will be more effective in attracting back to the city others who are exhausted or disillusioned with suburban life. But unless we begin now to deal with them, the trend of certain groups away from the city will continue—and probably at an accelerated rate. Certainly, in assessing the potential demand for medium-priced housing in the central city, an important variable is the success we have in creating and maintaining public schools which have an appeal to the families involved.

THE CLASS AND RACE MIX OF THE CITY TOMORROW

This analysis suggests that in northern and border cities there can be a degree of class and racial mixture compatible with attracting and holding middle-class whites. In the expensive and upper medium-rental apartments and sales houses this presents few problems of planning. The income structure assures only token participation by non-whites and of course eliminates the low-income group. If the desirable mix (from the point of view of maintaining large numbers of medium-income families) involves limited participation of low-income households, this too can be achieved be redeveloping or renewing areas large enough to establish their own identity and limiting the amount of low-cost housing. This however implies the responsibility for providing in attractive locations an adequate supply of low-cost units and cessation of such widespread dislocation of families as has typified urban renewal to date.

It is at the level of medium-cost housing that real problems arise. The non-white and particularly the Negro housing market includes a growing number of families ready, willing, and able to purchase or rent such shelter. If the market is open to them in only a few locations at any one time the "tipping point" may soon be reached in any one or two developments. As was indicated above, opening the suburbs to non-whites is one of the necessary prices for attracting and holding middle-income whites in the central city.[50]

Cessation of widespread dislocation of low-income families was suggested in the earlier discussion of high and upper-medium-cost housing. It was proposed there from the point of view of political expediency and equity. It is pertinent to the discussion of medium-cost housing for another reason. As long as large numbers of low-income families are uprooted by slum clearance they are a potential source for the displacement of middle-income families elsewhere in the community. This is especially true when they are colored and limited to a racially restricted market.

A final approach, applicable chiefly to conservation areas, is to perfect techniques for stabilizing racially transitional neighborhoods. To be effective they must be an element in a comprehensive program for expanding the supply of housing available to non-whites at all price levels. Also, it must be realized that there are some neighborhoods which, because of location in relation to the growth of areas of non-white concentration, will not respond to this treatment. This only illustrates that cities are not static institutions. Their physical facilities change and their people move. The problems of class and color can never be solved in any one neighborhood. Today they cannot be solved in the central city. They are problems of metropolitan areas.

If this analysis is valid, it has significance for the kind of cities we may expect in the next generation. While the size and squalor of slums may be decreased we shall not clear all of them. Poverty, rejection, and a certain amount of individual choice [51] will dictate their perpetuation. Through better schools—in terms of plant, quality of teaching and effective programs to reach low-income families—the economic and social status of many slum residents can be raised. If we perfect and apply techniques to give the newcomers a feeling of belonging and provide meaningful assistance to the normal as opposed to the problem family, there can be greater occupational, educational and residential mobility among this group. For these approaches to work, our urban populations will have to be less color-conscious; and anti-discrimination housing legislation affecting the suburbs

---

[50] This is a complex matter. It would operate as suggested above by (1) syphoning off some of the middle income demand for housing among non-whites from the central city; (2) removing the attraction of racial homogeneity from the suburbs; (3) reducing the snob appeal of racial exclusiveness since no area could assure it; (4) reducing the threat of "tipping" in any one racially open neighborhood.

[51] John R. Seeley, "The Slum: Its Nature, Use, and Uses," *Journal of the American Institute of Planners*, February 1959, pp. 7–14.

as well as central cities will be required. We need also to develop more tolerance to variations from established middle-class values and behavior.[52]

American urban centers will not soon, if ever, become a total of class and racial heterogeneous neighborhoods. Realistic and courageous planning, constant progress toward open occupancy, continued economic advancement on the part of the disadvantaged, progress in dealing with transitional neighborhoods, an expanding supply of housing suited to the family needs and pocketbooks of low-income and lower medium income households, good schools, and the development of techniques to upgrade at a reasonable cost much of the existing housing supply will enable our cities to develop and maintain neighborhoods with varying degrees of class and color heterogeneity. But most of these will be predominantly of one income level; some will be almost exclusively non-white; a few will have a small number of medium-income non-whites; and others will be integrated in varying degrees.

What of the central cities? They will survive. Indeed, their demise, largely on the same grounds cited as threatening them today, has been foretold many times in the past.[53] Of course, they will be different. For years to come they will have trouble attracting and holding middle-income white families with children. As long as there are private and parochial schools, some such households will remain. To the degree that redevelopment, renewal, and conserved neighborhoods, as well as areas which are left alone, become or continue to be identified as middle class, there will be middle-income whites with children in the central cities. Good public schools and other satisfactory public facilities will augment the number. Almost equally important will be the success we have in utilizing housing codes and other tools to raise the general level of housing, in developing realistic school programs to raise motivation and achievement in all schools, and in applying effective techniques for accelerating the occupational, residential, and social mobility of the growing number of newcomers who are entering and will continue to enter our cities.

[52] R. C. Weaver, "Human Values of Urban Life," *Proceedings of the Academy of Political Science*, June, 1960.
[53] Louis Winnick, *Facts and Fictions in Urban Renewal*, p. 18.

V. DESEGREGATION, INTEGRATION, AND ATTITUDE CHANGE

31. The Demography of Desegregation[*]

THOMAS PETTIGREW AND
M. RICHARD CRAMER

As late as the spring of 1965, only 2 per cent of all Negro public school students in the eleven states of the old Confederacy were attending desegregated classes. Therefore, even though the Civil Rights Act of 1964 calls for the desegregation of school districts, this selection by Pettigrew and Cramer is still timely. The article shows correlations between district desegregation by counties and a number of county characteristics. It indicates that degree of urbanism is directly correlated with desegregation,

[*] The authors wish to express their appreciation to the Harvard and Radcliffe assistants who aided immeasurably in preparing the data for machine processing: Miss Katherine W. Bolster, Mr. Richard S. Green, Mr. Peter Kane, Mr. Dennis S. O'Leary, Mr. James B. Peters, Mr. Richard D. Roark, Mr. John W. Sears, and Miss Anne Gayle Tanner.

SOURCE: *Journal of Social Issues*, Vol. 15, No. 4, 1959, pp. 61–71 (footnotes omitted and tables simplified). Reprinted by permission of the publisher and of the senior author.

Thomas L. Pettigrew is Associate Professor of Social Psychology in the Department of Social Relations at Harvard University. He is author of *A Profile of the Negro American*, and co-author of *Christians in Racial Crisis*. *M. Richard Cramer* is Assistant Professor of Sociology at the University of North Carolina.

354

while proportion of the Negro population is inversely correlated with it. A word of explanation for the reader unfamiliar with statistical methods: a correlation between two phenomena does not necessarily mean that either has caused the other; it means merely that they are associated. Correlational studies are often useful for calling attention to other related factors that may be more immediate causes of a phenomenon that is to be explained. For example, the proportion of a county's population that is Negro may be expected to exert great weight on the character of political participation and leadership there, and this factor, in turn, may have a more direct bearing on the county school system than does Negro population density as such.

Increasing evidence indicates that the South's pervasive pressures to conform to white supremacy norms form the principal factor underlying the region's racial intolerance (2, 11, 12, 15, and 16). This raises the problem of how these conformity pressures can be measured; one answer has involved the use of census materials.

One of the first demographic analyses of racial phenomena was made by the Southern Commission on the Study of Lynching (4, 17). The Commission's detailed investigation of the 21 lynchings of 1930 revealed that the areas with lynchings tended to be systematically different from those without lynchings. Later studies have successfully analyzed in demographic terms the patterns of segregationist voting in the South (6, 7, 8, 13). And, finally, census variables have been related to the school desegregation process in the border states (10), a project that has been extended and is more fully reported in this paper.

THE DEMOGRAPHY OF SOUTHERN RACIAL PHENOMENA

The factors that these demographic studies have consistently isolated as important in southern race relations can be conveniently catalogued into four interrelated classifications: variables related to (1) urbanism, (2) the Negro, (3) economic prosperity, and (4) traditionalism. Let us consider each of these separately.

URBANISM

Lynching, segregationist voting, and actual school desegregation are all closely linked to measures of urbanism. Thus lynching was a predominantly rural technique. Many southern cities have never had a recorded lynching[1]—e.g., Fayetteville in Arkansas; Durham, Wilmington,

---

[1] This is according to the Tuskegee Institute records of lynching since 1882.

and Winston-Salem in North Carolina; Amarillo and Austin in Texas; and Norfolk, Portsmouth, and Richmond in Virginia. And only one city, New Orleans (29 lynch victims since 1882), ranks among the areas of very high incidence.[2] Moreover, for a 30-year period in 14 southern states, the number of deaths by lynching per 10,000 population was inversely proportional to the size of the county; for example, a resident of a county of less than 10,000 people was in 60 times as much danger of being lynched as a resident of an urban county of 300,000 or more people (20).

Southern segregationist voting is generally related to urbanism, too. Ogburn and Grigg (8) noted that only 61% of the white voters in Virginian communities larger than 5,000 people, as opposed to 72% of other white voters in Virginia, supported a pro-segregationist issue in 1956. And after the effects of the Negro ratio variable are partialled out, urbanism is found to be negatively related to a 1956 Arkansas vote on segregation, though the correlation is small and not statistically significant (13).

Moreover, racist politicians in the South usually run better in the rustic regions than in the cities. Heer (6) has shown that Strom Thurmond's South Carolian vote by counties for president on the white supremist "Dixiecrat" ticket was positively related to the percentages of rural-farm whites ($+.37$); and Pettigrew and Campbell (13) have shown that Orval Faubus's vote by counties in the 1958 Arkansas gubernatorial primary was positively related to the percentages of rural-farm people in the county populations ($+.40$).[3] Key sums it up: "The growth of cities contains the seeds of political change for the South. In almost every type of analysis urban political behavior differs significantly from that of the rural areas. Apart from other political consequences of urbanism, cities seem to be less dominated in their political behavior than rural areas by consideration of the race question." (7, p. 673)

Cities are also more prepared to desegregate their public schools. A 1957 study (10) revealed that the county patterns of school desegregation in Kentucky and Missouri were highly associated with percentages of urban population. Thus *all* 24 counties in these states that were predominantly urban (50%+) had desegregated by May of 1957, while only about three-fourths of the partially urban (1%–49%) and slightly less than half of the totally rural counties had desegregated. Early school desegregation also occurred in the border cities of Washington, D.C. and Baltimore. And now, as the desegregation process creeps slowly into the middle South, token programs have started principally in the cities: Arlington, Norfolk, Charlottesville, Winston-Salem, Greensboro, Durham, Charlotte, Nashville, Fayetteville, and even Little Rock.

---

[2] Many of these victims in New Orleans, it should be noted, were white.
[3] The rural-farm correlation was only $+.17$ with the Faubus vote in the July 1954 gubernatorial primary when he made no antidesegregation appeal.

THE NEGRO

The relative numbers and condition of the Negro population in various areas are important data for all racial phenomena. Consider lynching again. Though the state of Mississippi as a whole and many Black Belt counties throughout the South have been the scene of a vast number of lynchings in absolute terms, the ratio of Negroes in the total population is actually *inversely* related to lynchings when they are calculated per 10,000 Negroes in the population (4, 17). That is, controlling for the size of the Negro community, counties with relatively few Negroes have tended to have the *highest* lynching rates. Early investigators thus concluded that the more stable and rooted racial traditions of the Black Belt acted as a paternalistic protection for the mass of Negroes who furnished the cheap labor required by the area's economy (4, 17).

But these same stable traditions make the Black Belt the bastion of segregationist sentiment. Again using the county as the unit of analysis, the Arkansas and Virginia segregationist votes correlated highly (+.64 [4] and +.67) with the Negro population percentages (8, 13). And the 1948 Thurmond presidential votes in Arkansas (7, p. 343) and in South Carolina (+.67; 6) and the 1958 Faubus gubernatorial primary vote in Arkansas (+.19; 13) also related positively with the proportions of Negroes in the population.

In addition, the two segregationist votes of 1956 in Arkansas and in Virginia were significantly associated with the county levels of Negro education. Even after the Negro percentage factor is partialled out, median years of Negro education correlates −.45 in Arkansas (13) and −.60 in Virginia (8) with pro-segregationist voting. Thus it is those counties with large percentages of relatively uneducated Negroes that form the core of racist political power in the South.

The Negro ratio variable promises to be of importance in the school desegregation process, too. Even in rural Kentucky, an area sparsely populated by Negroes, the Negro ratio factor is associated with educational desegregation. Only half of the rural counties of Kentucky with 6% or more Negroes had started desegregating their public schools by May of 1957, but over two-thirds of those with less than 6% had started (10). A similar trend is not discernible, however, in rural Missouri (10), a border-state with even fewer rural Negroes than Kentucky.

The crucial importance of these Negro variables is amplified by a number of additional studies. For instance, Blalock (3) has demonstrated that severe racial discrimination in many forms is centered in the Black Belt. Negro-white disparities in housing, education, and income are all

---

[4] As opposed to the Pearsonian coefficients routinely reported, this is a Kendall rank correlation coefficient.

correlated highly and positively with the non-white percentages of counties. That this blanket suppression is due in large degree to the steep traditionalism of the Black Belt is suggested by a variety of investigations. Dornbusch and Irle (5) have shown that the 1955 vote by presbyteries of the southern Presbyterians *against* union with the northern Presbyterians was correlated +.57 with the non-white percentages of the general population. And Key (7, p. 320) and Price (14, pp. 35–54) have both noticed southern counties with relatively few Negroes that politically behave quite similarly to the Black Belt; upon closer scrutiny, both observers discovered that these counties had usually had large numbers of Negroes before migration radically changed the scene. In short, the traditional, anti-Negro norms of the Black Belt are the important factor; these norms can even cling on in an area long after the county's racial condition has changed.

And these Black Belt norms have sharp effects on individual attitudes. One study randomly sampled white adults in four small southern towns, two in the Black Belt (38% and 45% Negroes) and two outside of it (10% and 18% Negroes). Respondents in the Black Belt were significantly more anti-desegregation (9) and more anti-Negro (11) than the other Southerners. Of particular interest, too, is the fact that these two groups of Southerners were *not* significantly different in their authoritarian, F-scale responses (11).

ECONOMIC PROSPERITY

Poverty has long been a southern fact of life. But when an area in the South does become more prosperous, it begins to enter the mainstream of American culture and all indices of race relations improve. Such prosperity, of course, is closely related to the other classifications—urbanism, the Negro, and traditionalism—but it is helpful to review the effects of economic variables directly.

The counties in which the 1930 lynchings occurred were generally very poor. Relative to their states' averages, these counties tended to be deprived in terms of *per capita* tax valuation, *per capita* bank deposits, *per capita* farm and factory income, farm ownership, and automobile ownership (4, 17).

Similarly, the economically backward areas tend to vote more heavily for segregation and racist candidates. In Virginia, the 1956 segregationist voting was correlated negatively with white family income (−.45) and positively with the percentage of families making less than $2,000 in 1949 (+.32, 8). In South Carolina, Thurmond's 1948 Dixiecrat support came largely from counties with relatively small percentages of non-farming whites in manufacturing (−.53, 6). These variables are not as clearly associated, however, with the 1956 and 1958 Arkansas votes, for rural prosperity is associated with high percentages of Negroes in Arkansas (13).

In both Kentucky and Missouri, the economically prosperous areas tended to desegregate their public schools first. Totally rural counties that had started their educational desegregation programs by May of 1957 had significantly larger family incomes, more manufacturing, more valuable farms, and greater proportions of homes with central heating and mechanical refrigerators than totally rural, segregated counties (10). Poverty breeds resistance.

TRADITIONALISM

Sections of the South that are rural, heavily Negro, and poor tend to be the most traditional, particularly in regard to race. So this classification, too, is by no means independent of the others.

Previously we noted that the *less* traditional areas tended to have the highest lynching rates, once the size of the Negro population is controlled. Lynching was typically a substitute for rooted racial norms; relative rates were highest in the "fringe" states, Florida, Oklahoma, Arkansas, and Texas, and lowest in the long-established "Old South" states, South Carolina, North Carolina, and Virginia.

In an effort to measure traditionalism statistically, investigators have employed two variables—population change and the percentage of white women in the labor force. A stagnant area, losing population over the years, is assumed to be undergoing fewer pressures for social change than a rapidly expanding area. Likewise, an area that has relatively few of its white women employed is assumed to be more traditional because of the historically-rooted sanctions in the South against white women formally entering the labor force. Population increase from 1940 to 1950, for instance, has been noted to be moderately and negatively related to both the 1956 Virginia segregationist vote (8) and the 1958 Arkansas primary vote for Faubus (13). The proportion of white women in the labor force was also negatively related to the 1958 Faubus primary returns (13).

Moreover, totally rural counties in Kentucky and Missouri that had begun their school desegregation programs by May 1957 had tended to lose significantly fewer people from 1940 to 1950 than those counties that were still tightly segregated (10). Inasmuch as these variables tap traditionalism, it appears that the more traditional sections of the South vote more solidly for segregation and a candidate like Faubus and resist school desegregation more effectively.

DEMOGRAPHIC CHARACTERISTICS OF BORDER-STATE
SCHOOL DESEGREGATION

Many writers have discussed the importance of the "New South" on race relations. "The Shore Dimly Seen" in 1946 by Ellis Arnall (1), former Georgia governor and an ardent proponent of southern industrialization, is now coming clearly into view. Urbanization, industrialization, and migration have been radically changing the face of the South. Indeed, these processes have been so rapid as to be disruptive; Vander Zanden (18, 19) has noted how this social disruption leads to virulent forms of resistance to racial equality.

But our brief review of demographic studies of race reveals the long-predicted, broader picture. It is the poor, traditional, rural areas with large percentages of uneducated Negroes that form the tinder for racial conflict. The very consistency of this pattern for a variety of racial phenomena suggests its use as a predictive instrument for school desegregation. This is a preliminary report of efforts to develop demographic formulae for the county-by-county order of accomplished educational desegregation.

One of the first findings was that each state has to be analyzed separately. Apparently, the political leadership of the various states differs so widely in respect to race relations that county-by-county predictions across states is impossible. Further, the demographic characteristics of the southern states vary sharply.

A county is defined as "desegregated" when at least one of its previously all-white public schools enrolls a Negro student. And all counties with less than 100 Negroes in 1950 are eliminated from the sample. With these criteria, five border states—Texas, Oklahoma, Missouri, Kentucky, and West Virginia—had a sufficient degree of school desegregation and enough counties to be examined in detail.

Twenty-two variables, all of them tapping one or more of the previously discussed classifications, were initially tested against the county order of public school desegregation in each of the five states.[5] All of them yielded at least modest relationships in the expected direction for most of the states. But the basic two variables of previous research were again found to be important: urban percentage and non-white percentage. Table 1 shows how these two measures, split crudely at their medians, are related to the first year of school desegregation in each of the tested states. With but one reversal, high urban-low Negro ratio counties tend to integrate the earliest, mixed counties are intermediate, and low urban-high Negro ratio counties are the latest.

---

[5] These twenty-two variables were: percentage of urban dwellers, percentage of rural-farm dwellers, population of county's largest town, absolute number of Negroes, percentage of Negroes, median years of education of Negroes over 24 years of age, percentage of Negroes in the professions, Negro sex ratio, Negro median family income, white median family income, racial differential in median family income, median family income (both races combined), percentage of dwellings with central heating, percentage of dwellings with mechanical refrigerators, percentage of labor force in medical services, percentage of labor force in manufacturing, percentage of labor force in non-traditional industry (i.e., metal, mechanical, and chemical), percentage of white women in the labor force, percentage of population change from 1940 to 1950, median age of population, percentage of population either widowed or divorced, and percentage of people living in same dwelling in 1950 as in 1949.

Table 1: Counties with Some School Desegregation during the First Year [1]

	High Urban, Low Negro Ratio [2]		Low Urban–Low Negro Ratio and High Urban–High Negro Ratio Combined		Low Urban, High Negro Ratio	
		(N)		(N)		(N)
Texas	28%	(64)	8%	(61)	0%	(58)
Oklahoma	77%	(13)	87%	(31)	59%	(17)
Missouri	80%	(10)	74%	(35)	46%	(11)
Kentucky	60%	(15)	15%	(59)	0%	(18)
West Virginia	75%	(8)	47%	(19)	22%	(9)

[1] "First year" refers to the first year that any school desegregation took place within the state. This was 1954 for Missouri and West Virginia, and 1955 for Texas, Oklahoma, and Kentucky.

[2] "High" and "low" refer to the median splits for each state considered separately.

For more precise analyses, multiple regression methods are employed. Again, the county is the unit of analysis and each state a separate problem. The dependent variable, educational desegregation, is measured in terms of the year it occurred. Thus counties that desegregated at least one school during the state's first year of desegregation are assigned "1," during the second year a "2," and so on till those counties still segregated are arbitrarily assigned the next year that they could possibly desegregate.[6]

In addition to urbanism (U) and Negro ratio (NR), two other independent variables were tried in the final analyses: percentage of white women in the labor force (WWLF) and non-traditional industry (NI). In order to approximate normal distributions, a square root plus one transformation was performed on all four of these variables in all five states.[7]

Tables 2 and 3 present the correlational results. Once more, we see that the urban and Negro ratio percentages relate consistently to date of desegregation (Table 2). With coefficients ranging from —.13 in West Virginia to —.39 in Missouri, high urbanism relates to early desegregation.

[6] Improvements in future analyses can be made by using a somewhat different scoring scheme for desegregation. For instance, it is more realistic to assume that still-segregated counties will take four or five years, rather than one year, to alter their policies. Future work will thus increase the desegregation variance by randomly assigning still-segregated counties to a number of future years.

[7] This transformation led to satisfactory distributions with all of the predictor variables save urbanism. A considerable number of counties in each of the states are entirely rural and tend to skew the urbanism distributions. As a test of the effects of this property, Texas was analyzed completely in two different ways: once with all 182 counties of 100 or more Negroes, and once without the all-rural counties (leaving 148 counties). The results of the two analyses were extremely similar.

Table 2:   Demographic Correlations with Date of School Desegregation

DATE OF SCHOOL DESEGREGATION WITH . . .

	N	Urb.[1]	N–R	Urb. & N–R	WWLF	N–I	Urb., N–R & WWLF	Urb., N–R & N–I
Texas	182	—.27‡	+.40‡	.445‡	—.24†	—.05	.452‡	.446‡
Oklahoma	61	—.17	+.32*	.389†	—.33†	—.27*	.472†	.468†
Missouri	56	—.39†	+.36†	.591‡	—.43†	—.06	.629‡	.599‡
Kentucky	92	—.30†	+.17	.413‡	—.26*	—.40‡	.445†	.464‡
West Virginia	36	—.13	+.49†	.526†	—.11	—.37*	.557†	.553†

[1] "Urb." refers to the percentage of urban population; "N–R" to the Negro ratio; "WWLF" to the percentage of white women in the labor force; and "N–I" to non-traditional industry's percentage of the total labor force.
* Significantly different from zero correlation at the 5% level of confidence.
† Significantly different from zero correlation at the 1% level of confidence.
‡ Significantly different from zero correlation at the .1% level of confidence.

Table 3:   Partial Correlations[1] with Date of School Desegregation

DATE OF SCHOOL DESEGREGATION WITH . . .

	N	Urbanism	Negro Ratio	White Women in the Labor Force
Texas	182	—.12	+.37‡	—.08
Oklahoma	61	+.03	+.34†	—.29*
Missouri	56	—.24	+.49†	—.27*
Kentucky	92	—.19	+.34†	—.18
West Virginia	36	—.31	+.55†	+.22

* Significantly different from zero correlation at the 5% level of confidence.
† Significantly different from zero correlation at the 1% level of confidence.
‡ Significantly different from zero correlation at the .1% level of confidence.
[1] Each correlation is a partial correlation, holding constant the effects of the other two predictor variables.

And with coefficients ranging from .17 in Kentucky to .49 in West Virginia, high concentrations of Negroes relate to late desegregation. Urbanism and Negro ratio, when combined, yield multiple coefficients ranging from .389 to .591.

In an effort to improve this two variable relationship, the white women in the labor force and the non-traditional industry measures were added. The latter does not relate to desegregation in Texas and Missouri, and fails to improve the urban-Negro ratio multiple coefficients in those states.

WWLF, however, relates consistently to desegregation in all five states and tends to raise somewhat the multiple coefficients, particularly in Oklahoma.

Table 3 sheds further light on these relationships by providing the partial correlations of U, NR, and WWLF with desegregation. Save for Texas, the NR coefficients all rise when U and WWLF are controlled, but both the U and WWLF coefficients tend to shrink. The reasons for this become clear after inspection of Table 4's intercorrelations between the

Table 4: Intercorrelations of Prediction Variables

	N	Urb.–[1] N–R	Urb.– WWLF	Urb.– N–I	N–R.– WWLF	N–R.– N–I	WWLF.– N–I
Texas	182	—.21†	+.62‡	+.37‡	—.15*	—.01	+.37‡
Oklahoma	61	+.14	+.68†	+.49†	+.01	+.17	+.50†
Missouri	56	+.19	+.69‡	+.26*	+.12	—.06	+.33*
Kentucky	92	+.34†	+.71‡	+.46‡	+.45‡	—.11	+.49‡
West Virginia	36	+.13	+.73‡	+.64‡	—.17	—.24	+.76‡

[1] "Urb." refers to the percentage of urban population; "N–R" to the Negro ratio; "WWLF" to the percentage of white women in the labor force; and "N–I" to non-traditional industry's percentage of the total labor force.
* Significantly different from zero correlation at the 5% level of confidence.
† Significantly different from zero correlation at the 1% level of confidence.
‡ Significantly different from zero correlation at the .1 level of confidence.

predictor variables. First, two types of demographic patterns emerge. In Texas, the more typical southern pattern involving significant concentrations of rural Negroes results in a negative relationship between urbanism and Negro ratio. This means that the combined predictive power of these two variables is reduced in our desegregation problem. Note in Table 2 how the addition of urbanism with the Texas data raises the Negro ratio—desegregation coefficient from +.40 to only .445. For the other four states, positive associations exist between these two key variables. Thus, we need to develop at least two different basic formulae for predicting future school desegregation in the middle and deep southern states.

Note, too, in Table 4 that WWLF is highly related to urbanism, from +.62 to +.73. This explains why the partial correlations of these variables with desegregation were typically lower in Table 3 than the raw correlations of Table 2.

Table 5 presents the beta weights for the three-variable predictions of school desegregation. Urbanism, with standard deviations roughly four times the size of those for NR and WWLF, has consistently negative and small weights, save for the Oklahoma data. Negro ratio has consistently

Table 5:   Regression Weights for Three-Variable Prediction of Desegregation

RAW BETA WEIGHTS FOR . . .

	N	Multiple R	Urbanism	Negro Ratio	White Women in the Labor Force
Texas	182	.452	—.025	+.113	—.107
Oklahoma	61	.472	+.006	+.120	—.273
Missouri	56	.629	—.047	+.238	—.258
Kentucky	92	.445	—.053	+.250	—.218
West Virginia	36	.557	—.045	+.200	+.136

positive weights. And WWLF has negative weights, save for a reversal with the West Virginia data. But the multiple coefficients provided by these three predictor variables are still only moderately large, ranging from .445 to .629. Further work is now underway to find new variables and develop better predictive formulae on the border-states before applying the work to the rest of the South.[8]

APPLICATION OF PRELIMINARY FORMULA TO MARYLAND

Though further work needs to be done, a validating test of the present preliminary formula has been made on the school desegregation pattern of Maryland. This border-state was left out of our original analyses because it has only 23 counties with 100 or more Negro residents. But there is considerable desegregation variance in Maryland; the process began in 1954 in the city of Baltimore, and the state still has (at this writing) nine totally segregated counties.

Many of Maryland's rural counties have concentrations of Negroes. Consequently, for the 23 Maryland counties analyzed, there is, as in Texas, a negative correlation (—.48) between the urban and Negro percentages. Hence, the beta weights for Texas (Table 5) were employed for Maryland. Surprisingly, the resulting correlation between the county scores and the actual desegregation pattern is higher than the previous correlations—.72.

One explanation of this higher coefficient is that Maryland's desegregation pattern provides greater variance than the other five border-states. This suggests that higher relationships may be found in the future for the middle and deep South states, all of which seem likely to have a slower and more protracted school desegregation process than the border South.

[8] Predictions for the middle-South, where the desegregation process is just now beginning, must await the 1960 census data.

SUMMARY

Many observers of southern race relations are particularly impressed by the importance of conformity pressures on the attitudes and behavior of individual Southerners. Yet these pressures vary widely in intensity throughout different parts of the South. This paper has offered demographic variables as a method of measuring these cultural pressures to conform and of studying their intra-regional variance.

A brief review is presented to indicate the demographic consistency of such southern racial phenomena as lynching, segregationist voting, and school desegregation. Repeatedly we have found these racial indices to be closely related to variables tapping urbanism, the Negro, economic prosperity, and traditionalism. More specifically, it is the poor, traditional, rural areas with large percentages of uneducated Negroes that form the core of racial conflict.

Taking the cue from this earlier work, a preliminary report is made of current efforts to predict the school desegregation patterns in the border-states. Five states are analyzed separately (Texas, Oklahoma, Missouri, Kentucky, and West Virginia), using counties with 100 or more Negroes in 1950 as the units of analysis. Three-variable multiple coefficients, employing urbanism, Negro ratio, and white women in the labor force as measures, varied from .45 to .63. An application of a tentative regression equation to Maryland's desegregation pattern resulted in an even higher relationship—.72.

Further refinement of these border-state analyses will be made; then, after the publication of the 1960 census data, demographic predictions of school desegregation in the middle-South states will be undertaken.

References

1. Arnall, Ellis G. *The Shore Dimly Seen.* New York: Lippincott, 1946.

2. Black, Percy & Atkins, Ruth D. Conformity versus prejudice as exemplified in Negro-white relations in the South: some methodological considerations. *Journal of Psychology,* 1950, 30, 109–121.

3. Blalock, H. M., Jr. Per cent non-white and discrimination in the South. *American Sociological Review,* 1957, 22, 677–682.

4. Commission on the Study of Lynching. *Lynchings and What They Mean.* Atlanta: Commission on the Study of Lynching, 1931.

5. Dornbusch, S. M. & Irle, R. D. The failure of Presbyterian union. *The American Journal of Sociology,* 1959, 64, 352–355.

6. Heer, D. M. The sentiment of white supremacy: an ecological study. *The American Journal of Sociology,* 1959, 64, 592–598.

7. Key, V. O. *Southern Politics.* New York: Knopf, 1949.

8. Ogburn, W. E. & Grigg, C. M. Factors related to the Virginia vote on segregation. *Social Forces*, 1956, 34, 301–308.

9. Pettigrew, T. F. Desegregation and its chances for success: northern and southern views. *Social Forces*, 1957, 35, 339–344.

10. Pettigrew, T. F. Demographic correlates of border-state desegregation. *American Sociological Review*, 1957, 22, 683–689.

11. Pettigrew, T. F. Regional differences in anti-Negro prejudice. *Journal of Abnormal and Social Psychology*, 1959, 59, 28–36.

12. Pettigrew, T. F. Social psychology and desegregation research. *American Psychologist*, in press.

13. Pettigrew, T. F. & Campbell, E. Q. Faubus and segregation: an analysis of Arkansas voting. *Public Opinion Quarterly*, 1960, 24, 426–447.

14. Price, H. D. *The Negro and Southern Politics*. New York: New York University Press, 1957.

15. Prothro, E. T. Ethnocentrism and anti-Negro attitudes in the deep South. *Journal of Abnormal and Social Psychology*, 1952, 47, 105–108.

16. Prothro, E. T. Social psychology of the South: challenge without response. *Journal of Social Issues*, 1954, 10, 36–43.

17. Raper, Arthur F. *The Tragedy of Lynching*. Chapel Hill: University of North Carolina Press, 1933.

18. Vander Zanden, James W. The Klan revival. *The American Journal of Sociology*, 1960, 65, 456–462.

19. Vander Zanden, James W. Desegregation and social strains in the South. *Journal of Social Issues*, This issue.

20. Young, Earl F. The relation of lynching to the size of political areas. *Sociology and Social Research*, 1928, 12, 348–353.

32. Education, Prejudice, and Discrimination: A Study in Readiness for Desegregation

MELVIN TUMIN, PAUL BARTON,
AND BERNIE BURRUS

The previous selection demonstrated that rates of desegregation could be accounted for in terms of the demographic characteristics of political units as wholes. The following paper, in contrast, identifies characteristics of

SOURCE: *American Sociological Review*, 23, 1958, pp. 41–49. Reprinted by permission of the American Sociological Association and of the senior author.

Melvin Tumin is Professor of Sociology and Anthropology at Princeton University and author of, among other works, *Desegregation*. At the time this paper was written Professor Tumin's collaborators were graduate students at Princeton University.

individuals *that affect their* attitudes *toward desegregation. In a North Carolina county known for its relative liberalism on racial matters (it has a Quaker background and is the seat of several colleges), the better-educated and more prosperous were less likely to have staunchly segregationist views. Later data from public opinion polls generally support these findings, for they show that throughout the South, the younger, better-educated, and higher-income groups are more likely than those who are older and less well off to think that school desegregation is inevitable. A more general, but perhaps even more relevant, finding was reported in a Gallup poll of May 23, 1965: in 1963, 61 per cent of white southern parents would have objected to sending their children to a school where a few of the students were colored, but by 1965 the proportion objecting had dropped to 37 per cent.*

Earlier notions of the relation between prejudice and discrimination held them to be closely interdependent. Discrimination, it was often assumed, was practiced by the prejudiced person and could not be eliminated except as prejudice was first removed.[1]

More recent research and theory have been very persuasive, however, in the suggestion that there exists between the attitude of prejudice and the action of discrimination a gap in which a variety of facilitating or inhibiting factors can be interposed. In short, between private feeling and public action there is room for the play of other factors which significantly influence the extent to which feeling will be translated into matching action or will be repressed on behalf of other values. Law, custom, conscience and informal community restraints are the types of factors which can and have been interposed.[2]

Even the most ardent advocates of legal action will admit, however, that it is questionable how enduring or stable are purely legal restraints in preventing the translation of prejudice into discrimination. Unless deeper commitments oppose prejudices, one must be seriously concerned.[3]

Yet we also know that prejudice will not easily, if ever, yield to the

---

[1] For a thorough review of the major viewpoints, see G. W. Allport, *The Nature of Prejudice*, Cambridge, Mass.: Addison-Wesley, 1954. For more specialized surveys of related problems, see J. S. Brunner and R. Tagiuri, "The Perception of People" in Gardner Lindzey (ed.), *Handbook of Social Psychology*, Vol. II, pp. 634–654, Cambridge, Mass.: Addison Wesley, 1954; and J. Harding, B. Kutner, H. Proshansky and I. Chein, "Prejudice and Ethnic Relations," *ibid.*, pp. 1021–1061.

[2] For analysis of the "vicious circle" and the effectiveness of interpositions at various points, see, for example, R. K. Merton, "The Self-Fulfilling Prophecy," Chapter VII, in his *Social Theory and Social Structure*, Glencoe, Illinois: Free Press, 1949; and R. M. MacIver's *The More Perfect Union*, New York: Macmillan, 1948.

[3] The best full-length analysis of the role of law in ethnic relations is Morroe Berger's *Equality by Statute*, New York: Columbia University Press, 1952. See also his excellent article, "Desegregation, Law and Social Science," *Commentary*, 23 (May, 1957), pp. 471–477; and his *Racial Equality and the Law*, Paris: UNESCO, 1954.

blandishments of rational evidence. Nor is emotional re-education a feasible public alternative. We are therefore led to seek other factors which may be invoked to help counterbalance the impulses and drives generated by emotionally-rooted prejudices, and which may effectively modify behavior without necessarily altering the prejudices themselves. If these factors are to become instruments of public policy, they must be able to be developed reasonably quickly and at relatively low cost.

A clue is given to us by the studies of the impact of formal education upon behavior in a variety of contexts. For the literature is rich with suggestions that as formal education increases there tend to occur noticeable shifts from:

(a) nationalism to internationalism, in political point of view;
(b) traditionalism to secularism, in general social philosophy;
(c) common sense to science, as acceptable evidence;
(d) punishment to reform, in penological theory;
(e) violence and direct action to law, as agents of policy;
(f) rigidity to permissiveness, in child rearing;
(g) patriarchy to democracy, in spouse relationships;
(h) anesthesia to creativity, in patterns of recreation.

A common feature of these changes is that they imply the development of an awareness by the individual that there are: (a) other places than his own locality; (b) other times than the immediate present; (c) persons other than himself and his immediate primary group; and (d) other values he cherishes as ingredients of other aspects of his self. In brief, the individual who experiences these changes has enlarged his perspectives on time, place, person and values. This enlargement, the literature suggests, occurs somehow as a result of prolonged exposure to formal education. In other terms, it is apparently through this process of enlargement of perspective that formal education produces the changes cited.

It seems likely, moreover, that these larger perspectives develop without any necessary or matching reduction in the emotional sets against which they are posed. In sum, these are *countervailing perspectives*.

How do they work? We suggest that they serve to restrain the individual from acting upon blind and immediate impulse in search of immediate gratification of a limited number of values. They urge upon him a certain greater caution and deliberateness, and the importance of keeping an eye on the long as well as the short run of events. The psychic bookkeeping of such an individual is thus rendered more complex and more balanced with respect to his consideration of the number and variety of alternative values. By orienting the individual to the needs and wishes of others, and to the prevailing mores in communities other than his own, they increase the range of reference groups which will be taken into account in his plans of action. In short, these countervailing perspectives, developed during the course of formal education, help produce an increasingly mature and socially responsible individual.

COUNTERVAILING PERSPECTIVES AND ATTITUDES TOWARD DESEGREGATION

These notions regarding countervailing perspectives were developed in the course of our effort to understand and analyze the findings in a study of readiness for and resistance to desegregation conducted in Guilford County, North Carolina, in the fall of 1956. The overall purpose of the study was to discover the major variables associated with different degrees of readiness for and resistance to desegregation, particularly of the public schools as ordered by the Supreme Court ruling.[4]

Faculty members and students in a Seminar on Methods of Research* spent several months planning the study, including an inventory of the literature, preliminary trips of reconnaisance in North Carolina, establishment of liaison facilities with various persons at the University of North Carolina (particularly the personnel of the Institute for Research in Social Science), the drawing of an area probability sample, pilot testing and pretesting the questionnaire, and numerous meetings during which hypotheses were worked out, the interview largely precoded, and training conducted in techniques of interviewing. Consequently, the interviewing went smoothly, with a satisfactorily low loss through refusals, considerable rapport, little disturbed by the fact that the interviewers were almost all northern students questioning Southerners about a delicate and topical issue.

THE SAMPLE

The final sample drawn consisted of 341 households, expected to contain White male adults in the labor force, 18 years or older. Two hundred eight, about 70 per cent, of these were in the urban areas of the County, and 133, about 39 per cent, were rural. The research target was 300 completed interviews. Actually, 287 were completed, of which 183, about 64 per cent, were urban and 104, over 36 per cent, were rural. Thirty-eight

[4] The important roles played by several persons in the conception and conduct of this study must be mentioned. Stephen K. Bailey, Director of the Graduate Program of the Woodrow Wilson School, was the moving spirit behind the initial formulation of the project and provided valuable advice and support throughout. Professor George E. Simpson of the Institute for Research in Social Science at the University of North Carolina afforded us invaluable aid, as did several other members of the institute. Mr. Robert Cutler and Mrs. Leila Mattson have helped significantly in all phases of the study. Professor Warren Eason of the Department of Economics at Princeton shared the direction of the field phases of the study.

* Generous support was provided by the Woodrow Wilson School of Public and International Affairs at Princeton University, under a subvention of the Carnegie Corporation.

interviews were lost due to refusal; 26 households were lost because of the absence of any eligible person. A preliminary comparison of the sample including substitutes with what the sample would have been like had it included all those originally selected, reveals that there is little likelihood that the final sample differed in any relevant characteristics from the original sample.

A large number of variables were investigated for their relevance to attitudes toward desegregation. But this study will focus almost exclusively upon various measures of education, as they relate to desegregation.[5]

THE EDUCATIONAL GROUPS

The amount of education of each respondent was ascertained as the number of years of school completed. The individual years were coded as such, but aggregates of years were later combined for easier analysis. These aggregates or groups, whose differences were analyzed, were made up as indicated in Table 1.

Table 1: Education

Group Number	Years of School Completed	Number	Per Cent	Mean Number of Years	S.D.
I	1–8	103	35.88	6.22	1.66
II	9–12	105	36.58	10.69	1.14
III	13 or more	71	24.73	15.36	2.13

In the following discussion, Group I is sometimes referred to as the grammar school or lower-education group; Group II as the high school or medium education group; and Group III as the college or higher education group.

MEASURES OF READINESS

The concept of readiness, as used in this study, has five related aspects, whose meanings are given by the nature of the measures employed. These measures are intended to test the quality of the individual's orientation, as involving: (A) an Image of the Negro; (B) an Ideology which defines the ideal type of social relationship the individual would like, if possible,

---

[5] Other variables have been analyzed and reported. See Melvin M. Tumin, "Exposure to the Mass Media and Readiness for Desegregation," *Public Opinion Quarterly*, 21 (Summer, 1957); and Tumin and Robert Rotberg, "Leaders, the Led and the Law: A Case Study in Social Change," *Public Opinion Quarterly*, 21 (Fall, 1957), and Tumin, "Readiness and Resistance to Desegregation: A Social Portrait of the Hard Core" (in press). Other reports, not yet in press, include "Imaginary vs. Real Children: Some Southern Views on Desegregation," and "Status, Mobility and Anomie: A Study in Readiness for Desegregation."

to have with Negroes; (C) the Sentiments he states he would feel in certain hypothetical contacts with the Negro; (D) the Actions he thinks he would take when faced with those hypothetical contacts; and (E) the Actions he thinks he would take in *one* situation of possible contact, specifically the question of desegregating public schools.

We view the Image and the Ideology of the Negro, as held by the White, as being more closely related to prejudice than to readiness to discriminate. Alternatively, we see the General Action Set (Scale D) and the Specific Action Set (Scale E) as being more closely related to readiness to discriminate than to the feeling of prejudice.[6]

The measures as they were actually employed consisted of five sets of questions, as follows:

A. IMAGE OF THE NEGRO

Here we asked the respondent:

So far as intelligence is concerned, would you say that, compared to Whites, Negroes are by nature: [7]

[6] Our concept of "readiness" involved some real difficulties. It does not make much sense to talk of readiness to be prejudiced, but it does make a good deal of sense to talk about readiness to discriminate. In effect, then, our five-fold distinction implies that all of the five aspects are to some degree indicative of readiness to discriminate. But some phases, namely Image and Ideology, and, to a lesser degree, Sentiment Structure, are clearly more within the meaning ordinarily given to the term "prejudice." By contrast, General and Specific Action Sets ask for much more of a commitment to a plan of action than are called for by the other phases; i.e., we view the Action Sets as being closer to the discrimination end of the continuum.

More detailed analysis of the relationships among the scales will be undertaken in a later study, in which we will consider problems raised by treating the scale scores as absolute values, the correlation among the scales, and other related matters.

[7] We have been doubtful about whether or not the words "by nature" served to elicit from the respondent his actual opinion about the biological make-up of the Negro relative to the White. In some cases, when we probed—and we probed in all interviews—it was clear that the respondent was talking about present characteristics, without any necessary reference to inherited biological traits. In other cases, it was equally clear that a definite biological trait was the reference. In veiw of the mixed evidence, we are forced to remain uncertain about the respondents' meanings. It may be that the way in which the college group veers off from the other groups, once the questions on Ideology are posed, reflect a belief in biological inferiority held by the latter as against a belief in socially determined inferiority held by the former. We would not hesitate to offer this interpretation if it were not for the fact that when plans of action are asked for, the groups' responses are as similar as they were in their Images of the Negro. One can interpret this re-occurrence of homogeneity to mean that whether or not the belief in Negro inferiority is based on biological assumptions does not seem to matter as much as one might expect; òr, one may prefer the interpretation that the beliefs about Negro inferiority do not in fact imply the assumption of biological inheritance in view of the ways in which all the groups become relatively homogeneous in their plans of action. Still other interpretations are possible. But there is little point in spelling these out. However the responses to the questions of Image are interpreted, certain events transpire in responses to other questions which could not be predicted from a knowledge of the former. If we identify the questions on Image and Ideology as "prejudice" and those on Action Set as "readiness to discriminate," then we may conclude that prejudice is not predictive of readiness to discriminate in this sample.

(1) Superior to Whites.
(2) The same as Whites.
(3) Inferior to Whites.
(4) Don't know, can't say.
(5) No answer, no information.

The same question was asked concerning responsibility, morality and ambition. Responses indicating the Negro to be superior or the same as Whites were classified as desegregationist. Answers stating that the Negro is inferior to Whites, or that the respondent couldn't say or didn't know, were classified as segregationist. Tests for scalability revealed that the items roughly satisfied the requirements of a Guttman type scale, yielding a coefficient of reproducibility of 92.51.

B. SOCIAL IDEOLOGY

C. SENTIMENT STRUCTURE

D. GENERAL ACTION SET

These three measures were developed from responses to a sequence of questions, as follows:

> Now, Mr. X, I would like to ask you a few questions about kinds of situations in which you might find yourself, and ask you how you would feel about these things. For instance, suppose you were eating in a restaurant (cafe, bar, soda shop) here in (whatever town is appropriate). Suppose then a Negro comes in and sits down and wants to be served. Suppose the proprietor serves him.
>
> (1) How would you *feel* about this?
> (2) What would you *do?* (Explore if he would leave, force Negro to leave, etc.).
> (3) Does it matter at all what kind of Negro it happened to be?
> (4) Would it make a difference if it were a number of Negroes instead of one?
> (5) Suppose all this happened not here in (———) but in (———)? (A larger city in North Carolina was named as the alternative place.) What would you do then?
> (6) Suppose all this happened in New York City while you were there on a visit. Then what would you do? (Explore the "why" if he would do differently.)
> (7) In general, how do you feel about Negroes eating with Whites? What do you think should be the way in which facilities are set up in public places? (Get his picture of how he would like to see the particular relationship handled in general, if he could make it whatever he wanted it to be.)

Responses to question 7 were used to construct the measure of Social Ideology (B). Responses to question 1 formed the basis for the measure of Sentiment Structure (C). Responses to question 2 were used to make up the General Action Set (D).

Space limitations forbid detailed indication of the range of responses. But it can be said that we were fortunate in the small number of responses of dubious indication of pro- or anti-segregationist sentiment. In such cases we were able frequently to resolve doubts by the materials given in response to questions 3, 4, 5 and 6.

The same seven questions were then applied to the following situations: A Negro buys a house on the same block as the White; a Negro is hired at the same job classification and works next to the White; a Negro is hired as supervisor and the White works under the Negro's supervision; a Negro enters a bus and sits next to the White; a Negro applies for membership in the White's church; the White encounters a Negro as a dinner guest at the home of the White's friend; Negro students are enrolled in the schools attended by the White's children. Each of these situations was treated in the same fashion as the restaurant episode.

These situations were then conceived as scale items by asking whether or not they constitute an order of increasing difficulty for Whites to accept, or to respond to in a desegregationist fashion. In testing for scalability, we found that the responses to the questions about permitting a Negro to live on the same block and joining in dinner at a friend's house where a Negro had been invited fell too far above the 80–20 per cent split to be used in a scale. The other six items—restaurant, co-work, Negro supervisor, bus-riding, church membership, and common schools—were more nearly satisfactory as scale items, holding for all three measures—Social Ideology, Sentiment Structure, and General Action Set.

E. SPECIFIC ACTION SET

This final set of questions was focussed on the issue of desegregation of the public schools. Although questions referring to the schools were included in Scales B, C and D, we felt that much more could be learned about this most topical issue if we concentrated upon it more specifically. Accordingly, each respondent was asked the following:

> Now, Mr. X, I want to turn for one last look at the schools in particular. As you know, this is the situation most people are excited and concerned about these days. And so I would like to get your attitudes on this matter.

> (1) Some people have suggested that the Supreme Court Decision ordering desegregation was wrong and that the states ought to be permitted to decide for themselves on this question. The proposal

Table 2:   Mean Scores and Standard Deviations of Three Educational Groups
on Five Attitude Scales

		EDUCATION GROUP		
Scale	Scale Limits	(I) 1–8 Years	(II) 9–12 Years	(III) 13 or More Years
(A) Image of Negro	0–4	$\overline{X} = 2.82$ $\sigma = 1.56$	$\overline{X} = 2.79$ $\sigma = 1.53$	$\overline{X} = 2.57$ $\sigma = 1.61$
(B) Ideology	0–6	$\overline{X} = 4.73$ $\sigma = 1.56$	$\overline{X} = 4.17$ $\sigma = 1.85$	$\overline{X} = 3.01$ $\sigma = 2.38$
(C) Sentiment	0–6	$\overline{X} = 4.09$ $\sigma = 2.07$	$\overline{X} = 3.69$ $\sigma = 2.26$	$\overline{X} = 2.78$ $\sigma = 1.83$
(D) General action	0–6	$\overline{X} = 3.50$ $\sigma = 2.22$	$\overline{X} = 3.04$ $\sigma = 2.49$	$\overline{X} = 2.45$ $\sigma = 2.23$
(E) Specific action	0–4	$\overline{X} = 2.39$ $\sigma = 2.40$	$\overline{X} = 2.08$ $\sigma = 1.33$	$\overline{X} = 1.75$ $\sigma = 1.28$

is to go through the process of getting an amendment to the
United States Constitution to take power away from the Supreme
Court. How do you feel about this kind of proposal to try to
amend the U. S. Constitution?

(2) In Texas, the Governor has threatened to withhold state
school funds from any school district which desegregates the
schools, i.e., which permits Negro children to attend the same
schools as White children. How do you feel about withholding
state money from school districts here in North Carolina, if and
when any of these districts start letting Negro and White children
go to school together?

(3) Some people have suggested that if need be, the public schools
ought to be closed altogether rather than have Negro and White
children go to school together. How do you feel about this?

(4) Once in a while you hear it said too, that if need be, people
ought to get together and resist with force any attempts to mix
Negro and White children in the same schools. How do you feel
about this?

In each case the respondent was asked to indicate whether he would: (1)
Strongly approve, (2) Approve, (3) Undecided, (4) Disapprove, or (5)
Strongly disapprove. Tests for scalability of these four items again roughly
satisfied the criteria, yielding a coefficient of reproducibility of 95.65.

EDUCATION AND ATTITUDES
TOWARD DESEGREGATION

We can now compare and contrast our three educational groups in terms of their mean scores on the five scales described above.

Certain problems of interpretation are raised here by the fact that the scales differ in the total ranges, Scales A and E ranging from 0–4 and Scales B, C and D from 0–6. Conversion of the means into standard scores according to standard formulae for such conversions is a highly dubious procedure in view of the fact that the standard deviation of the means would be based on a very small N. One way to avoid this difficulty is to express the means as the per cent of the total range of each of the scales at which the mean falls. In Table 3 . . . the converted mean scores are presented.

Table 3: Means of Three Educational Groups on Five Scales Expressed as Fractions of Their Ranges *

		EDUCATION GROUP		
Scale	Scale Limits	(I) 1–8 Years	(II) 9–12 Years	(III) 13 or More Years
(A) Image of Negro	0–4	56.40	55.80	51.40
(B) Ideology	0–6	67.57	59.97	42.99
(C) Sentiment	0–6	58.43	52.71	39.71
(D) General action	0–6	50.00	43.43	35.00
(E) Specific action	0–4	47.80	41.60	35.00

* E.g., the mean for the 1–8 group on Scale A is actually 2.82, which is 56.40 of the distance from 0–4, where this is counted as a 5-point range. The mean for the same group on the B scale is 4.73, which is 67.57 of the distance between 0 and 6, where this is counted as a 7-point range.

With these converted scores, it becomes possible to see more clearly the relationships among the scores. The following findings are singled out for special attention:

(1) On all the scales, the mean scores decline as formal education increases. That is, the higher the formal education, the more favorable the attitude toward desegregation.

(2) For all three educational groups, the mean scores decline from Scale B through E, with the exception of the college group, whose scores on Scales D and E are identical, in terms of per cent of the scale range.

(3) The relative position of the score on Scale A, which measures the Image of the Negro, is different in all three cases. For the 0–8 group it is third highest among its five scores; for the 9–12 group it is second; and for the college group it is first. But this is also true of the relative position of the scores on the other scales. Thus the . . . rank orders [Table 4] emerge, expressed according to the descending order of resistance to desegregation.

If we interpret these rank orders as reflecting degrees of resistance to desegregation, then we note that the deepest resistances are located in different spheres for each of the three groups, while the greatest permissiveness concerning desegregation occurs at the same place for each of the groups. But this type of interpretation must be supplemented, if possible,

Table 4: Rank Order of Resistance to Desegregation for Three Educational Groups on Five Scales

	EDUCATION GROUP		
Rank Order of Scale Scores	(I) 1–8 Years	(II) 9–12 Years	(III) 13 or More Years
1 (high)	Ideology	Ideology	Image
2	Sentiment	Image	Ideology
3	Image	Sentiment	Sentiment
4	General action	General action	General action
5 (low)	Specific action	Specific action	Specific action

by some notion regarding the logical sequence of these aspects of the orientation of the White to the Negro. Our scales are lettered sequentially to express such a notion. That is, we see Scale A, the Image, as preceding all other aspects. This is followed by Scale B, the Ideology of social relations, which is based in part upon this Image. When we ask our respondents to express their Sentiments, Scale C, in hypothetical situations of contact, they are induced, we believe, to evoke their Image of the Negro and their Ideology of social relationships, along with such other matters as may now enter into their calculations. The sequence continues with the introduction of a General Action Set, Scale D, followed, finally, by Scale E, the Specific Action Set.

We are doubtful about this postulated sequence only at one point: the relationship between the last two items. For we recognize that our General Action Set may be as much an artifact of the observer as a verifiable aspect of the orientation of the respondent. It seems warranted to infer, however, that a generalized predisposition to action has a high priority in the organization of the psyche.

Proceeding, then, on the assumption of a logical sequence as postulated, our interpretation of the findings of Table 3 develops as follows:

(1) The 0–8 group is not substantially more prejudiced, in its Image of the Negro, then the other groups. But when faced with the question of the type of social relations it would consider desirable, it appears to add to its unfavorable Image a host of augmenting factors, perhaps proceeding from the fears it entertains regarding Negro status-improvement. This augmented unfavorable image of the Negro is expressed on Scale B in a relatively high rejection of the Negro as a social partner. Not only is the 0–8 group uninhibited in its Ideology of social relations by countervailing perspectives, but new factors in the situation deepen its resistance to desegregation.

(2) The 9–12 group expresses in its Ideology of social relations a milder version of this same process. For this high school group also seems to invoke other unfavorable visions of the consequences of relations with Negroes, since it expresses in its Ideology score a higher degree of resistance to desegregation than is apparent from its Image score.

(3) The college group stands in sharp contrast both to the 0–8 and 9–12 groups in these respects. For its expression of rejection of the Negro drops, as we proceed from Image to Ideology, almost as sharply as the scores rise in the 0–8 group. This suggests that members of the college group take less account of their unfavorable Image and possibly of other invidious versions of the Negro when describing the kinds of social relations they ideally prefer.

This suggests further that for the college group, unlike the others, certain countervailing and balancing factors enter at this point (Scale B) to modify its unfavorable Image of the Negro. That is, in expressing an Ideology of social relations, an awareness is shown of what is possible, as well as ideally desirable. The sense of possibility appears to include considerations of cost and consequence which override, to some degree, emotion-laden prejudices associated with Ideology. The college group does not feel as unrestricted as other groups to be Ideological, in our sense of a cost-free vision of an ideal situation. It is more cautious, more restrained, more aware of the actual context of Negro-White relations.

Further understanding of the processes at work in these different groups is gained from examining the pattern of differences between their respective mean scores. Table 5 shows the results of t-tests of significance of difference between means.[8]

---

[8] Variances were pooled in the computation of t, but no tests were made for homogeneity of variance. There are discrepancies in the sizes of various standard deviations; overinterpretation of the statistical findings is clearly a danger. Similarly, our data cannot satisfy the conditions required for the application of the t-test as these are restated by

We note first that the groups do not differ significantly in their Images of the Negro: none of the t-values approaches the .05 level. In comparison with the t-values on the other scales, those for the scale of the Image are the least differentiated—as if the entire sample shared a common Image of the Negro. But on all other scales, the groups are heterogeneous, often to a significant degree.

The greatest heterogeneity is indicated by the scores for Ideology, in which the three groups differ significantly. Yet it will be recalled that on this scale, Groups I and II (0–8 and 9–12) is expressed their greatest resistance to the Negro; and the college group shows its second greatest de-

Table 5: T-Tests for Significance of Differences between Means of Three Educational Groups on Five Scales

Scale	Groups Compared	t =	p =
(A) Image	I vs II	.039	N.S.*
	I vs III	.316	N.S.
	II vs III	.277	N.S.
(B) Ideology	I vs II	2.40	.02
	I vs III	5.10	.001
	II vs III	3.41	.001
(C) Sentiment	I vs II	1.31	N.S.
	I vs III	4.28	.001
	II vs III	2.83	.01
(D) General action	I vs II	1.42	N.S.
	I vs III	3.00	.01
	II vs III	1.60	N.S.
(E) Specific action	I vs II	1.14	N.S.
	I vs III	2.23	.05
	II vs III	1.59	N.S.

* N.S. = not significant, i.e., less than .05.

Hanan C. Selvin in "A Critique of Tests of Significance in Survey Research," *American Sociological Review*, 22 (October, 1957), pp. 519-527. The formula for t which was used is:

$$t = \frac{\overline{X}_1 - \overline{X}_2}{\sqrt{\dfrac{sx_1{}^2}{N_1(N_1 - 1)} + \dfrac{sx_2{}^2}{N_2(N_2 - 1)}}}$$

$$\text{where } sx^2 = \Sigma x^2 - \frac{(\Sigma x)^2}{N}$$

gree of resistance. In short, the level of scores is high for each group, relative to its other scores. But here the group differences are greatest.

What does this suggest about the impact of education upon attitudes toward the Negro? Education does not appear to reduce resistance to desegregation. But whatever effects of education are at work seem to be sufficiently strong to distinguish the groups by significant margins.

Following the same line of interpretation, we note that the groups resemble each other closely in Specific Action Sets. Here the p-values for the levels of *t* suggest that only the 0–8 and college groups differ from each other significantly, and that while the other differences are not totally inconsequential, they are less impressive than any comparable set of differences except for those on Scale A, the Image. Thus the conclusion that education makes the least difference when the Image of the Negro is in question and the second least difference when specific patterns of action are called for is, we believe, warranted.

It is also noteworthy that the pattern of increasing similarity among the groups begins clearly to emerge on Scale D, the measure of General Action Set. At this point, the scores for the grammar and high school groups drop rather sharply from their relatively high points on Scale C, Sentiment. The college group scores also drop, but less so.

In summary: (a) The different education groups start out as relatively homogeneously resistant to the Negro in their Images; but (b) their scores then scatter, when Ideology is measured, so that while remaining relatively high they are not significantly different from each other. (c) The same tendency for relatively high but differentiated scores persists through the measures of Sentiment. (d) There is then a rather sharp drop for all the groups when General Action Sets are estimated; and (e) finally, the groups begin to merge into a more homogeneous universe, once again, when specific action plans are contemplated.

The important difference between the homogeneity on Scale A and on Scale E is that in the case of the former, the similarities occur at a relatively high level of resistance, whereas in Scale E the similarities are found at a relatively low level of resistance to desegregation. Morover, the convergence of scores at E is a function of the movement of the scores of the 0–8 and 9–12 groups toward the low level scores of the 13-plus group. Note that the scores of the college group undergo the greatest modification in the movement from Image to Ideology, and thereafter remain relatively constant, as compared with the much sharper drop in scores throughout the scales which is manifested by both the grammar and high school groups.

We may surmise then that the presumed effects of education for the college group at the level of Ideology are not paralleled in the grammar and high school groups until plans of action are called for. At this point, these groups too become aware of consequences and costs and fashion their answers accordingly.

This is not to say that the college group is not also affected by the call for action and the vision of consequences which is thereby invoked. It is to say, however, that the college group seems able to anticipate these costs and consequences long before it is called upon to face them. This is precisely the effect to be expected if countervailing perspectives "work," as we have earlier suggested. That is, they serve as anticipatory modifiers of social behavior. For they seem to be interposed between prejudices expressed in Images and other aspects of orientation toward the Negro, and thus to produce restraint early in the sequence of stages which leads ultimately to action.[9]

This finding has implications for prediction. If we know the college group's ideological vision of a social system, we have a more reliable measure of its probable actions in the future than in the cases of the high school and grammar school groups. For once the college group defines the situation in terms of its desires, it appears to cling to this model more closely than the other groups adhere to their desired models.

Our finding also has relevance for social policy. The probable behavior of less educated groups when action is called for is unlikely to be ascertained by asking them about their feelings concerning the Negro or about the type of social relations they would like. On these matters, they appear to feel relatively free to define both the Negro and their desired relations with Negroes with little regard for what is concretely possible.

Table 6: Some Selected Characteristics of Three Educational Groups

	EDUCATIONAL GROUP		
	I 1–8 Years	II 9–12 Years	III 13 or More Years
Median age	43.6	36.8	43.3
Median annual income	$3200.00	$4296.00	$7727.00
Per cent white collar	8.6	30.3	73.1
Per cent married	82.5	92.3	90.1
Per cent in major Protestant denominations	84.32	87.62	98.56
Per cent who attend church once a week or more	31.07	40.00	54.93

[9] For the information of the reader, the following materials [Table 6] on some selected characteristics of the three educational groups are presented. We make no effort in this report to use these data in our analysis, though they will be incorporated in a larger study.

33. Family Decision Making over Desegregation*

EUGENE A. WEINSTEIN AND
PAUL N. GEISEL

The speed with which desegregation occurs depends upon the willingness of Negroes to press for change as well as upon the willingness of whites to grant or accommodate to it. After allowing for the major parts played by government and other organizations in making desegregation possible, in the most immediate sense the consolidation of desegregation depends upon the willingness of Negroes themselves to be pacesetters, or upon their readiness to urge and allow their children to be in the vanguard of change. The following study, carried out among border-state Negro families whose children could have gone to desegregated schools if their families chose to have them do so, shows, inter alia, that parents who continued to favor segregated schools were the more alienated, and were the more likely to have lower social status. These findings are even more interesting when considered in light of certain parallel results reported in selections 22 and 24.

Many plans for school desegregation make enrollment in a newly desegregated school optional for the Negro child. The presence of such an option transforms the issue of integration for affected Negro families from a hypothetical moral problem to one in which either action or inaction has real consequences. These conditions provide an excellent natural laboratory for the social psychologist concerned with decision making, both as process and in terms of its attitudinal correlates.

Attempts to identify factors related to the choice to desegregate were made by Crockett (1) and by Garth (2). Both compared Negro high school students who elected to transfer to newly desegregated schools with those who decided to remain, Crockett in St. Louis, and Garth in Louisville. Crockett's study unsuccessfully attempted to isolate socio-economic and school achievement differences between the groups. Garth's study focused on more psychological concomitants. He discovered significant differences between the meaning systems of transferees and non-transferees, especially in the meanings of "White people" and "Integrated High School."

* The authors wish to express their thanks to the Social Science Research Council and the Vanderbilt University Institute for Research in the Social Sciences for Grants-in-Aid in support of this research. We also wish to thank Harry Allen, Mrs. Donna Ryan, and Mrs. Anne Welch for their assistance in the study.

SOURCE: *Sociometry*, 25, 1962, pp. 21–8 (footnotes omitted). Reprinted by permission of the American Sociological Association and of the senior author.

Eugene A. Weinstein is Professor of Sociology at Vanderbilt University. *Paul N. Geisel* is Assistant Professor of Sociology at the University of Pittsburgh.

In both studies, the person most directly affected by the decision, the student, also played a major role in making it. The present study is based upon Negro families in Nashville, where schools are under a grade-a-year plan starting from the first grade. At the time of the study, the first three grades had been desegregated. Thus, in Nashville, the person most directly affected by desegregation is likely to have the decision made for him by his parents. These parental decisions for their children are the focus of this study.

The quest for correlates of parental choice covered three major areas: (a) demographic characteristics of the parents; (b) the decision-making process itself, including variables characterizing the parental definition of the desegregation situation; and (c) more general attitude variables. Sets of descriptive hypotheses between choice and specific variables in each of the three areas were formulated.

In the first area, demographic characteristics, it was hypothesized that desegregated families would be of higher socio-economic status, come more frequently from urban areas, and less frequently from Deep South states than their segregated counterparts.

The decision-making process for the desegregated group was expected to be characterized by more affective involvement. They were expected more frequently to have a family discussion concerning the issue, to have the discussion take longer, and the decision made democratically. A choice for segregation was predicted to be more frequently made by the mother only, reflecting the traditional lower-class Negro matriarchal family organization. It was also expected that the decision would more frequently be made by default, i.e., the family would simply do and say nothing about the child's eligibility. The desegregated families were expected to be more interested in the general issue of school desegregation, to be more optimistic about its long range outcome, to perceive more reference group support for the decision to desegregate, and to expect the effects of desegregation on the child to be favorable.

Differences between the two groups were hypothesized in four broad attitude areas. The segregated families were expected to have less favorable attitudes toward education, to be less favorable toward Negro participation in social change in the South (pioneering), to be more alienated, and to identify themselves predominantly as Negroes, rather than Americans.

METHOD

A sample of 88 Negro families having children eligible to attend a desegregated school was drawn from a list compiled from a door-to-door survey of eligibility in affected school districts. In 50 of these families, the eligible child was enrolled in a segregated school. They represent a random sample of all such cases. In 27 cases, the child was enrolled (as of June, 1960) in a desegregated school. In 11 cases, a child had attended a desegregated school but had subsequently transferred to a segregated one. The last two groups represent all locatable cases of their respective types. It is estimated that no more than five to ten such cases were not located. The interviewing was done during the summer of 1960 by a trained Negro female interviewer. The mother was the respondent in all but six cases. Difficulty in arranging to contact both parents necessitated this restriction. There were no refusals to cooperate.

The 27 currently desegregated and 11 previously desegregated families were combined as "ever-desegregated" cases in the statistical analysis. The decision to do this was made prior to the analysis. However, in order to check on possible distortions resulting from combining, distributions for the three uncombined groups on all independent variables were compared. Generally, the drop-out group resembled the desegregated cases much more than the segregated. In no case would any relationship have been materially affected by combining in this manner. Analysis of the reasons for dropping out indicates that only three did so because of dissatisfaction with desegregation per se. This probably accounts for the observed patterns.

Table 1: Relationship of Selected Demographic Characteristics to the Decision to Desegregate *

Variable	r_{p-bis}
Deep South background	N.S.
Rural vs. Urban background	.30*
Mother's education	.32
Father's occupation	.28

* Correlations stated so that a high value on the variable, or the second named characteristic in a dichotomy, are associated with the desegregated group. Phi coefficients are reported for dichotomous independent variables.

FINDINGS

Table 1 summarizes the findings for the demographic variables. With the exception of regional background, all of the relationships are significant in the hypothesized direction using the .05 alpha level. Since all but six of the sample mothers spent most of their lives in a border state, there was no chance for this variable to covary with the decision. While the great majority of mothers also came from urban backgrounds, 11 of the 12 exceptions cluster in the segregated group producing the significant relationship.

The present study was somewhat more successful than Crockett's in finding socio-economic differences between the groups. There was a difference of over two years in the mean number of school years completed between the groups of mothers. Similarly, over two-thirds of the segregated fathers were in unskilled or semi-skilled occupations compared with about half in the desegregated group.

The results for variables characterizing parents' definitions of the desegregation situation and the decision-making process appear in Table 2. The predictions concerning the decision-making process generally did not hold.

Table 2:   *Relationship of Family Decision-making Variables to the Decision to Desegregate*

Variable	$r_{p\text{-bis}}$
No family discussion vs. family discussion	N.S.
Length of family discussion	N.S.
Sharing of responsibility for decision	.33*
Perceived support from friends	N.S.
Perceived support from kin	N.S.
Perceived support from minister	N.S.
Weighted index of reference group support	N.S.
Absence of perceived threat	N.S.
Degree of interest in desegregation issue	.64
Optimism concerning extent of future change	N.S.
Unfavorable vs. favorable effect on child	.33*

* Phi coefficients.

In over 90 per cent of all cases, there was some family discussion. The tendency for less time to be spent in discussion in the segregated group was not significant. The one hypothesis in this area that did hold partially was the difference in who had chief responsibility for the decision. In the majority of cases in both groups, the mother reported that both parents shared responsibility. However, the exceptions clustered heavily in the segregated group (divided equally between mother and father as primarily responsible.)

Exploration of the area of perceived support for and pressures against a decision to desegregate yielded no systematic differences. Each respondent was asked to indicate how favorable her friends, kin, and minister would be to her sending her child to a desegregated school. Generally, the amount of perceived support was low. In no case was significantly more support perceived in the desegregated group. In addition to the questions concerning reference group opinions, respondents were asked to indicate how important the opinion of each group was to her. The opinion ratings were weighted by the importance ratings and summed, producing a weighted index of reference group support. This also failed to discriminate between the groups. In fact, the direction of the difference was opposite to that predicted. The absence of differences in the amount of perceived difficulty for the family if the child was enrolled in a desegregated school is interesting. In only 16 of the 88 cases was concern expressed about social or economic threat and eight of these are simple reports of what did occur during the first year of the plan rather than perception of present possibilities.

The desegregated group showed a much higher degree of interest in the general issue of school desegregation. This correlation, the largest in the study, is not particularly surprising if one has any faith in a relationship between voluntary participation and affective involvement. Of course, the question of temporal priority between participation and involvement is a knotty one. This interpretation must also be tempered somewhat by the fact that education is also related to degree of interest in desegregation ($r_{p\text{-bis}}=.41$). However, the partial correlation, holding education constant, was not materially lower ($r=.59$). While more interested, the desegregated group was not significantly more optimistic concerning the future of school desegregation, as had been predicted. The majority of cases in both groups saw continued spread of token desegregation in the near future.

Finally, as expected, the desegregated group was more liable to see their decision as having favorable effects on the child.

Not reported in Table 2 are the parents' expressed motives for their decision. These were analyzed in detail in an earlier paper (8). The chief reason given by the desegregated parents was that the school is closer to their home. Since the desegregated school was also closer in all but two of the segregated cases, this factor could hardly be crucial in discriminating between the groups. The most frequent reason for not sending one's child was a surprising one, the presence of an older child in the family who was not eligible to attend the desegregated school. Nineteen of the 50 segregated parents were reluctant to separate the children. Further investigation of this serendipitous finding revealed that the problem of having to separate children was proportionately less frequent in the desegregated group. A significant Phi coefficient of .22 resulted from the 2 x 2 table. Even so, over one third of the desegregated cases had this problem and over a third of the segregated ones did not. It would appear that factors other than those involved in expressed motives account for the bulk of variation in the decision.

During the interview a questionnaire was administered containing items from the following four content universes:

Attitudes toward Education	4 items
Alienation	Srole's 5 items (7)
Attitudes toward "Pioneering"	5 items
Degree of Negro Identification	4 items

Kuder-Richardson reliabilities were computed for each of the four sets of items. The Education and Negro Identification reliabilities failed to exceed chance level so they were deleted from the rest of the analysis. In passing, it might be noted that the almost unanimously favorable responses to the Education items in both groups seems to account for the failure. Reiss and Rhodes (5) in a study of adolescent conformity found similarly high values placed on education by Negro adolescents.

Reliabilities of .38 and .83 were found for the Alienation and Pioneering scales respectively. The reliability for Alienation was lower than that found for white samples. McDill and Ridley (3), for example, found a Kuder-Richardson reliability of .72 for a sample of white, Davidson County, Tennessee, suburban residents. This may well be due to subcultural variation in item meanings, a problem for which empirical research is badly needed. For example, agreement with the statement, "There's little use writing to public officials because they really aren't interested in the problems of the average man," may well reflect more realism than alienation

Table 3: Intercorrelations among the Decision to Desegregate, Alienation, Pioneering, and Education

	1	2	3	4
1. The decision to desegregate	—	—	—	—
2. Pioneering	.32	—	—	—
3. Alienation	—.41	—.36	—	—
4. Education	.32	.24	—.18	—

for the Southern Negro. The reliability for Pioneering is very high for a five-item scale. Since it correlates significantly with the decision to desegregate, it may be a useful instrument in further research on Negro attitudes. The items and response categories appear in the Appendix.

Table 3 contains the correlations of Alienation and Pioneering with the major dependent variable. Since education is related to the decision to desegregate it is also included in the matrix.

The only non-significant correlation on the Table is that between Education and Alienation. This is highly surprising since the relationship between them is well established in the literature (4, 6). Correcting for attenuation due to the low reliability of the Alienation scale results in a correlation of —.29, still considerably below those in the —.50's usually found. It may be that, within the Negro subculture, alienation reflects a component of adjustment to minority group status that is relatively more independent of socio-economic status.

The Alienation and Pioneering correlations are both significant in the predicted direction. Partialling out the effects of education does not materially reduce either, the partial correlations being .26 and .39 respectively.

Discussion

While somewhat scattered, there does appear to be a good deal of internal consistency in the study's significant findings. This might be best illustrated by constructing ideal-typical characterizations of each decision group.

The segregated families are lower in socio-economic status, come slightly more frequently from rural areas, and more often would have to separate children if they enrolled the eligible child in a desegregated school. These variables account for but a small part of the variance in the decision. The chief differentiating theme between the groups seems to be in their adjustment to being Negro. The segregated families are more alienated, more apathetic to social issues, and, while generally favorable toward change in the pattern of race relations in the South, prefer others to be the trailblazers.

The fact of being Negro for the desegregated group does not isolate one from concern or involvement with the larger society. While one may not be satisfied with social conditions as they exist, the adjustment is not to withdraw but to work actively to change them. This is reflected in higher involvement in the desegregation issue, more highly favorable attitudes toward Pioneering and lower Alienation.

If a single variable were to be selected as being at the core of the differences, Alienation would be the most likely candidate. Its correlation with the decision is remarkably high considering the low reliability for this sample. Correcting for attenuation, the correlation would be .68, accounting for nearly half the variance. Attitudes toward Pioneering may be regarded as a specific reflection of Alienation, viewed in turn as a more general personality attribute. The study provides some empirical evidence for this. Based on the unattenuated correlations, holding Pioneering constant does not materially affect the correlation between Alienation and the decision to desegregate, (.68 vs. .63). However, when Alienation is held constant, the relationship between Pioneering and the decision washes out completely. By Durkheim, out of Srole, it appears that Alienation is the best predictor sociologists have found since S. E. S.

Summary

A sample of 88 Nashville Negro families having children eligible to attend desegregated schools was interviewed. In 38, the child was (or had been) enrolled in a desegregated school; in 50, the child was enrolled in a segregated school. The focus of the study was to discover correlates of this difference in parental response to desegregation.

Significant socio-economic differences between the groups were found, with the desegregated group being higher. Variables characterizing the decision-making process itself were generally similar in both groups. The major differences appeared to be attitudinal. The desegregated group showed considerably more interest in the general issue of school desegregation and thought it would have more favorable effects on the child. The segregated group was characterized by significantly less favorable attitudes toward "pioneering" in race relations, and was more socially alienated. These differences persisted when the effects of socio-economic status were statistically controlled.

References

1. Crockett, H. J. Jr., "A Study of Some Factors Affecting the Decision of Negro High School Students to Enroll in Previously All-White High Schools, St. Louis, 1955," *Social Forces*, 1957, 35, 351–355.
2. Garth, C. E., "Self-Concepts of Negro Students Who Transferred or Did Not Transfer to Formerly All-White High Schools," Paper read at the Annual Meeting of the Southern Sociological Society, Atlanta, April 23, 1960.
3. McDill, E. L., and J. C. Ridley, Unpublished Study of Residential Mobility in Davidson County, Tennessee.
4. McDill, E. L., "Anomie, Authoritarianism, Prejudice, and Socio-Economic Status," *Social Forces*, 1961, 39, 241.
5. Reiss, A. J., and A. L. Rhodes, "Are Educational Norms and Goals of Conforming and Delinquent Adolescents Influenced by Group Position in American Society?", *Journal of Negro Education*, 1959, 28, 262–266.
6. Roberts, A., and M. Rokeach, "Anomie, Authoritarianism, and Prejudice: A Replication," *The American Journal of Sociology*, 1956, 61, 356.
7. Srole, L., "Social Integration and Certain Corollaries: An Exploratory Study," *American Sociological Review*, 1956, 21, 709–716.
8. Weinstein, E. A., and P. N. Geisel, "The Negro Family's Decision to Desegregate," *The Negro Educational Review*, 1961, 12, 4–11.

34. Union vs. Neighborhood in a Tension Situation*

DIETRICH C. REITZES

It is true that some people who are prepared to discriminate in one area of their social lives are prepared to discriminate in others. More precisely, however, a large body of research findings shows that many Americans are more likely to discriminate in those areas of their lives that are generally regarded as more intimate, involving more nearly private concerns. These results from research into "social distance" attitudes also help support Gunnar Myrdal's ideas about what he called "the rank order of discrimination." This selection indicates that workers who accept Negroes on the job are not necessarily prepared to accept them as neighbors. One could suggest a number of reasons for the difference in attitudes. For instance, neighboring involves cross-sex contacts; or men in low-level occupations may measure their prestige more by their homes than by reference to their colleagues. The author of this selection emphasizes that in different roles, as workers and as residents, men may belong to different organizations that define similar social circumstances in quite different ways. It can be a gross oversimplification to take account of one organization that represents one set of role concerns while failing to note that other organizations may be representing other sets.

Much of the current work in the field of "race relations" is limited by the assumption that behavior in racial contact situations is structured by the attitudes of individuals as such. As a result racial relations are often interpreted from the perspective of the individuals who constitute the group. Two corollaries follow: One is that changes in race relations are to be brought about through changes in the individuals' attitudes: the other is that once changes have occurred in the person's attitudes in one situation, similar changes in other situations will also occur. Thus it is often felt that individuals who work with Negroes in the plant or cooperate with Negroes in the union will also accept Negroes in other situations. When observation reveals that many individuals accept Negroes in one situation reject them in others, this is interpreted as an "inconsistency" in the individual's behavior.

* The writer is greatly indebted to Mr. Joseph D. Lobman for the conceptual framework of this study.

SOURCE: *Journal of Social Issues*, Vol. 9, No. 1, 1953, pp. 37–44. Reprinted by permission of the publisher and of the author.

Dietrich C. Reitzes is Professor of Sociology at George Williams College. He is the author of *Negroes in Medicine*.

It is the theme of this paper that this basic assumption has to be re-examined. This paper rests on the premise that human society is not a mere aggregation of individuals, and that the present and anticipated behavior of people in society will depend primarily on the kind of *organization* that exists in the given area of conduct. It follows too that an understanding of individual behavior in most situations is predicated on understanding how deliberately organized groups define those situations.

Certainly a focus on the group is necessary both in the work and community setting. At work the individual is incorporated in large organizations which mediate between him and management. Within the organization a hierarchy of officers and committees formulate policies, establish objectives, decide on strategy and tactics.[1]

A parallel development is taking place in the community. The residential neighborhood is the special locale in which individuals attempt to realize such interests as the protection of property values and personal and social deference. In terms of these interests their activities are mobilized and collectively shaped. These interests bring individuals together in organizations and cause the members to reflect in themselves, as individuals, the *raison d'être* of the group.

The key question is to what extent are attitudes a "product" of group membership. Our contention is that these deliberately organized groups structure and define the situation for the individual and offer him ready and available definitions of behavior.[2] Individual behavior under such conditions, therefore, cannot be explained in terms of personal attitudes toward minority groups. In the community or neighborhood it is the property owner's association which provides us with the key to the actions of individuals in situations of racial contacts. In the plant it is the union.

We tested this thesis in the midwest by analyzing the rejection or acceptance of Negroes in a residential neighborhood and on the job. The two situations mentioned involved the same white individuals. The white individuals all lived in a residential neighborhood which had a pattern of strong rejection of Negroes, and yet the same individuals participated in a union which strongly accepted Negroes on an equal basis.

The analysis was made in terms of the collective definitions of these situations by the neighborhood organization, the union and management respectively. The study of individual behavior was preceded by an intensive study of the two situations involved, with particular emphasis on their organizational structure.

---

[1] Herbert Blumer, "Sociological Theory in Industrial Relations," *American Sociological Review*, 1947, v. 12.
[2] Joseph D. Lohman and Dietrich C. Reitzes, "Note on Race Relations in Mass Society," *American Journal of Sociology*, 1952, 58, 241–242.

The Neighborhood

We found that in the center of the organizational pattern of the neighborhood—let us call it Steelside—was the property owner's association, called the Civic Club. The main objective of the Civic Club was to keep Negroes out of the community. The president of the Club stated: "Now we generally don't talk about that freely, but actually the main purpose of the Club is to keep up the bar against the colored element moving in here. That was the purpose when it was first founded and that is still the purpose today."

The Civic Club claims to reflect and carry out the wishes of the people in the neighborhood. Actually, however, it is more accurate to state that the Club *formulates* the sentiments and *directs* the actions of a large portion of the population on *certain* issues, namely those dealing with the residential neighborhood. This became obvious when we studied the operation of the Club in detail. Attendance at meetings was very small and the actual control of the organization lay in the hands of a few individuals who made all important decisions.

The influence of the Club, however, could not be judged by its membership or attendance at meetings. A study of the entire neighborhood revealed that all other neighborhood organizations followed the Civic Club's leadership in its rejection of Negroes in Steelside. There were definite and clear lines of communication between the other organizations and the Club. This enabled the Club to mobilize the entire neighborhood against Negroes whenever necessary.

The Civic Club was able to mobilize individuals because of the interests of the individuals in the neighborhood. These interests centered around property values and social acceptance, and the Club was effective because it provided the individual with well formulated statements, reasons and justifications for his specific acts in specific situations.

The neighborhood itself reflected the success of the Civic Club's activities. At the time the study began, in 1948, no Negroes lived in Steelside. Several Negroes had attempted to move in, but were repelled by force, including such instances as burning down back porches, etc. Impending sales of homes to Negroes were prevented through pressure on the owners or their agents.

A short time before the study was made a major racial disturbance occurred in a near-by community when Negroes sought to move into that area. Individuals living in Steelside participated in that disturbance, and a number were arrested by the police. There was some evidence that the Civic Club was active in arousing the individuals in its own area and sending them to the scene of the disturbance.

The Work Situation

Many of the people who lived in Steelside worked in industrial plants which are located just outside of the neighborhood. To study the work situation we selected two factories which had the largest number of employees from Steelside.

The individual and collective interests in the work situation differ, of course, from the interests in the neighborhood. The key organizations are the company and the union. The local union was part of an international affiliated with the CIO. On all three levels, the local, the parent union and the national CIO, there was a clear-cut policy of non-discrimination.

This policy of equality for Negroes, however, was not considered as an end in itself but was definitely and consciously related to the larger union objectives. This is illustrated by a statement of the local union organizer:

> We are an industrial union and we learned years ago through bitter experience that we cannot afford to have any disruption or break in our Negro-white relationships among the workers. They are all workers faced with common problems for which the union fights and on which they have to stay together.

Management, too, had a policy of non-discrimination. One plant was part of a large progressive-minded heavy manufacturing company which had pioneered a policy of integrating Negroes into its labor force. The second plant, belonging to a different company, had a policy, too, of employing Negroes, and reported that such equality created no special problem.

Thus in the work situation the effective organizations defined Negro-white contact on the basis of equality. The interviews clearly revealed that as far as race relations were concerned the white workers were primarily influenced by the union policy and definition of the situation. Therefore, in the analysis of individual behavior, we have emphasized the union rather than management.

The situation in the plants and union hall reflected this formal policy. Neither plant had segregated facilities. Locker rooms, lunch rooms, shower rooms, and toilets were shared by Negroes and whites; Negroes participated fully in union activities, and several held important elective offices.

The Interviews

It was against this background of the community and work situation that the data were analyzed. We interviewed 151 white persons all of whom lived in Steelside, worked in the two plants mentioned, and belonged to the union.[3]

The interviews were conducted in the interviewees' homes, and the individuals were told that it was a general community study. No special emphasis was placed on "race relations." Our questions were directed to ascertaining the involvement of the individual in the group life of the neighborhood, on his rejection of Negroes in the neighborhood, on the involvement of the individual with union activities and his acceptance of Negroes on the job. We used open-ended interview questions. Our main effort was to get the individual to describe situations to us, and particularly to describe his own activity in these situations. We felt that by emphasizing descriptions of situations, we would get not only information about the situation but also the individual's own definition of the situation which would provide the key to his actions. This proved to be the case. Thus by asking the respondent: "Do any Negroes live here?" we would get not only factual information but also almost invariably the respondent's concept of Negroes as neighbors.[4]

Tables I to III are based on ratings made from the completed interviews. Table I indicates the relationship between "involvement in the collective existence in the neighborhood" and "rejection of Negroes in the neighborhood." (The value of chi-square for this table is 79.90. In order to be significant at the one per cent level a chi-square of only 13.27 is required.) This indicates that there is a definite positive association between these two factors.

---

[3] Over 90 percent of the workers in the plants were members of the union. Their names and addresses were obtained by selecting from the union membership lists those members who lived in Steelside. In one local we were able to make this check ourselves and selected all union members in the neighborhood. In the other local we did not have access to the list but had a union member do the selecting for us. We attempted to interview all individuals so selected. However, in 51 cases we were unable to contact the person. We have no reason, however, to believe that the loss of those cases biased our results.

[4] In order to test our hypothesis the completed interviews were then rated. To do this objectively we extracted from every interview all the information available pertaining to (1) the respondent's involvement in the collective existence of the neighborhood, (2) his rejection of Negroes in the neighborhood, (3) his involvement in union activities, (4) his acceptance of Negroes on the job. These data were recorded separately for each category. Then we graded one group at a time marking each case "high," "medium," or "low" in accordance with established criteria. In order to check the objectivity of our own judgments we submitted the first 44 cases to three other judges. These judges were given the extractions and the criteria for judgments. The judges agreed with the writer in better than 90 per cent of the cases so that it was felt that this procedure was not necessary for the balance of the cases. However, we did compare the balance of the cases with the first group and found that the associations between the four areas did not change significantly in the cases which were not checked by other judges.

Table I: Relation between Involvement in Collective Existence of the
Neighborhood and Rejection of Negroes in Neighborhood

REJECTION OF NEGROES IN NEIGHBORHOOD	INVOLVEMENT IN THE COLLECTIVE EXISTENCE OF THE NEIGHBORHOOD			
	High	Medium	Low	Total
High	56	9	3	68
Medium	8	36	18	62
Low	1	8	12	21
Total	65	53	33	151

Table II: Relationship between Involvement in Union Activities and Acceptance of Negroes at Work

ACCEPTANCE OF NEGROES AT WORK	INVOLVEMENT IN UNION ACTIVITIES			
	High	Medium	Low	Total
High	45	19	?	66
Medium	7	47	13	67
Low	0	6	12	18
Total	52	72	27	151

Table II indicates the relationship between "involvement in union activities" and "acceptance of Negroes at work." The value of chi-square for this table is 86.45—while a chi-square of only 13.27 would have indicated significance at the one per cent level. Thus this table also indicates high association between these two factors.

The most significant finding is the one regarding the relationship between "rejection of Negroes in the neighborhood" and "acceptance of Negroes on the job." This relationship is shown in Table III. (The chi-square test cannot be applied to this table since the expected value in some of the squares is less than 5. Inspection of the table indicated, however, that the distribution of cases is almost random.) Tables I and II show clearly the strong association between individual behavior and the organizational structure of the situation. Table III shows the inadequacy of explaining this behavior in terms of individual attitudes. Thus only 11 of the 68 cases which were rated as showing "high" rejection of Negroes in the neighborhood showed "low" acceptance of Negroes on the job, while 31 persons who strongly rejected Negroes in the neighborhood showed

Table III: Relationship between Rejection of Negroes in Neighborhood and Acceptance of Negroes at Work

ACCEPTANCE OF NEGROES AT WORK	REJECTION OF NEGROES IN NEIGHBORHOOD			
	High	Medium	Low	Total
High	31	25	10	66
Medium	26	32	9	67
Low	11	5	2	18
Total	68	62	21	151

"high" acceptance of Negroes on the job. Also only 10 of the 66 cases showing "high" acceptance of Negroes at work indicated "low" rejection of Negroes in the neighborhood, while 31 of these cases showed "high" rejection in the neighborhood.

The three tables show that knowing a person's behavior toward Negroes in one situation does not enable one to predict that person's behavior toward Negroes in another situation. But knowing the organizational definition of a situation and the involvement with this organization, prediction of behavior becomes possible.

It should be emphasized that the interviews clearly indicated that the Negro issue as such was not the determining factor in either the involvement of the individual in the community or in the involvement of the individual in the union. The controlling interests in the neighborhood were social acceptance and property values, and on the job they were wages, security and working conditions. It is in terms of these specific interests that organizations mobilized the individuals and directed their actions.

IMPLICATIONS OF THE STUDY

The findings of this study are in agreement with the hypothesis that in modern mass society the basis for individual behavior in situations of racial contacts becomes increasingly the *definition of the situation provided to the individual by deliberately organized collectivities.* This organizational structuring is effective to the extent that it defines the situation for the individual in terms of his specific interests in the situation.

These findings have important implications for tactics in the field of race relations. A labor union with non-discriminatory practices might be concerned with the race relations pattern in the community and attempt to influence it. In that case, the non-discriminatory behavior of union members on the job notwithstanding, it cannot be assumed that they will also follow the union's policies when it takes a stand on community issues. What is required is that the union leaders be fully aware of the organizational structuring of the community and in the development of their tactics take this into account.

Our own study provides some illustrations of this point. A few years before the study was conducted, the issue of public housing came up in the neighborhood. We interviewed the man who was at that time the president of one of the locals. He stated:

> The union, that is, the national office, decided to come out in favor of it [a public housing project]. They told me that as president of one of the locals in this area I had to make an official statement in favor of it. Well, I refused. So they called me down to the national office and put me on the carpet. But I told them that we are property owners and that our property values would go down if the project would be built. I know that on that issue I had more support among the membership than the national office, so I never came out favoring [the project].

Another illustrative incident: Shortly before our study was made, a nearby neighborhood was the scene of a near race riot. During this period the Publicity and Education Director of one of the locals wrote a letter to the local newspaper attacking the paper for its anti-Negro position. This letter was written on union letterhead and the signature included his position in the union. The members of the local reacted immediately and strongly against this "interference" by the union in local affairs. The author of the letter was severely criticized. The executive council and the president of the local had to write letters to the paper stating that the Publicity Director had acted as an individual and that his position did not represent the sentiments of the local.

The union can be effective if it can so define the community situation that non-discriminatory behavior would serve the interests of the people involved. This is, of course, less difficult when the community organizations are weak and more difficult when they are strong. The specific tactics would depend on the specific situation. The union can indicate to the individuals involved that non-discriminatory behavior in the neighborhood can serve the individuals' interests better than discriminatory behavior. It can explode the myths used by the neighborhood organizations promoting discrimination. Thus the union can point out that property values do not necessarily decline when Negroes move into a neighborhood, that crime does not necessarily increase, etc. This means that in order to be effective in the neighborhood, the union would not only have to use the same tactics that are effective in the work situation, but be prepared to enter into the neighborhood itself.

35. A Study of Desegregation

MARIAN RADKE YARROW

It is frequently assumed that equal-status contact can change the attitudes of members of different racial or ethnic groups so that group members will understand and accept one another. As stated, that assumption is too general, but adding two qualifications can refine it a good deal. First, the contact should take place in an atmosphere in which constituted authority clearly favors close cross-group contact; second, members of both groups must be able to feel that they are not in competition for scarce values. The selection that follows discusses a situation in which these conditions were met, revealing that in a relatively brief period of time, interracial contact did change the attitudes of white toward Negro children, and of Negro children toward themselves, in a more positive direction.

Imposed desegregation offers a natural situation for exploring the hypothesis that: "change in the behavior of individuals and groups can be brought about by a change in the social situation in which they are required to function," without preceding changes in attitudes and beliefs. Desegregation can be conceptualized as a social psychological problem involving a conflict between external forces and internalized norms—the situation requiring performance at variance with existing norms of interpersonal relationships. Going beyond the general hypothesis of situational influences, we are asking to what extent does the changed social environment bring about changes in individuals and in group functioning and at what levels of response does conformity or non-conformity to situational expectations take place?

In the present paper the "social situation" with which we are dealing is the total camp setting, with segregated and desegregated children's groups. The desegregated situation imposed equality in all areas: equality of responsibility and authority of leaders of both races, equality in interpersonal relationships among leaders, and equality in the physical setup of living facilities. Congenial interpersonal relationships among the counselors and the counselors' acceptance of all children supplied the models and the expectations for interracial relationships on the children's level. The coun-

SOURCE: *Journal of Social Issues*, Vol. 14, No. 1, 1958, pp. 8–9, 21–8, passim. Reprinted by permission of the publisher and of the senior author.

Marian Radke Yarrow is Chief, Section of Developmental Psychology, Laboratory of Socio-Environmental Studies, National Institute of Mental Health. In addition to numerous articles on ethnic and other aspects of social psychology, she is co-author of *They Learn What They Live*. John D. Campbell is also with the Laboratory of Socio-Environmental Studies, while Leon J. Yarrow is Research Psychologist at the Family and Child Service.

selors came to desegregrated groups with the experience of preceding segregated sessions. They had no special training for leading racially-mixed groups but they were motivated to have integrated groups succeed.

To assess individual and group functioning, analyses were made in terms of several different levels of response:

1. *Behavior*. The detailed recordings of specific items of behavior were translated into categories of interaction along dimensions of affiliation, nurturance, fear, domination, aggression, etc. The direction of behavior, whether toward oneself, members of one's own race or of the other race, was recorded.

2. *Social perceptions*. Children's descriptions of and judgments about the other children in the cabins were obtained.

3. *Group properties*. Characteristics of group functioning such as degree of cohesiveness, subgroupings, group crises, etc., were studied.

4. *Psychodynamic processes*. This label is used to cover a variety of assessments involving inferences concerning motivations, causal sequences in interaction, defense mechanisms, etc.

. . . . .

SOCIOMETRIC AND GROUP ROLES

The harmonies and tensions which exist side by side in the desegregated group raise a number of questions. Are cohesive cabins and individual tensions maintained together by the children's remaining highly conscious of their racial identity but deciding to "play it" politely? Or has the group with the lower social status outside of camp simply adopted or accepted a similar lower position at camp and thus maintained a peace? Or have social relationships developed in the cabins on camp-relevant and personality-relevant lines, with race in a recessive role but one none the less contributing to individual insecurities and conflicts? Children's preferences for one another (and their rejections) provide some clues.

Each child ranked his cabin mates on their desirability as friends. From rankings, the relative status positions of white and Negro children in the eyes of their peers were derived; and from children's first choices the nature of mutual friendships was examined (friendship defined as two children selecting each other as best friend).

A racial status structure is reflected in the ranks assigned to white and Negro children. . . . Significantly higher ranks are given to white children. Since average differences may be the result of small tendencies to up- or down-grade a given racial group, or may reflect sharp status contrasts, the ranks within each cabin were inspected. In nine of the sixteen cabins in which the children were interviewed the status differential is marked;

white children initially hold the top two or more ranks with one or more Negro children in the bottom ranks. In seven of the cabins the grading is not so distinct—both white and Negro children are in upper and lower ranks. At the end of camp the status differential is lessened. Only one cabin retains the clearly differentiated ranking with only white children at the top ranks and Negro children at the bottom.

This differential racial preference, however, does not serve as an adequate predictor of specific friendships that develop. When A chooses B and B chooses A, one assumes that a degree of positive communication and empathy between two children is present. Does this kind of empathic relationship develop as frequently in desegregated groups? Mutual choices occur no less frequently in desegregated than in segregated groups. On first interviews, 45 per cent of the children in segregated groups are in mutual pairs, each choosing the other as likely best friends; 35 per cent are in mutual pairs on the interview at the end of camp. Approximately half of the original pairs are stable over time. In desegregated groups, 44 per cent and 33 per cent on first and second interviews respectively are mutual best friends. A third of the initial choices are stable over time. Of the friendship pairs in desegregation, 44 per cent include a white and a Negro child. These pairings develop despite the general racial status differential shown in the preference data. To assure that mutual pairs of like and unlike race did not represent qualitatively different configurations, each friendship pair was examined in terms of the kinds of attractions and relationship between the pair members. Similar skills at camp, physical proximity in cabin, common interest in "boy friends" or "girl friends," etc., ran through both types of pairs. Seldom are the members of mutual pairs in a supra-subordinate relationship to one another. (There are four such pairs.) Friendships appear to be much the same whether of like or unlike race composition.

The sociometric data examined are consistent with other aspects of interaction in the children's groups. They again reveal harmonies and disharmonies in the relationships of children of the two races. From the status and friendship data, it is apparent that the predominant picture in the camp, that of cohesively functioning groups with accompanying individual tensions, does not stem from static subgroup relationships. Neither of the suggested alternatives—of each subgroup's playing it politely, or of the minority group's passively accepting a subordinate role—fits the picture.

As the various elements of preference and behavior are fitted together, the processes of adaptation to new norms become apparent. The outside-of-camp status of white and Negro, with the Negro's self-devaluation is felt in cabin life. This coexists with behavior that in large measure is not according to status lines. Over time, the status (preference) lines become less distinct and less divergent from behavior, more nearly approximating the equal-status relations expressed in their actions. Internal balances within the groups change over time. As we know, groups in general exist and develop with balances of various sorts between disintegrative and integrative processes. Even the more cohesive groups at times must manage conflicting influences within them. Differences between segregated and desegregated groups seem to lie in the nature of the counterforces and balances in group living rather than in any singularly different performance and relationship. There are many more counterforces in desegregation than in segregation. In desegregation there are fluctuations in adherence to extra-camp and intra-camp racial norms. There are inconsistencies in behavior—conformity and resistance to conformity, racial status differentials and individual friendship associations. Compatible participation is carried on but at a somewhat heightened cost of personal tensions. An elaboration of the cognitive elements in these responses further fills in the pattern of adaptation to new norms.

BEHAVIOR, COGNITION, AND AFFECT

Children's perceptions of one another can now be examined in the context of behavioral interaction. Measures of cognitive content consist of the "free" descriptions of peers, and responses to "guess-who" questions about peers. The responses were analyzed with reference to the race of the perceiver and the perceived child. Few descriptions, as gestalts, are dominated by racial stereotypes. This is in contrast to the many findings from attitude studies based on questions about race in the abstract (such as, what are Negroes [whites] like?). It would appear that face-to-face contact and attention to the individual of the other race decrease the potency or permissibility of verbalized stereotypic generalizations.

The descriptive categories for peers of own and other race are remarkably comparable in aspect of sociability, conformity, and affiliation. We know from the behavior that white and Negro children are providing highly similar behavioral stimuli. This similarity is not distorted in perceptions of one another. Possibly concern about intergroup relations may be involved in the tendency for both Negro and white children to be more sensitive to independent, assertive behaviors in children of the other race. . . .

Indirect effects of racial stereotyping are evident in other trends. Initially heightened sensitivity or alertness to behaviors involving aggression and domination appears in both Negro and white children in desegregated groups when describing cabin mates. The concern varies depending on the race of perceiver and perceived. White children are specially alerted to aggressive behaviors in describing Negro children; Negro children with regard to other Negro children. Thus, for white children, comments on aggressive characteristics rise from 15 per cent in segregated groups [65 children] to 53 percent in desegregated settings [63 children] when the object of description is a Negro child. Their reports on aggression in other white children (17 per cent) do not increase in desegregation.

The responses of Negro children suggest concern on their part as to how Negro children manifest or control aggressive impulses. Their reports on aggressive behaviors of Negro peers are 29 per cent in segregation [55 children], 48 per cent in desegregation [57 children]. Alertness to the same dimensions in their white peers occurs in 33 per cent of the cases. Similar increases occur in the reporting of rebellious and non-conforming behavior in desegregation. The screen of racial stereotypes or stereotyped expectations may account for these emphases, for the behavior of Negro children and white children is not sufficiently different to account for these differences in perceptions.

The orientation of Negro children toward impulse control in the presence of white children is reflected elsewhere in the cognitive data. In self-choices on "guess-who" descriptions, Negro children avoid identifying themselves as aggressive actors. On "who gets mad easily" Negro children rather freely choose themselves in segregated groups (25 per cent of the girls and 16 per cent of the boys). In desegregated settings none of the Negro girls and 8 per cent of the boys choose themselves for this characterization. Further, only 7 per cent of Negro children in segregated groups name themselves as the child who "helps others out"; in desegregated groups, 25 per cent do so.

The "guess who" characterizations of cabin mates reflect patterns of choice linked with the race of the child chosen. This linkage, however, is not one in which boys and girls of each race show identical biases; indeed, boys and girls respond quite differently. Boys do not tend consistently on initial and final interviews to over- or under-choose peers of either race on given characteristics. . . . Girls (both Negro and white), on the other hand, tend consistently to name a Negro girl as "afraid and shy." In a similar fashion, social sensitivity ("sizing up others") is attributed to white girls.

Children's perceptions of others vary not only in the particular characteristics of behavior they describe but also in the depth or complexity of their judgments of other children. Complexity varies in the degree of differentiation of another's characteristics, the degree of insight or concern with his motives, and the degree of interpretation of causal factors underlying behavior. The white and Negro children's free descriptions of each other were analyzed in terms of level of complexity. Ratings were made on a seven point scale; the lowest level of organization characterized by fragmentary descriptions, the highest level being organized interpretations of the characteristics of the child. Ratings of complexity of interpersonal perceptions were compared in segregation and desegregation, and in cross-race and within race perceptions.

More complex interpersonal perceptions appear in desegregated than in segregated settings suggesting more intensive cue-seeking in this more ambiguous situation. (These differences approach but do not reach statistical significance.) In desegregation, white children make more complex searching appraisals of Negro cabin mates (the more ambiguous objects) than of white cabin mates, at beginning and end of camp. Negro children, on the other hand, make fuller descriptions of members of their own race initially, at the time when their behavioral passivity is most pronounced, and when they are hypersensitive about aggression control in their own group. However, at the end of camp the Negro children, too, are attending more closely to the characteristics of children of the other race.

SUMMARY OF ADAPTATION PROCESSES
AND CHANGES OVER TIME

If the gross picture of social relationships in the desegregated camp is placed against the history of precamp experience, the children's rapid and smooth acceptance of the new social-racial expectations is a major change. This immediate adjustment is the more impressive when we see in initial contacts not only behavioral conformity but also much personalization of peers in children's perceptions of one another (as opposed to viewing one another predominantly as racial objects—although some element of this latter clearly exists). But children's preferences, feelings, and tensions are not as fully congruent with the desegregated setting as are their behaviors and perceptions.

If a cross-section of subjective and overt reactions to the situation is examined, the inconsistencies in adaption become apparent, within each level of individual response (behavioral, cognitive, affective) and among the various levels. While friendly associations develop, passing reverses and cleavages occur as well. Participation by some children is maintained anxiously. Friendships form across racial lines although preferential position of the white children exists. Both realistic and stereotyped selectivities run through the children's appraisals of their cabin mates.

Some of the longitudinal developments of these patterns can be assessed over the two weeks of contact. After this period of living together in an environment supporting equalitarian relations, how successfully were the groups functioning? Although the question is a logical one to pose, success and failure are not unitary, and evaluation cannot adequately be simplified to these terms. The children's experience over time is a process of consolidation of initial adaptions, attempted reconciliations of incompatibilities, and for some children, sharpened conflicts. The camp experience has the effect of "shaking up" the child's patterned reactions to racial groups. The two weeks of camp were not sufficient, generally, to effect wholly settled adjustments. Moreover, how new patterns evolve varies by child and by subgroup. Yet some general trends are evident.

If the experience of integration is successful in reducing social distance between the Negro and white children, one would expect that race as a criterion (conscious or unconscious) for assessing friendship should exert less influence at the end of two weeks. The findings support this. Although at the end of camp the children still tend to prefer their white cabin mates as friends, there is a statistically significant drop in the extent to which they are the favored group.

The children describe each other much more critically (reporting on aggression and non-conformities) after two weeks than in their first interviews. This increasing criticism, however, takes place in segregated as well as in desegregated groups. The significance, racially, in the desegregated groups is that the negative reports are not directed disproportionately to the children of the other race.

Among the white children changes during the two weeks are not dramatic or completely consistent. The major shift is in their friendship assessments of their Negro peers. At the end of camp, in the eyes of the white children their Negro peers were significantly more desirable as friends than they had been earlier in the session. Indeed, at the end of camp, white and Negro campers were about equally desired as friends by the white children.

One of the more significant effects of the equalitarian culture of the camp is the effect upon the Negro children's concept of their own race and on their own personal self-esteem. This is demonstrated in several ways. Their over-sensitivity to unfavorable behavior in Negro peers is decreased. There is a generally systematic tendency for them to describe other Negro children in more favorable terms than initially. Among the Negro girls there is a lessened tendency to reject other Negro girls on friendship ratings. The experience does not result in a conflict-free situation for these children, but the picture they hold of their own race, and of themselves, is markedly altered during their camp stay.

What effect does the camp experience have on children's acceptance of the *idea* of desegregation, and on their anxious anticipations regarding intergroup relationships? In general, at the end of camp, the experience of integrated camping was viewed favorably by the children (76 per cent wanted camp to continue longer). They had anxiously coped with the new situation. Many of their fears had probably not been realized in the actualities of camp. Possibly their favorable responses at the end of camp indicate less apprehension and readier acceptance of interracial contacts.

The two-week experience cannot be viewed as completing a process of change in norms of intergroup relations for either racial group. It provides the first steps in the process of reorganizing beliefs and feelings.

36. Residential Proximity and Intergroup Relations in Public Housing Projects*

DANIEL M. WILNER, ROSABELLE P. WALKLEY,
AND STUART W. COOK

Selection 35 made clear that under appropriate conditions, equal-status intimate contact between whites and Negroes could reduce prejudiced attitudes. The following selection shows that the extent of the reduction depends in large measure on the extensiveness of opportunities for close contact. Where whites and Negroes live in proximity to one another, under objectively equal housing conditions, neighbors have a better chance to get to know one another well, and prejudice decreases more markedly. It is important to keep in mind that this study deals with public *housing, where issues relating to considerations of prestige and of property values are less likely to arise than in communities where the housing is predominantly private. For more complete discussion of these last points, see Weaver's paper, selection 30.*

A major hypothesis underlying the studies reported here is that prejudice is a product of social learning, that it is transmitted through the prevailing folklore and supported by existing social arrangements, many of which carry the connotation that Negroes are different from, and inferior to, white persons. Negroes tend to live in segregated, often deteriorated, residential districts. White persons are more often employers or patrons, Negroes more often servants; white persons are more likely to hold the skilled jobs, Negroes (sometimes with no less training) to hold the unskilled jobs. From observation of the prevailing social patterns, the white person draws the conclusion that the two races are different in social worth. At the same time, he develops negative feelings toward Negroes as a group, and adopts certain unfavorable stereotypes purportedly characteristic of all Negroes. The two processes reinforce each other; the stereotypes are used

* The authors are greatly indebted to Claire Selltiz for assistance in preparing this article.
SOURCE: *Journal of Social Issues,* Vol. 8, No. 1, 1952, pp. 45–69, passim. Reprinted by permission of the publisher and of the senior author.

Daniel M. Wilner, a psychologist, is Professor of Public Health in the School of Public Health at the University of California at Los Angeles. *Rosabelle Price Walkley,* a sociologist, is Associate Research Behavioral Scientist and Lecturer at the same institution. *Stuart W. Cook* is Professor of Psychology at the University of Colorado.

to justify the social practices, and the practices provide social support for the stereotypes and negative feelings.

The prevailing social patterns, it is assumed, operate in still another way to perpetuate prejudice. By limiting the opportunities for contact under circumstances which favor the perception of similarities between Negro and white persons, they reduce the possibility that stereotypes will be corrected through observations which belie their validity.

If prejudice develops out of, and is reinforced by, social separation of the races, it may be expected that under certain conditions where this separation does not occur, favorable changes in attitude of one group toward the other will take place. A number of conditions which might be expected to contribute to such change may be hypothesized: (a) when members of the two groups occupy the same or equivalent roles in the situation (have the same type of jobs, are organization members with the same rights and responsibilities, are tenants in housing of about the same type and quality or own homes of about the same type and quality, etc.); (b) when the individuals from the two groups who are in close proximity are similar in certain background characteristics (socio-economic status, education, age, etc.); (c) when the situation is such that it leads to the perception of common interests and goals—or at least does not introduce objective sources of competition and conflict; (d) when the social climate within the situation is not unfavorable to interracial association.

. . . . .

CHOICE OF PUBLIC HOUSING PROJECTS AS A SETTING

Several characteristics of public housing projects which accommodate Negro and white residents make them a particularly appropriate setting for investigation of these hypotheses about relationships between proximity, interracial contact, social climate, and ethnic attitude.

A bi-racial housing project provides a setting in which there is a strong likelihood of varying kinds of at least minimal face-to-face contacts between white and Negro residents. Moreover, when interracial contacts do occur, they occur between whites and Negroes who are like one another in various important characteristics—a circumstance that is due to the nature of the policies governing the public housing project. Thus, regulations regarding minimum and maximum income limits tend to condense the range of incomes of all residents, regardless of race. Priorities given to veterans of World War II tend to result in a large proportion of adults under forty; some projects built since 1946 house veterans almost entirely. A consequence of similarity of age of the adults is, of course, similarity in the age range of the children in the project. Furthermore, all tenants face much the same problems. There is a single management with published rules and regulations applying to all residents alike. White and Negro housewives not only have similar problems concerning children, but must avail themselves of common or identical facilities in the course of their everyday activities. Finally, in the interest of harmony within the project, the management must at least discourage open friction between the racial groups, though it may or may not actively encourage friendly association between them.

Furthermore, housing projects provide "natural" variations of two factors believed to be crucial: proximity, and certain aspects of social atmosphere. In some projects all the white families live very near Negro families, and in others all the white families live quite far from Negro families, with relatively little variation in distance from Negroes within a single project. Within other projects, the differences in distance may be greater, especially when Negroes represent only a small proportion of the project population.

One aspect of occupancy pattern may be assumed in certain circumstances not only to affect proximity but in addition to carry connotations about social norms. Assignment of white persons to separate and distinct areas in which there are no Negroes may carry for some of the white persons in them certain of the connotations of segregated practices in the larger community—that there is an intrinsic difference between Negro and white, and that closer proximity and association are not desirable. On the other hand, assignment of white and Negro families to apartments in the same buildings or to buildings near one another without sharp demarcation runs counter to the connotations of usual segregated social arrangements.

Public housing projects, then, offer a setting in which certain conditions believed to be conducive to the development of favorable attitudes (equivalence of roles within the situation and similarity of background characteristics) are relatively constant, while variation occurs in other factors (degree of proximity, and social connotation of the physical arrangements). Such a setting provides an opportunity to investigate the effects of these latter factors.

. . . . .

THE PLAN OF THE TWO STUDIES

. . . With regard to occupancy pattern, two projects of Study A[1] were integrated and two were *area*-segregated; in Study B,[2] two projects were

[1] Study A was conducted by Morton Deutsch and Mary Evans Collins in the spring of 1949. For a full report, see *Interracial Housing: A Psychological Evaluation of a Social Experiment*. Minneapolis: University of Minnesota Press, 1951.
[2] Study B was conducted by the present writers in the spring of 1951. The complete report of this study is to be found in *Human Relations in Interracial Housing*. Minneapolis: University of Minnesota Press, 1955.

integrated and two were *building*-integrated. (These terms will be defined in greater detail below.) With regard to racial proportions, the projects of Study A had between 40 per cent and 70 per cent Negro residents, whereas all the projects of Study B had a much smaller proportion (approximately 10 per cent) of Negro residents.

The data were collected by means of intensive interviews with white housewives in each of the projects. In Study A, 400 interviews were obtained, approximately 100 in each of the four projects. In Study B, there were more than 800 interviews, approximately 200 in each of the four projects. The interviews lasted from one to two hours, during which many issues concerning Negro-white relations in the project were discussed. The interview schedule used in Study B was derived from that used in the earlier study and was similar to it in major respects. Certain adaptations were made in view of the different project conditions.

In presenting the data in the following pages, we shall make comparisons between persons living various distances from Negroes, although it is apparent from the foregoing that in the housing projects studied another potentially important factor occurs simultaneously with and is sometimes indistinguishable from actual physical proximity. We may array the women in the projects of the two studies in terms of their physical proximity to Negroes as follows:

a. Women in the integrated projects of Study A. Almost all these women lived next door to Negroes.

b. Women living near Negroes in the projects of Study B. In the integrated projects these women lived in the same building with Negroes (usually only one Negro family in the building); about a quarter of these women lived immediately next door to a Negro family. In the building-segregated projects these women lived in buildings adjacent to buildings which housed frrom four to eight Negro families.

c. Women living relatively far from Negroes in the projects of Study B. In the integrated projects these women lived in all-white buildings sometimes relatively near, sometimes quite far from mixed buildings which housed, for the most part, a single Negro family. In the building-segregated projects these women lived in buildings not adjacent to Negro buildings and sometimes at considerable distance from them.

d. Women in the area-segregated projects of Study A. All these women lived in all-white areas, most at a considerable distance from Negro buildings.

The physical distance from Negroes of each of these groups of women is greater as we progress from the integrated to the area-segregated projects of Study A. If the hypotheses stated earlier are correct, we should expect a corresponding progression with regard to extent of contact with Negroes and attitude toward Negroes. The women in the integrated projects of

Study A, being physically closest to Negroes, we should expect to have the most extensive contact with them and the most favorable attitudes; we should expect the likelihood of intimate contact and of favorable attitude to decrease in each succeeding group.

CONTACT BETWEEN WHITE AND NEGRO RESIDENTS

. . . . .

It should be noted that, in presenting findings throughout this paper, the two integrated projects of Study A have been combined, as have the two area-segregated projects. Similarly, for Study B the respondents living "near" Negroes (in mixed buildings) in the two integrated projects have been combined into a single group, and contrasted with the combined group of respondents from both integrated projects who lived in all-white buildings. There has been an analagous combination of "nears" and "fars" in the two building-segregated projects. These groupings have been made in the interest of simplicity of presentation. Only summaries of main results are given for Study A. . . . Findings of Study B, although also condensed, are given in somewhat more detail.

Statistical tests of differences between groups being compared have been made in both studies. With regard to Study A, any difference mentioned as existing between the integrated and area-segregated projects is significant at the 95 per cent level of confidence. With regard to Study B, any difference mentioned as existing between "near" and "far" proximity groups occurred in the indicated direction in all four projects. Most of the differences reported were significant at the 95 per cent level of confidence in at least three projects, and several of them in all four; the cumulative significance is, of course, considerably higher.

Physical closeness . . . increases the likelihood of encounters under conditions conducive to recognition, greeting, and conversation. Whether such encounters lead to the development of more than casual acquaintanceship and to the actual choice of friends is dependent, of course, on a number of other factors. Nevertheless, our prediction was that those white housewives who lived near Negroes would be the group most likely to extend their contacts in the direction of increasing intimacy. The data from both studies support this prediction.

STUDY A

The women interviewed in Study A were asked to name the five persons they knew best in the project. Two fifths of the women in both integrated projects mentioned at least one Negro resident among those they knew best. In sharp contrast, none of the women in the area-segregated projects included Negroes in their lists. Thus, this fairly general measure indicates that a considerable number of those who have an opportunity to make friends with Negroes do so. It is also clear that where white women live at a distance from Negroes, interracial friendships are not formed—at least in the type of social climate which characterizes area-segregated housing.

Study A also explored certain behavioral indicators of intimacy of inter-racial contacts. Women in the four projects were asked whether they engaged in any of four general types of activity with Negroes, each of which presupposed considerable intimacy: visiting back and forth, helping one another out (caring for children or for the sick), informal club activi-ties, and going out together (shopping, etc.). No fewer than half the women who lived as neighbors in the same buildings with Negroes (i.e., in the integrated projects) reported at least one such type of contact with their Negro neighbors. Only five women out of the two hundred in the area-segregated projects reported engaging in such activities with Negroes.

STUDY B

The evidence from Study B similarly supports our hypothesis of the rela-tionship between bi-racial proximity and intimacy of bi-racial contact. White women in the four projects of Study B were asked to describe the extent of their contacts with Negroes in the project. Some reported that, although they passed Negroes in the street, they had no further contacts —not even an exchange of greetings. Others reported that they at most greeted Negroes during casual encounters. A third group customarily stopped for more or less extended conversations about a variety of topics. Finally there were those who engaged in neighborly associations involving relatively intimate relationships. These neighborly associations included activities such as those described in connection with Study A—visiting, helping one another out, and doing a variety of things together. Table 1 shows, for both integrated and building-segregated projects, the relationship between these different types of contact and the relative nearness to one another of Negro and white tenants.

In the integrated projects of Study B (where about 10 per cent of the tenants were Negroes), among white housewives living in mixed buildings the number reporting a given type of contact increased at each level of intimacy—from 10 per cent with no contact to 42 per cent with neighborly association. Among white housewives in all-white buildings in these proj-ects, the reverse trend was found: consistently fewer reported contacts with Negroes at each increasingly close level of intimacy.

Similarly, in the building-segregated projects (also having about 10 per cent Negro tenants), white women who lived near Negroes were more likely than those who lived farther away to report the closer kinds of asso-ciations with Negroes. In addition, when we compare the white women

Table 1:   Degree of Proximity and Extent of Contact

	TWO INTEGRATED PROJECTS (LOW NEGRO-WHITE RATIO)		TWO BUILDING-SEGREGATED PROJECTS (LOW NEGRO-WHITE RATIO)	
Extent of Contact with Negroes	Mixed Buildings (N=186)	All-White Buildings (N=252)	Near Negro Building (N=135)	Not Near Negro Building (N=233)
No contact	10%	37%	5%	21%
Exchange greetings, but no more	22	30	26	44
Extended conversations in chance encounters, but no more	26	19	43	26
Neighborly association (visit, help one another out, do things together)	42	14	26	9

living near Negroes in the building-segregated projects with those living in mixed buildings in the integrated projects, we find considerably fewer reporting the closest type of contact—neighborly association.

Two additional factors may be related to the development of contact between the races: the climate of white opinion in the project regarding friendliness with Negroes, and elements in the white housewife's own background which might predispose her either to seek out or to avoid Negroes in the project.

THE CLIMATE OF OPINION CONCERNING
WHITE-NEGRO FRIENDLINESS

Recognition of prejudice as a social phenomenon makes relevant an investigation not only of the extent and kind of interaction between whites and Negroes, but also of the social supports for the interaction. We may expect that a powerful influence on the white housewife will be the opinions of her white friends and neighbors in the community. These opinions may be made known to her in many ways. She learns how neighbors feel about an issue by listening to them express their views, by overhearing their instructions to children, and, probably most important of all, by observing their interaction with Negroes.

We have already learned how distance from Negroes is related to this interaction; and the frequency with which the interaction occurs may in itself be considered as an objective indicator of the climate of opinion. We may pursue the investigation further, however, by inquiring about the white housewife's own perception of the situation—whether she thinks interaction with Negroes is approved or disapproved.

STUDY A

The white housewife in the four projects of this study was asked to antici- pate the reactions of white friends in the project to her own potential or actual friendliness with Negro residents. Almost half the women in the two integrated projects reported the feeling that their friends would favor friendly interaction with Negroes, compared to only 15 per cent who reported anticipating hostility. In contrast, only 4 per cent of the women in the area-segregated projects reported their friends as favorable, while more than half anticipated hostility.

STUDY B

Answers to a similar question in the four projects of Study B reveal differ- ences dependent on proximity in each of the four projects; differences which, as expected, were not as marked as in Study A. Half of the women who lived near Negroes in the low-ratio integrated projects perceived their friends as approving friendly interaction with Negro residents; 36 per cent of the women living farther away had similarly favorable expectations. In the low-ratio building-segregated projects, 42 per cent of the white residents living in the vicinity of Negro buildings, compared to 24 per cent living in areas with no Negro buildings, anticipated favorable reactions from friends in the project. That these expectations were based, in part at least, on observation of the extent of Negro-white association taking place in the project is apparent from the fact that many more of the women living near Negroes than of those living farther away reported observing contact between other white persons and Negroes in the project.

INITIAL ATTITUDE AS AN INFLUENCE
ON EXTENT OF INTERRACIAL CONTACT

．．．．．

The data from both studies, when summarized, make possible an estimate of the relative influence upon the level of interracial contact of initial atti- tude, on the one hand, and interracial proximity and social climate on the other: (1) When white persons live at a distance from Negroes and are separated sharply from them, as in the area-segregated projects of Study A, the latter factors appear to be almost completely dominant; interracial contacts of the more intimate types are unlikely, regardless of original attitude. Even the woman who has previously lived near or worked beside

Negroes finds the physical and social barriers such as to discourage inter-racial contacts. (2) These same factors remain dominant, though less so, when white persons live near Negroes, as in the integrated projects of Study A and in the mixed buildings and adjacent buildings of Study B. While such persons differ somewhat in the extent of contacts they have with Negroes, depending on their original attitude, in all projects in both studies considerably more than half of the white persons living near Negroes—whether more or less favorable to Negroes at the outset—report contacts with Negroes in the projects which extend at least to the level of street conversations. (3) When the distance from Negroes is intermediate between those extremes, as in the all-white buildings or areas of Study B, the white person's initial attitudes takes on more importance as a factor in the type of contact she has with Negroes. In other words, in situations where the physical arrangements neither necessitate nor preclude interracial contact, leaving greater scope for the operation of individual preference in establishing and extending contacts with Negroes, the latter factor may have noticeable effects.

· · · · ·

BELIEFS ABOUT NEGROES IN THE PROJECT

In the projects of both studies, Negro residents are not very likely to con-form to the typical stereotypes held by many white persons; moreover, for reasons already mentioned, they are in many ways very much like the white residents. Within a project, the white residents with the greatest opportunity to observe these similarities are those who live near Negroes. As a result, such residents might be expected to hold fewer stereotyped notions than the white residents who live farther away from Negroes.

STUDY A

During the course of the interviews, white women in the projects of this study were encouraged to talk about the Negroes in the project. Many of their comments ascribed positive or negative attributes to the Negro resi-dents. Considerably more women living in the integrated than in the area-segregated projects mentioned positive attributes: "helpful," "polite and respectable," "sociable and friendly," etc. On the other hand, more women living in the area-segregated projects than in the integrated projects ascribed negative attributes to Negroes—described them as "low class," as having ill-mannered and destructive children, as making trouble and as being aggressive.

The white housewives in this study were also asked, "Are they (Negroes in the project) pretty much the same as the white people who live here or are they different?" About four fifths of the women in the integrated projects, in contrast to less than three fifths in the area-segregated projects, replied that Negro residents in the projects were the same as the white residents.

STUDY B

A slightly different technique was used in Study B to obtain an estimate of women's beliefs about Negroes. They were asked to indicate, on the basis of their experiences with both races in the project, who was superior—white or Negro residents—or whether they were both the same, in such matters as cleanliness, the upbringing of children, care of community property, intelligence, ambition, and trustworthiness. Women living near Negroes were more likely than those living farther away to report the races equal in these characteristics.

Four of the items on which the women compared the races were combined into a scale. Of the women living in mixed buildings in the integrated projects, 39 per cent rated Negro and white equal in all characteristics included in the scale, and only 18 per cent rated them equal in at most one characteristic; of women in the all-white buildings, the corresponding percentages were 25 and 35 respectively. Of the women living near a Negro building in the building-segregated projects, 32 per cent rated Negro and white equal in all characteristics, and only 13 per cent rated them equal in at most a single characteristic; of women *not* living near a Negro building, the corresponding percentages were 23 and 33 respectively. It is clear that women living far from Negroes were, on the average, twice as likely as women living near Negroes to occupy the more prejudiced end of the scale.

•   •   •   •   •

THE MEANING OF THE DIFFERENCES IN
ATTITUDE AMONG PROXIMITY GROUPS

The differences between proximity groups in the various dimensions of attitude . . . may be interpreted as indicating that white women living near Negroes had *changed* in a favorable direction in their attitudes toward Negroes during their tenancy in the project, while white women living farther away either had changed less or had not changed at all. This interpretation is based on the supposition that if similar distributions of original attitudes occurred among the white residents in the proximity groups being compared, then the more favorable attitudes of the white housewives living near Negroes represent a change from their original attitudes. . . . as far as could be determined, the women living relatively close to and relatively far from Negroes within any given project of Study B were similar in their initial attitudes, and . . . the slight differences in estimated initial attitudes between the residents of the integrated and area-segregated projects of Study A were not sufficient to account for the differences in extent of interracial contact and in ethnic attitudes at the time of the study. It is this contrast—essential similarity of estimated attitudes between the proximity groups at the time they moved into the projects, and differences between the proximity groups after they had been living in the projects—which leads us to conclude that change has taken place in one group (the women living near Negroes) and not in the other (those living far from Negroes), or, at any rate, that the former have changed more than the latter.

Further evidence for the interpretation that the more favorable attitudes on the part of white women living near Negroes reflect *changes* in attitude is found in the white housewives' own reports of their present feelings about Negroes compared to their former feelings. In both Study A and Study B, the white housewives were asked whether "their ideas about colored people" had changed since living in the project. In Study A, three fifths of the women in the integrated projects, compared to about one quarter of those in the area-segregated projects, reported favorable change in their attitudes toward Negroes. In Study B, both in the low-ratio integrated and the low-ratio building-segregated projects, not quite half of the women living near Negroes reported changing in a favorable direction while, again, this was true of only a quarter of the women living farther away.

In both studies, women who were originally unfavorable in attitude (and who therefore had greater possibility for change in a friendly direction) were more likely to report change of attitude. In Study A, more than three quarters of the white women in the integrated projects who reported themselves originally unfavorable said they had changed in a favorable direction; this was true of about one third of the originally unfavorable women living in the area-segregated projects. In Study B, the findings were similar. Among women reporting themselves originally unfavorable to Negroes, almost twice as many living near Negroes as living farther away reported changing in a favorable direction; in the integrated projects the proportions were about two thirds and one third respectively, and in the building-segregated projects, four fifths and two fifths respectively.

. . . . .

The process becomes even more clear when we take into account the perception of social climate with regard to interracial association. Of *all* the women, regardless of degree of physical proximity, those most likely to hold Negroes in high esteem were the ones who both engaged in extended street conversation or in neighborly associations with Negroes *and* perceived the social climate as favorable to interracial association. The proportion of such women was twice as great among those living near Negroes as among those living farther away. On the other hand, the persons most likely of all to hold Negroes in low esteem, regardless of proximity, were those who had no contacts with them or, at most, exchanged casual greetings *and* who perceived the social climate as unfavorable to interracial association. The proportion of such women was twice as great among those living far from Negroes as among those living closer to them. We may now formulate an explanation of the attitude differences between proximity groups: *These differences may be largely accounted for by the differences in the proportions of women in the different proximity groups who have relatively intimate contacts with Negroes and perceive these contacts as socially approved, and, as a result, change in their attitudes.*

The two studies thus provide strong support for a hypothesis that has gained increasing acceptance in recent years: that contact among racial groups of equal or nearly equal socio-economic class and status-roles is a favorable condition for the modification of ethnic attitudes. The data from these studies indicate that this is particularly likely to be the case in situations where the social climate supports such contact.

Speculation about the process which takes place in the interaction of these factors suggests that contact may be viewed as both cause and effect of favorable attitude change. An originally hostile white woman who finds herself visiting back and forth with a Negro neighbor does not at that point alter her attitude in a favorable direction. Such relatively intimate neighborly behavior already reflects some attitude change. Upon repetition of the activity, the change which has already taken place is reinforced and then extended. The relationship between contact and attitude modification is thus seen to be similar to that which is characteristic of all social *processes*, a dynamic interaction among the components. Attitude is not the only aspect of this process that undergoes change in the course of time; the nature of the contact changes as well.

Both the extension of contact and the attitude changes, we may hypothesize, are supported if the social climate is perceived as favoring association between whites and Negroes. If one major source of prejudice, as we have assumed, is assimilation of social norms which characterize Negroes as inferior and contact between whites and Negroes as undesirable, it seems reasonable to suppose that a potent dynamic for attitude change is conformity to new social norms which embody approval of interracial association.

VI. THE SEARCH
FOR NEGRO IDENTITY

37. Color and Identity
Conflict in Young Boys

EUGENE B. BRODY

As Brody indicates at the outset of this selection, a good deal of research indicates that color consciousness develops quite early among Negro children. Partly because of the visibility of racial differences, intellectual and emotional overtones of race frequently become part of an individual's basic identity. This tendency is more pronounced in Negro than in white youngsters, for whites are more likely to be able to take their race for granted, especially if they do not have much contact with Negroes.

Many of the Negro youngsters discussed in Brody's paper provided materials showing that they were depressed about their color, that they equated blackness with weakness and badness, and that they felt constrained to suppress the hostility (in the interview setting, it was expressed

SOURCE: *Psychiatry*, 26, 1963, pp. 188–200 (with some descriptive material on individual cases omitted). Reprinted by permission of the publisher and of the author. Copyright © 1963 by the William Alanson White Psychiatric Foundation.

Eugene B. Brody is Professor of Psychiatry and Director of the Psychiatric Institute at the University of Maryland School of Medicine. He has published widely in the fields of physiological, clinical, and social psychiatry.

indirectly in the form of play) arising as a consequence of their feelings of futility and relative worthlessness.

Do not generalize the results of this study too far. Its sample consisted of emotionally disturbed children and their mothers. Without a corroborating comparative examination of healthy boys and their mothers, it would not be legitimate to assert that conflicts over color somehow caused rather than reflected emotional difficulties. Nevertheless, Brody's examination is of special interest because it demonstrates that children can develop uncomfortable color consciousness from their mothers' attitudes, even when this development runs counter to the mothers' conscious intentions. As reprinted here, the selection omits descriptive material on some individuals, but the analysis is complete.

Although there is published evidence indicating that many young Negro children wish that they were white, there is little literature concerning the role of mother-child interaction in the development of such a wish, or the way in which the child deals with it. This paper reports observations of: (1) young Negro boys' perceptions of themselves as white or Negro, and (2) their mothers' deliberate but unwitting indoctrination regarding their color status. The observations were made as part of a series of studies concerned with the influence of sociocultural factors on character and psychopathology. Such factors appear to be prominently related to problems of self-definition, especially to how a person sees himself in relation to others.

EARLIER STUDIES

The first study of the series concerned a segment of Baltimore's Negro population presenting obvious and extreme identity problems—a group of schizophrenic young men admitted to a segregated state mental hospital.[1] These patients denied their color, their social and economic status, and their sexual prowess, substituting fantasies of having lighter skin and greater prestige, wealth, or potency. They often seemed to be saying: "I don't like who I am," "I don't know who I am," "I am not the person I seem to be," or "I am not the person you think I am."

For these young men, as in Eric Erikson's formulation,[2] achievement with real cultural meaning—and the sense of reality that comes from a way of life which is an individual variant of a stable group identity—were out of reach. This was partly because there is no American Negro culture, in the sense of a stable, well-defined, socially transmitted system of behavior

[1] E. B. Brody, "Social Conflict and Schizophrenic Behavior in Young Adult Negro Males," *Psychiatry* (1961) 24:337–346.
[2] Erik H. Erikson, *Childhood and Society;* New York, Norton, 1950; pp. 397 and 208.

patterns covering all major life areas, and partly because Negroes are not as yet permitted free access to the white culture. The patients' families, their primary agents of socialization, were not total participants in the general white American culture. Thus, while the patients were growing up, they were not able to acquire within their families a set of norms, behavioral referents, or social response patterns congruent with those of the surrounding society. Inasmuch as the families themselves were fragmented and reflected the efforts of the minority group to accommodate to the majority,[3] they possibly could not offer a child a set of internally consistent or stable patterns for interaction either within the family group or within the Negro social world. One way of looking at these difficulties is summarized by Shibutani: "When participating in societies in which the component group norms are not mutually consistent, it becomes progressively more difficult for any man to integrate his various self-images into a single unit."[4]

A second population which has been studied with respect to problems of self-definition consists of Negro college students.[5] These persons are upwardly mobile in terms of social and economic status. They are conscious of their rights as American citizens and of what has been denied them in the past. They are beginning to achieve new identities for themselves as citizens of the wider United States community rather than solely as inhabitants of the Negro social world. This developing marginal status has many inherent identity problems, which are reflected in their attitudes and sometimes in maladaptive behavior patterns.[6]

SAMPLE

The children most available for the study described in this paper were those attending the clinics associated with the Psychiatric Institute of the University of Maryland. These constitute a special population which, through maladaptive modes of problem solving, may reveal conflicts that are present but less significant for others. Each child has at least one concerned and presumably sensitive parent. The parents ranged from unskilled

[3] See Robert L. Derbyshire, Eugene B. Brody, and Carl Schleifer, "Family Structure of Young Adult Negro Male Mental Patients: Preliminary Observations from Urban Baltimore," *J. Nervous and Mental Disease* (1963) 136:245–251.
[4] Tamotsu Shibutani, *Society and Personality*; Englewood Cliffs, N. J., Prentice-Hall, 1961; p. 246.
[5] R. L. Derbyshire and E. B. Brody, "Personal Identity and Social Distance in Negro College Students," presented at annual meeting, Amer. Psychiatric Assn., Toronto, May 11, 1962.
[6] R. L. Derbyshire and E. B. Brody, "A Functional Analysis of American Negro Marginality," presented at annual meeting, Eastern Sociol. Assn., Philadelphia, April 7, 1962 (in press, *Internat. J. Social Psychiatry*).

laborers or domestics with some grammar school education to white-collar workers who had graduated from Negro colleges.

It is possible that issues surrounding color are more apparent in neurotically disturbed Negro children and their mothers than in less disturbed children. However, the question of whether conflicts concerning color and racial identity stimulate neurotic responses, or whether the disturbances themselves aggravate and are reflected in color-identity problems, is unclear.

Boys were selected for study, in part because of the tendency for Negro families to have a matriarchal structure. Most of the fathers of the nineteen boys who were investigated were grammar school graduates, laborers or artisans, and the mothers were economically important to the family. In six cases no father or father substitute lived with the family, although in all six the boy saw his father occasionally or maintained an irregular relationship with one or more of the mother's male friends (sometimes called "daddy"). In four other cases the mother was divorced and remarried, so that in ten of the families the mother provided the only consistent parental relationship. This was also true in a less dramatic way for the remaining nine cases, in which the child's biological father was a member of the family group.

Kardiner and Ovesey, and Frazier have presented evidence that the American Negro man has had a significant problem in maintaining his masculine status, not only because of the structure of his family but also because of the emasculating pressure of the white society, against which effective retaliation has, heretofore, been impossible.[7] It seems plausible, then, to assume that problems related to color will be more apparent in boys than in girls.

The hypothetical emasculation may begin with the little boy's awareness that his father and father-surrogates are vulnerable in relation to white males. The studies of Goodman and of Clark and Clark indicate that discrimination on the basis of color, recognition of the difference in power and prestige between Negroes and whites, and an uneasy preference for being white can be demonstrated in four- to five-year-old Negro nursery school children.[8] For the present study, therefore, the age range from six to ten was selected, in order to provide subjects in whom the capacity to

---

[7] Abram Kardiner and Lionel Ovesey, *The Mark of Oppression: A Psychosocial Study of the American Negro;* New York, Norton, 1951. E. Franklin Frazier, *Negro Youth at the Crossways;* Washington, D. C., Amer. Council on Education, 1940.

[8] Mary Ellen Goodman, *Race Awareness in Young Children;* Cambridge, Mass., Addison-Wesley Press, 1952. K. B. and M. K. Clark, "The Development of Consciousness of Self and the Emergence of Racial Identification in Negro Preschool Children," *J. Social Psychol.* (1939) 10:591–599. K. B. and M. K. Clark, "Skin Color as a Factor in Racial Identification of Negro Preschool Children," *J. Social Psychol.* (1940) 11:159–169. Kenneth and Mamie Clark, "Emotional Factors in Racial Identification and Preference in Negro Children," *J. Negro Education* (1950) 19:341–350.

discriminate was well developed, and who had passed through the initial problems of becoming accustomed to school, but were not yet involved in adolescence. Consecutive clinic admissions of grammar school boys were admitted to the study group over a period of several months with a frequency determined in part by the available time of the investigators. The prolonged period of study was also a function of the nature of the clinic population, which was predominantly white and within a slightly older age range. One five-year-old first grader was inadvertently included. His behavior was not significantly different from that of the others.

METHOD

Preliminary interviewing was carried out with seven boys, two white and five Negro, and their mothers. On the basis of these interviews a procedure was developed which was utilized with a study group of sixty additional people, eleven white and nineteen Negro boys and their mothers. The interviewers were white, which poses an obvious methodological problem. However, it was not possible to clearly identify the particular consequences of the interviewers' color, and in an earlier study of adult Negro patients no differences were observed in data gathered by white and Negro psychiatrists.[9] The possibility that special stresses may also be imposed upon Negro children by an interviewer of the same color is indicated by Clark's observation of the highly emotional reactions (weeping and evidence of marked anxiety) of Negro children when he required them to choose between Negro and white dolls.[10] No such reactions were observed during the course of the present study.

Two sets of observations were made on each subject, about one hour each and approximately one week apart. For the mothers the sessions consisted of interviews, for the boys they consisted of directed play. Each mother was first interviewed with an essentially unstructured technique aimed at gathering general information concerning her perceptions of her son and his problems, her husband and other family members, and her life situation. In the second interview attention was specifically directed to her attitudes toward race and color and her attempts to train her son in these respects.

The boys, in both sessions, were engaged in play with white and Negro male hand puppets following a predetermined scheme. The puppets were made of soft, pliable rubber and dressed in business suits. They were similar except for skin and eye color (the Negro was brown-skinned and dark-eyed; the white was blue-eyed) and conventional Negroid or Cauca-

---

[9] See footnote 1.
[10] K. B. Clark, discussion, Crownsville State Hosp., Md., November, 1961.

soid features. The boy was initially allowed to play with both puppets. At the beginning he was asked what he wanted to be when he grew up; which puppet resembled and which was different from him, his parents, and siblings; and in what way they were different. After a period of free play he was then given the choice of keeping one puppet while the interviewer took the other. Finally, the interviewer switched puppets with the boy. After another period of free play he was asked, "If this one [white] were white and this one [Negro] were Negro, then what would they do?" If the boy did not spontaneously make a clear statement of preference regarding the puppets, he was asked about this. At the end of each puppet play period he was also asked about the relative strength, goodness, and mood of each puppet. The sessions were observed through a one-way mirror and most were tape recorded, with typescripts made for later study.

RESULTS

The findings, confined to those possible after observations of the nineteen Negro boys and their mothers, do not permit statistical generalizations. They are presented to indicate the variety of individual ways of dealing with color-identity problems that are present in this population.

Table 1 summarizes reactions of the twelve boys who evidenced color-conflict, gives several features of each mother's behavior, and indicates whether or not a significant problem in communication existed between mother and son. The attitudes of mothers and sons are illustrated with verbatim statements from the interview and puppet play situations. Table 2 similarly describes the seven boys, and their mothers, who evidenced no color conflict. Obviously, it cannot be said that these seven had no conflict concerning color, but any such feelings, if present, were not clearly expressed during the course of the study.

Table 1:   Mothers and Sons with Evidence of Color Conflict *

. . . . .

RR, Age 7.

W: Resembles father; fighting, superior, powerful, hard to placate. N: Later assumes W's role and kills W. Refers to puppets as "white boy" and "black boy." Kills both puppets in midplay but then denies W's death and says, "I'm going to try to kill that black one now." A lion will first eat "the black one" but then both; "white" first since "black" has three guns to protect himself.

Mother of RR.

No discussion of intrafamilial color range. Group reactor. Denies boy's conflicts about color. Probable communication problem. Generally distrustful and

* W represents white puppet; N represents Negro puppet.

laconic in interview, doesn't believe that issues surrounding color, or her feelings about anything have any effect on her son, especially on his current school problems. Often punishes him harshly, physically or by deprivation.

·   ·   ·   ·   ·

GT, Age 8.

W: Resembles self and mother. Some fighting with W winning, though later N stabs him in the back. Great emphasis on N's facial characteristics: Chocolate ice cream is spilled on N's face and "People say they don't like a chocolate face. That's bad." Later, "N has a rash, would like to get rid of it . . . a face like Frankenstein, used it to scare W away . . . under the dark face is like a girl . . . face was painted white." When playing with W says, "I have a face now. It's white." Later, speaking of N: "He has two faces. One is white. It is hidden in his hair. It has no mouth, nose, or ears, only eyes so nobody won't know it and can't see it."

Mother of GT.

Concerned with intrafamilial color range. Individual reactor, but conscious of tendencies to be sensitive to group reaction. In conflict. Denies boy's conflicts about color. Probable communication problem. "He doesn't seem to be conscious of race at all." Although children are aware of color shadings he "is only aware of this from the standpoint of a color chart . . . it is only color itself." When he asked her about a newsphoto of a Negro man being beaten, she said: "Some people are mean. Color has nothing to do with it." If he were to press her about the meaning of skin color, she would tell him: "It is true that there are different races . . . but it is not race that is important . . . the pigment of your skin would make no difference." She speaks of Jews, Germans, and Poles in her area.

KW, Age 7.

W: Resembles self, father, sisters. Fighting prominent in second visit with W attacking; later has a snake bite W and says N would win. N is also "bad." Preoccupied with color: He has been called "Black Stuff" and "Blackie." "Blackie is the color of my shoes, that's a name that makes me mad. . . . I feel that sad about being dark-skinned. I felt that way since I was a baby." When called this he fights and is mad; when mad he feels bad and sad. He doesn't like to have the N puppet on his right hand "because I'm a light-skinned person, and I'm supposed to have things that are light-skinned, and I like to be like a . . . like a white . . . I mean if somebody took a picture of me and made a puppet just like me I'd want it light-skinned not dark-skinned."

Mother of KW.

Concerned with intrafamilial color range. Individual reactor, but very conscious of race and ethnicity. Denies son's color problem, though later acknowledges he may have an "inward" one that he has never expressed to her. Probable communication problem. She does "not feel that the question of color bothers K at all" although he did once tell her that he was white. As for herself, "It has never been a problem . . . if I carry myself in the right way it doesn't make any difference what color you are . . . if everyone is dignified color doesn't matter." When children have asked her about newspaper accounts of race riots she said, "There is good and bad in everyone; color doesn't make any difference." Has also noted, "The gentile and the Jew and the Irish and all that . . . everybody has their own class . . . there are different races of white people . . . and . . . brown races that are not considered Negro as well as white races not considered pure white." Has told this to other children, but "The occasion has never arisen to explain to K."

KH, Age 6.
W: Resembles brother. Friendly puppet interaction, but W is drunk, hit on head "by a light-skinned person," has more money, is happy, might "knock N out," while N is sad. At first says he likes W best, that W resembles him but finally: "N is more like me . . . I'm dark-skinned . . . light skin is the best . . . light is prettier . . . light skin is too light . . . I never wanted to have a light skin."

Mother of KH.
Concerned with intrafamilial color range, but without strong emphasis. Individual reactor. Recognizes son's concern with color, though does not state it as a problem. No obvious communication problem. Has told him when he has wondered why some people are colored and some are not: "That's life, there are all nationalities."

. . . . .

---

*Table 2: Mothers and Sons without Evidence of Color Conflict**

JCL, Age 10.
W: Resembles mother and sisters. Likes N best because he resembles him more. Generally innocuous play with no apparent uncertainty re identity.

Mother of JCL.
Concerned with intrafamilial color range. Individual reactor though very sensitive to issues concerning color. Denies that he has a color problem, but at the same time says integration has made him nervous and reports frequent questions about color. Probable communication problem. "I try to teach him to be proud of his race." As to significance of color differences: "It never really occurred to my mind to ask him any things like that . . . never occur to him either, feelings . . . difference between one and the other. I mean I don't have any feelings like that and neither do my children . . . he doesn't feel no prejudice or bitterness toward the other race . . . because we had white and colored living all around us." "I try to raise my children different . . . to believe in no difference between race, creed, or color . . . I don't want my children to grow up with hate in their hearts or a feeling that they are handicapped because they are colored." In response to the boy's question about a librarian she told him he is not concerned with the boy's color. He also asked

---

* W represents white puppet; N represents Negro puppet.

if it is harder for a colored man to succeed than a white man. She said, "It depends on the man . . . color is only skin deep . . . depends on how you carry yourself as an individual that will give you respect and affection from people around you." In her neighborhood whites are more prejudiced against Jews, she says, than Negroes.

. . . . .

DD, Age 10.

W: Resembles whole family, including self. A stiff, constricted performance with little spontaneous activity. Innocuous interaction. Told mother that he was bored, and that the white puppet was "too faded."

Mother of DD.

Concerned with intrafamilial color range. Individual reactor but very color conscious. Denies any color problem, but says that D called her "dirty colored." Probable communication problem. Very light-skinned, as is D. Says that she doesn't categorize people as white or Negro although "I am more uncomfortable among Negroes as a group" and "People who pass as white are very unhappy." "I haven't trained the children to anything colorwise knowingly, you know, coming out and saying black is black and white is white. Color hasn't even entered our family." As a child heard about Wops, Polacks, and niggers, "but it didn't mean anything to me . . . the word 'nigger' wasn't permitted in our house." In junior high school she stayed overnight with white girls and vice versa, but not when older. "I think of myself as being me, just me, that's the way I feel rather than white or Negro."

. . . . .

RD, Age 10.

W: Resembles self. N stronger, smarter, richer, and a better driver than W. N is happy and the best man. Generally friendly puppet interaction. Is, however, sensitive to color, indicating that he is like W because he is lighter skinned than other family members.

Mother of RD.

Concern with intrafamilial color range. Individual reactor. Recognizes that son once asked her about color. No obvious communication problem. Differentiates between "regular all colored neighborhood" and a lower-class one. Has a friendly relationship with a white woman who often takes R out with her son and is more interested in him than "some of the colored." Is interested in possible sexual attraction of whites and Negroes, with special reference to a white woman in her area with a colored husband. "A colored man would not want a light woman because his children would be too white."

. . . . .

TH, Age 10.

W: Resembles nobody. Stiff, somewhat laconic, but friendly puppet interaction. In second session N and W are even friendlier and W invites N to dinner.

Mother of TH.

No concern with intrafamilial color range. Probably a group reactor. Tends to be a denier of possible color problems. Probable communication problem. Will not talk about color because doesn't regard it as related to son's difficulties. Notes that the school has some but "not too many white children," that T plays "pretty good" with one white boy; is concerned about several white girls who "play with the colored children." T, whom she regards as "bad," told her nothing at all about his visit to the clinic.

. . . . .

BOYS' BEHAVIOR

Puppet Play Evidence of Color-Conflict Judgments about the presence or absence of significant color-conflicts were made on the basis of the nature of the boys' play with the puppets and of their comments about the state of being Negro or dark-skinned, in comparison with the state of being white or light-skinned. Each boy listed as exhibiting color-conflict either directly stated his wish not to be Negro or his unhappiness about being Negro or gave some less direct indication of not being fully able to accept his reality status. The indirect indications included negative valuations of color, anxiety-laden uncertainty and shifting feelings about color status, or the playing out of situations in which the Negro puppet was made to be weak, inferior, or bad in comparison to the white—play patterns that might reasonably be considered to imply strong tendencies to reject a Negro identity.

The boys' statement of their own or relatives' resemblance to the white puppet were not used in making the judgment as to color-conflict because many families included a range of skin color. In eleven of the twelve color-conflict cases, however, the boy said that one or more family members resembled the white more than the Negro puppet; in three instances the boy included himself. Only three of the seven boys exhibiting no evidence of color-conflict stated such a resemblance to family members; two of these three included themselves.

Three of the twelve color-conflict boys, EB, KW, and UD, stated directly that they wished they were white or that they were unhappy about being Negro. KW added, "I feel sad about being dark-skinned; I felt that way since I was a baby."

Less positive statements of similar significance included those by PS and by GT, who said, "People say they don't like a chocolate face. That's bad."

Greater vacillation is suggested by KH, who valued light skin but said he did not want it. In a somewhat similar vein, JL spoke of the Negro puppet's shifting thoughts and feelings about being white or colored. Examples indicating conflict with even less clear-cut rejection of Negro status include EJ, whose Negro puppet's friends told him not to like white people. The two puppets then fought with each other; white won the battle, and the boy referred to the Negro puppet as "bad." Later, however, he reversed his initial preference for the white puppet. MW, who referred to the white puppet as good and the Negro as bad, later reversed his statement, and also indicated an internal-external conflict.

Six boys in the color-conflict group referred to the Negro puppet as "bad," and three of these also called it "sad" in response to the interviewer's direct question. A fourth, KH, who said that the white puppet might "knock out" the Negro, referred to the latter only as being "sad."

Significant fighting occurred at least once in the puppet play of eight of the twelve color-conflict boys, and five of the eight fighting Negro puppets were described as "bad," "sad," or both. In some instances the white puppet was initially victorious, strong, unbeatable, and knowledgeable. Nonetheless, the defeated Negro puppet might be labeled as "bad" because he was a fighter. Sometimes a shift occurred, so that the Negro puppet had his turn, but as the victor he tended to be more vicious and murderous, was less apt to win in direct face-to-face combat, and employed some magical or special technique such as judo to gain his ends.

In contrast, only one of the seven boys evidencing no color-conflict, JW, exhibited marked fighting behavior. He stated a strong preference for the Negro puppet, who was good and dominant while the white was "bad" and "sad." JF engaged in some fighting play, with the two puppets, evenly matched, being called "bad" in turn. RD regarded the Negro puppet as superior to the white one. He, like the others, demonstrated a pattern of friendly puppet interaction.

Resemblance of Boy or Family Member to White or Negro Puppet   Four of the nineteen Negro boys viewed their fathers as resembling the white more than the Negro puppet; five said that they themselves, and eight said that their mothers, resembled the white more than the Negro puppet. Only six, that is, about one-third of the boys, saw themselves and all members of their families as more closely resembling the Negro than the white puppet and of these six, two expressed some uncertainty, leaving only four of nineteen boys who identified themselves and both parents as unequivocally Negro.

Six of the eight boys who regarded their mothers as resembling the white puppet portrayed friendly or even affectionate activities rather than fighting between the two puppets. In these six instances the white puppet was not portrayed as superior to the Negro.

Symptomatic Behavior   There was no apparent relation between the absence or presence of color-conflict in the puppet play, or the form which it took, and the nature of the complaint bringing the boys to the clinic.

One boy, FO, who expressed marked dislike for white children in his integrated school did not reveal this in his play, which was characterized by friendly relations between the two puppets.

Intrafamilial Color Range Seven of the nineteen mothers indicated that intrafamilial color range was a significant issue for them. They reported without being specifically asked that differences in shading from dark to light between themselves, their spouses, and their various children were topics of concern in conversation in the family.

Group Reactors and Individual Reactors Although independent judges were not used to rate the mothers, inspection of typescripts of interviews and of the written descriptions of observations through the one-way mirror permitted a rough division of the mothers into two groups.

The largest group included thirteen mothers who seemed to view themselves and whites in individual human terms rather than as representatives of color classes. They are called "individual reactors." Six of these mothers described emotionally meaningful work and neighborhood relationships with individual white people. The difficulty in assessing this kind of attitude is indicated by the fact that eight of the thirteen individual reactors, including three of the six who had had reciprocal emotional relationships with whites, were highly conscious of and very sensitive to issues surrounding color. Two of these also expressed marked awareness of social class and ethnic differences in general among members of non-Negro as well as Negro groups. It seems likely that for these verbally expressive color-sensitive mothers the individual reactor attitude reflected a basically intellectual rather than emotional viewpoint.

Five mothers were labeled "group reactors." They identified themselves and whites more in terms of class membership than of individual characteristics, and usually were more defensive and suspicious in the interview. The remaining mother gave so little information that it was impossible to classify her in this respect, but her reticence and defensiveness suggested a group reactive attitude.

All of the seven mothers reporting a significant intrafamilial color-range sensitivity were rated as individual reactors and four of these were very sensitive to questions surrounding color. Only six of the remaining twelve mothers were individual reactors.

Mother-Son Communication Nine mothers responded to the interviewers' questions with direct statements illustrating their attempts to train their sons in regard to color. Six responded by discussing their own attitudes only, and the remaining four avoided the question or denied its significance.

Eight of the nine directly responding mothers were regarded as individual reactors, and the sons of seven of the nine were in the color-conflict group.

An example of a direct response is that of the mother of EB, who said that he liked white people and did not like himself. Working against the odds presented by her antiwhite sister and shade-sensitive husband, she trained EB to use a white friend's proper name, at the same time pointing out their similarities except for color. In this instance there was no obvious communication problem between mother and son, although the intra-familial conflict was more clearly presented than usual.

An example of a response in terms of her own attitudes is that of the mother of DW, who cast the white puppet in superior roles and regarded the Negro puppet as bad, sad, and mean. She denied the presence of any conflict in DW, and then made a series of contradictory statements about herself. The estimate that a probable communication problem existed between mother and son was made partly on the basis of her denial of any possibility of color-conflict in DW, and partly on the basis of the inference that she transmitted conflicting attitudes to him through her words and behavior. Thus, while her attitude would prohibit free communication from him regarding his doubts and conflicts about color and would indicate that she did not consider this a legitimate matter for discussion or even for concern, she would simultaneously transmit her sensitivity about her possibly inferior status and her underlying hostility toward whites—in short, her obvious intense concern with the issue of color.

In many other instances, while it was possible to define a conscious message about color deliberately offered by mother to son, it was also possible to define another message transmitted through action, attitudes, and feelings, rather than words. The most frequently encountered conscious message was to the effect that "People are all the same inside," or "We are all human," or "People are what they are and skin color is unimportant." The implied, simultaneously transmitted, unconscious message, mediated through affective and behavioral cues, was essentially: "While I tell you that people are the same inside, I expect you to behave as though this is not true, and, in fact, I don't believe it myself. People are divided into classes; they are not the same; we are different." This message was reinforced by such inherently self-contradictory overt statements as: "It's nicer to call someone brown than black," or "There's no difference between the races, white is white and colored is colored."

Congruence between Puppet-Play Attitudes and Mothers' Reports of Sons' Attitudes   The obvious difference between some mothers' reports of their sons' attitudes and the attitudes as revealed in the puppet play raised a question as to the frequency with which this disparity occurred. Only six of the nineteen mothers made statements recognizing some color-conflict in their sons; nine denied its existence in one way or another; and in four cases no definite statement was made.

Of the six mothers who described their sons in color-conflict terms, four had sons who expressed clear conflict about color status in the presence of the interviewers, and a fifth was included in the color-conflict group despite less clear evidence. Of the nine deniers, five had sons who expressed such conflict. Of the four mothers who could not be classified in this way two had sons in the color-conflict group. All recognizing mothers were individual reactors; four of the nine denying mothers were group reactors.

Although it is clear that many mothers deny the existence of apparently marked color problems in their sons, there was no clear-cut relationship in this group between the mother's denial and the way in which the boy expressed his problem. However, some suggestive tendencies were apparent. Thus, the mothers of seven of the twelve color-conflict boys (58 percent) gave direct responses to questions about their attempts to train their sons regarding color, while only two (28 percent) of the seven mothers of no color-conflict boys gave such responses. Nine (75 percent) of the color-conflict mothers were individual reactors (including five who showed evidence of marked color sensitivity) while four (57 percent) of the no color-conflict mothers were listed as individual reactors. Slightly more of the former (67 percent) had apparent communication problems with their sons than did the latter (57 percent). The significance of recognizing or denying a son's color-conflict is especially unclear in view of the fact that a boy who exhibits no conflict in the course of puppet play may, during his daily life, present his mother with nothing of this nature for her to "recognize." In fact, 57 percent of the mothers of no color-conflict sons were classed as deniers, as compared with 42 percent of the mothers of color-conflict sons; while 41 percent of the mothers of color-conflict sons were classed as recognizers, as compared with 14 percent of the mothers of no-conflict sons. When the mothers who expressed neither denial nor recognition are taken into account, six of the seven mothers (86 percent) of no-conflict boys denied or made no statement about their having color as a problem, while this was true for seven (58 percent) of the twelve mothers of boys showing clear-cut conflict.

The division between the two groups of mothers—individual reactors and group reactors—was more sharply defined on grounds other than their sons' apparent color-conflict. The label of individual reactor may have encompassed a cluster of characteristics. Thus, seven of the thirteen individual reactors were women who discussed the range of color shades within their family (although only two of these considered their sons to suffer from color problems). Individual reactors were inclined to report deliberate attempts to train their sons in regard to perceiving their color status. In contrast none of the group reactors presented intrafamilial color range as an important issue, none specifically acknowledged color problems in her son, and only one reported indoctrination of her son in regard to color.

DISCUSSION

The data make it clear that many of these Negro boys do have significant conflicts involving anxiety or guilt-laden wishes to be white rather than Negro. In this sense some may be considered uncertain as to their identities. Some seem to have little ambivalence or uncertainty, and clearly noted their wish to be white and their depressed feelings about being dark-skinned.

The possible significance of aim-inhibited hostility in the development of identity problems is suggested by the much higher frequency of fighting play in the color-conflict group and the boys' tendency to label the fighting Negro puppet rather than the white as "bad" or "sad."

For most boys, apparent uncertainty was also suggested by statements that they, their parents, or siblings resembled the white rather than the Negro puppet. These statements of resemblances, as well as other evidence of conflict, may reflect: (1) a reality-oriented wish to be the more powerful white and to abandon the less rewarding Negro identity; (2) a tendency to identification with the aggressor as a way of dealing with the powerful white world, particularly as it is known through the attitudes and feelings of parents; (3) a tendency to deal with hostile feelings developed in relation to the white world (usually mediated through the parental relationship) by turning them against the self. It may be inferred that hostility and conflict apparently directed toward a symbol of the white world (the puppet or, more abstractly, "skin color") is, at an unconscious level, often directed against the parent.

The overt dominance of the white puppet over the Negro may reflect the boy's perception of the Negro male as ineffective in relation to the white. Adams, in particular, has pointed out that the Negro child whose parent presents a picture of insecurity and impotence in the face of social reality might ". . . turn to the white group for identification as a defense against his anxiety, but that at some point he will inevitably encounter a final rejection."[11]

The more frequent statement that mother rather than father resembled the male puppet may have reflected the son's perception of her as the dominant parent, and the one to whom, therefore, he ascribed the white

[11] Walter A. Adams, "The Negro Patient in Psychiatric Treatment," *Amer. J. Ortho-psychiatry* (1950) 20:305–310; p. 308.

role. In this respect it is interesting that in the four instances in which the father was classified with the white puppet, the boy classified himself similarly, differentiating himself and father as members of a group to which mother did not belong. This was true in only two of the eight instances when mother was grouped with the white puppet. There was no correlation between statements of resemblance of one or another parent to the white or Negro puppet and the physical presence or absence of a fulltime father in the family.

The mothers, like the sons, exhibited varying degrees of conflict about the color of their skin and their status and role as Negro. Those with several children of differing shades of skin coloring appeared to make a significant effort to view other people in individual terms, rather than solely as representative of the class of Negro or white. The individual reactors in general were more likely to regard their sons as suffering from problems around the question of color and to report deliberate attempts to train their sons to deal with potential problems around color, particularly insofar as the problems might impair the sons' self-esteem. This is compatible with the fact that more than half of the individual reactors appeared to be very sensitive to questions regarding color and in some cases to ethnic issues in general; it may be inferred that their attitude was one requiring conscious self-discipline and some intellectual work on their parts.

The intellectual approach of the individual reactors, who may be more adaptive and secure in the sense that they are possibly less massively repressed, may be related to the finding that their sons did not themselves exhibit less evidence of color-conflict. In general, mothers of sons without evidence of color-conflict were not likely to report its presence and were more likely than mothers of overtly conflictual sons to deny its presence. This, along with a less marked tendency to be individual reactors, suggests that these mothers share with their sons similar avoidance mechanisms for dealing with the anxieties incident to being Negro in Baltimore. Although mothers of the color-conflict group were readier to instruct their sons regarding color, the nature of their instructions and their other attitudes aften revealed a great deal of anxiety and sensitivity about color coupled with a tendency to deny its real significance in their lives. Thus, it seems probable that for mothers of both groups of boys the denial of the significance of color differences is a security operation reflecting considerable sensitivity to this issue. Those boys exhibiting marked evidence of conflict in their puppet play, however, would appear to have been less successful in utilizing their mothers' defensive maneuvers, which were apparently less massive and more verbal-intellectual, and to have suffered from greater problems in communication with their mothers. There is no evidence to indicate the limits of this generalization or its possible relevance to the future mental health of the boys concerned.

The function of Negro mothers as models for their sons, and the impact of their communications regarding color have been emphasized in this discussion. It seems unlikely that a relationship with a mother as the most important power, however secure, can be an adequate basis for the development of a stable social identity in a boy, whether in terms of sex, color, or other significant element.

38. Youth and Social Action: Perspectives on the Student Sit-In Movement

JACOB R. FISHMAN AND
FREDRIC SOLOMON

The following selection analyzes the reasons why Negro youngsters participate in nonviolent demonstrations against what they perceive as racial injustices. The paper's additional interest for sociology stems from its statement of connections between present conscious motivations and historical experience, and between demonstrations per se and the more general political processes they are designed to affect. Participation in a nonviolent demonstration may satisfy a variety of personal needs, but an observer should not assume that each participant has precisely the same motivations, or that each satisfies his needs in precisely the same manner. Some may look forward to the fellowship and feeling of solidarity; others to the chance of proving their bravery and demonstrating their manhood. Some may wish to vent repressed hostility; others may be more interested in impressing their girl friends. In short, it is characteristic of collective movements to crystallize sentiment, bringing together individuals who do share a desire for a common goal but who receive various idiosyncratic rewards through their activity in pursuit of it.

This is the initial report of a study of the psychodynamics of adolescent and student participation in public, risk-taking activities for racial de-

Source: *American Journal of Orthopsychiatry*, 33, 1963, pp. 872–82. Copyright © the American Orthopsychiatric Association, Inc. Reproduced by permission of the Association and of the senior author.

Jacob R. Fishman and *Fredric Solomon* are members of the Department of Psychiatry at Howard University Medical School, where Dr. Fishman is also Director of the Howard University Center for Youth Studies.

segregation. The major participants in this movement have been Negro and white college students in the Southern United States. Their most dramatic and perhaps most effective weapon has been a form of public passive resistance known as the sit-in demonstration. Indeed, the whole movement has come to be known as the student sit-in movement, and the term has quickly become part of our contemporary culture.

The original targets of these demonstrations were variety stores, which customarily welcome Negro patrons in most departments but exclude them from service at lunch counters. The first student sit-in took place on February 1, 1960, when four freshmen at an all-Negro college in Greensboro, North Carolina, deliberately decided to request service at such a segregated lunch counter (18). When service was denied them because of their color, they refused to leave; instead they remained seated, reading schoolbooks and Bibles. Since that time demonstrations have spread through many parts of the country where such policies are in effect and have been aimed at all kinds of segregated public facilities.

There are several possible results from a sit-in. At one extreme, the segregation policy may be promptly ended and the students served. At the other, the demonstrators may be heckled and assaulted, or arrested, jailed and charged with trespassing or disorderly conduct. Whatever the outcome, the pattern of social crisis is always the same: The students aggressively cross the color line, and then passively allow the consequences to rest on the co-operation of other like-minded people and on the decisions of civic authorities and businessmen in the dominant white majority. In the space of three years the South has witnessed thousands of demonstrations, which have also included boycotts, picketing, mass marches, hunger strikes of jailed students and the "freedom rides" on interstate buses. As of April, 1961 (before the freedom rides), demonstrators had numbered in the tens of thousands and had been active in some 75 Southern towns and cities. Three thousand five hundred demonstrators had been arrested; of these, an estimated 95 per cent were young people of both sexes in their teens or early twenties, both Negro and white.[1]

These demonstrations have resulted in the desegregation of more than 5,000 eating facilities, as well as hundreds of libraries, places of recreation and churches. The local, national and international news media have provided wide coverage, and the impact has been felt on campuses all over the country. For the Southern United States, this has represented a rate of social change far more rapid than any it has known since the Negro people were emancipated from slavery nearly 100 years ago (6, 17, 21). In view of the social significance of this student movement, an understanding of the psychodynamic background and motivation of these young

[1] Statistics provided by the Congress on Racial Equality, New York, N. Y.

people should illuminate some of the relationships among personality, society and social change.

During the past two years we have studied the development of this movement, particularly in the Washington, D. C., area. The present paper represents our tentative psychosocial formulations of some motivational and personality factors in these students. Further data collection and analysis is under way (5, 18–20). This report focuses mainly on young Negroes, whereas future papers will deal more extensively with the white student demonstrators, as well as with opponents and supporters in surrounding communities. Reports have already been presented on the very first of the organized sit-in demonstrations (18) and on the dynamics of nonviolent action (20).

Picketing demonstrations in the Washington area have on occasion attracted as many as 200 participants, including, at one point in the summer of 1960, five United States Congressmen. However, the decision-making core of regular demonstrators consisted of about 40 students, calling themselves "NAG," "Nonviolent Action Group." They felt this name exemplified the group's determination to "nag the conscience of the community." (It also symbolizes the recurrent theme of a passive-aggressive, persevering style of action.) White and Negro students, both male and female, were about evenly represented in the group. The average age was 18 years and six months, most members having completed one year in college, with little or no comparable prior experience with interracial organizations. In its first year of activity, the group succeeded in desegregating about 25 facilities, including restaurants, lunch counters, a movie theatre and the area's only amusement park. In addition, they were an important factor in stimulating the development of a council on human relations in suburban Montgomery County. During the course of these activities, about 100 arrests of demonstrators were made by local authorities. Several members of the original group later went on to become involved in freedom rides and other risk-taking actions for desegregation in the Deep South (20).

Seventeen students (7 Negroes and 10 whites) in the Washington group were interviewed both individually and in groups. Three others (2 young Negro men who were major leaders, and one young white woman) were interviewed individually in some depth over a period of six months. Of primary interest in the interviews were those factors leading up to a student's decision to involve himself in a public, risk-taking activity for desegregation; a second focus was on family background and parental reactions to the student's participation. The demonstrators readily volunteered to discuss these and related matters, and two of the young Negro leaders have continued to maintain close contact with us (20). In addition to interviews, direct observations were made of demonstrations and other group activities, and public reaction was followed through the extensive coverage of the local news media.

EMERGENCE OF A NEW SOCIAL CHARACTER

One of the 19-year-old Negro students recalled his reaction, which was typical, when he read the newspaper report of the very first organized sit-in in Greensboro, North Carolina. He and his friends at Howard University "all rejoiced, and we all felt the opportunity was here; and the fact that college students were doing it is one of the powerful reasons for participating ourselves . . . but more than anything . . . we all realized we had been *wanting to do something* and now was the time." Many of these students remembered that they first began "wanting to do something" in 1954 when they first heard about the Supreme Court decision for school desegration; the student quoted above was 13 years old at that time, as were most of the young demonstrators in this study.

Thus it was at the threshold of their adolescence that the United States Supreme Court ruled unanimously that the segregated schools these youngsters had been attending were illegal. The Court had decided that systems of separate schools for Negroes and whites were inherently unequal because they generated in Negro students "a feeling of inferiority as to their status in the community that may affect their hearts and minds in a way unlikely ever to be undone." A unique and significant precedent was set in the use of statements of psychologists and social scientists to support this ruling.

This Supreme Court decision immediately received widespread publicity, discussion, denunciation and praise. It was apparent from talking to all of our Negro subjects that its message had been deeply imprinted on their minds and outlook. This public and legal recognition of the desirability of desegregation and its possible achievement in the near future was an experience in the adolescent development of these young people quite different from that of their parents and older siblings. They felt that the older generation had come to accept segregation and social inferiority as the natural order of things. They were aware of the Southern tradition that, when dealing with white people, one should present the appearance of a contented subordinate. However, feeling that desegregation was now their right, these students experienced increasing frustration with its painfully slow implementation and with the seeming hypocrisy of adults who paid lip service to principles but took no risks for implementation. Such feelings were intensified by the contrast of their own situation with that of many African peoples who were aggressively achieving independence and total public recognition as adults in the family of nations.

Many observers have pointed out that the psychosocial history of the

Southern Negro has been largely characterized by his need to suppress and displace elsewhere his feelings of hostility toward the dominant whites (1, 15, 16). Similarly he has had to suppress and displace any motivation to compete in economic and social spheres. He has been forced to assume a manifest role of passivity and submission, a role which has its social roots in economic and legal dependency on the white majority as well as in fear of punitive retaliation for overstepping color boundaries. These characteristics are expressed and further reinforced through the incorporation by the Negro of certain aspects of Christianity—especially the child-like trust in God, acceptance of one's lot in life, turning the other cheek and a belief in a happy afterlife coming to those good Christians who suffer and endure (15).

Outbreaks of this bottled-up aggression in the South through crimes directed against whites have been dealt with traditionally in an extraordinarily harsh manner, for example, lynchings. Crimes within the Negro community, however, have received greater toleration from the white authorities, who viewed them as the behavior of irresponsible children who could be taught no better. The inhibited anger against the whites commonly has been turned on the self and displaced into the greatly disguised, stereotyped patterns of laziness, apathy, passivity and unreliability. The hostile roots of such behavior have been so well masked and denied by the defensive operations of both racial groups that, until very recently, the prevalent Southern white's view of the Negro was that of a rather irresponsible but essentially contented child. The Negro's needs were thought to be amply taken care of by a paternal system of social relationships modeled on the traditions of slavery. It comes as a real shock to many Southerners to see a discontented Negro forcefully displaying his discontent in a public, vocal manner. This confrontation is very threatening to some white Southerners, as shown in some of their violent reactions to sit-ins.

The Negro student in the sit-in movement proves he is neither childlike nor contented. The protests are neither indirect nor patient, as tends to be the behavior of the older generation. At the same time they express publicly the frustration and resentment that has been so long hidden. Through the force of the moral and democratic principles they invoke to justify their action, they channel aggression into a positive identification with the traditional ego-ideal of the white majority, as well as with that of the world community. Using the terms of Erich Fromm, we may describe this as the emergence of a new social character for the Southern Negro (8). One prominent white Southern politician has remarked, "These kids seem to be completely new Negroes, the likes of which we've never seen before." This new social character has emerged from the psychological reaction of adolescent members of a social group to changed external realities. It is built upon certain long-standing personality and cultural traits shared by the group's members, as well as the changing events, ideas and circumstances around them.

IDENTITY FORMATION AND "PROSOCIAL ACTING OUT"

Along with these factors of changing social history and new social character, an additional perspective is necessary to understand the student sit-in movement. One must take into account certain features of the developmental and group psychology of late adolescence—with special emphasis on interrelationships between action and identity formation. As Erik Erikson has intimated, the unique needs and strengths of late adolescence frequently focus on the social and intellectual crises of the era, translating issues into the ideology and action of the youth movement. Thus ideology and social action may have a fundamental role in the development of identity in adolescents.

We have already remarked the childlike nature of the Negro stereotype in the eyes of the white Southerners (vividly symbolized in the custom of hailing any adult Negro male as "Boy," instead of "Mister" or "Sir"). Until recently the Negro could either accept that role, or move to the North. In the South he has been largely denied the opportunity to express normal aggressive and masculine strivings through dignified and respected occupations in the general society and in competition with the white male. Under these conditions the Negro male is degraded and depreciated and cannot serve as an adequate ego ideal or model for identification for his children (20).

The young Negro demonstrators are acutely aware of the lack of adult identity that has characterized their fathers in the South. Both the conscious and unconscious strivings for potent male identification became very apparent in talking to them. In 1955, Rev. Martin Luther King led the entire Negro community of Montgomery, Alabama, in a boycott of the city's transit buses; after one year's struggle, the buses were desegregated (13). This occurred when many of the students were only 15, two years after the Supreme Court had told them that their anger against segregation was justified and sanctioned. Young people all over the South were vastly impressed with the Montgomery boycott. They felt it was a lesson in the practical and emotional "advantages of direct action" in expressing legitimate Negro discontent.[2] King became the image of an assertive Negro male assuming freedom of action with dignity, and achieving respectful recognition through successful struggle with the white community (that

---

[2] It is interesting to note reports that indicate a sharp decline in the incidence of crime among the Negro population of Montgomery, Alabama, during the year of the boycott (11).

is, male community). In a sense he became the figure the Negro adolescent wished his father might have been, and as such he was incorporated as part of the ego-ideal. Three years later, soon after leaving home for college, Negroes were acting on the dictates of this identification model through the sit-in. Thus, for the late adolescent in the vanguard of the sit-in movement, the search for recognition as an adult that so characterizes his age group has been intimately interwoven with the struggle of Southern Negroes as a social group for recognition as mature human beings. For the 19-year-old student, then, the creation of a new social character for his people has become identical with the development of his own personality as a young adult.

As part of their struggles to achieve emancipation and identity, many of the Negro students seem to display significant ego-syntonic processes that suggest an acting out through the sit-ins of early childhood frustrations and parental conflicts and wishes. Although the concept of acting out has been used primarily in connection with certain forms of antisocial behavior (10) and problems of psychotherapy (9), data in the current study suggest a more general role for acting out in character and identity formation (5, 18). This is illustrated in the following description of B., a seemingly typical, poor, ambitious 19-year-old male Negro college freshman from the Deep South who became a leader of the Washington group of demonstrators. The data and formulations are based on a six-month series of research interviews and subsequent followup.

B. was brought up in a matriarchal family in which his step-father was absent most of the time, or jobless and degraded when home. His real father had left when he was still an infant. He is the oldest of eight brothers and sisters. His mother worked as a domestic for a white Southern family. He grew up feeling contemptuous and resentful of his father, but guilty about this resentment and perhaps responsible for the father's failures and absences. B. has ambivalent feelings toward his mother whom he fantasies really loved him most, but was forced to give prime attention to his younger siblings as well as the white family that employed her. He wore the white family's cast-off clothing. His mother was quite harsh with him if ever he expressed resentment about their status or about white people. She told him that they must know their place, and it would do no good to antagonize the whites. She feared losing the meager job which was their only source of income. He associates the lives of his parents with submission to the white community, and displaces onto this social submission much of the resentment, frustration and deprivation he experienced within his family. At the same time he recognizes his parent's passive-aggressive ambivalence to the whites and the different levels of meaning in his mother's prohibitions against open hostility. This perception helps him develop an idealized image of his parents in which they are really eager for and capable of self-assertion (which would mean more love, attention and recognition for him); but their self-assertion is blocked by circumstance or fear.

B.'s decision to participate in a sit-in demonstration was at first quite impulsive, with a great deal of subsequent rationalization. His personal involvement and dedication have been intense, and actions result in much discharge of affect, as anger and depression are transformed into elation. This discharge of affect is related not only to the stimuli of immediate circumstances but also to symbolic mastery of childhood frustrations. Thus, on the one hand, he acts out his longstanding resentment of his parents derived from his repeated experiences of deprivation and displacement as a youngster, which he now sees as a consequence of his parents' social role. On the other hand, when he takes risks and tests the retaliatory dangers of which he has been warned by his family, he may threaten his mother, but he also wins her secret approval. He thereby enhances his self-esteem as an autonomous, masculine adult. He has acted out his family's suppressed resentment of the social system in a dignified and passive-aggressive manner and has responded to his mother's fantasied need for a socially potent male. (It is of interest that, in follow-up interviews two years later, he reports that his whole family has "come around" to open support of his activities.) It can be inferred that for some adolescents acting out has an important role in identity formation and progressive development of ego functions.

In an historical context, B. feels "caught between Uncle Tom and Jim Crow." Uncle Tom represents the internalized ambivalence of his parents in telling him he must be passive. Jim Crow represents the traditional pattern of segregation and sanctions applied by the whites, which also thwarts his aggressive strivings. He is able successfully to act out unconscious parental hostility to the whites that they themselves have been unable to express overtly. Consciously he has an idealized image of what his parents "really" feel or ought to feel about what is right. He also perceives that he is acting according to the dictates of the conscience of the total community and that he is doing what others fear, hesitate or are "too hypocritical" to do.[3] This perception of the super-ego or conscience of the community and of his parents allows him to rationalize his rebellion against his own family thereby decreasing guilt and anxiety. He feels he is doing what his parents (and the nation) really want him to do but they are afraid to say so openly. We have found similar dynamics in all but two of the young white demonstrators as well. One after another they reported that their parents were both definitely against racial segregation

---

[3] An interesting parallel may exist between the messianiclike feelings and identification of this young Negro leader and those formulated about Moses by S. Freud (7).

and definitely against doing anything about it. Some were consciously aware of the mixture of anxiety and pride their parents felt about their activities. As it were, they are acting out the conscience of the community.

The acting out of suppressed parental wishes and problems of deprivation, frustration and moral ambiguity has been frequently reported in the psychodynamics underlying adolescent delinquency and antisocial behavior (10). However, the acting out we have observed here is consciously based on moral imperatives, that is, on the perceived super-ego or conscience of the community, which becomes incorporated into the individual and group functional self-image. Since this perception began in childhood and, as we have shown, was dramatically reinforced during early adolescence, it becomes part of the ego-ideal; action based on its dictates becomes an important source of self-esteem. Therefore, we suggest the term "prosocial" acting out to describe this behavior (5). This distinction is important. Delinquent acting out is described as antisocial precisely because of its opposition to the morality of the community. Acting out occurs through the delinquent's rebellion against severe super-ego dictates or in the framework of defective super-ego development (for example, "lacunae") (10). In prosocial acting out, however, the ego-ideal and resultant functional self-image are much more in accord with the dictates of the community morality and conscience. Those involved in the latter require some level of social or moral approval, and their goals are rationalized in the direction of social welfare. This allows a gratifying and self-enhancing resolution of emotional conflict and social identity formation. They feel they are "doing society's work for it." The answers to the typical adolescent questions of autonomy, time perspective, work and ideals (2) are vastly different in these two forms of behavior. However, the dynamics seem to have many similarities. It may be that a more detailed understanding of the differing determinants of these two adolescent pathways would have significant implications for the social health of a community, as well as for a new approach to the prevention and treatment of delinquency.

One aspect of the group dynamics of acting out is worthy of note here. Through the conversion of their own anger into a seemingly passive and pious stance these students threaten the bigoted and volatile defenses of the white extremists. In so doing, the demonstrators accomplish a remarkable psychosocial feat, much to their advantage. The white extremists are provoked by the young Negroes to act out for them the very anger and resentment that they (the Negroes) have themselves felt. However, the anger and violence have now been externalized and projected onto the "aggressor," so that the students feel guiltless and even exhilarated in their justifiable indignation. It also helps win the sympathy of the observing public and reduces the fears of whites that Negroes intend to retaliate violently for past suppression (13). This is probably a prominent feature of the dynamics of nonviolent action as a political weapon.

It is extremely important for these young students to be able to express publicly and directly their discontent and indignation against restriction, dependency and inequity. It allows them to identify their aggressive strivings for independence and recognition, which are intrinsic to the adolescent phase of development, with their desperate need for social emancipation and equality. These demonstrations are certainly aggressive. However, the dignified, well-disciplined, nonviolent style of the student action is calculated to be an effective propaganda weapon that will encourage the more moderate white southerners to accept some measure of desegregation, as well as win the sympathy and support of news media and public in other parts of the country. The students are also keenly aware of the attention they receive in news media in other parts of the world; they are surprisingly sophisticated in their political and social awareness. Although they are preoccupied with the task at hand, they readily identify with students and movements for recognition and emancipation in other parts of a total world community.

IDEOLOGY AND IDENTITY

The use of nonviolent resistance means that the students will picket, set-in, ride buses and use facilities that are segregated, but they will not resist when heckled, attacked or arrested. It is consciously conceived of by many as a pragmatic political weapon applicable to the problem of segregation, and is consistent with Christian religious training. Although Biblical and Christian teachings and the traditions of Ghandi and civil disobedience are incorporated into their ideology as formulated by Martin Luther King (13), these students are generally not pacifists. This is exemplified in the remarks of B., who was very much committed and dedicated to the principles of nonviolence in the sit-in. Soon after quoting from the Scriptures and Ghandi in support of nonviolence, he went on to talk with pride of his own personal ambitions to be a jet pilot in the U.S. Air Force.

At the same time, the philosophy of nonviolence is consistent with the long tradition of minimizing offense to the white community. It is a natural outgrowth of the traditional passive and submissive role in the face of white domination and potential retaliation. The internal prohibition against hostility to the whites is deep-seated; this hostility is more readily expressed by first being transformed into love for those who hate you. This process reduces guilt and anxiety and makes easier the students' departure from parental stereotypes; yet at the same time it allows them to identify with the parental religious ego-ideal. The ideology helps the adolescent maintain super-ego control over angry impulses while simultaneously internalizing an ego-ideal of love and respect for all human beings including the enemy, which in turn enhances the sense of identity and self-esteem. This illustrates the connection of ideology and identity formation for many adolescents (3).

In one sense, then, the sit-in can be described as a passive-aggressive act. For a few it provides the arena for masochism and martyrdom. For all it is a demand to be seen, heard and recognized. As is usual with adolescent movements, it is never anonymous. Names are freely given and no one hides his face when pictures are taken. However, one should not underestimate the intensity of the aggression and hostility being channeled here, especially in the Negro students. We did not need to probe very deeply to find resentment and hostility built on layers of social and personal frustration in the demonstrators we interviewed. The aggression is manifest in the very circumstance that they are coercing people to accept or react to the accomplished fact of sitting-in at a segregated establishment, as well as in the evident satisfaction at stirring social turmoil by what seems to be such a small, quiet initial action; moreover, this is done frequently in areas where the violent and explosive potential of white segregationists is well known.

In our interviews with them, all these students, both Negro and white, saw its high moral purpose as a major feature of their activity. Desegregation and the philosophy of nonviolent resistance are seen primarily as moral rather than political principles (20). As Erikson has pointed out in describing the process of ideology formation in adolescents (3), these students take literally the moral commitment of the community and, denouncing what are perceived to be the hypocrisies of the current social and political situation, demand a substantial change. Here the goals of conscience of the students represent not only the traditional Christian morality of the nation but also the well-known and basic American social and political principles of equal rights and freedom of choice. Thus the Negro sit-in youth thinks of himself as more Christian than the white community in the South. He also thinks of himself as more in accord with the highest principles of American democracy than the white hecklers on the sidelines. He derives considerable ego support from thus identifying with the ideals of the white majority and a great feeling of compensatory gratification from the experience of superior moral dedication. This helps him offset traditional feelings of racial inferiority that have been so long a part of the Southern milieu.

Although the ideology is highly moral, this is by no means an intellectual movement. There is a heavy orientation to action and work, even to the point of impatience with prolonged intellectual discussion. During the organization of the first sit-in in the Washington area, the original students, in recruiting others in their dormitory to join them, used as their rallying cry, "There's work to be done." Again and again there was an emphasis on getting down to the work at hand, the picketing or sitting-in, with a minimum of fuss or preliminary discussion. A great deal of gratification was derived from their sense of dedicated work, and it undoubtedly has an important function in the formation of individual and group identity (2). However, it also illustrates the impulsive urge to immediate action so characteristic of adolescent time perspective and so different from that of the older generation. This sense of immediacy is exemplified in the students' frustration with "plenty of ideals but no action." Such an action orientation leads to considerable risk taking. Since deciding to take a risk is done by an individual student quite on his own (albeit with group support), such a decision helps to develop a feeling of autonomy, as well as proving bravery and the willingness to endure suffering on behalf of one's principles (4). The mutual experience of action, risk taking and injury does a great deal to solidify the feelings of unity and identity of the group and to assure individual loyalties. Thus the sit-in groups derive great strength from their experiences in jail or in the midst of hostile crowds.

The assertion of freedom of choice in one's own behavior is interestingly parallel to the emphasis on freedom of choice in the principle of desegregation. For example, an 18-year-old white girl with a mixed group being arrested at a suburban bowling alley asked simply, "If these are my friends and I want to bowl with them, why should we be arrested?" For this girl, the need for freedom of choice and action so typical of the adolescent has become identical with the strivings of Negroes in the community at large.

It seems that an element of renunciation of former dependency gratifications is almost always present in the process of growing up. As they approach maturity, social groups as well as individuals must lose some of the security of their former social and economic relationships. A young person feels most free or independent only after having done something active and aggressive to win that independence. In this context, perhaps an "independent" identity can never be freely given—it must be at least partially *taken* by adolescents and, possibly, by young nations as well.

In summary, we would emphasize that one can find in the student sit-in movement patterns of adolescent identity strivings similar to those in many other adolescent groups. These young people, however, are caught on a wave of psychosocial transition and upheaval. For the Negroes, inferiority, submission and deprivation are their childhood experience; passive-aggressive resolutions their heritage; Christianity their moral background; the Supreme Court decision and the coming of age of new African nations part of the tempo of change. Through these influences, are filtered the typical internal pressures and new ego capacities of early and late adolescence. Public action for social goals is their way of at least temporarily resolving issues of identity formation, conscience and aggression. They see themselves as prodders of the national conscience, and derive satisfaction and self-esteem from this role. As a result, they have been forced into synthesizing a new social character with its new problems and anxieties, with its risks and violence, but also with a vitality and optimism for a future that they feel they have had a hand in shaping.

Recent student activities in this and other countries suggest that the motivation and psychodynamics of student involvement in political and social action represents an important area of study (14, 19, 22). Such studies may help in understanding the effects of social change and crises on personality and identify formation, as well as the converse effects of adolescent striving for recognition and identity on social and political change.

References

1. Dollard, J. 1939. Caste and Class in a Southern Town. Harper & Bros., New York, N.Y.

2. Erikson, E. 1956. The problem of ego identity. J. Amer. Psychoanal. Assn. 4(1): 56–121.

3. ———. 1958. Young Man Luther. W. W. Norton & Co., Inc. New York, N.Y.

4. ———. 1962. Youth; fidelity and diversity. Daedalus 91(1): 5.

5. Fishman, J. R. and F. Solomon. Prosocial Acting out. In preparation.

6. Fleming, H. 1960. The new South and the sit-ins. J. Intergroup Relations 2(1): 56–60.

7. Freud, S. 1934. Moses and Monotheism. Hogarth Press. London, Eng.

8. Fromm, E. 1941. Appendix: Social character and social process. In Escape from Freedom. Farrar & Rinehart. New York, N.Y.

9. Greenacre, P. 1950. General problems of acting-out. Psychoanal. Quart. 19: 455–467.

10. Johnson, A. M. and S. A. Szurek. 1952. The genesis of antisocial acting-out in children and adults. Psychoanal. Quart. 21(3): 323–343.

11. Kahn, T. 1960. Unfinished Revolution (Pamphlet). Igal Rodenko, Printer. New York, N.Y. : 28.

12. Kardiner, A. and L. Ovesey. 1951. The Mark of Oppression: A Psychosocial Study of the American Negro. W. W. Norton & Co., Inc. New York. N.Y.

13. King, M. L. 1958. Stride Toward Freedom: The Montgomery Story. Harper & Bros. New York, N.Y.

14. Laquer, W. Z. 1962. History of the German Youth Movement. Basic Books, Inc. New York, N. Y.

15. Myrdal, G. 1944. An American Dilemma. Harper & Bros. New York, N.Y.

16. Powdermaker, H. 1943. The channeling of Negro aggression by the cultural process. Amer. J. Sociol. 48: 750–758.

17. Rexroth, K. 1960. The students take over. The Nation. 191(1): 4–9.

18. Solomon, F. and Fishman, J. R. Identity formation and crisis in student demonstrators against racial segregation. Presented at the Annual Meeting of the American Psychiatric Association, Toronto, Canada. May 7, 1962.

19. ———. Youth and social action: students participating in a large "peace"

demonstration. Presented at the Annual Meeting of the American Ortho-psychiatric Association, Washington, D.C. March, 1963.

20. ———. Non-violence in the South: a psychosocial study. Presented at the Annual Meeting of the American Psychiatric Association, St. Louis, Mo. May 6, 1963.

21. Wilson, J. Q. 1961. The strategy of Negro protest. J. Conflict Resolution. 5(3): 291–303.

22. Youth: change and challenge (a symposium). 1962. Daedalus 91(1).

39. A Contemporary Revitalization Movement in American Race Relations: The Black Muslims

JAMES LAUE

The prominence of dissident sects espousing nationalistic and racialistic doctrines in a framework of religious orthodoxy has been one of the more dramatic concomitants of Negro Americans' contemporary protest against racial injustice. The Nation of Islam, known colloquially as the Black Muslims, is the best studied of these sects. The Muslims do not veil their antipathy toward white men, but they are apparently able to harness and redirect it into a sense of pride in their own group. Their rituals and unique cosmology, their assumption that they are linked to a great cultural tradition alien to the Western world, and their esprit de corps all serve to develop, maintain, and intensify a new sense of racial identity in their members.

Laue's discussion provides a general description of this group and of the relationship between its religious doctrines and its social position. He also suggests that the Muslims can be used to illustrate more general processes that are characteristic of social movements among lower-status groups eager to discover a basis for reshaping their identity.

Rarely do empirical cases seem so made-to-order for a particular socio-logical theory as does the Black Muslim movement for Anthony Wal-lace's formulation of the "revitalization movement."*

---

* The reference is to Anthony F. C. Wallace, "Revitalization Movements," *American Anthropologist*, 58, 1956, pp. 264–81. Ed.

SOURCE: *Social Forces*, 42, 1964, pp. 315–23 (footnotes omitted). Reprinted by permission of the University of North Carolina Press.

James Laue is Assistant Professor of Sociology at Emory University.

The "Lost-Found Nation of Islam in North America" is a mushrooming sect of Negro Americans led by some of the country's angriest young men. A politico-religious organization preaching black nationalism and claiming "hundreds of thousands" of members throughout the United States, the Muslim movement is productively viewed in Wallace's revitalization terminology as a "deliberate, organized, conscious effort by members of a society to construct a more satisfying culture." There is no question that Negro Americans have been trying to do this since slave times; the Black Muslims stand out as a contemporary and highly organized example of this effort.

Although black nationalist groups have been a force in United States racial patterns for most of the twentieth century—particularly in the northern ghettos—interest in the Muslims is only now beginning to grow among American social critics, popular pulp writers, and social scientists. The first scholarly work on the movement was C. Eric Lincoln's *The Black Muslims in America*, published in 1961. Then in 1962 E. U. Essien-Udom's *Black Nationalism: A Search for an Identity in America* appeared.

While Lincoln and Essien-Udom give considerable attention to the historical and psychological dimensions of the movement, the specifically sociological implications are yet to be explored. In this paper, then, Wallace's theory is juxtaposed with what we know about the Muslims in hopes of clarifying the theory and operationalizing it as a guide for sociological research on the Movement.

A NOTE ON METHOD: I AM A "GRAY"

Since I am a "gray" (or "grayboy"—the hep Negro's terminology for the white man, signifying status as a mutation from the pure black), I cannot get into Muslim temple meetings. It is hardly necessary to say that this is a decided research disadvantage! Research on the movement in the past three years has taken me into a number of temple-type situations, however; one of the chief sources of information presented in this paper has been participation in a number of informal discussion groups with several young Muslim members.

Combined with this participant observation have been documentary research on Muslim publications, analysis of various semi-popular articles and television programs, and attendance at public meetings regarding the movement. On two occasions I have seen the Muslims' musical tragicomedy, *Orgena* ("A Negro" spelled backwards), finding in the two performances differences which are presented later in this analysis. The most productive forms of research, finally, have been interviews and dialogue with leaders and students of the movement, among them Minister Malcolm X, [then] heir apparent to the top position in the movement.

The Theory of Revitalization Movements:
"...A More Satisfying Culture"

Wallace's definition of a revitalization movement as a "deliberate, organized, conscious effort by members of a society to construct a more satisfying culture" implies an organismic analogy and the corollary principles of stress and homeostasis. Society is seen as an organic system which is constantly exposed to stress induced in its component subsystems. The total system maintains itself by providing mechanisms sufficient to handle this stress.

Wallace finds each member equipped with what he calls a "mazeway"— a mental image of self, society, nature, and culture through which values operate in maintaining social order. "Whenever an individual who is under . . . chronic stress receives repeated information which indicates that his mazeway does not lead to action which reduces the level of stress, he must choose between maintaining his present mazeway and tolerating the stress, or changing the mazeway in an attempt to reduce the stress. . . . It may also be necessary to make changes in the 'real' system in order to bring mazeway and 'reality' into congruence. The effort to work a change in mazeway and 'real' system together so as to permit more effective stress reduction is the effort at revitalization; and the collaboration of a number of persons in such an effort is called a revitalization movement."

Wallace sees six types of movements reported in the literature which can be classified under the revitalization rubric:

> *Nativistic.* emphasis on elimination of alien persons, customs, and values.
> *Revivalistic.* emphasis on re-institutionalization of customs and values thought to have been in the mazeway of previous generations.
> *Cargo Cults.* importation of alien values, customs, and material into the mazeway via a ship's cargo.
> *Vitalistic.* importation of foreign elements, but ships and cargo are not the necessary mechanisms.
> *Millenarian.* an apocalyptic world transformation engineered by the supernatural.
> *Messianic.* participation of a divine savior in human flesh in the mazeway transformation.

The most prominent historical cases to which Wallace points are the origins of Christianity and Islam, and the Ghost Dance and the Peyote cult of American Indian tribes.

Revitalization movements move through five ideal-typical stages in what Wallace calls the "processual structure":

I. Steady State. Chronic stress within the system varies within tolerable limits as culturally recognized techniques for satisfying needs operate efficiently.

II. Period of Increased Individual Stress. "Individual members of a population . . . experience increasingly severe stress as a result of the decreasing efficiency of certain stress-reduction techniques." The population may, according to Wallace, be "'primitive' or 'civilized,' either as a whole society or a class, caste, religious, occupational, acculturational, or other definable social group." Some of the elements responsible for lowering efficiency of stress-reduction mechanisms may be changes in the physical environment, military defeat, socio-economic distress, political subordination, acculturational pressures, and epidemics.

III. Period of Cultural Distortion. Individual maladjustments combine to produce internal cultural distortion. "The elements are not harmoniously related but are mutually inconsistent and interfering." Stress reproduces itself and anxiety rises as the incongruities of the mazeway are perceived. Life is no longer meaningful.

IV. Period of Revitalization. Total cultures or subsystems on the way to disaster are frequently rescued—or, at least delayed—by the revitalization movement. The theory specifies six functional problems at this point: mazeway reformulation, communication, organization, adaptation, cultural transformation, and routinization.

V. New Steady State. A new *Gestalt* is in operation, both for the members of the revitalized group and the host and/or neighboring cultures. Wallace's formulation here clearly implies that the movement has been institutionalized.

THE MUSLIM MOVEMENT TODAY:
"THOSE WHO KNOW AREN'T SAYING"

The Muslim movement, according to the most accurate guesses, encompasses less than 100,000 members (some estimates run as low as 5,000) organized in some 80 "Temples of Islam" throughout the country. Muslim leaders do not release exact membership figures—and their refusal to do so adds to the aura of uncertainty about Muslim strength which gives the movement so much leverage in the American racial situation today. "Only Allah knows," smiles Malcolm X, who, like most Muslims, has rejected his "Christian name" and substituted the symbol of an unknown quantity. "Those who know aren't saying, and those who say don't know!"

But the sociological significance of the movement has less to do with numbers than with mood—the militant mood and new sense of urgent activism growing in Negro Americans at all class levels in the last decade. For while the number of fully participating members is uncertain, there is no uncertainty about the way hundreds of thousands of Negroes respond to the Muslims' stark and straightforward articulation of "the problem" and its causes—white evil and intransigence. There is no question that Negroes have been ready to hear this for a long time.

LEADERSHIP

There is no doubt that Malcolm X is the Muslims' driving organizational force. But the movement is formally centered around the Messenger, the Prophet of Allah—the Honorable Elijah Muhammad. The Messenger, a Georgia-born, light-skinned man in his middle sixties, is the ideal-typical shaman; he is believed to have a mystical association with God himself, and "believes in and follows Allah 100 percent."

MEMBERSHIP

Membership is predominantly male and lower class. Selected men belong to the Fruit of Islam, a "secret army" which acts as a security force at temple meetings and speeches by the leaders. The FOI is rigorously trained in military tactics and strategy and, while it will not initiate aggression, it responds with force to any encroachments on its honor. One FOI member was killed and many injured in a recent struggle with police who attempted to break up a temple service in Los Angeles. The FOI is thus symbolic of the Muslim prescription to "act like a MAN!"—and by such an orientation the leaders are working to restore the Negro male emasculated by American discrimination to the head of a patriarchal family structure.

HISTORICAL DEVELOPMENT

The Muslims are one of a long line of black nationalist groups which have made the scene (in the words of the Brothers) in America in the last half-century. A number of these groups work the streets of Harlem and other northern ghettos today; the Muslims are the largest. The most important forerunners of today's Muslim movement were the Moorish Science Temple movement of Noble Drew Ali and the Universal Negro Improvement Association of Marcus Garvey—a "Back to Africa" group. Both hit their peak in the World War I era, and have small followings today.

Today's Muslims stem most directly from the work of Wallace D. Fard, who appeared in Detroit in 1930 as the incarnation of Allah. Elijah Poole, who had recently moved to Detroit, ". . . came under the spell of Fard, who, he recalls gratefully, took him 'out of the gutter . . . and in three-and-a-half years taught (him) the knowledge of Islam.'" Re-named "Elijah Muhammad" by Fard, the enthusiastic migrant established a mosque in Chicago in 1932, where he later sheltered Fard from the police. When Fard disappeared in 1934 (there were rumors that Muhammad had induced Fard to offer himself as a human sacrifice), Muhammad was the logical successor. Under his guidance, the movement grew slowly and maintained a position among the many sects competing for the marginal, disgruntled

Negro. Malcolm X was converted while in prison in 1947 (many Muslim members are former convicts, addicts, and social derelicts), and his organizational ability and quick wit have been central to the movement's phenomenal growth in the last few years.

VALUES: THE RELIGIOUS-HISTORICAL IDENTITY

The Muslims claim to be a branch of orthodox Islam, accepting most of the Koran and ". . . only the parts of the Bible which are divine." The Genesis story of the creation is true—for the white man only—and the Muslims have the date placed somewhere around 6,000 years ago. But the black man was created 66 trillion years ago, and the white man is only here as the result of an albino mutation produced by an evil black scientist who succeeded in breeding out the pure black strain.

Muhammad preaches black nationalism (which is often interpreted as black supremacy) and black union against the white world. "The white man has robbed you of your name, your language, your culture, and your religion," Muslims are told. Through this treacherous stripping of the "so-called American Negro" of his heritage, the white man has succeeded in subjugating the black man—whose *real* language is Arabic, whose *real* religion is Islam and whose *original* homeland is the Nile valley in Northern Africa. "The white man was still living in caves in Europe and eating meat raw while our forefathers lived in luxury in flourishing civilizations on the banks of the Nile," continues the Messenger.

VALUES: THE SECULAR PROGRAM

The Muslims say they want several states of their own to set up a separate black nation. If the United States does not repent for its treatment of this nation-within-a-nation, Allah will strike down the oppressor. The Armageddon date was originally set for 1914, but Allah granted a 70-year extension.

I am convinced from a number of conversations with Muslim leaders, however, that what they *really* want is access to the vices and virtues enjoyed by white Americans. The Muslims' Puritanical ethical prescriptions place them in the mainstream of the dominant American middle class value system. Members are enjoined to run their businesses like the white man, protect their women, abstain from alcohol and tobacco, and give generously to the "church" (many Muslims donate one-third of their livelihood to the temple). And nowhere is the neat, well-mannered, humble model of an American family attending church better exemplified than in the Muslim family going to three or four temple meetings per week. Significantly, the demanding discipline of the Muslims has made them more successful than any other civic, religious, or governmental agencies in social rehabilitation of Negro convicts, prostitutes, addicts, alcoholics, disorganized families, and slum homes. But also significantly, the wave of press attention to the movement has chosen to play down these achievements.

Muslim women are placed on a pedestal (and are the subject of a song popular in the movement, "Black Gold") while the white man is blamed for the long history of miscegenation under slavery and segregation. Many women in the movement enroll in the Muslim Girls Training and General Civilization Class, where they are ". . . taught how to sew, cook, keep house, rear their children, care for their husbands, and how to behave at home and abroad."

RITUAL BEHAVIOR

Temple meetings are quite subdued compared to many lower-class Negro religious gatherings. Members are searched before entering the mosque, and are not admitted if they have alcohol on their breath. Some altar settings present the star and crest of Islam opposite a silhouetted lynching scene backed by the American flag and the cross, with a sign asking, "Which Will You Choose?" Sermons are customarily long. In addition to temple attendance, most orthodox followers bathe and pray five times a day.

AESTHETIC EXPRESSION

Minister Louis X of Boston, a former calypso singer, is the artist of the movement; *Orgena* is his product. The show has played in most of the large Eastern cities, including return engagements in New York and Boston. It depicts the glorious ancient culture of the black man, his enslavement by white colonializers and slavetraders, and the trial of the white man—who finally confesses that he is the devil, and is dragged off stage under the death sentence. The play is punctuated by several of Minister Louis' songs, including "A White Man's Heaven is a Black Man's Hell," which presents Muslim theology attractively backed by a calypso beat. A recording of "White Man's Heaven" is now in national circulation by the movement, and acts as a potent recruiting force.

THE MUSLIMS AS A REVITALIZATION MOVEMENT: THE SHAPING OF A SUBSTITUTE IDENTITY

The Muslim movement is one of several alternative avenues of expression for the angry, sensitive, disillusioned Negro in America today. He is thoroughly Americanized at the value level, but frustrated at the personality level because of lack of institutionalized channels of cultural achievement. While the closed-system nature of the dominant white culture in the nineteenth century dictated clowning, self-hate, and neuroticism as adjustive techniques, the more aggressive channels of protest safely available today include enhanced striving, in-group aggression, prejudice against out-groups, and militancy. The particular cluster of mechanisms demonstrated in the Muslim movement involves all of these, plus denial of membership-substitution of identity as a "Muslim" for identity as a "Negro."

The psychological stances represented by these reactions are all part of the Black Muslims' unique mazeway. They have been translated into a coherent movement, which exhibits elements of five of the six types of revitalization movements Wallace suggests:

The *nativistic* phase of the movement emphasizes elimination of the white slave-master and his evil system, to be replaced by an all-black nation-within-a-nation—in which contact with the white's alien customs and values is neither desirable nor possible.

Consequently, in *revivalistic* fashion the Muslims hope to institute patterns of ancient Islamic society as they idealized it—an example of the Golden Age approach of every people who have ever suffered cultural disorganization.

From our perspective on the "outside," we can also call the Muslim movement a *vitalistic* effort, stressing importation of foreign elements. But it is clear that the Muslims do not accept this "importation" terminology, for the germ of the core-values they espouse is inherent in every black man, they say; he is phylogenetically a Muslim, and automatically superior to his white counterpart.

The *millenarian* emphasis of the movement is very strong. Minister Malcolm and the Messenger state time and again that Allah will engineer a Babylon-type demise of the white man if he does not repent in time.

And, while Fard was the official incarnation and Muhammad only a shamanistic prophet, Muslim leaders know that many members do not make the distinction, and indeed view the Messenger as a *messianic* figure actually participating in the divine.

Viewing sociological theory as an organizing, economizing, and operationalizing endeavor, we may now specify the points of congruence and variation between Wallace's outline of the "processual structure" and the historical development of the movement:

I. STEADY STATE

While the terminology of "steady state" and "new steady state" which Wallace uses may be a necessary theoretical distinction, it implies too much of a revolutionary character for the revitalization movement, and suggests an almost qualitative split between steady state, the flux phase, and steady state. For societies and their subgroups are *never* in a state which can be differentiated as "steady" when compared to another given state. Groups and ideologies dance in and out of power and influence, forming a dynamic matrix whose continuity is violated if we arbitrarily slice out chunks surrounding certain "movements." Social changes in the "movement" form should not be conceptualized as mutations of a former order (which the *"new* steady state" terminology implies), but rather as logical maturations with discernible etiological bases. We would do better to label these periods simply "stage one" and "stage two"—with the intervening processes seen as mediating developments leading to the new stage of systemic equilibrium.

Viewed in this light, it is appropriate to specify some of the dynamic social patterns which bred and nurtured the Muslims. Most obvious is Negroes' irrepressible dissatisfaction with their disproportionate share of the benefits from the expanding American economy—benefits which are paraded before all citizens every day via the mass media. Equally important is the failure of the old philosophical and religious systems to provide meaningful rationalizations for Negroes' non-attainment of deeply internalized democratic goals. The tight white opportunity structure becomes intolerable when a minority member is able to objectify his position and see what he is being denied. And finally—but by no means exhaustively— the emergence of African nations is *the* most specific model for American Muslim militancy today. Muslim leaders press for an identification with the African spirit of black revolt but carefully avoid any implication of actually returning to African ways, thus avoiding Garvey's mistake by recognizing that Negro Americans are too thoroughly middle class in their values for any "Back to Africa" approach to succeed.

II. PERIOD OF INCREASED INDIVIDUAL STRESS

I am saying, then, that the "breakdown of stress-reducing mechanisms" for Negro Americans has been occurring since the first slave arrived, and that the breakdown has led to protests of varying intensity throughout the years. In the last few years American society has not been able to provide stress-reducers at a rate rapid enough to satisfy its increasingly heterogeneous population structure. The system has not been able to institutionalize deviant channels of adjustment as they have appeared.

Negro Americans have experienced in varying degree the status-deprivation of which we talked in the last section. But, as Wallace rightly points out, the initial consideration of a substitute mode of adjustment often *increases* stress because of lack of feedback about the effectiveness of this alternate stance. The Muslims have avoided this pitfall by some highly successful advertising of the restructured identity they offer. They have worked in prisons and on the streets of Harlem and other large cities, first convincing potential converts of their totally deprived state as "so-called American Negroes," then presenting a totally new identity, ready-made and ready to put on. It is an active, life-consuming identity, not a "pay-your-membership-fee-without-necessary-commitment-to-action" stance, which for years has been the folk-level format of the now threatened and allegedly non-militant NAACP.

III. PERIOD OF CULTURAL DISTORTION

Regressive individual responses to deprivation long have been at a level which produces distortion in the Negro subculture. Crime, alcoholism, addiction, prostitution, and family disorganization have made their mark on the Negro American community. Mr. Muhammad's missionaries have capitalized on this cultural distortion, winning many of their converts from the lowest planes of society. "Look at these acts you committed as a Christian, as a so-called Negro," preach the ministers. "Then look at *our* people, who have rejected their slave-master and their slave religion, and have thrown off the vices taught by the blue-eyed devils."

IV. PERIOD OF REVITALIZATION

The first important functional task in revitalization is *mazeway reformulation*. Wallace proposes that this reformulation generally depends on a restructuring of elements and subsystems already current in the system—elements which are articulated, combined, and operationalized by the prophet as guides to action. While the Muslims claim to preach a doctrine entirely alien to America, their position becomes a thinly-veiled acceptance and rephrasing of American ideals, as suggested above.

The revitalization period usually originates in ". . . one of several hallucinatory visions by a single individual. A supernatural being appears to the prophet-to-be, explains his own and his society's troubles as being entirely or partly as a result of the violation of certain rules, and promises individual and social revitalization if the injunctions are followed and the rituals exercised." Muhammad *did* receive instructions from a supernatural being (Fard), but as far as we can determine, it was in-the-flesh and not hallucinatory communication.

After "the dream," the prophet moves to *communicate* his insights, fulfilling the second functional requirement of the revitalization process. The two doctrinal motifs hypothesized for this stage are manifested by the Muslims: ". . . that the convert will come under the care and protection of certain supernatural beings" (Allah); and that "both he and his society will benefit materially from an identification with some definable new cultural system" (Islam, of the Black Muslim variety). Disciples readily assume the responsibility for communicating the word; in the Muslim case, followers like Malcolm X and Louis X have become recruitment agents with charisma at least equal to that of the Messenger—although neither of them would (or could) admit it, of course.

Wallace's discussion of the *organizational* phase of the revitalization stage hinges on what Weber calls the problem of succession: the prophet must transfer his charismatic qualities to other individuals and the organization to effect legitimation of his cause. Muhammad is certainly regarded as an unquestionable authority, sanctioned by the supernatural. His movement has already moved out of the cult stage, since the leadership structure is sufficiently developed to ensure its maintenance when Muhammad dies, even though a good deal of conflict may result as the hierarchy adjusts. The disciplinary action of the Fruit of Islam, the unifying force of *Orgena* where ever it is produced and the organizational ability of Minister Malcolm combine to give the Muslim movement a solid bureaucratic structure that makes Negro rights organizations and lower class religious groups envious.

Perhaps the most important phase of the revitalization process is *adaptation*, and it seems to be the major area of the theory upon which elaboration is necessary. Wallace suggests three aspects of this process: doctrinal modification, political and diplomatic maneuvers, and force. Muslim doctrine has undergone drastic modification in the last few years as the membership has broadened, but, contrary to the theory, most of the alterations have been engineered by Malcolm X rather than the prophet.

Some of the major doctrinal modifications which may be seen in the Muslims' sect-to-church drive are:

(1) The black supremacy doctrine is being softened in an effort to attract Negro intellectuals. A former *Orgena* focus on problems of the Negro in America, for instance, is now tempered with strong emphasis on colonialism in Asia and Africa. In fact, it now is "colonialism" rather than "the white man" which is sentenced to death in *Orgena*.

(2) Relationships with other Negro rights groups are improving. Malcolm X has called former NAACP legal head and now Federal judge Thurgood Marshall a "twentieth century Uncle Tom" loudly and often, but the Muslim leader has accepted a number of speaking engagements at local NAACP chapters in the last two years. Too, former vehemence against the sit-ins and Martin Luther King, Jr., was absent in a recent television debate which found Minister Malcolm consciously trying to tone down his criticism for a national audience. And following the Los Angeles police slaying of a member in 1962, the Muslims readily cooperated in a protest rally with the NAACP, the Congress of Racial Equality, and local Negro ministers—indicating a new level of synthesis not possible only a few years earlier when the Muslims had reached neither their current level of national prominence nor their desire for a broader-based "church" status.

3. Muslims are re-emphasizing the religious character of the movement in response to charges that the Islamic orientation is merely a gimmick and cloak for political motives. Minister Malcolm's Harvard Law School Forum speech in 1961 focused around the Muslims as a *religious* movement—a radical change from an address at Boston University a year earlier.

At the same time, the Muslims are not condemning Christianity with their former gusto—at least publicly—as exemplified in open debates and the most recent performances of *Orgena*.

In discussing force as an adaptive technique, Wallace suggests that as organized hostility develops, emphasis in the movement frequently shifts from cultivation of the ideal to combat against the unbeliever. I find this ingroup ideal vs. outgroup combat syndrome more cyclical than lineal, however. For a time, the main task of the Fruit of Islam was ". . . guarding the Black Nation against 'trouble with unbelievers, especially with the police.' " In 1960 and 1961, with the environment perceived as less hostile, the emphasis had moved back to ingroup solidarity and uplift, including policing errant members and performing as a drill team at performances of *Orgena*. But more recently, in response to increased extra-systemic challenge from prison wardens and police as the movement seeks to expand, the FOI has redirected its efforts and training toward outside forces.

The Muslim movement today is clearly in the "adaptive" phase of revitalization, and promises to remain there for several years. The proposed phase of *cultural transformation*—acceptance of the movement as a legitimate mode of social adjustment by a controlling portion of the host population —may come rapidly if the Muslims continue to adapt their doctrines in true third party style.

Routinization—the tragedy that befalls all revolutions—occurs on both integrative (internal) and adaptive (external) planes, although the theory stresses only the integrative aspects of this process. For Wallace, routinization takes place only after the desired transformation has occurred. Perhaps the gravest immediate challenge to rapid rationalization will occur when the ailing Muhammad dies, for a power struggle between Malcolm X and others is certain unless the Messenger makes a definite pronouncement regarding his legitimate successor.

V. NEW STEADY STATE

After my earlier strong objections to the nondynamic implications of "steady state terminology" and analysis of the Muslims as professional discontents, we may conclude that the Nation of Islam cannot logically reach anything resembling a "new steady state"; it would go out of existence first.

There is one more aspect of the theory which deserves clarification— Wallace's qualification that the revitalization terminology is best applicable to a movement which is completely successful. His position here indicates that his data and interpretations derive necessarily from "dead" movements —a characteristic of postdicting which sociology has found hard to overcome. This approach would thus limit analysis considerably, since many powerful and socially disruptive movements do not reach even the adaptive phase. The Muslim movement, on the other hand, is one of a number of researchable in-process movements that offer a dynamic context in which theory can be checked as it is built.

The success or failure of a revitalization movement depends largely on the relative "realism" of the doctrines, according to Wallace. I think that this formulation must be modified to include the *degree to which the leaders make known their doctrinal positions to power elements of the host population.* Many movements fail, says Wallace, because wildly unrealistic predictions which do not come true result in mazeway disintegration of the members. The Muslims have learned this lesson well: they purposely keep predictions and interpretations vague to save themselves embarrassing re-fencing later. More and more in the last years, Malcolm X has been hedging on questions concerning relations with other groups, black supremacy, the battle of Armageddon, and the Muslim action plans for the future. He is ever-ready with "Only Allah knows," to counter a prying or threatening question regarding the nature and destiny of the movement.

PROSPECTS FOR FUTURE RESEARCH:
"PRETTY SOON, MAN"

The Muslim movement is becoming increasingly aware of its public face —and particularly its image with intellectuals. In the next few years, then, the movement should be more and more amenable to social scientific research. The chief requirement for the social scientist who wishes to successfully execute such research, of course, is the proper skin color! Even these barriers may be loosening, however, for recently when I half-jokingly asked Malcolm X, "When are you going to let me in to a temple meeting?" he half-seriously replied, "Pretty soon, man. Maybe pretty soon."

Now that the facts concerning the etiology of the movement are surfacing, a major longitudinal research study charting the sect's drive toward institutionalization is called for. Here, for instance, the Weberian may find a twentieth-century case of an underdeveloped nation-within-a-nation (the Negro subculture in American society) already exhibiting the religiously sanctioned asceticism to which Weber attached such great importance as motivator and justifier of this-worldly economic activity.

Intensive comparative studies are also needed. As one hypothetical framework for this kind of research, we can view the Muslim movement as analogous in origin and development to the Peyote cult. Antecedents of both Peyotists and the Muslims were aggressive and uncompromising in their orientation to the host population. Indian Ghost Dances at the turn of the century were harsh and unrelenting ritual rejections of the encroaching white culture; earlier black nationalist groups like the Garvey and Moorish Science movements were soon doomed to obscurity by their failure to adapt even marginally to the host population. Just as the emergence of the Peyote cult offered a more readily syncretic alternative for frustrated and hostile Indian Americans, so the Lost-Found Nation of Islam presents today a workable and sufficiently flexible identity for an ever-expanding group of militantly disenchanted Negro Americans.

VII. AND THE FUTURE?

40. Liberalism and the Negro: A Round-Table Discussion

JAMES BALDWIN, NATHAN GLAZER,
SIDNEY HOOK, GUNNAR MYRDAL,
AND NORMAN PODHORETZ

The last and longest selection in this book raises many questions and reaches few conclusions. Still, it is a fitting end-piece for discussions of areas that, still changing, are the subject of different policy orientations and deliberations. In matters of ethnic and racial relations, men of different persuasions seem readier to express hopes for the future than to make specific predictions about it. Each participant here demonstrates that his own interests and perspectives, even his own most carefully considered judgments, differ from those of other men of good will who sit with him to discuss issues of mutual concern. The symposium shows that thoughtful

SOURCE: *Commentary,* 37, (March, 1964) pp. 25–42. Copyright © 1964 by the American Jewish Committee. Reprinted by permission.

James Baldwin is the essayist and novelist whose works include *The Fire Next Time* and *Another Country.* *Nathan Glazer,* as noted for selection 11, is Professor of Sociology at the University of California at Berkeley. *Sidney Hook* is Professor of Philosophy at New York University and the author of *From Hegel to Marx* and *The Paradoxes of Freedom.* *Gunnar Myrdal,* as noted for selection 3, directs the Institute for International Economic Studies and is the author of *An American Dilemma.* *Norman Podhoretz,* who wrote selection 23, is the editor of *Commentary.*

459

men, assumed by others to share similar points of view, cannot achieve consensus in deciding the best ways to try to accomplish change in patterns of intergroup behavior in a democratic fashion. Assessment of the various proposals and rebuttals in this selection will hopefully lead the reader to stretch his own thinking further, calling on him to use materials from earlier selections to arrive at his own opinions.

A brief summation cannot really do justice to the statements of all the major participants in the symposium. However, because the selection is so long, and because the contributors occasionally introduce points of view somewhat tangential to the main thread of the discussion, the reader will probably find it helpful to know something about the selection before reading it.

Podhoretz, the moderator of the discussion (and author of selection 23 in this volume), can assume at the outset that well-known liberals will desire more extensive federal government participation in programs designed to alleviate racial inequities and poverty. Obviously, not all sectors of American political opinion share that desire.

But after making allowances for the participants' similar points of view about this general matter of public policy, one can easily see that their opinions about the present and future character of American race relations differ sharply. Hook and Myrdal (the latter to a more limited extent) are assimilationists who think the future of the American Negro lies in sharing society's rewards and participating more fully in its dominant cultural patterns. Glazer and Baldwin are more nearly pluralists. They believe that in American society separate class, racial, and ethnic groups each retain some distinctive characteristics for long periods of time. As Glazer sees it, these groups are sometimes in harmony and sometimes in conflict; whenever it can, each group will form coalitions with others in order to maintain or improve its own position as much as possible. Furthermore, in a complex society, large organizations and associations are more concerned with their own purposes and administrative exigencies than with abstract principles of justice and morality.

Baldwin goes much further, for he thinks that of all the groups in the American pluralistic pattern, the Negro group is the only one that has been kept from joining in these power coalitions. Critical of more than white institutional patterns, he is also impatient with white liberals. Baldwin finds liberals hypocritical and suffering from a limited perspective. To draw an analogy, his advice to them is like that of the physician who tells his patients they may have to undergo a relatively brief period of intense pain in order to be cured of more chronic difficulties. The problem of the white liberals, as Baldwin sees it, is their unwillingness to consider that they may have to threaten their own status and security by changing the character of the institutions and organizations from which they derive psychic support and gainful employment, in order to allow Negroes a genuine opportunity for finding their own place in the society. Baldwin insists that his views have been shaped by his own situation, and by his connection with the historical process that for generations has subjected Negroes to discrimination and judgments of categorical inferiority. Not trusting white America's claim that it is moral, he finds himself disagreeing sharply with Hook, who seems to feel it is not necessary to perform radical surgery on society's values and institutional structure. Instead, for Hook, reforms that permit existing principles to be put into practice more effectively are what are most needed. Such reforms should urge us to begin to use, and then should capitalize on, what Hook thinks are enormous but still-untapped reservoirs of acceptance and justice.

Myrdal also believes that a strong sense of morality can be an important force for social change in American society, but he places more weight on the necessity for revamping the economy in order to provide everyone in the society with a decent livelihood. Through this means, marked differences in incomes and life-styles would still exist, but each individual would have the chance to seek his own level and to try to improve it. According to Myrdal, any such program of economic change would have to include poor and untrained whites as well as poor and untrained Negroes, for crash efforts devoted exclusively to improving the Negro situation would be politically infeasible.

The final editorial comment in this book is cautionary: Each participant in the symposium has been affected by the perspective of his respective discipline. In addition, although all of the contributors may seem to be spokesmen for particular points of view, they are in fact individuals who are not necessarily representative of groups with which they might appear to be identified.

NORMAN PODHORETZ: I think it may be fair to say that American liberals are by now divided into two schools of thought on what is often called the Negro problem—though it probably would be better to use the term that Professor Myrdal used as the title of his famous book, and to speak not of a Negro problem but of an American dilemma. On the one side, we have those liberals whose ultimate perspective on race relations (as David Danzig puts it*) envisages the gradual absorption of deserving Negroes one by one into white society. At its most extreme, this position has sometimes looked forward to an eventual merging of the two races, though of course that possibility has rarely been discussed in public among liberals—and for very good reason, as I am here to testify. Over the past two or three years, however, a new school of liberal (or perhaps it should be called radical) thought has been developing which is based on the premise—to quote Danzig again—that "the rights and privileges of an

* "The Meaning of Negro Strategy," *Commentary,* February 1964.

individual rest upon the status attained by the group to which he belongs." From this premise certain points follow that are apparently proving repugnant to the traditional liberal mentality (if one can judge by New York *Times* editorials and the statements of presumably liberal politicians like Governor Rockefeller and the late President Kennedy). For the traditional liberal mentality conceives of society as being made up not of competing economic classes and ethnic groups, but rather of competing *individuals* who confront a neutral body of law and a neutral institutional complex. At any rate, the newer school of liberal thought on race relations maintains that the Negro community *as a whole* has been crippled by three hundred years of slavery and persecution and that the simple removal of legal and other barriers to the advancement of individual Negroes can therefore only result in what is derisively called "tokenism." This school of thought insists that radical measures are now needed to overcome the Negro's inherited disabilities. Whitney Young of the National Urban League, for example, has recently spoken of a domestic Marshall Plan, a crash program which he says need last only ten years, in order to bring the Negro community up to a point where it can *begin* to compete on equal terms with the white world. Other Negro leaders have similarly talked about 10 per cent quotas in hiring, housing, and so on. . . . The slogan "preferential treatment for Negroes" is the most controversial one that has so far come up in this discussion. . . .

There is, then, a conflict within the liberal community on the question of race relations; that much seems obvious. And the conflict is exacerbated by certain economic considerations that Professor Myrdal, in particular, speaks of in his new book, *Challenge to Affluence*. . . . Mr. Hook, while you may not be an expert on race relations, you are most certainly an expert on the principles of liberalism, and so I think I'll ask you to start.

SIDNEY HOOK: Well, let me begin by referring to an experience I had thirty years ago, when I was on the executive committee of the American Workers Party, which was certainly dedicated to the proposition that society consists of competing economic groups. We had sent our organizers to the South, and one night, at a meeting of our executive committee, the organizer from Texas appeared. He had succeeded in organizing councils of unemployed workers among the whites and Negroes, and the question then developed as to how and under what circumstances to arrange the first meeting. It turned out that the white members had refused to come to a meeting unless the seating were segregated, and our organizer was now reporting back to us for instructions. Now, all of us were liberals, all of us were socialists—indeed left-wing socialists—and we were faced with a dilemma, because if we insisted upon banning segregated seating at that meeting, there would be no organization and no possibility of getting the reforms we were working for. Well, the decision was made to have the first meeting, at least, segregated—in the hope that when these unemployed workers got together, they would, in recognition of their common interests and common struggle, abandon segregated seating in the future. It didn't work out that way because there was no future: the opposition to any kind of council of the unemployed, segregated or desegregated, was too strong. I cite this story to illustrate the fact that a conflict of principles can arise whether you take the traditional, liberal-individualistic point of view or the social group-conflict point of view.

To me, the case against discrimination rests fundamentally on ethical premises. The justification of formal rules of equality lies in the hope that such rules will further both the economic and the ethical equality of human beings—and I define this ethical equality as an equality of concern on the part of the community for each individual within it to develop his capacities to their greatest reach, for each individual to become a fully developed person. From this perspective, I do not see any conflict with the traditional principles of liberalism, as I understand them, in the idea of a *temporary* crash program to improve the position of the Negro community.

Let us imagine that an earthquake or some other disaster has taken place in a neighboring city followed by an influx of the population from that region to ours. I think it would be perfectly compatible with our commitment to democracy to make special provision for the people involved— individuals who had been disadvantaged, who had suffered more than members of our own community—so long as the provision were temporary. There might be some relative injustice to some other individuals in our community who were also in need, but any moral order of priority would have to recognize the greater need. We have done comparable things in the past. In the 30's, there was an influx of refugees from Germany to the United States. Very often these immigrants were given vocational opportunities that others in the community may have been just as qualified to fill. But no one thought it was unjust to provide special opportunities for them, because their need was more urgent, sometimes desperate.

The other day I read that James Farmer had proposed a program to the President involving vast measures of remedial educational enrichment for deprived children. Now to be sure, those who would profit most by a program of this kind would be Negro children. It isn't because they are *Negro* children that we ought to support this program; it's because they are deprived children. They have been disadvantaged more than other children, their need is greater, and therefore they are morally entitled to special treatment. This is how we can achieve the level of ethical equality I was talking about a minute ago. I draw the line only where I think a respect for the personality of Negroes requires that it be drawn. It is well known that in some institutions like the Bronx High School of Science, and in certain other special schools for the gifted, the number of Negro students in relation to the school population is small. Some of my friends have argued that in order to establish a proper balance, in order to provide equal educational opportunity for the Negro student, he should be given a special status in those schools—which means that standards should be lowered or waived altogether; otherwise, the argument runs, it would take too long for the imbalance to right itself. This seems to me to be objectionable on many grounds. I consider a program which would lower the standards of *achievement* for Negroes as tantamount to regarding them as second-class citizens. We have a moral responsibility to provide the educational opportunities that Negroes need to achieve the full measure of their own potential. But to say to the Negro in a spirit of patronizing friendliness, "Well, if you can't make the grade we set for the whites, we'll lower it for you," is an expression—perhaps an unconscious expression—of the kind of chauvinistic attitude which in the past all genuine liberals have deplored. Negroes have just as much right, for example, to be treated by adequately trained physicians as whites. Under present conditions, unfortunately, this depends upon there being many more Negro physicians in practice. And although it may take time for a sufficient number of Negro physicians to be trained— unhappily there are not many more today than there were twenty or thirty years ago—the measures required to counteract that situation do not entail a lowering of professional and intellectual standards. What is needed is a program to create greater educational opportunities for those now deprived, and to mobilize the nation's resources at the most strategic points towards that end.

PODHORETZ: Mr. Baldwin, you've had some unkind words to say about liberals, if I remember rightly. Do you still want to say them? How does the situation look to you—especially in terms of what Mr. Hook has just said?

JAMES BALDWIN: I don't want to sound—as I'm told so often I do sound —bitter or disaffected, but I do think that there's a very real problem in talking, as Mr. Hook was just doing, about ethical considerations in a society which is essentially *not* ethical. I might be perfectly willing to be one of the first Negroes to be accepted either here or there; I might even be perfectly willing to wait ten years or a generation to be fitted into American civilization, or American society, if I really felt that one *could* be fitted into it as it now is, as it's now constituted. But to my mind, you see, before one can really talk about the Negro problem in this country, one has got to talk about the white people's problem. The German refugees that Mr. Hook mentioned and all the other immigrants who have come to these shores and who have gotten or not gotten preferential treatment were nevertheless looked on by the bulk of the American community as white people, and they never served—at least not in the memory of any man living—the same function that American Negroes have served. I don't think we can discuss this properly unless we begin at the beginning. And the beginning is that Negroes were a source of cheap labor and everything white people did thereafter in relation to Negroes was a way of justifying this. I think it can be said, and I think that most liberals would finally have to agree, that the presence of the Negro here is precisely what has allowed white people to say they were free; and it is what has allowed them to assume they were rich. There is a sense in which one can say that the history of this country was built on my back. I don't mean that other people didn't pay for it too, but I do mean that the economy would be very different today if I hadn't built the railroads for nothing, if I hadn't picked the cotton for nothing—if, in fact, my role weren't to keep on doing all that, in effect, for nothing. After all, part of the reason there is a battle going on in the Deep South (to leave it only there for the moment) is that as the Negro starts voting and becomes economically free, the power of the Southern oligarchy will obviously be broken and the South is apt to become a very different place. And if the South becomes a different place, so will the rest of the nation.

Now, to get back to preferential treatment and ethics and morality: from a certain point of view, it doesn't matter whether you send Negro kids to the Bronx High School of Science or to any other school, indeed; and it doesn't matter what you teach them about ethics and morality there. Because those kids don't live in school, they go home. I went to DeWitt Clinton High in New York; I wasn't a bad student; and I got along very well with my playmates and all that jazz. Nevertheless, when the school day was over, I went back into a condition which they could not imagine; and I knew, no matter what anybody said, that the future I faced was not the future they faced. So inevitably, as graduation time approached, what had looked like a friendship broke up and we went our different ways— because the forces of our society drove us in different ways. Clearly, in terms of the American mythology and in terms of any realistic assessment of my future, I was going to be a porter, and they were not.

What I am trying to say is that you can't hope to invest a child with a morality in school which is going to be destroyed in the streets of Harlem— and every Negro in America lives in one or another version of Harlem. Until we can deal with the question of *why* Negroes are kept in ghettos and *why* white men move out when Negroes move in; until we can deal with the question of *why* precisely in a free country we allow the South to dictate to the federal government; until we face our responsibilities as citizens of this country quite apart from the Negro problem, I don't see that we can begin to talk about the Negro problem with any hope of clarity.

PODHORETZ: Mr. Glazer, as a sociologist who has studied what is called in the trade the acculturation of immigrant groups, do you agree with Mr. Baldwin that this whole problem begins with cheap labor?

NATHAN GLAZER: I'll get to that point eventually, I suppose, but I'd rather talk about liberalism first, because I see a number of very serious problems in connection with that word. Liberalism assumes the existence of certain mechanisms for the solution of problems: it assumes reasonable-ness; it assumes also a kind of good will; it assumes an acceptance of the principle of the fundamental equality of all men. But none of these assump-tions applies in the South. Let me read you a newspaper clipping I've brought with me: "A group of housewives in Jackson, Mississippi charged in a bitter hearing today that their children are being subjected to brain-washing by textbooks that teach them that prejudice is wrong. The women also contended that the school books introduce pleas for world government, and try to further a belief in the brotherhood of all people."

Now this seems to me a real challenge to the American Creed—to use a term that Dr. Myrdal made famous—and it raises a question similar to the one that the appearance of Nazism in Germany raised for liberalism in the 1920's, or for that matter that the Southern defense of slavery raised for this country in the 1850's. What does liberalism do or say in the face of what seems to be a mass commitment to evil, or at least to a point of view that doesn't enforce on those who hold it an obligation to work to-ward any improvement?

Having mentioned the worst problem, I would now like to speak about the big cities of the North which seem to be the major context for our discussion here. Unfortunately what happens in the big cities of the North is colored by the fact that they're part of the same country as Mississippi and Alabama. Maybe it would have been better if we hadn't fought the Civil War at all, and could now take the same attitude to the South as we do to South Africa—because I do think that the Southern kind of position just can't be found in the North. Regardless of their behavior, people in the North won't even admit to poll-takers that they are prej-udiced—or anyway very prejudiced. Now even if this is hypocrisy, a case of the homage that vice pays to virtue, it's still true that the American Creed does prevail in the North. Bills can be passed; whites and Negroes can confer together on what ought to be done about discrimination; you can get a Fair Employment Practices Law; you can get a Fair Housing Law. Of course, many Northern Negroes see all this as not only illusory but as some sort of farce. The assumption seems to be that the people who run the Fair Employment Practices Law aren't doing their job or that the law itself is irrelevant. So Negroes in New York, for instance, insist on jobs by demonstrating in the streets and chaining themselves to cranes, while the political authorities run around trying to do something about it. But I'm convinced that the Fair Employment Practices Law isn't a farce. In New York they have a big budget; they check personnel procedures and application forms (in the big organizations anyway); they act pretty quickly on complaints. And they get results—Negroes *do* get jobs. But the results aren't good enough—at least not good enough to make the Negroes feel that the political order is responsive to their real situation and their needs.

Then take the case of housing. It's not a matter of "tokenism," nor can you talk about an exclusive power structure, when a Negro, Robert Weaver, heads the Federal Housing and Home Finance Agency in Washington, or when a Negro runs or is second in command of a local housing commission (he's usually one or the other), and when 30 per cent of his staff is Negro. Despite what the *Amsterdam News* says about those Negroes—that they've sold out, that they're Uncle Toms, or what have you—if not for an accident of fate, they might today have been on the staff of the *Amsterdam News* writing editorials themselves. Anyhow, I know something personally about the housing situation since I worked for Mr. Weaver for a year in the Housing and Home Finance Agency. There's no question that probably four-fifths of the Negroes in New York City (and other cities as well) live under awful conditions; a small number, of course, live in nice houses in Queens, and a much larger number (about one-sixth or one-seventh) in public housing projects. Now, it's hard enough to deal with the demand for "Freedom Now" in general, but how do you even deal with the demand for Freedom Now from rats, from vermin, from crowding, from garbage? How do you provide good housing conditions *now?* People with perfectly good credentials, both racial and libertarian, have been struggling with such matters for a long time, and they have to contend with conflicts of interest —this, I suppose, brings us back to Mr. Baldwin's point about the power structure and the economy—that no one seems able to overcome. It isn't Mr. Weaver's fault or the fault of any other administrator. There are some cities, for example, which could build far more public housing than they are currently doing. Why don't they? Well, one of the reasons is that this housing would be available to Negroes, and the white people of those cities don't want Negroes living near them. But that's only the beginning. There is also the question of money. We don't have adequate funds for public housing. Two per cent of all housing in this country is public housing as against something like 30 per cent in England and similar percentages in other countries. Americans don't like public housing, and one of the reasons they don't like it is that they put all sorts of restrictions into the law to make sure that it will be awful. Nobody ever quite says this, but the idea is that while the poor may be entitled to safe, decent, and sanitary housing, they aren't entitled to live as well as *we* do.

The Northern problem, then, is not a problem of laws or of formal equality. Negroes in the North vote, they go to school, they get jobs, there aren't any repressive or discriminatory statutes on the books. But formal equality simply hasn't worked to produce actual equality, or rather it has been working too slowly. It's ridiculous that there should be only one Negro principal out of six hundred or eight hundred in New York City. The *Amsterdam News*, looking at such a figure, says that the Board of Examiners discriminates. I myself feel sure that the Board of Examiners doesn't discriminate—not in the way the *Amsterdam News* means. They have tests which for a lot of reasons Negroes find hard to pass: the school system, like everything else, is a bureaucracy, and Negroes haven't yet been able to penetrate it.

Now let me come back to an important point that James Baldwin brought up. The formal equality that prevails in this country has always been accompanied by a great order of inequality that doesn't apply only to Negroes, though Negroes are its worst victims. Traditionally, there have been ways of dealing with this problem, and these ways have worked well enough to prevent ethnic and race wars from breaking out. One of them has been the provision of formal equality itself: formally we take no cognizance of differences among groups. Informally, however, cognizance has always been taken of these differences. We set up "balanced" tickets, we make sure that different groups are represented on boards, commissions, and so on. Of course, all this comes about as a result of pressure from these groups—pressure that elicits an intelligent or a civilized response from someone in power. Sometimes the man in power, like the mayor of Detroit, is clever enough to give a job to a member of the pressure group before he is asked for it, or before the pressure group even thinks of asking for it. In my opinion, this is a reasonable procedure. American democracy has always been a hazardous thing. The official idea—call it hypocritical if you will—is that we are all alike and can live together in harmony. But everyone knows that we are all different and want to live apart—which we do. The Jews live apart, not only because they are often socially excluded, but also because they themselves want to maintain their separateness. The same is true of the Catholics: they want a certain amount of contact with other groups, but not that much, and they do many things to insure their separateness, including the maintenance of a very expensive parochial school system. This, then, is the American group pattern. The problem for Negroes is not that they are outside the pattern, but that they have been very badly off within it. And this too poses a challenge—a challenge of another sort—to liberalism.

PODHORETZ: Mr. Myrdal, to what extent do these matters we're discussing seem to you a problem of laws—some that can be made, and others that can be removed? I know that you have some ideas as to what is likely to happen so far as the legal situation is concerned in the next ten years.

GUNNAR MYRDAL: Let me start a little further back with the ideological framework that you sketched in before, because I don't feel myself at home at all within that framework, and most American liberals I know, Negro and white, don't fit into it either. You tell me that there are now two schools of thought. The first believes that if the Negroes are given their rights, they can move up one by one, and eventually you will have an integrated society. Then there is another school which says that society is made up of groups and not of individuals, and that it is the whole group which must be moved up. I don't see those two positions as the real alternatives. Certainly as a liberal, I believe that all laws and rules that discriminate against Negroes must be done away with, and I personally am optimistic enough to believe that within the next ten years all such laws and rules will in fact disappear. But we should not be so stupid as to think that this by itself will solve the problem. It won't. Prejudice will continue to exist even if the legal and institutional basis for it is removed. And not only that, but since the Negroes are poor—and since they have a higher proportion of illiteracy, of school dropouts, and the rest of it— other things besides the removal of prejudice are needed to lift the group. To that extent, I agree with the second school of liberal thought that Mr. Podhoretz was talking about—except that I don't understand why they should speak of the *Negro* group. I don't think Negroes are going to be given preferential treatment and I think it would be most unfortunate if they were—though Professor Hook is probably right in saying that there are individual cases in which preferential treatment might work. But on the whole, what is needed, of course, is to lift *all* the poor people at the bottom, the people I call the "underclass" or the submerged group, out of poverty and everything that poverty implies. And this means—as Mr. Baldwin said—remaking American society. I think it would be most unfortunate to try to get a kind of Marshall Plan specifically for the Negro. There are several reasons. Politically, I doubt that it would be possible to push such a plan through—if only because white people today simply do not have a bad conscience over the fact that Negroes were brought here into slavery a long time ago. My ancestors were the Vikings, who were of course a murderous crowd—murdering, raping, and enslaving people. And yet you'll find the average Swede or Norwegian almost proud when he talks about the Vikings. The point is that ancestral guilt doesn't work, and it certainly won't work in America where the underclass includes so many other groups —the Puerto Ricans, the Mexicans, and the poor whites in all the big slums in the big cities, and the small slums in the small cities and the rural slums in the country. Improving the lot of this whole submerged group has become a very acute problem for America, and it is only in that larger setting that the Negroes will be able to achieve anything more than formal equality. Furthermore, looking just at the practical side of the whole matter, anyone with any sense knows that it's not possible to solve the Negro housing problem as a *Negro* housing problem. For one thing, you could never get the money; and even if you could get the money, I doubt that it could technically be done. I think the same is true of education: you'll have to get rid of all your bad schools and improve the *whole* educational system.

Of course at the moment the Negroes are the only active part of the submerged group. The others—the Mexicans, the Puerto Ricans—are just quiet. The Negro rebellion—it seems to me very interesting that this should have happened—is an exception to the general rule that America has the least revolutionary proletariat in the world. But when the situation of a rising group is aggravated by unemployment, you inevitably get a revolutionary situation; and now you've got one in America. This doesn't mean, however, that something preferential ought to be done for the Negro group alone. For the last six years I've been working very hard on development problems in Southeast Asia, and I've seen something of how a policy of preferential treatment works out in practice. There is India, for example, where, as you know, the Untouchables constitute a much larger group than the Negroes do in America. The Untouchables for some time now have been given preference in employment, in education, in voting, and in many other areas. But when you look at all this closely, you find that it really amounts to nothing more than tokenism, because it affects only a very tiny minority of the Untouchables. And in addition, it also contributes to stabilizing the situation of caste in India, just as, I am sure, preferential treatment for Negroes would tend to make firmer and more lasting the differences among groups in America. And there I am liberal in Mr. Podhoretz's first sense—both in believing that all formal discriminatory rules and laws must be eradicated and in looking forward to a society which is color blind. I've seen places in America—a few university campuses, for instance—where people already move around together and don't notice who is Negro and who is white.

HOOK: May I ask you a question at this point, Dr. Myrdal? It seems to me that a dedication to the long-range goal of remaking all of society is not responsive to the *specific* problems which exist here and now. Let's take your illustration of India, for example. In India not only are special considerations given to the Harijans, but there is, I believe, an *unofficial* policy that 10 per cent of all civil service posts be set aside for Moslems until such time as the number of Moslems in the civil service shall be proportionate to the number of Moslems in the population as a whole. This plan has a time limit built into it. It was designed to meet a specific situation, and was an indication of the willingness of the Indian government to make provision for the special, disadvantaged situation of the Moslem, and particularly to assure the Moslem that he was not outside the national community. I do not think such a policy—which has probably lessened the danger of subversion and civil war in India—is incompatible with liberalism.

MYRDAL: Well, you give the argument for this kind of thing, but you know, Gandhi was always against it. Furthermore, it's dangerous, because it can lead to a situation where people who are less qualified are preferred to people with better qualifications.

HOOK: It depends upon how *critical* the situation is—and, of course, I am assuming roughly equal qualifications. But these are not the only measures to be adopted. I agree that it is essential to move toward the improvement of the economic situation. As a socialist, I take it for granted that we are trying to move in that direction. But economic improvement alone does not eradicate discrimination.

Here I want to go back to the fundamental question that Mr. Baldwin raised about whether we are an ethical society. Of course, no society has historically been organized on the basis of ethical principles, but I don't think we can understand how any society functions without observing the operation of the ethical principles within it. And if we examine the development of American society, we certainly can say that we have made *some* progress—not enough progress, to be sure, but progress nevertheless—by virtue of the extension of our ethical principles to institutional life. If we want to explain the progress that has been made in the last twenty years by minority groups in this country—not only the Negroes, but other groups as well—I believe we have to take into account the effect of our commitment to democracy, imperfect though it may be. After all, one of the justifications for having laws against discrimination on the books is that after a while people begin to regard the law as the determining norm in their lives. I can't see how we're going to achieve what Professor Myrdal has in mind if we don't assume that the direction we should be moving in is ethical as well as economic.

BALDWIN: I must say that I don't myself necessarily take it for granted in this context that one is always moving in an ethical direction.

HOOK: One should.

BALDWIN: Well, I'm not sure that one can. I'd like to. But what strikes me here is that you are an American talking about American society, and I am an American talking about American society—both of us very concerned with it—and yet your version of American society is really very difficult for me to recognize. My experience in it has simply not been yours. God knows I have no desire to say that we have made *no* progress, though I have certain attitudes of my own about it. For example, as far as I can tell, the progress that has been made in the last twenty years has not been mainly due to the application of ethical principles but to the fact that the country has been extremely prosperous (without further examining what that prosperity really means). When the economic level of the country as a whole rose, obviously the Negro level rose more or less proportionately with it. And this created, among other things, those kids in the streets who were raised in relative security and therefore had a different attitude toward the world than we did who were raised in the Depression. Besides, by the time these kids were sixteen or seventeen, the black people of America were no longer at the mercy of the American vision of black people, because there were now other black people in the world who escaped the definitions which American Negroes had always been taught and more or less forced to live with. Now that is, if you like, progress. But looking at it as a black American citizen, looking back at the entire record and speaking not as a sociologist but as a writer, I don't see that there's been any real change in American attitudes: I'm delighted to know there've been many fewer lynchings in the year 1963 than there were in the year 1933, but I also have to bear in mind—I have to bear it in mind because my life depends on it—that there are a great many ways to lynch a man. The impulse in American society, as far as I can tell from my experience in it, has essentially been to ignore me when it could, and then when it couldn't, to intimidate me; and when that failed, to make concessions. The way white Americans look on each other is not the way they look on the black population here. You simply can't get around that fact.

HOOK: Mr. Baldwin, we have lived, of course, in different worlds, but perhaps not so far apart. I grew up in a Brooklyn slum before the First World War, and I was just thinking of the difference between Mr. Podhoretz's experience as he described it in his *Commentary* article last year,* and my own. I went to a school where the hero was a Negro teacher, a man by the name of Jim Harris. He was a hero primarily because he could kick a football over the school building. But he was also *my* hero because he was the man who gave me, so to speak, my educational start. At the same time there were race riots going on in Brooklyn, not reported in the press. On the basis of your experience, Mr. Baldwin, you say that the attitudes of the American people to the Negro haven't changed. But on the basis of my experience, I say that the attitudes of large sections of the American people *have* changed. Things that were practiced when I was young would be regarded as intolerable today. In Coney Island, for instance, there was a horrible game: I mention it only as a symbol of many other things. For a nickel you got three hard balls that you could throw at a Negro who served as the target. I remember being consoled by my father who told me that it really wasn't a Negro who was the target but a white man dressed in black face—as if that made any difference. Today, of course, such a thing would be regarded as an outrage. The whole moral tone has improved, and part of the new attitude toward the Negro is a reflection of the burgeoning consciousness of more and more whites that the democratic legacy was betrayed in the past by the way Negroes were treated. These whites haven't got a sense of collective guilt, but they do have a greater sense of responsibility than most people had when I was young. And this, it seems to me, is of the first importance to recognize. A kind of revolution of rising expectations has taken place—expectations as to what decent conduct should be—and it flows, I think, primarily from education. That's why I would continue to put the main emphasis on education.

PODHORETZ: Mr. Baldwin, this seems to me a crucial point. Did you

* "My Negro Problem—And Ours," February 1963.

literally mean to deny a minute ago that there have been important changes in white attitudes toward Negroes in the last twenty years?

BALDWIN: Well, I have to repeat that, yes. But could I come back to it in a moment after I talk about two other things? One is the concept of rising expectations. I think that concept applies to immigrant groups, and we've talked a great deal about immigrant groups here—that is, people who came to this country voluntarily and who managed, once they got here, to achieve a way of life and a whole attitude toward reality and toward themselves which they could not have achieved if they had remained wherever they came from in Europe. In that sense it is perfectly true that the idea of rising expectations is part of the American experience: you leave the famine-ridden farm in Ireland, you come to America, you fit into the American scene, you rise, you become part of a new social structure. But that is only the European immigrants' experience. It is not the Black experience. I did not one day decide to leave my farm and come to America. I was brought here. I did not want to come. And when I got here, I did not, like the Irish and the Jews and the Russians and the Poles and the Czechs and the Italians, immediately find myself in a slum and then by hard work and saving my pennies rise out of the slum into a position of relative economic security so that my idea of reality changed. That is not the black experience in this country, and there is no point in pretending to ourselves on any level whatever that it *is*. The black experience is entirely different. You find yourself in a slum and you realize at a certain point that no amount of labor, no amount of hard work, no amount of soap is going to get you out of that slum.

Which brings me to the second thing I want to talk about—education. Any Negro born in this country who accepts American education at face value turns into a madman—*has* to. Because the standards that the country pretends to live by are not for him, and he knows that by the time he starts pledging allegiance to the flag. If I had believed, if any Negro on my block had really believed what the American Republic said about itself, he would have ended up in Bellevue. And those who did believe it *did* end up in Bellevue. If you are a Negro, you understand that somehow you have to operate outside the system and beat these people at their own game—which means that your real education essentially occurs outside of books. You cannot believe, as Americans apparently do believe, that George Washington chopped down that cherry tree and said "I cannot tell a lie." You know better. And so what you have to do is educate yourself. I think it might be useful to turn the proposition we've been discussing around for a minute, and instead of talking about giving Negroes preferential treatment, talk about giving *white* people preferential treatment for the purpose of enabling them to learn their own history. Because what you discover as a Negro child in school—and certainly later—is that you are not in the history books. It doesn't demand a vast amount of perception to discover *why* you are not in the history books. And then you realize that if *you* are not in the history books, a great many other things must be left out of the history books too, including everybody else in the country.

GLAZER: But that's not the point. Sure—everybody else has been left out too, and they know it.

BALDWIN: I'm not sure they know it.

GLAZER: Of course they know it.

HOOK: They know it because they read about it in the books.

GLAZER: No, they know it the same way Negroes do—because they've been left out of the books. The Jews aren't in the history books, the Italians aren't there, the Japanese aren't there, the Czechs aren't there. In fact, the immigrants are only there to explain how the cities became corrupt. So this is a society in which we all learn to live on two levels—the level on which we say that there's equality in America, that we all have the same chance to get ahead, that we're all going to get our rightful share; and that other level on which we know perfectly well that somebody always has an advantage, that some groups are more privileged than others, and that some people have better connections than others. I don't think the first level is a complete phony. Since the assassination of President Kennedy, a lot of the Irish in Washington have been very sad for more than the obvious reason. They know that many of them will be leaving, even though it may take a year or so. But why were there so many in the first place? Was it a plot? A conspiracy of the power structure? Of course not—these were the people the late President was comfortable with. This is American society—the part that never gets written about and that everybody knows about. Politicians certainly know about it, and they act on it when they make up tickets and appeal for votes.

Let's look at it this way: on the one hand, this country does too much through laws, much too much, and one of the problems is that you can't get rid of them when you need to, because they all represent complex compromises. But on the other hand, very important things are done in America without any legal authority. Now there, I think, the Negro revolution has reminded people of the failures of sense and of awareness which they have been guilty of. It's ridiculous that New York doesn't have thirty Negro school principals by now. But I'm convinced that the reason has more to do with blindness than with prejudice as such. In general no one paid enough attention to the fact that the lower class was becoming mostly Negro in the cities. Now they're paying attention.

HOOK: Do you think there's been progress in the last twenty years?

GLAZER: Oh, that's a complicated story. Yes, in a way. If you look at income figures, Mr. Baldwin, you have to conclude that a lot of Negroes must have believed "that stuff" and not gone crazy. Twenty per cent of the Negroes in New York have white-collar jobs; that figure must mean something. As far as white attitudes are concerned—yes, there's been progress in the sense that there's been a decline in violent attitudes and violent feelings. What they've been replaced by is another question. The ethical quality of American life is least evident among people talking to each other in places like bars and private homes. But it does come into effect wherever the groups have to get together—where the politicians get together, where heads of school systems get together, and so on. Then they remember the American Creed. But the whole thing is very perilous. Look at the public-opinion polls. Down below hardly anybody wants equality or is in favor of civil liberties, and they want to take the vote away from the Communists. But up above they remember the American Creed. And the system works because there's enough power at the top to keep it going. Is that progress? I don't know. But I think that's the way things work in America.

PODHORETZ: Mr. Myrdal, you had a comment to make on this question of the ethical element in American life, didn't you?

MYRDAL: Well, what I believe is that this country succeeds in living a very sinful life without being deeply cynical. That is the difference between Europe and America, and it signifies that ethics *means* something here. And it is because ethics means something here that I feel certain there are going to be changes in the law within the next ten years. It's true, as Mr. Glazer says, that the ethical element operates particularly within institutions, and the higher the institution the more perfectly it operates. A local labor union may stand for discrimination, but the national association won't; it will be more liberal because it represents a greater investment of American ideals. On the other hand, of course, your ethical American will very happily ignore many things around him which are bad, and he is particularly ready to follow his ethical principles to their logical conclusion when it doesn't cost too much. The civil rights things don't cost very much. But improving the real situation of Negroes and poor people generally *would* cost money. Now, as an economist, I think I can prove that in the *end* it wouldn't cost money, because it would mean the utilization of wasted resources, and the utilization of wasted resources has to make a society richer. Still, there is all this superstition about the budget in this country, and getting around it really presents a messy problem.

As to white attitudes toward Negroes, yes, I do believe that there have been changes. But you know, no upper class ever gave up its monopoly or its privileges out of ethical principles; the submerged group needs power to force its way in, and it is this that makes the ethical principles prevail. In a place like Bloomington, Indiana, they have slums that are exactly like Harlem, but the people living in them aren't Negroes, they're "Kentuckians," old-American stock who have migrated from the Appalachian region. They live in shacks, they have a high crime rate, there's a lot of prostitution and gambling, they get only occasional work. But nobody cares. Many people in Bloomington probably aren't even aware that such slums exist in their town. And there, of course, the Negro rebellion helps—it helps to make people conscious of the extent to which poverty is still a problem, and it helps activate the better part of the American heart.

So power is important, but attitudes and ethical principles count also. And where the Negroes are concerned, they count enormously, because the Negroes don't have enough power. I had a visit the other day in Stockholm from a Negro sociologist, a professor from California, who said that he didn't believe at all in my idea that the better part of the American heart was on his side. "But brother," I said to him, "you are only one-tenth of the American people, a poor tenth, and you are powerless; if the whites wanted to, they could dump you all in the ocean or they could buy up some old plantation land somewhere in Mississippi and pen you up in it. They can do whatever they like with you." "No, no," he said, "what about the Supreme Court?" "Well," I answered, "if the whites, who are 90 per cent of the population, wanted to change the Constitution, they could dump the Supreme Court in the ocean too." So what the Negroes have to rely upon in the end is that America *is* its institutions, and that the highest of these institutions will act when they come under pressure. And when they act, they will act according to certain principles, which, like Professor Hook, I call ethical.

PODHORETZ: Mr. Baldwin, what do those institutions look like to you, as a Negro? First, do you have any real faith in them to operate against the resistances, and particularly the second-line resistances, that have been developing in the North? And second, how seriously do you want us to take your statement that there have been no attitude changes? What about that 20 per cent Mr. Glazer was referring to who are not in Bellevue, but who are assimilated, acculturated, embourgeoised, or whatever nasty word you want to use?

BALDWIN: Mr. Glazer doesn't go to cocktail parties with them. I know about that 20 per cent; my point about progress would be the same even if the figures were higher. No matter how well they may get along in the office with their fellow workers, they are not white, and they still lead different lives from white people, and in the main they don't tell the truth to white people. Mr. Hook talks about ethics, but when he says ethics, I read attitudes. And I know about the attitudes that Americans have toward justice, freedom, and equality, and I understand that no self-respecting white American on a certain level is about to say what he feels about Negroes—and indeed, I'm sure he doesn't feel much about Negroes, I'm sure that by now he knows that my body odor is no worse than anyone else's. But the gap between your institutions (assuming now that they're ethical) and the people in the streets is what has created the danger in which we stand now and the urgency of our situation. You and I around this table and everyone in this room may agree that our institutions are really working to liberate the Negroes. But the *Negroes* don't believe it. And given their history, given their experience and their actual situation, they have no reason to believe it. They would have to be willing to be betrayed one more time by the people on the top who say, "Wait, and we'll take care of you tomorrow," and tomorrow means the 20 per cent Mr. Glazer is talking about, while the other 80 per cent are still in jail.

Who created this pressure on the institutions, after all? It was the people in the streets, disaffected and despairing, who forced whatever changes have taken place within the last six years; it was the people who got their heads broken and were put on chain gangs. Six years in and out of jail is not easy. If America were really a more ethical society, this price would not have been demanded. And it's certainly not through being paid yet.

PODHORETZ: May I reformulate the question for everybody around the table? I think it's unfortunate that the word ethics came into the discussion.

HOOK: That's a very peculiar observation.

PODHORETZ: Maybe so, but I think it ought to be possible to discuss the question without reference to how good or how bad anybody's intentions are, and therefore I'd like to reformulate it in the following manner. Have we by now arrived at a point where it is beginning to be conceivable that the Negroes as a people, as a community, will take their place within the next five or ten or fifteen or twenty years as one of the competing groups in the American pluralistic pattern? By a pluralistic pattern, I mean precisely one which is made up of *groups*, each competing for a share of the pie and each getting about as much of the pie as its political, economic, and intellectual power can get for it. Until pressure was brought by those people on the streets, it was not, in my opinion, conceivable that such a thing would happen. Now I believe that it is conceivable. Do any of you agree?

HOOK: I think it all depends on what we ourselves do. To take the position (which seems to me almost implicit in Mr. Baldwin's words) that it's hopeless, that the more things change the more they remain the same, may have a tendency to paralyze our ethical impulses. Our real problem— and this is how I interpret ethics—is to work on all the specific projects by which we can bring our Negro fellow citizens into the "kingdom of democratic ends."

PODHORETZ: What about the kingdom of jobs?

HOOK: I'll come to that. But in answer to Mr. Baldwin and to set the record straight, I want to point out that the Supreme Court desegregation decision of 1954 was handed down before there was any pressure from the streets. Of course the Supreme Court has played a very unhappy role, from Dred Scott to the nullification of the Civil Rights Act of 1875; if that act had been upheld in 1883, discrimination could have been abolished a long time ago. But let's not dwell too much on the past. The 1954 decision was a tremendous reversal, and it did not come about as a consequence of pressure from the streets. Nor were the actions of two American Presidents in sending soldiers to enforce the rights of individual Negroes—something which, when I was young, would have been hard to imagine—the consequence of mass pressure from the streets.

Now to return to the specific instance of jobs. One of the problems we encounter here is trade-union opposition to jobs for Negroes. Many of us fought for labor in the past, and now we discover that some of our friends in the labor movement are opposed to sharing jobs with Negroes. Well, what is one to do? Does one deplore it and let it go at that? Certainly not. It seems to me one should press for legislation which would deny the use of federal services to any trade union that discriminated against Negroes. There are very few unions that could survive a law of this sort. Applying the same pragmatic approach to every other point, it should be possible to do some creative thinking instead of throwing in the sponge whenever we encounter a particular problem which is very stubborn. Sometimes we have to go slowly. It's a mistake, for instance, to try to integrate the schools by bussing white children from long distances into Harlem; this does neither the schools nor the children any good, and it creates unnecessary obstacles to other measures which favor the common goal. In answer to your question, then, Mr. Podhoretz, as to what the next ten or twenty years have in store for us, I should say it depends entirely upon our own intelligence and our own courage.

PODHORETZ: Mr. Baldwin, is it conceivable to you that the Negroes will within the next five or ten or twenty years take their rightful place as one of the competing groups in the American pluralistic pattern? Or is something more radical—or perhaps less radical—more likely to happen the way things are going now?

BALDWIN: In the first place—I want to say this particularly to Mr. Hook —I don't feel at all hopeless. One can't afford to. But I'm afraid I have to keep coming back to the same thing. Because the whole structure interlocks. In itself it's a very interesting fact, though a sinister one, that trade unions should object to Negroes being in them and working side by side with white workers. But that's not the only problem. The problem is that the economy cannot provide enough jobs for everybody—I mean white people now—and so when the Negroes come along and ask for jobs, we get, as we have now gotten, into a very dangerous situation which could precipitate chaos. If this is so—and we all know it is—then we have to take a very hard look at the economy and do whatever has to be done to revise it. Or take legislation: even if we got from the federal government a law prohibiting trade unions from discriminating against Negroes—and any such law is a long way off—it would still have to be enforced, and that has to be done by the people, really. How much time can a man spend in court to get a job or a house? Now since the law is so far off, and since there is no guarantee that we'll get it or that it will be enforced if we do get it, Negro men chain themselves to cranes and lie down on airports to dramatize the situation and, if necessary, to immobilize the country. At bottom—and I'm very serious about this—it is not a Negro problem. It is not what is happening to the Negro that is so terrible. It is what is happening to the whole country that is so terrible. That's why when you ask about the Negroes in the next five or ten or fifteen years taking their place as a competing group and getting their share of the pie, I can't answer directly. I can't put it that way to myself. What pie are you talking about? From my own point of view, my personal point of view, there is much in that American pie that isn't worth eating.

PODHORETZ: O.K., that's you, but what about your fellow Negroes? Wouldn't they be perfectly happy to eat everything in that pie? You said in *The Fire Next Time* that Negroes wonder whether they want to be integrated into a burning house, and at that point—as someone observed— you were speaking as an American social critic rather than as a Negro. Now the question is, is it the Negroes who feel that the house is burning and that the pie is rotten, or is it only James Baldwin?

BALDWIN: I think this: terrible things have happened to white people as a result of our history and terrible things have happened to Negroes. One of the things that has happened to Negroes is that they themselves have acquired such habits of inferiority and have evolved such a way of life—which, whatever else one says about it, is more vivid than the bulk of white American lives—that they have become in some sense accustomed to their oppression. I don't mean that they accept it or that they like it, but they *know* it. *They know it.* They do not call the cops as other American citizens do; they don't have the same expectations.

GLAZER: Yes, they do call the cops.

BALDWIN: Not at all. They don't.

GLAZER: They call the cops. One of the biggest demands in Negro slums around the country is for more police protection and better police protection. Maybe they don't like the police, but they want them. Look at the newspapers, talk to the people. They certainly demand the cops.

BALDWIN: No, but let's be clear about this. It depends on who you are talking about now. Who wants them?

GLAZER: A lot of Negroes do.

PODHORETZ: The cops are part of the pie. I think we can agree on that, so we get back to the same question.

BALDWIN: Before we get back, I want to say one thing. At least in Harlem and on the South Side of Chicago, the two Negro communities that I more or less know, the complaint about the cops is that they don't protect the property, they don't protect the lives. One can be robbed in Harlem three times a week and nothing will ever happen. Now if they're asking for cops, they're not asking for what you think they're asking for. They're asking for police protection. It is not the same thing.

HOOK: I'd like to pursue the question that Mr. Podhoretz asked as to whether James Baldwin is speaking for himself or for most Negroes. If I read his most recent book properly, he actually believes that all Negroes hate white people; at least that's how some people have interpreted him. But that's not true for the Negroes I know, and it can't be true for Negroes who have married whites.

PODHORETZ: It depends on your theory of marriage.

HOOK: There's Dickens's idea that since all things wear off in time, it's best to begin marriage with a little aversion. Anyhow, I think some of us have a tendency to drug ourselves with rhetoric when we speak of attitudes. There are people who say you either have to love Negroes or kill them. I don't love *all* white people. Why should I love *all* Negroes? I think we drug ourselves with rhetoric when we advocate wholesale solutions like total intermarriage to make color disappear. It seems to me this is an insult to the Negro population.

PODHORETZ: Are you referring to my article on the Negro problem?

HOOK: Well, the proposal you made there is a variation of an old one. Bruno Bauer in the 19th century said that the best way for Jews to get their civil rights was to stop being Jews. But the conception of democracy—which, as I keep repeating, is fundamentally an ethical conception—is that we can live peacefully together with our *differences*. It's enough to have friendship and respect for one another without necessarily loving one another; and of these, respect is more important than friendship because friendship is personal, while respect is the basis on which all the moral and political obligations we have to one another as human beings rests. I want to say again, I find a good deal of the discussion concerning the Negro problem these days very rhetorical and unnecessarily inflammatory; much of it puts obstacles in the way of progress. I saw a television program the other night called "Confrontation." I was horrified to discover that the only feeling many white people had toward the Negroes who are moving into their communities was one of resentment; they had no notion whatever of their own elementary human responsibilities. We as educators have failed to make an impact upon communities of this sort. But were they to become familiar with the doctrine that all Negroes hate whites and to believe it, they would have some justification for their attitude. I think, then, that we owe a responsibility to the problem, to ourselves, and to our fellow citizens to speak bravely, eloquently, but without exaggeration.

PODHORETZ: If I'm not mistaken, Mr. Baldwin and I have both just been charged with irresponsibility. I'm the moderator and not a participant, so

I'll resist the temptation to answer, but I think Mr. Baldwin ought to have a chance.

BALDWIN: Let me say one more time, I don't hate white people. I haven't got the time, I haven't got the energy, I have other things to do. And as far as I know, Mr. Hook, I never said that all Negroes hate white people either. What I *have* said is that I cannot imagine any Negro in this country who has not for at least one of the twenty-four hours of a day hated all white people just because they were on his back. That is not the same thing as saying all Negroes by definition hate whites. Negroes do have every reason, let's face it, to be extremely bitter and distrustful toward white people, and that is part of the burden of what I am trying to say.

But I don't know why we don't face the question of power here. For example, the real victims in the Deep South are the white Southerners. Those people, ignorant and pathetic and miserable as they are, are at the mercy of the Southern oligarchy. It is one of the most cunning bargains ever struck in history. Men like Senator Eastland—in fact, that whole lot in Washington—batten on those people and keep them in their prison. Now we could, of course, take mobile units down there and educate them, but we also have to get rid of the people in power in Washington whom they serve. In other words, there is a power structure that has to be examined.

PODHORETZ: We have an economist and a sociologist with us here. Maybe they can examine it for us. Mr. Myrdal?

MYRDAL: As an economist, I would rather talk about what I believe is the really fundamental thing—the rate of economic progress. Even if this is a group society, and the Negroes exert their power as a group, and because of the American ethos (which I think is important) all discriminatory rules are abolished—if you don't get your economy moving, you will be stuck no matter what laws you make. The primary condition for the progress and for the group actions we are talking about is to get the American economy moving. But I don't think you can get it moving—and here we have the connection between the race problem and poverty problem—until the whole submerged group is given more purchasing power and the education and training they need to compete more successfully on the market. America is not only a pluralistic society, it is also a society made up of individuals. And when you talk about individuals, the economic argument comes in. And I, for one, think that the economic argument is very important.

GLAZER: I agree—the economic argument is absolutely essential. Being the sociologist here, though, I want to make two more points about power. It was said earlier a number of times that trade unions object to Negro workers getting in. But it isn't the trade unions who object, it's the workers. Not that they object to working side by side with Negroes; a white family may move away when a Negro family moves in, but no white worker (except maybe in the South) ever left his job because a Negro moved in. This is a great strength, and it means that you can do a lot with jobs that you can't do with housing. So it isn't a matter of workers insisting on *segregation;* it's that they are defending a monopoly. This is the point I want to raise about the whole power situation. To get the country moving —to develop the higher expenditures which would make for a higher rate of economic growth—involves measures all of which affect monopolies. For example, we don't, I assume, have enough skilled workers in this country. But the skilled workers don't think so; they think it's fine that plumbers make fifteen thousand a year, and they'll fight to the death against the notion that there should be twice as many plumbers—whether Negro, white, Jewish, Chinese, or anyone else—with salaries stopping at ten thousand. Or take the case of education. The experts insist that we need more money for education, much more money; I'm not so sure money is the problem in this area, but in any event, there's no way of getting it locally, so it has to come from the federal government. What stands in the way? Not so much the right wing as the difficulty of giving money to the public schools without giving it to the Catholic parochial schools. Health insurance is another example. You can look at the issue abstractly in terms of the Right versus the Left, but what really is happening is that a private and special interest—namely the AMA—is holding on to a certain kind of monopoly which it interprets to its own advantage. My point is that this country is very feudal, which is why the discussion in terms of ethics seems to me almost irrelevant to the way things actually happen. From this perspective the reconstruction of American society raises problems that look to me almost as apocalyptic as Mr. Baldwin's —the breaking of traditional monopolies which have played a very important role in American history.

HOOK: How do you expect to motivate the attack on monopolies without appealing to the ethical consciousness of all groups in the population? How do you think the AMA will ever be forced to make these concessions? I mean, granted that you have to fight monopolies, with what instruments are you going to fight them?

GLAZER: Ethical instruments, among all others. But I think the most valuable instruments are political—you have to find different interest groups which for various reasons form a coalition to effect a certain change.

HOOK: How about the powerless? Suppose they haven't got power to fight power?

GLAZER: That brings me to my very last point: the illusion of powerlessness. When I talk to someone who works on the highest levels in Washington and he says he doesn't have any power, I wonder who's crazy. But of course everybody has power; everybody has *some* power. The problem is putting it together and using it.

PODHORETZ: On that singularly unapocalyptic note, I think we'll close the discussion around the table and open the floor to questions. Mr. Charles Silberman.*

SILBERMAN: Mr. Baldwin, speaking not long ago, before a group of teachers at P.S. 180 in New York, you were asked what is the role of the white liberal in social change, and your answer was, "There is no role for the white liberal, he is our affliction." I wonder if you could amplify that.

BALDWIN: I was talking about what I take to be a certain missionary complex on the part of white liberals, whose assumption basically seems to be that I am much worse off than they are and that they must help me into the light. Now, that's a perfectly honorable thing to feel, but historically it has been an affliction to Negroes. My own attitude toward the Bible, for instance, is still somewhat ambiguous because the people who brought it to me didn't themselves believe it. What I want to say here, though, is this: in general, the level of American experience—as I read it, as I have experienced it living here for all the years that I've been alive— seems to me much less dense, much less interesting, and finally in some way much below that of most Negroes that I have had to deal with. White Americans impress me as being far more hopeful, far more innocent, far more irresponsible, far less aware of the terrible, black, ugly facts of life than black people can afford to be. I don't mean this as a level of sensibil- is entirely possible that you can't help me. Because I have had to find out ity, I mean it as a matter of experience. I said at that meeting of school- teachers that if you don't know what Ray Charles is singing about, then it some things that white Americans do not know and that they must find out. I had to lose my virginity very early, and most white Americans still cling to it. It's on this basis that I called white liberals a kind of affliction— there is something impertinent in the assumptions they make about me. After all, I have watched the way most white people in this country live. I have worked in their kitchens and I have served them their brandy, and I know what goes on in white living rooms better than white people know what goes on in mine. And what I repudiate is the idea that I should learn how to live that way. I can get through my morning without a psychiatrist —so far—and if I had to choose between the way most white Americans live and my spareribs and my watermelon, then I would take my spareribs and my watermelon. Of course, it's a choice I refuse to make.

HOOK: I'm a white liberal. It seems to me Mr. Baldwin is here confusing white people and white liberals. The white liberals I know do not ask him to share any particular kind of culture. The white liberals I know are fighting for his right as a human being to make his choice as to what kind of culture he wants to live in. The white liberals I know do not define democracy as an equality of sameness, of identity, but as an equality of difference. And that's why I criticize the sentimentalists who say that

---

* Mr. Silberman is a member of the Board of Editors of *Fortune*.

everybody either has to be like the whites, or that everybody has to be like the Negroes. I want to have as much difference as possible, but difference on the basis of political and social and ethical equality. This is what I mean by saying that Mr. Baldwin, who is one of the most eloquent voices of our time, sometimes speaks in a way which makes a common struggle for common values difficult. He speaks of responsibilities which we white liberals recognize. But what about the Negro's responsibility? What about the responsibility of the Negro intellectual? If he develops a myth of collective guilt, as Mr. Baldwin has done in his recent writings, then he's doing a disservice to the whole cause of liberalism. Our minds have already been too poisoned by the doctrine of collective guilt, and the Negroes themselves have often suffered because of it. The white liberals I know do not feel responsible for actions which they couldn't control. There's a difference between collective guilt for the past and collective responsibility in the present, for such responsibility can ultimately be brought home to each individual's door.

SILBERMAN: Mr. Baldwin, since you said that there is no role for the liberal, could I ask you how this radical reconstruction of American society that you insist is necessary, can take place? Are the white conservatives going to do it?

BALDWIN: I have a very definite idea in my mind when I talk about a white liberal. These may not be the liberals you know, Mr. Hook, but they are the liberals I know. They are the people who nowadays, for example, say to me: "Jimmy, what are you crying about? You've *made* it." Now it seems to me that such a statement reveals a terrible set of assumptions. I happen not to have a Cadillac, but the liberal assumption is that I want one. The liberal assumption is that once you arrive at a certain level of social and economic status in American life, there's nothing left to worry about. What I mean by a liberal is someone who accepts these mechanistic terms and someone, furthermore, whose real attitudes are revealed when the chips are down—someone who thinks you're pushing too hard when you rock the boat, who thinks you are bitter when you are vehement, who has a set of attitudes so deep that they're almost unconscious and which blind him to the fact that in talking to a black man, he is talking to another man like himself. What I am calling for, asking for, hoping for, is that when I walk into a room, people will not immediately assume that I want to talk about civil rights. Maybe I don't want to talk about civil rights. The man who assumes that I always do doesn't mean me any harm, he's not my enemy, he's not a wicked man at all. He just has a certain set of reflexes which control him. He doesn't know what this does to the Negro he's talking to, who is aware that he is not being talked to as he would be talked to if he were white, simply.

As for collective guilt, I'm not anxious to make people feel guilty, I don't think there's any point to that. But I do think—and perhaps I should preface this by saying that I am a writer, that I can't lie about what I see—I do think that one of the things that has been absolutely crucial to American history can almost be summed up in the metaphor of a black corpse or a black presence or a black horde which everyone in one way or another agreed not to look at. One sees in the South, for example, an effort on the part of an entire population to deny what they know they have done. One is not interested in accusing any given person of any given crime. That is not the point. The point is that these crimes are committed, and have been committed for generations now, in the name of white Americans. So you can't now say, "My neighbor can be lynched and he's also innocent," and still say that you're not responsible. Do you see what I mean?

HOOK: Yes, but I don't agree. A man is responsible for the things that he can control, for the things that he can avoid doing. Those people in the South today who turn their eyes away from the Negro problem are responsible for the situation to the extent that they can relieve it. But they are not responsible for the initial acts which developed the situation in which they find themselves. People in some communities in the North who have never come into contact with Negroes find it incomprehensible to be charged with guilt. They can be charged with responsibility for not playing a greater role, for not taking a more active part in the political process. But there's a tremendous difference between responsibility for a problem which we run away from and collective guilt for the crimes of racists. The only way we can go forward is to focus on problems and to try to solve these problems intelligently. The greatest guilt an individual, white or black, can have in this matter is refusal to use his intelligence. Intelligence may not be enough, but there's no substitute for it, here as elsewhere.

PODHORETZ: Mr. Kenneth Clark.*

CLARK: How do I—a Negro in America who throughout his undergraduate years and the early part of his professional life identified himself with liberalism—how do I now see American liberalism? I must confess bluntly that I now see white American liberalism primarily in terms of the adjective, "white." And I think one of the important things Negro Americans will have to do is learn how they can deal with a curious and insidious adversary—much more insidious than the out-and-out bigot. And this is not easy. But let me give you some specifics. In this very room, about twenty-four hours ago, a group of social scientists, liberal social scientists, met to talk about how they could be more effective in the study of race relations. The chairman of the department of social psychology at a major university in America said that he had got some money to do something in the area of race relations. So what did he do? He and his department decided that they would not hire anybody who had done any research in race relations;

---

* Mr. Clark is professor of psychology at CCNY.

they would hire somebody who had done extremely good experimental work in the psychology of visual perception. When I heard that, I suspected, as a Negro—bitter, distorted—that maybe one reason they did not invite anyone who had done work in race relations was that they might have had to think of a Negro. If I had said this, I would have been accused of bigotry, my liberal white friends would have been unable to understand why I had violated the code of affability.

Second, liberals are predominant in the field of social work. In New York City a situation has existed in our ghettos that is now beyond the capacity of social workers to deal with. Liberal social workers are unable to understand that they are being described as irrelevant, that they have to be ignored and bypassed if the Negro community is to do something about its predicament. Anyone who says this to them is exaggerating. If he's a Negro, well, they have to handle him a little delicately. He can't be rejected completely, but he's a little peculiar.

Third, the public schools in New York City are not headed by bigots, they're not headed by people who say outwardly, "I believe that Negroes are inferior, that they can't learn"; they're headed by liberals. Most principals in the New York City public schools and most of the principals in Harlem schools say, "I am a liberal, I vote the Democratic ticket." Some of them might even say, "I'm a little socialist-inclined." But the fact is that these schools are woefully inferior, Professor Hook. They are not getting better; the evidence is that they are getting worse and worse. And the people who are directly responsible for this are self-identified liberals.

Fourth, our unions, our liberal unions. One could almost set it down as a rule that the more liberal the reputation of a union, the worse the predicament of Negroes in that union will be. We could go right down the list of areas of American life that are not controlled by out-and-out bigots, but that are controlled by individuals who define themselves as liberals, and find that the predicament of the Negro in each of these areas is incomprehensible. One must then conclude—or I must conclude—that there's a peculiar quality to American liberalism. With all due respect to my friend and former colleague and boss, Professor Myrdal, I have come to the conclusion that so far as the Negro is concerned, the ethical aspect of American liberalism or the American Creed is primarily verbal. There is a peculiar kind of ambivalence in American liberalism, a persistent verbal liberalism that is never capable of overcoming an equally persistent illiberalism of action. And so I am forced to agree with James Baldwin that so far as the Negro is concerned, liberalism as it is practiced—I am not talking of it as it is verbalized—*is* an affliction. It is an insidious type of affliction because it attempts to impose guilt upon the Negro when he has to face the hypocrisy of the liberal. The Negro doesn't have to feel guilty when he faces out-and-out bigotry. Mr. Baldwin has been put on the defensive all throughout this discussion by people who don't want to be made uncomfortable by him. Professor Hook, is, in effect, saying: "Jim, don't make me uncomfortable. Don't make me face the fact that my Negro friends. . . ." I almost expected Professor Hook to say, "My Negro cook. . . ."

HOOK: Oh, I've never had a cook.

CLARK: All you've been saying to Mr. Baldwin is: "Don't make me have to look behind my own facade. Don't let me have to find out that my Negro friends aren't really giving it to me straight." I'm glad that James Baldwin is around, because he's helping some of the rest of us cope with this difficult problem of facing the American liberal with the fact that in relation to the Negro he has never been as liberal as he likes to profess.

GLAZER: I think it's all very well to say that. Of course, we can read the same sort of thing all the time in the Negro press; it's a widely held point of view. But that doesn't mean that it's right, or that it fits the facts. I don't know how long James Dumpson has been head of the Department of Welfare in New York. What's wrong? Is he being sabotaged by his white assistants? I don't know exactly how many of the social workers employed by the city of New York are Negro—probably about a quarter or a fifth. Are they an affliction? They aren't white, of course, but they're all undoubtedly liberal. No, the problem isn't the psychology of the white liberal. The problem is institutions. The Department of Welfare isn't a *white* institution, it's an *institution*, and a Negro like James Dumpson is as limited by it and responsible for it as any white commissioner would be. And if social workers are irrelevant, as Kenneth Clark says they are, it's not because they're white social workers, or because they're liberals; the problem is social work itself. When Mr. Clark talks about education, and says that the schools are worse today than they were eight or ten years ago, I can well believe him. But is it because they're run by white liberals? Of course not. There are a hundred other reasons: the changes in the student body, the difficulty the Board of Education has in dealing with its own Board of Examiners, its own bureaucracy, and so on down the line. If the Board of Education begins to do a better job under Calvin Gross, it won't be because he's white or liberal, but because he can find a way to manipulate and manage that institution. Maybe a Negro could do it too, and maybe a Negro couldn't. Many people think that my former boss, Mr. Weaver, hasn't found a way to handle the Federal Housing and Home Finance Agency. I don't quite agree with them, but in any case it has nothing to do with his being a Negro. Negroes tend to assume that many of these problems have to do with their being Negro. But the truth is that the problems are a product of the kind of unwieldy institutions we have, the kind of feudal country we have, the kind of recalcitrant special interests that have developed—among them Negro interests. And so we all fight it out. There's certainly a role for the white liberal and the white intellectual—and the Negro liberal and the Negro intellectual—to play, and that is to figure out how to break these bottlenecks in the way of a rational approach to the solution of problems.

As for the people in the streets demanding jobs, I spent a good part of my year in Washington looking for Negroes our agency or others could hire. Now certainly this was partly because there were Negroes in the streets. But that's the way things happen in America. In Chicago they look for Poles to give jobs to, because they're worried about the Polish vote. The situation isn't all that different with Negroes.

HOOK: I just want to supplement that remark with respect to universities. The universities that I am acquainted with, and I have seen many—are today trying to recruit qualified Negroes for their teaching staffs. Every informed person knows this. The overwhelming majority of people who teach in American universities are liberal and are free of the discriminatory attitudes we have condemned here. The fact that you can't find many Negroes among them doesn't prove that they are hypocritical. Perhaps there exists a chairman of a psychology department who stupidly believes that a background in the psychology of perception is the proper qualification for a chair in race relations. Perhaps his stupidity is only a pretense for his prejudice, but if so, he is not representative of the universities.

Now of course, the kind of white man who will talk to Mr. Baldwin only about civil rights is someone who is to be condemned, because he is treating Mr. Baldwin as the representative of a group and not as a human being. He is like the people who tell you that they love Jews. Next to anti-Semites, I most despise philo-Semites who profess to love Jews as such. And there are some people who profess to love Negroes as such. I would not call such people liberals at all. But what Mr. Clark is talking about is something quite different. He's delivered himself of a serious indictment for which he has given no convincing bill of particulars at all.

PODHORETZ: Mr. Lionel Abel.*

ABEL: I want to address this question to you, Mr. Baldwin, but not for the purpose of putting you on the defensive, as Mr. Clark intimated. The main reason most of the questions have been addressed to you is that you made the most provocative remarks. As for my question, its purpose is really clarification. I'm struck by the fact that you stress the particularity of the Negro experience. You stress it in two ways—you stress it negatively: the greater ignominy of the Negroes, who were brought to this country against their will; and you also stress it positively: the greater vivacity or density of Negro life. In both ways you separate Negroes from white people. But then you also say that you want to change the foundations of American society in order to solve the Negro problem—that is, a true solution

---

* Mr. Abel is a playwright and critic who contributes frequently to *Commentary*.

of the Negro problem, you believe, will require a thorough renovation of American life. In that case, why do you stress the particularity of the Negro experience?

BALDWIN: It is not *I* who stresses Negro particularity; it is not *I* who insists on the separation of the Negro experience. Even if I did not say those things, it would still be absolutely true that Negroes came here against their will, and that they were chained, and that they were a source of cheap labor. It would also be true that it is not because *I* decided to live in a ghetto that I'm living in one, but because the white republic decided to put me there and keep me there. Nothing that has been said here, as far as I've heard, contradicts my major premise, which is simply this: that in terms of my own experience and the experience of people around me, the liberal record is a shameful record. And the reason it is so shameful is that white liberals—with some exceptions—have been unable to divest themselves of the whole concept of white supremacy and that this concept is reinforced by all the institutions in which power is located. This is why I say that in order for the Negro to become an American citizen, all American citizens will be forced to undergo a change, and all American institutions will be forced to undergo a change too. These institutions, which are established, can only begin to operate to free me and all other Americans by changing. There is no possibility, for example, of the Church in this country accepting me into it as a Christian without becoming a different institution itself. Mr. Abel has implied that I'm trying to have my cake and eat it too—that I stress Negro particularity in terms of its ignominy and then in terms of its vivacity. But I think we all know that a people who are oppressed, and have been oppressed so long, evolve certain techniques for survival—among them things like spareribs, dancing, and watermelon. Now I also happen to think—this is my *own* opinion about my republic— that most of the people in it are terribly divorced from any sense of themselves, I mean their bodies, who they really are. They mainly live by attitudes, and no longer even know how to conduct their private lives: look at what they do to their children. Speaking again only for myself, I do not intend to live that way. I repudiate most of the standards by which Americans live, and I don't see any hope—not for *my* freedom, but for *our* freedom, as long as we live by these standards.

PODHORETZ: Mr. Shlomo Katz.*

KATZ: Mr. Baldwin, even assuming that the changes you want were to take place, do you think that it would ever be possible for eighteen or nineteen or twenty-two million American Negroes to eradicate from their memory their specific, particular, unique history in the United States—a history which the rest of the population did not experience? If such a

---

* Mr. Katz is editor of *Midstream*.

thing were possible, then, of course, we could talk about a wholly new society. But if it is not possible, then won't there be new separations which in their own turn will engender differences leading again to discrimination?

BALDWIN: It seems to me that there's an assumption revealed in the very way you phrase the question. The history which the Negro endured coming to this country and in this country was not only endured by *him*; it was endured on another level by all the white people who oppressed him. It is, Mr. Hook to the contrary, a collective history. I was here, that did something to me. But you were here on top of me, and that did something to *you*. What happened to the Negro in this country is not simply a matter of *my* memory or *my* history; it's a matter of *American* history and *American* memory. As a Negro, I cannot afford to ignore or deny or overlook it, but the white American necessity is precisely to deny, ignore, and overlook it. Now what I would like to see happen in some day to come is a fusion between what I remember and what you remember. Then there will be no question about our separation. We are really one people and—this is part of our problem, in fact—we spend all of our time denying it.

As for discrimination and prejudice, I'm not so utopian as to suppose that we will ever arrive at a state when people will not discriminate against each other, will not be prejudiced against each other. My complaint here is that you have the power to enforce your doctrine; your vision of me you have the power to make real. I don't care if you don't love me; I just don't want to be kept in a ghetto because you don't love me. I don't care if I live to be a thousand years old and you don't love me; but I want you to let my children go. And since what happened to me here happened to you here too, this cannot be done if we try to go our separate ways to do it.

HOOK: I'm not sure that Mr. Baldwin's answer actually meets Mr. Katz's question. Even if we succeeded in reconstructing American life, there would still be Negroes with memories of their past. There would still be Jews with memories of their past. That's not the point. The important thing is whether the individual would be free to identify himself with a group or not. Let us at least try to distinguish our problems. We are fundamentally concerned here with the freedom of the human being to develop his personality and to make his own choices. That freedom should be open to everybody. The kind of culture he wants to live in, the kind of life he wants to live—all that is something to be decided subsequently. Not all whites have a common attitude to their children, Mr. Baldwin. There is a great deal of variation in white attitudes and in white modes of behavior which you don't recognize. And I suspect that there is more variation in Negro life and in Negro attitudes than you yourself have articulated. When I read Ralph Ellison, I get a sense of other dimensions in Negro experience as important as the dimensions you have discussed. In the early 30's, when we were all trying to convert the country to socialism, there were some people who said, "Why do you want to bring the values of a machine civilization to the workers? After all, such a civilization is antipathetic to the best human ideals." But to men who were unemployed and whose families were starving, this was an irrelevant criticism. The "existentialists" of those days often made fun of the ambition to live like people in Flatbush, and to have clean homes. But that's what the workers wanted, no matter what the critics said.

BALDWIN: I get your analogy, Mr. Hook, but I talk about the culture because in fact the culture cannot give the workers of today—these black workers, these black people—*anything at all* without changing. It is not a question of my deciding, after I have been accepted, what kind of culture I will live in. It is now impossible for this culture as it is to give me any place to live at all.

MYRDAL: You can say a lot against the white liberals, sure. With a situation like this the whole people becomes a little sick. Certainly there are a lot of rather queer elements in race relations. We can read about them in studies, and Mr. Baldwin writes about them as a novelist. But nevertheless, Mr. Baldwin, you will have to rely upon the liberals because, as somebody said before, it's not the conservatives who are going to fight for the bigger reforms which must be made—to eradicate poverty and everything that poverty implies, to create a fully mobile society where everyone can get ahead through education and hard work, to liberate the *whole* submerged group. The first thing to be done is, of course, to settle this civil-rights business, even if you and I are quite clear that that alone will not solve the problem. The way history is now proceeding, we don't have a very long time ahead of us, and therefore it is really necessary to speed up your efforts to get the reforms through—reforms which cover the whole broad field of how a young man grows up in America if he belongs to the submerged group. But to speed things up, you will have to rely on the liberals—even if sometimes they are not too clear and too courageous, and even if they need you to give them a push. I think the most encouraging thing which has happened in America in recent years is the rebellion of the Negro group, because that rebellion will help the liberals to get into power and do the job that has to be done.

PODHORETZ: Mr. William Phillips.*

PHILLIPS: I agree with much of Mr. Baldwin's criticism of American liberalism, and I'm beginning to wonder whether I'm the only white person here who does. Mr. Baldwin spoke of the necessity for a radical transformation of society in order to wipe out discrimination (and to do a few other good things, I hope, too). I'd like to ask him, though, to be concrete and tell us what kind of radical transformation he has in mind. And I'd also like to ask Mr. Hook, conversely, whether he really believes that we can achieve genuine desegregation without some radical transformation of our society.

---

* Mr. Phillips is co-editor of *Partisan Review*.

HOOK: To achieve total desegregation, we would indeed have to make very important modifications in American society. As a socialist, a democratic socialist, I take for granted that the problem of poverty still remains to be solved. But I think I've learned something since my early socialist days, and that is that the solution of economic problems is not a cure-all, especially for racial problems. There are some Negroes today who are not economically deprived, and yet they are discriminated against and made to feel that they're not part of the human race. The better off they are, the more sensitive they are to the patterns of discrimination.

I return to what I'm surprised to find so many of you consider irrelevant —namely, the ethical foundations of democracy. Anybody who has raised a family knows what I mean when I say that the good family is one in which there is an equality of concern on the part of the parents for the development of all their children. It's absurd, of course, to make literal comparisons between the family and the community. But the analogy emphasizes the fact that if you believe in equality of concern, it doesn't follow that you must also believe in mechanical equality for everybody at every point. The concern is always for the person, for his individual needs. As applied to the problem we're discussing here, this means not only economic change, but educational change, psychological change. I don't ever anticipate a society in which human beings are going to be happy. Every society finds its own forms of unhappiness. But I do want a society in which the institutions are not so geared as to impose a burden of unnecessary unhappiness upon the people who live under them. The tragic estate of man remains what it is under any system. Let us not add social impediments to it.

PODHORETZ: Mr. Baldwin, do you want to have the last word? Our time has almost run out, so it looks like you're going to get it whether you want it or not.

BALDWIN: When I talk about a radical transformation of society, I have in mind several very concrete things. I have in mind, for example, that if one really intends to eliminate ghettos, one has to be prepared to deal with the banks, the real-estate boards, and the other groups and pressures which in fact create the ghettos and keep the children in prison. To deal with these power groups is obviously to undertake a radical transformation. Dr. Myrdal is right—Negroes are not the only submerged and oppressed people in our society. My hope is this, and I think it is our only hope: that when *all* the submerged, when *all* the oppressed, when *all* the penalized, and when *all* the subjugated are finally liberated, then we too will be liberated by the new energy that will be released into the mainstream of American society.